ADVANCES IN FAMILY PSYCHIATRY

Advances
in
Family Psychiatry

Volume II

Edited by

JOHN G. HOWELLS

INTERNATIONAL UNIVERSITIES PRESS, INC.
New York

Library of Congress Cataloging in Publication Data

Main entry under title:

Advances in family psychiatry.

    Includes bibliographies and indexes.
    1.   Mentally ill — Family relationships.   2.   Family.
3. Family psychotherapy.   I. Howells, John G.
[DNLM: 1. Family therapy. WM430.5.F2 A244]
RC455.4.F3A37   616.89'156   78-13895
ISBN 0-8236-0101-3 (v. 2)

Contents

FAMILY DIAGNOSIS

FAMILY SYMPTOMATOLOGY

Family Psychotherapy

Vector Therapy

Preface

Volumes in the series *Advances in Family Psychiatry* are planned to appear at intervals, depending on the availability of worthwhile material in the field. Volume II, as was its predecessor, is a selection culled from a large number of papers collected recently at the Institute of Family Psychiatry. Selection for the volume is based on a paper having merit, being innovative, and being appropriate for clinicians. Each volume is not a textbook, but a reflection of the growing points in the field. The world's literature has been searched for suitable work, so that we have contributions from Australia, Canada, India, Norway, Tasmania, the United Kingdom, and the U.S.A., all by distinguished family clinicians. Sometimes a significant paper has been found in a journal not usually read by family clinicians.

As with its predecessor, the high quality of this volume has been guaranteed by an abundance of material. Certain fields, notably family psychotherapy, have produced a veritable flood of work, and much care has been needed to discriminate in the choice of papers. Systematic investigation is the life blood of family psychiatry, as will become increasingly apparent with each succeeding volume in the series.

As was explained in Volume I, family psychiatry embraces more than the narrow field of family therapy, which, as the term suggests, emphasizes therapy; thus, the series considers theoretical aspects, family psychopathology, family diagnosis, family symptomatology, and vector therapy as well as family psychotherapy.

It is a pleasure to record my thanks to Mrs. M. Livia Osborn for her efficient and enthusiastic help in every stage of the compilation of this volume.

Theoretical Aspects

Choosing contributions on this aspect of family psychiatry proved exciting. Here quality supplants quantity.

The first chapter addresses itself to clinical research and the theme is then elaborated by contributions on a new model for marital work, primary health care, the family life cycle, rarely discussed ethical concerns, and, finally, a model for family functioning from a prominent family center.

Theoretical Aspects

Research in Family Therapy

MELVIN R. LANSKY

Problems of research in family therapy partake of all difficulties inherent in any psychotherapy research: uncertainty of outcome criteria, choice of pertinent variables for study, the effects of interchangeability of therapists, comparability of samples with controls and with samples from other studies. Each of these problems, difficult enough in any setting, becomes more pronounced when whole families are considered. From a research perspective these difficulties become compounded to the point where methodologically thorough investigations would require designs that surpass any possibility of implementation. Another basic problem for family therapy is the lack of even a generally accepted point of view from which to approach a methodological evaluation of family treatment. For these and perhaps other reasons, the actual body of research on family therapy is scant.

I believe the situation is nonetheless workable, and suggest a point of view toward research in family therapy that emphasizes psychopathology. Meaningful statements about family therapy must start with the notion that specific difficulties faced by the family — whether seen as predicaments, illness, emanations of pathological personality organization, or provoked by habitual transactions between members of the family — may profitably be studied together with the specific techniques or measures felt necessary to respond to them. This point of view is not the prevailing one in family therapy circles today, and therefore some explanation using an historical perspective is in order.

Family therapy evolved out of studies beginning in the early 1950s which attempted to assess the role of the family in the etiology of schizophrenia (Lidz and Lidz, 1945; Lidz, Fleck, Cornelison, et al., 1965; Jackson, 1957; Wynne, Rycoft, Day, et al., 1958). An early supposition

Melvin R. Lansky, M.D., is Adjunct Associate Professor of Psychiatry, UCLA School of Medicine, Los Angeles, Calif.

3

was that the family system itself could cause major psychiatric disorder in the absence of illness or prepsychotic personality organization in the patient. The discovery of the exploitation of the difficulties of the designated schizophrenic by other family members gave rise to such a reactive antipathy on the part of some researchers to the notion of patienthood that the evolving field of family therapy has tended to swing to eschewing the notion of patienthood or illness altogether. There has been emphasis on the organization of the whole system around designating, creating, and enforcing the defectiveness in one member and, accordingly, a reluctance to accept that either illness or personality organization in individual members of the system has relevance. While the search for the specific and convincing etiological role of family dynamics in any major psychiatric disorder has been strikingly unsuccessful, the antimedical and anti-individual bias remains. The antimedical and antipsychoanalytic outlook of the family therapy movement has gained in momentum by the attraction to the field of therapists by and large not mindful of traditional professional affiliations.

Also since the early 1950s, the discovery of potent psychopharmacologic agents — the major tranquilizers, tricyclic antidepressants, and lithium carbonate — has stimulated rethinking of psychiatric diagnosis to the point where elaborate research criteria have been developed (Feighner, Robins, Guze, et al., 1972), and diagnosis consistent with categorization in terms of course of illness and treatment response has seemed like an attainable goal. The new "Kraepelinianism" has been opposite in direction to that of the family therapy movement so that the fields barely, if ever, communicate and advances in one are seldom brought to bear on work in the other. The advance of the medical model has also been augmented by convincing genetic evidence (notably, adoption studies of monozygotic twins) that has convincingly demonstrated constitutional factors in the etiology of most major psychiatric disorders. During the same period of time there has been increasing optimism about psychoanalytically treating patients who do not have typical transference neuroses and who are characterized by a personality organization centered around defenses that reinforce splits in the ego. These include the vast category of borderline personalities and some narcissistic disturbances (Kernberg, 1967, 1975).

There is, then, an expansion of more or less solid psychiatric and psychoanalytic knowledge, acquired over the last 25 years, that has gone counter to the main thrust of interest of family therapists. Furthermore, many family therapists have yet to assimilate the notion that family research has failed to demonstrate any exclusively etiologic role of family process; and other research has established beyond reasonable doubt the presence of constitutional and genetic factors in the major psychiatric syndromes. In short, there are individuals whose illness cannot be seen solely in terms of victimization by family process.

The defeat of the assumption of etiological primacy of family process by no means gainsays the (also well established) fact that families may compound, reinforce, and perhaps precipitate many features of illness. The need for family therapy and judgments as to its effectiveness are by no means undercut by any etiologic discoveries about illness. The role of the family system in containing the illness and perpetrating it under some circumstances does not depend on the assumption that a disturbed family caused the disorder in the first place. Likewise, it is not a tenable premise for the conduct of family psychotherapy that it consists solely of the reversal of a process that caused psychiatric disturbance; and it cannot be maintained—for research purposes especially—that "family therapy" is a definite thing that can be studied without further description. There is no notion of "family therapy" the same for any psychiatric disorder any more than there is an "operation" the same for any surgical disorder.

There is a great range of approaches to family difficulties in which no major illness of psychotic proportions or major personality disturbance manifested by significant splits in the ego is in evidence. In such situations any number of ameliorative approaches may exploit the givens of the therapy setting, i.e., willingness to see a problem, willingness to appear together to work on it, and willingness to talk to a professional—all of which favor a good outcome with any approach—together with the general features of any psychotherapy (Frank, 1973), i.e., emphasis on explicit communication, dependency gratification, or fantasies of protection by the therapist that engender a permissive attitude toward self-discovery and assertiveness. More nonspecific support is added by the presence of significant others in a protective, nonjudgmental, facilitative environment with an emphasis on explicit communication.

One way out of the research impasse posed by the vast number of variables in family therapy and the lack of uniformity in approach is emphasis on the study of which psychopathological features do well with which technical procedures (Eissler, 1953). This point of view has a heavy emphasis, deliberately weighted here, on technical measures that have some chance of being isolatable enough to be studied in the treatment of families containing at least one member with a psychiatric disturbance of major proportions. The approach fails to deal with variables not directly organized around major psychopathology, and accordingly it fails to consider research which compares different approaches to therapy and nonpathological predicaments of families. It does have the advantage of drawing attention to specific alterations in technique posed by specific pathological situations.

It is an assumption here that the field of psychotherapy with families who do not present major psychopathology is not sufficiently organized to isolate variables for study. It is also an assumption that some techniques in family treatment of patients with major pathology may be assembled for the beginnings of research scrutiny. The research attitude, then, will be basically organized around psychopathology rather than psychotherapy. The discussion is divided into three sections concerned with schizophrenia, the affective disorders, and borderline conditions.

FAMILY THERAPY IN SCHIZOPHRENIA

It was with the attempt to study the intrafamilial milieu of the schizophrenic in the search for the etiology of schizophrenia that the field of family therapy began in the early 1950s. Prior to that time, Lidz and Lidz, noting a high preponderance of disturbed family members of hospitalized schizophrenics, expanded on a previous postulate that a relationship with a "schizophrenic" mother was of possible etiologic significance (Lidz and Lidz, 1945). The fact that many such mothers also had nonschizophrenic offspring necessitated a deepening of the family etiologic hypothesis beyond the simple noxious effect of the mother. A number of groups began to study the whole family environment of the presumably schizophrenic patient. These groups, all working somewhat simultaneously, were Wynne and his co-workers, Murray Bowen, Lidz and Fleck at Yale, and Bateson and his co-workers in Palo Alto.

Wynne et al. (1958), in collaboration with Singer and others, described in detail disturbed patterns of communication in disturbed families. He coined the terms "pseudomutuality" and "pseudohostility" for the peculiar patterns of relatedness in such families, and the "rubber fence" metaphor to describe the system's holding on to the victim as well as the victim's impulsive return to the system.

Murray Bowen (1960), starting from the study of whole families hospitalized for lengthy periods of time, developed a hypothesis of the development of schizophrenia as a compounding of immaturity projected through marriages over at least three generations. The most vulnerable child is likely to absorb some immaturity from even a relatively normal marriage. This child, more dysfunctional than either parent, will tend to marry someone of similar dysfunction, producing a union with even more immaturity to be absorbed by its most vulnerable off-spring. By this declension of immaturity, according to Bowen, a schizophrenic is eventually formed.

Lidz and his collaborators (1965), in a more psychoanalytic framework, have evolved a series of studies pointing to a violation of sexual and generation boundaries in the families of schizophrenics, prohibition of extrafamilial socialization, and the importance of "marital schism" and "marital skew." Marital schism, an open rift in the marriage of the patient, is said to be more prominent in the families of female schizophrenics. Marital skew, the attempt to mask the deep disturbance in one parent by compensatory functioning and distorted communication in the other is more prominent in males.

Bateson, Jackson, Weakland, and Haley (1956) formulated the "double bind" theory modeled on Bateson's observations of animal play, which presumed to outline the genesis of the thinking disturbance in schizophrenia by the programming of the patient with conflicting injunctions, one at a higher level of abstraction than the other, and another which precludes leaving the emotional field. Double bind is commonly mistaken to be the simple presence of conflicting injunctions. The authors' intent, however, was to point out something much more complex. As a result of conflicting injunctions at different levels of logical types, there would presumably be a learned inability to meta-communicate. This is a failure of the sort of function noted by Bateson in which animals can discern whether a particular activity is transmitting a message (play, courtship, defense) on a different conceptual level than the actual moves in the activity.

All of these early studies were hypothetical in that they asked: What must the intrafamilial situation be such that the transmission of schizophrenia is entirely interpersonal? Disclaimers notwithstanding, all of the earlier studies seem to be attempts at etiologic investigation. None of the studies deal adequately with the notion of diagnosis, and at least one refers to acute reactive schizophrenia (Wynne et al., 1958), an entity which today would be more likely to be considered schizophreniform than truly schizophrenic. The weakness of the design of these early investigations, their dubious diagnostic criteria, and the overwhelming evidence of genetic factors in the etiology of schizophrenia may be summarized: there is virtually no convincing evidence that the family process in itself can cause schizophrenia.

The presumption that the family process may cause schizophrenia is unwarranted, as is the presumption, implicit or explicit, that alteration in the family process in the course of therapy may alter the fundamental features of the illness. The odium for the patient role shared by so many systems theorists has tended to blind family therapists to situations where real residual illness exists. There has been a tendency to avoid the schizophrenic patient rather than to adapt theory to the task at hand (Lansky, 1977).

An exception to this general tendency is an elegantly designed and executed study by Brown and his co-workers, who have shown convincingly that the amount of negatively expressed emotion in families of schizophrenics at the time of admission is positively correlated with rate of relapse (Brown, Birley, and Wing, 1972). The authors are careful to distinguish data pointing to expressed emotion (EE) as a variable independent of initial disturbance and highly related to relapse if contact with such relatives exceeds 35 hours a week of face-to-face contact. The authors conceive of an optimal arousal level for schizophrenics, compared to which the patient's course of illness may be adversely affected by under-stimulation (excess social withdrawal) or overstimulation (one manifestation of which is sustained exposure to high EE levels in the family). If replicable, such a study suggests that behavioral manipulation of the interpersonal stimulus barrier may be an important independent treatment variable related to outcome.

Work of Laqueur (1972), Norton, Detre, and Jarecke (1963), and more recent work by Lansky, Bley, McVey, et al. (1978), suggest that working with groups of families may have distinct advantages over working with one family alone. The advantage is gained by what Laqueur has called identification constellations, the ability of group members to identify with those in similar positions in other families (Laqueur, 1972). A collective ego strength that is not possible in other ways can be developed. Mothers identify with mothers, fathers with fathers, patients with patients, so that both confrontation and support can be stronger in the presence of a feeling of shared support in a common predicament. Risk-taking and experimentation across families can be tried before the same issue is handled within the family. A mother can explore her feeling with other mothers that she has been to blame for her son's illness. A young schizophrenic may reveal drug refusal or a return of symptoms to find that other schizophrenics have had the same experience but been too frightened to reveal it.

Another vitally needed research investigation concerns those at risk for schizophrenia—the offspring of schizophrenics in particular. The study of risk of manifest schizophrenia is in an early stage, and understandably must precede the study of the effect of preventive intervention on those at risk. These studies of preventive intervention will, by the nature of the question being asked, require great lengths of time to yield meaningful results.

FAMILY THERAPY IN THE AFFECTIVE DISORDERS

Considering the prevalence and importance of the affective disorders, there are remarkably few studies of family treatment in carefully diagnosed patients with such disorders.

The most prominent of the scant reports prior to the last few years is the study by Cohen and her co-workers which examined the families of 12 cases of manic-depressive psychosis (Cohen, Baker, Cohen, et al., 1954). The work is a compilation of observations on data from psychoanalytic treatment. The authors note the use of the future manic-depressive to meet prestige needs in families where the lack of prestige is often blamed on the father. The study gives the impression that little more than a few modifications in intensive insight therapy are required with such patients to increase empathy by the interpretation of the defensive use of "conventional barriers to emotional interchange"; by awareness of the dependency, transference, and countertransference issues involved; and by the setting of limits. Despite its broad scope and ambitious intent, Cohen's study is woefully inadequate in presenting a convincing account of manic-depressive symptomatology and family constellation, and it deals even less with effective treatment of any sort. Characteristically of studies in the 1950s, the preoccupation with psychogenesis precludes adequate attention to management of features of the disorder which in all likelihood are biologically determined.

In the last decade, significant research into the genetics and classification of affective disorders (Gershon, Dunner, Goodwin, et al., 1971), together with an understanding of the role of antidepressants and lithium carbonate in managing such disorders, has made the search for etiologic explanation entirely within the family outmoded and it has created a need for more specific treatment strategies — family and otherwise.

A series of papers from the National Institute of Mental Health produced detailed descriptions of the plight of the married manic as observed in couples who were grouped homogeneously for diagnosis (Ablon, Davenport, Gershon, et al., 1975; Davenport, Gold, Adland, et al., 1977). Themes of fear of recurring mania, hostility between spouses, massive denial, symbiosis, and dependency are noted. These themes may or may not be specific for manic-depressive psychosis. Also notable is the high frequency of weak or absent fathers. While the finding of ineffectual fathers is reported throughout the spectrum

of psychopathological disturbances, the investigators do note significant separations (over six months before the patient's sixteenth birthday) in a large percentage of manic patients. Married male manics
divorce less often than married females. Because of the difficulty of
engagement in treatment and the disruption in heterogeneous groups,
the authors recommend homogeneous conjoint group therapy. This
specific technique offers anxiety reduction; support for disclosures
otherwise not possible; more effective problem-solving opportunities;
alteration of rigid views; reduction in anxiety about genetic transmission; support of medication efforts; and more group tolerance of intimacy (Davenport et al., 1977).

Greene and his co-workers studied marital treatment in situations
where one spouse had a primary affective disorder (PAD) (Greene,
Lustig, and Lee, 1976). They noted a low incidence of divorce, which
they attributed to the conscious or unconscious selection of an overcontrolling mate with whom a deep symbiosis was possible. The authors
proposed a number of specific treatment techniques:

1. They emphasized the importance of preventive work, and of
cautioning patients with PAD about the risks of marriage on both
spouse and children.

2. Deployment of the unaffected spouse as an assistant therapist
was a major thrust. Some 90 percent of the couples were able to
manage without regular therapeutic modalities: this was enhanced if
the nonaffected spouse was counseled about the illness.

3. Group therapy was avoided because of the difficulties posed by
the PAD patient's permeability of ego boundaries, which might not be
perceived by the other group members. (The authors apparently did
not consider the possibility of groups homogeneous for diagnosis or
predicament to deal with that very problem.)

4. The authors noted that 64 percent of their sample had considered suicide and 43 percent had attempted it. This, of course, dic-
tates special concern and the use of hospitalization when suicide risk is
unmanageable.

In virtually all cases of manic-depressive illness, the family is confused about which of the patient's demands are to be reasoned with and
which are not. An accent on the family's knowledge of the disorder
early in the treatment may be valuable (Lansky, 1977). This technique
may have varying degrees of applicability to other affective disorders,
depending on the extent to which the psychopathology can be seen
apart from an intensely symbiotic collusiveness that depends on the
symptomatology for its homeostasis (Lansky, in press).

The scarcity of research on family therapy in major affective disorders is striking. Perhaps recent attention to the need for clarification of our understanding of mood disorders will open new possibilities for distinguishing family treatment of major affective disorders from less discrete entities such as families dealing with depression in a colloquial sense (rather than a diagnostic one) or families with a suicidal member.

For the suicidal patient, special attention to the therapist's anxiety and its origin in the totality of the family's communication is crucial. Failure to experience anxiety about suicide by the family or by the patient will result in the therapist feeling responsible for the possibility of suicide and perhaps that he is the only one worried about it (Straker, 1958). Pointing to communication in the system which attempts to relocate responsibility (and hence anxiety) is central in family therapy practice at any time. Nonetheless, such metacommunication deserves special emphasis with the suicidal patient. The recognition of and discussion of anxiety in the therapist may be a strong factor in the decision to take drastic steps dealing with the suicidal risk.

As with schizophrenia, therapy research directed at prevention of dysfunction in children of parents with affective disorders can only follow studies of risk. Many anecdotal and several systematic studies indicate that developmental difficulties attendant on having a depressed nurturant figure may be much more severe than previously anticipated and may add to the genetic vulnerability of the child (Cohler, Gruenbaum, Weiss, et al., 1977).

FAMILY THERAPY IN BORDERLINE DISORDERS

The confusing but tenacious term "borderline" has recently acquired central significance in its own right, mostly in psychoanalytic circles, and in relation to addictive behavioral, marital, and sexual disorders in other contexts.

Of the many usages of borderline, two can usefully be distinguished: (1) a prepsychotic or nondecompensated psychotic character organization, and part of the schizophrenic spectrum (Goldstein and Jones, 1971; Goldstein and Rodnick, 1975; Hoch and Polatin, 1949) and (2) a character organization consisting of splits in the ego and mechanisms to reinforce splitting, and which is under the dominance of oral aggressive rage and defenses against it (Kernberg, 1967, 1975).

Borderline in the sense of a nondecompensated psychotic disorder on the schizophrenic spectrum has been the subject of family research concerned with schizophrenia. This research regards such conditions as literally on the borderline of what is schizophrenic and what is not. Prominent in the family investigation of such disorders is the UCLA Family Project under the leadership of Rodnick, Goldstein, and their co-workers. Some early results with a comparatively small sample size have shown that adolescent psychopathology as well as parental transactional style may be seen to be a predictor of young-adult diagnosis (Goldstein and Rodnick, 1975). The UCLA group has found that in the absence of bizarre adolescent symptomatology and parental communication deviance, there is usually mild to minimal pathology in the same patients as young adults. One unanswered question concerns the possibility that both the bizarre symptomatology and the parental transactional style may indicate an already existent disorder and not just a predisposition. (The authors clearly have guarded against contamination of the data by manifest psychosis.) The UCLA project has been carefully designed and can be expected to yield more significant results as the observation time and sample size continue to increase.

In the sense that borderline refers to character pathology organized around low-level defensive operations reinforcing splitting (Kernberg, 1967, 1975, 1976), there is increasing but still inadequate recognition of the implications of such personality organization on the conduct of treatment. Specific technical problems are posed by such personality organization, which may be said to be the major pathology requiring attention separate from — and in many cases more basic than — any specific symptomatology.

The features of borderline disorders, as distinguished from less severe pathology, include: ego splitting, an unusually punitive conscience (Klein, 1948, 1952), the tendency to form all-encompassing symbiotic dyadic relationships or to avoid them by schizoid mechanisms, and persistent feelings of anger and entitlement (Lansky, in press; Murray, 1964).

The notion of splitting sometimes refers to ego states that may coexist within the same person in alternation and without affecting each other (Kernberg, 1975, 1976). This has important consequences for the theory and practice of therapy since difficulties usually occur with one ego state characterized by extreme affective intensity, closeness to the immediate situation, and imperviousness to therapeutic influence; whereas therapy may occur in another ego state, calmer and more accessible, but without influence on the first. An example is the aggressive destructiveness in an alcohol-related split which often is unaffected by anything in the sober state. Another sort of splitting within the family describes the collusive process whereby one family member carries disowned traits for the others and is felt to be the only locus of such parts

(Dicks, 1963, 1967; Johnson and Szurek, 1952; Shapiro, Zinner, Shapiro, et al., 1975; Zinner and Shapiro, 1975). When these parts are disowned and there is collusion around the role of carrier of the disowned parts (alcoholic, failure, madman, or others), the splitting within the family requires more than just an understanding of the conscious advantages served by locating the symptom in one person. The conceptual apparatus provided by the object relations theory (Fairbairn, 1952) forms, in essence, a psychodynamic theory of vicariousness in which disowned traits are split off and felt to belong to the scapegoat alone.

The primitive conscience (Klein, 1948) operative in borderline personality disorder is not confined to savageness of self-reproach; it includes a terror of responsibility (and dismal estimates of one's ability to assume it), and an inner feeling of basic emptiness and defectiveness. Avoidance of mortifying humiliation at being exposed as defective is a major defensive concern operative at all times. Such a conscience necessitates the phantasied evacuation and relocation of bad parts at all costs. In family systems where there is some advantage for one member to accept the evacuated parts, a steady state of such activity is stabilized in the scapegoat role.

In borderline disorders, the understanding of personality organization, collusion in the family system and the symptom itself are crucial because a difficulty may be addressed on any of these levels and meaningful family therapy research must address the chosen level of intervention. Some typically borderline pathological situations are not always seen as such: these include difficulties often treated symptomatically as addictive disorders, including alcoholism, behavior disorders, marital difficulties, and sexual dysfunction.

The addictive disorders and alcoholism may be seen as a wide spectrum of pathological conditions underlying common symptoms. Substance abuse cannot be dealt with in any simple way. The abuser may be medicating a psychosis or an affective disorder; or tension, anger, or feelings of emptiness in a borderline condition. The symptom may serve to insure the primary psychological gain of keeping a more frightening realization from awareness. Schizophrenics may take marijuana and attribute their psychosis to the drug. There may also be a secondary gain of dependency gratification, compensation, or avoidance of responsibility. There are defensive and expressive features in the symptom itself that can often be understood in the immediate systems context of the family (Davis et al., 1974). There is always the necessity of acquiring a therapeutic understanding and an evaluation of the techniques to be employed specific to each case. If the manifest symptom is so overriding that it precludes addressing anything else, then techniques may include the use of pharmacologic agents (Antabuse, methadone, narcotic antagonists), manipulative control of the abuse substance by hospitalization or other means, or protective custody. If the use of drugs or alcohol represents an attempt at self-medication, appropriate medication can be instituted. If the patient's symptomatic toxic state is seen to be a split-off state, techniques appropriate to borderline families may be instituted together with techniques to control the symptom. Only then can the more usual system approach, i.e., looking at the function of the symptom in the system, be effectively employed.

One of the promising pioneering works in family theory was done by Johnson and Szurek (1952), who coined the term "superego lacunae" for the propensity of conscience in children that allows them to enact repressed wishes of the parents. This promising hypothesis was supported by evidence that major behavioral pathology in children sometimes abates when the parents alone are treated. Indeed, every family therapist knows that behavior disruptions are often an attempt by children both to exploit and to control a marital rift between their parents. What has been shown by research in other areas, however, is that behavior disorders often endure. Masterson's studies on families of borderline adolescents show that deeper pathology remains despite transient amelioration in the behavior disturbance (Masterson, 1976). There is a pressing need for more outcome studies to indicate what sorts of behavior problems remain at risk despite symptomatically successful remission after family therapy. It may be that family involvement will prove, for some individuals at least, to be a first step toward long-term treatment in which they might otherwise be too impulse ridden to engage. Evidence for this possibility is widespread, although largely anecdotal.

For marital disorders without major pathology, a wide variety of family therapy approaches is available and effective. If, however, there are phenomena indicative of character pathology which is organized around splitting and the pervasive use of defensive operations such as contempt, disdain, arrogance, or blame, then the attempt to facilitate communication within the family will often be stalemated by overreactivity and blaming. There will be a general inability to learn from the therapeutic experience because of fear of exposure of inadequacy or loss of relationships, both of which are not so pervasive in less pathological families. Techniques such as the intergenerational approach, orchestration of communications through the therapist, and eventual long-term individual therapy, may be necessary.

The same considerations apply to brief conjoint treatment of sexual dysfunction, the technique developed by Masters and Johnson (1970). Their extremely high success rates were probably influenced by sample biases that selected the couples without major psychopathology. In an unselected sample (Lansky and Davenport, 1975), couples with good prognosis seemed to be those whose defensiveness was secondary to the symptom. Where the symptom served as a distancing maneuver, in marriages characterized by preoccupation, contempt, depression, and blame, such treatment was invariably unsuccessful. In short, although the brief treatment of sexual dysfunction is of proven effectiveness with some couples, it must be staged as part of the overall treatment program and is probably of no avail if major psychopathology is present.

Conclusions

This chapter has attempted to develop a psychopathologically based research attitude for the study of family therapy. Research demonstration of the efficacy of family therapy is beyond the scope of this attitude; I have assumed that family therapy is a well-established therapeutic modality. My major thesis is that special situations may require specific technical procedures based on psychopathological understanding of the situation. Although any sort of predicament or illness may require techniques developed from a therapeutic understanding, this discussion has centered around the techniques adapted to major psychopathology within the family system. The emphasis on technique that is organized around psychopathology may provide a basis for researching a field with an almost uncontrollable amount of variables and little agreement about what those variables are.

There are problems with the attitude presented. Major psychopathology is a designation based on medical and individual models, and the transplantation of such notions to family systems thinking cannot be glibly presumed. However, it is no violation of the systems notion to think of a family system with a schizophrenic, manic, or depressed member. In cases of borderline pathology, Murray Bowen's (1960) reminder that spouses have remarkably similar levels of underlying differentiations of self despite outward differences, as well as object relations theorists' notions of the whole family as a solitary ego (Shapiro et al., 1975; Zinner and Shapiro, 1975), may serve to bridge the gap.

Meaningful research on family therapy must start from more than one point. The present viewpoint draws very little from research into the actual conduct of psychotherapy — family or otherwise — and ignores such factors as variability in empathy, adjustment of reinforcement contingencies, specifics of the relationship with the therapist, and so forth.

In addition, there is specific knowledge about families of patients with major psychopathology — parents, spouses, offspring, and siblings — that must find its way into research designs of the future along with the important factor of outcome. One very promising way to proceed with family therapy research would be a systematic examination of treatment failures, but such an effort unfortunately has scarcely begun (Lansky, 1975; Masters and Johnson, 1970; Masterson, 1976). This method has many advantages. Not only is the clinician reminded of the incompleteness of his current attitude toward technique, but the very focus on treatment failures initiates a research attitude that questions both tacit and explicit assumptions about psychopathology, course of the disorder, and its amelioration by the techniques used. Groups of phenomena that may elude other kinds of research come quickly to the fore when unsuccessful cases are reviewed and compared both to each other and to successful cases. Patterns can be seen that have unique advantages to the investigator in terms of hypothesis formation and further study. In this way, the "stumbling block" of one theory provides the "cornerstone" for the next (Freud, 1933, p. 104).

REFERENCES

Ablon, S., Davenport, Y., Gershon, E., et al. (1975), The married manic. *Amer. J. Orthopsychiat.*, 45:854–866.

Bateson, G., Jackson, D., Weakland, J., & Haley, J. (1956), Toward a theory of schizophrenia. *Behav. Sci.*, 1:251–264.

Bowen, M. (1960), A family concept of schizophrenia. In: *The Etiology of Schizophrenia*, ed. D. D. Jackson. New York: Basic Books.

Brown, G. W., Birley, J. L. T., & Wing, J. K. (1972), Influence of family life on the course of schizophrenic disorders. *Brit. J. Psychiat.*, 121:241–258.

Cohen, M. B., Baker, G., Cohen, R., et al. (1954), An intensive study of twelve cases of manic-depressive psychosis. *Psychiat.*, 17:103–136.

Cohler, B. J., Gruenbaum, H., Weiss, J. L., et al. (1977), Disturbances of attention among schizophrenic, depressed, and well mothers and their young children. *J. Child Psychol. Psychiat.*, 18:115–135.

Davenport, Y., Gold, P., Adland., M., et al. (1977), Family dynamics and manic-depressive illness. Paper presented at the annual meeting of the American Psychiatric Association, Toronto.

Davis, D., et al. (1974), The adaptive consequences of drinking. *Psychiat.*, 37:209–215.

Dicks, H. (1963), Object relations theory. *Brit. J. Med. Psychol.*, 36:125.

———— (1967), *Marital Tensions*. New York: Basic Books.

Eissler, K. R. (1953), The effect of the structure of the ego on psychoanalytic technique. *J. Amer. Psychoanal. Assn.*, 1:104–143.

Fairbairn, W. R. D. (1952), *Psychoanalytic Studies in the Personality*. London: Tavistock.

Feighner, J., Robins, E., Guze, S., et al. (1972), Diagnostic criteria for use in psychiatric research. *Arch. Gen. Psychiat.*, 26:57–63.

Frank, J. (1973), *Persuasion and Healing*. Baltimore: Johns Hopkins.

Freud, S. (1933), New introductory lectures on psycho-analysis. *Standard Edition*, 22:1–182. London: Hogarth Press, 1964.

Gershon, E., Dunner, D., Goodwin, F., et al. (1971), Toward a biology of affective disorders. *Arch. Gen. Psychiat.*, 25:1–15.

Goldstein, M. & Jones, J. (1971), Adolescent and familial precursors of borderline and schizophrenic conditions. In: *Borderline Personality Disorders*, ed. P. Hartocollis. New York: International Universities Press, 1977.

_____ & Rodnick, E. (1975), The family's contribution to the etiology of schizophrenia. *Schiz. Bull.*, 14:48–63.

Greene, B., Lustig, N., & Lee, R. (1976), Marital therapy where one spouse has a primary affective disorder. *Amer. J. Psychiat.*, 133:827–830.

Hoch, P. & Polatin, P. (1949), Pseudoneurotic forms of schizophrenia. *Psychiat. Quart.*, 23:248.

Jackson, D. D. (1957), The question of family homeostasis. *Psychiat. Quart. Suppl.*, 31:79–90.

Johnson, A. & Szurek, S. (1952), The genesis of antisocial acting out in children and adults. *Psychoanal. Quart.*, 21:323–343.

Kernberg, O. (1967), Borderline personality organization. *J. Amer. Psychoanal. Assn.*, 15:641–685.

_____ (1975), *Borderline Conditions and Pathological Narcissism*. New York: Aronson.

_____ (1976), *Objective Relations Theory and Clinical Psychoanalysis*. New York: Aronson.

Klein, M. (1948), The early development of conscience in the child. In: *Contributions to Psychoanalysis*. London: Hogarth Press.

_____ (1952), Notes on some schizoid mechanisms. In: *Developments in Psychoanalysis*, ed. J. Riviere. London: Hogarth Press.

Lansky, M. & Davenport, A. E. (1975), Difficulties in brief conjoint treatment of sexual dysfunction. *Amer. J. Psychiat.*, 132:177–179.

Lansky, M. R. (1977), Establishing a family-oriented inpatient unit. *J. Operational Psychiat.*, 8:66–74.

_____ (in press), On blame. *Internat. J. Psychoanal. Psychother.*

_____ Bley, C., McVey, G., et al. (1978), Multiple family groups as aftercare. *Internat. J. Group Psychother.*, 28:211–224.

Laqueur, H. P. (1972), Mechanisms of change in multiple family therapy. In: *Progress in Group and Family Therapy*, ed. C. J. Sagar & H. S. Kaplan. New York: Brunner/Mazel.

Lidz, R. & Lidz, T. (1945), The family environment of schizophrenic patients. *Amer. J. Psychiat.*, 106:332–345.

Lidz, T., Fleck., S., Cornelison, A., et al. (1965), *Schizophrenia and the Family*. New York: International Universities Press.

Masters, W. & Johnson, V. (1970), *Human Sexual Inadequacy*. Boston: Little-Brown.

Masterson, J. (1976), *Psychotherapy of the Borderline Adult*. New York: Brunner/Mazel.

Murray, J. (1964), Narcissism and the ego ideal. *J. Amer. Psychoanal. Assn.*, 12:477–511.

Norton, N., Detre, T., & Jarecke, H. (1963), Psychiatric services in general hospitals: A family-oriented redefinition. *J. Nerv. Ment. Dis.*, 136:475–484.

Shapiro, E. R., Zinner, J., Shapiro, R. L., et al. (1975), The influence of family experience on borderline personality development. *Internat. Rev. Psycho-Anal.*, 2:399–412.

Stewart, R. et al. (1975), An objective relations approach to psychotherapy with marital couples, families and children. *Fam. Proc.*, 14:161–177.

Straker, M. (1958), Clinical observations on suicide. *Can. Med. Assn. J.*, 19:473.

Wynne, L., Rycoft, I., Day, J., et al. (1958), Pseudomutuality in the family relations of schizophrenics. *Psychiat.*, 21:205–220.

Zinner, J. & Shapiro, E. (1975), Splitting in families of borderline adolescents. In: *Borderline States in Psychiatry*, ed. J. Mack. New York: Grune & Stratton.

Marital Conflict and Marital Intimacy: An Integrative Psychodynamic-Behavioral-Systemic Model

LARRY B. FELDMAN

Repetitive cycles of nonproductive marital conflict[1] are a major cause of psychological distress (Gurman and Rice, 1975), physical injuries (Gelles, 1972), and violent deaths (Wolfgang, 1958) and are frequently a major impetus for the initiation of marital therapy. At present, the multiple factors that stimulate and maintain conflictual cycles are poorly understood. In the present paper, a clinically derived conceptual model of one common dynamic pattern underlying many conflictual marriages will be presented and illustrated with a clinical example. This model is not intended to be all-inclusive. It is the writer's belief that many different factors play a role in the stimulation and maintenance of marital conflict cycles; the present model focuses on some, but by no means all, of these factors. The main theses of the present model are:

1. Repetitive, nonproductive marital conflict behavior is purposive (goal-directed) and is maintained by a particular pattern of reinforcement (Kanfer and Phillips, 1970) and negative feedback (Watzlawick, Beavin, and Jackson, 1967).

2. From an intrapsychic perspective, one major goal of conflictual behavior is to prevent the emergence into conscious awareness of in-

Larry B. Feldman, M.D., is Assistant Professor, Division of Family Studies, Department of Psychiatry, Northwestern University Medical School.

The assistance of Eleanore Feldman, M.S.W., Jean Goldsmith, Ph.D., Jack Graller, M.D., Charles Kramer, M.D., William Pinsof, Ph.D., and Miriam Reitz, A.C.S.W., is gratefully acknowledged.

[1] Following Bach and Wyden (1968), marital conflicts are defined as nonproductive when they cause psychological and/or physical hurt, decrease interpersonal trust, and fail to generate constructive changes in subsequent marital interaction.

19

tense unconscious anxiety that has been stimulated by an actual or anticipated increase in interpersonal intimacy. From an interpersonal perspective, the goal is to decrease the level of (actual or anticipated) intimacy.

3. Once conflict behavior is triggered, the level of verbal and/or physical destructiveness begins to escalate. This escalation is maintained within system-specific limits by two factors: (a) the emergence of conflict-generated anxiety, and (b) the reemergence of a fundamental need for intimacy. When the combined intensity of these two forces exceeds that of intimacy anxiety, conciliatory behavior is stimulated, leading to the eventual reemergence of intimacy. This is temporarily gratifying, but soon the intimacy begins to stimulate anxiety, and defensive conflict is again triggered.

The entire circular process is diagrammed in Figure 1. In this diagram, the major components of this intimacy-conflict cycle are connected by solid lines, with arrows indicating the direction of movement around the circle. The dotted lines illustrate the pathways of reinforcement and negative feedback by means of which system homeostasis (Watzlawick et al., 1967) is maintained. In the following sections, each aspect of this diagram will be considered in detail.

INTIMACY

Intimacy is characterized (Random House Dictionary, 1968) by (a) a close, familiar, and usually affectionate or loving personal relationship; (b) sexual relations; (c) detailed and deep knowledge and understanding arising from close personal connection or familiar experience. The level of acceptable (tolerable) intimacy in a marital relationship is determined by the complex process by which an interpersonal system is "calibrated" or "set" (Watzlawick et al., 1967). As two people develop a relationship, they communicate, overtly and covertly, a set of expectations, desires, needs and fears regarding the kind of relationship they want. Over time, this process leads to the creation of implicit and explicit relationship rules (Jackson, 1965) that define a range of acceptable deviation for a variety of interactional behaviors. Once these rules have been created, the system is said to be calibrated or set. One important dimension of a marital system's calibration is the degree and limits of acceptable intimacy.

From an intrapsychic perspective, relationship rules are compromises between the wishes (conscious and unconscious) and fears (conscious and unconscious) of the two interacting individuals. The wish for intimacy has its roots in the most fundamental needs of the human

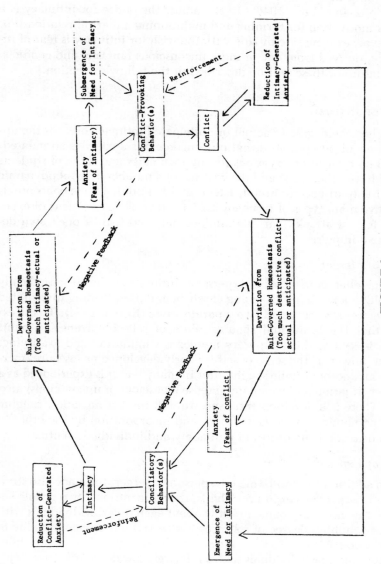

FIGURE 1
Intimacy-Conflict Cycle

organism — to be held, touched, comforted, and nourished. In infancy, when these needs are not fulfilled, babies fail to develop and may even die (Spitz and Wolf, 1946). In the adult, the desire for intimacy is a major motivation for forming and maintaining a marital relationship. However, existing side by side with the wish for intimacy is fear of intimacy, derived from one or more unconscious fantasies and conflicts. The nature of these will be described in the following section.

FEAR OF INTIMACY

When the degree of actual or anticipated intimacy exceeds the upper limit of acceptable deviation, unconscious anxiety is stimulated. Based on clinical observations (of my own cases and those of students that I have supervised) and the writings of a number of psychodynamic theorists (particularly Freud, Klein, and Erikson), I have conceptualized five main types of intimacy anxiety: fear of merger, fear of exposure, fear of attack, fear of abandonment, and fear of one's own destructive impulses.

Fear of Merger

One characteristic of interpersonal intimacy is that it periodically stimulates a relative weakening of self-boundaries, leading to a limited and temporary merger of two separate selves (Kuten, 1974). To the extent that the individual spouses' sense of self-cohesiveness (Kohut, 1971) is secure, this temporary merger is stimulating and gratifying. When, however, the sense of self is poorly developed or insecure, merger with another (while sought after in many ways) is experienced as a danger situation and stimulates intense (conscious or unconscious) anxiety. There is a developmental spectrum of merger anxieties, ranging from psychotic fears of engulfment and incorporation by the other to more neurotic fears of loss of autonomy and individual identity.

Fear of Exposure

In addition to stimulating interpersonal merger, intimacy also stimulates interpersonal exposure. This is, the more intimate two people become, the more they come to know about each other. Individuals with a relatively high degree of self-acceptance and self-esteem are able to experience such exposure as intimacy-enhancing and relatively nonthreatening. For individuals with a relatively low degree of self-acceptance and self-esteem, however, exposure is highly threatening. Such individuals are intensely afraid of being exposed as weak, inadequate, repulsive, etc., and of experiencing the marked sense of inferiority and shame they fear would accompany such exposure. When this fear is stimulated, it leads to a defensive wish (usually unconscious) to avoid or terminate intimate interaction.

Fear of Attack

This form of anxiety is generated when current interpersonal experiences stimulate unconscious wishes and fears associated with one or both of two major developmental periods: the period of developing basic trust versus mistrust (Erikson, 1950) and the Oedipus/Elektra period (Freud, 1916–1917).

During the period of basic trust versus mistrust, the fundamental issue is whether or not the human environment is experienced as warm, nurturing, and dependable. When it is, a sense of basic trust in oneself and the world is developed. When it is not, overwhelming frustration stimulates intense aggressive, destructive impulses that are projected onto environmental figures, leading to fears of persecutory attack and annihilation (Klein and Riviere, 1964). These fears persist at an unconscious level and become a significant factor in determining the structure of later intimate relationships.

The major conflicts of the Oedipus/Elektra period involve sexual impulses and wishes in relation to the opposite-sex parent and aggressive impulses and wishes in relation to the same-sex parent. These impulses and wishes generate intense anxiety, stemming (in part) from fear of genital mutilation or castration by a jealous and vengeful same-sex parent. In the course of normal development, these wishes and fears are successfully repressed and/or sublimated (Freud, 1916–1917). When development is impaired, however, they continue to exert a powerful negative effect on current life experiences, particularly those involving interpersonal intimacy.

When interpersonal intimacy exceeds acceptable limits, one or both of these two forms of attack anxiety may be aroused. In general, preoedipal (persecutory) anxiety is more likely to be prominent in individuals with more severe impairment of psychological development (psychotic and borderline personalities), and oedipal anxiety is more likely to be prominent in less severely impaired individuals (neurotics).

Fear of Abandonment

As with fear of attack, fear of abandonment also has oedipal and preoedipal roots. Preoedipal fear of abandonment has been discussed by Freud (1926) as fear of loss of the love object. In Freud's formulation, emphasis is placed on the feeling of being overwhelmed and helpless when the love object is gone. In those adults whose childhood has been marked by excessive or traumatic separations, an unconscious link between intimacy and loss is created. As a result, experiences of intimacy stimulate unconscious fears of being traumatically separated from the intimate other. One way of defending against this anxiety is to reduce interpersonal intimacy, and one way of reducing intimacy is to generate conflict. In the Oedipus/Elektra period, one major source of anxiety is the previously described fear of attack by a jealous and enraged same-sex parent. However, this developmental period also stimulates a very different type of anxiety, having to do with fear of abandonment by a defeated and vanquished same-sex parent. The dilemma facing the child is that to the extent that she or he is successful in winning the rivalry with the same-sex parent, the much needed love and support of this parent will be lost. Normally, this anxiety is mastered by means of identification with the same-sex parent (Freud, 1916–1917). In pathological development, it persists unconsciously and is stimulated whenever unconscious impulses derived from the Oedipus/Elektra period are aroused.

Fear of One's Own Destructive Impulses

The importance of the role of anxiety aroused by one's own aggressive, destructive impulses in relation to intimate others has been particularly emphasized by Klein and Riviere (1964). In her conceptualization of depressive anxiety, Klein suggests that during the depressive-position phase of development, there is increasing awareness of the parent(s) as "whole objects" who can be both gratifying (good) and frustrating (bad). This awareness is of special significance during those times when, in response to frustration, the infant becomes enraged at the "bad" parent(s). Klein suggests that at those moments, intensely hostile and destructive fantasies emerge, connected with impulses to injure or destroy the frustrating object. These, in turn, lead to intense fear of losing the good object as a result of one's own destructive impulses (depressive anxiety). When depressive anxiety has not been resolved during the course of childhood development, it becomes a powerful potential stimulus for defensive behavior in adult intimate relationships.

CONFLICT

When unconscious fear of intimacy reaches a level at which it threatens to break through into conscious awareness, defensive conflict behavior is mobilized. The actual methods by which overt conflict is triggered vary from couple to couple, but in general this takes the form of one spouse saying or doing something that diminishes or threatens the self-esteem of the other. This leads to an equally defensive-attacking response by the second spouse, and an escalating spiral of attack and counterattack is generated. With some couples the roles of initiator and responder are fairly fixed; with other couples there is a more or less random fluctuation. In either case, both spouses are equally anxious, equally defensive, and make an equal (though not necessarily identical) contribution to the initiation and promulgation of the conflict.

REDUCTION OF INTIMACY-GENERATED ANXIETY — EMERGENCE OF NEED FOR INTIMACY

At some point during the course of a conflictual episode, as interpersonal distance increases, intimacy anxiety begins to diminish. As this happens, the conflicting spouses begin to experience the reemergence of a wish for intimacy. As noted previously, this wish is a fundamental one whose roots are very deep. Thus, when interpersonal conflict has sufficiently reduced the level of intimacy anxiety, there is a natural upsurge of the basic need for intimacy.

CONFLICT-GENERATED ANXIETY

At the same time that intimacy anxiety is being reduced and a wish for intimacy is beginning to reemerge, the conflict itself stimulates anxiety. This anxiety is most often connected with fear of abandonment and/or fear of loss of control of one's own aggressive impulses. These anxieties stimulate what Klein and Riviere (1964) have described as a need for reparation, a wish to repair the ambivalently loved (and hated) other. This wish, in turn, stimulates interpersonal moves toward reconciliation.

CONCILIATORY BEHAVIOR

When the combined intensity of conflict-generated anxiety and the reemergence of intimacy needs exceeds that of intimacy-generated anxiety, conciliatory behavior is initiated by one or both spouses. As with conflict-provoking behavior, the particular form of conciliatory behavior varies from couple to couple. Frequently some form of reparation is involved in the conciliatory process. This may be verbal (e.g., "I'm sorry I hurt your feelings"), behavioral (e.g., giving a gift), or both. If each partner has reached an approximately similar psychological state, such initiatives lead to the reinstatement of intimacy. When there is a discrepancy, and the noninitiating spouse is still feeling defensive, the conciliatory initiative will be rebuffed, and another round of conflict set in motion. Eventually, the balance of forces shifts in both spouses, and the conciliation process is carried to completion.

While the conciliation process leads to the temporary cessation of hostility, it does not lead to any basic changes in the intrapsychic and interpersonal roots of the conflict-generating process. Therefore, repetitive cycles of destructive, nonproductive conflict continue to occur.

REINFORCEMENT AND NEGATIVE FEEDBACK

The mechanisms that maintain the repetitive cycles of nonproductive conflict are reinforcement and negative feedback. Reinforcement is the process by which the consequences of an act increase the probability of the recurrence of that act in the future under similar stimulus conditions (Kanfer and Phillips, 1970). In the intimacy-conflict cycle, reinforcement is especially significant in regard to conflict-provoking behavior and conciliatory behavior. As indicated by the dotted lines in Figure 1, the major reinforcer for both of these acts is anxiety reduction. Conflict-provoking behavior leads to the reduction of intimacy-generated anxiety; conciliatory behavior leads to the reduction of conflict-generated anxiety. As a result of these reinforcement contingencies, the probability of the future recurrence of conflict-provoking and conciliatory behavior is maintained at a high level.

Negative feedback is the process by which deviations from the limits of system calibration are counteracted, in this instance by means of communication (overt or covert) to discontinue the deviant behavior (Watzlawick et al., 1967). In the intimacy-conflict cycle, the two major deviations occur when either intimacy or conflict exceeds acceptable limits. When the former occurs, conflict-provoking behavior is generated, resulting in an implicit message to stop intimacy behavior. Likewise, when conflict behavior exceeds acceptable limits, the emergence of conciliatory behavior is a signal to stop conflicting. By means of these negative feedback signals, both intimacy and conflict are maintained within implicitly agreed-upon limits. However, there is a tendency for these limits to change over time, with the acceptable level of intimacy becoming reduced and the acceptable level of conflict increasing. As this happens, there is an increasing possibility of a destructive positive-feedback spiral, or "runaway," leading either to the destruction of the marriage or the physical injury or death of one or both of the spouses.

THERAPEUTIC IMPLICATIONS

The major therapeutic implication of the intimacy-conflict model is that repetitive, nonproductive marital conflict behavior is a multidimensional phenomenon and that the treatment of conflictual couples should be based on a detailed understanding of both the interpersonal and the intrapsychic aspects of this process. Once this understanding has been obtained, a variety of therapeutic strategies and techniques can be usefully employed to promote constructive change.

Often, it is important to direct early therapeutic interventions toward improving communication, especially in the area of conflict management. Such techniques as behavior rehearsal, modeling, and contracting (Eisler and Hersen, 1973) are useful for this purpose. The major goals of this phase of the work are to diminish the likelihood of a destructive conflictual "runaway," and to create an atmosphere in which an exploration of each spouse's intimacy anxieties can be undertaken.

As early as possible, detailed histories of each spouse's experiences in his or her family of origin are obtained. These histories are then utilized as the foundation for an ongoing examination of the transference connections between the current marital system and the two families of origin. As therapy progresses, each spouse's dreams become particularly important vehicles for exploring the nature of their unconscious transferences. I have found it very useful to ask spouses to write down their dreams routinely and to note when the dream occurred, thus developing a cumulative record of each spouse's unconscious wishes, fears, and conflicts. This record can be related to ongoing interactions in the spouses' lives, including those interactions that occur during the therapy meetings.

As the nature of the intrapsychic and interpersonal dynamics of the marriage are explored, the spouses not only become more aware of their own wishes, fears, and defenses, but they also (and equally important), become more aware of the wishes, fears, and defenses of the other. This increased understanding promotes the development of empathy, concern, and trust, which are essential components of lasting intimacy.

During the course of therapy, the behavioral focus and the intrapsychic focus combine and alternate with each other. The overall process of change in successful marital therapy with conflictual couples involves a series of mutually reinforcing changes in both behavioral and intrapsychic dynamics. As the overt conflictual behaviors of the two spouses become less destructive, the possibility of intrapsychic exploration becomes available. As this process is successful in diminishing the degree of intimacy-anxiety in both spouses and in promoting the development of empathy and trust, intimate behavior becomes more frequent and longer lasting, and conflict behavior becomes less frequent and less destructive. Eventually, a new equilibrium is established in which both genuine intimacy and constructive, problem-solving forms of conflict resolution contribute to the ongoing development of each spouse and of the marital system.

CLINICAL ILLUSTRATION

To illustrate the observational foundations for the intimacy-conflict model and the applications of the model to concrete clinical situations, a detailed clinical example will be presented and discussed.

Mr. and Mrs. X had been married for eight years at the time they began marital therapy. Their major presenting problem was a chronic pattern of repetitive, nonproductive conflict that began shortly after they were married. At various times, these conflicts had generated a wide variety of interpersonally destructive behaviors, including sarcasm, insults, name-calling, and (occasionally) physical violence (pushing, hitting, slapping, etc.). When therapy began, the frequency and intensity of the conflicts had been increasing.

During the course of Mr. and Mrs. X's therapy, the nature of the intrapsychic and interpersonal forces that stimulated and maintained their conflictual cycles became increasingly clear. To illustrate the nature of these dynamics, the categories of the intimacy-conflict model will be utilized as a conceptual framework within which the observational data will be presented.

FEAR OF INTIMACY

As therapy progressed, evidence of intense intimacy anxiety in both spouses emerged. Mr. X's anxieties were primarily fear of exposure, fear of attack, and fear of his own destructive impulses; Mrs. X's anxieties were primarily fear of merger and fear of abandonment. The existence of these anxieties was inferred from a variety of clinical observations, including the information that the spouses presented about their families of origin, their transference reactions, and especially their dreams. Because of the central importance of dreams as a vehicle for understanding unconscious dynamics, some of Mr. and Mrs. X's dreams will be presented in detail, along with my interpretations of the dreams.[2]

[2] As with all dream interpretations, the ones to be presented are inferential. They are offered as hypotheses whose validity, while by no means proven, has been supported by a variety of observations — the spouses' associations to the dreams, their transference reactions to each other and the therapist, memories of early experiences, etc.

Mr. X

Dream No. 1. Mr. X is alone in bed when his sister-in-law (his wife's older sister) climbs into bed with him, and they begin to have a very pleasurable sexual experience. They are interrupted, however, by the entrance of Mrs. X, her sister's husband, Mrs. X's mother, and other members of Mrs. X's extended family. Mr. X feels exposed, ashamed, guilty, and fearful of being either physically attacked or verbally ridiculed by his older and stronger brother-in-law.

Interpretation. I view this as essentially an oedipal dream, in which Mr. X's fear of exposure of his incestuous impulses toward his mother (symbolized in the dream by his sister-in-law), his feelings of weakness and powerlessness in relation to his father (symbolized in the dream by his brother-in-law), and his fear of attack from his father are all highlighted.

Dream No. 2. This example is actually a sequence of three dreams that occurred on successive nights while Mr. and Mrs. X were visiting Mr. X's parents. On the first night, Mr. X dreamt that he was to star in a TV show. During rehearsal, a woman is coaching one of the other male stars, and Mr. X feels jealous. Then the show starts, and Mr. X feels his performance is poor. He feels exposed, humiliated, and angry at the woman for choosing to coach the other man instead of him. The next night, Mr. X dreamt that his wife had cancer and was dying. On the third night, Mr. X had two dreams — in the first, he had been arrested and was in jail awaiting trial; in the second dream, he was stopped by two policemen on the street, backed against a wall, and searched.

Interpretation. In the first dream of this sequence, Mr. X's possessive wishes toward his mother (the coach) and jealousy of her attentions toward his father (the other male star) are highlighted. In the second dream, murderous impulses toward his mother (symbolized by his wife) are in the foreground. The sequence of the first and second dreams suggests that Mr. X is unconsciously struggling with unresolved hostility toward his mother as a consequence of her frustration of his oedipal desires (by choosing his father over him). This aspect of the Oedipus complex has been emphasized particularly by Kohut (1971) in his discussions of narcissistic rage. In the third dream, Mr. X's anxiety and guilt feelings are central. Again, the sequence suggests that a major stimulus for these emotions is unresolved hostility toward his mother.

Mrs. X

Dream No. 1. Mrs. X is in a house with a large number of people. Mr. X calls on the telephone and he is angry and impatient. He says,

"Where are you?" Mrs. X says she doesn't know what he's talking about. Mr. X goes on, "You're supposed to pick me up. You messed up my schedule, so I had to stay here at the office, where I'm spending the night." Then Mr. X hangs up the phone. Mrs. X looks around the room and notices that people are walking around. Then somebody picks up some food so a man can eat quickly and leave.

Interpretation. Mrs. X's fear of being abandoned by Mr. X because of his rage at her for failing to live up to his expectations (particularly in the area of meeting his instrumental needs) is the major theme of this dream. The connections between the dream and Mrs. X's experiences in her family of origin were readily apparent. During much of her childhood, Mrs. X was embroiled in a pattern of repetitive conflict with her parents, especially her father. In most instances, these conflicts began when Mrs. X failed to perform some expected function (e.g., doing the dishes, turning off the lights, etc.) to her father's satisfaction. On a number of occasions, the conflicts escalated to a point where Mrs. X's parents threatened to throw her out of the house, and on at least one occasion they actually did so.

Dream No. 2. A prima donna is giving a concert, and everyone is scurrying around to please him/her (it was not clear in the dream whether the prima donna is a man or woman). Mrs. X is assigned to the task of going to the fish store to get fish to cook. She feels bossed around but follows orders, gets the fish, and begins to cook it. As she's cooking, she feels angry and exploited.

Interpretation. This dream highlights one of Mrs. X's major unconscious conflicts—idealization versus exploitation. The figure of the prima donna symbolizes Mrs. X's wish to attach herself to (merge with) an idealized figure from whom she can derive a vicarious sense of self-cohesiveness and self-esteem (Kohut, 1971). As demonstrated in the remainder of the dream, however, this wish is opposed by the fear of exploitation by the idealized other. This conflict played a major role in Mrs. X's relationship with her husband in which she alternated between idealizing him and feeling exploited by him. The origins of this conflict in Mrs. X's relationship with her father emerged very clearly during the course of therapy.

Conflict-Provoking Behavior as a Defense Against Anxiety

The primary evidence for the hypothesis that conflict-provoking behavior is (at least in part) a response to anxiety about interpersonal intimacy consists of observations of regularly recurring behavioral sequences in which conflict behavior short-circuits the build-up of intimacy (actual or anticipated). Two particularly clear examples of this pattern occurring between Mr. and Mrs. X are the following:

On the first occasion, Mrs. X had made a sexual advance by asking Mr. X if he would be interested in making love later that evening. This was, at the time, fairly unusual behavior for Mrs. X, a fact about which Mr. X had often complained (e.g., "How come I'm the one who always takes the initiative in our sex life?"). Thus, Mrs. X's sexual initiative represented a direct gratification of an often-expressed wish of Mr. X's, and there would seem to be good reason to expect Mr. X's subsequent behavior to reflect pleasure and gratitude. In fact, precisely the opposite took place. He be became grouchy, irritable, and preoccupied with thoughts about his business. Eventually, this behavior ignited Mrs. X (who was extremely sensitive about being "ignored" or "taken for granted"), and a prolonged and heated argument ensued. Needless to say, there was no sex that night or for many nights to follow. In discussing this experience some weeks after it happened, Mr. X remembered experiencing a powerful but vague sense of anxiety following Mrs. X's sexual advance.

In the second example, Mr. X had been behaving in a very considerate and nurturing way toward his wife. Over the years of their marriage, the relatively low frequency of this type of behavior had been a major complaint of Mrs. X's. On this particular occasion, she responded to Mr. X's attentions by asking him: "How come you're being so nice to me? Did I do something right? Are you feeling guilty about something?" Such a response would be disconcerting to anyone but was guaranteed to infuriate Mr. X, who was extremely sensitive about being criticized or accused of wrong-doing. Therefore, it was highly predictable that Mr. X responded to Mrs. X's statement with angry withdrawal, and another cycle of conflict was underway.

CONFLICT AND RECONCILIATION

Once a conflict had been precipitated, the subsequent sequence of events was highly predictable. Angry accusations and blaming statements were exchanged, sometimes accompanied by sarcasm, name-calling, and (occasionally) pushing, hitting, or slapping. This would be followed by a period (lasting from a few hours to a few days) of hostile withdrawal, during which the spouses would either not speak at all or would do so in a cold and distant way. Eventually, one of them would break the ice and indicate a wish to make up. Sometimes this led quickly to a reconciliation; at other times, two or three cycles of approach and withdrawal were necessary before a reconciliation was effected.

This, then, would lead to a period of no conflict, during which the level of intimacy would begin to build, until a new stimulus would trigger another round of conflict and reconciliation.

DISCUSSION

The model of marital conflict and intimacy described and illustrated in the previous sections of this paper is congruent in many ways with other recent efforts to integrate psychodynamic and social-learning theory (e.g., Dollard and Miller, 1950; Sloane, 1969; Wachtel, 1977). Of particular importance is the work of Wachtel (1977), who presents a compelling model of human behavior based on the notion of intrapsychic and interpersonal feedback loops. Building on the work of Dollard and Miller (1950), Wachtel places particular emphasis on the role of unconscious anxiety as both a stimulus of, and a response to, maladaptive (defensive) interpersonal behavior. A central postulate is that defensive patterns of behavior reinforce the persistence of anxiety by eliminating opportunities for new learning to take place. Specifically, they prevent the individual from learning (via extinction) that the original childhood danger situation (real or fantasied) that stimulated the development of the anxiety is not, at least at present, a realistic threat. Thus, intrapsychic anxiety stimulates interpersonal defensive behavior, and this in turn reinforces the persistence of the anxiety. From a therapeutic point of view, Wachtel strongly urges the integration of active, behaviorally oriented techniques (e.g., systematic desensitization, behavior rehearsal, modeling, etc.) with psychodynamic interventions (exploration, reflection, interpretation, etc.).

When applied to the phenomenon of marital conflict, Wachtel's analysis leads to some very fruitful insights. As noted in the delineation of the intimacy-conflict cycle, unconscious anxiety in relation to interpersonal intimacy is seen as a major stimulus of interpersonal conflict behavior. Of equal importance is the notion that repetitive cycles of interpersonal conflict behavior are a major cause of the persistence of intimacy anxiety. Because the episodes of conflict interrupt the development of intimacy, they block opportunities for "natural desensitization" to take place and thus contribute to the perpetuation of the anxiety. Over time, an intrapsychic-interpersonal feedback loop is generated, in which anxiety and interpersonal conflict are mutually reinforcing.

In agreement with Wachtel, I believe that the major therapeutic implication of an integrative conceptualization of human behavior is the great value of combining behavioral and psychodynamic methods of assessment and intervention. Marital and family therapy offer particularly fruitful opportunities for such an integration. The presence of multiple family members provides a context in which such interpersonal technqiues as behavior rehearsal, behavior-contracting, and modeling can be readily utilized to promote behavior change directly. At the same time, intrapsychic work (particularly dream and transference interpretation) offers unique opportunities for loosening up longstanding patterns of anxiety and defense that have been contributing to the continuation of maladaptive patterns of behavior and for promoting the development of empathy and trust. The integrated combination of behavioral and psychodynamic interventions offers, in my opinion, far greater therapeutic leverage than either approach by itself.

References

Bach, G. & Wyden, P. (1968), *The Intimate Enemy.* New York: Morrow.
Dollard, J. & Miller, N. (1950), *Personality and Psychotherapy.* New York: McGraw-Hill.
Eisler, R. & Hersen, M. (1973), Behavioral techniques in family-oriented crisis intervention. *Arch. Gen. Psychiat.*, 28:111–116.
Erikson, E. (1950), *Childhood and Society.* New York: Norton.
Freud, S. (1916–1917), Introductory lectures on psycho-analysis. *Standard Edition*, 15 & 16. London: Hogarth Press, 1963.
———— (1926), Inhibitions, symptoms and anxiety. *Standard Edition*, 20: 75–174. London: Hogarth Press, 1959.
Gelles, R. (1972), *The Violent Home.* Beverly Hills: Sage.
Gurman, A. & Rice, D., eds. (1975), *Couples in Conflict.* New York: Aronson.
Jackson, D. D. (1965), The study of the family. *Fam. Proc.*, 4:1–21.
Kanfer, F. & Phillips, J. (1970), *Learning Foundations of Behavior Therapy.* New York: Wiley.
Klein, M. & Riviere, J., eds. (1964), *Love, Hate, and Reparation.* New York: Norton.
Kohut, H. (1971), *The Analysis of the Self.* New York: International Universities Press.
Kuten, J. (1974), *Coming Together — Coming Apart.* New York: Macmillan.
Random House Dictionary of the English Language (1968), New York: Random House.
Sloane, R. (1969), The converging paths of behavior therapy and psychotherapy. *Amer. J. Psychiat.*, 125:49–57.
Spitz, R. & Wolf, K. (1946), Anaclitic depression. *The Psychoanalytic Study of the Child*, 2:313–342. New York: International Universities Press.
Wachtel, P. (1977), *Psychoanalysis and Behavior Therapy: Toward an Integration.* New York: Basic Books.
Watzlawick, P., Beavin, J., & Jackson, D. D. (1967), *Pragmatics of Human Communication.* New York: Norton.
Wolfgang, M. (1958), *Patterns in Criminal Homicide.* New York: Wiley.

Unified Health Services
and Family-Focused Primary Care

STEPHEN FLECK

Well over 25 years ago the United Nations and the World Health Organization asserted the unity and indivisibility of health, yet medical dichotomizing in practice and theory remains with us (Balint, 1957; Binger, 1945; Dubos, 1968). Progress toward achieving optimal human health has been neither uniform nor holistic. Modern medicine began its rapid, albeit jerky and discontinuous march toward scientific clarification of illnesses and scientific foundation of treatments some six score years ago. It has, consequently, become attractive and practical to favor categorical programs, either for those illnesses which have arrived or nearly arrived in the scientifically documented and treatable sphere, or in response to acute and urgent needs like epidemics. Some forms of ill health, however, have suffered a reverse fate during this period; because of unpleasantness, continuing inaccessibility to explanatory causal chains and great manpower requirements for adequate but not necessarily scientific treatment, they have been relegated to the back burners and, in the case of mental illness, even to the backwoods (Dingle, 1973; Pasamanick, 1972).

While the treatment or management of the severely mentally disturbed throughout human history is a far from glorious chapter of human behavior, and while such patients often have not even been admitted to the circle of ill people deserving of care and sympathy, the dichotomy between physical and mental illness is recent and parallels the discovery of infectious agents and the subsequent scientific elucidation

Stephen Fleck, M.D., is Professor of Psychiatry and Public Health, Department of Psychiatry, Yale University School of Medicine, New Haven, Conn.

The editorial assistance of Ms. Rebecca Saletan is gratefully acknowledged.

of metabolic disorders and deficiency states. In ancient Persia no such distinction was made when Al-Rashi cured the king of his paralysis by making him violently angry. Physicians know that chronic illnesses are crucially affected by psychosocial and emotional parameters, but rarely pay much heed to these parameters in practice and treatment, having learned little about them in their medical education. The emphasis in medical schools on specialization and scientification of medicine and on painstaking study of organs and body systems has left the psychiatrist by default as a kind of caretaker of the human side of practice, at least in large medical centers where most students learn their trade (Fleck, 1966; Linn, 1964; Vandervoort and Ransom, 1973).

The general hospital, however, is a poor locus for health care. Hospitals are disease-oriented institutions prepared for complicated emergencies of any sort, that have become increasingly economically wasteful in the routine care of self-limited diseases, or for health promotion and preventive programs. Likewise, hospitals with major teaching tasks are possibly least equipped, prepared, or inclined to undertake routine outpatient services, primary or health care. The surgeons want to use their expensive hardware for complex operations, the internists look for diagnostic problems, the obstetricians want to deliver babies, not abort fetuses, and the psychiatrists want major psychoses for their wards and neurotic but educated patients for their outpatient clinics. The reasons for these predilections are not capricious. They derive from the teaching and research missions of academic staffs who are equally concerned with rendering optimal patient care, but not for unselected patient populations (Lucente and Fleck, 1972; Vandervoort and Ransom, 1973).

Primary medical care and health care must be extended to all people — the well and the unwell, the poor and the rich, the misfits and the powerful. Complete medical and health care to all people cannot and need not be rendered only by physicians. It takes teams to do all the screening and routine care for reasons of economy — economy of manpower, of skill resources, and of money.

Observations of medical practice indicate that some of what general physicians do during their 60-hour weeks and some of what they do not do could and ought to be done by physician-associates, nurse-clinicians, public health nurses and social workers. In this way family-focused medicine can also be practiced even if physicians on the team want to see only individuals and eschew group work or family treatment per se. However, they must understand the principles of family dynamics and of intrapersonal, interpersonal, and social systems as they operate to maintain balances between cells and their components on one hand and the human and nonhuman environments on the other. It is these balances between tissue integrity and environmental impacts which determine, aside from a subjective sense of well-being, the differences between what we label illness and health respectively or abnormal and normal developments (Dingle, 1973; Dubos, 1968).

Between the individual and the larger environment, increasingly populated with humans and increasingly dangerous to humans, stands the family, responsible for personal development and integrity. Promoting and safeguarding family health therefore must be part of individual and societal health programs, and unless this is done all these interrelated systems must suffer. Any community (neighborhood) health service, therefore, should be so organized that it can render family health care and nurture the family as carefully as we calculate feeding formulae for infants (Beloff, 1968; Royal College of General Practitioners, 1967).

The outstanding lesson of the first decade of the community mental health center development seems to be that it was the right idea in the wrong specialty. All the organizational ideas and principles which underlie the mental health center for total care to a population with five nuclear service areas—emergency, consultation, inpatient and partial hospitalization, and community participation in leadership and administration—all these are sound, except for the lack of emphasis on the family as a clinical focus. More importantly, all this should apply to health and medical care based on a neighborhood health station or "human services center" with mental health or psychiatry as one element in the total care spectrum; instead, mental health centers have been confronted with all health and related social problems, as if they could function like primary care providers. Out on a limb without other health and medical supports, often disconnected from social agencies and caught in sociopolitical crosscurrents, many centers have floundered from having neither the equipment and design to render all the clinical services demanded and needed, nor the staff prepared to cope knowledgeably with necessary sociopolitical advocacy tasks (Group for Advancement of Psychiatry, 1968; Whybrow, 1972).

Many mental health professionals are latter-day veterans of such community health battles before the establishment of neighborhood health stations, followed by health maintenance organizations. Nothing in medical history, which usually is ignored anyway, has so dramatically illustrated the un-wisdom of categorizing and fragmenting health care as have these experiences of the last decade. A New York City politician put it in a nutshell when he indicated that he was

not going to vote another penny for mental health until the kids' teeth
were fixed. One important lesson professionals can learn from this is
that they must observe the boundaries of knowledge and competence
and not redefine a specialty or profession in response to identified and
urgent needs, many of which drastically affect health and psychosocial
well-being. But slum housing, school inadequacies, political ill will
and discriminatory practices, especially discriminatory law enforcement, are not primary health problems. These social and political
shortcomings have long been known to the public health officer, but
traditionally have not deterred him from doing first things first, namely
establishing preventive programs and health surveillance while tending
to related sociopolitical problems through negotiation and collaboration with community leaders and legislators. He limited his role to that
of consultant to political operations without functioning as a part of
them or becoming a care agent (Elliott, 1964; Group for the Advancement of Psychiatry, 1968; Whybrow, 1972; and Unpublished Data
from Connecticut Mental Health Center).

The mental health center experience has demonstrated that health
and medical care as systems (and as human values) are interrelated
with sociopolitical systems as well as with basic biomedical disciplines.
As disciplines, psychiatry and other mental health professions constitute a bridge between the basic scientist-clinicians and the sociocultural agents concerned with human development and welfare. The family
in turn is a bridge between every individual and his community.

Besides unifying and integrating health services, not only care delivery systems but also preventive and health-promoting programs, we
must also change the exclusive focus on the individual and view the
family as the basic clinical and health-promoting unit. Having paid
only lip sevice to the idea that medical care and health problems have
been familial through the ages from the Hippocratic oath to the recent
establishment of the Academy of Family Practice, we must now recognize in practice that, genes and integral physiological and metabolic
development aside, family patterns and organizations have great impact on health and disease (Ackerman, 1958; Bruch, 1940; Ehrenwald,
1960; Grolnick, 1972, Lidz, Fleck, and Cornelison, 1965; Meissner,
1966; Richardson, 1948; Tuckman and Regan, 1967; Winnicott, 1965).
Amplified by family therapy experiences, a body of knowledge about
the family as a system now exists (Ackerman, 1958; Fleck, 1972;
Howells, 1963; Lidz, 1963).

THE FAMILY AND HEALTH

The modern family, especially in its nuclear form in developed societies, is less engaged in survival tasks in the sense of basic life essentials than it was in the past or still is in agricultural nations. The family has become a system whose cohesion and function depend primarily on the interpersonal and affective relationships within it in the pursuit of its basic tasks, which as far as societies are concerned remain primarily preparation and introduction of the younger generation into adulthood. As the basic social and interpersonal system, the family's operation must be understood and be subject to clinical scrutiny, like any other organismic or environmental system which has a bearing on health and disease. Whether or not parents are constrained by economic, nutritional, social, or other vicissitudes, society expects them, and they usually intend, to cope with the basic family tasks. These are nurturing and teaching relationships and the utile and symbolic communication modes of the culture, and guiding the emancipation of young people into adult society. Although adulthood may be very different in different cultures in terms of economic independence, educational goals, and geographic and emotional distance from the family of origin, all societies expect young people at a certain age to become full-fledged, gender-typical, productive participants in societal life, who in turn procreate and provide continuity for that society and its culture (Erikson, 1964; Fleck, 1972; Lidz, 1963; Winnicott, 1965).

Clinicians and health professionals must assess this family system as functional or malfunctional at particular phases of its evolution, and as healthful or pathogenic at a particular stage or task performance. "Healthful" here emphatically includes not only physical health and development but also age-appropriate emotional and psychosocial competence of all family members. The teaching of health behavior is among these family tasks. Parents function also as coping models during crises and stress, and as gender-specific role models in their own daily behavior, especially with each other, i.e., how they live as a couple and as parents. For instance, certain neurotic defense patterns are apt to be repeated from generation to generation. Parental exploitative behavior toward society can be learned in the family, as can addictive propensities or pathological suspiciousness of the world around the family (Ehrenwald, 1960; Grolnick, 1972; Lidz et al., 1965).

Although the family as a unit of clinical investigation and research has come into its own only in recent decades, cumulative clinical evidence has made it imperative that health professionals always be concerned with the functioning of family systems (Richardson, 1948).

Assessment of the family system must be both cross-sectional and longitudinal. The "Family History" must be more informative than a list of various relatives, their ages and the diseases they have conquered or succumbed to. It must include the history of the marriage and marital adjustment, the planning or not-planning of offspring and the couple's adjustment to becoming a family. Role configurations in the household as well as the nature and possible sources of role conflicts must be noted, for instance significant differences in the spouses' background values and cultures (Blood, 1963; Group for the Advancement of Psychiatry, 1954; Kreitman, 1964). Direct observations of family behavior in the home or as a group in a clinic setting will also reveal such conflicts, besides being the only way in which to observe communication modes, parental leadership qualities, the question of age-appropriate behaviors, or the possible scapegoating of a member (Fleck, 1972; Howells, 1963; Jackson, 1966).

Furthermore, examining the family as a system requires attention to task performance in system terms, i.e., how the previously cited general tasks are defined and performed with respect to the age-related needs of all members and how a sense of family boundary and identity is effected and managed. Neither social psychiatry nor social medicine can become substantive without such comprehension and the clinical skills to deal with this basic social system — the family (Howells, 1963; Richardson, 1948; Vandervoort and Ransom, 1973).

All this leads to several considerations of the family's roles in health and disease. One facet is that health is a goal whose achievement depends very much on health behavior, which like all behavior is shaped to a crucial extent in the family system. Public health agents are acquainted with conflicts between the family unit and specific health measures such as universally imposed vaccination, flouridation of water supplies, or getting an identified dangerous patient to a psychiatrist or into a mental hospital. Yet, other forms of prevention are clearly, albeit less directly, dependent upon family influences. It may be true that there is no form of addictive behavior that does not have some roots in early family experiences and relationships. Eating habits may be the most important potentially addictive behavior from a preventive standpoint. It is now clear that a great deal of cardiovascular disease could be prevented by more healthful diet, one of the few issues that cuts across all socioeconomic classes even though the reasons for injudicious eating may be different among the poor than among the very affluent. Exercise and leisure time utilization are not only important family functions, but also important opportunities for learning lifelong healthful habits. The preventive value of regular physical activity has been elegantly demonstrated in a number of studies, especially in England (Morris, 1973a, 1973b).

Besides health behavior of this type, more tangible measures like seeking specific preventive health care, annual visits to the pediatrician and dentist, or following up indications of school-identified defects or handicaps, are also learned in the family. Consequently, one of the important functions of any health service worthy of its name is to promote positive health behavior in family units beginning with marital and reproductive health care and guidance prior to marriage. Effective preventive medicine requires attention not only to adequate prenatal care, particularly to the future mother's nutrition, but also to the spouses' preparation for parenthood, including the wholesome spacing of children, who preferably are not produced until the marriage is at least a couple of years old. With one-third of children presently being born within the first year of marriage and a large percentage even within less than nine months, the area of marriage and reproduction is obviously a much neglected field in which health behavior can be improved (Beasley et al., 1971; Caplan, 1960; Christensen and Bowden, 1953; Clark et al., 1968; Group for the Advancement of Psychiatry, 1969, 1973; Luban-Plozza, 1972; Wolfe and Ferguson, 1969).

A community health approach is not complete without knowledge and understanding of the implications and vicissitudes of broken or one-parent families; of incidences of child abuse; of the nature of underachievement and underperformance in formal education; of school failures among the underprivileged; of undernurtured and underattended children; or of addictive behavior of epidemic proportions among the young (Dykman et al., 1970; Fleck, 1964; Francis, 1969, 1971; Gil, 1971; Howells, 1963; Minuchin, 1967). All these conditions, among others, involve the family system, although they may not lead to a specific psychiatric diagnosis in any one family member. Yet such family malfunctioning is real all the same and requires remedial measures. Clinical attention to such families, as families, can also prevent further psychosocial and biological aberrations and deficiencies. Yet the family as a system is not isolated. This system interacts with other social systems which are as crucial to family existence and welfare as is the family to societal functioning (Fleck, 1964; Group for the Advancement of Psychiatry, 1973; Howells, 1963; Luban-Plozza, 1972; Winnicott, 1965).

FAMILIES AND SCHOOL SYSTEMS

Family and related systems' dysfunctions are often ignored when a clinically diagnosable health problem exists in individuals of whatever age. Then the diagnosed condition likely will determine the course of remedial action and treatment, if any. Next to the family the school is the most important social system involved in human development. But when a school underachiever is, typically, referred to remedial classes or tutoring, possibly based on a psychological or medical examination and diagnosis, the familial roots of his disability may well be ignored. Such a limited approach may seem practical but actually borders on malpractice in the face of our knowledge that a diagnosed condition in a particular family member, especially a child, while deserving of treatment, may be only a relatively minor and surface manifestation of a malfunctioning family system.

A community health service should therefore be prepared in manpower and competence to do much more than respond to specific and often temporary complaints brought forth by an acute illness, or refer an underachiever or a disturbed and disturbing chool schild to a psychologist or a mental health agency for specific determination of the nature of the difficulty without making any effort to look at the systems in which the difficulties occur and arose over time. This neglect arises more often from our lack of resources and clinical competence than from ignorance that these are the systems, the family and the school in this case, which need to come under clinical scrutiny. Teachers, for instance, are quite aware that their interaction with a particular child may produce difficulties, but are equally aware that often the child who has trouble at home manifests it in school, whether or not the problem is recognized in the home. It is time that we viewed any school health or adjustment problem not only as an indication to establish an individual diagnosis but also as an equally urgent indication to examine the relevant social systems (Dykman et al., 1970; Francis, 1969, 1971; Minuchin, 1970; Waldrop and Bell, 1964).

To do so we must have agencies prepared to proceed in this fashion, so that interventions can extend beyond putting the child on medication or through a course of behavior modification, to exploring the role and possible deficiencies of the family system. Moreover, if the family contains more than one child, failure to examine this system will also withhold preventive measures from other family members; thus, each and every symptom must be viewed as an opportunity not only to remedy but to modify related conditions that may adversely affect other family members. The same view applies to the school system, whose role in a pupil's difficulties must be assessed not only for that child's sake, but also because school policies or a teacher's behavior may be detrimental for many students. We would not undertake surgery without examining the cardiovascular or respiratory systems, and we should not treat any patient without examining the significant social system or contexts in which malfunction occurred. H. B. Richardson (1948) in a much-neglected study told us 25 years ago: "To say that patients have families is like saying that the diseased organ is part of an individual."

THE FAMILY IN DISEASE AND TREATMENT

To the concepts of psychosomatic illness and somato-psychic and somato-psychosomatic syndromes we must add the clinical considerations of familio-somatic and somato-familial disorders (Beasley et al., 1971; Grolnick, 1972; Howells, 1963; Lindemann, 1950; Mechanic, 1965; Meissner, 1966; Minuchin, 1970). In brief, any illness produces or aggravates familial stress, and familial vicissitudes can produce or complicate illness. Among the 13 most stressful life events related to any disease in the Holmes-Rahe Scale, all but three are family events. The three "exceptions" are jail term, being fired from work, and retirement, events which also carry a stressful impact on families. It should be recalled that these stress factors were established on the basis of large population surveys here and abroad, prospectively as well as retrospectively with regard to disease events (Rahe et al., 1967). Furthermore, there are good studies indicating a connection between desirable health behavior and conjugal role structure, and also the adverse impact of low socioeconomic status and family instability on health, not to mention the documented familial aberrations encountered in the backgrounds of many psychiatric patients (Bruch, 1940; Jackson, 1966; Lidz et al., 1965).

Somato-familial and familio-somatic mechanisms also play an important role in treatment. Treatment can at times be effective, whether or not the patient is considered as a person who also lives and works in relevant social contexts, if the condition is one for which essential causal factors are known and specific treatment is available. For instance, if an antibiotic has been proven to be effective against a patient's infecting agent, this antibiotic will control the infection whether the patient is sad or happy or whether or not his family likes him or her. However, family behavior often matters because prescribing what should be done does not mean that it will be done unless we ascertain that patients can, and are motivated to, apply the treatment and can do so without interference from significant others for whatever reasons. As psychiatrists and mental health professionals know, illness or disability can constitute secondary gain, motivating individuals in a countertherapeutic direction. We also know that families may channel and focus their system pathology onto one member whose illness therefore must be preserved rather than cured for the sake of such a family's equilibrium. Unless the affective and interactional forces in the group are realigned, treatment interference or sabotage of rehabilitation is likely to occur or continue (Jackson, 1966; Lindemann, 1950; Minuchin, 1970).

Viewing the family as the clinical unit in treatment, in addition to appropriate individual examination and prescription as indicated, must be part and parcel of modern practice whoever the primary care agent may be. Most of the highly prevalent chronic disability is not caused by diseases amenable to specific scientific treatment, and therefore the functioning and reactions of the family system are of major relevance (Balint, 1957; Dingle, 1973; Fleck, 1949; Richardson, 1948). Rheumatoid arthritis, mental illness including addictions, and cardiovascular disease, all chronic or intermittently remitting diseases, constitute over three-quarters of all ailments besetting our population, and in all of these, family attitudes and functioning matter greatly because they intertwine with the course of these conditions and with the course of treatment.

Every health worker, physician and surgeon included, must understand and attend to the stressful repercussions on the family of a member's illness, acute or chronic, which affects not only other family members, but which acutely and over time can change all facets of family dynamics. A husband and father who suffers a myocardial infarction may drop out not only as a breadwinner, but also as an active sexual partner to his wife, as the leader of the group or as an active companion of his teenage children. Whether through organic limitations or somato-psychic anxieties, he may regress psychically as well as socially and become dependent on his family in tangible and emotional spheres. A mother, briefly confined with childbirth, may seemingly return to the family fold in her previous roles, but if the baby happens to be handicapped and difficult, or if she is depressed, the older children and her spouse may find that she has only very partially resumed her roles with them. A defective new member can be integrated into the family group only at the expense of everybody's attention and energy and of reduced need-fulfillments from the mother for the rest of the family. Public health nurses are well acquainted with such familial repercussions and those of almost any illness or recovery period (Beloff et al., 1968; Fleck, 1949); physicians, especially hospital-based specialists, often are not, at least not firsthand. Obviously, adequate care must include clinical care of the patient and the family whether such care is rendered by an individual practitioner, by a clinical specialist, a health team, or through outreach from a neighborhood health center.

Community health agencies or "family physicians" therefore must be prepared for these contingencies — to evaluate and treat if indicated the patient *and* the relevant systems in which he or she lives and moves. This cannot be done if such an agency has to dichotomize instead of integrating all facets of treatment services and medical competence within its own team and through appropriate networks of special agencies and consultants (Elliott, 1964; Royal College of General Practitioners, 1967, 1970).

AGING AND DYING

Family attitudes and behavior are of particular concern in the case of the aged. Aging itself is a tissue process, not necessarily a particular disease, although aged people are at high risk for most degenerative and malignant illnesses. The two-generation nuclear family is generally unsuited economically and often emotionally to care for aging grandparents in the home. The elderly themselves usually prefer to have their independent abode and life for as long as possible, especially if spouses can be together, and if their respective disabilities do not prevent caring for each other. Although they prefer to live near children and grandchildren, isolation of elderly people is a common and serious problem (Bell, 1973; Group for the Advancement of Psychiatry, 1971; Luban-Plozza, 1972).

In the U.S.A. more than 1,000,000 people over 65 reside in nursing homes or chronic care facilities, either because their disabilities demand it or because neither family nor community resources to support them in home situations exist. Many of these patients are mentally disturbed with or without specific physical disabilities. Another 100,000 or more reside in mental hospitals where they usually receive minimal care or attention and suffer many indignities.

In the last decade many such patients have been returned from the large mental hospitals to communities, but not always to better care. However, it has been found that families if extant can become reinvolved in the care of such patients, and that attention to, and support for, families caring for an aged member can prevent his or her institutionalization. Because such people often need medical as well as psychiatric treatment and surveillance, however, ready access to an agency providing integrated medical support for the patient and his or her family is essential (Bell, 1973; Group for the Advancement of Psychiatry, 1971).

Equally important is clinical attention to a family with a fatally ill member, whether at home or in an institution. Dying is as natural an event and eventuality as is birth. For the latter event we have created an entire specialty, but the medical student may have his first encounter with dying as a clinical clerk, unprepared and without guidance. He learns from dead bodies, about death rates, and a great deal about prolonging and saving lives, but usually nothing about death as a process and a life event. Mourning used to be a common experience for families when life expectancy was less than half a century and when infant and child mortality were high. Now most people become parents and many even grandparents without ever having experienced a death in their immediate families. Even then, death occurs away from home, in hospitals or nursing homes, if not altogether in a different locality in this mobile nation.

The family tasks in this connection are less those of facing death than of coping with dying and mourning. Dying patients depend on their families' mastering the situation, not only for care and nurture, but for their final separation. The propensity on the part of families and professional staffs to withdraw from this situation has been well documented (Weisman, 1972). Guiding families and the dying patient-member towards this separation, allowing them to grieve and share their sorrow is also part of family medicine and psychiatry. Obviously mental health professionals cannot participate and contribute to such care if they are locked into separate facilities, maybe miles away from the general hospital or nursing home (Group for the Advancement of Psychiatry, 1971; Richardson, 1948; Weisman, 1972).

Coping with dying and mourning are important preventively, because it has been found that unresolved guilt and depression in a parent, traceable to the death of one of his or her parents, is a common source of chronic family disturbance (Fleck, 1972).

Psychiatric Aspects of a Family Focus

In psychiatric illnesses as such, the foregoing facts stand out even more clearly. Neurotic and unwholesome behavior traits of parents often reappear in their children (Bruch, 1940; Ehrenwald, 1960; Howells, 1963), but even more important are the severe deficiencies in family task performance in the backgrounds of many psychotic patients. In the families of young schizophrenic patients such deficiencies include, among others, faulty marital coalitions, especially schismatic and skewed relationships, failure to observe generational boundaries, inappropriate modeling of gender-typical roles by parents, and aberrant communication patterns including the transmission of irrational or unrealistic ideation (Lidz et al., 1965). Family disturbances related to severe affective disorders have not been established as clearly as with schizophrenic patients, except that overemphasis on family prestige and success, traumatic separation experiences, and familial or communal discrimination have often been found particular burdens for depressed individuals.

This is not the place to discuss these pathological family frames in detail. The correlation of particular family-wide disorders and particular diagnostic entities, however, is less important to health care and treatment than are the examination and evaluation of basic family functions and task performance with regard to both wholesome and pathogenic aspects (Fleck, 1972). Yet the patient's treatment and recovery involve his or her family in crucial respects. Hospitalization itself often depends on, and affects, the family — they may resist it or precipitate it; they may interfere or cooperate with the staff at the hospital; they may remove the patient from the hospital prematurely against advice in order to regain their earlier equilibrium which included the psychotic member, or eject him from the family group, leaving his treatment and rehabilitation entirely to the hospital staff and such community resources as can be marshaled in the patient's behalf (Lidz et al., 1965, chapter 16).

Mental health teams and psychiatric staffs must also be alert to their own system deficiencies which can alienate patient families as well as community agencies. Boundaries among mental health service systems and between them and other health and community services often impede rather than facilitate patients' smooth passage from one care system to another (Astrachan and Levinson, 1976; Bell, 1973).

The feasibility and effectiveness of treating psychiatric problems in the context of primary care agencies or general hospitals has been thoroughly established (Detre et al., 1961; Fleck, 1966; Linn, 1964; Reding and Maguire, 1973). The mushrooming of psychiatric units in general hospitals and of psychiatric liaison services in teaching centers during the past 25 years is an institutional reflection that emotional and neurotic disorders are being treated more often by nonpsychiatric physicians than by mental health professionals. Only among the poor has the mental health center development brought about new or additional services by, as noted above, concentrating on population sectors and neighborhoods where practically no health services other than the nearest hospital emergency room existed. There, as in other general hospital units, medical, surgical, and psychiatric patients have coexisted for years. Without elaborating further, or endorsing every level or type of care in these units generally, we note that such care and practice can be fully adequate if emergency room staffs work as a team, if ward personnel are taught and guided by psychiatrists and other mental health professionals, and last but not least, if the unit is family-oriented (Fleck, 1966; Lindemann, 1950; Linn, 1964).

Systematically conceived primary "medical" care, however, must include not only the initial management and triage of mental disorders but also family-oriented preventive services. The latter encompass reproductive services including abortion and possibly sterilization (laparotoscopy and vasectomy) as well as care for the aged and aging including the dying patient and his family, if any. Clinical competence is required not only for individual care and treatment but also for assessment of family functioning and therapeutic attention and intervention on a group level.

The neighborhood health station or health maintenance organization should interlock with more categorically oriented medical services, nursing homes, halfway houses, social agencies and the general medical center where more complicated illnesses are diagnosed and treated. Such health stations should also collaborate appropriately with other community services such as the schools, the courts, housing authorities, and welfare departments. All these community subsystems are involved in health and illness so that the family-focused health center becomes another subsystem in the arena of human and humane services.

REFERENCES

Ackerman, N. W. (1958), *The Psychodynamics of Family Life*. New York: Basic Books.

Astrachan, B. M. & Levinson, D. J. (1976), Entry into the mental health center: A problem in organizational boundary regulation. In: *Task and Organization*, ed. E. Miller. London: Tavistock.

Balint, M. (1957), *The Doctor, His Patient and the Illness*. New York: International Universities Press.

Beasley, J. et al. (1971), Evaluation of national health programs IV, Louisiana family planning. *J. Pub. Hlth.*, 61:1812–1825.

Bell, W. G. (1973), Community care for the elderly: An alternative to institutionalization. *Gerontol.*, 13:349–354.

Beloff, J. S. et al. (1968), Organization of a comprehensive family health care program [Yale Studies in Family Health Care II]. *J.A.M.A.*, 204:355–360.

Binger, C. A. L. (1945), *The Doctor's Job*. New York: Norton.

Blood, R. O. (1963), The husband-wife relationship. In: *The Employed Mother in America*, ed. F. I. Nye & L. Hoffman. Chicago: Rand McNally, pp. 282–305.

Bruch, H. (1940), The family frame of obese children. *Psychosom. Med.*, 2:141–206.

Caplan, G. (1960), Emotional implications of pregnancy and influence on family relationships. In: *The Healthy Child*, ed. H. C. Stuart & D. G. Prugh.

Cambridge: Harvard University Press, pp. 72–82.

Christensen, H. T. & Bowden, O. P. (1953), The time interval between marriage of parents and birth of their first child, Tippecanoe County, Indiana. [Studies in Child Spacing II]. *Soc. Forces*, 31:346–351.

Clark, M. et al. (1968), Sequels of unwanted pregnancy. *Lancet*, 2:501–507.

Detre, T. P. et al. (1961), An experimental approach to the treatment of the acutely ill psychiatric patient in the general hospital. *Conn. Med.*, 25:613–619.

Dingle, J. H. (1973), The ills of man. *Scien. Amer.*, 229:76–84.

Dubos, R. (1968), *Man, Medicine and Environment*. New York: Praeger.

Dykman, A. et al. (1970), Children with learning disabilities: Conditioning, differentiation, and the effect of distraction. *Amer. J. Orthopsychiat.*, 40:766–782.

Ehrenwald, J. (1960), Neurosis in the family. *Arch. Gen. Psychiat.*, 3:232–242.

Elliott, R. W. (1964), Further developments in the health service and cooperation with general practitioners. Unpublished report, County Council of the West Riding of Yorkshire.

Erikson, E. H. (1964), *Insight and Responsibility*. New York: Norton.

Fleck, S. (1949), Emotional effects of a long-term illness on the family. *Pub. Hlth. Nursing*, 41:463–466.

———— (1964), Family welfare, mental health and birth control. *J. Fam. Law*, 3:241–247.

———— (1966), Psychiatry in the general hospital, *Conn. Med.*, 30:650.

———— (1972), The role of the family in psychiatry. In: *Human Behavior*, ed. A. M. Freedman & H. Kaplan. New York: Antheneum, pp. 408–431.

Francis, H. W. S. (1969), The unification of the health services and the school physician. *The Medical Officer*, 122:259–263.

———— (1971), The school physician and the emotional hazards of the school. *Publ. Hlth. London*, 85:286–294.

Gil, D. G. (1971), Violence against children. *J. Marr. Fam.*, 33:637–648.

Grolnick, L. (1972), A family perspective of psychosomatic factors in illness: A review of the literature. *Fam. Proc.*, 11:457–486.

Group for the Advancement of Psychiatry (1954), *Integration and Conflict in Family Behavior*. Report No. 27.

———— (1968), *The Dimensions of Community Psychiatry*. Report No. 69.

———— (1969), *The Right to Abortion: A Psychiatric View*. Report No. 75.

———— (1971), *The Aged and Community Mental Health: A Guide to Program Development*. Report No. 81.

———— (1973), *Humane Reproduction*. Report No. 86.

Howells, J. G. (1963), *Family Psychiatry*. Springfield, Illinois: Thomas.

Jackson, D. D. (1966), Family practice: A comprehensive medical approach, *Compr. Psychiat.*, 7:338–348.

Kreitman, N. (1964), The patient's spouse. *Brit. J. Psychiat.*, 110:159–173.

Lidz, T. (1963), *The Family and Human Adaptation*. New York: International Universities Press.

———— Fleck, S., & Cornelison, A. R. (1965), *Schizophrenia and the Family*. New York: International Universities Press.

Lindemann, E. (1950), Modifications in the course of ulcerative colitis in relationship to changes in life situations and reaction patterns. In: *Life Stress and Bodily Disease*, *Proc. A. Res. Nerv. & Ment. Dis.*, 29:706–723.

Linn, L. (1964), Some aspects of a psychiatric program in a voluntary general hospital. In: *Handbook of Community Psychiatry and Community Mental Health*, ed. L. Bellak. New York: Grune & Stratton, pp. 126–143.

Luban-Plozza, B. (1972), Preventive medical and psychosocial aspects of family practice. *Internat. J. Psychiat. Med.*, 3:327–332.

Lucente, F. E. & Fleck, S. (1972), A study of hospitalization anxiety in 408 medical-surgical patients. *Psychosom. Med.*, 34:304–312.

Mechanic, D. (1965), Perception of parental responses to illness: A research note. *J. Hlth. Hum. Behav.*, 6:253–257.

Meissner, W. W. (1966), Family dynamics and psychosomatic processes. *Fam. Proc.*, 5:142–161.

Minuchin, S. (1967), *Families of the Slums*. New York: Basic Books.

_____ (1970), The use of an ecological framework in the treatment of a child. In: *The Child and His Family*, ed. E. J. Anthony & C. Koupernik. New York: Wiley, pp. 41–57.

Morris, J. N. (1973a), Four cheers for prevention. *Proc. Roy. Soc. Med.*, 66: 225–232.

_____ et al. (1973b), Vigorous exercise in leisure-time and the prevention of coronary disease. *Lancet*, 1:333–339.

Pasamanick, B. (1972), The human services-non-system: Where do we go from here? Presented at the 24th Institute on Hospital and Community Psychiatry, St. Louis, September 26.

Rahe, R. H. et al. (1967), A longitudinal study of life changes and illness patterns. *J. Psychosom. Res.*, 10:355.

Reding, G. R. & Maguire, B. (1973), Non-segregated acute psychiatric admissions to general hospitals. *New Eng. J. Med.*, 289:185–189.

Richardson, H. B. (1948), *Patients Have Families*. New York: Commonwealth Fund.

Royal College of General Practitioners (1967), Family health care. London: The Team.

_____ (1970), Present state and future needs of general practice. Reports from General Practice XII, 2nd ed. London.

Tuckman, J. & Regan, R. A. (1967), Size of family and behavioral problems in children. *J. Genet. Psychol.*, 3:151–160.

Vandervoort, H. T. & Ransom, D. C. (1973), Undergraduate education in family medicine, *J. Med. Ed.*, 48:158–165.

Waldrop, M. F. & Bell, R. Q. (1964), Relations of preschool dependency behavior to family size and density. *Child Devel.*, 35:1187–1195.

Weisman, A. D. (1972), *On Dying and Denying*. New York: Behavioral Pub.

Whybrow, P. C. (1972), The use and abuse of the "medical model" as a conceptual frame in psychiatry. *Internat. J. Psychiat. Med.*, 3:333–342.

Winnicott, D. W. (1965), *The Family and Individual Development*. London: Tavistock Publications.

Wolfe, S. R. & Ferguson, E. C. (1969), The physician's influence on the non-acceptance of birth control. *Amer. J. Obstet. Gyn.*, 104:752–757.

Fixation and Regression
in the Family Life Cycle

LAURENCE R. BARNHILL
and DIANNE LONGO

In spite of the obvious fact that families differ significantly depending on their current stage of the family life cycle, most of the family literature focuses on intervening in ongoing family interaction without specific attention to family developmental issues. While it is understandable that general principles of family intervention needed to be developed before more specific variations and elaborations could be elucidated, our work with distressed families suggests the need to increase the specificity with which our assessments and interventions are tailored.

As an example of the state of the field, Weakland et al. in 1974 discussed impasse points in family interaction and development. The concept is not a new one, being a formulation of principles that can be accepted by many, if not most, family therapists. Briefly stated, the assumption is that the family can function adequately until it is stressed or forced to change; at that point the family can become "stuck" in rigid patterns. Outside intervention is often useful so as to upset the pathological pattern—thus allowing the flexibility needed for new problem solving and growth (see also Haley, 1964; Whitaker, 1972). Once freed from stuck patterns and the resulting pessimism and pain, the family is able to cope relatively successfully with its problems. If a future "stuck point" emerges, the family can remobilize re-

---

Laurence R. Barnhill, Ph.D., is Coordinator of Outpatient and Emergency Services, South Central Mental Health Center, and Adjunct Assistant Professor, Department of Psychology, Indiana University, Bloomington, Indiana.

Dianne Longo, R.N., M.S., is Post-Master's Fellow, University of Washington, School of Nursing, Seattle, Washington.

The authors wish to express appreciation to Dr. Harout Babigian and the staff of the University of Rochester Medical Center Emergency Department who facilitated our identifying and working with these families.

sources or seek further outside intervention (see also Camp, 1973). Thus, rather than "curing" a family, a respectable goal of family therapy can be to loosen rigid patterns and thus, to get the family problem-solving mechanisms working again. This approach is also quite compatible with the Family Crisis Intervention approach developed by Langsley and colleagues in Denver (1968).

While this is an interesting and often useful paradigm for family intervention, it is clear that it is a general framework lacking details about how families differ according to their stage of development. Family sociologists, while not focusing on modifying family functioning, have provided more detailed tools with which to understand the differences, as well as general similarities, between families. Especially useful in family crisis therapy is the incorporation of the time dimension, as seen in the family developmental approach by Hill (1964) and others. This perspective can provide additional details and clarity on the developmental needs and tasks of the family, the sequencing of roles, and the process of changing family norms: "Any research [or clinical work, we would like to add] which seeks to generalize about families without taking into account the variation due to the stages of family development...will have tremendous variance unaccounted for" (Hill, 1964, p. 190).

Both Hill and Hansen (1960) and Rodgers (1962) have reviewed and critiqued various models in the family development approach. Hill (1964) cites Duvall's (1957) nine stage schema as a widely used and relatively sound framework. The schema is based on three sets of readily available data: numbers of positions in the family, age composition of the family, and employment status of the father. The stages of the family life span, each of which then forms a "distinctive role complex," are as follows:

I. Establishment (newly married, childless);
II. New parents (infant-3 years);
III. Preschool Family (child 3–6 years and possibly younger siblings);
IV. School Age Family (oldest child 6–12 years, possibly younger siblings);
V. Family with Adolescent (oldest 12–19, possibly younger siblings);
VI. Family with Young Adult (oldest 20 until first child leaves home);
VII. Family as Launching Center (from departure of first to last child);
VIII. Postparental Family, The Middle Years (after children have left home until father retires);

IX. Aging Family (after retirement of father) [Hill, 1964, p. 192].

For our own clinical uses we have modified stages V and VI to the following:

V. Family with Early Adolescent (oldest 12–16, possibly younger siblings);

VI. Family with Late Adolescent (oldest 16–20 until first child leaves home).

This alteration was made in order to delineate more clearly the various family developmental tasks, specifically to take into account the increased freedom of youth 16 years and older.

While numerous other family life cycle frameworks have been developed and are clearly possible, these nine stages have been found to be clinically useful as well as based on a wide survey of theoretical and empirical work. Perhaps of most pragmatic clinical relevance is the concept of each stage as a "distinctive role complex" (Hill, 1964). This concept implies that the family must undergo considerable change in the transition from one life stage to another. Thus, the transitions have become thought of as "normal family developmental crises" (Rapoport, 1965).

It is clear that many other external and internal stresses (in addition to developmental changes) can lead to a request for treatment. A focus on these transition points, however, is useful and important in three ways. First, *most or all* families face such crises, so more information about them can have wide applicability. Second, these transitions *are* important in many clinical cases: the majority of families referred to our family treatment unit have appeared "stuck" at a particular stage or transition point. Third, even if a developmental transition does not appear to be the major factor in the disturbance, the life cycle stage nearly always *interacts* with the problem and thus becomes a relevant factor.

FIXATION AND REGRESSION IN THE FAMILY LIFE CYCLE

In exploring the relevance of family life cycle transition points to identified family difficulties, we have found useful the psychodynamic concepts of fixation and regression. Here, however, we are not referring to individual psychological functioning but to the developmental stages of the family unit. Addressing the family unit with the traditional concepts of fixation and regression is not difficult. Just as in the case of the individual, it is possible to hypothesize that families pass through and resolve the conflicts of each stage with varying degrees of success.

Since 100 per cent success at resolving the conflicts is rare it can be assumed that there will be some partial fixation on unresolved issues at one or several of the life cycle stages. Growth and change continue inexorably, however, and the family must continue to move on if it is to meet the new challenges ahead. The conflicts can then become sealed over, though vulnerable points can be left behind.

It is possible then to conceive that under a later situation of stress (internal, external, or both) the family can regress to previous levels of functioning. With the experience of stress it becomes likely that old, unresolved conflicts from the partial fixation can become uncovered and alive again. Thus, as if it is not enough for the family to deal with one difficulty, another conflict is reawakened, together with the old unsuccessful patterns of coping with the stress. The rigid, unsuccessful patterns are relived, leading to frustration, a sense of helplessness, and an increasing sense of urgency until the family appears for help, quite "stuck." Concepts of family life cycle development then become important to the family worker who needs to be able to identify not only the *current difficulty* but also the *fixation* point issues which are being dealt with by the family at the same time.

It can be seen that such conceptualization utilizes crisis theory as well as psychodynamic and family dynamics concepts. It is a tenet of crisis theory that the therapist need not only deal with the current situation, but also, to some extent, with whatever unresolved issue has turned a "stress" into a "crisis." Many such unresolved issues in individuals are well known, especially the importance of unresolved grief (Lindemann, 1944). Another point of crisis theory that appears relevant is Caplan's (1964) hypothesis that dealing with the unresolved past issue as well as the current stress can leave the individual (and family) "better" than before. Thus, though the focus may be on the current difficulties, attention to the fixation point can leave the family at a higher level of functioning than before the crisis, in that the family may now be less vulnerable to future stress.

Some of our families have presented with a clear and overt stress as a precipitant and we use problem-solving intervention around that issue. Many of our families, however, present with an internal family stress or a precipitant that appears merely to be the last straw before breakdown. These latter families we conceptualize as being involved in a family life cycle transition that has not been successfully managed as yet. Since they are in acute distress, however, and not just patiently working on their conflict, we assume also a significant regression to a previous level of functioning. This is called the "partial fixation" point since it had been sealed over with some success for years.

FAMILY LIFE CYCLE TRANSITIONS

It may be noted that the focus of our work is not generally on the stages per se but rather on the transition from one to the next. Rather than dealing with Duvall's basic stages, then, we have had to formulate the key principles of the *transition* points. It is clear that this approach (below) is just a beginning of the process of identifying the key issues in the transitions. The nine transitions, then, leading to the nine stages, we have tentatively conceptualized as follows:

0-I. *Commitment.* In the transition to stage I (establishment) we include late courtship, wedding, honeymoon, and preparenthood. The major process for the developing family is of breaking away from the family of origin and developing a lifelong commitment to the new family. This commitment needs to change over time and is a fertile point for partial fixations: "I'll stay with you as long as. . ." being the actual contract as opposed to the stated one of "till death do us part" (Solomon, 1973).

I-II. *Developing New Parent Roles.* In the transition from the husband-wife to mother-father roles, several new interrelated roles need to be developed. The shift from spouse to parent, within both the nuclear and extended families, necessitates role transitions for numerous family members. Both dynamic and spatio-temporal issues are involved in the acceptance of the newborn in the family (Barnhill, Rubenstein, and Rocklin, 1979; Solomon, 1973).

II-III. *Accepting the New Personality.* As the child passes from the stage of infancy to that of childhood, the family needs to allow the development of the new individual personality in addition to the normal dependency of the newborn.

III-IV. *Introducing the Child to Institutions Outside the Family.* As the child become older she or he needs to establish independent relationships to such institutions as school, church, scouts, sports, etc. The family needs to deal with the individual's adjustment and to cope with the new environmental feedback (Signell, 1972).

IV-V. *Accepting Adolescence.* With the onset of puberty and early adolescence, numerous role transitions and developmental issues need to be faced. The necessity of developing a sexual identity for the adolescent, as well as the individual's integration into peer group culture, are some of the critical issues modifying family relationships.

V-VI. *Experimenting with Independence.* As the oldest child is moving into late adolescence and young adulthood, the family needs to allow independent, counterdependent, and adult strivings to emerge. Increased mobility, sexual experimentation, and the need for making initial career plans require a gradual lessening of the primary ties with the family of origin (Stierlin, 1974).

VI-VII. *Preparations to Launch.* Acceptance of the independent adult role of the first child requires several role transitions in order to permit the child to leave the family nest and move toward developing his or her own family of progeny. This transition thus can overlap transition 0-I for the following generation.

VII-VIII. *Letting Go — Facing Each Other Again.* After many years of family focus on child rearing, it is a major transition for the parents to let go of the children and to face each other as husband and wife alone again. This requires, as well, that children be able to leave the parents to themselves. In addition, the development of the new roles of grandparent (for the parent) and parent (for the children) in a new three-generation arrangement is generally required.

VIII-IX. *Accepting Retirement and/or Old Age.* Retirement requires the married couple to cope with a role transition toward an entirely new life style excluding career plans, goals, and responsibilities. The second generation family, often freed by now from early childhood care of their own offspring, must begin to plan for caring for the older, as well as the younger generation.

Case Examples

The families we wish to discuss are those that have presented with some difficulty in managing a transition phase, concomitant with a regression to earlier stages of family development.

Family A

Family A came into treatment requesting assistance for their 18-year-old daughter who had developed the symptom of banging her head with ashtrays and other hard objects or hitting her head against the wall and/or the floor if deprived of such objects. She was the youngest of three siblings; the other two children had left home and established their own families of progeny quite some distance from the parental home. She often had her "fits" or "spells" after arguments with her boyfriend with whom she was living part-time, and who exploited her financially to support his developing business in illegal drug traffic.

Her father had developed an ulcer a few years previously and had recently recovered from a heart attack. He was due for retirement within three months after the family presented themselves at the medical center emergency room. Mrs. A, who seemed to be of an hysterical

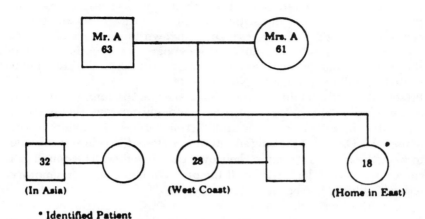

FIGURE 1
The A Family

temperament, was in generally good health. In the last year, however, she had gradually increased her nightly beer consumption to nearly steady drinking from dinner to bedtime. The couple had no hobbies or joint activities except evening TV and a weekend drive.

The events precipitating the request for consultation were as follows: The daughter had sold her dental assistant's tools (bought by the parents for her training program) for money to give to her boyfriend. After using up the money, the boyfriend attempted to "throw her out" of his place, sending her back to the parental home. She became hysterical, throwing herself to the ground and repeatedly striking herself with objects. After several hours of attempting to calm her, the frightened parents called the family physician who recommended the emergency room. Shortly thereafter, the parents appeared with their bruised daughter quietly in tow.

Developmentally, the A family was having significant difficulty coping with two simultaneous life cycle transitions: VII–VIII, Letting Go — Facing Each Other Again, and VIII–IX, Accepting Retirement. While each of the individuals in the family had significant personal difficulties, it seems possible that some resolution could have been found by the family if they had been able to deal with the transition issues in a more ordered and sequential manner. That is, the two simultaneous transitions appeared to be more than the family could tolerate and the extreme symptoms appeared. It was not sufficient, however, to explore ways that the parents could "let go" and develop an interest in each other, as well as explore means of structuring their postretirement time, though it was necessary to cover these areas. First, some understanding and resolution of the dangerous acting out needed to occur. Utilizing our own impressions of the interaction as well as some family historical data, we hypothesized that the behavior could be conceptualized as a regression to a fixation point in early childhood, Stage II, New Parents (with infant), or Stage III, Preschool Family (child making friends outside the family). We thus relabeled the "spells" as "tantrums" and encouraged the parents, especially the father, to insist upon certain orderly behaviors in the household. Once this pressing situation was altered, an effort was made to have the parents structure their own time together. The daughter's career plans were dealt with as if the problem had been a "temporary setback" which, indeed, it had become.

Lest this particular family seem "too easy," it might be worth noting that they initially dropped out of treatment immediately after symptom remission. It was not until the second time around, after a "relapse," that we were able to alter the marital structure. The second request followed a "suicide attempt" during which the daughter tried to strangle herself with a bathtowel in the kitchen of the home. She was angry at her mother's drinking which was then addressed more seriously in a marital session. Linking Mrs. A to peers for increased social interaction provided alternative behaviors and allowed Mr. A room to develop new interests of his own.

Family B

Family B came to the emergency room as their "last chance" after previous involvement with a family service agency and police. Their oldest boy, and second oldest child, Jack, 13, had taken the family car after an argument with his mother. He had picked up a friend and escaped from a pursuing neighbor in a 65-mile-an-hour chase by passing a truck on a curve. The parents felt they had little or no control over the boy and were hinting that the only solution would be placement and/or juvenile detention.

The only ally that Jack could muster in the sessions was his older sister Brenda, 15, who sided with him on adolescent freedom issues because the parents snooped on her every relationship with boys. Brenda, however, was quite irritated at Jack's behavior with her so she was quite willing to join in attacking him as well. There was also an occa-

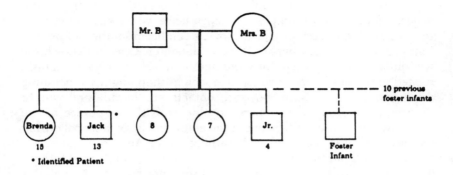

FIGURE 2
The B Family

sional sense that his father, who grew up from age eight in an orphan-
age, relished his son's daring escapades. Additional stress was placed on
the family by Jack's poor school performance and a series of minor dis-
ciplinary problems at school. The school had suspended him and he
was currently at home involved in a home tutor program.

The other family stress that appeared to be a possible precipitant
was the mother's hysterectomy two months previously. This appeared
to be of greater significance when considered in the context of the family structure and life style. (See Figure 2.) With the extreme emphasis
placed on infant care in this family, the hysterectomy served notice
that the parents could no longer experience the remnants of Stage II,
New Parenthood (including childbearing and infancy), at least with a
natural child of their own. They had compensated somewhat by a
series of temporary infant placements but their own children were getting older and they needed to address new issues. This fixation point
was clearly noted by Mrs. B when she stated she did "better" with infants and had "more difficulty" when the children "developed their
own personalities."

In the family's struggle to accept and cope with adolescence, transition IV-V, the family had appeared to regress to Stage II coping techniques. That is, Jack was back in the home and was being watched "like
a hawk" by the mother in order to protect him and the family. These
coping techniques, however, were not successful with an adolescent,
and the pressure-cooker exploded on a regular basis. Both family life

cycle transitions of "weaning" the parents from infants and allowing adult striving in the older children needed to be dealt with simultaneously. Since Jack's attempts at independence were too frightening to the family, the easiest way of achieving conflict resolution of adolescent issues was by focusing on the older daughter. Once addressed, she was quite willing to accept the focus and both parents were given tasks related to facilitating her adolescence such as shopping trips, planning driving lessons, negotiating boy-girl contacts, etc. Parallels relevant to the son were brought up where possible, and the assistance of the school was sought to get Jack out of the house and back in school during the day, giving everyone more breathing room. An additional necessary focus of treatment in this family was a consideration of the father's difficulties in dealing with an adolescent son since he went through this period himself without a father.

FAMILY C

Addressing stages earlier yet in the family life cycle, Family C presented when the husband arrived at the information desk seeking psychiatric hospitalization for his wife. Upon referral to the emergency room, Mr. C's request for hospitalization was found to be related to: (1) Mrs. C's "nerves" — she was on a minor tranquilizer for anxiety in public situations, and (2) Mr. C's discovery that Mrs. C was seeing another man. Mr. C's family of origin had known of the contact for several months and his brother eventually told Mr. C when Mrs. C did not respond to the brother's insistence that she end the extra-marital contact. Though the shocked husband accepted the wife's story that the relationship was platonic — just "coffee and talk" — thoughts of divorce nevertheless arose and precipitated a struggle for position with regard to possible custody of their three-year-old child. A complicating factor and additional precipitant was Mr. C's vasectomy one year previously, which could leave him childless for life if Mrs. C obtained custody in a divorce.

Conceptualizing the dominant issue of Stage II as New Parenthood (including childbearing and infancy), it becomes clear that the C family is in transition II-III, with an abrupt end to Stage II interaction patterns being inevitable. The vasectomy became a significant problem to this family as they faced this transition, because both now felt they wanted another child of their own. The reasons for Mrs. C's drift away to contact with a male friend were never clearly expressed during treatment. With the life cycle stress and the "other man" precipitant, however, both partners became so isolated that we were clearly struggling

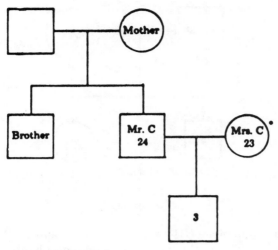

* **Identified Patient**

FIGURE 3
The C Family

with the 0-I Commitment transition as well. There was no indication of problems in the I-II Accepting Parenthood transition as both spouses were more than willing to assume parenting responsibilities.

Further indications of a regression to the Commitment phase were evidenced by the family's move to Mr. C's parents' home and his shift of primary alliance back to his family of origin. His brother had threatened Mrs. C's life if she sought custody of the child, though Mr. C defended his brother saying that it "was just a joke." Our first step was to encourage the couple to move back to their own home in order to limit the conflict as much as possible to the marital couple. This was not easy as even after the move, Mr. C's mother continued surveillance of the trailer until stopped by Mr. C. This allowed a less complicated consideration of the transition toward a recommitment. Effective problem-solving was not possible, however, until their pattern of mutual blame for the vasectomy was eased by shared mourning for the lost potential of future children. This latter experience provided the first closeness observed between the couple and allowed them to focus ahead on other normative marital conflicts.

FAMILY D

The D family provides some variation on our theme. Though they were

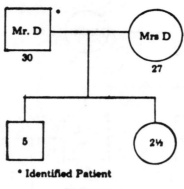

FIGURE 4
The D Family

also in a transition phase (III-IV), the transition appeared unrelated to
their difficulties. They did, however, show considerable evidence of
partial fixation at stages I and II as well as regression, though the latter
appeared due to external stresses. The couple presented to the emergency room with the stated difficulty of Mr. D being unable to handle
work stresses and his self-depreciation. The family physician played
some role in their referral as he had recommended evaluation for hospitalization of Mr. D due to either "paranoid schizophrenia" or "manic-
depressive psychosis." Both spouses, in fact, were working so hard to
identify Mr. D as the patient that a more traditional view would likely
have been an "acute schizophrenic episode" or worse. While Mr. D was
indeed confused, depressed, and exhausted, we were hopeful that brief
outpatient contact might be helpful especially since similar therapy
had been beneficial to them three years previously just before the birth
of their second child.

     Mr. D's work stresses were, indeed, at least part real as his co-
worker had just quit and he was trying to do the work of both to keep
his shipping and receiving room in order. Why he had worked himself
to exhaustion did not become clear until late in the second session after
a good night's sleep and a couple of days off from work. The precipitant
appeared to arise from a casual flirtation at work that apparently got
an eager response from a female co-worker of Mr. D. Since he had
quite traditional values, Mr. D became guilt-ridden (and apparently
frightened by the response) and told his wife, who became upset and
turned to her parents for support. Mr. D began working "like a de-
mon," returning exhausted from work and full of self-recriminations.
As the pair became further isolated, Mr. D began to speak of "not de-

serving" to be married to his wife, to the point of asking his father-in-law to beat him and considering leaving his family. This frightened Mrs. D further and she became more dependent on her own family of origin and eventually, the family physician.

Consideration of the family of origin of each spouse yielded numerous conflicting and rigid expectations of the spouses for themselves and for each other. This focus allowed renegotiation and reaffirmation of their commitment to each other (0–I transition). After dealing with this regression, the life cycle transitions II–III (Accepting the New Personality) and III–IV (Child Contacts with Outside World) emerged as relevant to the family. As the younger child, age two-and-a-half, began to develop more autonomy and the older child, age five, was about to begin school, the parents could no longer focus their interactions on a dependent infant and preschooler. They needed to renegotiate their marital relationship and develop new goals. Consideration of the latter transition points led the therapists to focus on other ways for Mrs. D to spend her time and use her increased freedom, as well as for her to support her husband regarding his work stresses.

CONCLUSIONS

Watzlawick et al., in their book, *Change* (1974), persuasively argue that students of human behavior can learn much about change in human behavior by observing naturally occurring changes in human relationships. Our team has found the structured family crisis therapy approach to be an excellent vantage point from which to observe and study, as well as intervene in, relationships in a state of flux. Of significant theoretical utility in such study is the concept of family life cycle stages and transitions as explored by family developmental theorists. Family life cycle transitions are important not only because of their frequent relationships with family crisis, but also because they are issues which all families face. Thus, the knowledge to be gained from them can have wide applicability.

REFERENCES

Barnhill, L., Rubenstein, G., & Rocklin, N. (1979), From generation to generation: Fathers-to-be in transition. *Fam. Coord.*, 28:229–235.

Camp, H. (1973), Structural family therapy: An outsider's perspective, *Fam. Proc.*, 12:269–278.

Caplan, G. (1964), *Principles of Preventive Psychiatry*. New York: Basic Books.

Duvall, E. (1957), *Family Development*. Chicago: Lippincott.

Haley, J. (1964), Research on family patterns: An instrument measurement.

Fam. Proc., 3:41–65.

Hill, R. (1964), Methodological issues in family development research. *Fam. Proc.*, 3:186–206.

———— & Hansen, D. (1960), The identification of conceptual frameworks utilized in family study. *Marr. Fam. Liv.*, 22:299–311.

Langsley, D., Kaplan, D., Pittman, F., Machotka, P., Flomenhaft, K., & DeYoung, C. (1968), *The Treatment of Families in Crisis*. New York: Grune & Stratton.

Lindemann, E. (1944), Symptomatology and management of acute grief. *Amer. J. Psychiat.*, 101:141–148.

Rapoport, R. (1965), Normal crises, family structure and mental health. In: *Crisis Intervention*, ed. H. Parad. New York: Family Service Association, pp. 75–87.

Rodgers, R. (1962), *Improvements in the Construction and Analysis of Family Life Cycle Categories*. Kalamazoo: Western Michigan University.

Signell, K. (1972), Kindergarten entry: A preventive approach to community mental health. *Comm. Ment. Hlth. J.*, 8:60–71.

Solomon, M. (1973), A developmental, conceptual premise for family therapy. *Fam. Proc.*, 12:179–188.

Stierlin, H. (1974), *Separating Parents and Adolescents*. New York: Aronson.

Watzlawick, P., Weakland, J., & Fisch, R. (1974), *Change: Principles of Problem Formation and Problem Resolution*. New York: Norton.

Weakland, J., Fisch, R., Watzlawick, P., & Bodin, A. (1974), Brief therapy: Focused problem resolution. *Fam. Proc.*, 13:141–168.

Whitaker, C. (1972), Process techniques of family therapy. Unpublished manuscript, University of Wisconsin.

Ethical Concerns in Family Therapy

PAULETTE M. HINES
and RACHEL T. HARE-MUSTIN

Increasing attention is being directed today to the fact that the objectives of change agents may interfere with individual privacy and human rights. The ethical concerns of which psychotherapists must be aware are compounded and made more complex in instances in which they intervene with an entire family in therapy.

This article is an effort to call attention to ethical problems that may arise in the context of family therapy. Family therapy at present is more of an orientation than an agreed upon set of procedures (Montalvo and Haley, 1973); some family therapists conduct interviews with an entire family, others with various subgroups or with subgroups and the entire family concurrent with individual therapy for a given family member. It is important to recognize that the therapeutic relationship with the family implies a contract with and a responsibility to each member.

Despite increasing concern about ethical practice and patient rights, a review of the literature yields a surprising dearth of guiding ethical principles that may be used by practicing family therapists. Some principles, such as competence, which is the ethical issue par excellence, apply in all therapies (Hare-Mustin, 1974). Family therapists must first ask themselves what training or supervision they have had in this modality that qualifies them to use it. We have singled out three major areas of ethical concern for consideration: (a) the goal of maximizing the growth of the entire family, (b) the issue of confidentiality, and (c) the myth of valueless thinking.

Paulette M. Hines, Ph.D., is on the staff of the Rutgers Community Mental Health Center, Piscataway, New Jersey.

Rachel T. Hare-Mustin, Ph.D., is Director, Community Counseling Program, Villanova University, Villanova, Pa.

Maximizing the Growth of the Entire Family

In family therapy, the therapist attempts to maximize the growth of the family as a whole, as well as that of individual family members. Frequently, within the confines of the therapy hour, the therapist may encourage direct expression of negative affect and evoke and escalate family confrontations as well (Minuchin, 1974). Although family members may be fully aware of each other's hostile feelings, they may not be accustomed to direct verbalizations of hatred, especially in the presence of nonfamily members. The therapist who encourages the expression of anger but is not concerned with preventing these behaviors from occurring outside the therapy room (Mace, 1976) runs the risk of promoting family dissolution and early termination of the therapeutic contract. The therapist can guard against family disintegration by inoculation, that is, by alerting the family during the initial stage of therapy to the stresses that may be expected in resolving long-term conflicts.

Breaking down a family's mode of interaction, promoting change in one family member, or change in an area of familial functioning may evoke new or increased distress and dysfunction in other family segments. Different family members at various stages may need added support, if not concurrent individual therapy. An alliance with any family member when it is at the expense of other members, regardless of how psychologically healthy they appear to be, must be carefully weighed against overall goals. The therapist may have stated or implied a position of nonalignment when establishing the initial therapeutic contract, which is now being violated.

A frequently voiced question arises from consideration of the family member being seen by the therapist in individual therapy. Whose interest is the therapist ethically bound to serve? Some therapists (Grosser and Paul, 1964) espouse the view that if the progress of the patient seen in individual treatment is of primary concern and is dependent upon family participation, the clinician must try to involve the family in treatment. Family therapists seem not to have given adequate attention to the basic issue of requiring all family members to participate. As Silber (1976) has pointed out, the prevailing "therapeutic ideology" is that we assume all persons can and should benefit from therapy. However, legal questions are being raised as to whether a person has a right *not* to be treated. This could very well apply to reluctant adult and adolescent participants, as well as children brought to family therapy sessions. Recent concern for children's rights is long overdue. Issues of informed consent are especially difficult when children are involved (Smith, 1976). Similar questions arise in cases in which there appear to be irreconcilable differences between family members. The therapist must examine the situation critically, for dissolution of the family unit may prove to be beneficial for some but not for other family members.

Another issue is the possibility that family members may suffer from embarrassment, a high level of anxiety, and a loss of respect in the eyes of other family members as a result of disclosure of failures in family therapy session discussions. Grosser and Paul (1964) considered this to be a quasi-ethical concern. They asserted that parents are often relieved when others in their family realize that they are not omnipotent and faultless. In the case of more controversial subject matter (e.g., sexual difficulties), Minuchin (1974) believed the therapist should protect the spouses' privacy. Therapists differ in the boundaries they wish to place around different subsystems in the family, but they should always be aware of the ethical, as well as the treatment, issues involved in including or excluding various family members.

CONFIDENTIALITY

Within the family system, different members vary in their capacity to be open and honest. Information may be transmitted to the therapist in family subgroups or individual sessions by persons unwilling to reveal information when the entire family is assembled. Thus, therapists often find themselves in possession of information that could be therapeutically employed for the well-being of the entire family system.

Whether the therapist has avoided or has encouraged a confidential relationship, the issue is: Do family members have the right to question the therapist and receive information about another member? Mariner (1971) advanced the position that prior agreement on the part of all involved is necessary before communication of information revealed to the therapist is released — and then only to very close family associates. Guidelines for those conducting growth groups suggest that information on such issues as confidentiality should be made available in writing to prospective participants (American Psychological Association, 1973).

There are several modes of action available to therapists who announce their stands on "privileged communications" at the onset of therapy (Committee on the Family, 1970). First, they may state at the beginning of therapy that they will not keep secrets. When family members reveal information that another member or they themselves are in imminent danger, the therapist may need to inform the family in order to elicit their aid. The California Supreme Court recently judged that a therapist must inform an intended victim (Whiteley and Whiteley, 1977), so such disclosure may become a matter of law rather than solely an ethical issue. Whether cases of marital infidelity should be revealed also has ethical as well as treatment implications. Therapists who advocate nonsecrecy may find it hard to maintain such positions when the consequences for all participants are thoroughly examined.

A second option open to the therapist in regard to confidentiality is to accept confidences with the intent of working with a family member's resistance to openly revealing information to the family. The therapist may help such persons to reveal their secrets to the family or may seek the person's permission to use the information in family sessions. The therapist who follows the second line of action, as well as one who encourages or accepts individual confidences and vows to keep secrets isolated from the family, may be confronted with the same dilemma. Privileged communications cannot help but bias the way the therapist perceives the family, as well as the interventions she or he chooses to make. Thus, it is an open-ended question about how honest the therapist is to promise absolute confidentiality to a family member.

Problems also arise with relatives outside the family therapy group. Mariner (1971) suggested that besides informing the person who phones that his or her information may be used in therapy, the person should be informed that the patient or family must be apprised of the call. Extreme caution in telephone conversations where the caller's identity is not certain is advised.

There appears to be a gap between what therapists perceive their legal position to be and what it actually is in regard to the issue of confidentiality (Marsh and Kinnick, 1970). Privilege refers to immunity from criminal and/or civil action for what one says or refuses to say. It may be absolute or conditional. Recent court decisions (e.g., Ziskin, 1971) leave no room for doubt that the privileges granted to many psychotherapists are at best conditional.

The courts are becoming increasingly involved in conflicts that arise between psychotherapists and their clients. Therapists are being required to support their claims of "accepted and proficient practices" with the establishment of peer review organizations. Although professional groups have developed ethical standards to guide their conduct (see American Psychological Association, 1977), it appears that "unless ethical and professional standards promulgated by professional associations afford adequate safeguards to members of the general public, said standards afford little or no protection to the professional from either criminal prosecution or civil (malpractice) action" (Roston and Sherrer, 1973, p. 271).

The Myth of Valueless Thinking

As London (1977) has pointed out, we can no longer question the powerful influence of the therapist's values but can only decide the manner in which those values are permitted to influence the therapeutic transaction. For a therapist to tell a family what is "good" is different from the therapist's facilitating a family's own ability to clearly assess their options (Engelhardt, 1973). "Can the individual family member also be considered a captive of the therapist's notions of how a family should be changed" (Boszormenyi-Nagy and Spark, 1973, p. 363)? The personal and professional values that provide direction for therapists' manipulations (e.g., assertiveness, autonomy, emotional closeness) may conflict not just with one person's value system but with those of the entire family. Therapists are often unaware of the extent to which their own personal and professional values govern therapeutic moves, to the exclusion of recognizing the uniqueness of the family situation and the net effect of disturbing the family system. Behaviors which therapists seek to change may appear pathological when viewed in a traditional context but have adaptive value within the family's own ecological setting.

Dishonesty on the part of therapists may often be fully recognized by clients according to Halleck (1963). Consider, for instance, the suggestion that impulses are easily modified. Adolescents, especially, recognize that success in this world is not dependent upon such restraint and that conformity may or may not lead to resolution of the adolescent's difficulties. Therapists may unwittingly encourage in their clients certain behaviors that would not be in their best interests from a legal point of view. This is especially true when there are marital conflicts or custody issues that might lead to litigation among family members (Hare-Mustin, 1976; Robitscher, 1972).

Therapists need to direct their attention to the impact that stereotypes based on gender, social class, ethnicity, and education may have on their motivation to initiate and continue treatment with a family, on their choice of interventions, and on their interpretation of unsuccessful outcome (Sabshin, Dressenhaus, and Wilkerson, 1970). Patients may be labeled *resistant* and *poor risks for therapy* for numerous reasons. It is ethically incumbent upon therapists to examine how their expectations and biases may ultimately lead to fulfillment of their prophesies. This is not to say that one can ignore empirical evidence and clinical experience which indicate that the personality characteristics of certain clients, especially as they interact in family systems, make them unlikely to benefit from particular methods of psychotherapy. We, however, do feel justified in pointing out the tendency of some therapists to characterize any person or family who does not respond to their method of treatment as psychologically unsophisticated. Therapists must examine the long-term significance of the labels they use and the extent to which these labels follow from an inability to deal with value systems different from their own.

Conclusion

A review of the literature indicates that relatively little attention has been directed to ethical issues in family psychotherapy. This fact is congruent with the lack of systematic ethics training in most graduate programs and the growing involvement of the courts in resolving conflicts between therapists and their clients. Family therapists, in particular, must increase their awareness of the multiple means by which their actions may impinge upon the rights of the persons they seek to serve. As Hobbs (1965) has pointed out, ethics is not just a guide to conduct but "the very essence of the treatment process itself" (p. 1508).

There is not only a need for increased awareness but also for expansion of existing guidelines. Several proposals may be considered toward this end.

1. Ethical training should be an integral part of professional training programs (Shore and Golann, 1969).

2. Workshops, seminars, and in-service training should be employed to facilitate discussion and development of feasible ethical guidelines.

3. Present ethical principles should be spelled out sufficiently to be of value in the day-to-day endeavors of family therapists.

4. Ethical standards are empirically derived and thus become dated; they should be periodically updated (Hobbs, 1965).

5. Therapists must continually scrutinize themselves regarding their honesty, competency, stereotypes, and biases.

6. Family therapists must utilize the knowledge of persons in other disciplines, particularly in regard to the legalities of therapy (Marsh and Kinnick, 1970).

7. The formulation of policies to be presented to legislators should be a major focus of psychotherapy conventions.

In summary, the ethical issues involved when one intervenes in the world of the family are exceedingly complex; they may never be totally agreed upon nor resolved. However, it is ethically incumbent upon family therapists to continually examine the complex ways their interventions can affect the lives of family members.

References

American Psychological Association (1973), Guidelines for psychologists conducting growth groups. *Amer. Psychol.*, 28:933.

—— (1977), *Ethical Standards of Psychologists*, rev. ed. Washington, D.C.

Boszormenyi-Nagy, I. & Spark, G. M. (1973), *Invisible Loyalties*. New York: Harper & Row.

Committee on the Family (1970), The field of family therapy. *Group for the Advancement of Psychiatry*, 78:594–603.

Engelhardt, H. (1973), Psychotherapy as meta-ethics. *Psychiat.*, 36:440–445.

Grosser, G. & Paul, N. (1964), Ethical issues in family group therapy. *Amer. J. Orthopsychiat.*, 34:875–884.

Halleck, S. (1963), The impact of professional dishonesty on behavior of disturbed adolescents. *Soc. Work*, 8:48–56.

Hare-Mustin, R. T. (1974), Ethical considerations in the use of sexual contact in psychotherapy. *Psychother.*, 11:308–310.

—— (1976), The biased professional in divorce litigation. *Psychol. Women Quart.*, 1:216–222.

Hobbs, N. (1965), Ethics in clinical psychology. In: *Handbook of Clinical Psychology*, ed. B. Wolman. New York: McGraw-Hill.

London, P. (1977), *Behavior Control*, 2nd ed. New York: New American Library.

Mace, D. R. (1976), Marital intimacy and the deadly love-anger cycle. *J. Marr. Fam. Coun.*, 2:131–137.

Mariner, A. (1971), Psychotherapists' communications with patients' relatives and referring professionals. *Amer. J. Psychother.*, 25:517–529.

Marsh, J. & Kinnick, B. (1970), Let's close the confidentiality gap. *Personnel Guid. J.*, 48:362–365.

Minuchin, S. (1974), *Families and Family Therapy*. Cambridge: Harvard University Press.

Montalvo, B. & Haley, J. (1973), In defense of child therapy. *Fam. Proc.*, 12:227–244.

Robitscher, J. (1972), The new face of legal psychiatry. *Amer. J. Psychiat.*, 129:315–321.

Roston, R. & Sherrer, C. (1973), Malpractice: What's new? *Prof. Psychol.*, 4:270–276.

Sabshin, M., Dressenhaus, H. & Wilkerson, R. (1970), Dimensions of institutional racism in psychiatry. *Amer. J. Psychiat.*, 127:787–793.

Shore, M. & Golann, S. (1969), Problems of ethics in community mental health: A survey of community psychologists. *Comm. Ment. Hlth. J.*, 5:452–460.

Silber, D. E. (1976), Ethical relativity and professional psychology. *Clin. Psychol.*, 29:3–5.

Smith, M. B. (1976), Conflicting values affecting behavioral research with children. *Amer. Psychol.*, 22:377–382.

Whiteley, J. & Whiteley, R. (1977), California court expands privilege debate. *APA Monitor*.

Ziskin, J. (1971), Psychology and the law. *Prof. Psychol.*, 2:202–204.

The McMaster Model
of Family Functioning

NATHAN B. EPSTEIN, DUANE S. BISHOP,
and SOL LEVIN

Family therapy has become an increasingly popular mode of treatment over the last two decades (Epstein and Bishop, 1973; Group for the Advancement of Psychiatry, 1970; Gurman and Kniskern, 1978; Haley, 1971; Olson, 1970; Zuk, 1971). Its acceptance has not been limited to psychiatry and other mental health fields, for it has been increasingly viewed as an important development by Family Medicine (Comley, 1973; Epstein and McAuley, 1978; McFarlane et al., 1971a, 1971b; Patriarche, 1974; Stanford, 1972) and by Pediatrics (Finkel, 1974; McClelland et al., 1973; Tomm, 1973). Training programs and study curricula in family therapy have grown tremendously in the last 10 years, and reports of a significant amount of research have also appeared (Glick and Haley, 1971; Gurman and Kniskern, 1978; Olson, 1970).

Despite this explosive growth and popularity, the diagnosis of a family who seeks mental and/or general health services is still basically restricted to clinical judgment, and this demands a conceptual model of family functioning. Literature reviews expose the general diversity of conceptual models of family functioning, indicating the lack of a generally accepted conceptual framework within which to perform a family assessment. With many schools and models represented in the literature, the onus for detailing the models and their development lies with the proponents of each approach. This presentation details the further development of one approach — the McMaster Model of Family Functioning.

N. B. Epstein, M.D., F.R.C.P., is Professor and Chairman, and Duane S. Bishop, F.R.C.P., is Assistant Professor, Section of Psychiatry and Human Behavior, Brown University — Butler Hospital, Providence, R. I.

Sol Levin, F.R.C.P., is Professor and Chairman, Department of Psychiatry, Northeastern Ohio Universities College of Medicine, Akron, Ohio.

Background for the Model

A conceptual framework, The Family Categories Schema (Epstein, Sigal, and Rakoff, 1962) originally developed in the course of a study of 110 "non-clinical" families, formed the basis of thinking for the current model (Westley and Epstein, 1969). Significant development and revision of the original concepts have taken place, such that the approach requires a new statement.

An important aspect of this conceptual model is its clinical utility. It has been developed and used extensively in a variety of psychiatric and family practice clinics (Comley, 1973; Epstein and Westley, 1959; Guttman et al., 1971, 1972; Postner et al., 1971; Rakoff et al., 1967; Sigal et al., 1967; Westley and Epstein, 1960) and by therapists who treated families as part of a large Family Therapy Outcome Study (Guttman et al., 1971; Santa-Barbara et al., 1975; Woodward et al., 1974, 1975, 1977). The framework has also been used in a Family Therapy Training Program[1] and found to be readily teachable. We make no claim that this is "the" model of family functioning. While not addressed to all aspects of family functioning, the model does focus on certain aspects which we have found important in dealing with clinically presenting families. The model deals with the full spectrum of family functioning from health to pathology and, therefore, should allow the placement of a given family's functioning on this spectrum.

Values have a great effect on the judgment and evaluation of behavior, and they have to be taken into consideration using this model. The great deal of cultural variation that occurs affects the behavior of people living in groups, and has to be understood and handled with care by practicing clinicians. When dealing with families we operate on Western Judaeo-Christian values which emphasize the optimal development of each human being. Any number of other systems may provide a value base, and might be equally valid. We do not try to impose our own values, but believe that those behavioral scientists working in the field should be prepared to state the value base on which their approach rests (Epstein, 1958).

The model of family functioning is based on a systems approach as described by Epstein and Bishop (1973):

> In this approach the family is seen as an 'open system' consisting of systems within systems (individual, marital dyad) and relating to other systems (extended family, schools, industry, religions). The

[1] The Family Studies portion of the Clinical Behavioral Sciences Program, McMaster University, Faculty of Health Sciences, Hamilton, Ontario.

unique aspect of the dynamic family group cannot be simply reduced to the characteristics of the individuals or interactions between pairs of members. Rather, there are explicit and implicit rules, plus action by members, which govern and monitor each other's behaviour. The significance for therapy is the fact that the therapist is not concerned with what it is in the family which produced pathology in the individual, but rather with the processes occurring within the family system which produce the behaviour which is labelled pathology. Therapy on this basis is directed at changing the system and, thereby, the individual. The concepts of communication theory, learning theory, and transaction approach are drawn on, although the infra-structure remains the systems model [p. 176].

Or, in Spiegel's words, "the ancient and honourable problems of the relation of one to the many can be solved only by finding a pattern in which the many appear as parts of the one" (1971, p. 38).

Spiegel outlined the differences between self-action (intra-psychic process), interaction, and transaction. Olson (1970, p. 509) has also elaborated on this and cites Dewey and Bentley's (1949) definition of the differences between interaction and transaction. A recent article by Ritterman (1977) also addresses the differentiation.

The aspects of systems theory which underlie the model to be presented can be summarized as follows:

1. Parts of the family are related to each other.
2. One part of the family cannot be understood in isolation from the rest of the system.
3. Family functioning is more than just the sum of the parts.
4. A family's structure and organization are important in determining the behavior of family members.
5. Transactional patterns of the family system are involved in shaping the behavior of family members.

THE McMASTER MODEL OF FAMILY FUNCTIONING

Before going into an elaborate discussion of family functioning, it is important to reiterate our assumption that, "The primary function of today's family unit appears to be that of a laboratory for the social, psychological, and biological development and maintenance of family members" (Epstein et al., 1976, p. 1411). In the course of carrying out these functions, families deal with a number of tasks which we group into three areas: *Basic Tasks, Developmental Tasks,* and *Hazardous Tasks.* Basic tasks are instrumental in nature and include such fundamental issues as the provision of food and shelter. Developmental tasks encompass those family issues that arise with the natural processes of growth which we differentiate into two sets: those associated with the individual developmental stages that each family member goes through, e.g., infancy, childhood, adolescence, middle and old age crises, and those associated with family stages, such as the beginning of the marriage, the first pregnancy, the birth of the first child, and so on. Developmental concepts and family functioning have been referred to by a number of authors (Berman and Lief, 1975; Brody, 1974; Group for the Advancement of Psychiatry, 1970; Hadley et al., 1974; Scherz, 1971; Solomon, 1973). Berman and Lief (1975) have integrated both individual and family developmental stages and the individual and family tasks appropriate to each stage. Scherz (1971) has focused on the interaction of family and child development stages, and Solomon (1973) has clearly laid out the developmental stages that a family goes through. A significant and recent literature, therefore, supports the consideration of developmental tasks and family functioning. The hazardous tasks area includes the crises that arise in association with illness, accidents, loss of income, job changes, moves, etc. There is a substantial family literature dealing with these topics (Berman and Lief, 1975; Comley, 1973; Hill, 1965; Langsley and Kaplan, 1968; Minuchin and Barcai, 1969; Parad and Caplan, 1965; Rapoport, 1965).

FAMILY DIMENSIONS

The McMaster Model of Family Functioning considers family functioning in the following dimensions: Problem Solving, Communication, Roles, Affective Responsiveness, Affective Involvement, and Behavior Control.

Some groups studying family functioning conceptualize much of family behavior as occurring within a single dimension such as communication (Bateson et al., 1956; Watzlawick et al., 1967; Weakland et al., 1974; Westley and Epstein, 1969) or role behaviors (Parsons, 1951; Parsons and Bales, 1955; Spiegel, 1971). In contrast, the McMaster Model of Family Functioning does not focus on any one dimension as the foundation for conceptualizing family behavior. We feel many dimensions need to be assessed for fuller understanding of such a complex entity as the family. Although we attempt to clearly define and delineate the dimensions, we recognize the potential overlap and/or possible interaction that may occur between them. Further clarification will undoubtedly result from our continuing research.

Each dimension will now be defined, and a summary of the concepts is outlined in Appendix A.

Problem Solving

The problem-solving dimension is defined as a family's ability to re-solve problems to a level that maintains effective family functioning. A family problem is seen as an issue that threatens the integrity and func-tional capacity of the family, the solution of which presents difficulty for them. Not all "problems" are considered, as some families have on-going, unresolved difficulties that do not threaten their integrity and function.

Problems are subdivided for clinical utility into *instrumental* and *affective* types. Instrumental problems are the mechanical problems of everyday life such as financing and housing problems. Affective prob-lems are those related to feelings. Clinical experience has shown that families may have problems restricted to the affective area, whereas in-strumental problems are almost always coupled with problems in the affective sphere. It is possible, of course, to identify problems that pre-sent an overlap of the instrumental and affective components, and the dichotomy is, therefore, not complete.

We postulate that families who have difficulty in resolving both in-strumental and affective problems function least effectively, those who have difficulty in resolving only affective problems are more effective, and families who resolve both types are most effective in their problem-solving functions.

Effective families solve most problems rapidly, easily, and without much thought, so that at times there can be some difficulty eliciting and detailing the problem-solving steps they go through. Families that present at clinics, however, bring at least the presenting problem as an unresolved difficulty. It is important, therefore, to analyze the steps at-tempted toward problem resolution. As an aid to clarifying the stages in this process, our model includes a sequential listing and operational definition of the components to be considered as follows:

1. Identification of the problem.
2. Communication of the problem to appropriate resources within or outside of the family.
3. Development of alternative action plans.
4. Decision regarding a suitable action.
5. Action.
6. Monitoring that action which is taken.
7. Evaluation of the success of the action.

The *problem identification* stage includes consideration of who identifies the problem. Is the pattern consistent or inconsistent? Does it vary with the type of problem (affective or instrumental, children, house, finances, etc.)? This stage also requires a judgment as to whether the family correctly identifies the problem. Families frequently displace real problems onto less conflicted areas which are then identified as *the* problem. The *communication of the problem to the appropriate resources* stage considers to whom the identified difficulty is communicated and whether that resource is an appropriate one. The third stage considers the type of *alternative action plans* developed and how they vary with the nature of the problem. The fourth stage embodies the *decision regarding a suitable action.* Do they decide, or don't they? Is there real consideration given to alternatives, or do they bypass this stage and act in a predetermined manner? This stage also considers whether those who will ultimately be involved in the action are informed of the decision. The fifth stage of *action* embodies consideration of the degree to which the family carries out the alternative they have decided on. A range of possibilities exists for a family having decided on a suitable course of action: the family may not act at all, may act in only a limited way, or may carry out all aspects of the action. We obviously view the latter as the most effective end of the range. The sixth stage addresses whether or not the family built in an accountability mechanism to *check that decisions they have taken are,* in fact, *acted on and carried out.* The last stage is an *evaluation of the success* of their problem solving. Does the family review what happened in an attempt to learn from the situation and evaluate which mechanisms are proving most successful? Are they able to recognize inappropriate problem-solving behavior when it has occurred?

It is postulated that the more effective a family's functioning the more stages of this process they can negotiate. Families with marked difficulty may not even be able to identify the problem. It is further postulated that it may be only exceptional families that carry out all of these steps (i.e., there may not be many families that actually carefully evaluate the mechanisms they use and the success of them).

COMMUNICATION

We define communication as how the family exchanges information. The focus is solely on verbal exchange. We are fully aware that this definition is constricted. Nonverbal aspects of family communication are tremendously important but are excluded here because of the methodological difficulties of collecting and measuring such data for research purposes at this point in time.

Communication is also broken down into instrumental and affective areas. Although there can be overlap between the two areas, clinical experience has shown that some families can have marked difficulties with affective communication while functioning very well in the area of instrumental communication, but the reverse is rarely, if ever, seen.

In addition, communication is assessed along two other vectors. These are the *clear versus masked continuum* and the *direct versus indirect continuum*. The former focuses on the clarity with which the content of the information is exchanged. Is the message clear, or is it camouflaged, muddied, vague, and masked? The latter considers whether the message goes to the person for whom it is intended.

It is possible on the basis of the two continua to arrive at four *styles of communication*. The first style would be *clear and direct* communication. An example of this for the affective communication of anger about Joe, an accountant, would be, "Joe, I'm angry at you because. . ." The second style is *clear and indirect* communication. Here the message is clear, but how it is intended for is not. Following on the previous example, the communication would be, "Accountants sure make me angry when. . .", a message that might or might not be intended for Joe. The third style is *masked and direct* communication. Here the content would be unclear but would be directed to the person for whom it is intended. Our example would be, "Joe, you look terrible today!" The fourth style is *masked and indirect* communication. Here the content of the message and for whom it is intended are both unclear. Our example now becomes, "You know, accountants give me a pain!"

It is postulated that the more masked and indirect the overall family communication pattern, the more ineffective the family's functioning will be, while the more clear and direct the communication, the more effective it will be. It is further postulated that masked and/or indirect communication invites a similar response from the recipient of the message.

The understanding of communication as we define it does not exclude, and indeed the clinical situation may at times require, consideration of such other variables as content, the potential for multiple messages, and checking whether the communication sent is appropriately attended to and interpreted by the receiver, etc. These considerations are consonant with the principles of communication as outlined by Lederer and Jackson (1968).

ROLES

The definition given to family roles is: Family roles are the repetitive patterns of behavior by which individuals fulfill family functions.

The present model breaks family functions again into instrumental and affective areas, with all of the implications previously mentioned. In addition, the functions are broken down into two further spheres— *necessary family functions* and *other family functions*. Necessary family functions include those that the family will have to address repeatedly if they are to function well and can be made up of instrumental, affective, or mixed types. Other family functions are those that are not necessary for effective family functioning but come up in the course of the life of every family to a greater or lesser degree. Some consideration of each group of functions is important.

Necessary family functions. Our model identifies five groupings of necessary family functions. The functions considered as part of *provision of resources* embody those tasks associated with the provision of food, clothing, money for the family, etc., and are largely instrumental. *Nurturance and support* functions, on the other hand, are affective in nature. This grouping includes the need for the family to make provision for comforting, reassurance, and support of the family members. The function *sexual gratification of marital partners* is self-explanatory. *Life skills development* functions refer to the adults as well as the children, and embody instrumental and affective components. The associated tasks become highly operative around the development of life skills. Examples would be the functions necessary to help a child start and get through school, the functions necessary to help an adult pursue a career or a vocational interest, and the functions required to maintain the level an individual member has achieved in personal development. The area of *maintenance and management of the family system* considers such management functions as leadership, decision-making, and those associated with maintaining the family boundaries and with maintaining standards.

Other family functions. Families may also develop functions that are unique to them. These can be adaptive or maladaptive. For example, where vacations would otherwise be impossible, a foster child's payments being used to pay for the annual family holiday could mean that the child is fulfilling an adaptive and unique function—the provision of holidays, whereas a common example of a maladaptive unique function is that of scapegoat. By definition this would be the development in the family of a functional process which involves a family member(s) becoming the active recipient on a continual basis of negative affect and/or negatively perceived attributes. The functional process serves the special purpose of providing a displacement mechanism as a means of avoiding conflicts in other more threatening areas.

In considering the role dimension, two further concepts are

considered. These are *role allocation* and *role accountability*. *Role allocation* incorporates the concepts of the assignment of responsibilities for family functions, whether such allocations are appropriate, and whether the allocation process is carried out implicitly or explicitly, by dictum or by open, free discussion. Attention is given to whether the allocated responsibilities are appropriately spread out and shared among the family members or whether they are unduly laden onto one or another overburdened member. Thus, it would not be reasonable to expect a six-year-old to take a major leadership role or for a young child to take over major functions relating to younger siblings — functions that are more appropriate for the parents. *Role accountability* involves the process of a family member being made accountable for the responsibilities which he/she has been allocated. Such accountability reinforces the commitment to and the effectiveness of the job being done.

To understand the role dimensions in a family it is important to specify the family functions (necessary or other), to ascertain whether the family has allocated the responsibilities for these functions appropriately, and whether there are appropriate mechanisms built in for accountability. The more functions that are adequately fulfilled and the clearer the allocation and accountability processes, the healthier the family.

AFFECTIVE RESPONSIVENESS

Affective responsiveness is defined as the ability to respond to a range of stimuli with appropriate quality and quantity of feelings. The focus is on the pattern of the family's responses to affective stimuli. (How they let each other know about those feelings is not considered in this dimension but within that of affective communication.)

The responses are divided into two classes, *welfare feelings* and *emergency feelings* (cf. Rado, 1961). Welfare emotions are exemplified by responses such as love, tenderness, happiness, and joy, and emergency emotions by fear, anger, sadness, disappointment, depression, etc. The appropriateness, quality, and quantity of the responses of the family and its various members to affective stimuli are considered. A family which can respond appropriately with love and tenderness but never with feelings of anger, sadness, or joy would be considered restricted and somewhat distorted. Further, it is postulated that the children in such a family would develop affective constriction which might strongly influence their personal development. The more effective the family, the wider the range and the more appropriate will be their responses in terms of quantity and quality for the given situation.

We are aware that factors related to cultural variability may have a marked and important influence on the affective responsiveness of families. Though time and space do not allow us to elaborate on this at this point, consideration obviously must be given to the issue of cultural differences within the confines of our definition.

Affective Involvement

The dimension of affective involvement is defined as the degree to which the family shows interest in and values the activities and interests of family members. The focus is on how much and in what way family members can show an interest and invest themselves in each other. There is a range of possible involvement along a spectrum as follows:

1. Lack of involvement
2. Involvement devoid of feelings
3. Narcissistic involvement
4. Empathic involvement
5. Overinvolvement
6. Symbiotic involvement

At one end of the spectrum is *lack of involvement* designating those situations where family members show no interest or investment in each other. Their only involvement is their shared physical and instrumental surroundings and functions, and they are much like a group of boarders. A second level on the spectrum is *involvement devoid of feelings*. This applies to those situations where there is some interest but little investment of the self or feelings in the relationships. The interest and investment is demonstrated only when demanded, and even then may be minimal. Another level is *narcissistic involvement*, which occurs when the investment in others is primarily egocentric and there is no feeling for the importance a particular situation holds for others. The most effective level is *empathic involvement* in which the investment in others contains feelings centered in the importance of a particular situation for the other. Family members can demonstrate a true affective concern for the interests of others in the family even though they may be peripheral to their own interests. The next level is *overinvolvement*, represented by an overintrusive, overprotective, overly warm type of involvement. The opposite end of the scale is designated *symbiotic involvement*, a label for those pathological states where the involvement is so intense that the boundaries between two or more individuals are blurred. Symbiotic involvement is seen only in seriously disturbed relationships, and at its most extreme individuals respond as one and there is marked difficulty in differentiating the boundaries of individuals.

The affective involvement dimension, therefore, considers a range of styles from a total lack of involvement at one end to an extreme involvement that blurs individual differentiation at the other. Empathic involvement is viewed as the most effective form, with involvement designations moving to either end of the spectrum implying increasingly ineffective forms of functioning.

BEHAVIOR CONTROL

The behavior control dimension is defined as the pattern the family adopts for handling behavior in three specific situations — physically dangerous situations, situations involving the meeting and expressing of psychobiological needs and drives, and situations involving socializing behavior both inside and outside the family. There are a number of obviously physically dangerous situations where the family will have to monitor and control the behavior of its members. Family members obviously attempt to meet and express a number of psychobiological needs and drives, including eating, sleeping, eliminating, sex, and aggression, and the family will adopt patterns for the control of such behaviors. Families also develop methods of controlling interpersonal socializing behavior between the family members as well as that involving people outside of the family. The inside/outside distinction is made because the pattern of acceptable behavior in each area may differ.

This definition embodies more than a consideration of child discipline. There are dangerous situations such as running into the road, playing in dangerous surroundings or with matches, etc., that apply to children. An equal number of examples exists for adults and might include behavior such as suicide attempts and reckless driving. It is important, then, to consider *all* family members' behaviors in each of these situations when conceptualizing the dimension of behavior control.

For each of these previously mentioned three areas, families develop a standard of acceptable behavior and of how much latitude they will allow in relationship to the standard. The standard and latitude for acceptable behavior determine the *style of behavior control*. The four styles of behavior control are classified as follows:

1. Rigid behavior control
2. Flexible behavior control
3. Laissez-faire behavior control
4. Chaotic behavior control

Rigid behavior control designates those situations where the rule involves a very constricted and narrow standard that allows little latitude or room for negotiation and change despite the context of situations. *Flexible behavior control,* on the other hand, involves a reasonable standard and reasonable amount of flexibility, given the context. One dictionary definition of laissez-faire is, "a philosophy of practice characterized by a usually deliberate abstention from direction or interference, especially with individual freedom of choice and action" (Webster's, 1969). *Laissez-faire behavior control* follows this definition and designates those situations where the standard or rule is not an issue because total latitude is allowed and anything goes. One dictionary definition of chaos is, "a state of things in which chance is supreme" (Webster's, 1969), and this applies to the style of *chaotic behavior control* in which the family shifts in a random fashion from rigid to flexible to laissez-faire styles so that family members are not aware which standard and latitude will be applied at any given time. Flexible behavior control is considered the most effective form and chaotic the least effective.

To maintain their style of behavior control, the family will develop a number of functions to enforce what they consider acceptable behavior. These are considered part of the role dimension and, in particular, systems maintenance and management functions.

Conclusion

There is no generally accepted model of family functioning which allows assessments to be performed in the course of family therapy practice. This article reviews the McMaster Model of Family Functioning now being used successfully in a number of clinical settings and teaching programs. Recent elaboration and clarification of the model further justifies its publication. A more detailed discussion of the literature will follow in a monograph planned for the future. Our current research and work toward the development of a family assessment device based on the Model will add to the understanding and knowledge of the Model and allow testing of the validity of the hypotheses presented in this paper.

The increasing demands for accountability from psychotherapists regarding their psychotherapy require clear statements of models and approaches. In our experience this model is clinically useful, teachable, and provides a framework which family therapists can consistently use to conceptualize their work with families.

Appendix A

Summary of Dimension Concepts

Dimensions	*Key Concepts*
Problem Solving	Affective and Instrumental problems

Problem Solving

Affective and Instrumental problems
Seven stages to the process:
1. Identification of the problem
2. Communication of the problem to the appropriate resource(s)
3. Development of action alternatives
4. Decision of one alternative
5. Action
6. Monitor that action is taken
7. Evaluation of success

Postulated:
Most effective — carry out all seven stages
Least effective — when cannot identify
(stop before stage #1)

Communication

Affective and Instrumental areas
Two independent dimensions:
1. Clear vs. masked
2. Direct vs. indirect
Above two dimensions yield four patterns of communication as follows:
1. Clear and direct
2. Clear and indirect
3. Masked and direct
4. Masked and indirect

Postulated:
Most effective — Clear and direct
Least effective — Masked and indirect

Roles

Two family function types — Necessary
                            — Other
Family functions also broken into Affective and Instrumental areas
Necessary family function groupings are:
1. Provision of resources
2. Nurturance and support
3. Adult sexual gratification
4. Life skills development
5. Systems maintenance and management

Role functioning is assessed by considering how the family *allocates* responsibilities and handles *accountability* for them.
Postulated:
Most effective—All necessary family functions have clear allocation to reasonable individual(s) and accountability built in
Least effective—Necessary family functions are not addressed and/or allocation and accountability not maintained

Affective Responsiveness

Two groupings—Welfare emotions
—Emergency emotions
Postulated:
Most effective—Full range of responses appropriate in amount and quality to stimulus
Least effective—Very narrow range (one or two affects only) and/ or amount and quality distorted, given the context

Affective Involvement

A spectrum of involvement with six styles identified:
1. Lack of involvement
2. Involvement devoid of feelings
3. Narcissistic involvement
4. Empathic involvement
5. Overinvolvement
6. Symbiotic involvement
Postulated:
Most effective—Empathic involvement
Least effective—Symbiotic involvement and Lack of involvement

Behavior Control

Applies to three situations:
1. Dangerous situations
2. Meeting and expressing of psychobio-

logical needs and drives (eating, drinking, sleeping, eliminating, sex, and aggression)
3. Interpersonal socializing processes inside and outside the family

Style is determined by the standard and latitude of what is acceptable in each of the above. Four styles are defined:
1. Rigid behavior control
2. Flexible behavior control
3. Laissez-faire behavior control
4. Chaotic behavior control

To maintain the style, various techniques are used and implemented under role functions (systems maintenance and management)

Postulated:

Most effective — Flexible behavior control
Least effective — Chaotic behavior control

REFERENCES

Bateson, D., Jackson, D. D., Haley, J., & Weakland, J. (1956), Towards a theory of schizophrenia. *Behav. Sci.*, 1:251–264.
Berman, E. M. & Lief, H. I. (1975), Marital therapy from a psychiatric perspective: An overview. *Amer. J. Psychiat.*, 132:583–592.
Brody, E. M. (1974), Aging and family personality: A developmental view. *Fam. Proc.*, 13:23–37.
Comley, A. (1973), Family therapy and the family physician. *Can. Fam. Physician*, 19:78–81.
Dewey, J. & Bentley, A. F. (1949), *Knowing and the Known*. Boston: Beacon.
Epstein, N. B. (1958), Concepts of normality or evaluations of emotional health. *Behav. Sci.*, 3:355–343.
_____ & Bishop, D. S. (1973), State of the art — 1973. *Can. Psychiat. Assn. J.*, 18:175–183.
_____ Levin, S., & Bishop, D. S. (1976), The family as a social unit. *Can. Fam. Physician*, 22:1411–1413.
_____ & McAuley, R. G. (1978), A family systems approach to patients' emotional problems in family practice. In: *Family Medicine: Principles and Applications*, ed. J. H. Medalie. Baltimore: Williams and Wilkins.
_____ Sigal, J. J., & Rakoff, V. (1962), Family categories schema. Unpublished manuscript prepared in the Family Research Group of the Department of Psychiatry, Jewish General Hospital, in collaboration with the McGill Human Development Study.
_____ & Westley, W. A. (1959), Patterns of intra-familial communication. *Psychiatric Research Reports 11, American Psychiatric Association*, 1–9.
Finkel, K. (1974), Personal communication.

Glick, I. D. & Haley, J. (1971), *Family Therapy and Research: An Annotated Bibliography of Articles and Books Published 1950–1970.* New York: Grune & Stratton.

Group for the Advancement of Psychiatry (1970), *The Field of Family Therapy.* Report No. 78.

Gurman, A. S. & Kniskern, D. P. (1978), Research on marital and family therapy: Progress, perspective and prospect. In: *Handbook of Psychotherapy and Behavior Change: An Empirical Analysis,* 2nd ed., ed. S. L. Garfield and A. E. Bergin. New York: Wiley.

Guttman, H. A., Spector, R. M., Sigal, J. J., Rakoff, V., & Epstein, N. B. (1971), Reliability of coding affective communication in family therapy sessions: Problems of measurement and interpretation. *J. Consult. Clin. Psychol.,* 37:397–402.

——— ——— ——— Epstein, N. B., & Rakoff, V. (1972), Coding of affective expressions in conjoint family therapy. *Amer. J. Psychother.,* 26:185–194.

Hadley, T. R., Jacob, T., Milliones, J., Caplan, J., & Spitz, D. (1974), The relationship between family developmental crisis and the appearance of symptoms in a family member. *Fam. Proc.,* 13:207–214.

Haley, J. (1971), A review of the family therapy field. In: *Changing Families: A Family Therapy Reader,* ed. J. Haley. New York: Grune & Stratton.

Hill, R. (1965), Generic features of families under stress. In: *Crisis Intervention: Selected Readings,* ed. H. J. Parad. New York: Family Services Association of America.

Langsley, D. G. & Kaplan, D. M. (1968), *The Treatment of Families in Crisis.* New York: Grune & Stratton.

Lederer, W. J. & Jackson, D. (1968), *The Mirages of Marriage.* New York: Norton.

McClelland, C. Q., Staples, W. I., Weisberg, I., & Bergen, M. E. (1973), The practitioner's role in behavioral pediatrics. *J. Pediat.,* 82:325–331.

McFarlane, A. H., Norman, G. R., & Spitzer, W. O. (1971a), Family medicine: The dilemma of defining the discipline. *Can. Med. Assn. J.,* 105: 397–401.

——— O'Connell, B., & Hay, J. (1971b), Demand-for-care model: Its use in program planning for primary physician education. *J. Med. Ed.,* 46: 436–442.

Minuchin, S. & Barcai, A. (1969), Therapeutically induced family crisis. In: *Science and Psychoanalysis, Vol. 14: Childhood and Adolescence,* ed. J. H. Masserman. New York: Grune & Stratton.

Olson, D. H. (1970), Marital and family therapy: Integrative review and critique. *J. Marr. Fam.,* 32:501–538.

Parad, H. J. & Caplan, G. (1965), A framework for studying families in crisis. In: *Crisis Intervention: Selected Readings,* ed. H. J. Parad. New York: Family Services Association of America.

Parsons, T. (1951), *The Social System.* Glencoe, Ill.: Free Press.

——— & Bales, R. F. (1955), *Family Socialization and Interaction Process.* Glencoe, Ill.: Free Press.

Patriarche, M. E. (1974), Finding time for counselling. *Can. Fam. Physician,* 20:91–93.

Postner, R. S., Guttman, H. A., Sigal, J. J., Epstein, N. B., & Rakoff, V. (1971), Process and outcome in conjoint family therapy. *Fam. Proc.,* 10:451–473.

Rado, S. (1961), Towards the construction of an organized foundation for clinical psychiatry. *Compr. Psychiat.*, 2:65–73.

Rakoff, V., Sigal, J. J., Spector, R., & Guttman, M. A. (1967), Communication in families. Unpublished manuscript.

Rapoport, L. (1965), The state of crisis: Some theoretical considerations. In: *Crisis Intervention: Selected Readings*, ed. H. J. Parad. New York: Family Services Association of America.

Ritterman, M. K. (1977), Paradigmatic classification of family therapy theories. *Fam. Proc.*, 16:29–48.

Santa-Barbara, J., Woodward, C. A., Levin, S., Streiner, D., Goodman, J., & Epstein, N. B. (1975), The relationship between therapists' characteristics and outcome variables in family therapy. Paper presented at the Canadian Psychiatric Association, Banff, Alberta, September.

Scherz, F. H. (1971), Maturational crises and parent-child interaction. *Soc. Case.*, 52:362–369.

Sigal, J. J., Rakoff, V., & Epstein, N. B. (1967), Indicators of therapeutic outcome in conjoint family therapy. *Fam. Proc.*, 6:215–226.

Solomon, M. A. (1973), A developmental, conceptual premise for family therapy. *Fam. Proc.*, 12:179–188.

Spiegel, J. (1971), *Transactions*. New York: Science House.

Stanford, B. J. (1972), Counseling — A prime area for family doctors. *Amer. Fam. Physician*, 5:183–185.

Tomm, K. (1973), A family approach to emotional problems of children. *Can. Fam. Physician*, 19:51–54, 60.

Watzlawick, P., Beavin, J. H., & Jackson, D. D. (1967), *Pragmatics of Human Communication*. New York: Norton.

Weakland, J., Fisch, R., Watzlawick, P., & Bodin, A. M. (1974), Brief therapy: Focussed problem resolution. *Fam. Proc.*, 13:141–168.

Webster's Seventh New Collegiate Dictionary (1969), Based on Webster's Third New International Dictionary. Toronto: Thomas Allan & Sons Ltd.

Westley, W. A. & Epstein, N. B. (1960), Report on the psychosocial organization of the family and mental health. In: *Decisions, Values and Groups, Vol. 1*, ed. D. Willner. New York: Pergamon.

———— ———— (1969), *The Silent Majority*. San Francisco: Jossey-Bass.

Woodward, C. A., Santa-Barbara, J., Levin, S., Goodman, J., Streiner, D., Muzzin, L., & Epstein, N. B. (1974), Outcome research in family therapy: On the growing edginess of family therapists. Paper presented at the Nathan W. Ackerman Memorial Conference, Margarita Island, February.

———— ———— ———— ———— ———— & Epstein, N. B. (1975), Client and therapist characteristics related to family therapy outcome: Closure and follow-up evaluation. Paper presented at the Society for Psychotherapy Research, Boston.

———— ———— ———— Epstein, N. B., & Streiner, D. (1977), The McMaster Family Therapy Outcome Study III: Client and treatment characteristics significantly contributing to clinical outcomes. Paper presented at the 54th Annual Meeting of the American Orthopsychiatric Association, New York City, April.

Zuk, G. H. (1971), Family therapy during 1964–1970. *Psychother.: Th. Res. Pract.*, 8:90–97.

Family Psychopathology

The understanding of psychopathology opens the door to precise diagnosis and effective therapy. This is true in the family field also. Psychic family group mechanisms have to be identified and clarified. Here are presented significant contributions that carry our understanding further on disturbed communication, deviant family interaction, role structure, episodic discontrol, intergenerational transmission, and the ecology of the dysfunctioning family.

Communication in the Family of the Asthmatic Child: An Experimental Approach

R. WIKRAN, A. FALEIDE, and R. M. BLAKAR

INTRODUCTION

Childhood asthma is now predominantly classified as a psychosomatic suffering (cf. Pinkerton and Weaver, 1970). The reason why it has been so difficult to gain insight into illnesses such as childhood asthma is the multifactorial causes (Aas, 1969a; Pinkerton and Weaver, 1970). Aas lists the following types of factors: biochemical, infectious, circulatory, ventilatory, psychogenic, allergic, and "unknown" factors.

Asthma in childhood may be precipitated, aggravated, and prolonged by various factors, and the influence of the same factor seems to vary from patient to patient, and over time within the same patient. However, there seems to be somatic predisposition in all cases of childhood asthma (Freeman et al., 1964; Feingold et al., 1966; Aas, 1969b). But there is no one-to-one relation between the physical basis and the severeness of the asthma (Jennings et al., 1966). Somatic as well a psychic factors may maintain the asthmatic condition (Block et al., 1964).

Rolf Wikran is Clinical Psychologist, Opdol Hospital, 6450 Hjelset, Norway; Asbjorn Faleide and Rolv Mikkel Blakar are on the staff of the Institute of Psychology, University of Oslo, PBox 1094 Blinden, Oslo 3, Norway.

We are grateful to Dr. Sorland, Cardiologic Department, Associate Professor Dr. med. Kjell Aas and Dr. Dag Nilsson, Section on Allergy at the Pediatric Department, Rikshospitalet, Oslo, and The Allergic Institute, Voksentoppen, Oslo, for their kind assistance regarding the subjects. This research has been supported by the Norwegian Council of Social Science and the Humanities under grants B.60.01–85 and B.60.01–100 given to Rolv Mikkel Blakar. The authors are indebted to Kjell Aas and Finn Askevold for valuable comments on an earlier version of this paper.

A comprehensive presentation of the projects of which the present study is an integral part is available in Rolv Mikkel (1980), *Studies of Familial Communication and Psychopathology: A Social-Developmental Approach to Deviant Behavior*. Oslo: Universitetsforlaget; New York: Columbia University Press.

Since the early 1950s there has been a fundamental change in attitudes toward psychopathology in general. There has been an increasing tendency to conceive of psychopathology as a product of the communication/interaction in the family and close environment, and not only as predominantly genetically determined individual states (Ruesch, 1951; Bateson et al., 1956, 1963). This redefinition *in terms* of communication initiated a lot of research, and various theories were developed (for reviews, see Mishler and Waxler, 1965; Handel, 1967; Framo, 1972; Riskin and Faunce, 1972; Jacobsen and Pettersen, 1974; Blakar, 1976, 1978, 1979a). It has to be mentioned, however, that the explanatory value of the substantial part of these communication-oriented studies on psychopathology is questionable (cf. Schuham, 1967; Riskin and Faunce, 1972; Blakar, 1974, 1975d, 1978, 1979b).

In therapy as well as in research there has been an increasing tendency to adopt a communication perspective and conceive of the family as a system and not work exclusively with the identified patient. Even in connection with different somatic illnesses some writers have argued in favor of such a strategy. In the summary of the survey "A Family Perspective of Psychosomatic Factors in Illness: A Review of the Literature," Grolnick (1972) concludes: "But the above viewpoint goes beyond the simple psychosomatic-organic dichotomy. One must consider whether a given family needs a member's illness, whether that illness be schizophrenia, alcoholism (Albee's "A Delicate Balance"), endocrine pathology, or whatever" (p. 479).

The purpose of the present paper is twofold: First, the literature on childhood asthma will be reviewed in order to see whether any support, direct or indirect, may be found for adopting a communication perspective in gaining insight into childhood asthma. Secondly, an exploratory experimental study of the communication pattern and efficiency of the asthmatic child's family will be presented.

It has to be emphasized that we conceive of the communication perspective as a supplementary perspective. The communication perspective exclusively will never be sufficient to understand bronchial asthma in childhood (cf. Blakar and Nafstad, 1979a).

REVIEW OF THE LITERATURE

When reviewing the literature, one has to be aware of all the methodological pitfalls in the psychosomatic asthma research (cf. Purcell, 1965; Feingold et al., 1966). Having reviewed more than 200 studies from 1950 on, Freeman et al. (1964) conclude: "In general the yield from all the effort expended to date is small indeed" (p. 565). On the other hand, no other alternative than a critical use of the available literature seems reasonable in the present case.

The most relevant literature fell naturally under the following three headings: (1) personality traits of the asthmatic child, (2) the mother-child relationship, (3) the milieu of the asthmatic child. The present review is not intended to give a general overview of the literature on childhood asthma. However, the literature is reviewed to see what support there may be for adopting a communication perspective on childhood asthma.

Personality Traits

There has been postulated a dependency conflict in the asthmatic child's relation to his mother (French and Alexander, 1941). A sensation of being avoided by, or separated from, the mother may provoke an asthmatic attack. This attack would thus represent a symbolic cry-out for the mother (French, 1939). Such an explanation may sound like a slogan. On the other hand, Sperling spells this out as a "psychosomatic relation" where the child is avoided only when being in good health and in proper function, claiming to be independent, but, in contrast, is rewarded and cared for when ill and helpless (Sperling, 1955). Several researchers support this hypothesis (Miller and Baruch, 1957; Block, 1969). Alcock (1960) studied four groups of children using the Rorschach projective technique. She found the asthmatic child to manifest a conflict typically centered around the object-relation and strong emotional loading that did not find an adequate outlet.

In discussing this psychoanalytic interpretation, Pinkerton and Weaver (1970) claim that this "approach/avoidance-conflict" is only one particular way of conceiving of what they more broadly suggest is an implicit "aura of ambivalence" present in the family situation. We assume that this ambivalence will affect the familial interaction, and result in confused and indirect communication.

In a heavily controlled study conducted by Garner and Wenar (1959) the psychosomatic children in general showed less capacity for social behavior than the controls, and they demonstrated less ability to give vent to intensive reactions and direct expressions of feelings. Furthermore they were more suspicious than the children in the control groups.

Moreover, both Alcock (1960) and Garner and Wenar (1959) call attention to the cumulation of emotional loading. It is not unlikely that one may find corresponding latent tensions within the family communication system.

The Mother-Child Relationship

As is the case in developmental psychology in general, research on childhood asthma has focused almost exclusively on the mother-child relation, and has tended to ignore the influence of the father, of the parental interaction, etc.

Garner and Wenar (1959) hypothesized that children with psychosomatic disorders lack "mothering." Roughly this means that mother and child are not operating in harmony with each other, and the mother is not able to meet the child's needs in an adequate manner. Through observations of the mother-child relationship in connection to differential diseases, they found in psychosomatic illnesses an almost negative interaction, i.e., the mother-child relationship was both close and frustrating. Their interaction was flavored by competition. This was most typical for the mother. In interpreting the results, Garner and Wenar maintain that the child is still a part of the mother's "self." The child has not learned to differentiate himself from the mother. Block et al. (1964) reached an analogous conclusion. Abramson (1954) describes the parents and child as "engulfing" each other. Thus this close and undifferentiated relationship seems to be typical for the whole family.

But the mother-child relation is not established in a social vacuum. As Titchener et al. (1960) comment in connection with ulcerative colitis: "We are of the opinion that colitigenic mothers are not born nor even made in their own childhood. Their ways of relating to their children come into being *in the family situation* and their special relationship with future ulcerative patients are largely determined by the dynamics of the family environment" (p. 129). In this connection one of our own studies (Faleide, 1969) is of particular interest. We found that traumatic events in the grandparents' generation seemed to have severely hindered the emotional development of one or both of the parents. One may thus tend to say that the asthmatic symptom of the child is the third generation's reaction to the first (grandparents') generation's conflict.

In clinical work with asthmatic children, we have noticed three characteristics typical of their familial situation. They live under constant emotional repression, in an atmosphere of unclear communication, in which their symptoms are being rewarded (Faleide, 1973). Furthermore, Ackerman (1958) discusses a correlation between inconsistent role expectations and unclear communication in the surroundings on one hand, and psychosomatic symptom formation of the child on the other. Mitchell et al. (1953) claim that the parents of the asthmatic child are inhibited in their emotional expressions. They also found that the parental interaction is characterized by the mother's domination and the father's withdrawal. Block et al. (1966) found deprivation to be a dominant trait in the mothers. In our clinical practice we have often noticed the father's "blindness" regarding the mother's needs (Faleide and Vandvik, 1976).

ALTERED ENVIRONMENT

It has been known for a long time that some children lose their asthmatic symptoms immediately upon hospitalization (Coolidge, 1956; Tuft, 1957; Peshkin and Abramson, 1959). Thus Tuft (1957) concluded with regard to the asthmatic child that "the conclusion seems inescapable that this relationship to his parents or his environment represented by his parent played the dominant role in the continuation of the former state of asthma" (p. 252).

A study by Long et al. (1958) lends support to Tuft's conclusion. A group of chronically ill asthmatic children hospitalized during an attack were tested for sensitivity to house dust. When symptom-free, the children with sensitivity to house dust were exposed to dust collected from their own homes. None of them reacted with asthmatic attacks.

In Purcell et al.'s (1969) study, parents and siblings of asthmatic children were removed from home, and lived in a hotel for two weeks. The patients were cared for in their own homes by substitute parents, thus keeping the physical surroundings almost perfectly constant. On the basis of interviews with the parents, it was predicted beforehand which children would become symptom-free. The predictions were based on whether the attacks were related to emotional factors. All the children predicted to be positive responders improved significantly during this experimental family separation. Taken together, the studies of Long et al. (1958) and Purcell et al. (1969) strongly indicate that social factors in the family are active in initiating and maintaining asthmatic attacks.

It has been claimed that the children who become symptom-free through hospitalization (rapidly remitting, [RR]) have a more psychogenic asthma than the steroid-dependent ones (SD). Indeed, many of the RR-children reported emotional factors as precursors of an attack (Purcell, 1965), although on the whole, both RR- and SD-children often considered complicated, interpersonal conflict situations in the family to be the precipitator of asthmatic attacks.

Kluger (1969) found it characteristic of the social system of the chronically ill patients that they exploited their physical illness as a medium for communication and interaction. Meissner (1966) describes somatic expressions of disharmony in the familial system of psychosomatic patients. Thus somatizing often seems to be the expression of conflicts in the family of the asthmatic child.

In his communication theory of psychosomatic diseases, Ruesch (1951) holds that the psychosomatic patient has learned to put greater value on his physical than on his psychic processes. Hence the body has acquired great communicational value.

Finally, Kluger (1969) noticed that all the members of the family show less social activity than would normally be expected, taking the age of the child and the socioeconomic status of the family into consideration.

In conclusion, then, on the basis of the literature it seems reasonable to assume that the communication typical of the family of the child with severe asthma is unclear and characterized by ambivalence, and in particular that overt and open discussions in connection with conflicts are avoided.

EXPERIMENTAL APPROACH

The above exposition of the literature has clearly demonstrated that a systematic examination of communication patterns in the family of the asthmatic child might represent a substantial contribution. As was demonstrated in the above review, on the basis of the literature rather specific hypotheses about the communication in such families could even be proposed. However, at the present stage of research it would seem more reasonable to conduct exploratory, though systematic, studies with the purpose of identifying and describing *qualitative* characteristics of the communication typical of such families, rather than of testing specific hypotheses. For a more general program on communication-oriented studies on psychopathology, see Blakar (1974, 1978, 1979a).

Every communication-oriented study on psychopathology — irrespective of which diagnostic categories one chooses to study — is immediately confronted with two substantial problems: First, there is the vague or even entire lack of relevant communication theory (cf. Riskin and Faunce, 1972; Blakar, 1975a, 1976, 1978, 1979a). Secondly, there is the serious lack of adequate methods (cf. Grinker et al., 1968; Haley, 1972; Blakar, 1974, 1978, 1979a; Blakar and Nafstad, 1979b).

The choice or development of methods in this field should ideally be based on an explicit theory of communication, and knowledge about families with psychopathological members. Regarding the latter, Haley (1972) concludes in his recent review of the field:

If we accept the findings of the research reported here and assuming it is sound, evidence is accumulating to support the idea that a family with a patient member is different from an "average" family. As individuals, the family members do not appear different according to the usual character and personality criteria. Similarly, evidence is slight that family structure, when conceived in terms of role assignment or dominance, is different in normal and abnormal families. On process measurements there is some indication of difference: Abnormal families appear to have more conflict, to have different coalition patterns, and to show more inflexibility in repeating patterns of behaviour. *The most sound findings would seem to be in the outcome area: When faced with a task* on which they must co-operate, abnormal family members seem *to communicate their preferences less successfully, require more activity and take longer to get the task done* [p. 35; italics added].

Our own expectations concerning the communication in the family of the asthmatic child (cf. the above review) would also point at the suitability of a cooperation task. And we felt that an experimental situation of the type envisaged by Haley would be a good point of departure.

THE METHOD AND ITS BACKGROUND

Starting from general social-cognitive theory on language and communication (Rommetveit, 1968, 1972; Blakar, 1970), we designed a method directed toward an identification of some *prerequisites for* communication (Blakar, 1973). The ideas behind the method were further inspired by various studies of communicational breakdowns, especially those typical for children (e.g., Piagetian studies on egocentrism), but also analyses of "usual" misunderstandings and how they occur (e.g., Ichheiser, 1970; Garfinkel, 1972). For a detailed presentation of the theoretical basis of the method, see Blakar (1972, 1973, 1975b, 1978, 1979a).

The idea behind the method was simple in the extreme, but in practice very difficult to carry out. The fundamental idea was to try to create a communication situation where one of the preconditions for (successful) communication was *not* satisfied. If one were able to create such a situation, one would be able to study at least: (1) the impact of that particular variable on communication, (2) the potential "missing requirements or preconditions" to which the subjects would attribute the resultant communicative difficulties, and (3) what the subjects actually do in order to try to "improve" their communication when it goes astray.

Perhaps the most basic precondition for successful communication to take place at all is that the participants have *"a shared social reality,"* a common "here and now" within which exchange of messages can take place (Rommetveit, 1972, 1974; Blakar, 1975a; Blakar and Rommetveit, 1975; Rommetveit and Blakar, 1979).

From what has already been said, an ideal experimental situation would then be one where two (or more) participants communicate with each other in the belief that they are "in the same situation" (i.e., have a common definition of the situation's "here" and "now"), but where they are in fact in different situations. In other words, we should try to create a situation where each participant speaks and understands what is said on the basis of his own particular interpretation of the situation, and falsely *believes* that the other (others) speaks and understands on the basis of that very same interpretation as well (cf. everyday quarrels and misunderstandings).

This is not the place to elaborate on the theory or explain the development of the method in any detail. Here it is sufficient to say that by relatively simple means we successfully created a communication situation of this type (Blakar, 1973). Concretely, the situation is as follows: Two persons, A and B, are each given a map of a relatively complicated network of roads and streets in a town center. On A's map two routes are marked with arrows: One short and straightforward (the practice route) and another longer and more complicated (the experimental route). On B's map no route is marked in. A's task is then to explain to B the two routes, first the simple one, then the longer and more complicated one. B will then, with A's explanations, try to find the way through town to the predetermined end-point. B can ask questions, ask A to repeat explanations, or to explain in other ways, etc. The experimental manipulation is simply that the two maps are not identical. There is an extra street added on B's map. So no matter how adequately A explains, no matter how carefully B carries out A's instructions, B is bound to go wrong. The difference between the two maps has implications only for the complicated route, however; the practice route is straightforward.

The practice route was included for three reasons: (1) to get the subjects used to the situation, (2) to strengthen their confidence in the maps, and (3) to obtain a sample of their communication in the same kind of situation, but *un*affected by our experimental manipulation (a "before-after" design).

The two participants sit at opposite ends of a table with two low screens hiding their maps from each other. The screens are low enough for them to see each other and have natural eye-contact (cf. Moscovici,

1967; Argyle, 1969). Everything said is tape-recorded, and for certain analyses the tape must be transcribed afterwards. For a more detailed presentation of the method and its theoretical background, see Blakar (1973).

Clinical Application of the Method

A study in which students served as subjects (Blakar, 1972, 1973) convinced us that the experimental manipulation was successful. The most interesting observations from this first study were: (1) It took an average of 18 minutes from the start on the experimental route *before* any doubt as to the credibility of the maps was expressed. During this time the subjects communicated under the false assumption that they were sharing the *same* situation (the same "here"). (2) Moreover, the situation proved successful in throwing light on (a) how the subjects "diagnosed" their communicative difficulties, and (b) what kind of "therapeutic" tools they had at their disposal in order to repair and improve their communication. The experimental situation appeared to make great demands upon the subjects' powers of flexibility and ability to modify their communication patterns, and also upon their capacity to decenter and see things from the other's perspective.

It was the latter findings in particular that led to the idea that the method could possibly be used to illuminate communication deficiencies in families with psychopathological members. And an exploratory study demonstrated that the method was sensitive with respect to differences in the communication of parental couples with and without schizophrenic offspring (Solvberg and Blakar, 1975).

In the present study we chose to focus upon the parental communication patterns. This for two reasons: First, we did not want to have the patient himself present, as possible differences could then be "explained" as a function of special considerations being made for the patient member. Secondly, the parents create the basic dyad of the family, the child being born into a milieu created by the parents.

It is essential to emphasize that a study of this type cannot say anything definite with respect to *causality* (cf. Blakar, 1974; Blakar and Nafstad, 1979a). On the other hand, there can scarcely exist any longer good reasons (i.e., in communication-oriented family research) for thinking in terms of simple chains of causality; one has to regard the family as a complex system (Jackson, 1959, 1965, 1966, 1967; Watzlawick et al., 1967; Jacobsen and Pettersen, 1974; Blakar and Nafstad, 1979a). Even though the parents do play a conclusive role in the constitution of the family system, there is no doubt that the childhood asthma, with its severe and often dramatic attacks, strongly influences the personality and the familial situation and interaction (cf. Holthe, 1972). For example, Neuhaus (1958) and Alcock (1960) hold different positions as to whether the typical personality traits are one of the consequences or one of the causes of chronic asthma.

Since the communication task given each couple is in principle unsolvable, we had to decide upon the criteria for terminating the experimental session beforehand. In earlier applications of the method, the following set of criteria was used (Solvberg and Blakar, 1975, p. 523):

1) The task would be considered as successfully finished as soon as the error was correctly localized and identified. 2) The task would also be considered resolved if and when the route was correctly reconstructed to the point of the error and one or both of the subjects insisted that the maps were not identical, and hence that there was no point in going on. (In this connection it has to be emphasized that the experimenter was instructed to neglect all suggestions that something might be wrong and give the impression that everything was OK as long as possible; see Blakar, 1973, p. 418). 3) Furthermore, if no solution according to criteria (1) and/or (2) was reached within 40 minutes, the communication task would be brought to an end. The subjects would then be shown the discrepancy between the maps and told that the task was in reality unsolvable. The 40-minute limit was chosen on the basis of earlier experiments (Blakar, 1973) and pretests with married couples of the same age and social background as the subjects to be. 4) Finally, it was decided that if the task should cause the couple too much emotional upset, the experimenter should stop and reveal the introduced error to them.

Re-analyses (Moberget and Reer, 1975; Endresen, 1977) of tape-recordings from preceding studies, however, have revealed two problems concerning these criteria: First, the experimenter could, according to criterion (2), accept the task as being solved, and consequently reveal the error to the couple in cases where careful examinations of the tape-recording (particularly the subjects' spontaneous comments afterwards) could throw doubt as to whether or not they had really resolved the communication conflict. Naturally, this would result in a loss of essential information. Secondly, it happened in some cases that merely one of the spouses revealed the deceptive maps, while the other one would show great surprise when the error was afterwards uncovered by a direct comparison of the two maps. This type of solution, which has been classified as an *individual* solution (Hultberg et al., 1976), is very different from cases where the two of them both are firmly convinced about the error (a *social* solution). Again, if the experimenter *too* readily accepts an individual solution, we would lose the chance to study how the spouse with insight about the deception would convince or fail to convince the other. Actually, this phase could be very revealing as to factors such as power and control. In order not to lose such critical information, we decided that the experimenter should "press" the couples as much as possible toward criterion (1) and not accept solutions according to criterion (2). Furthermore, the experimenter would hesitate to accept individual solutions and see whether the couple could reach a joint conclusion.

In order to simplify comparison between various couples the distribution of the two differential maps to the spouses had to be standardized. In order to play against culturally determined male-dominance, we gave the map with the routes marked in to the wives, so the husbands had to follow the directives and explanations of their wives.

SAMPLES AND MATCHING

Of basic theoretical importance is the selection of controls. There has been much diffuse theorizing due to random selection of controls, in particular the so-called "normal" family has been uncritically used as control (Haley, 1972; Blakar, 1975c; Blakar and Nafstad, 1979b). To make sure that the couples would be as comparable as possible, we had to select controls that were parents to a severely ill child, but where there should be no theoretical reason to expect any connection between the disease and the pattern of communication within the family. Parents to children with severe, chronic heart disease satisfy these criteria, and have frequently been used as controls in studies on asthma (Neuhaus, 1958; Glaser et al., 1964; Purcell, 1965; Grolnick, 1972).

For this study, then, we decided to use the two following groups of disorders. In group A (asthma) the patient member had the diagnosis bronchial asthma, strictly used, and the patients were aged from 7–11 years, because this is a relatively stable period. We had to select severe asthmatics so that the reactive factor was to be comparable with the corresponding factor in the heart disease group.

Congenital heart disease represents a stable condition, so for the two groups to be comparable, we aimed at as much stability in the A-group as possible. In establishing the heart disease (HD) group several diagnoses were included, but all had a congenital physical heart defect. The two groups were satisfactorily matched with respect to relevant background variables such as age, number of years of marriage, education, employment, social group, annual income, domicile, living conditions, number of children and their sex and age (for further details on the matching, see Wikran, 1974, pp. 55–61).

HYPOTHESES

Even though the present study is highly exploratory, hypotheses concerning degree of efficiency as well as qualitative differences were set forth. Regarding the possibility of *testing* specific hypotheses, the very nature of the experimental method is essential (cf. Blakar, 1974, 1978, 1979a). The method consists of two apparently similar, but in reality highly different, communication tasks. Whereas the first one is simple and straightforward, the second induces a communication conflict.

The following rather general hypotheses may in fact be considered tentative conclusions based on the above review of the asthma literature, and are in accordance with Haley's views (cf. the above quotation):

1. Couples from Group A will communicate less efficiently than those from Group HD. And this difference in efficiency will be most pronounced on the experimental route, where, due to the induced communication conflict, a critical reevaluation of and change in patterns of communication is required. In other words, the Group A couples will have *more problems* and use *longer time* in solving the experimental route where the communication conflict is induced.

2. Qualitative differences between the communication in Group A and Group HD will be revealed, and such differences are expected whether the communication situation is simple or complicated. On the basis of the literature, the communication of the Group A couples is expected to be more rigid, unclear, and replete with ambivalence. Furthermore, the Group A couples will tend to avoid open — and potentially clarifying — confrontation in conflict situations (also with respect to the experimentally induced communication conflict).

3. Finally, it is supposed that the qualitative differences (2) will throw light on and partly explain the differences in efficiency of communication (1).

RESULTS AND DISCUSSION

As was the case in the earlier studies with student subjects (Blakar, 1973; Stokstad et al., 1976, 1979) and married couples (Solvberg and Blakar, 1975) all the couples became absorbed and involved in the communication task.

Let us start by examining the communication on the simple practice

TABLE 1
TIME SPENT AND NUMBER OF RETURNS
TO THE STARTING POINT ON THE TRAINING ROUTE

Couple No.	A-1/HD-6	A-2/HD-7	A-3/HD-8	A-4/HD-9	A-5/HD-10
Asthma group	–* 27 times	54 sec 1 time	37 min 31 sec 14 times	3 min 49 sec 2 times	5 min 37 sec 2 times
Heart disease group	2 min 46 sec 1 time	2 min 27 sec 1 time	2 min 17 sec 1 time	3 min 0 sec 1 time	6 min 48 sec 1 time

* A-1 did not master the training route within 40 min.

route where they are not being influenced by the experimental manipulation. The most striking observation in Table 1 is the wide within-group variation found in the A-group. Group A is actually divided into two separate sub-groups: A-2, A-4, and A-5 with a mean of 3 minutes 27 seconds, which is almost identical to the Group HD, which used a mean of 3 minutes 29 seconds, and the two couples A-1 and A-3, demonstrating an extremely inefficient communication.

A direct comparison with the previous study on parents with and without schizophrenic children (Solvberg and Blakar, 1975) shows how inefficient the communication in this sub-group (A-1 and A-3) really was. The parents of the schizophrenic patients (S-group) used a mean of 4 minutes 50 seconds (ranging from 2 minutes 5 seconds to 9 minutes 56 seconds), whereas the parents of the controls (N-group) used 4 minutes 57 seconds (2 minutes 2 seconds to 8 minutes 52 seconds). That the HD-group and the other A sub-groups (A-2, A-4, and A-5) were a little more efficient than the S- and N-groups is likely to be due to their younger age and higher socioeconomic level.

Of the nine couples who started on the experimental route (A-1 did not manage the training route within 40 minutes, and consequently was not started on the experimental route), eight couples managed to solve the experimental route according to the predetermined criteria. All five HD-couples managed, whereas only three of the A-group couples succeeded. As would be expected from the practice route, it was A-3 which did not succeed within the 40-minute limit. If the time the "solvers" used is examined, no difference is found between the two groups. The three A-group solvers used a mean of about 30 minutes, and the five HD-couples a mean of about 32 minutes.

Such a dichotomy in the A-group did not come as a surprise. First, on the basis of the multifactorial causality (see above), a rather heterogeneous group had to be expected. Secondly, as part of the training of the experimenter (cf. Wikran, 1974, pp. 53–55), among others three A-couples were tested. Two of them resolved the induced communication conflict, whereas the third one did not.

However, the division into sub-groups made our A-group sample of five too small even for this exploratory study. Before qualitative analysis of the communication could reasonably be carried out, we had to enlarge the material in order to see how real such a dichotomy of the A-parents was. An enlargement of the sample was also required in order to get an idea of the relative distribution over the two sub-groups. Hence, as an additional study, as many A-couples as possible within our time limits were run. When we were obliged to stop experimenting, nine additional A-couples had been run.

All of them managed the practice route; mean time was 4 minutes 27 seconds, ranging from 42 seconds to 8 minutes 38 seconds. On the experimental route six couples managed, whereas three did not resolve the induced communication conflict. In Table 2 the distribution of "solvers" and "non-solvers" in our total A-sample of 17 couples is given. With respect to efficiency of communication, about one-third of the A-couples demonstrate an inefficient communication, whereas the rest of the group communicate as efficiently as the controls (HD- and N-groups). This distribution holds whether we look at the total sample or at each of the different part-studies (pretraining, main experiment, additional sample). Among the six "non-solvers" are two couples who in addition demonstrated real problems in mastering the simple communication task (i.e., the practice route).

From a general methodological point of view the controls (HD-group) are very interesting indeed. The argument then goes as follows: Blakar (1972, 1973) developed a method to study some prerequisites for communication. Solvberg and Blakar (1975) proved the method to be sensitive with respect to differences in communication of parents with and without schizophrenic offspring. Against this it may be argued that no communication patterns specific to parents of schizophrenic offspring had been revealed, but that it had merely been demonstrated that parents of severely ill children experience this experimental situation differently from control groups, i.e., that the demand characteristics of the situation are different for the two groups (cf. Haley, 1972; Blakar, 1975c; Blakar and Nafstad, 1979b).

In contrast to the N-group, but on a par with the S-group parents, the HD-parents *knew* that they were participating in the experiment *because* they were parents of severely ill children. As far as we can tell, the HD-parents did *not* deviate from the N-group in the previous study.

TABLE 2
DISTRIBUTION OF "SOLVERS/NON-SOLVERS" IN THE
THREE SUB-SAMPLES OF A-GROUP COUPLES

Sample	Solvers	Non-solvers	Total
Pretraining sample	2	1	3
Experimental sample	3	2	5
Additional sample	6	3	9
Total	11	6	17

The communication pattern found by Solvberg and Blakar in couples with a schizophrenic offspring can therefore not be said to be typical of the communication of parents to children with *all types* of severe illnesses.

It has to be mentioned that Hultberg et al. (1976) in a study applying this same method found that the pattern of communication in couples being parents to borderline patients deviated both from the pattern found in couples having a schizophrenic offspring and from that found in the parents of the normal controls. (For a general analysis of demand characteristics in this kind of research, see Blakar and Nafstad, 1979b.)

FURTHER QUALITATIVE ANALYSIS

In order to corroborate the above findings and to make an attempt at identifying qualitative characteristics specific to the communication of the group-A parents, the following analyses were conducted:

1. A communication-oriented student trained in clinical psychology was given the 10 tape-recordings (five A and five HD) from the main experiment, and asked to describe the interaction and, on the basis of her descriptions, to predict which of the couples had an asthmatic child and which had a heart-diseased child.

2. Detailed casuistic descriptions of the communication process applying the conceptual framework of social-cognitive communication theory were worked out for each of the 10 couples. Some of the more central concepts in this analysis are: *Egocentrism* versus decentration and taking the perspective of the other (Piaget, 1926; Mead, 1934; Mossige et al., 1976, 1979; Blakar et al., 1978); the type and quality of the *contracts* monitoring the communication process (Rommetveit,

1972, 1974; Blakar, 1972; Moberget and Reer, 1975; Glennsjo, 1977); *attribution* of communicative difficulties (Heider, 1958; Ichheiser, 1970; Hultberg et al., 1976; Haarstad, 1976). For more coherent presentations of the conceptual framework applied in this analysis, see Blakar (1974, 1975a, 1978, 1979a).

In the blind-scoring procedure, the scorer correctly identified four of the five group-A couples. To a certain extent it was thus possible to identify the A-couples on the basis of their mere interaction in the present experimental situation. A closer examination of the scorer's descriptions showed that the core cues on which she relied when identifying a couple as being a group-A couple were unclear communication and the husband's withdrawal.

On the basis of the casuistic descriptions worked out of the couples' communication, we were able to identify some qualitative aspects which seemed typical of the sub-group (the one-third) of the A-group couples demonstrating the inefficient communication. These qualitative aspects of their communication pattern, furthermore, seem to shed some light on *why* their communication failed so totally. In summary, the most significant characteristics of the communication of this sub-group were: The spouses of these couples proved to be highly *egocentric* and demonstrated very limited abilities to take each other's perspective. Their egocentrism was in particular revealed by their not seeming to "listen" to and take into account what the other said. Moreover, their tolerance for *vague* and *unclear* communication seemed very high, and the tendency to *pretend that* they understood each other was predominant. Although this represents more of an interpretation than an observation, the high anxiety that seemed to be present for (open) conflicts and confrontations has to be mentioned in this connection. Everything is done to *avoid* potential conflicts, and arising conflicts are being *covered up*. Interaction sequences characterized by *pseudo-agreement* were thus frequently observed in these couples. The active avoidance of potential conflicts resulted in an almost total *ignorance of testing* with respect to the information being exchanged. And their communication was characterized by "inactivity," e.g., an almost total lack of questions and fewer proposals than in the other couples. And little or nothing is done in order to find the causes of the communicative difficulties (*attribute*) encountered in the present situation. Another outstanding aspect of these couples was the *rigidity* of the complementary relationships. For a presentation of more casuistic material illustrating their pattern of communication, see Wikran et al. (1979).[1]

---

[1] As an integrated part of our general research program (see Blakar, 1978, 1979a; Blakar and Nafstad, 1979a, 1979b), the communication of asthmatic children *together with* their parents is presently being studied in this standardized communication conflict situation. In this ongoing study (by Vassend and Valstad), the parents are given the map with the routes marked in, and they are directed to explain the routes to their (asthmatic) child.

REFERENCES

Aas, K. (1969a), *Allergiske Barn*. Oslo: Cappelen.
_____ (1969b), Allergic asthma in childhood. *Arch. Dis. Child.*, 44:1–10.
Abramson, H. A. (1954), Evaluation of maternal rejection theory in allergy. *Ann. Allergy*, 12:129–140.
Ackerman, N. W. (1958), *Psychodynamics of family life*. New York: Basic Books.
Alcock, T. (1960), Some personality characteristics of asthmatic children. *Brit. J. Med. Psychol.*, 35:133–141.
Argyle, M. (1969), *Social Interaction*. London: Methuen.
Bateson, G., Jackson, D. D., Haley, J., & Weakland, J. H. (1956), Toward a theory of schizophrenia. *Behav. Sci.*, 1:251–264.
_____ _____ _____ _____ (1963), A note on the double bind—1962. *Fam. Proc.*, 2:154–161.
Blakar, R. M. (1970), *Konteksteffektar i sprakleg kommunikasjon*. Unpublished thesis, University of Oslo.
_____ (1972), Ein eksperimentell situasjon til studiet av kommunikasjon: Bakgrunn, utvikling og nokre problemstillingar. Mimeographed, Institute of Psychology, University of Oslo.
_____ (1973), An experimental method for inquiring into communication. *Eur. J. Soc. Psychol.*, 3:415–425.
_____ (1974), Schizofreni og kommunikasjon: Forelopig presentasjon av ei eksperimentell tilnaerming. *Nordisk Psykiatrisk Tidsskr.*, 28:239–248.
_____ (1975a), Psykopatologi og kommunikasjon. Mimeographed, Institute of Psychology, University of Oslo.
_____ (1975b), Human communication—an ever changing contract embedded in social contexts. Mimeographed, Institute of Psychology, University of Oslo.
_____ (1975c), Schizofreni og kommunikasjon: Vidareforing av var eksperimentelle situasjon. *Tidsskrift for Norsk Psykologforening*, 12(8):16–25.
_____ (1975d), Double-bind teorien: Ei kritisk vurdering. *Tidsskrift for Norsk Psykologforening*, 12(12):13–27.
_____ (1976), Kommunikasjon og psykopatologi: Ei kritisk vurdering av dette forskningsomradet. *Tidsskrift for Norsk Psykologforening*, 13(6):3–18.
_____ (1978), *Kontakt og konflikt*. Oslo: Pax.
_____ (1979a), Familial communication and psychopathology. In: *The Structure of Action*, ed. M. Brenner. Oxford: Basil Blackwell.
_____ (1979b), Statistical significance(s) versus theoretical clarification: A comment on the Doane-Jacob & Grounds dispute. *Fam. Proc.* (in press).
_____ & Nafstad, H. E. (1979a), Familien som ramme for studiet av psykiske lidingar og avvikande atferd: Nokre generelle teoretiske og metodologiske problem. In: *Anvendt og klinisk psykologisk forskning: Problem, utfordringar og valg av referanseramme. Tidsskrift for Norsk Psykologforening*, Monography no. 5, ed., R. M. Blakar and H. E. Nafstad.
_____ _____ (1979b), The social sensitivity of theory and method. In: *Social Method and Social Life*, ed. M. Brenner. London: Academic Press.
_____ Paulsen, O. G., & Solvberg, H. A. (1978), Schizophrenia and communication efficiency: A modified replication taking ecological variation into consideration. *Acta Psychiat. Scand.*, 58:315–326.

───── & Rommetveit, R. (1975), Utterances in vacuo and in contexts: An experimental and theoretical exploration of some interrelationships between what is heard and what is seen or imagined. *Internat. J. Psycholing.*, 4:5–32.

Block, J. (1969), Parents of schizophrenic, neurotic, asthmatic, and congenitally ill children. *Arch. Gen. Psychiat.*, 20:659–674.

───── Harvey, E., Jennings, P. H., & Simpson, E. (1966), Clinicians' conceptions of the asthmatogenic mother. *Arch. Gen. Psychiat.*, 15:610–618.

───── Jennings, P. H., Harvey, E., & Simpson, E. (1964), Interaction between allergic potential and psychopathology in childhood asthma. *Psychosom. Med.*, 26:307–320.

Coolidge, J. C. (1956), Asthma in mother and child as a special type of intercommunication. *Amer. J. Orthopsychiat.*, 26:165–176.

Endresen, A. (1977), *Modell för lösning av kommunikasjonskonflikt.* Unpublished thesis, University of Oslo.

Faleide, A. (1969), Haldningar og meiningar hos foreldre til astmabarn. Ei sporjeskjema undersokjing. Mimeographed, Institute of Psychology, University of Oslo.

───── (1973), Vurdering av psykoterapeutiske metoder ved astma bronchiale hos barn. Individualterapi. Mimeographed, Institute of Psychology, University of Oslo.

───── & Vandvik, J. H. (1976), Samtalegruppe med astmatiske barns foreldre. *Tidsskrift for Den Norske Laegeforening,* 22:1140–1142.

Feingold, B. F., Singer, M. T., Freeman, E. H., & Deskins, A. (1966), Psychological variables in allergic disease: A critical appraisal of methodology. *J. Allergy*, 38:143–155.

Framo, J. L., ed. (1972), *Family Interaction: A Dialogue Between Family Researchers and Family Therapists.* New York: Springer.

Freeman, E. H., Feingold, B. F., Schlesinger, K., & Gorman, F. J. (1964), Psychological variables in allergic disorders: A review. *Psychosom. Med.*, 26: 543–575.

French, T. (1939), Psychogenic factors in asthma. *Amer. J. Psychol.*, 52:86–101.

───── & Alexander, F. (1941), Psychogenica in bronchial asthma. *Psychosom. Med. Monogr.*, 4:1.

Garfinkel, H. (1972), Studies of the routine grounds of everyday activities. In: *Studies in Social Interaction*, ed. D. Sudnow. New York: Free Press.

Garner, A. M. & Wenar, C. (1959), *The Mother-Child Interaction in Psychosomatic Disorders.* Urbana: University of Illinois Press.

Glaser, H. H., Harrison, G. S., & Lynn, D. B. (1964), Emotional implications of congenital heart disease in children. *Pediat.*, 33:367–379.

Glennsjo, K. B. (1977), *Marital schism og marital skew — en kommunikasjonsteoretisk tilnaerming.* Unpublished thesis, University of Oslo.

Grinker, R. R., Werble, B., & Drye, R. C. (1968), *The Borderline Syndrome: A Behavioral Study of Ego-Functions.* New York: Basic Books.

Grolnick, L. (1972), A family perspective on psychosomatic factors in illness: A review of the literature. *Fam. Proc.*, 11:457–485.

Haarstad, B. E. (1976), *Anorexia Nervosa. En eksperimentell studie av familiens kommunikasjon.* Unpublished thesis, University of Oslo.

Haley, J. (1972), Critical overview of present status of family interaction research. In: *Family Interaction: A Dialogue Between Family Researchers and Family Therapists*, ed. J. L. Framo. New York: Springer.

Handel, G., ed. (1967), *The Psychosocial Interior of the Family*. Chicago: Aldine.

Heider, F. (1958), *The Psychology of Interpersonal Relations*. New York: Wiley.

Holthe, H. (1972), *Foreldres beskrivelse av sine astmatiske barn, pa noen atferds — og personlighets — variabler*. Unpublished thesis, University of Oslo.

Hultberg, M., Alve, S., & Blakar, R. M. (1976), Patterns of attribution of communicative difficulties in couples with a "borderline," a "schizophrenic" or a "normal" offspring. *Informasjonsbulletin fra Psykopatologi og kommunikasjonsprosjektet*, no. 6, 4–63.

Ichheiser, G. (1970), *Appearances and Realities: Misunderstandings in Human Relations*. San Francisco: Jossey-Bass.

Jackson, D. D. (1959), Family interaction, family homeostasis and some implications for conjoint family psychotherapy. In: *Science and Psychoanalysis, Vol. II: Individual and Family Dynamics*, ed. J. Masserman. New York: Grune & Stratton.

———— (1965), Family rules. *Arch. Gen. Psychiat.*, 12:589–594.

———— (1966), Family practice: A comprehensive medical approach. *Compr. Psychiat.*, 7:338–344.

———— (1967), The individual and the larger contexts. *Fam. Proc.*, 6:139–147.

Jacobsen, S. M. & Pettersen, R. B (1974), *Kommunikasjon og samarbeid i den schizofrenes familie*. Unpublished thesis, University of Oslo.

Jennings, P., Block, J., Harvey, E., Nurock, A., Simpson, E., & Yarris, J. (1966), Two components of the allergic process compared: Allergic potential and severity of asthma. *J. Allergy & Clin. Immun.*, 39:148–159.

Kluger, J. M. (1969), Childhood and the social milieu. *J. Amer. Acad. Child Psychiat.*, 8:353–366.

Long, R. T., Lamont, J. H., Whipple, B., Bandler, L., Blom, G. E., Burgin, L., & Jessner, L. (1958), A psychosomatic study of allergic and emotional factors in children with asthma. *Amer. J. Psychiat.*, 114:890–899.

Mead, G. H. (1934), *Mind, Self and Society*. Chicago: University of Chicago Press.

Meissner, W. W. (1966), Family dynamics and psychosomatic processes. *Fam. Proc.*, 5:142–161.

Miller, H. & Baruch, D. W. (1957), The emotional problems of childhood and their relation to asthma. *Amer. J. Dis. Child*, 93:242–245.

Mishler, E. G. & Waxler, N. E. (1965), Family interaction processes and schizophrenia: A review of current theories. *Merrill-Palmer Quarterly of Behaviour and Development*, 11:269–315.

Mitchell, A. J., Frost, L., & Marx, J. R. (1953), Emotional aspects of pediatric allergy — the role of the mother-child relationship. *Ann. Allerg.*, 11:744–751.

Moberget, O. & Reer, O. (1975), *Kommunikasjon og psykopatologi: En empirisk-teoretisk analyse med vekt pa begrepsmessig og metodologisk avklaring*. Unpublished thesis, University of Oslo.

Moscovici, S. (1967), Communication processing and the properties of language. In: *Advances in Experimental Social Psychology, Vol. III*, ed. D. Berkowitz. New York: Academic Press.

Mossige, S., Pettersen, R. B., & Blakar, R. M. (1976), Egocentrism versus decentration and communication efficiency in the communication of families containing schizophrenic members. *Informasjonsbulletin fra psykopatologi og Kommunikasjonsprosjektet*, no. 4, 4–53.

—— —— —— (1979), Egocentrism and inefficiency in the communication of families containing schizophrenic members. *Fam. Proc.* (in press).

Neuhaus, E. C. (1958), A personality study of asthmatic and cardiac children. *Psychosom. Med.*, 20:181–186.

Peshkin, M. M. & Abramson, M. A. (1959), Psychosomatic group therapy with parents of children having intractable asthma. *Ann. Allerg.*, 17:344–349.

Piaget, J. (1926), *The Language and Thought of the Child*. New York: Harcourt Brace.

Pinkerton, P. & Weaver, C. M. (1970), Childhood asthma. In: *Modern Trends in Psychosomatic Medicine 2*, ed. O. W. Hill. London: Butterworths.

Purcell, K. (1965), Critical appraisal of psychosomatic studies of asthma. *N. Y. State J. Med.*. 65:2103–2109.

—— Brady, K., Chai, H., Muser, J., Molk, L., Gordon, N., & Means, J. (1969), The effect on asthma in children of experimental separation from the family. *Psychosom. Med.*, 31:144–164.

Riskin, J. & Faunce, E. E. (1972), An evaluative review of family interaction research. *Fam. Proc.*, 11:365–455.

Rommetveit, R. (1968), *Words, Meanings and Messages*. New York: Academic Press; Oslo: Universitetsforlaget.

—— (1972), *Sprak, tanke og kommunikasjon*. Oslo: Universitetsforlaget.

—— (1974), *On Message Structure*. London: Wiley.

—— & Blakar, R. M. (1979), *Studies of Language, Thought and Verbal Behavior*. London: Academic Press.

Ruesch, J. (1951), Communication and mental illness: A psychiatric approach. In: *Communication*, ed. J. Ruesch & G. Bateson. New York: Norton.

Schuham, A. I. (1967), The double-bind hypothesis a decade later. *Psychol. Bull.*, 68:409–416.

Solvberg, H. A. & Blakar, R. M. (1975), Communication efficiency in couples *with* and *without* a schizophrenic offspring. *Fam. Proc.*, 14:515–534.

Sperling, M. (1955), Psychosis and psychosomatic illness. *Internat. J. Psycho-Anal.*, 36:320–326.

Stokstad, S. J., Lagerlov, T., & Blakar, R. M. (1976), Anxiety, rigidity and communication: An experimental approach. *Informasjonsbulletin fra psykopatologi og kommunikasjonsprosjektet*, no. 3, 6–36.

—— —— —— (1979), Anxiety, rigidity and communication: An experimental approach. In: *Studies of Language, Thought and Verbal Communication*, ed. R. Rommetveit & R. M. Blakar. London: Academic Press.

Titchener, J. T., Riskin, J., & Emmerson, R. (1960), The family in psychosomatic process. *Psychosom. Med.*. 22:127–142.

Tuft, H. S. (1957), The development and management of intractable asthma of childhood. *Amer. J. Dis. Child.*, 93:251–254.

Watzlawick, P., Beavin, J. H., & Jackson, D. D. (1967), *Pragmatics of Human Communication*. New York: Norton.

Wikran, R. J. (1974), *Kommunikasjon og samarbeide mellom astma-barnets foreldre*. Unpublished thesis, University of Oslo.

—— Faleide, A., & Blakar, R. M. (1979), Kommunikasjon og samarbeid mellom astmabarnets foreldre: Ei eksperimentell tilnaerming. In: *Barn — med astma. Ei psykologisk utgreiing*, ed. A. Faleide. *Tidsskrift for Norsk Psykologforening*, Monograph no. 4.

Family Interaction and Communication Deviance in Disturbed and Normal Families: A Review of Research

JERI A. DOANE

Investigators in the field of human psychopathology are becoming increasingly impressed by the role of the nuclear family in the etiology and maintenance of various psychiatric disorders, particularly, schizophrenia. Theories of family psychopathology vary widely in the emphasis placed upon the relative contributions of biological and environmental factors. However, most proponents of family-oriented approaches would agree that, at the very least, the nuclear family plays an important role in the development or prevention of psychiatric disturbance in the offspring. Over the past two decades, various theories were developed as to how the family exerts its detrimental influence. Bateson et al.'s double-bind theory (1956), Lidz' schismatic and skewed families (1973), Reiss' consensus-sensitive families (1971), Wynne's concepts of "pseudomutuality" and the "rubber fence," and more recently, Singer and Wynne's (1963) theory of disturbed focus of attention are among the major theories that inspired researchers to investigate the relationship of the family as a unit to psychopathology in its offspring. Mishler and Waxler (1965) have written a fairly comprehensive review of some of the major theories of family interaction.

Jeri A. Doane, Ph.D., is a member of the Department of Psychology, University of California, Los Angeles, Calif.

I wish to acknowledge gratefully the valuable suggestions of Dr. Alfred L. Baldwin, Professor of Psychology, University of Rochester, and Dr. James E. Jones, Assistant Professor of Psychiatry, University of Rochester Medical Center and Strong Memorial Hospital.

Research on the family is not, of course, a new idea. However, only in the past 15 years or so have investigators produced a substantial body of studies that employ direct observational methods involving systematic assessment of the family interaction as a unit. Several reviews of this literature have appeared recently (Goldstein and Rodnick, 1975; Jacob, 1975; Riskin and Faunce, 1972). Although each of these articles points to various shortcomings in the family interaction studies, Jacob's (1975) comprehensive review of this literature up through June, 1973, leaves the casual reader with a particularly discouraging view of the current state of affairs in family interaction research. Jacob reviewed direct observational studies that fell into four categories: dominance, conflict, affect, and communication clarity. Though his guidelines for improving methodology are indeed well-founded, his conclusions regarding substantive findings have raised eyebrows and tempers in the circle of family interaction researchers. With few exceptions, he concludes that the studies are inconsistent with one another and that because of methodological problems, it is virtually "impossible to untangle inconsistencies among studies..." (1975, p. 62). He goes on to state that "family interaction studies have not yet isolated family patterns that reliably differentiate disturbed from normal groups" (p. 56).

Jacob organized his review into four substantive areas: conflict, dominance, affect, and communication clarity. He further subdivided the conflict and dominance studies into: (a) quantitative process measures (verbal frequency measures such as talking time, interruptions, overlaps, duration of task, and so on); (b) qualitative measures (those requiring a judge to determine the occurrence and the quality or kind of event that has occurred); and (c) outcome measures (a measure that reveals the produce or outcome of a family's performance, such as number of agreements or disagreements on a resolution of differences task). He then divided the studies into those using schizophrenic families and those using disturbed nonschizophrenic families. Jacob then tallied comparisons providing evidence for or against a global construct, such as dominance, on the basis of accepting at face value the respective investigators' operational definition of the construct (e.g., high rate of interruptions = high conflict). In making his final conclusions regarding a given substantive area, he pulls together the different types of measures such as interruptions (a verbal frequency measure) and rates of disagreement (a measure that taps content). Not surprisingly, this kind of analysis yielded mixed results, and one wonders why he bothered to differentiate so carefully the different types of measures in the first place.

The purpose of the present review is to reexamine the family interaction literature in an attempt to reassess Jacob's argument that there are not as yet any family interaction patterns capable of differentiating disturbed from normal families. In addition, a substantial number of relevant studies published after Jacob's article are included. Studies of communication deviance, many of which do not entail direct observation of the family, are covered here on the grounds that this body of studies represents some of the most stable and powerful findings in the field. A substantive review would certainly be misrepresentative without consideration of this important work.

Unlike Jacob's article, the approach to the present review does not rely upon merely compiling cumulative counts of evidence for or against a particular global construct such as "dominance." Rather, the organizing principle is that of analyzing the various findings in order to differentiate pockets of consistency from areas on measures that are not particularly useful in discriminating disturbed from normal families. The various authors' operational definitions of the construct under study were not always accepted at face value. Rather, a sort of "armchair cluster analysis" was done by looking at each of the various findings and making an assessment as to how that finding fit together conceptually with other similar findings. Thus, a major goal of the present review is to identify dimensions of family interaction that appear to be promising areas of exploration for the future.

The studies covered are limited to direct observational studies, with the exception of the communication deviance studies. In addition, studies not employing a comparison or control group of some kind are not covered. Other than these considerations, no attempt will be made to differentiate studies on methodological grounds. The reader is referred to Jacob (1975), F. Jones (1973), and Riskin and Faunce (1972) for excellent discussions of methodological issues in family interaction research.

The review is organized in the following way:

I. Conflict and Dominance Studies
   1. "Pure-Process" Measures
   2. Family Structure (e.g., coalitions, conflict, flexibility)
   3. Family Harmony
   4. Family Efficiency and Effectiveness
II. Communication Studies
   1. Communication Deviance
   2. Acknowledgment, Clarity, and Conflicting Messages
   3. The Corrective Parent

CONFLICT AND DOMINANCE STUDIES

Conflict and dominance are two areas of study that have interested family researchers, theoreticians, and clinicians alike. Dominance, or lines of power within the family, was one of the earliest areas of exploration in studying the parameters of family interaction. Historically, the family of the preschizophrenic captured the attention of family interaction researchers, and concepts such as Fromm-Reichmann's "schizophrenogenic mother" were developed. Here, the mother is seen as powerful, dominating, and overprotective; the father as weak, ineffectual, and passive. Hypotheses such as this prompted researchers to ask such questions as: What is the nature of power distribution in abnormal families? Are abnormal families characterized by powerful mothers and weak fathers? Are mothers of schizophrenics noticeably more overprotective and dominating of their offspring than are mothers of other disturbed, nonschizophrenic offspring? Can one differentiate a discrete power structure in abnormal families different from that observed in normal families? Many of the early (as well as recent) attempts to delineate domains of power in disturbed families have relied upon measures of rates of verbal activity.

Conflict has been typically looked at from two perspectives: one, conflict among subsystems within the family, and two, total family (system-wide) conflict across diagnostic groupings. The first perspective raises such issues as: Do fathers of schizophrenics experience less conflict with their offspring than do fathers of normals? The second perspective deals with questions such as: Do members of disturbed families fight, argue, and clash with each other more than do members of normal families?

"Pure-Process" Measures

Traditionally, these measures have been used to infer evidence for such global constructs as dominance or conflict. The term "pure-process" here refers to four commonly used groups of measures of verbal activity that do not directly assess content of verbal productions (interruptions, talking time, number of statements received, and who-follows-whom). As such, each of these measures may reflect several very different dimensions of family interaction. A high rate of total family interruptions, for example, might reflect family conflict, or flexibility, or spontaneity. In light of their inherent lack of precision with respect to meaning, it is not surprising that they fail to provide sharp discrimination among family groups. And, because of their inherent vague referents, comparisons relying solely upon these measures are singled out here. Patterns of these measures are useful in operationalizing a content-free construct like flexibility-rigidity, but not constructs like dominance and conflict.

Interruptions

Included in this category are interruptions, simultaneous speech, and intrusions. This group of measures, although used widely as measures of conflict or power, appears to be quite limited in its ability to differentiate normal from disturbed families. Three studies found virtually no consistent or meaningful differences between types of families or among family members (Ferreira, Winter, and Poindexter, 1966; Lennard, Beaulieu, and Embry, 1965; Stabenau, Tupin, Werner, and Pollin, 1965) — the last significant only for a reduced amount of interruptions in schizophrenic sons. One study (Leighton, Stollak, and Ferguson, 1971) found more interruptions in clinic families than in normal families. Finally, three studies found that normal families exhibit more interruptions than disturbed families (Mishler and Waxler, 1968; O'Connor and Stachiowak, 1971; Riskin and Faunce, 1970).

Talking Time

Total talking time is frequently assumed to measure dominance within the family. Three studies showed virtually no differences between disturbed and normal families (Becker and Iwakami, 1969; Farina and Holzberg, 1968; Ferreira et al., 1966) — the last significant only for reduced talking time of the schizophrenic child. The two remaining studies (Leighton et al., 1971; Schuham, 1972), which included families of normal, clinic, and borderline offspring, both revealed a pattern of fathers of normals speaking more than mothers who in turn talk more than children. Disturbed families showed a lack of differentiation of patterns for parents and children or a reversal of mothers' and fathers' roles. Thus, although talking time does not always produce differences among families or family members, when it does, normal families show a hierarchy of Father > Mother > Child on the measure.

Number of Statements Received

Presumably, number of statements received reflects a measure of that family member's dominance within the family. The two studies reviewed here reveal no findings that would allow one to draw meaningful inferences with respect to dominance within the family. Murrell and Stachiowak (1967), in a study comparing clinic and normal families, found that although normal mothers received more statements than clinic mothers and older children more than younger children, there were no differences between parents of normals and parents of mentally retarded children. Finally, Murrell (1971) found no differences among statements received by members of families with a low-adjusted, an average-adjusted, and a high-adjusted child (all normals).

Who-Follows-Whom

This measure has been used to look at patterns of randomness or rigidity in families. When used as a pure frequency count, it does not seem to be adequate to discriminate families. Ferreira et al. (1966) and Haley (1967) both found no differences among a variety of diagnostic groups. An earlier study by Haley (1964) found that normal families were more random on this measure than were disturbed families.

Comment

In summarizing this section, it appears that these "pure-process" types of measures are not powerful discriminators of normal and abnormal families. Measures that tap content (to at least a minimal extent) would seem more likely candidates to reveal differences among families and family members. The next section on family structure looks at some of these measures.

FAMILY STRUCTURE

The area of family power distribution — hierarchical structure, lines of authority, and coalitions — together with the relative flexibility or rigidity of these types of constructs, is vastly confusing. An attempt is made here to reduce some of this confusion by dividing the studies into sections. Obviously, such compartmentalizing does not exist in the real world of families. However, it seems necessary to do so here in light of the wide range of measures used and the variability in types of comparisons made (intrafamily versus interfamily). Studies that rely solely on pure-process measures of the type discussed earlier (e.g., talking time, intrusions, attempted interruptions, length of speech, number of communications) are not included here on the grounds that the interpretation of these measures is too ambiguous. The studies reviewed in this section have used measures that seem relatively to be more direct indices of the constructs in question. Measures such as number of wins on a task, agreement-disagreement, predictability of speakers in sequence, and individual rankings of choice-fulfillment (the extent to which a member's initial preferences are incorporated into the group decision on a resolution of differences task) are included.

Passive Acceptance, Yielding, and "Dictatorial Decisions"

These measures have been used in studies attempting to assess dominance among family members. As their names suggest, they are rather narrowly defined measures. Studies using these particular indices are singled out here, as they differ from the rest of the studies to be reviewed in their rigid and restrictive definitions of dominant behavior. As such, they are best not compared with studies using "milder," less restrictive measures such as agreement-disagreement, number of wins on a task, and so on.

Comparisons using these narrow measures suggest that they are not sensitive enough to pick up differences among families. On the yielding measure, Farina and Holzberg (1968) found significant differences only for poor premorbid schizophrenic sons, whereas Becker and Iwakami (1969) found no differences at all between families of clinic and normal children. This same study reports no differences on passive acceptance. Finally, Ferreira and Winter (1965) found no differences on "dictatorial decisions."

Coalitions

A number of different studies employing families with a wide range of offspring psychopathology provide evidence suggesting that cross-generational coalitions are characteristic of disturbed families (Cheek, 1964; Lennard et al., 1965; Mishler and Waxler, 1975; Schuham, 1970). In Cheek's study (1964), mother and child agreement on a discussion task was higher than father-child agreement or mother-father agreement. Another study showed that, in schizophrenic families,[1] rates of father:child, child:father, mother:father, father:mother (where ":" means "directs communication to") communication are significantly lower than mother:child or child:mother rates (Lennard et al., 1965). Mishler and Waxler (1975) looked at the predictability of who-follows-whom in sequence and found that normal families were more likely to have more frequent mother-father coalitions (as measured by the likelihood that they would follow each other in the discussion). Schuham (1970) analyzed indices of support given and received between members of dyads and found that parents of borderline offspring were more impaired in coalition formation than were parents of normals. And when coalitions did occur, they were more likely to occur between father and index child than between mother and father.

[1] In order to avoid cumbersome language, the term "schizophrenic family" is used throughout the paper to refer to a family that contains a schizophrenic member; no etiological implications are intended.

Clinically, coalitions manifest themselves as alliances or bonds between two members of a family. Often the members are in coalition against another member or members on a wide variety of issues in the family. For example, a mother and eldest child may repeatedly side with one another in criticizing father, or they may unite on discipline issues involving a younger sibling against father's stance on the matter. Operational definitions of coalitions in family research are, of course, limited by the degree to which one can objectively measure such complicated family relationships. However, studies using measures such as differential rates of agreement or disagreement between and across dyads, relative support between dyads, predictability of speakers in sequence, and so on, provide data indicating that disturbed families deviate from normals by having a preponderance of parent-child coalitions. Normal families, on the other hand, are characterized by parent-parent coalitions. One early study by Haley (1962) does not support this conclusion. Using a button-pushing coalition game, he found that parents of schizophrenics were more often in coalition with each other than were parents of normals. It should be noted, however, that the nature of this particular task (button-pushing) may yield a conceptually different measure of coalition than do the more traditional verbal measures used in the other studies.

Thus, disturbed families seem to be characterized by weakness in the parental coalition and strength in corresponding parent-child coalitions. It is interesting to note that in one study of normal families, those with a low-adjusted child did not exhibit a clear-cut pattern of parent-child coalitions (number of times member spoken to and changes in member's opinion to agree with another [O'Connor and Stachiowak, 1971]). As the authors point out, this finding suggests that parent-child coalitions observed in clinic families may not yet be visible in families that are still functioning fairly well.

Parental Conflict

Lidz (1973) discusses the importance of the marital relationship in schizophrenic families and finds that it is frequently marked by schism (overt, bilateral conflict between spouses) or skew (a less overt type of conflict in which one parent dominates and the other abdicates in deference to the other). Both types of marital discord are thought to have profound impact on the offspring.

It is reasonable to expect that if disturbed families show a weak parental coalition and relatively stronger parent-child coalitions, the parents of the disturbed offspring ought to exhibit more conflict between them than do normal parents. Four different studies comparing parents of disturbed and normal offspring all support this conclusion (Caputo, 1963; Farina and Holzberg, 1968; Murrell and Stachiowak, 1967; Solvberg and Blakar, 1975). Conflict was operationally defined as: greater frequency of disagreement between schizophrenic parents than normals (Caputo, 1963); more rated expression of hostility between parents (Caputo, 1963; Farina and Holzberg, 1968); greater rated inability or unwillingness of clinic spouses to support each other (Murrell and Stachiowak, 1967); and greater unwillingness of schizophrenic spouses to listen to one another, greater tendency to ignore one another and express pseudo-agreement or "pleasing" than normals (Solvberg and Blakar, 1975). Schulman, Shoemaker and Moelis (1962) found no differences between clinic and normal parents on a conflict measure. However, it should be noted that they used a rather narrow and restrictive measure, "parent fights and argues with parent." Given that the task instruction in this study emphasized keeping the child interested in the task, it is not surprising that they found no differences.

Flexibility Versus Rigidity

Haley (1964) hypothesized that normal families would be more random in their interactions with one another, whereas disturbed families would deviate from this and be more "clique-ridden." He presented some data to support his theory, and a number of studies looking at his hypothesis followed. This random/nonrandom concept seemed to make sense. However, when analyzed from the standpoint of this dichotomous construct, the studies reviewed reveal conflicting results. Yet when one looks at the data from the slightly different perspective of a continuum of flexible (including but not restricted to randomness) to fixed or rigid, the studies provide strong support for normal and abnormal families differentiating along this dimension. In other words, perhaps normal families can be nonrandom (like abnormal families) but more flexible in their interactions *in relation to* abnormal families. Some of the "pure-process" types of measures cited earlier would seem to be more valid indices of constructs such as flexibility-rigidity, which by definition demand no inferences about content per se.

A total of 12 studies in all provide support for the notion that normal families are more flexible in their interactions with one another (Ferreira and Winter, 1968b; Ferreira et al., 1966; Haley, 1964; Herman and Jones, 1976; Leighton et al., 1971; Lennard et al., 1965; Mishler and Waxler, 1968, 1975; Murrell, 1971; Solvberg and Blakar, 1975; Winter and Ferreira, 1967, 1969). Operational definitions of flexibility in the studies cited include: evenness of distribution of who-follows-whom (Ferreira et al., 1966; Haley, 1964); balanced distribution of who-speaks-to-whom (Lennard et al., 1965); reduced predictability of speakers in sequence (Mishler and Waxler, 1975); low correlation between amount of silence across experimental tasks (Ferreira et al., 1966); higher rates of balanced triadic interaction than dyadic interaction (Herman and Jones, 1976); balanced rates of frequency of speech among members (Leighton et al., 1971; Lennard et al., 1965; Murrell, 1971; Winter and Ferreira, 1967, 1969); increased frequency of intrusions — one might expect that a family with rigid rules about who-speaks-to-whom-when would not allow a high rate of intrusions into the discussion (Lennard et al., 1965; Mishler and Waxler, 1968); higher frequencies of speech disruptions — the rationale here is the same as that for intrusions (Mishler and Waxler, 1968); less rigid distribution of roles in solving a joint task (Solvberg and Blakar, 1975). Although these measures appear on the surface to differ widely from each other, they are grouped together here because they share a common denominator: an index of flexibility of family functioning.

Abnormal families, on the other hand, show patterns of rigidity. Two exceptions were found. Murrell and Stachiowak (1967) found normal families to have less randomly distributed statements to one another than clinic families; and Haley (1967) failed to find differences between families on randomness of members' statements.

Comment

Several of the findings in this section are consistent with existing theories of family psychopathology. The findings that show disturbed parental coalitions and marital discord in disturbed families suggest that the marital relationship is an important variable in considering the pathology-producing impact of the family system. As mentioned above, Lidz, among others, has written extensively on this kind of linear model of family psychopathology in which the families of schizophrenics are characterized by either schism or skew, each of which has as its base a disturbed marital relationship. One result of this state of affairs is a lack of paternal leadership (Lidz et al., 1958). The results are also in accord with Haley's concept of disturbed power relationships (1963). And increased parental conflict in schizophrenic families is not inconsistent with Wynne's notion of "pseudomutuality," as this phenomenon is considered a characteristic of the family system as a whole.

The combination of increased parental conflict and parent-child coalitions leads one to speculate that the latter are less a direct cause of psychopathology in the family and more a result of family members attempting to replace the missing parental coalition with some form of leadership. Goldstein et al. (1976) report that a five-year follow-up of disturbed adolescents revealed no extended schizophrenia spectrum disorders in one of four groups of disturbed adolescents (passive-negative group). Interestingly, in another report using this sample, this group was the only one that did not show overt evidence of weak parental coalitions at the time of initial evaluation — i.e., neither parent overtly ignored the other (McPherson, Goldstein, and Rodnick, 1973).

Weakness in parental coalitions was found in a variety of types of disturbed families. Thus, although it may discriminate disturbed from normal families, it does not appear to isolate schizophrenia-producing families from other types. Nevertheless, one might speculate that the absence of a major parent-child coalition combined with a relatively stable mother-father coalition may operate to help prevent formal psychiatric disturbance in the offspring. Further research would be needed to explore this idea.

Traditionally, researchers have focused on evidence of either mother or father dominance within the family. Perhaps a more fruitful route is to look at lines of alliance within the family. The research reviewed here suggests that power *relationships* (coalitions, conflict between spouses, etc.) are more clearly delineated than are individual power figures in the family (e.g., the dominating mother; the weak, ineffectual father, and so on). It would seem that *who* is the most dominant or powerful member of the family is less important than whether an alliance between generations exists, thus giving the child relatively more of the power (and hence, responsibility) for the family functioning.

The notion of flexibility combined with parental leadership in normal families fits with both old-fashioned notions of parental dominance as well as research by Baumrind (1975) suggesting that a modified authoritarian ("authoritative") parenting style results in higher intellectual and social competence in children that does a laissez-faire approach.

Finally, the idea that disturbed families are rigid in their relationships and interactions with one another is consistent not only with observations of family therapists but also with theoretical positions such as that of Wynne. Wynne argues that families of schizophrenics have a disturbance in role structure — either roles are too rigid or are not clearly structured. Either situation functions to prevent the child from developing a clear sense of identity and autonomy.

Family Harmony

One problem in reviewing conflict measures in family interaction studies is deciding when to call a positive finding a measure of conflict and when to call it a measure of affect. The interpretation of findings showing conflict is difficult no matter how one labels it. For example, can one say that a family without conflict is truly normal? And, if not, how much conflict is necessary for healthy functioning of its members and how much is too much? Related issues involve defining conflict. For example, does disagreement among family members on a resolution of differences task indicate conflict or healthy individuation? Despite the confusion in this area, there do appear to be some conclusions one can draw regarding the relative harmonious functioning of disturbed versus normal families. The studies in this section are not necessarily representative of the general body of research involving family affect. Rather, they include a variety of studies of family harmony or discord and studies that would be grouped traditionally in the dominance or conflict areas.

Support

Measures of support are often not well defined in the literature. Support as used here refers to behaviors reflecting empathy, equality, genuine information-giving, genuine attempts at problem solving, and so on. Several studies measuring supportive behavior in families have found that normal families were more likely to exhibit support toward their members than were disturbed families (various indices of supportive behavior [Alexander, 1973b], expressiveness [Mishler and Waxler, 1968], acts of support [Schuham, 1970], and rated parental rejection and hostility toward the child [Schulman et al., 1962]). Furthermore, three of these studies revealed that while members of normal families are reciprocally supportive (e.g., positive correlation between M:C and C:M instance of support), members of disturbed families are not; in fact, they are frequently actively nonsupportive (Alexander, 1973a, 1973b; Schuham, 1970; Schulman et al., 1962). An interesting finding, however, was that parents of juvenile delinquents were much more strongly reciprocal with each other on support than were parents of normal children (Alexander, 1973a). This finding suggests that perhaps these types of parents use the child in some way to deal with their own relationship, a commonly reported observation among family therapists.

Spontaneous Agreement

Tasks that entail a family resolution of differences usually involve administering a list of questions to individual family members prior to requesting the family as a whole to come to a group consensus about the items in question. If one tallies how often family members' individual choices match each other, one obtains a measure of spontaneous agreement (SA). SA may be said to index family closeness, or the degree to which the family members share values, ideas, and so on. As such, it reflects a kind of baseline measure of family harmony.

Six studies employing families of normal and/or disturbed offspring (including schizophrenics, borderlines, neurotics, and juvenile delinquents) found that families of normal offspring exhibited higher SA than did disturbed families (Cheek, 1964; Ferreira and Winter, 1965, 1968a [trend but not quite significant]; Haley, 1967; Murrell, 1971; Schuham, 1972). Two of these studies analyzed SA among dyads, and found SA to be greater across all dyads in normal families (Cheek, 1964; Ferreira and Winter, 1965). Thus, this finding appears to be a system-wide phenomenon and characteristic of the family as a whole. One interesting finding was that regardless of age, the "well" child always shows greater SA with his parents than does the index child (Ferreira and Winter, 1968a).

Choice-Fulfillment

On a resolution of differences task, choice-fulfillment (CF) reflects the degree to which an individual family member's initial choices end up as the family's group choice. When one looks at the rate of CF for all family members together, a measure of general family satisfaction can be obtained and then compared with the rates for a more disturbed family. A family in which two of each member's choices are ultimately fulfilled may be different from a family in which only one member's choices become the group's choice.

Two studies comparing total family CF found that families of disturbed offspring have less CF than families of normals (Ferreira and Winter, 1965, 1968a). Murrell (1971) used only normal families with children subsequently rated as low-, average-, or high-adjusted and found no differences.

Comment

In summary, the studies in this section suggest a trend for disturbed families to be less harmonious in their functioning than families of normals. Not only do the family members start out with a lack of shared values and preferences, but they seem unable to have their needs (particularly for support) met once the members are interacting with one another. Further research is needed to determine whether this lack of harmony exists prior to (or in response to) the presence of a disturbed or "disturbing" child. A corollary to this picture of discord is that of impaired family decision-making and decreased task efficiency, the topic of the next section.

FAMILY EFFICIENCY AND EFFECTIVENESS

If the family truly operates as a system, then when one member is "disturbed," we would expect the entire family to be affected. In particular, we would expect the family to perform less well on a variety of tasks, especially those involving a group resolution of differences.

Three studies found that normal families are more productive than families of disturbed offspring on a variety of joint tasks (Murrell and Stachiowak, 1967; O'Connor and Stachiowak, 1971; Winter and Ferreira, 1967), whereas two studies found no differences (Hassan, 1974; Murrell, 1971).

Several studies present evidence that families with disturbed offspring are much less effective than normal families in dealing with the task at hand. Mishler and Waxler (1968) found that families with schizophrenic members were less effective in general in dealing with a resolution of differences task, with families of poor premorbids showing confusion about the task and families of good premorbids exhibiting rigidity in dealing with it. Furthermore, they found that normal families were more responsive to each other's verbalizations than poor premorbids, with good premorbids in-between. If members respond to each other in an acknowledging manner, one might assume they are at least hearing and possibly understanding what the other has said. This in turn might lead to more efficient problem solving. O'Connor and Stachiowak (1971) found that families of low-adjusted children communicated less well and often seemed to be confused about what was said, or implied. Solvberg and Blakar (1975), in a study of parents with schizophrenics and normals, found that the former exhibited an increased proportion of task-irrelevant talk. Glaser (1976) found the same thing using the entire family. And Friedman and Friedman (1970) found families of schizophrenics expressed more confusion, disorganization, and lack of goal orientation on a family TAT task than normal families.

Ferreira and Winter (1968b) found that decreased amount of information exchanged among family members was related to increasing psychopathology in the offspring, with members of schizophrenic families exchanging the least information. The decreased amount of information exchanged was true for all members, not just one or two dyads. Furthermore, they found that the measure was stable after a six-month interval. Interestingly, the amount of information exchanged correlated positively with the amount of choice-fulfillment for the family as a whole, with families of schizophrenics the lowest, maladjusted and juvenile delinquents in-between, and normals the highest. This type of finding suggests that ineffective communication may be at least partially responsible for the reduction in CF. In another study, using a similar sample, Ferreira and Winter (1965) found schizophrenic families to be more "chaotic" in their decision-making than the nonschizophrenic and normal groups. Finally, Farina and Holzberg (1968) and Schuham (1970) both found families with schizophrenic or borderline offspring to have significantly more difficulty reaching final agreement than did families of normals.

Comment

In concluding this section on family efficiency and effectiveness, it would appear that disturbed families are relatively inadequate in their ability to function effectively during a task imposed upon them from the environment. They are less productive, exchange less information, and have more difficulty making decisions that are based on the wishes of their members. The studies do not say anything, of course, about why this lack of effectiveness and efficient functioning exists. The next section, covering communication studies, begins to look at some hypotheses that might, at least partially, explain why a certain kind of disturbed family (that of the schizophrenic) seems to function poorly. The question remains to be answered by further research, however, of why families who produce disturbed offspring function less well. No doubt there are multiple reasons. And the causes behind the ineffectiveness of the juvenile delinquent's family and that of the schizophrenic's are likely to be quite different.

In summing up the studies reviewed up to this point, we can ask: What does the conflict and dominance literature have to say about dimensions of family interaction? It has been argued here that when pure-process verbal activity measures are excluded, meaningful dimensions of family interaction surface. We can speculate that in normal families, husband and wife are not in conflict much of the time and they are more likely to be in coalition with each other than with one of their children. There is likely to be a hierarchical structure of authority in the family with mother and father having more influence than child. The family members tend to have similar values and preferences, and they are actively supportive of one another. As a group, the family is able to function efficiently and effectively in situations imposed upon it from the environment. In general, the family system is marked by firm and smooth, but flexible, functioning.

At the other extreme are families with disturbed offspring. Marital discord is evident, with a corresponding breakdown in the parental coalition. As a result, the child is drawn into coalition with a parent and becomes enmeshed in cross-generational relationships that may be detrimental to its growth and development. The family tone is one of discord rather than harmony. The members lack a shared sense of values and closeness, and task-effectiveness is often impaired. Members tend not to support each other, and they frequently are actively nonsupportive. Patterns of functioning, in general, tend to be more fixed than those of normal families. More research is need to differentiate further dimensions of disturbance in families with schizophrenics from families with less severely disturbed offspring.

COMMUNICATION STUDIES

In contrast to studies reviewed up to this point, those in this section are grouped under "communication" because each of them deals with the nature of family communication per se. In other words, the primary aim in these studies is not to draw inferences about such global constructs as dominance or conflict, but instead to look at the stylistic components of the communication itself. Investigators cited in this section ask such questions as: What are the distinguishing features of the communicative styles of disturbed families? How clear and understandable is the communication? To what extent do the members understand what is being said? Do communicative styles differ systematically across diagnostic groups? Are members of disturbed families consistent in their communications, or do they tend to disqualify or negate them? The studies in this area are grouped for convenience into two sections: one dealing with the communication deviance studies and the other with studies looking at aspects of communication such as acknowledgment, clarity, and consistency.

THE SINGER AND WYNNE THEORY OF COMMUNICATION DEVIANCE

Communication deviance (CD) is a term coined by Singer and Wynne that refers to a set of defects and deviances in the communications of parents of schizophrenics. It emphasizes the manner in which family members convey that they are focusing their attention on the task at hand. Results from their studies using projective techniques show that parental forms and styles of communicating are related to thought disorder in the offspring. Cognitive and thinking disorders on the individual level are viewed as the counterpart of CD on the interpersonal level (Wynne, Singer, and Toohey, 1976). Singer and Wynne have stressed that if the efforts of two or more people to focus their attention in a conversation fail or become confused, the consequences for the rest of the communicative process will be profound (1965a). They believe that the communication in families of schizophrenics is disturbed at this attentional level, while that of borderlines, neurotics, or normals occurs later on after an attentional focus has been shared. Rather than being a subclinical manifestation of schizophrenia itself, CD has been shown to be a distinct measure that reflects the impact of the communication upon the listener (Wynne et al., 1976). The extent to which parents fail to communicate effectively is thought to be associated with the extent to which the child, who is dependent upon transactions with them, will become confused, lost, and distressed (Singer, 1967).

A projective test, usually the Rorschach, is used to elicit communications from the subject to the examiner. The form of style of the person's speech is emphasized rather than content. Communication deviance measures allow its proponents to classify parental communicative style into two types: "amorphousness," reflecting global, predominantly undifferentiated forms of thinking; and "fragmentation," in which some degree of clear differentiation is present, but in which are also reflected failures of interpretation at some level within the hierarchy. Thus, the fragmented form of CD is seen as a higher order of disturbance than amorphousness, in that at least some degree of differentiation is present in the former, while in the latter, the disturbance occurs earlier in the development at a point prior to differentiation. Singer and Wynne argue that the fragmented style is more often found in parents of a schizophrenic with a good premorbid history, while parents of poor premorbids more often exhibit amorphousness (1965a).

Singer and Wynne Studies of Communication Deviance

In 1963, Singer and Wynne published results from a study showing that their Rorschach and TAT CD measures could discriminate accurately among parental pairs of autistic, withdrawn, acting-out, and young-adult schizophrenic offspring. Results from the NIMH study (Singer and Wynne, 1965b) showed that parents of "frank schizophrenics" and "schizophrenics" could be differentiated reliably from both parents of borderlines and parents of nonschizophrenic neurotic indexes. Further, predictions of form of thinking (amorphous versus fragmented) were made with precision accuracy, as were predictions of severity of index symptomatology. These results were quite impressive considering that the predictions about offspring were done blindly from the typed transcripts of the parents' protocols. In addition, 80 per cent of parents of schizophrenics were discriminated from parents of normal offspring on a different type of task, the Object Sorting Test (Wild et al., 1965), and, using still a different source of material, Morris and Wynne (1965) were able to predict diagnosis of offspring and forms of thinking (amorphousness, fragmentation) by comparing parental communication styles from recorded excerpts from family therapy sessions.

More recently, Wynne et al. (1977) compared CD in 114 parental pairs with offspring ranging from normal to severely schizophrenic. They found that both severity of psychopathology in the parent(s) and parental CD each correlated with severity of offspring disturbance. Parents of schizophrenics were correctly identified on the basis of frequency of CD, even in cases where neither parent had a diagnosis of schizophrenia or "borderline" symptomatology. One interesting finding from this study was that frequency of communication deviance was higher in the nonschizophrenic parents than in their overtly schizophrenic offspring. These findings suggest that CD is not merely a subclinical manifestation of the psychosis itself. The results showed that parental CD scores rise increasingly with severity of illness of the offspring. Furthermore, scores for the parents of the schizophrenic group differ significantly from those of neurotics or normals.

In another recent study, Wynne et al. (1976) discovered that biological and adoptive parents of schizophrenics were indistinguishable on the CD measure. Again, all parental pairs with a schizophrenic offspring (regardless of biological or adoptive parental status) and those with nonschizophrenics were perfectly separated during prediction. This finding argues strongly against a purely genetic explanation of schizophrenia. And the authors conclude that their results support an interactionist view that CD may be a necessary but not sufficient condition for schizophrenia.

Finally, using two independent samples that included families of schizophrenics, borderlines, neurotics, and normals, Singer (1967) reports that parents of schizophrenics produced responses on the Rorschach that were judged significantly less visualizable than responses of normals.

OTHER COMMUNICATION DEVIANCE STUDIES

The association of parental CD and schizophrenia in the offspring has been documented by a number of other investigators. Hirsch and Leff (1971) attempted to replicate Singer and Wynne's NIMH study but admit to irregularities in their method of Rorschach inquiry. Nevertheless, they were able to differentiate significantly parents of schizophrenics from nonschizophrenics, although the separation was not as accurate as that found in Singer and Wynne's work. Hirsch and Leff found a correlation between word count and CD and concluded, therefore, that CD was an artifact of increased responding by parents of schizophrenics. This explanation seems highly unlikely, however, inasmuch as a number of independent studies have since found that CD continues to predict accurately even with words count partialed out (Glaser, 1976; Wild, Shapiro, and Goldenberg, 1975; Wynne et al., 1977).

Behrens, Rosenthal, and Chodoff (1968) used Loveland's (1967) Rorschach technique in a study of schizophrenics and normals. Using a modification of her criteria for scoring communicative content (clarity, grasp of the nature of the task and of other family members' comments, and family cooperation and coordination), they were able to identify correctly 80 per cent of the parents of schizophrenics. They found parents of schizophrenics to be deficient on a measure of ability to maintain a shared focus of attention.

A five-year, follow-up study of vulnerable adolescents at UCLA revealed a significant relationship between parental CD during adolescence and a follow-up diagnosis in the extended spectrum of schizophrenia (Goldstein et al., 1976). Furthermore, of the eight young adults who seemed to be improving, six had parents who were free from severe CD. These same authors also present evidence that CD may interact with other variables such as severity of adolescent behavior to heighten the probability of offspring becoming schizophrenic as young adults. J. E. Jones (1977), in another study, factor-analyzed CD categories from the TAT protocols of parents of high-risk adolescents and found that particular substyles of CD could reliably discriminate parents of hospitalized schizophrenics from parents of children who developed nonschizophrenic disorders.

Communication deviance studies have often been criticized because they have traditionally used parents of already schizophrenic offspring. Those studies employing nonpsychotic high-risk adolescents are particularly relevant with respect to this criticism. The UCLA high-risk studies cited above used adolescents without overt symptoms of psychosis. More longitudinal studies using high-risk families are needed.

Most recently, investigators have begun to look at communication deviance in the whole family. Shapiro and Wild (1976) looked at triads on a consensus Rorschach task, comparing families of schizophrenics, nonschizophrenics, and normal controls. The investigators looked at the product of the task rather than the communications themselves. To assess disturbance in shared focus of attention, they asked each subject individually to write down the response the family had just agreed upon. Their written responses were then scored for the degree of consensus, clarity, and complexity achieved. The scores significantly discriminated all three groups. Schizophrenic families had low scores, reflecting a lack of shared focus of attention.

A recent study of families of disturbed adolescents by Herman and Jones (1976) looked at the relationship between parental CD on the TAT and measures of family acknowledgment in triadic interaction on a Family Rorschach task. They found that high-risk families (those with parents scoring high on CD) exhibited fewer acknowledgment responses than did low-risk families (those with low parental CD scores). The fact that Mishler and Waxler (1968), among others, have found decreased acknowledgment characteristic of families of diagnosed schizophrenics makes this result even more interesting. The differences were evident for all family members. Thus it appears to be a system-wide phenomenon.

COMMENT

While the studies reviewed in this section provide strong evidence that communication deviance is a reliable instrument for discriminating parents of offspring with thought disorder, several questions remain to be answered by further research. For example, is CD a stable pattern? Does it persist over weeks, months, years? Is it manifested prior to a disturbance in the offspring, thus being an etiological factor? Or is it a response of the parents to a disturbed child? Which aspects of the index child's functioning are related to CD in the parents, and which are not? Can CD be used to predict thought disorder in high-risk families? More longitudinal high-risk research is needed to answer these and other questions.

Another relevant question is whether CD varies across experimental situations. A recent study by Glaser (1976) analyzed CD from the perspective of looking at its variation across different situations. Using families of schizophrenics, nonschizophrenics, and normals, Glaser analyzed CD on the Rorschach in the following three experimental situations: the individual members' protocols, a Spouse Rorschach, and a Family Consensus Rorschach. Thus, parental communication styles could be assessed when each is alone with a stranger, when they are alone with each other, and when they are in the presence of their disturbed offspring. Glaser found that CD is significantly greater in families of schizophrenics in all three settings. Furthermore, she found that more CD for both groups of families occurred in the spouse setting than in the family situation. Normal offspring and their siblings did best in a setting with a stranger (Individual), while schizophrenics did best in the Family Rorschach setting. The schizophrenic did not have a negative impact upon the CD scores of his parents (Family Rorschach). Rather, the parents actually improved their communicative style when with their psychotic offspring. This study suggests that parents may indeed play an etiological role in the development of thought disorder in their offspring.

ACKNOWLEDGMENT, CLARITY, AND CONFLICTING MESSAGES

In addition to the Singer-Wynne type of communication deviance studies, several others have also measured disturbed communicative styles. Among these are studies assessing acknowledgment, clarity, and validation.

Acknowledgment

Acknowledgment is a measure that reflects the degree to which a family member acknowledges a statement by another family member. The code ranges from total ignoring to full acknowledgment of the other's speech. One would hypothesize that schizophrenic families would exhibit much less direct acknowledgment of one another.

Mishler and Waxler (1968), in a large, well-controlled study, found that families of normals were higher on this measure than were families of poor premorbid schizophrenics. Families of good premorbids were in-between. Solvberg and Blakar (1975) found that parents of schizophrenics tended to ignore the other's active utterances more than normal couples do. McPherson et al. (1973) discovered that family patterns of acknowledgment varied across different groups of high-risk adolescent families.

Lennard et al. (1965) found that members of families of schizophrenics had fewer successful intrusions than normals. Riskin and Faunce (1970) showed that disturbed families changed topics more frequently, cut each other off, and shifted themes more frequently. Similarly, Stabenau et al. (1965), in a study of families of schizophrenics, juvenile delinquents and normals, found that schizophrenic families failed to acknowledge important themes.

Finally, Herman and Jones (1976) discovered that families at high-risk for schizophrenia (defined as presence of marked CD in the parents) used significantly less acknowledging responses in their interactions with one another than did families predicted to be at low-risk for schizophrenia. One interesting finding in this study was that while high-risk mothers appeared to dominate their family's interaction (increased monologues), they were in fact most often ignored by the others. Only one study produced no differences on acknowledgment between families of schizophrenics and nonschizophrenics (Glaser, 1976).

Clarity

Clarity measures the extent to which a communication is judged to be understandable and clear to the listener. It attempts to measure phenomena similar to CD but is actually a much more global construct and is typically measured in dichotomous fashion (clarity versus nonclarity). Several studies looking at clarity have found that disturbed families are more likely than normals to lack clarity in their communications with one another (Alkire, 1969; Behrens et al., 1968; Ferreira and Winter, 1968b; Friedman and Friedman, 1970; Riskin and Faunce, 1970; Solvberg and Blakar, 1975; Stabenau et al., 1965). Similarly, Beavers et al. (1965) found that mothers of schizophrenics produced a higher percentage of shifts of meaning and evasions in their communications than did normal mothers. The results of these studies dovetail nicely with those measuring communication deviance. However, it is important to note that while the Singer and Wynne measure of CD appears to be specific for thought disorder in the offspring, measures of clarity are not. Lack of clarity is found in nonschizophrenic disturbed families as well.

Conflicting Messages

Bugental et al. (1971) found that significantly more mothers of disturbed children produced messages containing evaluative conflict between channels (verbal, vocal, visual) than did normals. By evaluative conflict they are referring to statements that simultaneously convey friendliness or approval in one channel and unfriendliness or disapproval in another. The trend was the same for fathers but did not reach significance. These data are consistent with Bateson's double-bind hypothesis but suggest that conflicting messages may not be specific to schizophrenic families.

Hassan (1974) found that normal couples had maximal mutual validation between them, while parents of juvenile delinquents and schizophrenics had the least. She discovered that scales assessing disqualifications of the interactional context differentiated parents of juvenile delinquents and schizophrenics from the rest (ulcerative colitis, underachievement, and normal). Finally, a scale measuring closure and co-ordination (ability to share the other's focus of attention and to parti-cipate together) in the couples' interaction allowed separation of the ju-venile delinquent and schizophrenic parent groups. While parents of delinquents were marked by "disconnectedness" (paralled messages), parents of schizophrenics showed mostly "contextual blurring" (dubious logic, recurring tangentializations, an obliteration of the sense of mean-ingfulness, and a lack of closure and coordination). Hence, in the fami-lies of schizophrenics, a total interaction context is often invalidated.

These two studies provide further support for Singer and Wynne's argument that CD is related to thought disorder in the offspring. Studies that isolate different styles of communication for different diag-nostic groups, such as that by Hassan (1974), are particularly valuable for determining which types of disturbed communication are associat-ed with specific offspring outcomes.

Comment

The results presented in this section provide further evidence for the important role of communication deviance in family psychopathology. Communication deviance is a most promising measure for high-risk re-search, as it has been shown in several studies to be selective for thought disorder. Furthermore, it appears that this measure is capable of predicting offspring diagnosis even when severity of parental psy-chopathology is partialed out. Such a measure may turn out to be quite useful in unraveling the etiological-responsive question. The studies cited in the next section on the "corrective parent" suggest that the del-eterious effects of CD may be moderated by the presence of a relatively healthy spouse.

THE CORRECTIVE PARENT

Several of the studies cited in the communication section have pro-vided data supporting the hypothesis of the corrective parent. In fam-ilies with one parent overtly disturbed or disturbing, the deleterious effects of this parent's behavior upon the child may be reduced or offset by the presence of a relatively healthy, "counteracting" spouse (Singer, 1967). Thus, the "healthier" spouse may exercise a corrective influence in the family. This hypothesis is consistent with the stress that Singer and Wynne place on the role of the *interaction* between parents in dis-turbed families rather than on their individual psychopathology. Of the studies that have looked at the relative contributions of each spouse to the prediction of outcome in offspring, all present evidence that the "other" parent often has either a counteractive or aggravating influence (Hassan, 1974; Singer and Wynne, 1963, 1965b; Wild et al., 1965; Wynne et al., 1976). The data further suggest that presence of a counteractive parent operates to reduce the probability of a serious disorder such as schizophrenia.

If indeed it is the interaction between parents that is crucial to offspring outcome, we would expect improved discrimination of offspring diagnosis when data from both parents are used than if just the pathological parent's data are used. Six different studies support this hypothesis (Glaser, 1976; J. E. Jones, 1977; Singer and Wynne, 1963; Wild et al., 1975; Wild et al., 1965; Wynne et al., 1977).

COMMENT

Communication deviance by itself may not be sufficient to produce thought disorder in the offspring, at least when it is restricted to only one parent. Rather, it may interact with other variables such as the spouse's communicative style or the child's genetic predispositions to result in differing outcomes for the offspring. For the high-risk researcher, the model of the corrective parent may turn out to be an important variable to consider in predicting a wide range of offspring outcomes. Research designs that allow for comparison of the relative contributions of each spouse to outcome ought to be extended to other areas of family interaction besides communication deviance.

SUMMARY AND CONCLUSIONS

It appears that there are in fact several dimensions along which disturbed and normal families may be reliably differentiated. There are, of course, many variables that affect both comparability and generalizability of these types of studies (sex and age of child, developmental stage of the family, premorbid status, socioeconomic status, to name a few). A discussion of these issues is beyond the scope of this paper. Despite the difficulties inherent in family research, trends are evident.

There is much evidence to support the view that disturbed families are marked by a preponderance of parent-child coalitions and a corresponding weak parental coalition, as well as a conflicted marital relationship. There is some suggestion that families of delinquents and schizophrenics differ on this dimension in that the former may be rather rigidly organized, whereas the latter are characterized by unstable relationships and competition between parents for the child's support in dealing with issues surrounding the marital relationship. Thus, in treatment, it may be more valuable to look at how authority is handled rather than which individual family member has the most of it. This conclusion alone suggests that family therapy may be the treatment of choice for high-risk individuals. In any case, the evidence for cross-generational boundaries is consistent with both clinical observations (e.g., Minuchin, 1974) and theory (e.g., Lidz, 1973). Further research on the nature of coalitions in families will make it easier for the family therapist who works with high-risk families to determine when it is most advisable to strengthen coalitions and when it is better to loosen already existing rigid ones.

The studies reviewed also indicate that normal families have more flexible patterns of interacting, exhibit a greater level of general harmony or closeness, and are able to function more effectively on a variety of tasks. Perhaps teaching families communication skills may result in increasing the likelihood of their developing greater flexibility and harmony. There is some evidence that normal families are characterized by a flexible hierarchical structure, often father > mother > child. Building on the strengths of a potential "corrective parent" may be another way of reducing the impact of a rigid family system, a disturbed spouse, or a lack of parental leadership.

The communication studies argue strongly for deviant communicative style playing a crucial role in producing thought disorder in the offspring. It is hoped that high-risk researchers will incorporate this measure into further studies in order to test this hypothesis directly. For the family therapist, knowledge of communicative styles specific to types of disorder will help in evaluating, understanding, and planning treatment for a variety of disturbed family types.

The studies in total suggest that the marital relationship is indeed an important variable to consider in family research. Although studies of the whole family are certainly important, perhaps more attention should be paid to the impact the couple has on the family system.

In conclusion, it is hoped that this review offers a more optimistic outlook for the family researcher. It appears that measures designed or modified specifically for use with families, rather than small-group process measures of verbal activity, yield more meaningful and consistent results. Ultimately, high-risk family interaction studies will be useful in sorting out such complex issues as the responsiveness-etiological controversy. Additional family interaction research will contribute to family therapy outcome research by providing dimensions along which to differentiate disturbed and normal families, thus making possible the assessment of change. Further down the road, there is hope that studies of deviant and healthy families will allow us to prevent or offset the blossoming of severe psychiatric disorders in high-risk children.

REFERENCES

Alexander, J. (1973a), Defensive and supportive communications in family systems. *J. Marr. Fam.*, 35:613–617.
_____ (1973b), Defensive and supportive communications in normal and deviant families. *J. Consult. Clin. Psychol.*, 40:223–231.
Alkire, A. (1969), Social power and communication within families of disturbed and nondisturbed preadolescents. *J. Personal. Soc. Psychol.*, 13:335–349.
Bateson, G., Jackson, D., Haley, J., & Weakland, J. (1956), Toward a theory of schizophrenia. *Behav. Sci.*, 1:251–264.
Baumrind, D. (1975), The contributions of the family to the development of competence in children. *Schiz. Bull.*, 1:12–37.
Beavers, W., Blumberg, S., Timken, K., & Winer, M. (1965), Communication patterns of mothers of schizophrenics. *Fam. Proc.*, 4:95–104.
Becker, J. & Iwakami, E. (1969), Conflict and dominance within families of disturbed children. *J. Abnorm. Psychol.*, 74:330–335.
Behrens, M., Rosenthal, A., & Chodoff, P. (1968), Communication in lower-class families of schizophrenics: Observations and findings. *Arch. Gen. Psychiat.*, 18:689–696.
Bugental, D., Love, L., Kaswan, J., & April, C. (1971), Verbal-nonverbal conflict in parental messages to normal and disturbed children. *J. Abnorm. Psychol.*, 77:6–10.
Caputo, D. (1963), The parents of the schizophrenic. *Fam. Proc.*, 2:339–356.
Cheek, F. (1964), The 'schizophrenogenic mother' in word and deed. *Fam. Proc.*, 3:155–177.
Farina, A. & Holzberg, J. (1968), Interaction patterns of parents and hospitalized sons diagnosed as schizophrenic or nonschizophrenic. *J. Abnorm. Psychol.*, 73:114–118.
Ferreira, A. & Winter, W. (1965), Family interaction and decision-making. *Arch. Gen. Psychiat.*, 13:214–223.
_____ _____ (1968a), Decision-making in normal and abnormal two-child families. *Fam. Proc.*, 7:17–36.
_____ _____ (1968b), Informational exchange and silence in normal and abnormal families. *Fam. Proc.*, 7:251–276.
_____ _____ _____ & Poindexter, E. (1966), Some interactional variables in normal and abnormal families. *Fam. Proc.*, 5:60–75.
Friedman, C. & Friedman, A. (1970), Characteristics of schizogenic families during a joint family story-telling task. *Fam. Proc.*, 9:333–354.
Glaser, R. (1976), *Family, Spouse and Individual Rorschach Responses of Families With and Without Young Adult Schizophrenic Offspring.* Unpublished doctoral dissertation, University of California, Berkeley, Calif.
Goldstein, M. & Rodnick, E. (1975), The family's contribution to the etiology of schizophrenia: Current status. *Schiz. Bull.*, 1:48–63.
Goldstein, M., Rodnick, E., Jones, J. E., McPherson, S., & West, K. (1976), Familial precursors of schizophrenia and spectrum disorders. Paper read at the Second Rochester International Conference on Schizophrenia, Rochester, New York.
Haley, J. (1962), Family experiments: A new type of experimentation. *Fam. Proc.*, 1:265–293.
_____ (1963), *Strategies of Psychotherapy*, New York: Grune & Stratton.

———— (1964), Research on family patterns: An instrument measurement. *Fam. Proc.*, 3:41–65.

———— (1967), Speech sequences of normal and abnormal families with two children present. *Fam. Proc.*, 6:81–97.

Hassan, S. (1974), Transactional and contextual invalidation between the parents of disturbed families: A comparative study. *Fam. Proc.*, 13:53–76.

Herman, B. & Jones, J. E. (1976), Lack of acknowledgment in the family Rorschachs of families with a child at risk for schizophrenia. *Fam. Proc.*, 15: 289–302.

Hirsch, S. & Leff, J. (1971), Parental abnormalities of verbal communication in the transmission of schizophrenia. *Psychol. Med.*, 1:118–127.

Jacob, T. (1975), Family interaction in disturbed and normal families: a methodological and substantive review. *Psychol. Bull.*, 82:33–65.

Jones, F. (1973), Current methodologies for studying the development of schizophrenia: A critical review. *J. Nerv. Ment. Dis.*, 157:154–178.

Jones, J. E. (1977), Patterns of transactional style deviance in the TATs of parents of schizophrenics. *Fam. Proc.*, 16:327–337.

Leighton, L., Stollak, G., & Ferguson, L. (1971), Patterns of communication in normal and clinic families. *J. Consult. Clin. Psychol.*, 36:252–256.

Lennard, H., Beaulieu, M., & Embry, N. (1965), Interaction in families with a schizophrenic child. *Arch. Gen. Psychiat.*, 12:166–183.

Lidz, T. (1973), *The Origin and Treatment of Schizophrenic Disorders.* New York: Basic Books.

———— Cornelison, A., Carlson, D., & Fleck, S. (1958), Intrafamilial environment of the schizophrenic patient: The transmission of irrationality. *Arch. Neur. Psychiat.*, 79:305–316.

Loveland, N. (1967), The relation Rorschach: A technique for studying interaction. *J. Nerv. Ment. Dis.*, 145:93–105.

McPherson, S., Goldstein, M., & Rodnick, E. (1973), Who listens? Who communicates? How? *Arch. Gen. Psychiat.*, 28:393–399.

Minuchin, S. (1974), *Families and Family Therapy.* Cambridge, Mass.: Harvard University Press.

Mishler, E. & Waxler, N. (1965), Family interaction and processes and schizophrenia: A review of current theories. *Merrill-Palmer Quart. Behav. Develop.*, 11:269–315.

———— ———— (1968), *Interaction in Families: An Experimental Study of Family Processes and Schizophrenia.* New York: Wiley.

———— ———— (1975), The sequential patterning of interaction in normal and schizophrenic families. *Fam. Proc.*, 14:17–50.

Morris, G. & Wynne, L. (1965), Schizophrenic offspring and parental styles of communication. *Psychiat.*, 28:19–44.

Murrell, S. (1971), Family interaction variables and adjustment of non-clinic boys. *Child Develop.*, 42:1485–1494.

———— & Stachiowak, J. (1967), Consistency, rigidity, and power in the interaction patterns of clinic and non-clinic families. *J. Abnorm. Psychol.*, 72:265–272.

O'Connor, W. & Stachiowak, J. (1971), Patterns of interaction in families with low-adjusted, high-adjusted and mentally retarded members. *Fam. Proc.*, 10:229–241.

Reiss, D. (1971), Varieties of consensual experience. I. A theory for relating family interaction to individual thinking. *Fam. Proc.*, 10:1–28.

Riskin, J. & Faunce, E. (1970), Family interaction scales. III. Discussion of methodology and substantive findings. *Arch. Gen. Psychiat.*, 22:527–537.

_____ _____ (1972), An evaluative review of family interaction research. *Fam. Proc.*, 11:365–456.

Schuham, A. (1970), Power relations in emotionally disturbed and normal family triads. *J. Abnorm. Psychol.*, 75:30–37.

_____ (1972), Activity, talking time, and spontaneous agreement in disturbed and normal family interaction. *J. Abnorm. Psychol.*, 79:68–75.

Schulman, R., Shoemaker, D., & Moelis, D. (1962), Laboratory measurement of parental behavior. *J. Consult. Psychol.*, 26:109–114.

Shapiro, L. & Wild, C. (1976), The product of the consensus Rorschach in families of male schizophrenics. *Fam. Proc.*, 15:211–224.

Singer, M. (1967), Family transactions and schizophrenia: I. Recent research findings. In: *The Origins of Schizophrenia*, ed. J. Romano. Proceedings of the First Rochester International Conference of Schizophrenia. Amsterdam: Excerpta Medica Foundation.

_____ & Wynne, L. (1963), Differentiating characteristics of parents of childhood schizophrenics, childhood neurotics, and young adult schizophrenics. *Amer. J. Psychiat.*, 120:234–243.

_____ _____ (1965a), Thought disorder and family relations of schizophrenics. III. Methodology using projective techniques. *Arch. Gen. Psychiat.*, 12:187–200.

_____ _____ (1965b), Thought disorder and family relations of schizophrenics. IV. Results and implications. *Arch. Gen. Psychiat.*, 12:201–212.

Solvberg, H. & Blakar, R. (1975), Communication efficiency in couples with and without a schizophrenic offspring. *Fam. Proc.*, 14:515–534.

Stabenau, J., Tupin, J., Werner, M., & Pollin, W. (1965), A comparative study of families of schizophrenics, delinquents and normals. *Psychiat.*, 28:45–59.

Wild, C., Shapiro, L., & Goldenberg, L. (1975), Transactional communication disturbance in families of male schizophrenics. *Fam. Proc.*, 14:131–160.

_____ Singer, M., Rosman, B., Ricci, J., & Lidz, T. (1965), Measuring disorder styles of thinking. *Arch. Gen. Psychiat.*, 13:471–476.

Winter, W. & Ferreira, A. (1967), Interaction process analysis of family decision-making. *Fam. Proc.*, 6:155–172.

_____ _____ (1969), Talking time as an index of intrafamilial similarity in normal and abnormal families. *J. Abnorm. Psychol.*, 74:574–575.

Wynne, L. & Singer, M. (1963), Thought disorder and family relations of schizophrenics. II. A classification of forms of thinking. *Arch. Gen. Psychiat.*, 9:199–206.

_____ _____ Bartko, J., & Toohey, M. (1977), Schizophrenics and their families: Research on parental communication. In: *Developments in Psychiatric Research*, ed. J. M. Tanner. London: Hodder & Stoughton, pp. 254–286.

_____ _____ & Toohey, M. (1976), Communication of the adoptive parents of schizophrenics. In: *Schizophrenia 75, Psychotherapy, Family Studies, Research*, ed. J. Jorstad & E. Ugelstad. Oslo: Universitetsforlaget.

Role Structure and Subculture
in Families of Elective Mutists

KNUD GOLL

Elective mutism is defined as being able to speak but not using verbal communication except with members of the immediate family, and then only if no strangers are present. Elective mutism sometimes develops into total mutism. The patients are generally not considered psychotic (the mutists among schizophrenics are regarded as a special group). Usually elective mutism is looked upon as related to functional aphonia, although not the same phenomenon. This is evident from the almost regular, age-connected breakthrough in elective mutism (five to seven years), which is not seen in functional aphonia. Elective mutism must, of course, be kept separate from aphasia, which has its root in somatic cerebral diseases.

BACKGROUND

In my work on the children's ward of a psychiatric hospital in 1975, I met a boy, age 14, who had been an elective mutist for seven years (the last years totally mute). Several institutions and therapists had tried to cure him without result. Not one word had passed his lips.

After discussions with my wife and our children, we decided to take the boy to our home if his biological family could accept this procedure. The parents were willing, and after six months the boy began to speak.

In our work, we found the literature on this subject of help but not fully satisfying. Studying the boy, his problem, and his family struc-

Knud Goll, M.D., is on the staff of the Psykiatrisk Hospital, Risskov, Denmark.

The author wishes to express his appreciation to H. Myers, Viborg, Denmark, for his translation of this paper into English, and to J. Kristensen, amateur hypnotist, Struer, Denmark, for his help with three children (families A, B, and D).

ture, several points came up, resulting in a hypothesis that is the main theme of this paper. Let us look at the literature, starting with a venerable Danish legend. Then I will outline my hypothesis and present ten case histories in light of the hypothesis. Finally, I will describe the treatment of these cases and discuss therapeutic issues.

A LEGEND 1500 YEARS OLD

The oldest story of mutism I could find is written in *Danesaga* of Saxo (see Sakse, 1911). It can be retold briefly as follows.

Once upon a time there was a king of Denmark called Vermund. He was blind and very old. His son was named Uffe (or Offa) hin Spage (the meek, submissive, quiet). He was given this surname because he had never said anything but always went around with a sad, stubborn look on his face. He never did anything and was considered good for nothing.

Then one day a message came from the King of the Saxons suggesting that, since Vermund was weak and old, they combine their two countries. As an alternative, a single combat between the son of the King of the Saxons and a representative of the Danish people was proposed.

There was silence. Then suddenly Uffe said that he himself was willing to fight against the King's son if the son would bring with him the best Saxon warrior as his fellow fighter. King Vermund became angry. He asked who had spoken. Some men standing nearest to the blind king said that Uffe was the man who had spoken. King Vermund was offended and said that he did not like to hear impertinent falsehoods about his son, who could not speak. But the men assured the King that Uffe was the man who had answered the Saxons. Vermund asked Uffe why he had never talked before. Uffe replied that it had not been necessary because his father had ruled the country very well until that day.

In training before the day of combat, no sword was strong enough for Uffe. They all broke. But Vermund did not mention his own good sword, buried in the ground many years before, as his expectations of Uffe were not too great. But at last his men succeeded in persuading Vermund to reveal the place where the sword was hidden. But the king prohibited Uffe from trying out the weapon; it might break.

The day of the combat arrived. The river Ejder, which formed the border between the two countries, divided at a little islet, which was selected for the momentous fight. King Vermund moved his throne to the outermost edge of the riverbank and let the people know that he would drown himself if his son lost. Uffe fought his two opponents. On being told that his son killed the first one with a tremendous stroke, Vermund moved the throne back from the dangerous bank. When the second enemy fell, he wept openly. His joy was boundless.

This old story tells more about the mutist's situation than most modern papers on the subject. The mutist is living in the world of his parent's enemies. He has a symbiotic relationship to his father (or mother), who is blind to the mutist's possibilities to make a way of his own. The parent does not dare to reveal the place where the old sword is buried and talks about suicide when the mutist prepares for the big fight. Uffe's father is silent in two very important situations: when the enemies threaten him and when Uffe needs to know where the sword is hidden, the only weapon that can give the mutist a chance.

I was very impressed to find the mutist's family structure reflected in this old story. By the time I read it I had looked at ten mutists' files that disclosed almost the same family structure as that of our foster child and his biological parents. I will return to this point later, but first to the psychiatric literature.

Review of the Literature

Hesselman (1976) has published an excellent bibliography on mutism, as defined above. It refers to about ninety papers of the period from 1877 to 1973.

Parker et al. (1960) inclined to the opinion that mutistic children have been inoculated with the idea that the outer world and its inhabitants are formidable and alarming. They also believed that the parents have been mute (mutists), or silent, as a reaction to strangers. In 1962, Mora et al. reviewed the literature and found, among other things, fear of strangers, separation anxiety, symbiotic relationship between mother and child, and immature mothers as the most outstanding similarities. In 1971, Dummer presented a brilliant analysis of a case of functional aphonia that seemed to be related to elective mutism. A 17-year-old girl became totally mute in the course of a few hours. Perhaps because of the patient's advanced stage of development, she was able to present her problem and to offer much more material for analysis than elective mutists are able to in most cases. We find strong tensions in her family. The girl had been brought up by the maternal grandparents, who had a tense relationship with each other, and the patient's mother and grandmother were not on good terms either. The grandmother was the first victim of the patient's silence, which turned out to be total, only to be broken in hypnosis a couple of weeks later. She was then able to

tell about her constant worry about the tensions in the family. The
worrying tied up most of her resources and left her immobilized. Her
mother could not help her. She had herself returned from a failed marriage to her parents' home. As a model for her daughter, she was
passive and suspicious of the outer world. The therapist gave the
mother a foothold: "Get on! Learn to respect yourself. Then you will
be able to help."

Kehrer and Tinkl-Damhorst (1974) proposed a list of conditions
that seem to play a part in provoking elective mutism. They mentioned
organically determined speech defects and brain damage, but, beyond
this, most conditions could be referred to a family system characteristic
of the elective mutist. These conditions were seen mostly as factors provoking elective mutism by accumulation, not by creating an injurious,
self-perpetuating system harmful to *everybody* in the family. Perhaps it
is for this reason the authors tried behavior modification therapy —
without support from the parents. The sick family pattern persisted,
and the symptom (mutism) recurred as soon as the child returned to the
home. Since Reed's paper of 1963, many authors have tried different
forms of behavior modifications with success, but the prognosis seems
to depend on contact between home and institution (therapist).

Landgarten (1975) referred to a case of her own in which art therapy was used with success, but four months after termination the child
regressed. Landgarten did not have much contact with the mother. Art
therapy is described as encouraging the patient to express her feelings
through drawing and painting. The child did not want to draw her
own family, an unwillingness possibly founded on the fear of being a
traitor.

Rold Jensen (1975) tried not to put demands on the mute children
in his institution (for children with speech difficulties). I am grateful to
Jensen for having given me the opportunity to study his files. There are
good results, they seem to be lasting, and they are based on good contact with the home, contact that is initiated at the start of treatment
through a home visit.

Ruzicka and Sackin (1974) stand in a class of their own. They have
been brave enough to describe their own reactions and negative feelings arising from work with an elective mutist. Finally, I want to refer
to Bradley and Sloman (1975) who, according to Hesselman (1976),
have found 26 children with elective mutism among the children at 11
schools in Toronto, Canada. Twenty-three of these children were from
immigrant families who did not speak English at home.

In offering my hypothesis about the genesis of elective mutism, I am
indebted to Satir (1967), Richter (1971), Haley (1971), Manocchio and

Petit (1975), and others, especially Berne (1964), whose ideas about transaction and role playing have been an effective tool in my work as a family therapist. Jonsson (1974) has written about families who are suspicious of society. I find this author very convincing in his search for a new basis for his work with "outsider families."

HYPOTHESIS

In order to manifest itself, elective mutism requires two main factors: (a) a *society* that is able to produce and maintain outsiders and outsider groups, and (b) the *ghetto family*, which means a family with very little confidence in society. The family consists of individuals playing *four special roles*: (a) the *elective mutist* himself; (b) the *mutist model* (or models); (c) the *symbiotic partner*; and (d) the *leader of the ghetto family*. The roles usually require three persons, but sometimes only two, or occasionally even one individual. Let us have a closer look at the roles.

(a) The *elective mutist* himself (EM) is the identified patient of the system (see definition at the beginning of this paper). Often it is the teachers or the nurses at the kindergarten who are the first to identify the symptom. The role seems to find its player in any individual in the family, but children with speech problems due to minor cerebral damage, etc., seem to be the most likely candidates, and such speech problems are possibly reinforced by the situation.

(b) The *mutist model* (MM) is a family member whom the identified patient imitates by learning to use stubborn silence as a strong weapon. The MM is a refractory and reticent individual who is often a former elective mutist himself. Sometimes more than one person plays the role, and often one of them is the symbiotic partner.

(c) The *symbiotic partner* (SP) forms together with the EM an unhappy relationship, injuring both parties and depriving each of possibilities of growth. The EM and SP cling to each other, saying indirectly, "If you are not careful with me, I will get sick. If I get sick, we will both get sick, and we cannot even think of the dreadful things that might happen then. Let us stay together and be careful."

(d) The *ghetto leader* (GL) gets his name from the type of family to which the EM's family belongs—the ghetto family, which occupies a marginal position in society as a result of a number of factors: insufficient education, the parent's childhood in similar families (social inheritance), immigration, cultural gap, collision between different civilizations; even unsolved problems between the parents (with mutually unexpressed, angry feelings) are sometimes projected onto the outside world. The GL often sees his family (most of the time not consciously) as weak, poor, or badly educated, unable to make its way in a cruel world full of strong, beautiful, intelligent and clever strangers who draw together and leave outsiders alone. The GL has a fantasy that his family consists of strong, beautiful, clever persons in a society populated by stupid persons who have ulterior motives, who stick together, and who are capable of underhanded methods. The EM hears only the last part and reacts with mutism (the symptom having already been legalized by the model [MM]) from his first day in school. The ghetto family need not necessarily be poor or badly educated. It might be rich, but the GL always distrusts society and its official representatives (teachers, psychologists, etc.). In families in which the SP and GL are played by different persons, one may see bad or good relationships between them. If good, all GL's aggressions are projected outside the family, which is supposed to consist of angels.

CRISIS

Coming from the ghetto family with four pathogenic roles, EM steps into a crisis situation when starting at kindergarten or school — the first place where he is forced to make his own way. He feels he is among foreigners in a literal sense of the word. To *talk* to strangers means, in a way, to make friends — to be a traitor to the ghetto. He feels alone and weak. He is able to feel strong only in his fantasy, so long as he stays in the role of EM.

RESCUE

EM's new situation makes the society start a crusade to rescue the mute child from his "pathogenic" family. This is mostly without result unless the GL is won over, followed by the SP (and perhaps MM) and EM himself. Most teachers and therapists distrust the GL and the SP (and the whole family too), seeing the identified patient as captured in a snake pit. And now the magic ring is closed. Mutism implies a society in which families feel like outsiders.

As I see it, the main problem lies in the interaction between the ghetto family and society. EM is the victim.

CLINICAL MATERIAL

Elective mutism is a rather rare symptom, and I have worked personally with only four of these children, three from Jutland and one from Greenland. Two of these children were total mutists at the time of first contact. The four families are here designated A, B, C, and D, and it seems to me they all show the characteristic traits delineated in the above hypothesis.

FAMILY A

The mother's family of origin was dominated by the grandmother, and the mother seemed to have followed suit in her own family. She was a stubborn person and in disagreements would not give in, even in the face of clear evidence; she was able to get her own way regardless of the rest of the family. One of her methods was stubborn silence. The family replied to this with tolerant recognition. She was the MM. There were also signs of symbiotic patronizing and spoiling. The child, EM, ruled the family, especially the parents, with obstinate refractoriness. In spite of his seven years, he insisted on being held like a baby when answering the call of nature. He would not take off his clothes at bedtime, and the parents yielded to the boy, reporting (with a proud undertone) that he had slept with his clothes on. The mother, in particular, accepted this and was very protective. She continually reproached herself that an older brother of the EM had died in a traffic accident "because she didn't look after him properly." Although both parents had a somewhat symbiotic partnership with the EM, it is easy to point out the mother as the SP. One also had the impression of being confronted with a ghetto feeling in the family, both parents expressing their doubts about the skill of the child psychiatrists, psychologists, and teachers they were in touch with through the boy.

The boy was of course influenced by this view, and an educator reported a game in which a doll was put into the "hospital" by the boy. When asked if the doll would be all right, the boy answered with conviction that the doll could get well only if it was allowed to return home. There is reason to believe that the ghetto effect in this family came from pronounced solidarity in both parents' families of origin. The mother had the leader role in the family and was able to laugh in her husband's face, to his obvious discomfiture.

After putting the boy in several institutions, the family finally left him in an institution for maladjusted boys. He stayed there from his ninth to his thirteenth year without saying more than five or six words in all, despite the good reputation of the place. The boy was then referred to the psychiatric hospital in which I was working. At the start a colleague tried narcoanalysis; it was in vain. The family was more uncooperative than ever before, pointing to the bad results as reason to let the boy come home. Educators, psychiatrists, nurses, etc., understood the parents' frustration very well but also thought they heard an undertone of triumph.

FAMILY B

Anna was a girl of almost 15. She had not talked outside her home at any time and had been silent at home also when strangers were present. At age seven she was placed in an institution. She did not talk there, and visits home grew more and more infrequent, clearly increasingly avoided by Anna. At last she was a total mutist.

Her father was a skillful seal hunter who had always been a good provider for his big family; Anna had 15 siblings. A Danish film company once hired him to play a role as a seal hunter in a motion picture. During the shooting, a well-known and popular Danish star was very angry with him and called him a "typical Greenlander," adding some disparaging adjectives. The father became mute for three months, and the filming was abandoned. Anna's mother rarely said anything when strangers were around (both parents were MM).

The family's life style was rather retiring and isolated from the rest of the community. The children seldom appeared outside the house; one brother did not talk during the first months in school (another MM). Anna's father felt like an outsider as a seal hunter; the rest of the population in the little town had turned to more modern ways of earning a living. Further, the little community was intermixed with Danish "colonists," whose status might have seemed totally unattainable to most people living there. But Anna's father did not give in. He continued to perform his old role, and everybody wondered a little that he was able to return home every day with enough food to satisfy his big family (GL).

Her first day in kindergarten, six-year-old Anna sat passively staring with a blank expression on her face. The school's Greenlandish teachers had to lead her to her place in the classroom. She did not take her things out of her bag; she did not take off her coat. They gave her a pencil; she sat for hours, stiff, with the pencil in her hand just as it had been put there. She stood up and urinated without showing any reaction. She did not dare to make contact with her schoolmates. After three months the teachers gave up helping Anna. She was sent home, having withdrawn from a natural step in her development, which, until her first day in kindergarten, had been rather normal. (She had been able to sit up at the age of six months and walk alone before she was one year old, but started to talk only at four years of age.)

Soon Anna was placed in a children's home. Her new therapist, who was also the director, worked closely with the family, especially the father. She was Danish but had a great interest in the old Eskimo culture. She learned from him how to control a dog team, an art only rarely mastered by a Dane.

In the house of this energetic and warmhearted woman, Anna arrived as a totally passive girl who could neither eat nor dress nor go to the toilet by herself. For many months she moved around by crawling on the floor, able to talk only when she had a person to hold on to. When she was nine-and-a-half years old, she still did not talk and was referred to a child psychiatric facility in Denmark. Here she worked well at school but remained passive and mute. She was still so after returning to Greenland. From 10 to 12 years, Anna's movements and gestures became more normal, and she functioned socially in a normal way, only lacking language. (At home, with her parents, Anna's motor functions had appeared normal when she was playing with her siblings.)

During these years she had an unusual relationship with her father (SP), writing letters to him, telling him about her love for him, but also threatening suicide to "help him get rid of her." The father played three roles in the system (SP, MM, and GP).

This was the situation when Anna, at 14, came to Denmark for the second time along with her therapist (or rather foster mother), who again tried to contact a child psychiatric department. Anna was admitted and started school in the hospital. One has the impression that her therapist from Greenland did not trust this school, and perhaps the staff did not see the therapist in a positive light either. At any rate, contact between the two sides never really developed, and Anna did not start to talk.

FAMILY C

Here we have a long, drawn out story of a mutist who had been silent for about 10 years — throughout her school education. She was able to speak a few words now and then when alone with the family, but in class she hardly talked at all. Her mother had not talked to her father, probably because of anger against him that she was not able to express openly; their marriage ended in divorce. Further, the mother had been a mutist as a child until 17 years of age (MM), at which time she had had to shift for herself. Today the mother says she is glad that she started to talk, but she is not sure that her daughter is sufficiently *resistant* to stand such a drastic move. And the mother adds that she herself still does not feel safe enough among people to be convinced that it really is an advantage for her daughter not to be a mutist (GL). She does not want to put any pressure on her daughter because she sympathizes with her and is afraid of forcing her into a world where she might be destroyed (SP).

FAMILY D

In this family we have the most well-established people in the whole series. The father and the mother helped each other in their small factory. They were fortunate and possessed many material status symbols. They felt that their only problem was the youngest son, five years old. But under the surface the tensions were apparent. The family did not feel accepted in the village, where most people were small shopkeepers, farmers, and craftsmen. The family felt that the others thought the family was rolling in money without being compelled to work. The mother did not feel accepted by her husband (GL), who wanted her to have an abortion at the time she was pregnant with the boy, now the patient (EM). She supposed that her husband wanted a smart lady to represent the factory at sales exhibitions. Perhaps she was right to a certain extent. She felt responsible for the boy, and she wanted to protect him against an evil world onto which she seemed to project most of the anger she felt against her husband but did not give voice to. She was the SP and the MM as well, having been rather silent in the first years of their marriage, and even more so as a small girl.

The boy was sent to the children's ward of a general hospital. There he stopped talking even with his parents, except for whispering a word now and then. He was then referred to a child psychiatrist, who asked me to contact the family.

CASE RECORDS OF ROLD JENSEN

Rold Jensen, working at an institution for children with speech defects, has collected seven case records,[1] which means every elective mutist child coming to the institute between the years 1969–1973. The institution serves Nordjyllands *amt* (council), but it is well known that not every elective mutist living in a given area attends an institution like that.

These files contain every note about contacts with the family, the school, and the kindergarten and statements from psychologists, psy-

[1] The seventh case record, not included here, is identical to family A, which at the start of treatment many years ago was referred to Jensen's institution.

chiatrists, and other professionals as well. I have looked for the hypoth-esized roles of EM, MM, SP, and GL and for evidence of an existing family ghetto and unhappy interaction with the community.

Family E

Mother seemed shy, modest, and almost hid herself behind her hus-band at the first home visit (MM). She could not see any problem in mutism, as her two brothers (MMs) did not talk to strangers before they were eight and 10 years old. The patient, EM, who was six years old, sat on his mother's lap, sucking his thumb and whispering with his mother. After an operation for adenoids, he would not leave the home for a couple of months. The boy was admitted to the institution, but as soon as he got a little better, the mother (SP) wanted him home on some transparent pretext. She did not get her way at first, but the boy showed decreasing interest in school work and the teachers at the institution felt forced to let him go. The psychologists reported three drawings: one with a huge person, representing himself, another with a smaller person representing his mother, and still another with a small father. The father (GL) supported the mother and son about leaving the institution.

Family F

Both parents seemed to be self-conscious (MM). Every sibling, four in all, had been shy when younger (MM). Mother was described as un-happy, inhibited, and embarrassed when confronted with personal questions. She answered quietly and after a pause. By letter she ex-pressed herself brilliantly in a sort of cry for help. The father became more open after some conversations, but for the most part used empty phrases. Mother (SP) wrote, "L. is like me, she needs help." Mother was afraid that the child L. (EM) would experience the same difficul-ties as she herself already had. This family was an interesting example of "family ghetto." EM did not speak in kindergarten except on rare oc-casions, when she uttered a single word. But one day, relatives from Canada came to visit in Denmark, and the girl (EM) spoke and enter-tained by singing! The father (GL) then saw treatment as unnecessary, and the mother sided with him verbally (but not by letter).

Family G

Mother did not speak to strangers as a small girl, but this was never recognized as a serious symptom; eventually she started to speak spontaneously. Mother (MM) identified with her daughter (EM) and admitted that she overprotected her. Mother was SP too. The family was primitive but warm, and functioned well internally; confronted with the outer world (and its therapists), the father was uncooperative (GL). A family session was planned but never carried out. The picture of the family is rather negative; it remained mostly unknown territory, and the case was considered a failure.

Family H

The father was inclined to depressions and isolation from both family and society; he was the MM. When a loan was refused by the bank, he reacted for weeks with silent, depressed withdrawal. We found only vague signs of symbiosis, but the child (EM) was cross and childish when parents and staff were present at the same time. Her behavior was similar upon arriving home from kindergarten, perhaps a reaction against symbiosis with the mother (SP?). Mother was the GL, having not sent the child to kindergarten for the dubious reason that "it would never help the child."

Family I

The symptoms began while the child (EM) lived with her grandparents in her mother's original home. EM and grandmother (SP) slept in the same bed. This family, especially the grandfather (GL), saw kindergartens as "new-fangled nonsense" and were cool to the suggestion that the child be placed in one. The mother had been silent in the presence of strangers (MM) and still did not express her feelings and wishes. She felt indebted to her parents for helping her when she was unmarried and pregnant and when later she had no home for the child. During a conjoint family therapy session, however, it came out that she wanted her daughter (EM) to live with her. The grandmother (SP) reacted strongly against letting the girl do this. After therapy, the girl was able to solve the problem herself. She told the family that she wanted to live with her mother and her mother's new lover. After that, the symptoms vanished.

Family J

The father was very shy, especially when younger. At the time of his engagement to the mother, he did not dare to speak when they were together with strangers (MM). He admitted that he was not satisfied with himself and his achievements. EM, a girl, never asked for anything in the kindergarten. She expected to be served and remained seated, or even walked away, if not satisfied. Sometimes she cried in such a situation. The father had the best contact with the girl, who seemed to feel rejected ever since the birth of her little brother. Her mother (SP) let the girl dominate the family in a passive, stubborn fashion.

This family is interesting because there was no ghetto effect and, of course, no ghetto leader. The mother was trustful and cooperative, and the child soon started to speak, probably because the mother began to visit the kindergarten, showing the girl that she felt the personnel were trustworthy.

Families A–J

Seven of the EM roles were played by girls, three by boys. In seven of the families, mother had a similar role (MM). Indication or evidence of symbiosis was found in each family — the mother was SP in seven, the father in only one family, the mother's mother in one, and in one we have no evidence of a special SP role player. Signs of "family ghetto" were found in nine families, with strong evidence in six of these.

Two families were easy to help (I and J). In family I, the roles MM, SP, and GL were played by three different family members; in family J, the roles MM and SP were played by different persons and that of the GL was not played at all.

Two families were very difficult cases (A and B). The interaction between society and those families was highly disturbed, and the roles MM, SP, and GL were played by the *same* member of the family.

Discussion

This investigation is necessarily limited in amount of material — 10 families containing an elective mutist — because the symptom is infrequently encountered. It does seem, however, that the role structure of the 10 families is very much alike. Another limitation is the absence of consideration of biological factors, such as possible brain damage or inherited brain disease, that might cause delayed learning of vocabulary or speech defects, thus inhibiting the faculty of contacting people outside the family. The material contains six files from an institution for children with speech defects (seven records if family A is included, as above mentioned), and it is no wonder that some of these children are less than eloquent, even when speaking to the nearest family. Speech defects, however, are not constant factors in elective mutism. In family B, the EM (girl) began to speak seven years after she became totally mute. She spoke Danish without any defects and with a vocabulary appropriate to her age. But the girl's behavior upon starting school suggested psychosis, although the symptomatology responded well to her foster mother's patience and interest.

Though psychosis and speech defects do not seem to be constant factors accompanying elective mutism, the family roles of MM, SP, and GL do appear to be almost invariable characteristics of EM families. The question follows: Is this constellation of roles caused by the existence of the EM in the family, or does the family cause the EM's symptoms? According to modern family theory, the question is incorrectly posed. The role players keep each other in a sort of balance, resulting in a vicious spiral that aggravates everybody's symptoms and emphasizes the role pattern. EM causes SP and GL—and vice versa. For similar interactional patterns, see Watzlawick et al. (1967). But the situation is still more complicated. A similar vicious circle or spiral is established between society and the ghetto family; both elements are responsible for the pathogenic interaction. In this connection it is interesting to look at Bradley and Sloman (1975), who found a high frequency of elective mutism among immigrant families in Toronto, Canada. Treatment is complicated because the therapeutic institutions, their staffs and individual therapists, do not see themselves as parts of the sick interaction pattern. Indirectly they reinforce the subculture through their narrowly focused interest in the EM's symptoms, especially the mutism. And, often, family therapists work with the role pattern (SP + MM + GL + EM) long before they have even touched the interaction between culture and subculture (society and ghetto family). As professionals, I think we are all guilty. If we cannot cure the patient, we blame the family and project our unconscious feelings of insecurity onto the family with angry comments about their "sick" behavior. We tell our colleagues that our work is impossible in this or that case of elective mutism *because* the family counteracts the therapy. This behavior is the very problem, or part of it. I have never heard a surgeon say, "I cannot cure this appendicitis because the patient has inflammation of the appendix."

Perhaps we could go much further if we were not so busy "curing" and more eager to make the families feel safe and accepted as human beings. These families seem to contain a common substrate of low expectations in regard to every member of the community and to society, which is seen as consisting of strong and well-educated personalities, or at least of an intimate fellowship keeping out the ghetto family as a marginal group. This feeling of inferiority strongly colors the family's daily experiences, its thoughts about the future, its initiatives and successes. The ghetto family develops a collective symbiosis, an atmosphere in which growth, new insight, and experiments with new modes of emotional expression are doomed to wither. The family sticks to the familiar ways of emotional communication at any price. The identified patient continues to tread the same measure with the symbiotic partner, whether it is to the strains of criminality, hysteria, or mutism. Perhaps we ought not to wonder why mutist families produce mutists. We never wonder why Chinese children speak Chinese. Perhaps criminality and schizophrenia are just the emotional language of other types of ghetto families.

Future investigations ought to include families without treatment. We do not know exactly what happens to them and to their mute members. It may be impossible to find material on Danish or Scandinavian families that have not been the object of some kind of treatment. Kehrer and Tinkl-Damhorst (1974) write that elective mutism is unknown after the age of puberty, but the authors add that the children, if untreated, have to do without normal social contacts throughout their school days, and this is not at all acceptable.

We also need to investigate the frequency of elective mutism in specific populations and the way it is handled, by whom, its prognosis, etc.

TREATMENT

I have seen four families — two were cases of total mutism, derived from elective mutism (family A and B), and two of elective mutism that in family D threatened to become total mutism. The total mutism seems in families A, B, and D to be the result of aggressive feelings against the biological family, leaving the EM role player to therapists or institutions which were looked upon by both the patient and his family as strange and potentially dangerous.

FAMILY A

The classic form of conjoint family therapy had been tried, including family sessions in the home with as many members present as possible. The treatment had been without success, probably because the therapists did not concentrate on the relation between society (culture) and family (ghetto, subculture). Instead the therapy dealt mostly with internal communication in the family. This is an excellent model where the ghetto effect is not too distinct. Perhaps one's professional conscience does not really allow it, but at the start of therapy there is more to be gained by having a meal with the family or drinking a beer with the father (often GL). In such situations, it is possible to study the family's sense of humor, interests, emotional language, etc. The therapist learns to express himself more or less in the family's own style in order to seem less alien and threatening. In this phase it is important to confront the family with the therapist's own positive and negative feelings as provoked by the family. Unless this is done, the therapist cannot be accepted as anything other than a polite representative of a patronizing institution. The therapist risks being rejected one day with precisely the same politeness with which he introduced himself. For further enlightenment, see Kempler (1973).

After having tried to establish good contact with family A by more conventional methods, I became frustrated by their litany of complaints about the institution's neglect that they had uncovered during the boy's visits home on weekends. The list was long and tedious, consisting mostly of small spots on the boy's clothes and the like. I felt completely sure that my anger was provoked by the fact that the family was preventing me from taking up more serious subjects. Then I told family A that it was the most difficult and uncooperative family I had met for a whole year. It was true. After this the ice was broken.

Even this would not have been enough in the case of family A. After seven years of elective mutism, the boy had developed total mutism, and he was now so socially underdeveloped that his skills were only a parody of the accomplishments of most boys at the age of 14. His self-esteem suffered greatly. For many years people around the boy unconsciously considered him less than human, unable to think, because he never uttered a word. He escaped responsibility for the daily household tasks as a sort of secondary gain. All facial expression was extinct, apart from a pleading look in his eyes that provoked people to help him into helplessness. At first glance one really got the impression that this boy was subnormal with a low IQ.

Taking this boy in as a foster child, our first goal was to reinforce his self-esteem by teaching him new skills. We found inspiration in Glasser's book *Reality Therapy* (1974). The boy was confronted with his new family's disapproval when he refused to eat with us, to wash regularly, and to help in the kitchen as our own children did. He learned how to paint a door. We *demanded* these achievements of him, and in this way we showed him indirectly that we took it for granted that he was able to manage the duties required of him. During this period, the boy's facial expression became more open and his chewing muscles less tense — they were not visible through his cheeks any more. But after five and a half months he still did not speak to us. Every week his presence grew more and more unbearable. We could not help interpreting his silence as triumphant stubbornness, probably because in every other field we were successful by maintaining a policy of firmness, warmth, and unrelenting demands. But of course he was not really triumphing. The problem was that we were unable to *feel* his desire for help, probably because he was afraid to even think of speaking.

Then one day an amateur hypnotist dropped in. He is an engineer and a good friend of our family. As everything else had been tried, I said, partly for fun, that he, J. Kristensen, was the man to cure this "hopeless" boy. And so he was. After a few sessions, the boy began to whisper to his new therapist. Combined relaxation and suggestion, together with patience and sympathy, gave good results. Each session lasted about 20 minutes and was held in private. On the first occasion he opened his mouth and took a deep breath, and later he dared to expire through his mouth. After four to five sessions he dared to read aloud an easy text. Then came the day when I was allowed to listen. To make the boy read, my friend put me in the corner. Later he was able to read when we were alone. Then came the moment when the next person was invited to listen, and, after having read for every person in the family, he started to read aloud for one of his schoolteachers, and so on. Fourteen months later the boy was able to contact people himself, using the spoken word. He now goes to an ordinary school.

Of course we considered it of the greatest importance to keep in touch with the biological family of our foster child. The work with his social development has continued mostly in cooperation with his schoolteachers. After 20 months in our family, his willingness to speak became pretty normal, but it was quite clear that our foster child had certain speech defects that did not seem to disappear with time. A speech therapist is now working on these. As to the boy's IQ, we are still uncertain. We seem to see him waking up gradually, from month to month. About two years ago he tested at an IQ under 70, but this no longer is accurate.

We must not forget a special problem that showed up during treatment. It was when speech development started. We became jealous of the friend who gave us a hand but simultaneously provoked our anger against the boy and himself. After all we had been through, we found it unjust that we were not allowed to hear him speak. We had to discuss this problem with the therapist before treatment in order to calm down ourselves (and our foster son too). From that moment the therapy continued with success.

The biological family's distrust faded, but now and then the mother still asks anxiously if her son is ill. His progress in school interests her, but not as much as his imaginary weakness. Perhaps it is no wonder that his brother, two years younger, suffers from encopresis. He is still living with his parents.

FAMILY B

The EM was a 15-year-old Eskimo girl from Greenland. She was referred to the same hypnotist as our foster son, and the same procedure was used, this time with quicker results even though she too had been a total mutist for many years. There is no doubt that her Danish foster mother, a kindergarten teacher, had done two things already: (a) established good relations with the father, who was both the GL and the SP, by inducing him to teach her how to drive a dog sledge, thus encouraging him to feel safe and at ease with her; (b) began social training of the girl in the home of the foster mother (this was easier than before because of the good contact with the biological parents).

It is astonishing that a few hours' work was enough in this case to break the silence. Two hospitalizations in child psychiatric wards had been tried without improvement. As I see it, the hospitals started out with an enormous handicap because of the foster mother's half-conscious negative feelings about institutions owing to some school problems in her own childhood. Furthermore, a change of milieu was not what this EM needed. All that could have been achieved by this had already been achieved. The girl said subsequently that for a long time (several years?) she had thought that she was able to speak if she really wanted to. Later she really wanted to speak but became scared when she realized that it was impossible for her to do so. (Perhaps this change in her self-perception marked the point where the milieu therapy was complete.)

This girl spoke Danish from the beginning in spite of the fact that Greenlandic was the language she spoke before she became totally mute many years earlier. No speech therapist was needed.

FAMILY C

A family therapy session was held with the 17-year-old EM, her mother, a girlfriend, some teachers, and, last but not least, her father, who had left the family many years ago after a divorce. The father trusted the outside world in a natural way and showed the girl how to do so too; the mother had not been able to do that. Half a year later the former EM's new school reported that the result was lasting. The patient was reported to be talking "like a waterfall."

FAMILY D

The author has tried to carry through the therapy according to theory from the very beginning. First on the program have been home visits and the removal of the child to a new kindergarten of the SP's (mother's) own choice. The father became interested in the social training of the boy, who had been kept at a level of a three-year-old, though his real age is five. After four months, the boy began to speak aloud — at home. In the same period, the boy has been treated by a "zone therapist" found by the parents who have great confidence in her. According to their reports, the therapy includes painful massage of the feet followed by massage of tense muscles anywhere in the body. In this female therapist's office, the boy, perhaps for the first time in his life, has encountered his mother's acceptance of his ability and power to endure pain and thus indirectly a demonstration of her confidence in him. Week by week the boy is putting on weight, after having showed signs of light anorexia. He is also more free in his behavior in the kindergarten.

I had hoped to get further with the parent's interactional problems before working directly with their boy's elective mutism, but their impatience showed me that it was time for results. My cotherapist, J. Kristensen, did not obtain the same quick result he obtained in families A and B. The therapy was completed after a year and a half.

TREATMENT EXPERIENCE OF ROLD JENSEN

The files from Jensen are very convincing. Five of the seven EMs have been cured or at least improved, mostly through admission to a special kindergarten for children with speech defects. One child did not improve, probably because it was impossible to motivate the parents to let their boy stay till the result was reached. At first the therapists persuaded the parents to let him stay (to gain time), but it became obvious that the boy's achievements diminished and that this was the result of his parents' lack of confidence.

As mentioned, the seventh case is identical to my foster child. He was at the institution about eight years ago, and treatment began with good contact with the parents. But the institution at that time was not used to this type of problem. As no tangible result was forthcoming after a short time, the boy was referred to an institution with higher prestige, but without the parents' confidence. The treatment was, of course, fruitless.

Today the institution places great emphasis on careful home visits, the descriptions of which in the files give one the impression of a relaxed atmosphere that creates confidence in the institution. New hope, new optimism, and initiative is exited, and the ghetto structure seems to wither. None of the cured EMs have had symptoms for more than two years, and individual therapy, as in families A and B, has not been necessary.

THEORY OF TREATMENT

Since elective mutism seems to be primarily a symptom of a pathogenic interaction between the mutist's "ghetto family" and the surrounding, stigmatizing society, one strategy of treatment would be to break into the family's distrust of the outer world. But from the first moment, the therapist is seen as a representative of the alien society, whether he is aware of this fact or not. It is well accepted that no family therapist would dare try to help his own family with severe problems. He would seek advice elsewhere because he is part of the sick system himself. In a similar way, the therapist of a ghetto family needs somebody outside the system to help him — a supervisor, who is more necessary here than with most types of psychotherapy, I think.

It is the primary therapist's responsibility to describe the feelings that arise in his own breast when he sees the family. This material is therapeutic to the family if presented with correct timing. Kempler writes in his book *Gestalt Family Therapy* (1973) that the therapist must put forward both positive and negative statements, and preferably at the same time — for example, "I like your solidarity, but I don't like your distrust of me." (This example is constructed after Kempler's model and not directly taken from his book.) But often therapists move on tiptoe so as not to offend the "refractory" family. The result is a communication characterized by stiff "professional" smiles and a "sympathy" that reeks of pent-up aggression. Such behavior only reinforces the family's opinion that the representatives of society are not human beings of flesh and blood.

Once the *distrust is removed, social development* is often possible by putting the child into a new milieu (kindergarten, foster family, etc.) that eventually must instruct the biological family members on how to be good cotherapists.

If the child does not talk after several months, it will often be necessary to put the focus on the mutism itself. Here a new cotherapist will often be preferable because this therapy must proceed carefully by small steps, causing as little anxiety as possible. This sort of therapy is felt to be overprotective if one is accustomed to provoking confrontations about household responsibilities and the like, but the timing is different and the therapists must understand that they work with different problems and must not condemn each other's methods. The therapists have to work openly with the jealousy that is almost inevitable when the EM starts speaking to some persons but not to others.

Finally, the child must not return to his or her family before the family is able to let the EM have more responsibility or regression may occur.

REFERENCES

Berne, E. (1964), *Games People Play*. New York: Grove.

Bradley, S. & Sloman, L. (1975), Elective mutism in immigrant families. *J. Amer. Acad. Child Psychiat.*, 15:510–514.

Dummer, W. (1971), Psychogener Mutismus bei einer Jugendlichen. *Deutsch. Gesundheitesw.*, 26:563–567.

Glasser, W. (1974), *Realitetsterapi — Teori og Praksis*. Copenhagen: Nordisk.

Haley, J. (1971), *Changing Families*. New York: Grune & Stratton.

Hesselman, S. (1976), *Selektiv mutism hos barn*. Stockholm: Psykologiförlaget.

Jonsson, G. (1974), *Den Sociale Arvs Onde Cirkel*. Copenhagen: Fremad.

Kehrer, H. E. & Tinkl-Damhorst, N. (1974), Verhaltensterapie bei Elektivem Mutismus. *Acta Paedopsychiat.*, 41:34–44.

Kempler, W. (1973), *Gestalt Family Therapy*. Oslo: Nordahls Trykkeri.

Landgarten, H. (1975), Art therapy as primary mode of treatment for an elective mute. *Amer. J. Art. Ther.*, 14:121–125.

Manocchio, T. & Petit, W. (1975), *Families Under Stress*. Boston: Routledge & Kegan Paul.

Mora, G., De Vault, S., & Schopler, E. (1962), Dynamics and psychotherapy of identical twins with elective mutism. *J. Child Psychol. Psychiat.*, 3:41–52.

Parker, E. B., Olsen, T. F., & Throckmorton, M. C. (1960), Social casework with elementary school children who do not talk in school. *Soc. Work*, 5:64–70.

Reed, G. F. (1963), Elective mutism in children: A re-appraisal. *J. Child Psychol. Psychiat.*, 4:99–107.

Richter, H. E. (1971), *Familien som Patient*. Kobenhavn: Gyldendal.

Rold Jensen, O. (1975), Elektiv Mutisme. *Medlemsblad for Talepaedagogisk Forening*, 11:136–148.

Ruzicka, B. & Sackin, H. D. (1974), Elective nutism. *J. Amer. Acad. Child Psychiat.*, 13:551–561.

Sakse (1911), *Danesaga*. Kobenhavn: G. E. C. Gad.

Satir, V. (1967), *Conjoint Family Therapy*. Palo Alto, Calif: Science and Behavior Books.

Watzlawick, P., Beavin, J., & Jackson, D. D. (1967), *Pragmatics of Human Communication: A Study of Interactional Patterns, Pathologies and Paradoxes*. New York: Norton.

Episodic Dyscontrol
and Family Dynamics

HENRY T. HARBIN

This paper will present characteristics of patients with episodic dyscontrol who were seen at the University of Maryland Institute of Psychiatry and Human Behavior. The majority of these patients were adolescents treated with family therapy. In addition to violent outbursts, most of these patients had episodes of suicidal behavior. Most of the identified patients had EEG abnormalities (temporal lobe spikes and 6–14/second spikes) and showed evidence of soft neurological signs. Some patients took anticonvulsant medication or a tranquilizer. (It should be pointed out that, although most of the patients in this sample had some organic involvement, most patients with problems of violence do not.)

Violent behavior consisted of aggression directed at inanimate objects such as windows or furniture, aggression toward other people, sometimes with intent to kill, dangerous misuse of automobiles, and repetitive violence when drinking alcohol. Suicidal behavior sometimes occurred in conjunction with aggressive outbursts. For example, one patient put his hand through a window in an attempt to cut his wrist while he was angrily breaking up furniture.

A family therapy approach to violent behavior emphasizes the communicational meaning of the assaultive behavior and attempts to change the interactional patterns that maintain this dysfunctional symptom. Organic instability increases the vulnerability of the adolescent or young person to a multiplicity of family and developmental pressures, some of which may be of sufficient magnitude to lead to a

Henry T. Harbin, M.D., is Director of Psychiatric Education and Training, Maryland Mental Hygiene Administration and Assistant Professor, Institute of Psychiatry and Human Behavior, University of Maryland School of Medicine, Baltimore, Maryland.

163

dyscontrol episode. However, once the cycle of violence is set in motion, these episodes may take on an adaptive function for the family.
The dyscontrol episodes may serve as the final common pathway for
other family members' stresses, may be an attention-seeking mechanism for an individual, or may serve a protective function by shifting the
focus away from covert marital problems. It is important to evaluate
and weigh the overall mixture of intrapsychic, interpersonal, and organic variables that influence dyscontrol episodes before deciding on a
particular treating approach.

Typical Family Patterns

Overly Close Alliances

In reviewing cases treated in our hospital as well as families that
were only evaluated, I noticed certain repetitive family interaction patterns. A violent adolescent or young adult frequently has a close, almost
symbiotic, emotional bonding with one parent; the other parent is
usually only indirectly or ineffectually involved. Covert and overt
marital disturbances are almost always present with this constellation.
Of course, one of the major developmental tasks for the symptomatic
young person is separation from the family and increasing autonomy
from the parents. The parents themselves are usually struggling with
middle-age life crises, declining health, and identity confusion; these
issues are intertwined with the difficulties of the adolescent. The natural
ambivalence of the young person while separating will be exaggerated
due to the overly close relationship with one parent and will swing from
intense hostility to equally intense guilt and shame. The adolescent's attempts at separation invariably cause stress for the parents and siblings
as their dependency on the adolescent is disrupted.

The following case example shows the symbiotic relationship between a violent male adolescent and his mother. Therapy with this
family continued over a period of six months; at the end of this time the
therapeutic goals of cessation of violent outbursts, increased autonomy
for the adolescent, and reinvolvement of the father with the family had
been successfully reached.

A, a 17-year-old male, was referred because of several episodes of
violent behavior. His mother and father participated in outpatient
therapy. Both parents were frightened and concerned about what was
happening with their son. The mother was the dominant figure in the
sessions, and her questions and actions relating to her son were very intrusive. The father was somewhat passive and distant and seemed too

timid to intervene in child-rearing matters, thereby abdicating his role. A was particularly confused about his life goals and would swing from wanting to live at home to wanting to elope with his girlfriend. His first violent outburst occurred while he was with his girlfriend and was fantasizing about how much money he owed his mother and how he would never be able to pay off his debts to her. He became extremely anxious and began to smash chairs, threatened to hit his girlfriend, and finally broke a window with his hands. It required several people to control A, and he was hospitalized. He had only a sketchy memory and awareness of the events during his rage reaction.

It was subsequently determined that A had 6–14/second EEG spikes and he was placed on diphenylhydantoin. He was certainly in a situation in which his loyalties were split between his girlfriend, who was as domineering as his mother, and his mother, to whom he owed a much greater emotional debt. He seemed to be torn between the alternatives of either destroying himself or someone else as a response to this dilemma.

The following case also shows an overly close relationship between parent and child, but this time both parents are involved.

In this family the symptomatic person was the 19-year-old son, B, who had periodic outbursts of violence followed by suicidal behavior such as head banging and attempts at hanging himself while under the influence of alcohol. B also drove his automobile recklessly while drinking and had had several accidents. He was involved in a very hostile, dependent relationship with his mother and a more positive but symbiotic relationship with his father. The father was extremely dependent on his son and had great difficulty in setting limits for fear of hurting him or driving him away. The mother, however, was extremely hostile and rejecting at times. The marital relationship was chaotic, and there was a great deal of emotional distance between the spouses. B was unable to separate from home even though he had stated often that this was his only wish. Whenever he became angry with his parents for setting limits or disagreeing with him he would leave the house and get drunk; sometimes he became involved in provocative or assaultive actions with police when they attempted to arrest him or stop him for misusing his car. B had some evidence of brain dysfunction on EEG tracings.

In these examples and others, one sees the adolescent's alternations between exteme hostility toward self and others and extreme (mutual) dependency with the parents. Stierlin points out that guilt over leaving a home that is overly close can cause an adolescent to be overcome by self-destructiveness (1974). The psychopathology of the parents, the inability of the parents to negotiate their marital problems, the young person's confusion and fear about separating from home, the instability of the young person's central nervous system, and the poor self-esteem of both parents and child all add together to create a milieu in which episodes of behavioral dyscontrol can take place.

DISTORTIONS IN VALUE TRANSMISSION

Another frequently repeated pattern in these families is inconsistency in the values and limits concerning aggression transmitted by the parents to the adolescent or young adult. The parents may react very angrily to violent behavior at one time and then disqualify this limit by ignoring the same misbehavior another time. One parent may punish a certain behavior while the other parent subtly encourages it so that the child is caught in a covert conflict between the spouses. Other parents react to extremely violent behavior with a bland affect and seem afraid even to discuss punishments for these difficulties. This inconsistency in limit setting has been described in other families with delinquent adolescents; however, when delinquent behavior is violent this inability to set limits can be an extremely grave and dangerous problem. The following clinical example demonstrates the problem of parental inconsistency and how it can affect the offspring.

A 17-year-old girl and her family were referred because she had set two fires in an attempt to kill both her family and herself. During the first interview the parents seemed unable to hold their daughter accountable for her extremely destructive behavior. They seemed fearful of confronting her, as if they could not bring themselves to face the fact that their daughter had tried to murder them. Even when the therapist attempted to interject some of the missing affect and dangerousness of the situation, the mother responded that perhaps they should forget about the past and try to start over again. The 15-year-old brother of this adolescent girl also had frequent violent "accidents"; once he had cut his younger sister's lip. Even when he slugged his sister in the stomach at a family party and knocked her down, the parents did not see the need to punish him. This lack of parental follow-through of punishment was mixed with frequent verbal diatribes about the evils of disrespect and hostility. This inconsistency between words and behavior made it difficult for the children in this family to know where the limits were for their own drives, particularly their aggressive urges.

Many parents of children who are violent seem almost immobilized by guilt over their own seeming failure as parents. They feel that they are at fault for not having prevented the symptom through better parenting in the past. They feel that they have no right to be the authority in the present because of their past failures. The adolescent or young adult may exploit this shame by accusing the parents of past lapses in proper limit setting. The therapist may also unwittingly exacerbate this guilt by asking questions about the past and either clarifying or bringing into awareness mistakes that the parents made.

Another element that contributes to inconsistency in the transmission of values is the parents' fear of the young person's violence. This fearful reaction and consequent withdrawal by the parents from confronting the symptomatic behavior is most evident in one-parent families. The following examples show how this fear affected two patients whose fathers were not in the home and who lived with their mothers.

A rather large, heavyset 27-year-old man was living with his mother and two sisters. He had had several episodes of intrafamilial violence while under the influence of alcohol. He had hit and kicked both his mother and sisters over a two- to three-year period. The family sessions revealed that they had never even confronted this man with his behavior, largely because of their fear of him. In fact, the patient had not known about the extent of his violent actions because he had been drunk and his family had never told him. He responded with a great deal of shame to this confrontation and renewed his efforts to control his drinking.

A 19-year-old boy had repeatedly attacked his mother and sisters in the home. Twice the mother had to go to the hospital for treatment of injuries inflicted by the patient. However, she had never sought outside help in controlling her violent son. In fact, during one incident the patient himself called the police to come arrest him.

Psychotherapeutic Considerations

Before deciding on a treatment approach, it is necessary for the therapist to evaluate thoroughly the extent and nature of the violent actions and the degree of dangerousness, and to consider the necessity of a neurological workup. It is important to evaluate the family dynamics as well as the individual's problems. In my experience, a family therapeutic approach provides much more leverage than individual therapy because it makes the patient's most important interpersonal environment accessible to the therapist. Family therapy is particularly indicated when the aggressive act is directed toward another family member, unless, of course, the violent actions are of such magnitude that the person must be hospitalized or jailed.

In general, the therapist must be active and directive in attempts to change the violent symptoms. Haley (1973) and Minuchin (1974) have described strategies for actively changing behavioral symptoms via a shift in the family structure. One of the most immediate and primary interventions that a therapist should make with these families is to clarify and systematize the steps to be taken if another violent episode occurs. This therapeutic action will accomplish several goals: (1) it will decrease the parents' or other family members' fear because they will have a more clear and definite plan of action; (2) it will push the parents to confront a young person or adolescent who is acting out aggressive urges, thereby encouraging more open communication between them; (3) it will push the parents to be more consistent and specific in their limits with the adolescent, thereby leading to a clarification of the usually blurred generational boundaries; and (4) it will decrease the symptomatic person's fears of losing control by showing him that he can be managed by others in the immediate environment.

The parents need to be told that they should call the police if necessary, and that the young person can be taken to an emergency room or even to a correctional institution if he or she is completely out of control. Certain available members of the extended family or neighbors may be identified as persons who can be called upon to intervene in an emergency. The parents need the support of the therapist as an authority in order to help them reestablish their own authority over their offspring.

These actions by the therapist should be carried out during the first one or two sessions, particularly if the violence is life threatening. If a dyscontrol episode occurs during therapy, the family's handling of the matter should be examined in great detail, and any inconsistency or confusion should be remedied. After clarification of behavioral limits has been accomplished, the therapist can work on other underlying problems in the family, such as overly close alliances between parents and children, marital dysfunctions, or covert depression and suicidal thoughts in family members. It is important to keep in mind that whenever a sensitive problem for the family is being worked through, the potential for violence from the identified patient will increase.

When the symptomatic adolescent is diagnosed as having a seizure disorder and is placed on medication, family psychotherapy becomes more complicated. The diagnosis may intensify an already existing belief on the part of the parents that the adolescent is not accountable for violent behavior because he is physically "ill" and, therefore, not responsible for anything that happens. This may make it even harder for the young person to disentangle himself from the family. The therapist can help by pointing out that seizures of any kind are triggered by emotional conflicts and stress and that everyone in the family can work on coping with this stress in ways that will decrease the likelihood of a violent episode. A further explanation is also necessary: the adolescent or young adult must be told that he is responsible for whatever physical or personal damage is done during a dyscontrol episode regardless of whether there is a partial organic etiology. These dynamics were evident in the case of A mentioned above.

During family therapy, A had several more dyscontrol episodes. In one of these the parents called the police and neighbors to control their son and had him taken to the emergency room. The father then cleaned up the mess and repaired the broken furniture for his son. The therapist asked the parents not to do this in the future and had them clarify with the son that he was responsible for his behavior. At first A became angry and said that he had a medical problem and could not be responsible for his behavior. The therapist replied that it was true that he had a medical problem but that there was no one else to hold responsible for his behavior but himself and that this is what would happen. The next weekend A had one more violent episode, but this time he had to repair all the furniture and pay for the damage out of his own pocket. He did not like this, but he did not have any further dyscontrol episodes.

Another common problem in treating these families is the emotional reaction of the therapist. Violent individuals can stir up fear or intense anger in the therapist that can lead to countertherapeutic actions. Lion and Pasternak (1973) described in some detail the countertransference reactions involved in treating violent patients in individual therapy. One of the greatest dangers for the family therapist is that his emotional reactions are likely to be the same as those of the family members; this may lead to an intensification of conflict on both sides. The family therapist is not only reacting emotionally to the identified violent patient but also to the anxiety or denial of anxiety of the other family members. The therapist may withdraw and become paralyzed by fear that he is going to be attacked, just as some parents do, and thus be unable to effect positive action. He may react by scapegoating the symptomatic member and ignoring family pathology, thereby further isolating the violent person. It is important to have colleagues to consult with when treating these families in order to maintain a sense of objectivity and neutrality which can be easily lost in the face of such disturbing behavior.

REFERENCES

Haley, J. (1973), *Uncommon Therapy: The Psychiatric Techniques of Milton H. Erikson.* New York: Norton.

Lion, J. & Pasternak, S. (1973), Countertransference reactions to violent patients. *Amer. J. Psychiat.*, 130:207–210.

Minuchin, S. (1974), *Families and Family Therapy*. Cambridge, Mass.: Harvard University Press.

Stierlin, H. (1974), *Separating Parents and Adolescents*. New York: Quadrangle.

The Intergenerational Transmission of Family Violence: The Long-Term Effects of Aggressive Behavior

JOSEPH C. CARROLL

INTRODUCTION

Family violence is typically viewed as behavior which is learned in the context of family relations. Support for the position that being exposed to family violence as a child carries over to the treatment of one's own children is contained in the work of Gelles (1972), Levine (1975), Pizzey (1974), Silver et al. (1969), Steele and Pollock (1974), and Young (1964). However, except for Gelles's (1972) work, all of these authors relied on samples of particularly severe cases, using accounts of abused or abusive parents, or police, hospital, and medical records. Therefore, generalizing to the larger population from this empirical base is questionable. This lack of solid research evidence may account for the fact that there is no well-developed theory for the transmission of violent behavior. One goal of this paper is to contribute to the development of such a theory by suggesting variables which may determine why violence is transmitted across generations in some families and not in others. A second goal is to increase the generalizability of research evidence in this area by using a less selective sample to test the hypothesis that violence breeds violence. Using interviews that were designed to gather information on family backgrounds and family prob-

Joseph C. Carroll, Ph.D., is with the Department of Social and Behavioral Sciences, Colby-Sawyer College, New London, New Hampshire.

Data for this study were collected in 1973 under NIMH grant number 13050. The author is grateful for the helpful suggestions of Dr. Murray Straus, Dr. Richard Gelles, and Saundra Atwell during the preparation of this paper.

lems in general, subjects who mentioned that either husband-wife violence or overly severe punishment of children was a problem were compared to others who reported that these were not problems.

While lacking a well-developed theory of the transmission of violent behavior, the general area of intergenerational continuity provides some information as to how behavioral characteristics are passed down from generation to generation. According to Faris (1947) and Aldous (1965), parents' actions provide a "slow and unwitting apprenticeship" (Faris, 1947, p. 159) in which the young learn how to maintain social continuity, how to conduct social relations, and rear children. Aldous and Hill (1965) felt that the high social cohesion of the social bonds present in the family aids in the perpetuation of family values from generation to generation. Hill et al. (1970) found that with respect to value orientations about child-rearing and family behavior patterns over three generations, the phenomenon of discontinuity is more pronounced than continuity (p. 305). However, he also stated that extremes in leadership or lagging behind in terms of achievement are likely to be marked by continuity. Taken as a whole, the work of these authors only suggests that the cohesiveness of family relations provides an arena for the passing down of values and modes of behavior; it does not provide specific factors which may help or hinder the tendency to behave as one's parents did. Given the inadequate research on the intergenerational transmission of family violence, the intergenerational transmission of attitudes toward violence and the modeling of aggression were examined with the hope that specific factors would be discovered.

Indirect evidence for the continuity of violent behavior across generations was provided by studies which related violent experience in childhood to the approval of violence as an adult. Using a nationwide survey conducted by the President's Commission on the Causes and Prevention of Violence, Owens and Straus (1974) found that adults' approval of violence was as highly correlated with being a victim of violence as a child as was committing a violent act as an adult. Similarly, Adorno et al. (1950) and Lewis (1971) related severe family relationships with later punitive and hawkish attitudes. However, the link between experiencing violence in childhood and the approval of violent means of social control is not the same as that relating violent experience to the actual use of violence in adulthood.

The modeling of aggression may provide some insight into the intergenerational transmission of violence. Although they deal with short-term effects, Bandura (1962), Bandura and Huston (1961), Bandura et al. (1963), Baron and Kepner (1970), Harris (1973), and Nelson et al. (1969) found that aggressive behavior was imitated. Hoffman

(1960) studied parental discipline techniques and found that unqualified power assertion or a high degree of external coercive pressure by parents produced a need on the part of children to be assertive toward others. She felt that a highly coercive approach produces frustration, tension, and fear in the child and sensitizes the child to the effectiveness of power. One study that considered the long-term effects of exposure to violence was done by Eron et al. (1972). Through the use of cross-lagged correlations and path analysis, they showed that preference for televised violence at age eight led to aggressive behavior at age 13. Since actual exposure to violence may be a more powerful influence than television, its effect may be more likely to carry over into adulthood.

The indirect evidence for the intergenerational transmission of violence reviewed above suggests the following hypothesis:

1. The greater the extent to which physical violence is used on a child, the greater the chance that he or she will use violence on other family members as an adult.

Assuming that the hypothesis is supported, literature dealing with the modeling of aggression suggested some factors which may specify the above hypothesized relationship.

Hetherington and Frankie (1967) attempted to explain why a subject may identify with and imitate an aggressive model when the aggression is directed toward the subject. They proposed that identification with a hostile, dominant parent is most likely to occur when both parents lack warmth, because there is no escape to a nurturant and empathic parent. They also stated that a stressful, conflictive family relationship would increase the tendency toward defensive identification. The authors found that under high conflict, with both parents low in warmth, there was indeed a tendency for both boys and girls to identify with the dominant parent (1967, p. 124). This suggests that a lack of warmth and high stress in family relationships may positively contribute toward violent behavior in the next generation.

Another factor that may affect the transmission of family violence is the sex of the family members involved. Aldous and Hill (1965) and Hill et al. (1970) suggested that the transmission of violent behavior across generations is most likely to occur in same-sex linkages. They attributed this to the greater social cohesiveness of same-sex relations within the family. Hoffman (1960) and Sears et al. (1957) suggested that the mother is the parent more likely to be imitated. They found that mothers who punished their children more severely reported that their children showed more power assertiveness toward other children (Hoffman, 1960) and more aggression in the home (Sears et al., 1957).

The following three hypotheses suggest the manner in which warmth, stress, and the parent's sex may mediate the transmission of family violence from generation to generation:

2. To the extent that a child is subject to physical punishment and the family setting is characterized by low warmth, the child will be more likely to use family violence as an adult.

3. To the extent that a child grows up in a stressful family relationship and is subject to physical punishment, the child will be more likely to use family violence as an adult.

4. To the extent that one parent acts violently, a child of the same sex will be more likely to act violently as an adult.

SAMPLE

The sample used in this research was drawn from a larger study of what problems families face and how they handle these problems. Clientele at community guidance clinics who agreed to be interviewed composed about one-third of the original sample of 375 cases. The rest was a nonclinical control group selected randomly from city and town directories. All family problems that occurred during the three years prior to the interview were recorded.

For the purpose of this paper, two subsamples of cases were selected. The first consisted of all those who reported one or more incidents of violence toward a spouse (N = 23). The second sample was selected to serve as a nonviolent comparison group. A sample, rather than all of the nonviolent cases, was selected because funds and computer facilities available for this analysis limited the total number of cases to approximately 100, and 352 cases were not essential for purposes of the comparison to be made. The nonviolent group was therefore selected by first identifying all cases who were married, divorced, or separated during the three years prior to the interview. This was done in order to eliminate all those who would not have had the opportunity to engage in either husband-wife or parent-child violence. From this pool of married or recently divorced persons, a random sample of 77 cases was selected.

Had the data been available for all 77 cases, a total sample of 100 cases (23 violent and 77 comparison) would have been drawn on. However, the data for four of the comparison group cases were incomplete. The final sample therefore consists of 96 cases: 23 in which violence was known to occur, and a comparison group of 73.

MEASUREMENT OF KEY VARIABLES

VIOLENT EXPERIENCE AS A CHILD

Items from the Bronfenbrenner-Devereux Parental Activity Inventory[1] were indexed to provide a measure for this variable. The two items that measured the amount of physical punishment the respondent received as a child were "hit and slapped me" and "threatened to hit and slap me." Scores ranged from zero to eight for each parent with a mean of 1.56 for the father and 1.69 for the mother. The range of total physical punishment scores (father and mother combined) was from zero to 14 with a mean of 3.20.

PARENTAL WARMTH

The Bronfenbrenner-Devereux dimensions of nurturance and instrumental companionship were used to measure this variable. "I could talk with him or her about everything" and "Comforted and helped me when I had troubles" were the items that composed the nurturance dimension. "Taught me things that I wanted to learn" and "Helped me with schoolwork when I didn't understand something" were used to measure instrumental companionship. Combined index scores for parental warmth ranged from zero to 30 with a mean of 16.05.

STRESSFUL FAMILY RELATIONSHIP

The expressive rejection of the Bronfenbrenner-Devereux scale was used to measure this variable. The items composing this dimension were "Nagged at me" and "Scolded and yelled at me." Combined scores ranged from zero to 16 with a mean of 3.70.

USE OF VIOLENCE AS AN ADULT

During the interview respondents were read a checklist of problems that any family could have. The problems included various physical health ailments, husband-wife problems, parent-child problems, employment and financial problems, and personal problems such as depression, feeling unable to cope, and drinking too much. If respondents answered that either husband-wife violence or overly severe punishment of children were problems for them, the frequency of the prob-

---

[1] The Bronfenbrenner-Devereux Parental Activity Inventory is composed of 18 items which tap parent-child relations on the following nine dimensions: nurturance, instrumental companionship, principled discipline, prescription of responsibility, power, physical punishment, achievement pressure, deprivation of privileges, and expressive rejection. The possible responses for each item form a Likert scale with the responses and scores as follows: 0—never, 1—sometimes, 2—frequently, 3—usually, and 4—always or almost always.

lem was recorded.[2] The mean problem frequency for the entire sample was 0.604. This low mean was due to the fact that only about one-quarter of the sample had a frequency score of one or higher since most had not experienced these problems.

CONTROL VARIABLES

The respondent's sex, social status, marital happiness, amount of kin contact, and a psychological distress score were used as controls on the relationship between the experience of violence as a child and the use of violence as an adult. Social status was measured by the Hollingshead-Redlich two-factor index. Marital happiness was measured by the response to the request "Describe the degree of happiness, everything considered, of your marriage." The response to the question "In the last month, how often have you had contact with relatives, excluding those you live with, by getting together with them, telephoning them, or writing to them?" was used to measure kin contact. The psychological distress scale was a composite of 10 items gathered from the Midtown Manhattan Study (Srole et al., 1962) and the Army Neuropsychiatric Screening Test (Stouffer, 1948). These five control variables tap an individual's style of life, isolation from kin, and psychological well-being, all of which may be related to the tendency toward family violence.

FINDINGS AND DISCUSSION

INTERGENERATIONAL TRANSMISSION

A cross-tabulation of the amount of parental violence the respondent had been exposed to as a child with the mentioning of violence in the respondent's own family supported Hypothesis 1. Table 1 shows that 36.6 per cent of those who had experienced a high degree of parental punishment, compared to 14.5 per cent of those who had not, reported that physical violence was a problem in their own families (chi-square = 3.977; df = 1; p < .05; based on 41 families designated as having a high degree of first-generation punishment and 55 who had not).

Table 1 also shows that when the five control variables were introduced into the relationship, all 10 of the internal replications were

---

[2] Frequency scores may range from 0 to 5 with the following values: 0 — there was no problem at all, 1 — the problem occurred once a year or less, 2 — several times a year, 3 — at least once a month, 4 — at least once a week, 5 — almost every day.

TABLE 1
PER CENT REPORTING FAMILY VIOLENCE WAS A PROBLEM BY
AMOUNT OF PHYSICAL PUNISHMENT RECEIVED AS A CHILD,
CONTROLLING FOR SEX, SOCIAL STATUS, PSYCHOLOGICAL
DISTRESS, KIN CONTACT, AND MARITAL HAPPINESS

| Control Variable | N | | % reporting violence as a problem | | % difference (+ = high pun. greater) |
	Receiving high phys. punishment	Receiving low phys. punishment	High Pun.	Low Pun.	
None	41	55	36.6	14.5	22.2
Sex					
Male	14	24	35.7	16.7	19.0
Female	26	32	36.6	15.6	19.0
Social Status					
High	21	30	28.6	10.0	18.6
Low	19	26	42.1	23.0	19.1
Psychological Distress					
High	16	22	50.0	22.7	27.3
Low	24	34	25.0	11.8	13.2
Kin Contact					
High	21	25	28.6	16.0	12.6
Low	18	31	38.9	16.1	22.8
Marital Happiness					
High	26	45	19.2	13.3	5.9
Low	14	11	71.4	27.3	44.1

in the expected direction, which indicated a high degree of stability for the relationship between first-generation physical punishment and second-generation violence.

The only control variable that specified the original bivariate relationship to any great degree was marital happiness. Nearly three-quarters of the respondents who had reported a high degree of physical punishment as children and who felt that their own marriages were not particularly happy, reported that violence was a problem in their own families. On the other hand, a high degree of marital happiness was associated with fewer problems of family violence, even if the respondents had been exposed to a great deal of physical punishment as children.

WARMTH AND A STRESSFUL FAMILY RELATIONSHIP

Hypothesis 2 predicted that children from families characterized as low in warmth and who received a high degree of parental punishment, will be more likely to report a higher frequency of family violence in their own families. Table 2 presents the mean problem frequency scores of the four subgroups formed by the two dimensions of family warmth and parental punishment. As Hypothesis 2 predicts, the low warmth/high parental punishment families had the highest mean problem frequency. There was a significant main effect due to parental family warmth (F = 4.38; df = 1; p < 0.05; N = 96) but no other main or interaction effects. The fact that the low warmth/high punishment cell had the lowest mean frequency while interaction was not significant lends partial support for Hypothesis 2.

Hypothesis 3 predicted that children from families characterized as high in stress who had received a high degree of parental punishment will be more likely to report a higher frequency of family violence in their own families. Table 3 shows the mean problem frequency score for the interaction of stressful family relationships and parental punishment. As expected, the high stress/high punishment cell had the highest mean score. Also, the low stress/low punishment cell had the lowest mean frequency, lending support for Hypothesis 3. However, there were no significant main or interaction effects.

From the evidence presented in this section, it seems that low family warmth and the presence of a stressful family relationship do contribute to the transmission of violence from generation to generation. However, the fact that there was a main effect of warmth on problem frequency suggests that low family warmth may play a greater role in the transmission of family violence than a stressful family relationship.

SEX LINKAGES

Hypothesis 4 stated that the transmission of family violence is more likely to occur in same-sex linkages. To test this hypothesis, each parent's punishment score was cross-tabulated with whether or not a problem of violence existed and with the sex of the respondent.

Table 4 shows that same-sex linkages occurred most often. Males who received a high amount of punishment from their fathers were more likely to report that violence was a problem than females who were punished a great deal by their fathers. In fact, daughters who received less physical punishment from their fathers were more likely to report that violence was a problem than those subjected to a high de-

TABLE 2
ANALYSIS OF VARIANCE FOR VIOLENT PROBLEM FREQUENCY BY
PARENTAL PUNISHMENT AND PARENTAL FAMILY WARMTH

Parental family warmth	Parental punishment		Total
	High	Low	
High	.143 (14)	.346 (26)	.275 (40)
Low	1.190 (26)	.433 (30)	.784 (56)
Total	.823 (40)	.392 (56)	.572 (96)

TABLE 3
ANALYSIS OF VARIANCE FOR VIOLENT PROBLEM FREQUENCY BY
PARENTAL PUNISHMENT AND PARENTAL FAMILY STRESS

Parental family stress	Parental punishment		Total
	High	Low	
High	.923 (26)	.500 (14)	.774 (40)
Low	.857 (14)	.357 (42)	.482 (56)
Total	.899 (40)	.392 (56)	.604 (96)

gree of punishment. Overall, the difference between the father-son and father-daughter linkages was 16 per cent. The mother-daughter link was stronger than the mother-son link by 3.9 per cent. Comparing these percentage differences, it seems that the father has the stronger influence on the son, and the mother has the stronger influence on the daughter.

SUMMARY

Although it is generally accepted that family violence is learned in the context of family relations, there is no well-developed theory to ex-

TABLE 4
PER CENT REPORTING PHYSICAL PUNISHMENT WAS A PROBLEM
BY SEX OF THE RESPONDENT AND THE AMOUNT OF PUNISHMENT
RECEIVED FROM EACH PARENT

Sex of Respondent	N		% reporting violence as a problem		% difference (+ = high pun. greater)
	Receiving high phys. punishment	Receiving low phys. punishment	High Pun.	Low Pun.	
A. Physical punishment from *father* as the independent variable					
Son	21	15	28.6	13.3	15.3
Daughter	34	33	23.5	24.2	− .7
B. Physical punishment from *mother* as the independent variable					
Daughter	27	31	33.3	22.6	10.7
Son	13	25	30.8	24.0	6.8

plain, and very little solid research evidence to support this contention. This study suggested factors that may contribute to the intergenerational transmission of family violence. Also, a sample that was not primarily composed of serious cases was used.

The results of the study showed that there was a tendency for family violence to be transmitted from generation to generation. Also, low parental warmth and to a lesser extent the presence of a stressful family relationship in the first generation were factors that appeared to affect the intergenerational transmission of family violence. Finally, it was found that the transmission of family violence was more likely to occur in same-sex linkages. These results provide the potential for a future theory of the transmission of family violence.

REFERENCES

Adorno, T. N., Frenkel-Brunswick, E., Levinson, D. J., & Sandford, N. H. (1950), *The Authoritarian Personality*. New York: Harper & Row.
Aldous, J. (1965), The consequences of intergenerational continuity. *J. Marr. Fam.*, 27:462–468.
_____ & Hill, R. (1965), Social cohesion, lineage type, and intergenerational transmission. *Soc. Forces*, 43:471–482.
Bandura, A. (1962), Social learning through imitation. In: *Nebraska Symposium on Motivation*, ed. M. R. Jones. Lincoln, Neb.: University of Nebraska Press, pp. 211–269.

_____ & Huston, A. C. (1961), Identification as a process of incidental learning. *J. Abnorm. Exper. Psychol.*, 63:311–318.

_____ Ross, D., & Ross, S. A. (1963), Vicarious reinforcement and imitative learning. *J. Abnorm. Soc. Psychol.*, 67:601–607.

Baron, R. A. & Kepner, C. R. (1970), Model's behavior and attraction toward the model as determinants of adult aggressive behavior. *J. Personal. Soc. Psychol.*, 14:335–344.

Eron, L. D., Huesmann, L. R., Lefkowitz, M. M., & Walder, L. O. (1972), Does televised violence cause aggression? *Amer. Psychol.*, 27:253–263.

Faris, R. E. (1947), Interaction of generations and family stability. *Amer. Sociol. Rev.*, 12:159–164.

Gelles, R. (1972), *The Violent Home. A Study of Physical Aggression between Husbands and Wives.* Beverly Hills, Calif.: Sage.

Harris, M. B. (1973), Field studies of modeled aggression. *J. Soc. Psychol.*, 89: 131–139.

Hetherington, E. & Frankie, C. (1967), Effects of parental dominance, warmth, and conflict on imitation in children. *J. Personal. Soc. Psychol.*, 6:119–125.

Hill, R., Foote, N., Aldous, J., Carlson, R., & MacDonald, R. (1970), *Family Development in Three Generations.* Cambridge, Mass.: Schenkman.

Hoffman, M. L. (1960), Power assertion by the parent and its impact on the child. *Child Develop.*, 31:129–143.

Levine, M. (1975), Interparental violence and its effect on the children: A study of fifty families in general practice. *Medicine, Science, and the Law*, 14:172–177.

Lewis, R. A. (1971), Socialization into national violence: Familial correlates of hawkish attitudes toward war. *J. Marr. Fam.*, 33:699–708.

Nelson, J. D., Gelfand, D. M., & Hartmann, D. P. (1969), Children's aggression following competition and exposure to an aggressive model. *Child Develop.*, 40:1085–1098.

Owens, D. J. & Straus, M. A. (1974), The social structure of violence in childhood and approval of violence as an adult. *Aggres. Behav.*, 1:193–211.

Pizzey, E. (1974), *Scream Quietly or the Neighbors Will Hear.* Middlesex, Eng.: Penguin.

Sears, R. R., Maccoby, E. E., & Levin, H. (1957), *Patterns of Child Rearing.* New York: Harper & Row.

Silver, R. B., Dublin, C. C., & Lourie, R. S. (1969), Does violence breed violence? Contributions from a study of the child abuse syndrome. *Amer. J. Psychiat.*, 126:404–407.

Srole, L., Langner, T. S., Michael, S. T., Opler, M. K., & Rennie, T. A. (1962), *Mental Health in the Metropolis.* New York: McGraw-Hill.

Steele, B. F. & Pollock, C. B. (1974), A psychiatric study of parents who abuse infants and small children. In: *The Battered Child*, ed. R. E. Helfer & C. H. Kempe. Chicago: University of Chicago Press, pp. 89–133.

Stouffer, S. A. (1948), *The American Soldier.* Princeton: Princeton University Press.

Young, L. (1964), *Wednesday's Children: A Study of Child Neglect and Abuse.* New York: McGraw-Hill.

Ecology of Abusive and Nonabusive Families: Implications for Intervention

ALBERTO C. SERRANO,
MARGOT B. ZUELZER, DON D. HOWE,
and RICHARD E. REPOSA

Introduction

In recent years, child abuse has come to be considered a severe community problem which pervades all socioeconomic levels and ethnic groups. It appears that abuse is most often perpetrated within families between parents and children. The substrate for abuse lies within the personality characteristics of the abuser and the abused. It is often triggered by environmental stress factors. Because of the complex nature of abuse, there has been a tendency by researchers and clinicians to move from interpretations of single dimensions, such as biological, psychological, social, economic, etc., to consider a multidimensional view of the phenomenon. Many clinically oriented child abuse programs are

Alberto C. Serrano, M.D., is Professor of Psychiatry and Pediatrics, University of Texas, and Director of the Division of Child and Adolescent Psychiatry, University of Texas Health Science Center, San Antonio, Texas. He is also Executive Director of the Community Guidance Center of Bexar County.

Margot B. Zuelzer, Ph.D., is Assistant Professor of Psychology, University of Texas, and staff psychologist at the University of Texas Health Science Center and the Community Guidance Center of Bexar County.

Don D. Howe, M.D., is Assistant Professor of Psychiatry, University of Texas, and staff psychiatrist at the University of Texas Health Science Center and the Community Guidance Center of Bexar County.

Richard E. Reposa, M.S.W., is Social Work Supervisor and Department of Human Resources Special Projects Coordinator at the Community Guidance Center of Bexar County.

The authors would like to express their appreciation to Mr. Robin Morris for his valuable assistance in gathering and correlating the statistical data in this study.

presently looking at what is known as the "dynamics of abuse,"[1] including the parent-child relationship, the parents' own childhood experiences, the parents' personality dynamics, the quality of the marital
relationship, and the availability of a supportive network. Although as
yet unsupported by controlled research findings, these dynamics nevertheless seem to represent a clinical syndrome which has implications for
evaluation, diagnosis, and treatment of abusive families.

LITERATURE REVIEW

Abusive parents and abused children have been variously described
in regard to psychopathology and behavior deviance (Zalba, 1967;
Kempe and Helfer, 1972; Polansky et al., 1972; Gelles, 1973; Green,
1978). As the complex nature of abuse is increasingly recognized, the
importance of assessing personality dynamics within the context of parent-child interaction becomes apparent (Green et al., 1974). For instance, individuals with a certain personality structure, operating
under the burden of a painfully perceived childhood and immediate
environmental stress, might be likely to abuse the offspring whose temperament and behavior most readily elicits the unhappy childhood im-
agery of the past. Justice and Justice (1976) feature a continuous interactional model between host (parent), agent (child), and the social and
physical environment. The multiple correlational model by Young
(1977) links predisposing factors (early socialization experiences, early
abuse, role models, genotype, sex, etc.) with mediating factors (social
position, cultural values, psychological makeup of parents and child,
marital relationships, etc.) coupled with immediate precipitating situations (illness, arguments, child's misbehavior, etc.). Gil (1970, 1975)
has extensively discussed the multidimensional abuse phenomenon,
which he sees as causally related to varying combinations of social-environmental forces, pathological (group) interactional process, and individual psychopathology (Gil, 1966). He sees no absolute qualitative
difference between abusing and nonabusing families, but a difference
in degree (Gil, 1968).

Green (1976) addresses himself to implications for treatment of
abusive families. He advocates a multidisciplinary approach (not necessarily psychiatric) where he involves the parent in a corrective emotional experience with an accepting, gratifying, uncritical adult who
gives continuous reassurance and support during initial stages of the
treatment. The parents' own basic dependency needs have to be grati-

---

[1] National Institute of Mental Health (1977).

fied before "demands" can be placed on them. The therapeutic focus on the abused child needs a gradual and cautious approach to prevent the unleashing of jealousy and competitiveness on the part of the parent.

Purpose

The purpose of this study is to examine patterns of family interaction in 70 cases of child abuse and to discuss the implications for the treatment of the family. These 70 cases were matched with 70 nonabusive clinic cases for age level, sex, and primary diagnosis. Gil's hypothesis (1968) is tested that *"there is no absolute qualitative difference between abusers and non-abusers, but a difference in degree"* (p. 157).

Procedures

The 70 abusive families referred to the team had already come under the supervision of the Department of Human Resources (D.H.R.) because of verified chronic abuse and/or neglect. A designated staff person at D.H.R. screens all referrals to the team, which consists of a child psychiatrist, child psychologist, and senior psychiatric social worker. At evaluation, the team has a prebriefing with the caseworker to discuss the worker's present perception of family dynamics and his/her present intervention plans. The family is then interviewed by the team members in the presence of the worker. This involves taking an extensive family history and making detailed observations on family interaction. A "split" team-family evaluation approach is used (i.e., family members are interviewed together and separately by the team members; this may include parents together, parents separately, siblings together, siblings separately, etc.).[2] Great emphasis is placed on matching appropriate team members with certain family members for individual interviews. Members of the extended family are encouraged to participate. When a child has already been placed in a foster home, foster parents are interviewed separately from natural parents. After the evaluation, the team and the D.H.R. worker meet in a debriefing to discuss the family dynamics. Specific recommendations for further disposition and treatment are made. Relevant risk factors are weighed and considered, especially the parents' capacity for change. Disposition is discussed with the D.H.R. worker within the framework of the legal and social realities of the community. A detailed treatment plan is formulated and efforts are made to involve the extended ecological system of the child and family.

[2] For a detailed description of the team-family approach, see Serrano (1974).

The 70 families used in the control group were taken from the files of the Community Guidance Center, a psychiatric outpatient clinic for children and adolescents. This clinic has a family and social systems orientation. Referrals come from all economic strata and all ethnic groups representative of the local community. The overwhelming majority of cases seek treatment voluntarily.

RATINGS

Seven areas of family dynamics were rated on a four-point scale for degree of severity. These were (1) primary pathology; (2) family motivation to change; (3)husband-wife conflict; (4) family harmony; (5) parents' sensitivity to child's needs and capabilities; (6) parents' capacity to manage child's behavior; and (7) overinvolvement/underinvolvement.[3]

FACTORS ACROSS AGE GROUPS

Some common factors emerged across age groups with regard to abused children and their families. It should be noted, however, that although matched for age, sex, and primary diagnosis, the abuse sample and its controls could not be matched for income level. Both low- and middle-income abusing families showed severe disturbance in functioning, e.g., lack of motivation for change, marital discord, and lack of sensitivity to the child's needs. In the control group, however, only low income families ($0–7,999) showed severe disturbance in functioning, in contrast to middle-income control families, who showed mild to moderate disturbances. These findings underline Elmer's (1977) hypothesis that the stress and privation of lower-class membership may be as potent a factor as abuse in determining disturbed family interaction.

Change in residence, during the previous year especially in the younger abusive parents, was seen as an added contributor to isolation and lack of extended support systems such as neighbors or friends. Frequent moves by these families may be one style of keeping distance between themselves and the community because of their inability to make or sustain attachments. A predominant number of abusive parents had a history of severe psychiatric illness with hospitalization. This validated the team's clinical judgment that many of these parents were func-

---

[3] A detailed definition of terms used in the rating scale will be given upon request of the authors.

TABLE 1
PATIENT AND FAMILY CHARACTERISTICS
OF ABUSED/CONTROL SUBJECTS
(PERCENTAGE RATED OR ANSWERING AT EACH AGE AND LEVEL)
(N = 140)

	3–6 years	6–12 years	12+ years
PRIMARY PATHOLOGY			
Mild Child	0/10	3/3	0/20
Moderate Child	5/5	3/32	0/30
Mild Family	0/20	7/27	0/15
Moderate Family	30/65	30/32	20/20
Severe Family	65/0	57/6	80/15
X^2	21.58***	23.46***	21.89***
FAMILY MOTIVATION FOR CHANGE			
Exceptional	0/0	0/3	0/5
Average	10/75	7/57	10/65
Limited	55/25	50/33	30/15
Little or no	35/0	43/7	60/15
X^2	19.19***	21.91***	15.47***
HUSBAND-WIFE CONFLICT			
Mild	0/6	0/4	0/11
Moderate	0/28	10/52	15/47
Severe	100/66	90/44	85/42
X^2	7.56*	13.65***	8.22***
FAMILY HARMONY			
Appropriate	0/15	0/0	0/0
Mild	5/40	3/23	5/20
Moderate	35/40	33/57	20/50
Severe	60/5	63/20	75/30
X^2	17.82***	13.07***	8.23*

KEY: 10/22 = 10% of Abused Sample/22% of Control Sample
*P < .05
***P < .001
(3–6 N = 20/20; 6–12 N = 30/30; 12+ N = 20/20)

tioning at the borderline psychotic or severe personality disturbance level. Lack of ego strength, trust in others, and external support systems were reflected in a generally chaotic family history, isolation from extended family members, and chronic inability to seek help unless either court-ordered or legally committed. Thus, all of the abusive families had to be brought for evaluation and treatment by D.H.R. caseworkers, while approximately half of the mostly middle-class controls were self-referred, one third being referred by the family physician and the rest by school and community agencies.

Disturbed family interaction in the abuse sample took the form of chronic and intense conflict between children and parents and between marital partners. Multiple separations, divorces, and remarriages were interspersed with verbal and physical battles. Often, the children were drawn into these quarrels and locked into a no-win position, where everyone tended to lose. Abusive families showed repeated efforts to *maintain* dysfunctional family and marital ties. One or more of the parents tended to be severely overinvolved by often looking to the child for gratification of excessive dependency needs in a classic "role reversal" style. They tended to project their own feelings, and acted on their ambivalence by being punitive, rigid, and overcontrolling, as well as inconsistent and arbitrary. They showed little or no sensitivity to the child's needs, and were unable to manage the child's behavior in a consistent and nurturant fashion. The disturbance in family interaction appeared to manifest itself in different ways dependent upon the age of the child. Father- (or stepfather-) child overinvolvement in over half of the teenage sample involved sexual abuse. It occurred across low-and middle-income levels, with our study showing 47 per cent in the less than $4,000 income group and 29 per cent in the $16,000–20,000 income level. Three of these families were promiscuous across generational lines, with grandfather and father as well as male siblings involved. In all cases, there was overt or covert chronic conflict between husband and wife. The mother was seen as being in collusion by staying underinvolved and using massive denial. The children tended to be chronically depressed, and signaled their distress through running away, poor peer relationships, and delinquent behavior. Most of the teenagers had been forced to submit to sexual abuse since latency age, but chose not to reveal the involvement for fear of breaking up the family or to protect other siblings. Some of the girls, although feeling guilty over the involvement, were clearly ambivalent because closeness to their fathers was their only source of warmth in a cold, rejecting, and "conditional" family relationship. These adolescents would finally confide in a relative, neighbor, teacher, counselor, or friend after a seem-

TABLE 2
CLINICAL RATINGS OF PROBLEM AREAS
OF ABUSED/CONTROL SUBJECTS
(PERCENTAGE RATED BY EACH AGE AND SEVERITY LEVEL)
(N = 140)

	3–6 years	6–12 years	12 + years
PARENTS' SENSITIVITY TO CHILD'S NEEDS & CAPABILITIES			
Appropriate	0/10	0/7	0/10
Mild	10/45	14/23	0/35
Moderate	30/45	14/53	20/45
Severe	60/0	72/17	80/10
X^2	19.05***	19.85***	21.81***
PARENTS' CAPACITY TO MANAGE CHILD'S BEHAVIOR			
Appropriate	0/5	0/7	0/5
Mild	0/10	13/17	0/20
Moderate	30/85	17/66	15/40
Severe	70/0	70/10	85/35
X^2	22.6***	24.61***	11.44**
OVERINVOLVEMENT			
Mild	0/0	0/8	0/21
Moderate	7/100	9/71	0/64
Severe	93/0	91/21	100/14
X^2	26.26***	22.80***	25.59***
UNDERINVOLVEMENT			
Mild	0/20	0/37	0/0
Moderate	10/60	9/53	43/55
Severe	90/20	91/10	57/45
X^2	10.03**	26.99***	0.50

KEY: 10/22 = 10% of Abused Sample/22% of Control Sample
*$P < .05$ **$P < .01$ ***$P < .001$
(3–6 N = 20/20; 6–12 N = 30/30; 12 + N = 20/20)

ingly minor altercation with the father. Reaction by the parents at exposure ranged from denial to ambivalence to acquiescence. Mother tended to be upset, disbelieving, and primarily angry with the adolescent for "blowing the whistle" on the father.

Most control sample families differed in degree of disturbed interaction as well as in the resources, external and internal, which were available to their family units for resolution of interactional difficulties. Overinvolved nonabusive mothers tended to be moderately overcontrolling with their children, often seeing them as "the problem" when they tried to become more independent and thereby threatened the family equilibrium. Interestingly enough, the majority (63 per cent) of control group fathers tended to be underinvolved with their teenagers. Although this may reflect the work ethic of the primarily middle-class control sample, it may also be a reflection of the general distancing of fathers from their maturing children. In contrast to the majority of abusive families, internal resources could be utilized during treatment so that parents were able to use each other to manage the children's behavior more appropriately, provide more consistent structure, and take responsibility for assisting the children in constructive conflict resolution.

FAMILY AND SOCIAL SYSTEMS INTERVENTION

It is commonly accepted that the family is the basic social unit that supports the affective and instrumental needs of its members. Lewis et al. (1976) and Beavers (1977) describe that healthy families present a strong parental coalition, demonstrate open and clear communications among their members, and are able to share feelings openly with a predominance of positive affect. These families seem to have a wide repertoire of adaptive coping patterns and the ability to face crises creatively. They show respect for the autonomy of their members, along with a strong sense of solidarity. In our experience, healthy families are also able to recognize and to respect the basic developmental needs of children and adults and seem able to make flexible adjustment to family changes of equilibrium. Typically, these families have functional social networks (extended family, friends, neighbors, associates) which represent significant natural sources of emotional and instrumental support. These families also seem able to use well a broad range of community resources, including health, legal, religious, educational, and recreational social agents and agencies which are additional natural support systems.

In marked contrast, most abusive families present serious evidence of internal dysfunction and of social isolation. Often, many of the instrumental functions normally expected from families have been taken over by outside social agents. They also show considerable depletion of internal emotional resources and coping skills.

Control families in our study tended to fall in a mid-range category.

Even when they presented various degrees of impairment, they usually possessed more areas of strength than the abusing families. This consideration is of crucial value in formulating a treatment plan. Most of the control families were able to respond favorably to the relatively brief but intensive (10 to 12 sessions over a six-month period) family therapy offered at the Community Guidance Center.

In contrast, abusing families presented a picture in which the needs of the parents were primary to those of the children, often with enmeshment and blurring of generational boundaries. Their natural support systems were typically depleted or nonexistent. Even when the team was able to recognize some internal and external strengths, they could be mobilized only with considerable network coordination and over a longer period of time. The following case will illustrate in detail the role of the team in providing family treatment and facilitating the building of a support network.

Six-year-old Susie was one of three children from a middle-class Anglo family referred to the team with presenting problems of chronically "overactive" and attention-seeking behavior, a negativistic stance, and a low frustration tolerance with acceleration into self-punitive behavior or aggression toward others (i.e., biting or kicking of self or others). Physical abuse of Susie by her father was also reported. Susie had two younger siblings, ages four and two respectively, both girls. The parents demonstrated chronic marital and family problems due to low impulse control leading to periodic wife-battering by Mr. R., followed by numerous psychiatric hospitalizations involving reactive suicidal gestures by Mrs. R. Mr. R. had been physically abused as a child by his father, and Mrs. R. had been sexually abused by her stepfather between ages eight and 14, until she ran away.

Involvement with the family began early in 1977 and has included mental health and/or social service agency personnel, and D.H.R. casework staff. Both parents have been involved in individual psychotherapy with their own psychiatrists. In addition, the family has been seen in ongoing weekly family therapy and couples therapy by the team. Susie, who severely regressed in mid-year due to family stress and renewed physical abuse by her father, was concurrently admitted for residential treatment. The team and staff of the residential treatment center coordinate their intervention efforts to maximize the therapeutic impact on children and parents. The referring D.H.R. caseworker-convener, who has also been actively involved in ongoing family and couples therapy, was seen as crucial in building with the family a network of support. Specific efforts by her have included the mobilization of such services as preschool and day care placement for the children in order to allow Mrs. R. to seek full-time employment. This increased her self-esteem and helped minimize chronic financial problems in the family. Family therapy/couples therapy has focused specifically on decreasing the battering interaction in the marital relationship while upgrading Mr. and Mrs. R.'s parental competence. As the battering decreased and Mr. R. became able to find alternative means to deal with his anger, the couple went through various stages of "courtship." Even when the family balance shifted, the partners continued to act out their ambivalence verbally and physically. For instance, Mrs. R. began to escalate her self-destructive behavior in an effort to reengage her husband in the old, battering cycle. During the course of a treatment session involving the parents and Susie, Mrs. R. left the room and burned her wrist on the cottage stove of the residential treatment center, then returned to the session and engaged in slashing her wrist with a razor blade. The team stopped the self-destructive behavior by removing the razor, while at the same time containing Mr. R. in the room to deal with the rage he felt in response to his wife's behavior. They also redefined his wife's behavior as anxiety-based rather than "immature and bad." Meanwhile, Susie's therapist assisted her in dealing with reality-based anxiety that her mother would "do something dangerous to herself." Emphasis was placed on helping family members to cope with immediate events. Also, a clear message was provided by the caseworker that Susie would not be taken away from her family as a result. Finally, Mrs. R. was assisted in spending time alone with Susie at the close of the session with the very specific task of reassuring her that, although she (mother) had hurt herself, she (mother) would now take care of herself. Efforts were made throughout the session to support the mutually experienced feelings of anxiety which each had expressed in very different ways.

After a short psychiatric hospitalization, Mrs. R. was back with her husband and the two younger girls. She has resumed her full-time job and both marriage partners continue to work out their relationship. Both are "at a high," and Susie is slated to be discharged and returned home in approximately one month. Treatment at all levels is to be continued until a higher level of safety and competence is achieved.

Special Issues in the Treatment of Abusing Families

Let us remember that abusive families enter treatment under external pressure. On behalf of the child, the Protective Services worker joins the family to gather information that potentially may be incriminating to the adults and even the minors in the family. There are major transferential and countertransferential problems precipitated by this intervention. It has been well established that with a specialized program, most of the abusive families can be greatly assisted, if not rehabilitated (Justice and Justice, 1976). Green (1976) recommended that when necessary, psychiatric evaluations be performed independent of Protective Services personnel. In our experience, we find it most effective that a multidisciplinary mental health team work along with the D.H.R. staff. The team catalyzes the mobilization of a wide variety of supportive interventions aimed at enhancing the parents' competence with a variety of therapeutic, educational, and practical approaches.

Several specific aspects in our approach need further amplification. First, the abuse team includes the traditional disciplines and is available under contract by the regional unit of Protective Services, D.H.R., to consult with the staff and to assess and treat abusing families who have come under their supervision. The D.H.R. worker is the case manager and is assisted by the child abuse team in close collaboration. The worker is also encouraged to use the professional support of additional health, social, educational, and legal agents that can be mobilized as part of the network of community resources. By catalyzing the coordination of efforts of existing supports and facilitating the development of new ones, it is possible to make available a broad spectrum of therapeutic resources to assist the abusing families in their rehabilitation.

Most abusing families are long-term, frustrating cases which are often a countertransferential challenge. Even experienced clinicians struggle between not fostering excessive dependence or not precipitating premature terminations after some initial improvement, which may be acting out their impatience and frustration in response to family resistance. "Burn-out," a major problem with workers, is often relieved when consultation and team work are regularly available. Clinicians need objectively to recognize existing and potential healing resources that can be mobilized in individuals, families, and their natural social matrices. It is useful to know that abusing families often perceive "helpers" as abusing them. Indeed, their frequent demandingness, ambivalence, irresponsibility, and fragility make them easy targets for "professional abuse and neglect," which is less frequent in the control families.

This intervention model requires open and frequent communication across the social network. The incidence of interagency conflict (health care, educational, welfare, judicial, and others) has been surprisingly limited. Open communication, enthusiasm, considerable stamina, and optimism, along with a good sense of humor, are seen as essential in-gredients in maintaining the team's mental health as they deal with highly complex families, most of which are slow in achieving noticeable gains.

It is essential that the clinicians be clear about the boundaries of their role and their authority as they introduce themselves to the fami-ly as a support system that can assist the family in mobilizing potential resources. While the engagement of families is always technically complex, for these families to accept treatment is in itself a corrective emotional experience. We need to recognize and respect that most abusing families will initially resist the coercive aspects of the therapeutic engagement. Emphasis needs to be shifted toward family advocacy before the family starts to accept the team as a helping resource. This emphasis is essential to assess existing and potential strengths as well as liabilities. It is also important for the team to maintain enough objectivity so as to recognize when families are not improving their parenting skills and are unwilling or unable to change toward providing a home safe enough for children. Clinicians also need to be comfortable in the management of foster care and adoption when indicated.

In summary, the experience of this study tends to support Gil's hypothesis that there are mainly differences in degree between abusing and control families. Abusive families' limited ability to use internal and external resources makes it more effective to intervene through the *social system* to mobilize an extensive family-rehabilitative network. In addition to providing direct therapeutic intervention, the team assumes the role of facilitator, with the D.H.R. worker as case convener.

REFERENCES

Beavers, W. R. (1977), *Psychotherapy and Growth: A Family System Perspec-tive.* New York: Brunner/Mazel, pp. 19–41.
Elmer, E. (1977), A followup study of traumatized children, *Pediat.*, 59:273–280.
Gelles, R. (1973), Child abuse as psychopathology: A sociological critique and reformation. *Amer. J. Orthopsychiat.*, 43:611–621.
Gil, D. (1966), First steps in a nationwide study of child abuse. *Soc. Work Prac.*, 61–78.
———— (1968), Legally reported child abuse: A nationwide survey. *Soc. Work Prac.*, 135–158.
———— (1970), *Violence Against Children: Physical Child Abuse in the U.S.* Cambridge, Mass.: Harvard University Press.
———— (1975), Unraveling child abuse. *Amer. J. Orthopsychiat.*, 45:352–356.

Green, A. (1976), A psychodynamics approach to the study and treatment of child abusing parents. *J. Amer. Acad. Child Psychiat.*, 15:414–429.

_____ (1978), Psychopathology of abused children. *J. Amer. Acad. Child Psychiat.*, 17:92–103.

_____ et al. (1974), Child abuse: Pathological syndrome of family interaction. *Amer. J. Psychiat.*, 131:822–886.

Justice, B. & Justice, R. (1976), *The Abusing Family.* New York: Human Sciences Press.

Kempe, C. H. & Helfer, R. E., eds. (1972), *Helping the Battered Child and His Family.* Philadelphia: Lippincott.

Lewis, J. M., Beavers, W. R., Gossett, J. T., & Phillips, V. A. (1976), *No Single Thread: Psychological Health and Family Systems.* New York: Brunner/ Mazel, pp. 199–216.

Polansky, N. et al. (1972), *Child Neglect: Understanding and Reaching Parents.* New York: Child Welfare League of America.

Serrano, A. C. (1974), Multiple impact therapy — Current clinical applications. In: *Techniques and Approaches to Marital and Family Counseling,* ed. R. E. Hardy & J. B. Call. Springfield, Ill.: C. C Thomas, pp. 143–159.

Young, M. (1977), Multiple correlates of abuse: A systems approach to the etiology of child abuse. Paper presented at the American Association of Psychiatric Services for Children, 39th Annual Meeting, Washington, D.C.

Zalba, S. R. (1967), The abused child: A typology for classification and treatment. *Soc. Work,* 12:70–79.

Family Diagnosis

Precise diagnosis is a prelude to effective treatment. With time we fashion new tools to this end.

Here three contributors deal with general issues — labeling, parental attitudes to family assessment, and the family therapy record. Three further contributions consider new tools — Goal Attainment Scaling, the family behavioral snapshot, and family photographs and movies.

Relabeling and Reframing Reconsidered: The Beneficial Effects of a Pathological Label

HENRY GRUNEBAUM
and RICHARD CHASIN

Traditional labeling theory usually contends that pathological labels contribute to pathology and benign labels help alleviate it. However, it is likely that the role of pathological labels as the cause of pathology has been overstated and overgeneralized. Family therapists have probably overused the practice of substituting a benign label for a pathological label — relabeling. In fact, there are many families in which a pathological label applied to one family member may have beneficial impact on the family system, including that member. Five such cases are presented and labeling theory is reviewed. Definitions of the terms reframing and relabeling are suggested, and the differing implications of diagnosis and labeling theory are discussed.

The theory and practice of relabeling and reframing and their relation to labeling theory is a muddle. The confusion arises from one fact and two beliefs: (a) the fact that any label given to an individual either by a family or a therapist will have an effect upon him or her; (b) the belief that a pathological label inevitably causes or aggravates an individual's psychopathology; and (c) the corollary belief that a benign new label will be therapeutic. The cases we present will illustrate the fact but will provide exceptions to the two beliefs.

In each of the cases to be described, an individual who was part of a

Henry Grunebaum, M.D., is Director, Group and Family Psychotherapy Training, Cambridge Hospital, Cambridge, Massachusetts and Associate Professor of Psychiatry, Harvard Medical School.

Richard Chasin, M.D., is Co-Director, Family Institute of Cambridge, Cambridge, Massachusetts; Assistant Clinical Professor of Psychiatry, Harvard Medical School; and Assistant Clinical Professor of Child Psychiatry, Boston University School of Medicine.

marital or family system was relabeled as sick, and in each instance, the functioning of the system improved afterwards. It is well-known that relabeling a "designated patient" with a healthier label is a powerful tool often used with great effectiveness by family therapists. Very often this technique has the effect of helping the designated patient to escape from the burdens of the sick role, and this is sometimes called relabeling. It then permits the therapist to refocus attention to problems in the family system. The cases presented in this paper demonstrate that labeling a family member as a designated patient can also have beneficial influence on the family and alter the family system. Montalvo and Haley (1973) have discussed the fact that child therapy may be effective precisely because the child therapist accepts the family's labeling of a designated patient and works within this framework, although in ways that subtly subvert it.

Relabeling and reframing have been viewed by family therapists as a powerful technique for effecting change. For instance, Haley (1976) states, "There is a class of therapeutic situations in which the problem presented must be redefined as another problem before it is resolved" (p. 121).

Usually the redefinition in which family therapists engage is one in which a sicker, or less treatable, labeled condition is assigned a more benign or treatable label. Thus, it is typical, as Haley goes on to say, that ". . . a case of 'mental illness' may be redefined as one of 'bad behavior'. . . . It is not unusual for a clinician to define the psychiatric or medical problem of a child or adult as a misbehavior problem" (p. 121). Often this change can lead to more effective action on the part of the therapist, as in the case that Haley (1976) cites in which Minuchin (1970) redefines a child who is starving herself as an instance of a child's not minding—"The problem shifts from a child who is ill to parents who should pull together to make her mind (obey)" (p. 121). These examples from Haley are probably sufficient to make clear how family therapists view relabeling and its effect. But we may add that Watzlawick et al. (1974) have a whole chapter on Tom Sawyer who relabeled the onerous task of whitewashing as a privilege.

In practically all instances cited in the literature, relabeling involves the removal of a psychopathological term and its replacement by the term of "normal" or by a term that cannot be found in any lexicon of psychopathology. In the following cases, quite the opposite occurs — individuals are relabeled as pathological.

Some of these examples may appear merely to be a reversion to medical model, nonsystems psychiatry. However, in all instances, the systems approach was maintained. After the case summaries, we will examine labeling theory in greater detail.

CASES 1 AND 2

In each of two couples referred for conjoint therapy because of marital disharmony, it was gradually learned that one of the partners in each couple had significant mood swings, and a diagnosis of manic-depressive psychosis was made. In one couple, the husband repeatedly lost jobs when he became too exuberant and overinvolved in his work and was unable to set appropriate limits on his promises to clients. In the other couple, the husband would alternate between being so depressed that he could not work at all and becoming very active and unable to stop working in an effort to catch up on his backlog. His employer was aware of these cycles and their compensating nature. In each of these couples, the wife was distraught and ready to give up. Both men were encouraged to consult a psychopharmacologist, both were given lithium, and both responded well to this treatment. In both couples, work on marital issues was continued more effectively following the diagnosis of manic-depressive illness. The marital problems in each of the cases were not made worse but rather improved as the now "designated patient" improved. In addition, it was easier to carry out useful marital therapy after the change in diagnosis than it had been before.

CASE 3

A young man was admitted in late adolescence to a mental hospital following years of devoted efforts by his family to cure him of his problems. He had been given the label of "atypical development" as a preschool child (a diagnosis given to autistic and symbiotic children in the late 1950s for symptoms thought to be caused by faulty parenting, especially mothering). In an effort to foster normal development, he was seen for years in individual psychotherapy by experienced and caring therapists, and the parents were seen in casework. His siblings were encouraged to include him in their activities and to treat him as normal even though he had "problems." The patient, himself, was discouraged at the failure of his own efforts and was clearly psychotic on admission.

At a family conference, the diagnosis of mental retardation and chronic psychosis was made, and the family was encouraged to attempt, with the hospital, to find living and work settings for the patient that were compatible with his limited capacities. This new task was difficult for the family to undertake, for the previous label had offered the hope of an eventual cure. Gradually, relabeling was accomplished and at five-year follow-up, the family was in agreement that the family conference had been a turning point for both them and their child. The patient is now living in a less demanding situation and is much happier dealing with limited tasks at which he can succeed. The family felt that while they had initially been saddened, they were no longer confronted with impossible goals and felt more content with themselves. The siblings, in particular, spoke with great feeling of the burden of guilt that had been lifted from them.

CASE 4

A family was seen in consultation after their 19-year-old son had several hospitalizations for grossly inappropriate behavior. The family therapist, aware that the family had cared with great love and devotion for a mentally retarded sibling of the patient, told the family that the 19-year-old boy suffered from schizophrenia and would require help. The family was much relieved and told the therapist that they had never been told what was wrong with the patient and that they had thought he was "bad and just did not know how to behave properly." With their new understanding that he was sick, treatment efforts, both individual and family, were undertaken and seemed to move in a positive direction. In the two cases above, the labeling of the patient as mentally ill permitted more effective action and fostered improved family interaction.

CASE 5

An elderly woman was referred by her husband's therapist because of marital problems. She tried to work on these problems and to understand and respond to her husband's complaints about her and her behavior. Gradually, the therapist became aware that the husband was seriously depressed and endeavored to help the patient understand his response to retirement. However, the patient found herself increasingly angry at her husband who spent long hours alone hardly talking to her. Finally, when the wife reported that her husband had lost more than 20 pounds, the therapist realized that he was suffering from a severe depression. He told the wife that she was to treat her husband as a sick person who needed care. If he had complaints about the marriage, these could be viewed as the result of his depression and discussion of them postponed, although eventually they would have to be faced. The wife was much more able to help her husband after a diagnosis had been made. She brought meals to him and did not always respond to his anger with her own. She expressed her devotion and love rather than feelings of hopelessness about the marriage. The husband seemed to improve gradually, in part with the aid of this change in the couple system. He was clearly pleased with the change in his wife's attitude. At a later stage in this case, therapeutic work on the marital interaction became a central task, and the husband could no longer be viewed as sick.

This case illustrates that during the course of treatment a sick label may lead to improved family functioning at one stage, although, at another stage, a different frame of reference and label will be necessary.

Labeling Theory

Labeling theory emphasizes the social meaning of deviant behavior and the social consequences of that meaning. Scheff (1974), among others, contends that individuals manifest primary deviance that is but a normal variation or minor abnormality. He sees these primary deviations as "'amorphous,' 'unstructured,' and 'residual' violations of a society's norms" (1966, pp. 32, 82). These minor abnormalities are then labeled by social authorities, neighbors, or families as deviations that require viewing their possessor as a deviant. The consequences of this view are then the causes of secondary deviation, which is mental illness. This occurs when a person learns "the role style." Secondary deviation is therefore "the response to a response" (J. Murphy, 1976, p. 1019). The career of imprisoned juvenile delinquents and their learning to become hardened criminals is an example.

Lemart (1953), one of the pioneers in this branch of sociology, was influenced by his studies of stuttering, which he believed to be a pure case of secondary deviance; that is, all the pathology arises from the label. All children in learning speech exhibit some difficulties. In response to these difficulties, some parents insist that the children speak more slowly or carefully. This instance may make the child overly aware of his own speech and like the centipede who became paralyzed when asked which leg he moved first, these children have increasing speech difficulties. As Eisenberg (1977) says, "Stuttering is diagnosogenic" (p. 904). Support for this came from the belief that American Indians had neither a word for stuttering, nor stutterers. This, in fact, does not turn out to be true, but it is true that the absence of stuttering and of the word for it are associated with less stringent demands for verbal fluency.

Another useful example is that of blindness. J. Murphy (1976), in a paper entitled "Psychiatric Labeling in Cross-Cultural Perspective," cites Scott (1969) who found that some blind individuals so labeled by administrative authorities became involved with certain agencies, leading to processes of self-definition involving learned helplessness, but other, equally blind individuals not so labeled lived less helpless lives. Institutions for the blind differ in the extent to which they encourage acceptance or rejection of the deviant role, and these are reflected in the life styles of their clients.

At this point, it may be useful to consider the application of labeling theory to mental illness. Scheff (1974) states "that the studies he reviewed support labeling theory since they indicate that the social characteristics of the patient help to determine the severity of the societal reaction independent of the psychiatric diagnosis" (p. 449).

Among the studies cited, of particular interest is the now classic and much discussed "On Being Sane in Insane Places" by Rosenhan (1973), which illustrates how difficult it is for a normal person to shed the label of mental illness once it has been given. Scheff also cites research by Temerlin (1968), which demonstrates that the same interview will be evaluated differently depending on what the clinician is led to believe the client is, i.e., a mental patient, a job applicant, sane, or no data.

Scheff's main critic is Gove (1974), who cites various studies of mental hospitalizations and commitments to refute Scheff. He quotes Gouldner (1968) to the effect that most labeling theorists have sided with the deviant, seeing him as an underdog victimized by the social system. In fact, it is the position of R. D. Laing (1971) that the schizophrenic is the victim of the family. Gove (1974), in his review of the literature, states, "In the case of mental illness, the processes associated with hospitalization do not cause others to view the individual as deviant (they already do) but instead often redefine the deviance in a fairly positive way. For example...from that of being 'obnoxious and intolerable' to that of 'being ill and in need of help'" (p. 345).

Some proponents of labeling theory have been greatly influenced by cross-cultural studies. Many of them believe that mental illness is a myth like the belief in witches and that perhaps even holy men, shamans, and witch doctors are psychotics who have found a niche in these more tolerant cultures. In her recent work, J. Murphy (1976) states that these labeling theorists often "assume that the expanding body of data from non-Western areas has supported the relativist propositions put forth by Benedict (1934) that what we call 'Mental Illness' might be considered normal in a different culture or in a minority social class" (p. 1019).

However, J. Murphy concluded from her studies of Eskimo and

Yorubas that both these societies have concepts of, and words for, in-
sanity; that the incidence of these disorders is quite similar across all
studied cultures; and that the Eskimo and Yorubas sufferers are referred for treatment to native healers. These native healers have undergone long training and to quote an Eskimo, "When the shaman is healing, he is out of his mind but he is not crazy." The critical difference between the "healthy" individual and the mental patient is the ability to
control sensory perception and behavior. Interestingly enough, while
neither of these cultures has a single word for neurosis, neurotics are
viewed as treatable and in his practice, the native healer is likely to
have about 10 to 12 neurotics for every psychotic. In addition, Murphy
finds that mental patients are not venerated by the Eskimo or the
Yorubas but rather treated and protected with a mixture of compassion
and rejection reflecting human "ambivalence" much like that which
"occurs in Western Society" (1976, p. 1027).

On the other hand, Burton-Bradley (1963) on New Guinea and Rin
and Lin (1962) on Formosa found that the rates of schizophrenia in the
aboriginal populations were considerably below those in more "civil-
ized" members of the same group.[1] Waxler (1974) on Ceylon and H.
Murphy and Raman (1971) on Mauritius found that rates of recovery
were higher and residual defect less among natives. Clearly, it is to be
expected that the definitions of illness, its manifestations, its rates of
recovery will be influenced by the culture, which defines the boundaries of who is sick and healthy as well as the methods of treatment
and the level of functioning to be expected afterwards. Does this mean
that psychotic illness is diagnosogenic? We are inclined to believe that,
in schizophrenia, a primary defect and deviation probably precedes the
cultural processing that leads to secondary deviations and defects.

What are we to make of labeling theory in our understanding of
and work with families? At the outset, it may be useful to summarize
the conclusions arrived at in a recent review in the *Annual Review of
Sociology*. Here, Gibbs and Erickson (1975) conclude that labeling
theory cannot be reduced to testable propositions without confronting
numerous problems. The authors state, "It could be that the theory is
really only a definition — a deviant act which has occurred because of
reactions to previous deviance is called secondary deviance. Alternatively, the theory can be construed as asserting one genuine empirical proposition: some individuals commit deviant acts because of
reactions to previous deviant behavior. But the proposition cannot be

---

[1] We are grateful to Dr. Daniel Fisher for bringing some of the cross-cultural literature
to our attention.

falsified" (p. 32).

These authors go on to review the studies of Scheff (1974) and Gove (1974) and the many works they cite and conclude that there is no way of refuting the theory since there is no cut-off point at which the lack of impact of a label can be said to mean that the label has no effect. They conclude, and we agree, that "advocates of that [the reactivist] perspective have not thrown the baby out with the bath; rather they deny the infant ever existed. That infant is the hardly incredulous belief that being labeled deviant commonly has something to do with behavior prior to, and in that sense, [is] independent of reactions to it" (Gibbs and Erickson, 1975, p. 79).

We should like to suggest the following clarification of the terms reframing and relabeling. Reframing is a change in the frame of reference we use to look at some particular behavior. For example, in looking at an individual's symptomatic conduct, we may shift from a moral to a medical frame. An inevitable consequence of reframing is a change in label. Thus, in changing from an individual frame to a family frame, we change the label from "anorectic child" to "family with a parent-child coalition." Even though a relabeling has occurred, the process should be called reframing because the change of frame is the primary event and the change in label is a secondary consequence.

Relabeling should be reserved for those instances in which there is a change in label with no change in frame of reference. Thus, in changing a label from psychotic to neurotic, we stay within the health frame. Similarly, we stay within the family systems frame when we shift the label from "parents who cannot persuade a child to eat" to "a child who is losing weight for the whole family."

In working with families, we need to determine which frames of reference the family uses and what labels have been applied to behaviors, thoughts, and feelings within these frames. More importantly, we must determine the impact on the family members of the frames and labels used. In some families, the situation may be better for all if a member is labeled psychotic in the health frame rather than stubborn in the moral frame; it may be worse in others. When we take a history, we have an opportunity to evaluate the primary deviance and the amount of secondary deviance produced by framing and labeling by the family and others. We can learn what frames of reference a family typically uses and how they will respond to various labels within their frames. Watzlawick et al. have identified the information required for "the gentle art of reframing. Successful reframing needs to take into account the views, expectations, reasons, premises — in short, the conceptual framework — of those whose problems are to be changed" (1974,

p. 104). We can decide whether reframing or relabeling will decrease secondary deviance and produce other benign effects.

It is important to be aware that a family will typically consult a professional expecting that a certain frame of reference will be used but that a label may be changed. The consequences of employing an unexpected frame of reference should be considered before attempting it.

If clients knowingly choose a family therapist, they are more likely to be expecting a systems frame and may not so easily accept a pathological label for one family member. On the other hand, a number of families come with the question, "Is one of us the problem or is it all of us?" These families are more open to either an individual or a systems frame.

Reframing might "appear initially to be objectionably manipulative" (Rabkin, 1977, p. 90). Certainly, it is one of those interventions that can be used more with authority than through negotiation, more with cunning than with candor. The clients can easily be treated as objects, with the therapist's task to move them. However, it need not be used that way. Far from it. A therapist can reframe with openness and an attitude of mutuality and can be effective without risking the dehumanizing impact that covert manipulation can produce. The therapist can say, "If rather than looking at things that way, we were looking at them this way, what would be changed?"

SUMMARY

We have presented five cases in which giving a sick label influenced the family dynamics favorably. In these instances a medical diagnosis of an individual family member became the new label. However, diagnosing and labeling are different processes, even though at times they may lead to the same result, i.e., the same label. A diagnosis must be made within a given frame of reference. It is the name that inevitably is given to a quality or group of qualities inherent either in an individual (anorexia nervosa) or a schismatic family. Labeling, on the other hand, is relativistic, since it takes into account not only the accuracy of a name but also the effects of that name on the individual and family.

The reluctance to using pathological labels for individuals is quite understandable. However, there are instances in which the failure to do so can be damaging. There are many cases in which the family has been told that the identified patient is potentially normal and that the family is pathogenic. Such labeling may not only be unfair and inaccurate but also may lead to excessive expectations and guilt. In these cases, a pathological label for one member can relieve everyone, including that member, of paralyzing guilt and expectations and free the family to engage in constructive action. In general, the decision to use any label should be determined by its therapeutic impact. Sometimes labeling an individual as sick can have beneficial consequences.

REFERENCES

Benedict, R. (1934), *Patterns of Culture*. Boston: Houghton-Mifflin.
Burton-Bradley, B. B. (1963), Papua and New Guinea: Transcultural psychiatry, the first 1000 referrals. *Austral. N. Zeal. J. Psychiat.*, 3:130.
Eisenberg, L. (1977), Psychiatry and society: A socio-biologic synthesis. *N. Eng. J. Med.*, 296:903–910.
Gibbs, J. P. & Erickson, M. L. (1975), Major developments in the sociological study of deviance. In: *Ann. Rev. Sociol.*, ed. A. Inkeles, J. Coleman, & N. Smelser. California: Annual Reviews.
Gouldner, A. (1968), The sociologist as partisan: Sociology and the welfare state. *Amer. Sociol.*, 3:106–116.
Gove, W. (1974), The labeling theory of mental illness: A reply to Scheff. *Amer. Psychol. Rev.*, 39:242–257.
Haley, J. (1976), *Problem-Solving Therapy*. San Francisco: Jossey-Bass.
Laing, R. D. (1971), *Sanity, Madness and the Family*. New York: Basic Books.
Lemart, J. (1953), Some Indians who stutter. *J. Speech Hearing Disord.*, 18:168–174.
Minuchin, S. (1970), The use of an ecological framework in child psychiatry. In: *The Child and His Family*, ed. J. E. Anthony and C. Koupernick. New York: Wiley.
Montalvo, B. & Haley, J. (1973), In defense of child therapy. *Fam. Proc.*, 12:227–244.
Murphy, H. B. & Raman, A. R. (1971), Chronicity of schizophrenia in indigenous tropical people. *Brit. J. Psychiat.*, 118:489–497.
Murphy, J. M. (1976), Psychiatric labeling in cross-cultural perspective. *Science*, 191:1019–1028.
Rabkin, R. (1977), *Strategic Psychotherapy*. New York: Basic Books.
Rin, H. & Lin, T. (1962), Mental illness among the Formosan aborigines as compared with the Chinese in Taiwan. *J. Ment. Sci.*, 108:134–146.
Rosenhan, D. (1973), On being sane in insane places. *Science*, 179:250–258.
Scheff, T. J. (1966), *Being Mentally Ill: A Sociological Theory*. Chicago: Aldine.
——— (1974), The labeling theory of mental illness. *Amer. Sociol. Rev.*, 39:444–452.
Scott, R. (1969), *The Making of Blind Men*. New York: The Russell Sage Foundation.
Temerlin, M. (1968), Suggestion effects in psychiatric diagnosis. *J. Nerv. Ment. Dis.*, 147(4):349–353.
Watzlawick, P., Weakland, J., & Fisch, R. (1974), *Change: Principles of Problem Formation and Problem Resolution*. New York: Norton.
Waxler, N. (1974), Social change and psychiatric illness in Ceylon: An investigation of traditional and modern conceptions of disease and treatment. In: *Mental Health in Asia and the Pacific*, ed. W. Lebra. Honolulu: University Press of Hawaii.

Families: Parental Attitudes to Family Assessment in a Child Psychiatry Setting

P. G. CHURVEN

INTRODUCTION

The widespread awareness of the effects of family dynamics on children's disturbance has led psychiatrists to attend to the whole family system in both assessment and treatment of disturbed children. Ackerman and Behrens (1968) and Erikson (1965) describe the value of whole family assessment, whether or not family therapy techniques are to be used subsequently. In spite of the theoretical desirability of family assesment, professionals describe difficulty in practice. In departing from the traditional examination of mother and child, they may feel uncomfortable and intrusive in the presence of whole families. They express doubts as to the families' capacities to reveal themselves. Fathers and siblings of the disturbed child are thought to be unwilling to participate. Little is available in the literature on these specific issues, though there are some more general studies in related areas. As long ago as 1955, Redlich et al. described the problems caused by social distance between therapists and patients and the need to evolve new procedures suitable for class IV and V patients in particular. Jacobs et al. (1972) described an attempt to cope with the problem by education of patients and doctors. Friedman (1965) reviewed the literature in relation to therapy in the patients' home and described his own successful program.

This paper describes an examination of parents' attitudes and per-

P. G. Churven, M.B., B.S., M.R.A.N.Z.C.P., is Director of Child/Family Psychiatry at the Redbank House, Westmead, Australia.

The author wishes to thank Professor D. A. Pond for his continuing support and enthusiasm. The help and tolerance of colleagues and their patients at the London Hospital Department of Child Psychiatry was essential and invaluable.

formance in relation to family assessment. Home visiting as a strategy for family contact is also considered. The study is based on the following hypotheses:

1. Parents are prepared to undertake family assessment.

2. Home visiting may be required for family assessment.

3. Out of hours appointments may be required for family assessment.

4. The preparedness of parents to be involved in the assessment will increase with social class, self-initiated referral, and neurotic diagnosis of the child.

A survey was also made of the quality of information given to children about the appointment and the effect of previous psychiatric contact on subsequent attitude and performance.

Twenty-five families were interviewed at home, and their subsequent performance compared with that of 50 children referred to a clinic through normal channels. Some understanding of the particular community in which the study was undertaken is helpful in contemplating the overall significance of the findings.

The East End of London, a celebrated working class area, is in the process of considerable change. Willmott and Young (1957) have described the decrease in population by the migration of nuclear families to the new satellite towns and estates of London since the war. The resultant breakdown of traditional kinship ties produced stressful changes in family patterns. Predictably, these stresses are paralleled by lower birth rates and higher illegitimacy and infant mortality rates in relation to the national average (Watton, 1972). In addition to the demographic data about the area, there is a complementary literature about the community ethos. Searle (1973) has suggested that "There is a basic hostility to authority in most people living in the East End. The children and their parents know where the power lies. . . the children know particularly, because they are right on the end of it." The characteristics of this population should only serve to aggravate the problems for professionals examined in this study, since family intervention and other psychiatric approaches tend to be designed for a middle-class clientele. The families in this study had been referred to the London Hospital Child Psychiatry Clinic, part of a teaching hospital department of psychiatry, closely linked to the pediatric department. It is one of six child guidance clinics serving the borough, but as a teaching hospital clinic it also accepts referrals from outside the area.

METHOD

THE SAMPLE

Twenty-five families were selected from the clinic's new referrals and interviewed at the rate of two per week. Eligible referrals were defined by the following criteria: (1) no clinic contact in the past six months, (2) domicile in a specified area about the hospital (predefined on the basis of accessibility for home or clinic visit). Random numbers could not be used for sample selection because the clinic did not keep a long waiting list, and the flow of new referrals was unpredictable (varying from two to six per week). New patients were normally allocated to clinic staff at a weekly meeting and appointments then mailed. A research appointment letter was included with the clinic appointment for the first two new referrals considered at the meeting who fulfilled the criteria. There was no known alphabetical or other bias involved in this procedure. Two-thirds of referrals meeting the criteria during the period of the survey were included in the sample. Only one selected patient was excluded: a paranoid mother known to the social worker, in whom an interview might have produced complications for future treatment.

THE INTERVIEW

The research appointment letter requested the presence of both parents at home in the evening to participate in a survey of parental ideas about the child psychiatry service. They were interviewed prior to clinic assessment to ascertain their attitude unbiased by their experience of a particular assessment by a particular psychiatrist. The interviews were conducted at home in the evening to facilitate the father's presence.

The interview schedule was constructed from the hypotheses described; a proforma is appended. A pilot study of six interviews produced some rearrangement but no substantial change. A semistructured interview seemed most appropriate to this complex subject (Moser and Kalton, 1971). Interviewer bias was consistent to the extent that the author conducted all interviews. The schedule produced three types of data: (1) demography, (2) questions producing positive/negative answers (e.g., question 17), (3) open questions, which could be partially quantified by counting the number of responses (e.g., question 15).

At the parents' home the researcher explained the purpose of the research — to understand their needs more fully and improve our service. The identities of the interviewer and the psychiatrist they would see at the clinic were clarified. The author explained the form of the interview and the need for answers from both father and mother. It was emphasized that the child or family problems were to be dealt with later at the clinic assessment. Queries raised by the interview would be discussed after administration of the schedule. The presence or absence of children was left to the parents. The whole visit averaged 45 minutes.

Participation in the research and clinic assessment provided hard data for comparison with expressed attitudes. Diagnosis provided by assessing psychiatrists proved unfit for study: in the comparison group a wide variety of theoretical models was used; the classification of the index group failed to distinguish between neurotic and antisocial children due to a tendency to label antisocial behavior as "neurotic" on the basis of psychodynamic formulations. No children in either group were considered psychotic.

Results

All index mothers and all but one father participated in the research interview though a few fathers were late. The missing father had not been informed of the occasion by his wife. This provides some behavioral data consistent with the first three hypotheses. Parents seemed to relax and enjoy the interview once explanations were given. Children played about the room and cups of tea were routinely provided. The interview frequently led to queries about the families' role in the child's disturbance and the need for the fathers' participation. Fathers were told they would be welcome at the assessment, but that this was not currently a clinic policy or condition. Parents often attempted to initiate assessment and therapy but the interviewer persuaded them to await the clinic visit for exploration of their problems. In fact the interview schedule seemed an excellent tool for arousing interest in family therapy.

Table 1 shows the index and comparison groups to be comparable in terms of source of referral, sex distribution, and rates of immigration and divorce. The research visit produced improvement in subsequent clinic attendance particularly by fathers. It is noteworthy that index family attendance conformed exactly with the intentions stated at interview (question 10), whether or not they favored family assessment. This provides further behavioral data to support the predictive value of the attitudinal findings.

Table 2 provides most of the data relevant to the first hypothesis.

TABLE 1
CHARACTERISTICS OF INDEX AND CONTROL FAMILIES

Total no. of families	25	50
Social class	II. III. IV. V. 3 13 6 3	Not known
Referral source		
G.P.	15 (60%)	25 (50%)
Ped.	5 (20%)	14 (28%)
School	2 (8%)	6 (12%)
Court	1 (4%)	2 (4%)
Other	2	3
Immigrants	6 (24%)	8 (16%)
Divorced mothers	2 (8%)	4 (8%)
Step-parents	1	2
	Step-mother (4%)	Step-father (4%)
Child's sex	7F (28%)	18F (36%)
	18M (72%)	32M (64%)
Child attended clinic appointment	23 (92%)	37 (74%)
Father attended clinic appt.*	10/23 (43.5%)	3/46 (6.5%)

*Chi-square (11.385) 1 df, $P < 0.001$

Eighty per cent of fathers and all but one mother were prepared to participate in family assessment. Their actual performance is consistent with their attitudes: all the mothers and half the fathers of the positive group attended the clinic versus only 60 per cent of mothers and no fathers from the negative group. This underlines the fact that it was the fathers who were most reluctant to participate, contrary to the wish of their wives. Both attitude and performance are consistent with the number of reasons offered in favor (question 15) and against (question 16) family attendance, suggesting cognitive support for their attitudes. There is a tendency for positive parents to be of higher social class, to less often have antisocial children, and to initiate referral themselves, though numbers are insufficient for statistical analysis. This table clarifies the origin of referrals. Twelve of the 15 parents referred by general practitioners had gone to the family doctor purely to obtain a formal letter to the child psychiatrist. Furthermore, mothers managed the referral process in over 75 per cent of families (question 8).

Fifty-five per cent of positive parents said (in answer to question 18) they would spontaneously exclude siblings from family interviews (to

TABLE 2

THE RELATIONSHIP BETWEEN PREPAREDNESS FOR
FAMILY ASSESSMENT AND OTHER VARIABLES

	Positive group (prepared to be seen as a family)	Negative group (unprepared to be seen as a family)
Total no. (both parents agree)	20	5
Social class II	3	—
III	11	2
IV	5	1
V	1	2
Referral — Self	2	0
Self & G.P.	11	1
G.P.	1	2
Ped.	3	2
Police	1	0
School	2	0
Mean No. of reasons in favor of family assessment per family*	2.75	0.8
Mean No. of reasons against family assessment per family*	0.7	1.8
Child attended clinic appt.†	20	3
Father attended clinic appt.	10/19	0/4

*Chi-square (12.28) 1 df., P < 0.001.
†Fisher's test P < 0.05.

protect them), unless specifically requested to bring them. Eighty per
cent of negative families would spontaneously include the whole family. Thus their concept of relevant family does not account for parents'
attitudes to family assessment.

Table 3 provides data relevant to the second and third hypotheses.
Over 90 per cent of fathers and mothers prefer home visits though only
one third regard it as an essential requirement for seeing the whole
family. The preference for home visits related to feelings such as "we
feel relaxed and can really talk at home" and "you can see us as we really are." Convenience was not the issue and in fact the two families who
disliked home visits were negative to family assessment in any setting.
Evening appointments were required by one quarter of parents for

TABLE 3
ATTITUDE TO HOME VISITS AND OUT-OF-HOURS APPOINTMENTS

Sample size	25
Prefer home visit	92%
Dislike home visit	8%
No. for whom home visit essential for family assessment	32%
No. for whom out-of-hours essential	24%

TABLE 4
EFFECT OF PREVIOUS CONTACTS ON
ATTITUDES TO FAMILY ASSESSMENT

	Positive group (N = 20)	Negative group (N = 5)	Totals	Unsatisfactory experience in past
Previous psychiatric contact:				
Initiated for Father	1	0	1	—
Mother	2	2	4	2
Child	9	1	10	3
Previous social work contact	13	2	15	5

family assessment and most of these would also require home visiting.

Table 4 shows a surprisingly high number of prior contacts with psychiatrists and social workers. Previous experience with psychiatry did not seem a major variable in determining interest in family assessment unles it was grossly unsatisfactory. This applied to two mothers who had, themselves, undergone compulsory adult psychiatric assessment without treatment or follow-up. They remained hostile to any form of psychiatric contact for their children or themselves and accounted for the only two children of the index group who failed to attend the clinic.

In Table 5 parents' explanations to the index child about the child psychiatry appointment are classified into three groups. "Explanation" means that the parents gave specific information beyond telling the child of a visit to "a doctor." Sixty-four per cent of the children had been given no concept of the nature of a psychiatric assessment. Parents offered two main reasons for this failure: either they did not know enough about what psychiatrists did, or, they were afraid the child would embarrass them by telling neighbors. This latter fear is

TABLE 5
INFORMATION GIVEN TO THE CHILD
ABOUT THE PSYCHIATRIC APPOINTMENT

"No information"	"To see Dr."	"Explanation"
2	14	9

consistent with the finding that while parents discuss child management with friends they keep secret visits to psychiatrists (question 13). This indicates the stigma surrounding contact with psychiatrists. Interestingly, parents tended to address the interviewer as "mister" in their homes.

DISCUSSION

Questions of accuracy and replicability arise in studies of attitudes and need to be dealt with before the implications of the results are examined. Two tests of the degree to which parents' actual behavior conformed with their attitudes are inherent in the design of the study. First, the research interview involved both parents seeing a psychiatrist at home in the evening. Participation in itself served as partial behavioral test of hypotheses being examined. Second, subsequent clinic attendance conformed precisely with that predicted in the interview. That parents did what they predicted in these respects suggests that their other predictions might hold true.

The first hypothesis, that parents will accept family assessment is supported by three findings. Eighty per cent of sample parents said they would be seen as a family, and provided a significant number of reasons in favor of their attitude (Table 2). Third, their behavior was consistent with these attitudes — all parents except one father participated in the research interview and their subsequent clinic attendance improved significantly over the comparison group (Table 1). We are left to examine why the research interview produced these effects. There are three possibilities: the researcher himself, the content, or the fact that there was a research interview with both parents in the setting of their own home in the evening. The setting is considered specifically later.

The researcher was an experienced therapist and his Australian accent freed him of some class barriers. This does not explain the presence of the parents from the outset of the research interview. Nor is it likely to account for the improved clinic attendance since most patients were told they would be seeing another psychiatrist at the clinic. Furthermore, a semistructured, 30-minute interview limits the exhibition of the key therapeutic skills described by Truax and Carkhuff (1967). Similarly, the content of the interview seems insufficient to explain the findings, particularly in that the interviewer avoided discussion of the child's problems.

The research interview itself seems the major factor producing this degree of parental cooperation. It may have overcome some of the obstacles to client participation described by Mayer and Timms (1970). They argue that clients and workers often differ in judgment and perceptions: clients may perceive workers as "not interested" or "failing to understand them." Mayer and Timms (1970) propose that "working class clients are not introspectively inclined and expect the worker to play an active part in solving their problem." The interview schedule demonstrated interest and the home visit activity. This congruence provides one explanation of the effects of this study.

The second hypothesis that home visits are required for family contact is only partially supported. Only one third of parents regarded home visits as an essential condition of family assessment (Table 3). In subsequent clinic practice, the majority of fathers have attended in response to specific invitation. This suggests that the major obstacle to fathers' attendance is simply that, in this community, attendance at children's doctors is seen as part of the maternal nurturing role. Explicit invitations will often counteract this. However, 92 per cent of parents said they preferred home visits and virtually all cooperated with the research in that setting (Table 3). These findings are consistent with the researcher's subjective impression that families were more relaxed in their homes. Barnes (1973) and Friedman (1965) describe similar advantage of more contact with fathers and lower attrition rates. The preference might arise out of diminished fear of the stigma of psychiatric contact. A further explanation might be derived from Bowlby (1973). His thesis that fears of strangers and strange environments are natural phenomena which are normally resolved but which "neurotics" retain could explain the preference for the familiar in the often neurotic parents of disturbed children.

The third hypothesis is less well supported. Only 24 per cent of families regarded out of hours appointments as an essential requirement for family assessment. Most of these parents required home visiting as well (Table 3). It may be noted that this percentage matches the proportion of the comparison group who failed to keep their initial clinic appointment (Table 1). In contrast, all index families were seen at home out of hours and 92 per cent at the subsequent clinic assessment.

These findings suggest that most of those families who fail to attend clinic appointments will participate in home contact after hours. Alternative approaches to this problem are relatively cumbersome. Jacobs et al.'s (1972) plan of education of parents prior to seeing the psychiatrist still requires them to attend the clinic in the first place. Cartwright (1972) in his study of services for maladjusted children also demonstrated the need to fit clinics to parents' definition of acceptable service. He suggested child psychiatry "change its guise to counselling" and "work in an educational setting." Home visits to those who fail to attend a clinic may provide a simple alternative.

The fourth hypothesis cannot be properly explored since the small number rejecting family assessment precludes statistical analysis (Table 2). However, the table does suggest that general practitioners had not performed a diagnostic role for index families. Rather they simply wrote formal referrals at the parents' request. This practice may be questioned though the study does not indicate whether family doctors perform a filter function and treat a proportion of those requesting child psychiatry assessment themselves.

The high frequency of previous contacts with psychiatric workers (Table 4) shows that this sample was not a selected healthy middle-class group. The number of mothers who had had previous treatment is similar to Wolff and Acton's (1968) Edinburgh sample. This suggests the findings may be relevant to similar working-class communities. Previous experience with psychiatric workers had not informed parents of two important issues. The failure of the majority of parents to explain to their children the nature and purpose of the visit to the child psychiatrist augurs ill for the child's capacity to participate fully in the assessment (Table 5). Furthermore, just as fathers need specific invitations, so do siblings, or half the families will exclude them. Clinics might consider education of referring agents and phone contact with referred families as relevant strategies to deal with these recurring problems.

Professionals often perceive imcompatibilities between their sophisticated models and their patients' expectations and capacities. The problem may inhere not in the complexity of the theory, but in a failure to appreciate in detail the perceptions and attitudes of parents. Procedures may be developed without extensive public education or resiting of clinics. The attitudinal and behavioral data in this study suggest that the majority of parents will cooperate in family assessment if specifically invited. Most of those who fail to attend a clinic may cooperate in their home setting, out of working hours.

APPENDIX

Parent Attitude Schedule
(Answers obtained from both father and mother in each other's presence)

1–4. Name, Address, Age, Occupation
5. Who lives here?
6. Children—No., Age, Adoption?
7. Who first had the idea of your coming to the clinic?
Fa/Mo/G.P./School/Police/Other.
8. Who got the referral note from the G.P.?
Did not get one.
Yes.Fa/Mo/Other.
9. What did you think and feel when Dr . . . . referred you to Child Psychiatry?
10. Who is to come to the clinic appointment?
11. Have you had any help from other psychiatric clinics?
12. Have you seen Social Workers?
13. Has anyone you know well had help with their children?
14. If we asked you to be seen as a family what would you think/feel about it?
15. What advantages can you see in coming as a family?
16. What difficulties can you see in coming as a family?
17. Would you be prepared to be seen as a family?
18. Who would you have in a family interview?
Fa/Mo/Index Child/Other Sibs/Others.
19. How do you feel about clinic people coming to see your family at home?
20. Would they have to come to your home for a family interview?
21. How do you feel about clinics seeing families outside 9–5, the usual working hours?
22. Would they have to do this to see your family?
23. What sort of help would you like from the clinic?
24. What sort of help do you think the clinic will in fact give you?
25. What have you told your child about the appointment at the clinic?
Nothing/To see a Dr./Explanation.

REFERENCES

Ackerman, N. W. & Behrens, N. L. (1968), The family approach and levels of intervention. *Amer. J. Psychother.*, 22:5–14.

Barnes, L. S. (1973), Bringing family focused therapy to the residents of a low income housing project. *Amer. J. Orthopsychiat.*, 43:204–205.

Bowlby, J. (1973), *Attachment and Loss, Vol. 2: Separation.* London: Hogarth Press.

Cartwright, A. J. K. (1972), Exploratory studies into services for maladjusted children. Unpublished items, London Hospital Medical College.

Erikson, E. (1965), *Childhood and Society.* London: Penguin.

Friedman, A. S. (1965), Implications of the home setting for family treatment. In: *Psychotherapy for the Whole Family,* ed. A. S. Friedman. New York: Springer.

Jacobs, D., Charles, E., Jacobs, T., Weinstein, H., & Mann, D. (1972), Preparation for treatment of the disadvantaged patient. *Amer. J. Orthopsychiat.*, 42:666–674.

Mayer, J. G. & Timms, N. (1970), *The Client Speaks*. London: Routledge & Kegan Paul.

Moser, K. A. & Kalton, G. (1971), *Survey Methods in Social Investigation.* London: Heinemann.

Redlich, F. C., Hollingshead, A. B., & Belles, E. (1955), Social class difference in attitudes towards psychiatry. *Amer. J. Orthopsychiat.*, 25:60–67.

Searle, C. (1973), *This New Season*. London: Calder & Boyars.

Truax, C. B. & Carkhuff, R. R. (1967), *Towards Effective Counseling and Psychotherapy*. New York: Aldine.

Watton, R. W. (1972), Annual Report of the Medical Officer of Health. London Borough of Tower Hamlets, London.

Wilimott, P. & Young, M. (1957), *Family and Kinship in East London*. London: Penguin.

Wolff, S. & Acton, W. P. (1968), Characteristics of parents of disturbed children. *Brit. J. Psychiat.*, 114:592–601.

Clinical and Legal Issues
in the Family Therapy Record

NEAL GANSHEROFF,
IVAN BOSZORMENYI-NAGY,
and JOHN MATRULLO

In writing a family therapy record, the therapist must strike a delicate balance between including enough information to make the material clinically meaningful and useful and avoiding, as much as possible, the inclusion of material that may be legally damaging, shameful, or embarrassing to individual members of the family. When he makes an entry, the therapist should remember that the record may not always be left untouched in the file drawer. It may be needed by another therapist for continuity of care or used to satisfy accreditation standards. Or it may be subpoenaed as evidence in a malpractice or divorce suit or in a child custody case.

The family psychiatry department of the Eastern Pennsylvania Psychiatric Institute recently revised its format for keeping family charts and established guidelines for writing the charts. Those guidelines emphasize the need for therapists to consider four main, somewhat overlapping, aspects when writing records: hospital accreditation standards, clinical aspects, legal aspects, and respect for patients' privacy.

Therapists working in centers accredited by the Joint Commission on Accreditation of Hospitals must pay special attention to the commission's standards for writing medical records. Every two years the commission inspects those hospitals, including their medical records. If the records are considered completely unacceptable, hospitals can lose,

Neal Gansheroff, M.D., is Staff Psychiatrist, Philadelphia Psychiatric Center.

Ivan Boszormenyi-Nagy, M.D., is Director, Family Psychiatry Department, Eastern Pennsylvania Psychiatric Institute, Philadelphia, Pennsylvania.

John Matrullo, J.D., is Senior Attorney, Community Legal Services, Inc., Philadelphia, Pennsylvania.

221

and in fact some have lost, their accreditation. The standards are contained in the *Accreditation Manual for Psychiatric Facilities* and require, among other things, that "The medical record shall contain sufficient information to identify the patient clearly, to justify the diagnosis, to delineate the treatment plan, and to document the results accurately" (Accreditation Council for Psychiatric Facilities, 1972).

CLINICAL ASPECTS

Many therapists who may be quite adept at writing a meaningful, high quality record for an individual patient have major difficulties organizing and satisfactorily recording the wealth of complex, interrelated data obtained in treating an entire family. It is one thing to write a record on a single patient; it is quite another to write one about two adults, usually parents, and possibly several children that portrays each as an individual and yet conveys their complex nuclear- and extended-family relationships. If the records are to be meaningful, both individual and family data must be recorded.

Two basic questions should be asked to determine if the records will aid in the clinical management of the case and in a possible legal defense: Does the chart tell what is happening in the family, and does it justify a particular therapeutic or administrative decision? (Mills, 1965). As an illustration of such a justification, take the case of a therapist who, in the initial sessions, is faced with parents who want to focus only on their symptomatic child. He elects to postpone intensively exploring their marital relationship until later in therapy. He explains in the record that only a minimal marital history was obtained thus far because he felt that therapy might be jeopardized if that area were opened before the resistant parents were ready to discuss it.

Specific guidelines for family charts, as well as formats in which to include clinical material, have been established for the department's recently revised initial family report, progress notes, and closing summary. The formats were designed to be broad enough to be used by most therapists, even those with diverse orientations. Nevertheless, since any formats or guidelines will reflect, to some degree, the viewpoints of those who developed them, there may be some criticisms. The formats and guidelines are not intended to be the final word on family records, but rather elements that can be modified as new ideas are introduced and experience in using them is gained.

Initial family report. This report should contain the name of the family and of the therapist and the dates of the sessions. Under the heading "identifying information," the names and ages of all family members should be given, as well as their occupations, presenting problems, and source of referral. The next section is "history of presenting problem," followed by, unless the material is included elsewhere, one on "marital and family history."

Under the heading "characterization of family members," there should be pertinent information about race, religion, nationality, socio-economic status, developmental history of each member, the parents' families of origin and current relationships with them, and personality descriptions of each member in therapy. Under the heading "observations of family system" the therapist should record what goes on in the sessions, both verbally and nonverbally, between family members and between the family and the therapist. Main issues and themes should also be recorded here, as well as feelings evoked in the therapist.

A section on "dynamics and treatment plan" should include the therapist's understanding of each member, of the family system, and of how the presenting difficulties came about. Psychodynamics, societal, hereditary, and constitutional factors should also be included. The proposed type of treatment—for example, weekly family therapy or chemotherapy—and goals should be stated. Here the therapist may also give a prognosis.

Progress notes. These reports should state what is happening with the family relationships as well as with the individual family members in terms of important events in their lives and their emotional states. It should also include dates of therapy sessions, who attended them, how the members interacted, what was discussed, and the therapeutic approaches used.

Closing summary. This brief summary of the entire case should include an identification of the family members, the presenting problem, the treatment process, the outcome for the family as a whole and for each of the members, the reasons for termination, and the disposition. The date of the initial and final sessions or contact should also be included.

The essence of these formats is that people are individuals in their own right who significantly affect and are affected by their family members. Thus the formats provide for including valuable information about subjective experience and individual psychodynamics as well as a description of the family's systemic relationships.

LEGAL ASPECTS

Some therapists think of a clinical record as being used solely for clinical purposes. They should realize, however, that any member of the family may at any time become involved in a legal action. Divorce proceedings, child custody disputes, and certain other civil as well as criminal cases may arise during or after family therapy. In some instances the records may be subpoenaed.

What protection do therapists and patients have against having the records opened in court? It is the physician's or psychologist's ethical duty to keep confidential the information he has obtained about a patient in his professional capacity. In almost every state, such information is privileged and thus may not be disclosed in a legal proceeding without the patient's consent. A few states have extended the privilege to psychiatric social workers as well as physicians and psychologists.

Regardless of the professional degree of the family therapist or whether he is protected by privileged communication laws, family therapy and family-based record-keeping raise very special problems and legal issues. Privilege and confidentiality are affected by the type of legal case involved and by the sheer fact that more than one person is involved in the therapy. For example, a husband and wife go to a therapist for marital therapy. One later sues the other for divorce. One raises the issue of mental condition in either the claim or the defense. Most state courts would consider privilege to have been waived. But what if the other party did not want that information to be brought up?

Should one member of the patient-family have the right to waive the privilege to the detriment of other members of the family who may either still be in therapy or simply want their communications with the therapist to remain confidential? That issue has not yet been directly addressed by case law or statute. An argument could be made that the patient is the entire family unit and that each member must waive the privilege before the records can be examined. Although that argument may be used successfully in a divorce case (Ellis vs. Ellis 1971; Simrin vs. Simrin) its chances of success in a child custody case are slim because the court's primary concern is for the best interest of the child. Massachusetts law, in fact, explicitly denies privilege to any therapist in any child custody case in which either party raises the mental condition of the other party.

In sum, a general principle of law is that the court has a right to every person's evidence. The psychotherapist privilege is a justifiable exception but is strictly construed and is itself exception-laden. Most important, current law as it relates to family therapy, and records in particular, is at best unsettled. According to Slovenko, the test of relevance — not privilege — governs the right to nondisclosure (Slovenko, 1973, p. 67). Thus a therapist-family communication is best protected from disclosure by showing that the communication would have no relevance to the issues in the case.

Therefore, the therapist should be cautious about what information he includes in the records. For example, the admission by a husband that he is coming to family therapy sessions to make his case stronger in an anticipated child custody struggle might best be omitted from the record. If it is mentioned at all, the reference should be a vague one such as "Motivations for therapy were discussed." Certainly incriminating or conclusive statements such as "The wife is an unfit parent" should be avoided. How detailed the record should be will depend upon the setting in which the therapist works, the family problem being treated, and the type of litigation that could arise.

As a final precaution, each adult family member should be asked to sign an agreement that he understands that all of the communications are confidential and that the therapist will not disclose any communication unless all participating members join in the waiver. If each member does sign a release, the therapist must make sure that he did so knowingly and intelligently. But until the legislatures and the courts recognize the need for an absolute privilege for family therapists, this type of written agreement will provide very little protection in the event records are subpoenaed.

The lack of an adequate privilege law for family therapists has led some therapists to question whether they should keep any records at all. To be sure, accurate records are the therapist's best defense against a malpractice suit (Mills, 1965). Perhaps more important, accurate records ensure continuity of care. Nevertheless, many private practitioners keep no charts except the customary record of appointments and billings; others risk perjury by keeping two sets, one to be turned over in case of subpoena and the other for treatment.

PATIENTS' PRIVACY

In the course of an evaluation or therapy, patients may reveal various intimate aspects of their own or their relatives' past or current life. They generally do so with the belief that the information will be used by the therapist to help them and will not be passed on to others except in certain situations related to their treatment. To safeguard the patient's right to privacy, we recommend that certain damaging or embarrassing material not be written in the chart. Such material may include the details of sexual difficulties or an extramarital affair. In deciding how much, if any, of such private material should be included, the therapist should balance the need to have complete, useful records against the patients' right to privacy.

The more private the material is, the stronger must be the clinical reason for writing about it. We have found that an adequate description of the therapy process can be given without including details of exceedingly shameful or damaging material. It is more important to be clear about the strategy and management of the therapy than to be detailed about private matters.

REFERENCES

Accreditation Council for Psychiatric Facilities (1972), *Accreditation Manual for Psychiatric Facilities*. Chicago: Joint Commission on Accreditation of Hospitals.
Ellis v. Ellis, 472 S.W. 2d 741 (Tenn. App. 1971).
Mills, D. H. (1965), Hidden Legal Dangers of the Hospital Chart. *Hosp. Med.*, 1:34–35.
Simrin v. Simrin, 233 Cal. App. 2d 90, 43 Cal. Rptr. 376.
Slovenko, R. (1973), *Psychiatry and Law*. Boston: Little, Brown.

The Role of Goal Attainment Scaling in Evaluating Family Therapy Outcome

C. A. WOODWARD, NATHAN B. EPSTEIN,
JACK SANTA-BARBARA, and SOL LEVIN

One of the main issues facing researchers interested in evaluating any form of psychotherapy is the choice of methods for evaluating outcome. The purpose of this paper is to evaluate critically the contribution of Goal Attainment Scaling (Kiresuk and Sherman, 1968) to the evaluation of outcomes in the McMaster Family Therapy Outcome Study (Santa-Barbara et al., 1977a).

Measures of outcome status used in psychotherapy research have come under scrutiny and heavy attack in recent years. Psychotherapy outcome research has primarily relied on reports of patient functioning as rated by the patient and therapist involved in the treatment process. The appropriateness of relying on global reports of those directly involved in the treatment process has been repeatedly questioned (Garfield, Prager, and Bergin, 1971; Mintz, 1972; Paul, 1967). Patient functioning as measured by standard psychological tests using difference scores has also been a popular technique of assessing outcome, but its use has also been criticized. Standard rating scales assess outcome in the same way for all patients, regardless of those unique characteristics which brought them into treatment.

C. A. Woodward, Ph.D., is on the staff of the Department of Clinical Epidemiology and Biostatistics, McMaster University, Hamilton, Ontario, Canada.

Jack Santa-Barbara, Ph.D., is on the staff of the Research and Evaluation Service of Thistletown Regional Centre for Children & Adolescents, Rexdale, Ontario and the University of Toronto, Department of Psychiatry.

Nathan B. Epstein, M.D., F.R.C.P., is Professor and Chairman, Section of Psychiatry and Human Behavior, Brown University—Butler Hospital, Providence, R.I.

Sol Levin, F.R.C.P., is Professor and Chairman, Department of Psychiatry, Northeastern Ohio Universities College of Medicine, Akron, Ohio

In designing the present study, concern focused on (1) developing multifaceted indices of outcome; (2) including measures used in previous studies to allow for comparison; (3) using some measures of family functioning; (4) measuring whether or not the family was helped with the specific distressing behaviors that brought them into treatment; (5) use of follow-up assessment beyond treatment termination; and (6) assessment of outcome status by independent observers.

What was required was a measure that could assess family functioning as well as functioning of individual family members. Few adequate objective measures of family functioning are available. Objective, universal indices of family functioning (e.g., separation) are ambiguous. Therapists could readily give clinical anecdotes where separation of the patients was a treatment goal and would be viewed as a positive outcome, although in most cases their treatment goal was to improve the relationship between the parents. Indices of improved functioning centered around the unique problems the family presented. Furthermore, the type of family therapy practiced at the center where this study was conducted, is a systems-oriented approach (Epstein and Bishop, 1973) that focuses on interactions and transactions within the family. It was important that the measurement instrument chosen be able to reflect this orientation.

Goal Attainment Scaling (GAS) was chosen as a means of assessing outcome status because it deals with several of these concerns (Kiresuk and Sherman, 1968). GAS is a procedure for assessing client status on any number of dimensions (goal areas), in a way which is specific and unique to the individual client. Although used in a number of studies to assess individual therapy outcome, the procedure had not been applied to the evaluation of family therapy. It was felt that the individualized goals one could set by GAS would permit the uniqueness of each family's situation to be dealt with.

Given the lack of adequate, objective measures of family functioning, and the success of GAS, it was felt that this innovative means of assessing outcome could profitably be applied to family therapy. It could be used to measure family as well as individual functioning, could provide multiple indices each of which was particularly relevant to the family, and could be assessed by independent observers.

Table 1 presents a summary of the kinds of information about family therapy that GAS was expected to obtain, a list of GAS characteristics pertinent to the types of information desired, as well as the measurement characteristics of GAS available to provide the information. The level or range of goal attainment could be studied for families because a range of possible outcomes must be indicated by the goal

TABLE 1
INFORMATION AVAILABLE FROM GOAL ATTAINMENT SCALING

Information Desired	Related GAS Characteristic	Measure Used
Were treatment goals attained?	Explicit goal expectations	$\bar{x}$ goal attainment score
Were treatment goals exceeded or failed?	Range of goal expectations identified	Goal attainment score and its distribution
What kinds of goals are set for families?	Unique and explicit behavioral goals	Content analysis
Will different types of therapists set different goals?	Uniqueness of scales and flexibility of who sets goals	Content analysis

setter who constructs the scales.

Client deterioration, as well as improvement beyond therapist expectations, could be assessed from the distribution of goal-attainment scores. Content analysis of the goals could help clarify the areas of family functioning that therapists saw as important and amenable to change through treatment. The types of goals set by therapists of different disciplines and levels of experience could also be examined.

The use of GAS was also fraught with possible difficulties. Reliable and meaningful results had been reported for individual patients (Baxter and Beaulieu, 1974; Garwick, 1974a, 1974b). The adequacy of the technique for measuring outcomes in family therapy had not been tested. Family-treatment goals often involve change in distorted interaction patterns and were likely to be more complex than goals for individual patients. It was not at all clear whether therapists could translate what they mean by "improved communication" in a family into explicit, behavioral indices that were clinically relevant and could be reliably scored. In addition, relationship of this individualized measure, with unique psychometric properties, to other more global and standardized measures of outcome was not apparent.

The present paper will focus on the adequacy of GAS as a means of assessing outcome in brief family therapy, how well it met the initial objectives of the investigators, and its relationship to other measures of outcome.

METHOD

Details of the overall design and methods of the study are reported elsewhere (Santa-Barbara et al., 1977a). Briefly, 279 families were involved, each of whom had a child between six and sixteen years of age who was referred for academic and/or behavioral problems at school. All families received brief family therapy (mean number of sessions was nine).

PROCEDURE

The process of GAS results in a follow-up guide. The goal-attainment follow-up guide was constructed by the family's therapist, usually within the first few weeks of contact. When setting goals, therapists were instructed to consider the family's characteristics and problems, as well as their own ability to deal with such problems. In constructing a follow-up guide, the first step is to identify relevant goal areas in which change is expected. Next, the goal setter specifies in the most concrete terms possible what the expected outcome will be at the six-month follow-up. In addition, the goal setter specifies what expectations are less likely to occur, and which are more desirable (two levels) and which less desirable (two levels). The result is a five-point scale varying in both desirability and likelihood of occurrence. Any number of such scales may be constructed for each client. A minimum of three scales per guide was required for each family that participated in the present study. The relative importance of each scale was indicated by the therapist attaching weights to them if appropriate. The therapist also noted intake level (if it appeared on the scale), the informant(s) who were to be used at follow-up for determining the level of attainment of each scale, and the time period over which the scale should be scored (e.g., entire follow-up period, during the past month, during the follow-up interview, etc.).

A variety of training procedures was used to familiarize the 80 therapists who participated with the mechanics of scale construction. As the center operates in multidisciplinary teams, the team became a resource for teaching new members the technique. The research staff also developed a packet of information describing the rationale and mechanics of GAS, and monitored the technical adequacy (Garwick et al., 1972) of the follow-up guides. After checking for technical problems and negotiating their solution with the therapist when necessary, the follow-up guides were typed and all information identifying the therapist removed.

The clinical relevance of the scales was the therapist's responsibility. No formal checks on clinical relevance were made during guide construction by research staff. However, if the guide constructor was a student, the clinical supervisor was asked to review the guide with the student to ensure that scales were clinically relevant. For a small subsample of the guides, both the therapists and their clinical supervisors completed follow-up guides independently. This was done to check on whether guides completed by two therapists, both with knowledge of the family's situation, would have similar content and be scored similarly at follow-up.

The research staff contacted the family to set up the follow-up interview and sent the Goal Attainment Guide and other outcome measures to be scored during the interview to the follow-up worker available for the interview. Research staff scored only those goals that required information to be obtained from sources other than the family (e.g., school, police, family doctor). The seven women who served as follow-up workers came from a variety of backgrounds including social work, psychology, and public health nursing. Some had formal educational experience relevant to the task and had worked as interviewers for other research projects. None was associated with the center, and this was made clear to the families (Kiresuk and Sherman, 1968).

Follow-up interviews occurred in the family's home, and all family members were present. The follow-up worker was responsible for eliciting as much information as possible from the appropriate family member(s) to score each scale on the guide. After the interview, the worker recorded the level of attainment for each scale on the follow-up guide, rated the relevance of each scale to the family's mental health status at time of follow-up on a three point scale (relevant, partially relevant, or irrelevant), and commented on her ratings. An index of the follow-up worker's confidence that she had obtained enough information to score the scale appropriately was also obtained. The worker recorded her level of confidence in scoring each scale as high, moderate, or minimal.

Forty families were asked to participate in a second interview by a different follow-up worker to assess the reliability of scoring by follow-up workers. Thirty-five of the 40 families asked agreed to two separate interviews at different times.

The formula for normalizing the scores obtained on a follow-up guide (Kiresuk and Sherman, 1968) was used to derive a T-score for each scored guide. This formula considers the following factors: (1) number of scales designated by the goal setter; (2) level of goal attainment on the five-point scale; (3) expected overall intercorrelation among scales; and (4) the weighting given to each scale as an indicator of outcome. T-scores were computed for the level at intake and level scored at follow-up.

In order to examine the types of goal set by therapists and whether goals varied as a function of therapists' experience in family therapy or discipline, a schema for coding the content of the scales was developed. Initially, a subsample of 40 follow-up guides was used. Ten guides each were randomly selected from the highest, lowest, and midrange scores, as well as ten guides from those families who refused to be involved in the formal testing procedures of the study, but who remained in treatment. The 146 scales contained in these guides were coded according to the Family Categories Schema developed by Epstein, Sigal, and Rakoff (1962). This conceptual framework has been used as a teaching aid for family therapists at the center and elsewhere. After several discussions of specific scales, five major content areas and specific subheadings within each content area were defined. The 146 scales were then rated independently by three raters. Differences were discussed until there was either unanimity or a redefinition of a specific content area. This allowed the development of a manual for subsequent coding of a larger sample of the data. In all, 111 follow-up guides were randomly selected for content analysis. Reporter(s) for each scale (mother, child, etc.), participants in the scale (the actor[s]), and the arena (home, school, work, etc.) were also coded for each scale.

Results

Attainment of Treatment Goals

Goal-attainment follow-up guides were completed for 277 families. The level at intake was scored for all families in order to determine how far the families were from their expected goals at the start of treatment. The mean score at intake was 29.59 with a low standard deviation (5.54). Although the majority of families were identified as being about two standard deviations from their expected outcomes, very few families were rated as being as poorly off as they could be.

How well the families met their therapists' expectations is reflected in the distribution of post-goal-attainment scores obtained at follow-up (see Figure 1). The mean score for the full sample was 52.82 (s.d. = 12.35), very close to the expected theoretical mean of 50 and standard deviation of ten. The distribution of goal-attainment scores approximated a normal distribution, allowing the identification of families who failed to attain their therapist's goals as well as families who ex-

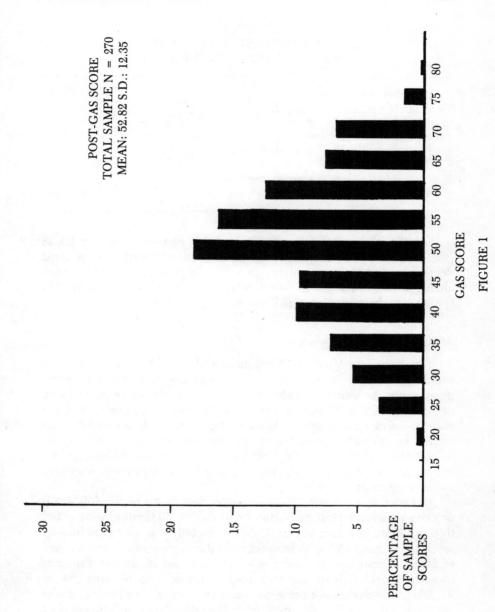

POST-GAS SCORE
TOTAL SAMPLE N = 270
MEAN: 52.82 S.D.: 12.35

GAS SCORE

FIGURE 1

TABLE 2
SOME CHARACTERISTICS OF GAS IN THE
FAMILY THERAPY OUTCOME STUDY

Total number of Goal Attainment Guides	277
Total number of scales constructed	1005
Mean number of scales per guide	3.6
Total number of scales scored	938
% of scales which follow-up workers rated as "RELEVANT"	86%
% of scales in which follow-up workers' confidence was "HIGH"	87%

ceeded the goals of treatment. The average change score was 23.38 (s.d. = 13.22). The majority of families changed about two standard deviations on the scale, although some showed considerably more change and a few actually deteriorated from their level at intake. On the whole, therapists were realistic in the goals they set.

ADEQUACY OF THE MEASURES

Given the complexity and uniqueness of the GAS procedures, it is important to consider the adequacy of this process from a psychometric perspective. As shown in Table 2, follow-up workers reported having high confidence in 87 per cent of the scales scored; 86 per cent of the scales were rated as relevant to measuring change or lack thereof in the mental-health status of the family. Further consideration will be given to the issue of the external validity of the goal-attainment guides below, in discussing their relationship to the other outcome measures used in the study.

In order to determine the inter-rater reliability of the follow-up workers who scored the goal-attainment guides, 40 families were asked to participate in a second interview conducted by a second follow-up worker. Of those asked, 35 families agreed and were interviewed a second time, about two to three weeks after the first interview. Product-moment correlation of the two goal-attainment scores was .84 (p < .001), and agreement between raters on scoring of individual scales was high. Of the 107 scales involved in the reliability study, 33 per cent were scored identically by both follow-up workers; 78 per cent were scored within one level (many within half a level); and 95 per cent were scored within two levels (see Table 3).

TABLE 3
RELIABILITY MEASURES OF GAS:
FIRST INTERVIEW vs. SECOND INTERVIEW*

Reliability of GAS when scored by two independent follow-up workers	$r = .84$
No. of days between 1st and 2nd follow-up	$x = 15.8$
	$SD = 9.7$
% of scales with perfect agreement	33%
% of scales scored within one level	78%
% of scales scored within two levels	95%

*n = 35 Guides; 107 Scales

Analysis of variance was used to assess whether goal-attainment scores differed as a function of follow-up worker. No significant difference was found (F = 1.25; d.f. = 6,268; p > .10), indicating that little of the variation in goal-attainment scores can be accounted for by differences among the follow-up workers.

Two follow-up guides, one constructed by the therapist and the other constructed by the therapist's clinical supervisor, were available for eighteen families. Both guides were scored at follow-up by the same follow-up worker. A product-moment correlation of the post-goal-attainment scores from both sources was .80 (p < .01), indicating high similarity in level of goal attainment as measured by both guides. Different goal setters, assessing the same family, produced guides scored similarly at follow-up.

The influence of number of guides constructed by the therapist on post-scores was also examined. Analysis of variance indicates that number of cases contributed did not significantly improve the therapist's ability to set realistic goals (F = 1.18; d.f. = 1,269; p > .10). The therapist's discipline (psychiatry, psychology, social work, or nursing) also did not affect post-goal-attainment scores (F = .47; d.f. = 3,267; p > .10).

The effects of the therapists' sex, level of expertise in family therapy (as rated by their supervisor, using the criteria developed by Cleghorn and Levin [1973]) and years of experience as therapists were also examined, using both analysis of variance and multiple-regression techniques. Few of these therapist variables had a major effect on, or were predictive of, a family's post-goal-attainment score. The therapists' sex and level of expertise in family therapy together accounted for less than two per cent of the variance in scores. It should be pointed out that these failures to find differences are encouraging, as they indicate that goal setters are taking into account their own ability to effect change in the family system. Differences would emerge only to the degree that one group or another was systematically optimistic or pessimistic. This is not to say that all groups set similar goals, as will be discussed below, only that the goals set by each group are realistic ones, attainable by the families they treat.

CONTENT ANALYSIS

One hundred eleven follow-up guides were randomly selected for detailed content analysis. Demographic, therapist, and treatment characteristics for families in this subsample were compared with those of the entire sample. No significant differences on any of these variables were found, indicating that the guides on which the content analyses were performed are representative of the guides from the entire sample.

Forty-three per cent of the 417 scales dealt with more than one family member, indicating it was possible to scale the kinds of family interactions meaningful to family therapists in their treatment of families. To determine how frequently the goal scales represented interactions between two or more people (rather than an individual's behavior), the actor(s) at the attainment level for each scale was identified. Table 4 indicates that the identified patient was most often seen as the sole actor (40.5 per cent of the scales), while interactions between mother and father accounted for the next largest proportion of scales (21.6 per cent); mother and father alone accounted for 8.9 per cent and 6.5 per cent of the scales respectively. Fifty-nine per cent of the scales involved the identified patient as one of the actors. Mother and father were involved as actors on scales with approximately the same frequency (42.9 per cent and 41.2 per cent respectively). Siblings were mentioned in 5.8 per cent of the scales, while people other than family members are rarely mentioned (2.5 per cent).

Table 4 also presents the most reliable reporters for these scales, according to the therapists. Mother was the most frequently chosen informant (41.7 per cent) for the behavioral goals, being so identified more than twice as often as was father (17.3 per cent). Outside of the family, school was most likely to be chosen as the source of information for a particular scale (12.5 per cent). In a few cases (2.4 per cent), the follow-up worker was asked to report on her own observations during the follow-up interview.

The vast majority of scales were concerned with behavior in the

TABLE 4
PROPORTION OF SCALES IN WHICH VARIOUS FAMILY
MEMBERS ARE ACTORS AND REPORTERS*

	Actor %	Reporter %
Identified patient	40.5	11.8
Mother and father	21.6	8.9
Mother	8.9	41.7
Mother and identified patient	4.6	**
Father and identified patient	6.0	**
Father	6.5	17.3
Identified patient, mother, father	4.1	**
Other	7.9	5.5**
Follow-up worker	—	2.4
School	—	12.5

*N = 111 follow-up guides, 417 scales (post-level)
**Other includes starred categories

home (67.1 per cent), while at least 14.9 per cent were involved with behavior at school. A relatively small proportion of scales were concerned with community/peer activities.

Results of the content analyses of 111 randomly selected follow-up guides are presented in Table 5. The majority of goals were concerned with role behavior (69.2 per cent); the largest subcategory is behavior management (14.6 per cent), which refers to any attempts by one family member to influence or control another's behavior. Many of the scales included in this category involved parents dealing with (controlling) their children, or with each other with respect to their children. Other scales describe the spouses' interaction (e.g., mother nags father x number of times per week). The discipline subcategory (11.6 per cent) refers exclusively to a child's behavior that is unacceptable to the family or to society (excluding the school). This area included not only disobedience and failure to do chores, but also such behavior as stealing, setting fires, and running away. It did not include the illegal use of drugs, which was coded elsewhere.

The involvement subcategory was identified as a goal area as often as was discipline (11.6 per cent). The amount of time various family members spend together was the most frequent content in this category. School behavior (10.7 per cent) takes in any discipline problem at school, including attendance, punctuality, and school phobias. Even

TABLE 5
PERCENTAGE OF SCALES AT THE ATTAINED LEVEL
IN VARIOUS CONTENT CATEGORIES*

Content Area	% of Total
Role Behavior	69.2
Behavior Management	14.6
Discipline	11.6
Involvement	11.6
School Behavior	10.7
Social Activities	8.0
Marital Roles	3.2
Other	9.5
Communication	19.7
Affective Communication	14.6
Clinical Symptoms	7.5
Miscellaneous	3.6

*Number of scales constructed = 412; number of cases = 111

when school performance (i.e., academic achievement) is added (less than 2 per cent), the proportion of scales constructed pertaining to these role behaviors is low. Given that one of the criteria for including a family in the study was that the identified patient had school-related problems, this is somewhat surprising. It appears that the therapists frequently identified goal areas other than those related to the presenting problem.

Social activities (8.0 per cent) covers a broad range of behaviors, from responsiveness and eye contact in the follow-up interview to socializing with friends at home and outside. Marital role (3.2 per cent) refers to scales depicting the fulfillment, or lack thereof, of emotional, sexual, and financial needs. Also included are issues of sharing daily household responsibilities. Other role behaviors, accounting for 9.5 per cent of the total, included such items as drug abuse, school performance, autonomy, and a miscellaneous category.

Communication was the next largest major content area, accounting for nearly 20 per cent of the 417 scales. Affective communication (14.6 per cent) concerns the exchange of information regarding the emotional aspects of family life. Fights between parents are also included. Instrumental communication (3.4 per cent) involves the exchange of information concerning mechanical aspects of family life.

The third major category, clinical symptoms (7.5 per cent) included enuresis and encopresis, somatic complaints, and depression, as well as issues of personal hygiene, substance abuse, including alcohol, and problems of self-esteem.

The remaining 3.6 per cent of the scales included problem-solving behaviors in terms of identification of problems, attempting solutions, etc., and a variety of other miscellaneous items.

The influence of the guide constructor's discipline (psychiatry, psychology, social work, nursing) on the type of goals set was examined. Nurses set goals related to change in clinical symptoms more frequently than any other group and were less likely to scale role behaviors overall (56.2 per cent) and discipline (4.2 per cent) and social activity (2.1 per cent) in particular. Behavior management was the most frequently scaled role behavior for all disciplines except psychology. Psychologists scaled school behavior twice as frequently (21.4 per cent) as any other group. Social activities were scaled as behavioral indices of goal attainment more frequently by psychiatric and social work staff (10 per cent of goals set) than by psychology (0 per cent) and nursing staff (2.1 per cent). All disciplines scaled affective communication more frequently than instrumental communication (14.6 per cent vs. 5.1 per cent, respectively). However, chi-square analyses of these content areas by discipline indicate that these differences are not significant.

In order to obtain an index of their level of expertise as family therapists, all therapists participating in the study were assessed using the schema devised by Cleghorn and Levin (1973). The relation between level of expertise and the content of goals constructed was examined. Therapists at the intermediate level scaled clinical symptoms twice as frequently (11.9 per cent) as did other therapists, and constructed more scales that fell into the miscellaneous category (5.9 per cent); only half the scales they constructed on communication involved affective communication (8.5 per cent).

The type of role behaviors scaled also tended to vary with level of experience. Behavior-management goals ranked first among students (19.4 per cent) and advanced beginners (14.6 per cent). Involvement was scaled at a disproportionately high level (20.4 per cent) by advanced therapists, who only rarely used discipline (5.6 per cent) and social activities (3.7 per cent) as indices of goal attainment. Chi-square analyses of these content areas by level of expertise were also nonsignificant, and these results are offered only to provide a description of the types of goals set by therapists at different levels of expertise.

RELATIONSHIP OF GOAL ATTAINMENT SCALING
TO OTHER OUTCOME MEASURES

To understand how GAS is related to other outcome measures, post-scores were intercorrelated with other outcome measures. These results are reported and discussed elsewhere (Santa-Barbara et al., 1977b). Briefly, goal-attainment scores correlate significantly with every other outcome measure at a low to moderate level (r's = .12 to .39; p < .05). The goal-attainment score is most highly correlated to how the family feels at the six-month follow-up regarding the problems that originally brought them into treatment (r = .39; p < .01). If a family reports feeling much better about their original problems, they are likely to have higher goal-attainment scores. It appears to be the best single predictor of outcome status. In addition, it also carries unique information.

Another way of assessing how goal-attainment scores relate to a broad range of outcomes is to examine extreme groups. The 36 families who attained the highest T-scores at follow-up were compared with 37 families with the lowest T-scores (see Table 6). The mean pre-post-T-score difference for the high scorers was 42.70 (s.d. = 6.87) while the low scorers' mean difference score was 4.05 (s.d. = 5.78). At closure, 24 per cent of the low scorers were seen by their therapists as deteriorating or not changing during treatment, as compared with only three per cent of the high scorers. High scorers were given good or excellent prognoses (59 per cent) more often than low scorers (35 per cent).

At follow-up, low scorers were also less likely to be satisfied with the services they received. Only 36 per cent said they were satisfied, as compared with 64 per cent of the high-scoring group. While 97 per cent of high scorers claimed to feel better or much better about the problems that brought them into treatment, only 54 per cent of low scorers felt this way. Low scorers were likely to say they felt worse (12 per cent) or the same (34 per cent). Recidivism among low-scoring families (46 per cent) was twice that of high scorers (22 per cent). Thus, low and high scorers differed significantly and in the expected direction on each measure of treatment outcome.

DISCUSSION

The goal-attainment scaling procedure has demonstrated its usefulness as an outcome measure in the study of family therapy. Despite the highly idiosyncratic behavioral goals set by the therapists, it proved to be a reliable and valid measurement device. The vast majority of goals

TABLE 6
COMPARISON OF HIGH AND LOW SCORERS ON
A VARIETY OF OUTCOME MEASURES

Outcome Measure	High Scorers %	Low Scorers %
At closure		
Therapist's perception of change:		
deteriorated or no change	3	24
Therapist's prognosis:		
good or excellent	59	35
At six-month follow-up		
Satisfaction with services:		
satisfied or very satisfied	64	36
How do you feel about the original problems now?		
much better or better	97	54
Type of recidivism:		
family doctor/school/other agency/ mental health professional	22	46

were scorable at follow-up with high confidence, and were judged to be a relevant reflection of the outcome status of the families treated. The high inter-rater reliability indicated that the follow-up workers' high confidence in scoring the scales appropriately is justified. Individual differences among follow-up workers were minimal and accounted for little variance in goal scores. Different therapists (students and supervisors) also tend independently to set similar goals, which were scored similarly by follow-up workers. Therapist characteristics (i.e., number of cases contributed, sex, discipline, years of experience and level of training in family therapy) also account for little variance in goal-attainment scores, indicating that therapists were able to accurately set realistic expectations for the families they treated.

GAS permits one to determine readily whether these individually tailored treatment goals were met by the families. In most cases, the goals were attained or exceeded by the families. The therapists who set the goals were fairly accurate predictors of expected level of goal attainment. This finding is particularly interesting in that their prognoses made at treatment closure tended to be poor predictors of the families' outcome status at follow-up (Santa-Barbara et al.,

1977b). These results suggest that if therapists rely on such private and subjective ratings as global prognoses, they are likely to learn little about the types of cases they treat successfully as opposed to those which are less successful. GAS, on the other hand, requires that more detailed consideration be given to specific indicators of success or failure, and can provide an important source of feedback to therapists concerning the long-term status of their treated families.

Goal Attainment Scaling results in a range of expectations that may be scored at follow-up. This characteristic of GAS allows one to determine the degree of goal attainment, rather than whether goals were simply attained or not. This range of outcomes makes it possible to carry out a more refined analysis of the client and treatment variables that relate to outcome status. As indicated above, families with high goal-attainment scores have more favorable outcomes on a variety of other measures than do families with low goal-attainment scores.

Content analysis sheds light on the types of goals used by therapists as behavioral indices of success of family treatment. It cannot be used to directly explicate the goals of short-term, systems-oriented family therapy itself. The categories obtained are not necessarily an accurate reflection of the goals of treatment or the problems as viewed by the family. For example, a presenting problem of school phobia might be assessed in terms of the parent's difficulty with affective communication. This would become the focus of treatment, yet the child's school attendance could be scaled by the therapist as an index of how well treatment proceeded. Conversely, inappropriate allocation of role behaviors could be seen by the therapist as the major problem, and become the focus of treatment and be scaled. Here the family may have viewed the problem as poor academic achievement by the identified patient. While the focus of systems-oriented brief family therapy is on transactions among family members, less than half the goals scaled involved more than one family member. This fact suggests that interactional goals are more difficult to scale. Content analysis, then, has its limitations in understanding the nature of the therapeutic focus. It is also laborious, and any coding schema cannot entirely capture the richness and diversity of goals set.

The major advantage of an individualized goal-attainment procedure is that it allows one to deal appropriately with the uniqueness of each case. The price for this flexible and useful idiographic approach is an absence of universal standards against which to compare the goals attained by patients. Although a family may have attained or surpassed the goals set by the therapist, this family may not be functioning well by any universal standard of mental health and pathology. Some families who exceeded their therapist's goals may not, in an absolute sense, be healthier than some who did not meet the goals set. This problem has led to the development of a health/sickness rating system based on a model of family mental health. Contents of the goal-attainment guides have been rated using this universal system to better understand the level of family functioning reflected in goal scores (Santa-Barbara et al., in preparation). Using the data (i.e., the specific behavioral expectations) generated by the GAS procedure in this way permits this highly idiographic approach to be integrated with a no-mothetic standard. Together, the goal-attainment scores and the health/sickness ratings of the specific content areas provide information basic to the evaluation of treatment outcome. GAS indicates how well a particular family does relative to reasonable expectations set for (or by) them. The health/sickness ratings indicate how individualized and relative goals relate to a more universal standard of family functioning.

Goal Attainment Scaling is a robust technique. Data have accumulated which suggest that, with careful attention to technical problems at time of scale construction, reliable and meaningful results can be obtained across a variety of populations, using different goal setters. However, the implementation process can be tedious (Santa-Barbara et al., in press) and goal setting takes time. In addition, procedures to examine the reliability of the data and the contribution of measurable sources of variance to the final goal scores are necessary. Despite being able to partial out the amount of variance contributed by follow-up workers and goal setters, the amount of residual error variance remaining in the present data is uncertain. However, it has been demonstrated that such error variance can be kept within acceptable limits (Garwick, 1974a). Sufficient true variance is present in the present data to demonstrate relationships to other outcome measures, and a significant difference across other outcome measures is found in groups with high or low goal-attainment scores.

The unique advantage of the GAS procedure is that it provides highly individualized information, which is especially pertinent to a particular family. This is an especially desirable characteristic, particularly in the area of family measurement, where no standardized device or procedure has earned widespread acceptance.

References

Baxter, J. W. & Beaulieu, D. E. (1974), Evaluation of the adult out-patient program. Hennepin County Mental Health Service. Program Evaluation Project Reports, 1969–1973, Chapter 9. Minneapolis, Minnesota, Program

Evaluation Resource Center.

Cleghorn, J. M. & Levin, S. (1973), Training family therapists by setting learning objectives. *Amer. J. Orthopsychiat.*, 43(3):439–446.

Epstein, N. B. & Bishop, D. (1973), Position paper—family therapy: State of the art. *Canad. Psychiat. Assn. J.*, 18:175–183.

———— Sigal, J., & Rakoff, V. (1962), Family categories schema. Unpublished manuscript. Family Research Group, Department of Psychiatry, Jewish General Hospital, Montreal.

Garfield, S. L., Prager, R. A., & Bergin, A. E. (1971), Evaluation of outcome in psychotherapy. *J. Consult. Clin. Psychol.*, 37:307–313.

Garwick, G. (1974a), A construct validity overview of Goal Attainment Scaling. Program Evaluation Project Reports, 1969–1973, Chapter 5, Minneapolis, Minnesota, Program Evaluation Resource Center.

———— (1974b), An introduction to reliability and the goal attainment scaling methodology. Program Evaluation Project Reports, 1969–1973, Chapter 3, Minneapolis, Minnesota, Program Evaluation Resource Center.

———— Grygelko, M., Makela, W., & Jones, S. (1972), Preliminary working paper on the manual for the standardized assessment of the Goal Attainment Follow-up Guide. Minneapolis, Minnesota, Program Evaluation Project, July.

Kiresuk, T. J. & Sherman, R. E. (1968), Goal Attainment Scaling: A general method for evaluating comprehensive community mental health programmes. *Comm. Ment. Health J.*, 4:443–453.

Mintz, J. (1972), What is "success" in psychotherapy? *J. Abnorm. Psychol.*, 80:11–19.

Paul, G. L. (1967), Strategy of outcome research in psychotherapy. *J. Consult. Psychol.*, 31:109–118.

Santa-Barbara, J., Woodward, C. A., Levin, S., Goodman, J. T., Streiner, D. L., & Epstein, N. B. (submitted for publication, 1977a), *The McMaster Family Therapy Outcome Study:* I—An overview of methods and results.

———— ———— Streiner, D. L., Goodman, J. T., & Epstein, N. B. (submitted for publication, 1977b), *The McMaster Family Therapy Outcome Study:* II—Interrelationships among outcome measures.

———— ———— ———— (in press), Marriage or mirage: Is a realistic marriage of clinicians, researchers and administrators possible in an evaluative research project. Evaluation.

———— ———— ———— Green, H. A., Bishop, D., & Epstein, N. B. (in preparation), A health/sickness index of family functioning.

The Family Behavioral Snapshot:
A Tool for Teaching Family Assessment

ISRAELA MEYERSTEIN

RATIONALE

Engaging a family in treatment is a complex process because of the multiple tasks the therapist must accomplish. While becoming sufficiently involved with family members to put them at ease and gain cooperation for work, the therapist is simultaneously attempting to evaluate family functioning as objectively as possible.

The impossibility of absorbing, let alone processing into meaningful data, all of the sensory information produced as a family demonstrates its interaction patterns is well known. For the beginning therapist, however, the demands of having to conduct an interview while reacting to ongoing family process can be quite overwhelming.

For this reason, a means of highlighting significant aspects of family functioning from an undifferentiated mass of interactional data would be valuable. It is hoped that the structured format of the Family Behavioral Snapshot will help the beginner to ask relevant questions, guide the interview actively, and be able to summarize his or her experience with a family in a useful way.

DESIGN

The Family Behavioral Snapshot is fashioned by ecological family systems thinking (Auerswald, 1968; Minuchin, 1970). Viewing the family as an "open sociocultural system in transformation" (Minuchin, 1974, p. 51), the Snapshot essentially treats three variables:

Israela Meyerstein, A.C.S.W., A.A.M.F.T., is in private practice in marital and family therapy, Allentown, Pennsylvania.

(a) Structure (i.e., the "anatomy" of a family, or the organization of its transactions); (b) Development (i.e., the structure of a family evolving over time in response to internal and external changes); and (c) Problem Solving (i.e., the "physiology" or manner in which a family adapts to and copes with stress).

Recent assessment literature (Fischer, 1976) supports the emphasis on dimensions of culture and development as vital contextual backdrops to the more standard intrafamily variables, such as structural descriptors, sanctions, controls, emotions, and needs.

Family problem solving, or how a family organizes itself around particular problems, is seen as the most useful entry point for understanding symptomatic behavior in context and for intervening into human dilemmas (Haley, 1976). In fact, attempts by family members to prevent, solve, or eliminate a problem are frequently seen as responsible for the persistence of symptomatic behavior (Weakland et al., 1974). For this reason, the Snapshot is problem-oriented and seeks to assess family participation: which members appear most invested in the problem as well as those who will pledge to work on it in treatment (Aponte, 1974).

The Family Behavioral Snapshot seeks as accurate a statement of the problem in the family's own words and language as is possible in order to grasp the realities experienced by family members (see section II, item B. and section V, item A. of the questionnaire, Appendix A). At the same time, the descriptive focus on here and now interaction links observable behaviors to theoretical constructs of family functioning with a minimum of inferential thinking about underlying family dynamics (Fischer, 1976).

Use of Tool

The Family Behavioral Snapshot is primarily a training tool for teaching family assessment and a guide to interviewing. As an assessment outline, the form identifies for further elaboration areas considered by one or more family members to pose difficulties in functioning. This includes problematic areas noted by the interviewer, whether or not acknowledged by the family. The beginner learns to view pathology as relative, residing in extremes of functioning, and to view problems within the context and unique culture of each family.

As an interviewing guide, the Snapshot leads the beginner through a structured interview. It is organized sequentially in a design similar to Haley's five stages of engaging a family during the initial interview (Haley, 1976). In section I, general information is gathered about family members and their life styles in an effort to get acquainted and establish rapport with the group. Section II focuses on the presenting problem. Section III's concern with developmental context and issues of family adaptation highlights the question, "Why now?" The section on family interaction (IV) evaluates the functionality of the family's structural organization. By this stage of the interview, interactional tasks are frequently assigned to test the resilience of observed interactional patterns. Finally, the therapist-family contract (see section V of the questionnaire) channels interview behavior in a positive goal-directed manner (i.e., "What would you like to see different in your family?") in order to achieve a measure of closure at the end of the interview.

CASE EXAMPLE

The Snapshot may be used in a variety of ways, depending on the inclination of the trainer. In this particular example, several beginning family therapy trainees observed through a one-way mirror as the trainer interviewed a family. The trainees, who had some acquaintance with concepts of family structure, development, and problem solving, but little experience applying them in clinical situations, were given the Family Behavioral Snapshot to fill out. A discussion followed the session, during which specific aspects identified by the Snapshot served as a guide in the evaluation of this family.

The J. family, a lower-middle-class black family, was referred for evaluation by the school counselor for problems with the eight-year-old son, Charles, who had been stealing in the classroom and at home. School officials felt his behavior represented just the "tip of the iceberg" in what they perceived to be a disturbed family situation.

The family members invited for the initial session included: Mother (36), Stephanie (12), Sharon (11), Charles (8), Shawn (4), and the mother's boyfriend, Johnnie Ray. The mother's boyfriend was included after a preliminary phone conversation with mother. Although the school had been unaware of his existence, it was later discovered that he had been helping to support the family for six years and was the father of the youngest son.

The use of the Snapshot helped to increase the trainees' awareness of the J. family's functioning in several key areas. First, it called attention to the hitherto neglected figures of the mother's boyfriend and the maternal grandmother, both of whom played significant roles in terms of suppporting or undermining mother's executive function in the family.

The data on the "family unit-in-society" revealed stable work histories of the breadwinners and adequate physical home conditions. Exploration of areas such as recreation indicated that there was sharing of family activities, and that role model identification existed along sex lines, all of which reflected considerable health in the joined family unit.

Careful examination of problem-solving patterns revealed that not only had the parents begun to work together in handling the identified patient's symptomatic behavior, with accompanying improvement in Charles (a fact which needed to be communicated to the school officials), but also that more than one problem was considered important to family members. The parents, when coordinated as a team, were quite capable of controlling Charles' behavior, yet the stepfather continued to allow the daughters to erode their mother's authority, thus maintaining the family turmoil, evidenced by incidents of stealing by the girls from mother.

The structural focus on general family interaction identified the split in parenting in a way that defined possible solutions. For example, the parents' inability jointly to impose limits on Shawn, the four-year-old son, led to his tyrannical position in the family. At the same time, the parenting capabilities of the adults showed that considerable strengths existed, which could be enhanced by a structural re-alignment.

Finally, eliciting family members' goals in an open-ended as well as specific way, led to new requests. Mother, for example, blurted out: "I'm so tired and can't relax; I can't get to spend time with him, except when I have trouble." Her wish to be relieved of her go-between role and to become closer with her disengaged man set directions for intervention strategy.

The data on the Family Behavioral Snapshot cannot always be covered in a single session. However, the Snapshot brings to the foreground the key areas of family functioning and points out avenues for future information gathering.

Summary Evaluation

The Family Behavioral Snapshot can have wide application in family therapy training because it is framed in language comprehensible to professional as well as nonprofessional interviewers. Because of its standardization of family process, the Snapshot can be useful in mental health clinics where there has been a theoretical switch-over to a family orientation without the accompanying changes in form and procedures. In such settings and in training, the problem-oriented Family Behavioral Snapshot is available as a tool whose potential value calls for implementation by clinicians.

APPENDIX A

PROBLEM-ORIENTED
FAMILY BEHAVIORAL SNAPSHOT

Instructions: Indicate existence of identified problem areas by marking as follows in box corresponding to item:

Place   0   (zero) to indicate area is not problematic.
Place   +   (plus) to indicate area is a problem by its presence or excess (i.e., too much, too frequent, overly, too high, etc.).
Place   −   (minus) to indicate area is a problem in its absence or insufficiency (i.e., too little, rarely, not enough, absent, or poor, etc.).
Place   ?   (question mark) to indicate not enough information is available; can't say yet whether it is a problem or not.

(Problem areas identified require further
specification and elaboration elsewhere)

I.   FAMILY ECOLOGICAL LIFE CONTEXT

A.   Family Membership:
(please include significant others, as extended family, neighbors, etc.)

(name)	(age)	(position, role in family)	(school or work — describe occupation)	☐
				☐
				☐
				☐
				☐
				☐
				☐

B.   Extended Kinship Network

Contacts with extended family   ☐
Social contacts by nuclear family members
with friends, peers outside home
    a. father   ☐
    b. mother   ☐
    c. children   ☐
    _____   ☐

☐
☐
_____   ☐
_____
Visitation by outsiders into home   ☐

C. Living Conditions

Amount of physical space in home   ☐
Income and socioeconomic level   ☐
Neighborhood life (i.e., safety, housing
conditions, availability of resources)   ☐

D. Work

Employment stability of breadwinner   ☐
Job Satisfaction:
    a. father   ☐
    b. mother   ☐
Work schedules permit family interaction   ☐

E. School

Educational background of parents   ☐
Academic achievement of school age children
                                                             ☐
_____   ☐
_____   ☐

Behavioral conduct of school age children
                                                             ☐
_____   ☐
_____   ☐
School (teacher/principal) — family relations   ☐

F. Recreation

Time spent in family activities (including meals) together   ☐
Hobbies, individual outside interests of family members
    a. father   ☐
    b. mother   ☐
    c. children
                                                             ☐
_____   ☐
_____   ☐
_____   ☐

Involvement in activities with children by:
    a. father   ☐
    b. mother   ☐
    c. siblings   ☐
Spouse activities alone without children   ☐

G.   Social Agency Helper Systems

Involvement with legal systems (i.e., police, jails, courts)   ☐
Dependence on income supplement, welfare (i.e., SSI)   ☐
Medical care of family members   ☐
Mental health system involvement:
     a. father   ☐
     b. mother   ☐
     c. children
         _____   ☐
         _____   ☐
         _____   ☐
         _____   ☐
     d. extended family   ☐
Institutionalization of family member   ☐

II.   FAMILY PROBLEM SOLVING   (Please fill in blank space
                                                corresponding to item)

A . Definition of the Problem

          Identified patient (name): _____
          Main presenting problem:
          (brief behavioral description) _____
          _____
          Family spokesman describing problem: _____
          Referral source: _____
          Duration of problem: _____
          Previous treatment attempts: _____
          (Describe) _____

B.   Family Participation (one-sentence behavioral description of how
     each family member views problem)

     Participant
     (name)   Description of problem
     _____   _____
     _____   _____
     _____   _____
     _____   _____
     _____   _____

C.   Attempted Solutions (one-sentence behavioral description of what
     each family member does to solve or handle problem when it occurs)

     Participant
     (name)   Attempted Solution
     _____   _____
     _____   _____
     _____   _____

_____ _____
_____ _____
_____ _____

Participant who appears most involved in identified patient's problem when it occurs: _____
Customer complaining most, sweating
about problem: _____

III. FAMILY DEVELOPMENTAL CONTEXT   (Indicate by X which areas appear to be current stresses to family unit)

A. Normative crisis
      Courtship   ☐
      Early marriage   ☐
      Birth of child   ☐
      Child entering school   ☐
      Adolescence   ☐
      Adolescent leaving home (empty nest)   ☐
      Middle marriage years   ☐
      Retirement and old age   ☐
      Death of spouse   ☐

B. Sudden change in family membership, size, organization
      Family member leaving
      (i.e., death, divorce, desertion, institutionalization)   ☐
      Family member entering (i.e., in-law, foster child,
      remarriage and entry of stepparent)   ☐

C. Exacerbation of idiosyncratic problem
      (i.e., retarded child, physical illness)   ☐

D. Sudden external crisis or disaster
      (i.e., fire, accident, disability, flood, loss of
      breadwinner's income, etc.)   ☐

E. Family explanation for why problem is occurring now_____
      _____
      _____

IV. FAMILY INTERACTION   (Indicate problem by + or −)

A . Family Structure

      Parenting (control, nurturance, guidance)
          Control
              Parents appear in charge of family as executive
              leaders
                  a. father   ☐
                  b. mother   ☐
              Delegation of responsibility to older children   ☐
              Effectiveness of control demonstrated by:
                  a. father   ☐

      b. mother   ☐

Strictness of discipline by:
      a. father   ☐
      b. mother   ☐

Parents consult each other to coordinate
decision making   ☐
Conflictual split over handling children   ☐
Conflict-resolution achieved within parenting unit ☐

Nurturance
Mother displays nurturance, affection, support
      a. to father   ☐
      b. to I.P.   ☐
      c. to siblings

         _____ ☐
         _____ ☐
         _____ ☐
         _____ ☐

Father displays nurturance, affection, support
      a. to mother   ☐
      b. to I.P.   ☐
      c. to siblings

         _____ ☐
         _____ ☐
         _____ ☐
         _____ ☐

Guidance
Mother provides information, guidance
      a. to father   ☐
      b. to I.P.   ☐
      c. to siblings

         _____ ☐
         _____ ☐
         _____ ☐
         _____ ☐

Father provides information, guidance
      a. to mother   ☐
      b. to I.P.   ☐
      c. to siblings

         _____ ☐
         _____ ☐
         _____ ☐
         _____ ☐

Marital functioning
Spouses display friendliness, warmth, mutuality ☐
Spouses display competition, disagreement   ☐
Spouses spend time alone away
      a. from children   ☐
      b. from each other   ☐
      c. from extended family   ☐
Conflicts handled within spouse unit   ☐

Conflicts involve triangulation of third
party (i.e., in-law, I.P., other sibling,
affair, lawyer, counselor)   ☐

Siblings
    Children are permitted own independent
    activities, interests:
        a. I.P.   ☐
        b. siblings
        _____   ☐
        _____   ☐
        _____   ☐
        _____   ☐

    Display of loyalty, affection, cooperation
        a. to parents   ☐
        b. to each other   ☐
    Display of aggression, disagreement,
    competition
        a. toward parents   ☐
        b. to each other   ☐
    Request affection, nurturance
        a. from each other   ☐
        b. from parents   ☐
    Request information, guidance
        a. from each other   ☐
        b. from parents   ☐
    Exert effective control
        a. over each other   ☐
        b. over parents   ☐

B.   Communication Patterns

    Spokesmanship
        Mother speaks for
            a. father   ☐
            b. I.P.   ☐
            c. children   ☐
        Father speaks for
            a. mother   ☐
            b. I.P.   ☐
            c. children   ☐
        I.P. speaks for
            a. mother   ☐
            b. father   ☐
            c. siblings   ☐
        Children speak for
            a. mother   ☐
            b. father   ☐
            c. each other   ☐
    Scapegoating of I.P.
            a. by mother   ☐

        b. by father   ☐

b. by father ☐
c. by siblings ☐
d. by external force (i.e., school, peers, etc.) ☐

I.P. viewed as "sick" (i.e., crazy, confused, infantile, helpless, retarded) and needing help, therapy ☐

I.P. viewed as "bad" (i.e., disobedient, mean, spiteful, criminal, beyond rehabilitation) and needing punishment ☐

Guilt, self-blame expressed by parents ☐

Blame, indignation expressed by parents ☐

C.   Family Affective Style and Organization

Expression of conflict, combativeness, anger, hostility
    a. between parents ☐
    b. between parents and children ☐
    c. between siblings ☐
    d. between family and therapist ☐

Expression of positive affect, warmth, friendliness
    a. between parents ☐
    b. between parents and children ☐
    c. between siblings ☐
    d. between family and therapist ☐

Tolerance of differences of opinion, autonomy
    a. between parents ☐
    b. between parents and children ☐
    c. between siblings ☐

Atmosphere of rigidity, closed unit, resistant ☐

Atmosphere of depression, sadness, hopelessness ☐

Atmosphere of utopian denial, avoidance or suppression of conflict ☐

Family members appear enmeshed (i.e., overly close, stuck, overconnected with each other) ☐

Family members appear disengaged (i.e., isolated, disconnected, apathetic towards each other) ☐

Family members appear underorganized (i.e., chaotic, leaderless, fluctuate between extremes of enmeshment/disengagement ☐

V.   FAMILY-THERAPIST CONTRACT

A.   Family Goals (i.e., one-sentence behavioral description of what each family member would like to see different in family; minimum acceptable change)

Participant   Goal Statement
_____   _____
_____   _____
_____   _____

_____   _____
_____   _____
_____   _____

B. List participants willing to pledge help in solving problem in treatment

_____
_____

C. List priorities of problems to work on in treatment

_____
_____
_____

REFERENCES

Aponte, H. J. (1974), Organizing treatment around the family's problems and their structural bases. *Psychiat. Quart.*, 48:209–222.

Auerswald, E. H. (1968), Interdisciplinary versus ecological approach. *Fam. Proc.*, 7:202–215.

Fischer, L. (1976), Dimensions of family assessment: A critical review. *J. Marr. Fam. Coun.*, 2:367–382.

Haley, J. (1976), *Problem-Solving Therapy: New Strategies for Effective Family Therapy*. San Francisco: Jossey-Bass.

Minuchin, S. (1970), The use of an ecological framework in the treatment of a child. In: *The Child in His Family*, ed. E. J. Anthony and C. Koupernik. New York: Wiley, pp. 41–57.

_____ (1974), *Families and Family Therapy*. Cambridge, Mass.: Harvard University Press.

Weakland, J. H., Fisch, R., Watzlawick, P., & Bodin, A. M. (1974), Brief therapy: Focused problem resolution. *Fam. Proc.*, 13:141–168.

Utilization of Family Photos
and Movies in Family Therapy

FLORENCE W. KASLOW
and JACK FRIEDMAN

Family therapists have developed a variety of techniques which are designed to elicit certain past experiences or bring the members of a family into touch with feelings they have toward one another as a carry-over from the past. Some techniques, such as mourning stimulation, rely upon verbal cues and associations (Paul, 1972). Various projective tasks, such as asking the family to plan an outing or vacation together or take a family Rorschach test, have been created for utilization when standard verbal, psychotherapeutic procedures are exhausted in order to stimulate therapeutic progress. Some techniques, like psychodrama, utilize reenactments of actual events (Moreno, 1923). Some therapists use positional and configurational arrangements of family members when doing family sculpting (Ferber et al., 1972; Papp et al., 1973). Underlying the use of such interventions is the assumption that the therapist's knowledge of the family's history and interactive patterns can be beneficial in understanding the family as it is now, and that family members, reexperiencing the past together, can better appreciate one another's feelings and gain mastery over unresolved conflicts.

In this article we will be describing a technique which has in common with the approaches mentioned above the evocation of past events and memories to uncover feelings about these happenings and relationships. We have designated this technique *Family Photo Reconnaisance*, as this label brings to mind the examination of aerial photographs by military intelligence for strategic purposes. Such microscopic examination of repeated aerial photos of the same geographic areas can

Florence W. Kaslow, Ph.D., is Dean and Professor at Florida School of Professional Psychology, Miami, Florida.

Jack Friedman, Ph.D., is Associate Professor, Department of Psychiatry, Jefferson Medical College, Philadephia, Pennsylvania.

This article, with minor modifications, is reprinted by permission from the *Journal of Marital and Family Therapy*.

yield unusual clues from seemingly mundane and almost unnoticeable details. In the same way, the self-conscious and specific examination of family photographs, slides, and movies can yield a wealth of data about the family's developmental history and the relationships of its members to each other.

The technique of employing family photographs and movies came about quite by accident. The first time that one of us used such material[1] was during a visit to the home of a family that had been in therapy for several months. There were the usual introductory quips about being bored with home movies and slides which followed a suggestion by the mother that the therapist see some pictures depicting the way the family had been in the past. Having already had the family in therapy enhanced the appreciation of the value of photographic materials. It was surprising how clearly the old photographs and movies revealed alliances and how accurately they characterized the emotional distance and closeness of different family members with one another. In the months that followed, the technique was used with several other families and it was understood that family pictures tend to be highly individualized (idiosyncratic) and reflect unique things about each family.

The coauthor of this paper was subsequently asked to utilize the technique to see if her experiences would corroborate her colleague's. After several years in which we both continued to experiment with and refine the technique, we made a presentation about the rationale, procedure, and results to our colleagues of the Family Institute of Philadephia in October, 1974. A number of them have since employed it and report similar valuable results. In our various training endeavors we each find this technique appeals to our students and they are quick to utilize it when it seems appropriate.

METHODOLOGY

If and when we are having difficulty reaching a family, or when they seem to be blocking on recall about significant past events and "important others" we may ask them to bring in photographs. If this occurs during a home visit, they may also offer to show slides or movies. Looking at these items jointly with the family may continue over sev-

---

[1] The coauthor first to employ family photographs was Jack Friedman, who began experimenting with this technique in 1968. When we first began using photo reconnaisance and sharing our observations and findings about its efficacy with other therapists, Akeret's *Photoanalysis* (1973) had not yet been published.

eral therapy sessions. Invariably we have found families respond favorably to this request as a sign of interest in them and their heritage and they find it an easy and pleasant one to fulfill. It is not complex and does not seem to evoke much anxiety; rather it proves of high interest value. We tend to use it with between 10 and 20 per cent of the families we see and have observed that it is a particularly worthwhile aid in the diagnosis and treatment of families that are not very articulate. Prodding memories by using family photographs in conjunction with having them develop family genograms elicits much repressed material and evokes forgotten affect attached to specific occurrences and people.

Observations of Photo-Taking Patterns

We have found a number of patterns regarding photo reconnaisance which are descriptive of a large majority of families:

1. Families tend to take photos at the time of particular, important events in the family's life cycle, such as weddings, births, birthday parties, holidays, vacations, and graduations. Ostensibly, these are pleasant happenings which mark milestones in the family's life history. Often the intended purpose of taking the picture is to enable the family, at a later time, to recall these special occasions and to assist the members in reliving the happy feelings.

2. Conversely, during periods of stress and family crisis, we note that there is a sharp drop in the number of pictures taken. This includes periods surrounding illness, death, family separations and fragmentations, and heightened conflict between different members and factions of the family.

Few parents take photos during the time of a child's incapacitation. There appears to be a pervasive aversion to photographing children who were handicapped, temporarily disfigured, in oxygen tents, casts, following surgery, or during use of dialysis machines for kidney ailments. There are some exceptions to these generalizations. For instance, parents seem to delight in photographing children with a black eye, especially in color. So too do they take pleasure in pictorially capturing developmental changes, such as loss of baby front teeth which will be replaced by second teeth. It may be that families have a tendency to take photos when the events or changes they are portraying represent progress.

Another exception occurs following surgery where positive change is anticipated. An illustration is a case where a teenage girl had plastic surgery, which in addition to correcting a deviated septum, was intended to give the nose a more esthetic appeal. The young lady and her parents took frequent photos during the weeks following surgery to show the wonderful changes that were occurring and to have a series of before, during, and after pictures. They happily displayed these to the therapist as have subsequent families in which a member has undergone successful cosmetic surgery.

3. Our experience has validated the commonly held notion that firstborns are photographed more than the siblings who come later. With each successive child there is a corresponding decrease in the number of photos taken. It may be that this reflects less of a need to make a fuss over certain events which the parents have previously experienced with the firstborn, such as baby's first steps, birthday parties, and first day of school.

Departures from this pattern may hold important hints for the therapist and ultimately for the family. In one case where the second child was photographed significantly more than the first, it was indicative of almost pathological favoritism for her as she was the blue-eyed, blond, pretty darling that her unattractive, older sister was not. She held out the promise of meeting the parents' dream for a beautiful, model child. Reversals from the trend may be partial evidence of a family secret, as when the eldest unphotographed child is illegitimate, handicapped, or disfigured.

4. People from all strata of society value and take photos and it is often a family activity. This generalization is based on our experience with white and black families spanning from poor inner-city urban areas to wealthy suburbs. It is inclusive of families from a variety of ethnic backgrounds such as Italian, Jewish, Puerto Rican, Chinese, and Irish. We have seen a wide range of difference in competence, mood, equipment, and photographic preference, but we have not yet found any families who have not taken, kept, and treasured their photos.

5. Size and prominence of pictures and portraits of family members hung in the house reflect attitudes regarding who is important enough to be captured in oil or in film and placed in a frame on display for all to see. Are there ancestors watching over and, if so, is it lovingly, critically, or with admonitions to uphold family traditions and not individuate? If there is a problem of sexual dysfunction, the therapist might ascertain who else is in the bedroom with the couple by observing pictures on the bureau or over the headboard.

VALUES INHERENT IN USING FAMILY PHOTOGRAPHS AND MOVIES

Over the period of the past eight years during which we have been utilizing this technique, we have noted a number of values accruing from its usage. Each is discussed separately and in sequence. Some case illustrations are provided.

1. *They provide much data of factual, historical significance.* The pictures reveal a great deal about who comprised and comprises the family; how the group has expanded or decreased over time; changes in how people look; where they lived and traveled; what kinds of activities they engaged in; who stood next to whom and who was included/ excluded; who was the family photographer; when and if this shifted and to whom; at what stages in the family's history pictures were and were not taken. In providing clues as to who has disappeared from the scene, who became the black sheep, outcast, or scapegoat, what the main alliances and splits are, who has gained or lost huge amounts of weight, and expectations for children, the pictures afford the therapist the opportunity to raise questions about obvious changes — what precipitated them, reactions to them, and consequences of them. In this way photographs become a key to understanding and unlocking family secrets, myths, skeletons, and projections. We use them as a basis for facilitating dynamic, interactional accounts in addition to the descriptive data (discussed by Akeret, 1973). Some of these points are exemplified in the case of Rita.

Case of Rita

Photo reconnaisance was used in the case of Rita, a 22 year old, and her family. In this family all of the male members were professionals, but the females remained in traditional "women's roles." There were no pictures of Rita in candid poses, none of her in dungarees or bathing suit. Instead she was always formally attired and carefully posed. The therapist remarked, after viewing several photographs, that she seemed almost to have a smile pasted on her face. The pictures usually showed her in a group receiving an award, giving an award, posing after some show or other special event. Even family pictures were posed, with Rita always well-dressed, her face bearing the pasted smile.

Her parents, in reacting to the pictures, remarked about how beautiful she looked then, how successful she had been. She had been popular and involved in many clubs, groups, and organizations. But Rita indicated that she felt empty, like a "posed cupie doll," unreal and without the feelings that should accompany success. Her mother reacted by remembering that she had been depressed and it became clear that somehow she had made Rita the recipient and bearer of her need to achieve fulfillment in life. In the photographs, mother also appeared posed and unreal looking, passing on to her daughter her own superficial way of appearing fulfilled. Rita was seeking to become a separate person who could be animated and genuine. The pictures created a backdrop for the climate in which this could occur.

2. *They help members retrieve memories and correct distortions.* Photographs are immutable. Unless parts have been destroyed, everyone is faced with an undeniable record of the past which is not amenable to the same distortions that verbalizations filtered through a memory screen and through conscious misrepresentations are. Children can visualize how their parents handled them during their early childhood, who preferred to be next to whom, who was present or missing. This is amply illustrated in the following case.

CASE OF MR. X. — AN "OFFENDER"

One of the problems most frequently encountered in doing therapy with "delinquents" and "criminals" is their total denial of responsibility for what has happened to them. There is an overriding tendency to project blame on parents or teachers, police, and other authority figures. They tell of gross deprivation, abuse, someone being "out to get me," and other disturbing cirucmstances. All is painted dull, dreary, and noxious. This is as true of the inglorious past as of the horrible present in a juvenile detention home or maximum security prison. It has proven extremely useful for the therapist to inquire if relatives might bring a photo album to the client and to join in a family therapy session on the next visiting day.

In one specific case where this occurred, the young man, Mr. X., a 20 year old "doing time," had totally berated his parents and told uncanny tales of his deplorable childhood. In his mind, he never had a good day; God and society had dealt him a completely negative deck. No one was more astounded than he was in a family therapy session when he began to recapitulate his life story as told in the photos. There were family visits to grandparents, Christmas dinners with neighbors, birthday parties, and other joyful events. The therapist's attention riveted on helping him see how distortions continued to permit him to project blame on everyone else and not confront his role in getting himself sent to prison. Mr. X. realized that his misperceptions led to his hiding behind unfounded criticism of "nothing to do" — the prison had many sports, a band, educational classes, group therapy sessions, work activities, and creative arts programs.

He further saw that not all cells were equally dreary — some inmates were able to create more liveable rooms with interesting personal touches. This became the key to opening up new horizons because of the several realizations fostered by pictures, namely, (1) each person is quite capable of at least partially shaping his own environment, (2) that he tended to both exaggerate and distort the facts, and (3) the responsibility for being and becoming something different and better lay within him — that he could no longer "cop out" by saying "it's all because of miserable upbringing."

3. *They stimulate interaction of family members, elicit emotionally charged material, and evoke affect in the "here and now."* Usually, all present react to at least some of the pictures quite spontaneously. They talk to each other, saying, "Do you remember?" or to the therapist, describing the event captured by the photographer. While they reminisce some abreaction occurs about meaningful past events, emotional reactions are triggered in the "here and now" which enable the therapist to seek access as to why the feelings expressed are weak or strong, positive or negative. Also, different accounts of the same picture or event become the basis for zeroing in on different perceptions, on underlying conflicts, and on the uniqueness of each family member.

4. *They expand member awareness of one another's personality and identity beyond the usual stereotypically perceived roles.* Pictures graphically depict that the family as a unit as well as each member individually has a history. Over time, at various stages in each one's life, they have played many roles. For example, the children can view their parents during their dating period and come to recognize that they have a bond to each other in their spouse-lover roles which preceded and is distinct from the parenting function. They may see now frumpy Mom as a former glamor girl or paunchy Dad as a once slender athlete. Other pictures may show different roles each is assuming in their contemporaneous life space outside of the family realm in the school or work world and thus enhance the esteem in which they are held.

5. *They illuminate the therapist on all of the above plus on values, interests, and talents of each member and how they respond to each other regarding the content of the pictures.* The therapist has an opportunity to analyze the kinds of things photographed; the amount of traveling the family has done, the type of outings they participated in, the diversity of interest versus narrow horizons, and to assess areas of strength and of past and potential growth.

6. *They sensitize each person to his own appearance.* Each person sees how he appears now, how he looks (looked), and why he may evoke the responses he gets. The therapist can observe and assimilate recent physical changes which may have disfigured or improved the

appearance of a family member. The actual film record militates against denial and strengthens the therapist's ability to work with each patient's body image and self concept.

7. *They aid the therapist in identifying critical times in a family's life cycle.* Periods of depression, crisis, disorganization, and rapid family change are often characterized by the absence of pictures. Gaps in the picture chronology can point to questions to be asked about loss, separation, disappointments, and grief.

8. *They elicit information regarding parents' expectations in the past, present, and for the future for their children and clarify how they often live out script messages* (Harris, 1967). The Nickois's case exemplifies this.

THE NICKOIS'S CASE

The original request was for marriage counseling. Mrs. Nickois was discontent in her marriage of five years. She was a vicacious, peppery, and somewhat chubby blond of 30 years. When she married Mr. Nickois he was living and working in a city several hundred miles away from his family of origin. He was a neatly attired "professional man," a moderately successful engineer who seemed ambitious. She was a teacher from another city and had assumed a great deal of initiative in their courtship. But, since it had been a "tale of two cities," they had only gotten to know each other superficially. Consequently, when they got married, they woke up to the fact that they were relative strangers.

Mrs. Nickois complained that her young husband was quite passive, particularly in relation to his family. About a year after their marriage, he had decided that engineering was less important to him than proving to himself that he could "make it" in his father's small retail business and he had insisted that they return to his home town. His fantasy was that his family would welcome his bubbling bride and that his father would willingly accept his input into the business. Since in the initial marital therapy sessions his real motivation for returning seemed obscure to both of them and because his memory of early childhood relationships and events was very vague, I suggested he bring in the family photo album. He had previously stated that he had received no attention or affection from his father. In looking through the album, pictures revealed he was more often held by his father than his mother and that his father's looks at him showed tenderness. Mother, by contrast, seemed haughty and remote. This enabled him to recall that the idea that father did not care for him came from his mother's comments and to realize that it reflected her way of undermining his original closeness to his father. In addition, his wife's contention that Mr. Nickois's sister had always been the favorite was not borne out by the pictures. Both children seemed to have fairly equal status as they appeared in a similar number of pictures marking similar developmental occasions. What seemed apparent was the general coolness of all parties.

The use of the photos helped Mr. Nickois realize that he had been drawn back to his home town and his family's small business, which in itself offered him little satisfaction, in order to try finally to acquire the love from his mother and approval from his father that they were unable to offer in earlier decades. Their own impoverished emotional state became apparent and Mr. Nickois was helped to see that they were unable to be giving, nurturant parents because of deficts in their own nature and not because he was unlovable. This new knowledge also freed his wife to stop pining for a loving acceptance from her in-laws. Both were able to turn more to each other for encouragement and approval, to focus on realistic meeting of needs in the present with less bemoaning of how unfair the past had been, and to reach some degree of acceptance of Mr. Nickois's parents as they are, rather than how they would like them to be.

9. *They aid in understanding the family role network.* For those who bring in a photo album, one can ascertain who has been the family recorder; with what care work has been done; whether it is a labor of love; whether it is labeled, sequenced, neat, and accurate; and when and of whom additions to the evolving family portrait are made.

SUMMARY

Of value to the profession as a whole is that photo reconnaisance bridges the gap between two dominant schools of thought (Kaslow, 1973) or opposing positions in psychotherapy on the role of historical data (the past) in the present and to the future. It utilizes pictures which recount the past as a stimulus and focal point in the present, to provide a sense of family history and continuity and a foundation on which to help the family plan a meaningful, less conflicted, and more satisfying future.

REFERENCES

Akeret, R. U. (1973), *Photoanalysis*, ed. T. Humber. New York: Wyden.
Ferber, A., Mendelsohn, M., & Napier, A. (1972), *The Book of Family Therapy*. New York: Science House.

Harris, T. (1967), *I'm OK, You're OK.* New York: Harper & Row.

Kaslow, F. W. (1973), Family therapy: Viewpoints and perspectives. *Clin. Soc. Work J.,* 1:196–207.

Moreno, J. L. (1923), *Theatre of Spontaneity.* New York: Beacon House, 1946.

Papp, P., Silverstein, O., & Carter, E. (1973), Family sculpting in preventive work with well-families. *Fam. Proc.,* 12:197–212.

Paul, N. (1972), In: *The Book of Family Therapy,* ed. A. Ferber et al. New York: Science House.

Family Symptomatology

Family psychopathology reveals itself in symptomatology which is an introduction to the family and its management.

Here family dysfunction is seen in three aspects of the neuroses— anxiety, separation anxiety, and epidemic hysteria. Three papers are devoted to the psychoses, covering aspects of the autistic child, the symptoms of schizophrenia, and genetic counseling in schizophrenia.

The Familial Prevalence
of Anxiety Neurosis

RUSSELL NOYES, JR., JOHN CLANCY,
RAYMOND CROWE, PAUL R. HOENK,
and DONALD J. SLYMEN

Compared to the exhaustive family studies of major psychoses, the family background of anxiety neurosis has been relatively neglected. This lack of attention is surprising considering the fact that the neurosis is one of the commonest mental disorders, occurring in at least five per cent of the population (Marks and Lader, 1973). It is also surprising in light of existing family history studies that point to an increased prevalence of the disorder among relatives of anxiety neurotics (McInnes, 1937; Brown, 1942; Cohen et al., 1951). Previous investigations indicate that roughly 15 per cent of parents and siblings, taken together, suffer from the same disorder. Studies based on family history data, such as these, probably underestimate the actual occurrence of the disorder. They are, nevertheless, important in establishing a familial predisposition to anxiety neurosis and in planning investigations based on data from interviews with family members. The present investigation provides additional family history data confirming the high familial prevalence of the disorder.

Russell Noyes, M.D., is Professor of Psychiatry, University of Iowa, College of Medicine, Iowa City, Iowa.

John Clancy, M.D., F.R.C.P., is Professor of Psychiatry, University of Iowa, College of Medicine.

Raymond Crowe, M.D., is Associate Professor of Psychiatry, University of Iowa, College of Medicine.

Paul R. Hoenk, M.S.W., is Research Assistant, Department of Psychiatry, University of Iowa, College of Medicine.

Donald J. Slymen, M.S., is Research Assistant, Department of Preventive Medicine and Environmental Health, University of Iowa, College of Medicine.

METHODS

The records of patients who had received a diagnosis of anxiety neurosis (or related diagnoses, e.g., hyperventilation syndrome) at the University of Iowa Hospital and Clinics between 1968 and 1972 were reviewed. From 1,024 records, a total of 155 cases were selected for study that met the following criteria for anxiety neurosis: (1) evidence of an illness characterized by either (a) relatively persistent generalized anxiety, nervousness, or apprehension; or (b) anxiety attacks occurring at times other than marked physical exertion or life-threatening circumstances; (2) at least five of the following symptoms occurring during periods of generalized anxiety or attacks: dyspnea or choking sensations, muscle aching or tension, sweating, flushing, or chills, chest pain or discomfort, fatigue or tiredness, insomnia, paresthesias, trembling or shaking, headaches, palpitations, nausea or vomiting, weakness, fainting or light-headedness, dizziness or vertigo, or abdominal pain or discomfort; (3) an illness of at least four weeks' duration; (4) an illness that does not meet criteria for any other psychiatric illness; and (5) an illness occurring in the absence of any physical illness that might account for symptoms (Noyes and Clancy, 1976).

A control group was selected from patients who had undergone surgical procedures at the University of Iowa Hospitals between 1968 and 1972. From 1,194 records, a total of 157 cases (34 herniorrhaphy, 40 appendectomy, and 62 cholecystectomy) were matched—as a group—for age and sex with neurotic subjects. For the sake of consistency, patients were excluded who suffered from physical illnesses that could have accounted for anxiety symptoms.

Structured interviews were completed by a social worker trained in psychiatric interviewing and blind to the status of subjects. Interviews were completed on 129 subjects and 140 controls. Detailed family history data were obtained from interviews together with pertinent follow-up information and screening for other psychiatric conditions. Whenever screening questions regarding first-degree relatives were answered affirmatively, an attempt was made to elicit a history of anxiety attacks and typical symptoms of anxiety neurosis in addition to information regarding other disorders. Psychiatric diagnoses, with the exception of anxiety neurosis, were made by one of the investigators according to criteria outlined by Andreasen et al. (1977). A diagnosis of "definite" anxiety neurosis required a history of the following: (1) chronic nervousness or apprehension, (2) attacks or spells of nervousness, (3) at least three of 15 criteria symptoms (as just listed), (4) treatment for an emotional disorder, and (5) no other physical or psychiatric illness that might account for symptoms. A "probable" diagnosis was made if two out of three symptom criteria (No. 1 through 3) were met and there was no evidence of other disorders that might account for symptoms (No. 5). The designation of "questionable" anxiety neurosis required only one symptom criteria (No. 1 through 3) together with an absence of other disorders (No. 5).

On the basis of interview data, 13 subjects were diagnosed as having other conditions that could have accounted for their symptoms; together with four from whom interview data were unreliable or incomplete, they were excluded from the study population. In a total of 112 subjects, the diagnosis of anxiety neurosis was confirmed at follow-up. These subjects composed the study group. Thirty surgical controls met the above criteria for anxiety neurosis at follow-up; when these were excluded, a surgical control group of 110 cases remained.

Anxiety neurotics included 63 women (56 per cent) and 49 men whose median age was 40 at the time of follow-up examination (Noyes et al., 1980). Surgical controls consisted of 59 women and 51 men with an average age of 39 at the time of follow-up. Subjects did not differ from controls with respect to age or sex, but came from lower social class as measured by Hollingshead and Redlich's (1958) Two-Factor Index of Social Position. The median age at onset was 25 years for anxiety neurotics and the median duration of illness at the time of initial examination was five years. As the latter figure indicates, subjects tended to be chronically ill. However, 24 per cent reported symptom-free periods during the course of their illness and 11 per cent were free of symptoms at follow-up (Noyes et al., 1980).

Morbidity risks for anxiety neurosis and depression were calculated by the Strömgren method and for alcoholism by the abridged Weinberg method (Slater and Comie, 1971, pp. 356–357). The age at onset distribution for anxiety neurosis used in these calculations was obtained from the follow-up study (Noyes et al., 1980). The age at onset distribution for depression was obtained from Winokur (1979) and for alcoholism from Amark (1951). Differences in morbidity risk between various groups of relatives were analyzed by means of a χ test with 1 df.

RESULTS

From a total of 919 first-degree relatives of anxiety neurotics, 114 were identified as having definite or probable anxiety neurosis. When those with a questionable diagnosis were included, the number increased to 160. Similarly, of 904 relatives of controls, 19 were diagnosed as having definite or probable anxiety neurosis; when questionable cases were added, the number rose to 37. The age-corrected morbidity risk for the disorder among relatives of anxiety neurotics was 18 per cent compared to three per cent among relatives of controls (Table 1). When questionable cases were included, the figures rose to 26 per cent and six per cent, respectively. These differences were statistically significant. The risk for the development of alcoholism was greater among relatives of anxiety neurotics than it was among control relatives (Table 1). Again, the difference, although small, was significant. However, the risk for depression, and other disorders that were diagnosed in small numbers, was not different for the two groups.

Table 2 gives the morbidity risk for anxiety neurosis among various relatives. The risk among female relatives was shown to be greater than that among male relatives in a ratio of approximately 2:1. When relatives with definite and probable diagnoses were included, the risk calculated for females was 24 per cent and for males 13 per cent. With the addition of questionable cases, these figures rose to 31 per cent and 21 per cent, respectively. This difference was statistically significant. The excess risk for females was identified among relatives of female, but not male, anxiety neurotics. Twenty-eight per cent of female relatives of definite and probable female anxiety neurotics were shown to be at risk compared with 19 per cent of female relatives of male neurotics. This type of difference in risk was observed among siblings of female subjects (26 per cent for sisters versus 12 per cent for brothers) but not among siblings of male subjects (20 per cent for sisters versus 19 per cent for brothers). A similar difference in morbidity risk was observed among relatives of female controls. Parents showed no greater risk of developing anxiety neurosis than siblings, although when questionable cases were included, risk figures of 30 per cent for parents and 23 per cent for siblings were obtained.

The morbidity risk for siblings increased according to the number of affected parents (Table 3). When relatives with definite and probable diagnoses were used in calculations, the risk for siblings was 44 per cent with both parents affected, 24 per cent with one parent affected, and nine per cent with neither parent affected. When questionable cases were included, the figures were 53 per cent, 29 per cent and 12 per cent, respectively. A similar increase was observed among the relatives of controls. The risk for siblings with one parent affected was eight per cent; with no parents affected, it was two per cent.

COMMENT

The data presented support previous findings of a high familial

TABLE 1
MORBIDITY RISK FOR ANXIETY NEUROSIS,
ALCOHOLISM, AND DEPRESSION AMONG RELATIVES OF ANXIETY
NEUROTICS AND CONTROLS

	Relatives at Risk*	Relatives Affected	Morbidity Risk, %
Anxiety neurosis (definite and probable)			
Subjects	619	114	18†
Controls	627	19	3
Anxiety neurosis (definite, probable, and questionable)			
Subjects	619	160	26†
Controls	627	37	6
Alcoholism			
Subjects	529	33	6‡
Controls	508	18	4
Depression			
Subjects	399	21	5
Controls	388	15	4

*Age corrected.
†P < .001.
‡P < .05.

prevalence of anxiety neurosis (Slater and Shields, 1969; Miner, 1973). Fifty-six per cent of anxiety neurotics in this study identified at least one first-degree relative as suffering from the same disorder. Cohen et al. (1951) reported that 67 per cent of their chronic patients identified at least one first-degree relative as having the same illness. As shown in Table 4, there is a striking correspondence between the prevalence of anxiety neurosis found in the present investigation and that demonstrated in earlier studies (McInnes, 1937; Brown, 1942; Cohen et al., 1951). Fifteen per cent of parents and siblings combined were found to

TABLE 2
MORBIDITY RISK FOR ANXIETY NEUROSIS
(DEFINITE AND PROBABLE)
AMONG RELATIVES OF ANXIETY NEUROTICS

Relatives	Relatives at Risk*	Relatives Affected	Morbidity Risk, %
Fathers	102	12	12
Mothers	103	28	27
Brothers	189	28	15
Sisters	151	36	24
Sons	39	4	10
Daughters	35	6	17
Parents	205	40	20
Siblings	340	64	19
Children	74	10	14
Males	330	44	13†
Females	289	70	24
Total	619	114	18

*Age corrected.
†P < .001.

TABLE 3
MORBIDITY RISK FOR ANXIETY NEUROSIS AMONG
SIBLINGS AS A FUNCTION OF THE NUMBER
OF AFFECTED PARENTS

Parents Affected	Subjects	Siblings at Risk*	Siblings Affected	Morbidity Risk, %
Neither	49	170	16	9
One	44	133	32	24
Both	9	36	16	44

*Age corrected.

TABLE 4
PREVALENCE OF ANXIETY NEUROSIS
AMONG PARENTS AND SIBLINGS OF ANXIETY NEUROTICS*

		Prevalence, %			
	N	Parents	Siblings	Combined	Controls
McInnes (1937)	50	15	15	15.0	4-5
Brown (1942)	63	21	12	15.1	0
Cohen et al. (1951) Chronically ill patients	67	36	13	15.8	0.4
Acutely ill patients	44	6	4		
Present study	112	19	14	15.5	2.7

*Figures not age corrected.

be suffering from the disorder, a figure identical to that reported in previous investigations. With age correction, the morbidity risk was found to be 19 per cent for the same relatives. Still, the percentage calculated including questionable cases (26 per cent) may prove closer to the actual risk because of the tendency to underestimate it using family history data and limited family awareness of an illness characterized by subjective distress but few outward manifestations (Noyes and Clancy, 1976).

The increased morbidity risk for alcoholism among relatives of anxiety neurotics confirms a similar observation made by Cohen et al. (1951). Of course, this risk was highest among male relatives, being 10 per cent for fathers and brothers of subjects compared to five per cent for the same relatives of controls. Cohen et al. (1951) found 12 alcoholics among 63 fathers (19 per cent) of their chronic patients. These investigators suggested that a number of alcoholic relatives might, on closer examination, be found to have anxiety neurosis. That a certain number of chronic anxiety neurotics may secondarily develop drug and alcohol dependence is a possibility supported by clinical observation (Woodruff et al., 1972). The failure to find an increased morbidity risk for other disorders suggests a degree of specificity in the transmission of anxiety neurosis that may not exist in other neuroses (Miner, 1973).

The finding of an increased morbidity risk among female relatives was expected since a predominence of females has been found in most studies of anxiety neurosis. And the risk ratio of 2:1 resembles closely the ratio of females to males in most populations studied (Marks and Lader, 1973). It also approaches the proportion of females to males among the subjects of this investigation. The localization of this increased risk among the female relatives of *female* subjects was unexpected and difficult to explain. Both Brown (1942) and Cohen et al. (1951) found more parents affected than siblings, an observation not confirmed in this study once figures were age corrected.

The potency of family influence on the transmission of anxiety neurosis was shown in the correlation between the risk to offspring and the number of parents affected (Table 3). Cohen et al. observed a similar correlation among their chronic patients. With neither parent affected they found a risk of six per cent, with one affected it rose to 15 per cent, and with both parents ill the risk increased to 43 per cent (Cohen et al., 1951).

The limitations of the family history method seem particularly evident in dealing with an illness that, even though chronic, usually involves little impairment and occasionally goes untreated. Although suitable criteria were established for the identification of anxiety neurosis in relatives, information was often limited, accounting for a sizable number of questionable diagnoses. In order to be suitable for genetic analysis, interview data appear to be required. Such data are currently being collected.

REFERENCES

Amark, C. (1951), A study in alcoholism. *Acta Psychiat. Neurol. Scand.*, 70(suppl.):1–283.

Andreasen, N. C., Endicott, J., Spitzer, R. L., et al. (1977), The family history method using diagnostic criteria. *Arch. Gen. Psychiat.*, 34:1229–1235.

Brown, F. N. (1942), Heredity in the psychoneuroses. *Proc. R. Soc. Med.*, 35:785–790.

Cohen, M. E., Badal, D. W., Kilpatrick, A., et al. (1951), The high familial prevalence of neurocirculatory asthenia (anxiety neurosis, effort syndrome). *Amer. J. Hum. Genet.*, 3:126–158.

Hollingshead, A. B. & Redlich, F. C. (1958), *Social Class and Mental Illness.* New York: Wiley.

McInnes, R. G. (1937), Observations on heredity in neurosis. *Proc. R. Soc. Med.*, 30:895–904.

Marks, I. & Lader, M. (1973), Anxiety states (anxiety neurosis): A review. *J. Nerv. Ment. Dis.*, 156:3–18.

Miner, G. D. (1973), The evidence of genetic components in the neuroses: A review. *Arch. Gen. Psychiat.*, 29:111–118.

Noyes, R., Jr. & Clancy, J. (1976), Anxiety neurosis: A five-year follow-up. *J. Nerv. Ment. Dis.*, 162:200–205.

—————— —————— Hoenk, P. R., et al. (1980), The prognosis of anxiety neurosis. *Arch. Gen. Psychiat.*, 37:173–178.

Slater, E. & Comie, V. (1971), *The Genetics of Mental Disorders.* London: Oxford University Press.

—————— & Shields, J. (1969), Genetical aspects of anxiety. In: *Studies of Anxiety*, ed. M. H. Lader. London: Royal Medico-Psychological Association, pp. 62–71.

Winokur, G. (1979), A family history (genetic) study of pure depressive disease. In: *Genetic Aspects of Affective Illness*, ed. J. Mendlewicz & B. Shopsin. New York: Spectrum Publications, pp. 27–33.

Woodruff, R. A., Guze, S. B., & Clayton, P. J. (1972), Anxiety neurosis among psychiatric outpatients. *Compr. Psychiat.*, 13:165–170.

Intergenerational Separation Anxiety in Family Therapy

ARTHUR L. LEADER

Union and separation, closeness and distance, love and hate, life and death are the hallmarks of the human condition. Conflicts, anxieties, and social and environmental pressures are a natural part of life. Even a state of contentment or homeostasis is the result of a delicate balancing or accommodation of these issues, often opposing forces, rather than their elimination. People, in their daily lives and especially at certain points along the psychosocial stages described by Erikson (1950), are generally struggling to maintain an equilibrium. Feelings and relationships tend to ebb and flow, involving shifting closeness and distance. Each person has his own dilemma in preserving his own unique identity while at the same time trying to accommodate his own self to others.

It is the author's belief that the kind and quality of this dilemma are centrally related to the universal phenomenon of separation anxiety and how this separation has been dealt with, especially in early life. Separation anxiety ranges from normal — a mild apprehension — to pathological — a fear of abandonment, annihilation, and death. In therapy, as in life, this issue becomes focal in many situations. Mandelbaum (1962) said, "Of all problems the social worker encounters in casework with parents and children, none is more significant than separation. But is it not true that separation is central to all life experiences?" (p. 26).

The professional literature, rich in discussion of this phenomenon, needs no extended elaboration here. The intent of this article is to discuss the impact of pathological forms of separation anxiety as it affects

Arthur L. Leader is Associate Director, Jewish Board of Family and Children's Services, New York, N.Y.

family members from one generation to another, stemming from experiences in family therapy.

Fear of Abandonment

One of the common forms of separation anxiety is the fear of abandonment. Individuals who grow up with a strong sense of deprivation tend to feel abandoned. They feel this way not only in relation to their families of origin, but also in relation to their nuclear family and others. They tend to replicate the theme of abandonment either through an unconscious seeking out or a provocation of abandonment. These people often anticipate and live on the edge of fear of abandonment. The neurotic repetitious pattern offers some measure of relief in confirming the consistency of one's image as the bad self and the others as cold and rejecting, therefore leading to no resolution.

It is a striking and pathetic phenomenon to see how those fearing abandonment ultimately are abandoned. Furthermore, those feeling abandoned, as they marry and become parents, find themselves, sometimes to their own surprise, psychologically abandoning each other or their children.

The emphasis in this article is on emotional or perceived abandonment rather than on actual abandonment — not on child placement or the desertion of a child through death, divorce, institutionalization, and so forth. Further, there is no implication that all people who experience fear of abandonment become disturbed or abandon others, or that all pathology has its origins in this phenomenon.

Among families engaged in treatment, what stands out clinically with extensive frequency and force is the fear of abandonment as a deep underlying current that has destructive consequences on intergenerational family interactions. These can be so devastating and overwhelming that families often keep their feelings in this area hidden, and therapists, too, have a tendency to avoid coming to grips with the same feelings. A similar sentiment is expressed elsewhere. Szalita (1968) said, "In reanalyzing patients, I usually find a neglect of the analysis of early losses of any kind, whether the death of grandparents, parents, siblings, friends, pets, or even loss of toys. Mourning and confrontation with death are not too popular themes in many analyses. The tendency to avoid feelings and thoughts on death is natural to man. It brings out the deepest helplessness in his destiny" (p. 7).

Pathological fear of separation or abandonment, although perhaps somewhat less severe than death, is sometimes experienced as the equivalent of death and is apparently not easy for the client or the therapist to face. The author's purpose, therefore, is to highlight the importance of the power and impact of the neurotic separation phenomenon on families and therapists, and the necessity for therapeutic focus on this issue.

FEAR OF SEPARATION

The "acceptance of self" has become a rather hackneyed expression in therapeutic quarters. Yet, it is a profound phrase — easy to express but difficult to carry out. Therapists in their daily work encounter clients of all ages who have not accepted themselves as separate persons, who have not emancipated themselves from their living or dead parents, who are merged with parents and their children, who do not know where they begin and others end, and who live for and through others and not themselves. This lack of boundaries and fusion leads to confusion of identity, role expectation, and performance. The parent who has not separated from his own parent often ties his child to himself in a similar manner in spite of a strong protestation that he will not let what happened to him happen to his child. Mitchell (1968) said, "The clinical evidence is overwhelming that the human being does not separate from what he needs but has never had, until he finds it or its equivalent." Through fortuitous living or through therapy some people are able to find what they need and to make appropriate separations. Perhaps more commonly, people cannot find what they need until they first come to terms with the issue of separation through their understanding and their feelings. In some instances, with help through family therapy, clients are able to reach a new accommodation or some form of psychological reunion with parents and then achieve a successful separation. In other words, contrary to what many adolescents and some of their therapists think, union must occur before true emancipation takes place. Forced separations are, of course, sometimes unavoidable and necessary, but they leave a trail of bitterness that results in fractured relations from one generation to another. The reality of separation, however, may leave a residue of sorrow and resentment all the more intense within the context of a conflict-laden relationship. Bowlby (1969) said, "A threat of loss creates anxiety, and actual loss sorrow; both, moreover, are likely to arouse anger" (p. 209).

The pathological fear of separation is so dreadful that it is difficult to face letting go — to confront one's own internal sense of loneliness, emptiness, inadequacy, selflessness. The resultant chronic anxieties and the diverse ways of coping with them, the need for tight control, the overt and covert fighting for breathing room, the impossible demands and subsequent frustrations, the acting out in behalf of another, the suppression of individual growth and creativity, and the reversal of roles are some of the prices that family members pay for the lack of separation.

Mitchell (1968) said, "In many instances the sense of belongingness is maintained only at a considerable cost to personal growth and fulfillment, because of the compelling need for being part of a whole, in adulthood as well as in childhood, and because of the inability to tolerate aloneness."

In discussing analytic patients, Szalita (1968) states that for some patients endless talking represents "a desire to have someone for one's own for as many hours as one can afford. It could very well be that behind the compulsion to talk is anxiety at the imminent separation — of being left alone" (p. 8). Some similarity of the reaction to death and to separation mentioned earlier is described by Fleck (1966): "The continuum of successive separations and their mastery by the family as well as by each individual in it can be extended to the issue of loss or death, but if no death occurs, separation experiences can serve to some extent as prototypes for shared grief and pain" (p. 316).

Scheflen (1960) also refers to the price paid and the death equivalent in severe separation anxiety or the threat of the disruption of pathological closeness: "Nearly all over-intense, immature relationships are maintained by mutual exploitation of separation and guilt feelings. Closeness is considered essential to life, and separation is unconsciously defined as the equivalent of death or of the loss of body parts or contents" (p. 5).

PSYCHOLOGICAL ABANDONMENT

In some ways psychological or perceived abandonment may be more difficult to assimilate than death because it does not have the finality of death. Therapists often find an endless search, in one form or another, for the elusive hoped-for closeness, the union, the abandoning parent, all the more pathetic because of the too common failure to find what one needs but cannot attain. The search may become a preoccupation or an obsession dominating the life of all family members. And tragically, the very self-absorbed intensity of the search and the resentment behind it often set up self-destructive barriers that interfere with even the finding of satisfying equivalents or substitutes. The search is complicated because it is often unconscious, and the seeker, unaware of his basic neediness, is in conflict over his right to gratification. He often ends up by pushing away positive gestures and sources of gratification. There then may erupt furious fights followed by futile frustration for the whole family.

It is even more complicated because the seeker, in dealing with the issue of pathological separation or abandonment as he establishes his own family, usually has the role of child, husband, and parent all at the same time. Many clients are still involved in symbiotic or hostile-dependent relationships to their parents, and, at the same time, they involve their spouses, sometimes their in-laws, and often their children in transferential relationships (Leader, 1975). These family members — spouses, in-laws, children — are not seen as separate persons in their own right but as substitute parents on whom to project unfulfilled needs. In turn, some of these family members often play their reciprocal part in the complementary cycle through a kind of parental nurturance, occasionally happily but mostly unhappily, and some refuse and remain at loggerheads either in open warfare or in sullen withdrawal.

The neurotic conflict tends to take two different directions. Persons dominated by a fear of abandonment tend in marriage to form either rather similar symbiotic relationships to spouses, to whom they cling tenaciously in an undifferentiated way, or serrated relationships in which the spouses often with complicity are repeatedly abandoning them emotionally. In either situation, the fear of abandonment, as a central driving force, perpetuates a basic sense of loneliness which has to be mediated at all costs. Thus preoccupied with their own internal needs, these people are in no position to relate to others as separate persons. They also can form tight, undifferentiated relationships with one or more children or can also abandon them, again not seeing them as children in their own right. In either situation, the children are essentially abandoned psychologically just as the parents perceive themselves as similarly abandoned. In the marital dyad and the child-parent relationship it is as if each member, in some way brushed with the theme of abandonment, is competitively trying to prove, usually unconsciously, that it is he who is the most abandoned. This competition results in a series of reciprocal reverberating reactions that are loaded with varying degrees of destructiveness that inhibit the growth of each family member and impair the functioning of the family as a whole. Clients caught in this crossfire are generally not in touch with their feelings and are unaware of the reasons underlying their reactive behavior and repetitive patterns. The feelings are too much to bear and have to be denied at considerable cost to every family member. The lack of awareness reinforces a rigid repetitious pattern which makes changes difficult to achieve. In fact, the more a family member strives to change the system, the more he is pressed into the old mold. In the following situation, it took a long time to involve the mother of several children in a therapeutic relationship:

> Mrs. B gave a continuous message to her children that growing up meant displeasing her and becoming her enemy. Part of her tenaciously clinging to old patterns was a response to the moves of her children toward greater separation and the extreme threat of abandonment it held for her. Finally, as she began to trust the therapist, she began to speak of her profound fear of abandonment and to admit that she bound her children to her in response to this fear. She said she herself needed too much mothering and was now concerned that she had been using the children to fill her own loneliness which was damaging to them.

Although studies are not available, it is the author's impression that, in the majority of families seeking help, the intergenerational theme of abandonment flows like a deep underground stream. Available records contain considerable references and clues to this phenomenon, although they are not consistently pursued — apparently because it is painful and *underground* to both client and therapist.[1] The fear of abandonment is often observed and even felt viscerally by client and therapist, but often the specific connections to past experiences and current linkages to parent, grandparent, spouse, and child are not acknowledged. Perhaps part of the reason for this is also related to the still prevalent tendency of focusing more on the individual than the family, as pointed out in the article by Minuchin et al. (1975) on family role in psychosomatic illnesses.

Case Illustrations

The following case illustrations present the effects of intergenerational abandonment:

Mr. and Mrs. M, on the verge of divorce, came in for marital counseling. It soon became apparent that their two young children were very disturbed, reactive mostly to the violent quarrels to which they had been exposed since birth. Both parents had been rejected by both of their sets of parents. During her childhood, Mrs. M's mother was quite depressed and unavailable to Mrs. M. Mr. M was a virtual outcast in his own home and learned early to make his own way in life.

---

[1] This is not to imply that appropriate treatment requires such pursuit in all cases.

The marital relationship centered on competitive striving for gratification of one's own neediness while simultaneously inviting, and certainly finding, abandonment. This abandonment was not only psychological but physical — both husband and wife would leave the house for several days at a time. Mrs. M was particularly rejecting of her young son at the time of his birth. Both parents, as indicated, in actually leaving the home not only abandoned each other, but also the children who in their fright reacted with symptom formation and disturbed behavior. Also there were numerous instances of psychological abandonment by both parents. This situation was complicated and even more upsetting to the chilidren because at times the parents were warm and responsive.

Mrs. M, not having separated from her mother in adulthood, for most of the marriage lived essentially through her husband, submerging her own identity. Out of her unsatisfactory relationship with her husband and her loneliness and longing for an emotional closeness she never had with her mother, she turned to her seven-year-old son and tried to make of him the confidant and parent she never had. This precocious youngster could not be a child. In family therapy it became clear that the child both relished and resented his role. Each child not only had his own set of problems but they frequently pummeled each other, with the younger, the more rejected child, usually being the aggressor.

Mrs. A, 34 years old, divorced for five years and the mother of three children aged 10, six, and five, requested help for Mark, her 10-year-old son. He was not getting along well in school or with his peers who consistently rebuffed him.

It became apparent that the central issue was Mrs. A's long-standing, conflict-laden relationship with her mother. Mrs. A was determined to prove her mother to be an uncaring, selfish parent in spite of her mother's obvious concern for her as expressed in numerous ways. The more her mother did for her, the more frustrated and angry she became, consistently yearning for the idealized deceased father. Mrs. A would then explode, withdraw, and accuse others, especially her mother, of abandoning her. She would then threaten her children with abandonment. Mark and the six year old, in their fright, tried hard to please her and constantly sought her approval and reassurance.

Because the daughter-mother conflict was of long standing, it was important to find out the precipitant to the current crisis. Apparently, Mrs. A had just suffered another in a series of abandonments by men friends, the latest by a man she had been seeing for one-and-one-half years.

Just as Mrs. A perceived herself to be abandoned by her mother and, in the early stages of treatment, by her therapist no matter what the therapist did, Mark in particular felt abandoned by his mother. He in turn acted out his similar dilemma by provoking his peers to abandon him.

Not only was Mrs. A's ex-husband similar to her mother, but he and her mother had developed a more positive relationship with each other than with her. As a result, she felt excluded and abandoned by both. Mark even tried to comfort his mother, but she could not accept that from him either.

As Mrs. A became more accepting of her own neediness, she stopped fighting the therapist and began seeing her mother in a more favorable light. She and her mother had a profound discussion in which they declared their need and love for each other. At the same time, Mrs. A curtailed her provocation of abandonment in others. She was more relaxed and less restrictive with the children and Mark's behavior improved considerably.

In some situations it takes time for the theme of abandonment to emerge. In others it presents itself early. In the following case illustration, the first interview revealed a substantial portrayal of the extent and influence of this theme.

Mr. and Mrs. J came in both feeling and looking overwhelmed. Mr. J quickly mentioned the possibility of a divorce. Overburdened by a boring job and demands from his wife, especially with respect to helping out with two young children, Mr. J said that it was not right, but he felt like splitting and then drew a parallel to his own father who deserted his mother and him when he was five years old. Mrs. J had responded to his absences and withdrawal with helplessness, depression, and destructive displacement in the form of extreme verbal and physical abuse of their five-year-old child. One of their major attractions to each other was their common bond — of the woman who felt unloved though not physically abandoned in her own family and the man who was psychologically abandoned in his family. Both had been fleeing from an intolerable home situation and now were on the verge of abandoning both each other and their children.

THE THERAPIST AND ABANDONMENT

Therapists are not immune from the manifestations of the pathological fear of abandonment: The naked confrontation of an underground stream that is apt to surface and drown the therapist as well as the client. The intensity of feeling, the primitive cry, the utter loneliness, the life and death quality, the submerged and sometimes outcropping of violence are at best not easy to take and can stir unresolved feelings about separation and abandonment in the therapist. Unless the therapist has worked out this basic issue in his own life or is at least aware of his own feelings in this area, he is likely neither to understand what is going on nor be sufficiently empathic with the terrors of his clients.

TREATMENT CONSIDERATION

It takes experience and skill to detect roadways and roadblocks to submerged feelings, but it is especially important that the therapist be emotionally ready to encourage, seek out, and stay with the emergence of the suspected theme and related feelings. A first breakthrough often follows the therapist's taking the initiative in supportively but firmly articulating the central issue and probable relevant feelings. The therapist with evidence and clues can make connections and formulate hypotheses about the critical importance of the separation theme.

FAMILY THERAPY

Family therapy provides a natural modality for the treatment of the phenomenon of abandonment, involving as it does so many family members across intergenerational lines. It is helpful to involve not only the children but at times the grandparents too. The advantage of family therapy is that more than one family member responds and, therefore, a more open and emotional exchange is generated. The family members, observing and testing the attitude of the therapist, feeling safe through his acceptance of their "dangerous" thoughts and feelings, are then freer to begin trusting him. In this very process, symbolically the family may feel that there is someone who cares, who is not frightened off by what is inside and between them, and who has the potential for not abandoning them.

In family therapy there is more opportunity for family members to act out the intergenerational separation theme. This acting out is helpful diagnostically, and the heightened emotionality thus created promotes greater therapeutic access. Also, the separation issue almost always expresses itself quickly between family members and with the therapist, resulting in a number of varying transferential relationships. The therapist can intervene during an actual living-out of an abandonment sequence — to help the family experience and recognize what they are doing on the spot rather than through a cooled-down recollection, to stop in motion the continuation of severe forms of abandonment, and to demonstrate that the therapist abandons no one. This intervention serves as a good model and provides relief through control of behavior heretofore uncontrolled.

If in some instances material about abandonment in life is not accessible, it tends to surface affectively within the client-therapist interaction because there generally is a fluctuating flow between closeness and distance. In family therapy this fluctuation is complicated because different family members are at different places with different reactions and receptivity. The family therapist, however, is in a position of making use of the differences. In fact, it is very useful to highlight these differences as a way of differentiating or making separate each family member's own perception and sense of himself. Moreover, the therapist is always on the lookout for budding differences in any areas. The pursuit of likenesses and differences among family members is almost always an exciting adventure, sometimes humorously relieving, that again serves to bring out individual differences. In this way, family members are able to come to terms with and hold on to their own separate selves. As they see themselves as different and take responsibility for developing their own separate selves, they are no longer apt to have the same need to play out the role of either the abandoned or the abandoner.

REFERENCES

Bowlby, J. (1969), *Attachment*. New York: Basic Books.
Erikson, E. H. (1950), *Childhood and Society*. New York: Norton, 1964.
Fleck, S. (1966), An approach to family pathology. *Compr. Psychiat.*, 7:307–320.
Leader, A. L. (1975), The place of in-laws in marital relationships. *Soc. Casework*, 56:486–491.
Mandelbaum, A. (1962), Parent-child separation: its significance to parents. *Soc. Work*, 7:26–34.
Minuchin, S. et al. (1975), A conceptual model of psychosomatic illness in children. *Arch. Gen. Psychiat.*, 32:1031–1038.
Mitchell, C. (1968), The therapeutic field in the treatment of families in conflict: Recurrent themes in literature and clinical practice. In: *New Directions in Mental Health*, ed. B. Reiss, New York: Grune & Stratton.
Scheflen, A. E. (1960), Regressive one-to-one relationships. *Psychiat. Quart.*, 34:692–709.
Szalita, A. B., (1968), Reanalysis. *Contemp. Psychoanal.*, 2(7):83–102.

A Clinical Report of Epidemic Hysteria in Six Members of a Family

H. S. NARAYANAN and A. S. MAHAL

Sirois (1974) has reviewed 75 distinct outbreaks of epidemic hysteria available in the literature during the past century. Among the symptoms observed by Sirois were convulsions, abnormal movements, and fainting headaches. Sirois also found that a number of these cases were from the lower socioeconomic strata. He has classified epidemic hysteria into five types: (1) sudden onset-explosive type; (2) explosive with an identifiable prodromal struggle; (3) the cumulative-outbreak type; (4) rebound outbreak; and (5) the large diffuse outbreak. In the third type (the cumulative-outbreak type), less than 10 persons are usually involved and transmission of symptoms occurs over a longer period of time—two weeks to one month—as a slow chain reaction. This type is often found in closed institutional settings.

The type of epidemic hysteria noted in this family is of the cumulative-outbreak type described by Sirois. Since Sirois (1974) could trace only three instances of epidemic hysteria occurring within the families in the last few centuries, the present report appears to be the fourth in the world and first of its type to be reported from India.

CASE MATERIAL

The family lives in a village 18 miles away from Bangalore. The family belongs to the lower socioeconomic class and their main occupation is agriculture. Though this is the only Tamil-speaking family, they have cordial relations with neighboring families.

H. S. Narayanan, M.D., is Assistant Professor of Psychiatry, National Institute of Mental Health and Neuro Sciences, Karnataka, India.

A. S. Mahal, M.D., is former Professor of Psychiatry, National Institute of Mental Health and Neuro Sciences, Karnataka, India.

Mr. Kri (husband of Mrs. Kri, who was an inpatient in the family ward) reported an outbreak of a strange disease in his younger brother's family in his village. The family consisted of nine members, that is, the informant's brother, his wife, their six children and one daughter-in-law. Of these, six members were affected with the same epidemic. The entire family was brought to the Mental Hospital, Bangalore (presently the National Institute of Mental Health and Neuro Sciences, Bangalore) and was admitted to the family ward on March 9, 1972.

All the affected members of the family would get an attack of a severe, spasmodic, hurried type of breathing lasting from five to 10 minutes. No sooner did one member get an attack than a chain reaction would follow and all of the other five would get the attack. The attacks would subside in all of them simultaneously.

Patient Mrs. Kup (wife of Mr. M. L., brother of Mr. Kri) suffered from similar episodes 16 years ago, which later induced a chain of similar symptoms in five other family members which was diagnosed as a hysterical outbreak.

Forty-year-old Mrs. Kup is an illiterate housewife who lost her parents at the age of 10 years. She was brought up by her aunt, who was reported to have treated her very affectionately. Her younger brother helps Mrs. Kup's family financially. She attained menarche at the age of 14 and was married at 16. She was disinclined to marry an illiterate villager. Soon after marriage, she pleaded with her husband to leave the village and live in the city. The husband did not agree. Mrs. Kup fell into a wide well in the presence of many people and the husband rescued her. Later, she agreed to live in the village.

Three years after marriage when she gave birth to a son, her sister became jealous as she only had daughters. Four years later, Mrs. Kup had a nightmare during pregnancy. In her dream the deceased sister attacked her and bit her chest. From that time, the patient started having pain in the abdomen, aches all over the body, and weakness. These symptoms used to be worse during subsequent pregnancies and on new moon days and full moon days. The symptoms lasted throughout the day. She and her family believed that the symptoms were due to her deceased sister's wrath.

When her second child was found dead one morning, the family also thought it was due to the sister's wrath. This reinforced her belief, and they started worshipping the deceased sister. A year and a half later, Mrs. Kup delivered her third child. She delivered two more children, each after an interval of a year and a half, but both died in infancy. Four years later she became pregnant for the sixth time. This time, she and her husband prayed at different temples that this child should be a female and should live.

During the fourth month of the sixth pregnancy, the patient one day had a burning sensation in the pit of her stomach. After 5–20 minutes, it ascended upward into her chest and brought on the same severe, spasmodic, hurried type of breathing. This was distressing and lasted for the next 10 minutes. Afterwards, she had no burning sensation but a vague pain all over the abdomen. She complained of pain all over the body and of weakness that lasted for the next two hours. The patient was fully conscious during the episode. From then on, she continued to have three or four every 24 hours, until she delivered the child. After the delivery, the attacks continued, but were less frequent in between pregnancies and more frequent during subsequent pregnancies and on new and full moon days.

Three months before admission to the ward her attacks increased in frequency. A peculiar feature at this time was that, along with her attacks, four of the six children and the daughter-in-law started getting attacks. At home one or the other experienced an attack which set off a chain reaction leaving all of them gasping. During such mass attacks people of her village used to gather around the house and show great concern and sympathy not only verbally but also by providing food, etc.

Other members of Mrs. Kup's family had attacks almost similar to the ones noted in Mrs. Kup and, in fact, these attacks often occurred simultaneously with very little interval between the affected members. Table 1 indicates the other members of the family who had similar attacks arranged in chronological order.

The unaffected members of the family are the husband of the index case (Mrs. Kup), aged 50 years, a son aged 19 years, and a daughter aged three-and-a-half years. These three were in good physical and mental health.

TABLE 1

Sl. No.	Case	Age	Sex	Time of origin of attacks	Relation to Mrs. Kup
1.	R.	8 years	Male	Since 2½ months	Son
2.	Mun.	20 years	Female	Since 3 months	Daughter-in-law
3.	Mut.	12 years	Male	Since 3½ months	Son
4.	Mu.	10 years	Female	Since 4 months	Daughter
5.	Mo.	16 years	Female	Since 5 years	Daughter

COMMENTS

The present study reports observations made regarding a rare phenomenon of epidemic hysteria in a rural family.

In this family, Mrs. Kup, aged 40 years, is the key person. Mrs. Kup transmitted the symptoms to her children. It was ego-syntonic for them, not only because they had similar backgrounds and experiences which led them to be sensitized to one another and think alike, but also because they had been extremely close and a strong emotional bond existed between them. Ehrenwald (1963a, 1963b) has described how psychological contagion may be conducive to the development of similar or dissimilar clinical symptomatology. When similar symptomatology occurred, he referred to it as "homonymic contagion." In Mrs. Kup's family, five other members developed similar illness in the form of a conversion reaction. Only the eldest son developed a different illness corresponding to what Ehrenwald called "heterominic contagion."

Mrs. Mun, daughter-in-law of Mrs. Kup, was the fifth person to develop symptoms. She was disliked by the mother-in-law, who did not allow her to purchase new clothes and made her work excessively. By developing the symptoms, she identified herself with the mother-in-law and other members of the family and derived secondary gain in the form of less work and more attention from the family. Her mother-in-law also became kind to her.

Sirois (1974) has stated that tension between members of the group leads to an epidemic. Faris (1964) proposes a convergent theory which holds that affinities shown by unstable individuals are responsible for outbreaks. To establish this view, it has to be shown what psychopathological traits index cases have, and whether affected and non-affected individuals in the group differ. Schuler and Parenton (1943) noted that their index cases were predominant figures in the group, like Mrs. Kup was in our study. The psychopathological trait in "index case" Mrs. Kup is quite notable. She is an extrovert and lacks control over her emotions. The children who continuously stayed with Mrs. Kup are highly suggestible. This can be seen very well when the family visited a temple; when the third son saw the priest possessed by God, he also started behaving as if he was possessed by God.

Mr. M. L., though head of the family and a hard working man, took little part in running the family and did not assume the role of leadership. Leadership was taken by sick Mrs. Kup who induced illness in the family. The outbreak of the conversion reaction in the family forced Mr. M. L. to assume leadership by taking them to temples and hospitals. He was assisted by his elder brother and his eldest son, who was also sick in a different way.

The nature of epidemic hysteria noted in the present family could be considered an example of the cumulative-outbreak type described by Sirois (1974). The latter has stated that other mechanisms in the interplay of individual and group factors could invoke the triggering by index cases of various conflicts in other members which are subsequently directed into a common pathway.

Waltzer (1963), in his description of a psychotic family, has stated that attitudes communicated to other family members may have the force of an illness. Ehrenwald (1963a, 1963b) observed that patterns of "homonymic contagion" seem to be much less frequent in marriage partners than in pairs of family relations, e.g., in parent and child, sibling and sibling — persons tied together by biological bonds. This is seen in the family under consideration, in which Mrs. Kup's husband was free from illness while all the other children except the youngest one, along with others who were staying in the family, developed illness.

This is the only Tamil-speaking family in the village that migrated from Tamil Nadu. Since Sirois (1974) has stated that isolation and cohesiveness are other group characteristics believed to be important in the conditions that lead to an outbreak of hysteria, this fact may have been important. The family gained more sympathy and assistance from most of the other people living in the village.

It was possible to admit all the members of the family to a family ward and to conduct a family group psychotherapy session with this family separately and along with other families in the ward twice a week. At the end it was found that they had sufficiently overcome their subjective feelings. As they were anxious to return home to attend to their agricultural duties, they had to be discharged. A follow-up was made by a personal visit by one of the coauthors (HSN) which revealed that the attacks were minimal during this period. Neighbors as well attested to the improvement.

REFERENCES

Ehrenwald, J. (1963a), Family diagnosis and mechanisms of social defense. *Fam. Proc.*, 2:121.

—— (1963b), *Neurosis in the Family and Patterns of Psychosocial Defense.* New York: Harper & Row.

Faris, R. E. L. (1964), *A Hand Book of Modern Sociology.* Chicago: Rand McNally.

Schuler, E. A. & Parenton, V. J. (1943), A recent epidemic hysteria in Louisiana High School. *J. Soc. Psychol.*, 17:221.

Sirois, F. (1974), Epidemic hysteria. *Acta Psychiat. Scand.*, Suppl. 252.

Waltzer, H. (1963), A psychotic family — folie a deux. *J. Nerv. Ment. Dis.*, 137:67.

Families of Autistic
and Dysphasic Children:
Family Life and Interaction Patterns

DENNIS P. CANTWELL, LORIAN BAKER,
and MICHAEL RUTTER

Since Kanner first described the syndrome of infantile autism in 1943, there has been a continuing controversy over the role of environmental influences, particularly family factors, in the etiology and pathogenesis of the condition. There is now good evidence that autistic children have a basic cognitive defect (Rutter, 1974) that is often associated with evidence of hereditary origin (Folstein and Rutter, 1977) or organic brain dysfunction, as indicated, for example, by epileptic fits (Rutter, 1971). Nevertheless, it remains possible that certain pathogenic psychosocial influences may interact with a biological defect to produce the syndrome of autism. This article is one of a series (Cox, Rutter, Newman, et al., 1975; Cantwell, Baker, and Rutter, 1977; Lennox, Callias, and Rutter, 1977) reporting a set of studies designed to investigate that possibility. The present report is primarily concerned with patterns of family life and parent-child interaction.

A number of writers have proposed that there may be deviant patterns of interaction between psychotic children and their parents. Too much stimulation, too little stimulation, inadequate structuring of the environment, lack of family roles and identities, and lack of shared family pleasure have all been postulated as figuring in the pathogenesis

Dennis P. Cantwell, M.D., is a Professor of Child Psychiatry at the University of California, Los Angeles, Department of Psychiatry, Division of Mental Retardation and Child Psychiatry.

Lorian Baker, Ph.D., is a Research Associate at the University of California, Los Angeles, Department of Psychiatry, Division of Mental Retardation and Child Psychiatry.

Michael Rutter, M.D., is a Professor of Child Psychiatry at the Institute of Psychiatry, London.

of childhood psychosis (Ward, 1970; Quay and Werry, 1972; Cantwell, Baker, and Rutter, 1978a).

Various uncontrolled observations have been used to suggest abnormalities in the families of "schizophrenic" children (Kaufman, Frank, Heims, et al., 1959; Esman, Kohn, and Lyman, 1959; Fraknoi and Ruttenberg, 1971). Others have failed to confirm these findings (Creak and Ini, 1960; Gittelman and Birch, 1967). However, little weight can be attached to either positive or negative findings in the absence of controls (Bender and Grugett, 1956; Klebanoff, 1959; Donnelly, 1960; Singer and Wynne, 1963; Ferreira and Winter, 1965, 1968; Holroyd and McArthur, 1976).

A detailed review of previous studies in this area can be found in a previous publication (Cantwell, Baker, and Rutter, 1978a). The findings as a whole are both contradictory and difficult to interpret. First, the groups studied have been diagnostically heterogeneous and often poorly defined. Few have been specifically concerned with infantile autism. Second, many of the measures have been of uncertain reliability and validity. Third, the control groups have been quite varied and frequently poorly matched. Parental functioning is likely to be influenced by the characteristics of the children as well as by the personalities and experiences of the parents. If the comparison groups of parents have children who differ greatly in either mental level or language skills, family functioning may well differ simply as a consequence of having markedly different children. The fact that one group has been labeled as "patients" whereas the other has not may also influence how parents and children interact. Fourth, most studies have failed to control for the sex of the children, but there are indications that family interaction may be affected by the sex of mentally ill offspring (Lidz, Fleck, Alanen, et al., 1963; Mishler and Waxler, 1968).

There was a need for a controlled study of a rigorously diagnosed group of autistic children with measures that were well designed to tap the aspects of parental functioning thought to be abnormal in autism. Because overt brain damage is most frequent in the case of mentally retarded autistic children, it appeared that psychosocial determinants should be most readily found in the case of autistic children of normal nonverbal intelligence. Goldfarb's (1961) findings support this supposition. Accordingly, a series of investigations were planned to compare such a group of autistic boys with an age-, sex-, IQ-, and language level-matched group of children with a specific developmental disorder of receptive language (Bartak, Rutter, and Cox, 1975; Cantwell, Baker, and Rutter, 1978b). Although the groups were closely comparable on the items used in matching, they differed very greatly in terms of the social and behavioral features characteristic of autism (Bartak, Rutter, and Cox, 1975, 1977).

A previous article reported an interview and questionnaire study of parental characteristics in these two groups of families (Cox, Rutter, Newman, et al., 1975); a comparison article reports a detailed analysis of mother-child linguistic interaction (Cantwell, Baker, and Rutter, 1977); while this article reports a detailed interview and home observation assessment of family life and interaction patterns.

METHODS

SAMPLE

The subjects of the present study consist of the families of 29 boys, aged six years and six months to 11 years and six months, with a nonverbal IQ of at least 70 and a disorder of language comprehension that had been present since infancy and that was not due to overt neurological disorder or peripheral deafness (fuller details of sample selection are given elsewhere [Bartak, Rutter, and Cox, 1975; Cantwell, Baker, and Rutter, 1978b]). Fifteen boys met the diagnostic criteria (Rutter, 1971) for infantile autism: a profound and general failure to develop social relationships, ritualistic and compulsive phenomena, and a serious disorder of language. The other 14 boys showed an uncomplicated receptive developmental language disorder; they are referred to as the "dysphasic" group. The two groups of boys were closely similar in age, nonverbal IQ, and level of speech (Cantwell, Baker, and Rutter, 1978b).

The original sample of children studied by Bartak and his colleagues (Bartak, Rutter, and Cox, 1975) consisted of 19 autistic and 23 dysphasic children. However, the dysphasic children tended to improve more in language and so, to better match the groups at the time of study, the six dysphasic children with least receptive language retardation were dropped from the investigation. Two autistic and two dysphasic children had moved overseas or were untraceable and could not be included. The families of two autistic children were unwilling or unable to participate in this part of the study. This left 15 autistic children and 15 dysphasic children for the follow-up study of families of which the present investigation forms a part (Cantwell, Baker, and Rutter, 1977; Cantwell, Baker, and Rutter, 1978b). At the last moment, one of the families of dysphasic children was unable to participate due to illness in the family, leaving a final subject population of 15 families of autistic boys and 14 families of dysphasic boys.

The parents and children were of closely comparable age in the two groups, but the autistic group contained a higher proportion of professional and managerial families (80 per cent versus 46 per cent).

Measures

Standard Day Interview

The standard day interview developed by Douglas and his colleagues (Douglas, Lawson, Cooper, et al., 1968; Lawson and Ingelby, 1974) was used to obtain a detailed account of the children's daily activities together with measures of the frequency, nature, and intensity of the children's interactions with other family members. With this technique, the interviewer takes the parents step-by-step chronologically through the events of the previous 24 hours (having previously ensured that the day was not atypical due to visitors, illness, etc.). Detailed information is obtained on a minute-by-minute basis with respect to what the child was doing, how long the activity lasted, who was with the child, the nature of any personal interactions, and whether any interruptions or additional events had occurred. A tape recording of the interview was made and transcribed for coding.

Four major groups of behaviors were used: activities (playing games, reading, etc.), basic care (eating, toileting, etc.), outings (shopping, visiting, etc.), and other (tantrums, nothing particular, etc.). All persons who had contact with the child were coded. Five different levels of interaction were coded: (1) concentrated, (2) continuous, (3) available, (4) available but not used, and (5) separate.

Concentrated interactions were those in which at least two of the following three conditions applied: (1) there was close physical contact between the child and the person concerned, (2) the child and the person concerned were sharing the activity, and (3) the child and person concerned were giving the activity and each other their full attention.

Continuous interactions were those that fell short of the criteria for "concentrated" but that involved the person giving the child a good deal of attention. This category was usually used for playing with other children, going out visiting, being visited, going out shopping, going for walks, and some mealtimes.

Available interactions were those that met one of the following criteria: (1) the child was being supervised, someone was around and easily reached, and contacts were possible such as through a doorway, (2) another child or adult was in the room and awake and was being talked to or approached, if only occasionally, or (3) there was a high intensity of interaction with someone else, but a third person was still around and available for interaction.

Available but not used interactions were defined as the child and another adult or child being in situations where contact was possible (as for available) but, despite an attempt by the other person, no interaction occurred.

Separate was scored if the child was alone and communication was only possible by shouting or crying or by the mother coming to the child or vice versa. If the child was inside, doors must have been shut.

A weighted qualitative interaction score for persons interacting with the child was obtained by giving a weighting of 4 for concentrated, 3 for continuous, 2 for available and available not used, and 1 for separate. The interaction score was then the sum of the products of these weights and the minutes of each type of interaction with the child. A weighted interaction score for the child was obtained similarly by using the child's minutes of interaction with the same weights, except that available not used was weighted 1 rather than 2. The reason for this is that available not used is equivalent to available from the perspective of the person *giving* the attention, but equivalent to separate from the perspective of the child *receiving* the attention.

In these various ways, the type, quantity, and quality of interaction could all be assessed. Douglas et al. (1968) have shown the measures to have a high interrater reliability and to agree well with similar measures obtained from direct observation.

Positive Interaction as Reported by Parents

A more global view of parent-child interaction that included less frequent, as well as everyday, activities was obtained by systematically asking the parent about all parent-child interactions that might be pleasurable to the child that had occurred over the previous week. The scale used was a slightly modified version of that developed by Brown and Rutter (1966). It has been shown to have a high interrater reliability (over + .90). Also, it has been found that there is good agreement (r = .72 to .78) between independent accounts from the mother and father.

Specific enquiry was made about playing games, reading to the child, roughhousing, doing things with the child, helping the child, the child helping mother or father, and outings with mother or father. An interaction was given a score of one point if it lasted an hour or less, and two points if it lasted an hour or more. Separate scores for these activities were obtained for mother and father together with a total score for all positive interactions over the course of a week.

Ittleson Scales

The Ittleson family interaction scales were developed by Behrens et al. (1969) to measure qualitative aspects of family relationships, parent-child interaction, and style of child care. The data for rating the scales derive from observations made by one of us (D.C.) during a four- to six-hour home visit that included a family mealtime. During the visit, parents were encouraged to adhere to their usual family routines as much as possible. Mothers and fathers were separately evaluated according to eight seven-point scales concerning spontaneity of interactions, decisiveness, consistency of emotional relatedness, mode of relating to the child, control of the child, imposition of routines, anticipation of the child's needs, and meeting the demands of the child. Behrens et al. (1969) provide anchoring descriptions for points 1, 3, 5, and 7 on the scales. In each case, 1 represents very poor functioning and 7 is optimal. Interrater reliability is reported as generally good; validity is based on a patient sample using comparisons with the judgments of caseworkers who have treated the families over a prolonged period (Behrens et al., 1969).

Time-Sampled Measures of Mother-Child Interaction

During the four- to six-hour period of home observation, 90 minutes were set aside for the systematic observation of mother-child interaction, using quantitative measures developed by Hemsley et al. (1978). The 90-minute period was chosen as one in which the mother was free of obligations (such as cooking a meal) and would normally be with her child. No restrictions were placed on activities, and mothers were asked to do whatever they would normally do at that time.

The observation schedule included 36 categories of behavior, 17 for the child's activities and 19 for parental behavior. Behavior was rated every 10 seconds on specially constructed sheets laid out for minimal hand movement and association of related categories. Each sheet was divided into 12 time periods, giving a total observation time of two-minutes continuous recording per sheet. After each two-minute period, there was a 30-second rest pause. Each observation session lasted for about 90 minutes, including time spent talking with the mother, setting up equipment, and allowing both mother and child to become accustomed to the observer's presence. Forty minutes of actual recorded time was obtained during each observation session. Details on the development, reliability, and validity of the observation schedule are outlined more fully elsewhere by Hemsley et al. (1978).

Eysenck Personality Inventory

Lastly, both parents completed the Eysenck Personality Inventory (Eysenck and Eysenck, 1964). This measure was chosen because it specifically examines introversion, which has been linked by some authors to parents of autistic children. Other measures of personality had already been obtained in an earlier part of the investigation (Cox, Rutter, Newman, et al., 1975).

RESULTS

STANDARD DAY MEASURES

Table 1 reports the standard day findings on the types of activities undertaken by the children in the two groups. As expected from the nature of the children's handicaps, marked differences were found. Whereas autistic children engaged in no cooperative games with people (such as cards or board games), dysphasic children did so for more than an hour a day on average. Autistic children also watched very little television, whereas dysphasic children did so for more than two hours a day. In contrast, autistic children spent much more time playing on their own and more time being read to, looking at books, or listening to or reciting rhymes. There were no other statistically significant differences between the groups.

The kinds of interactions (concentrated, continuous, etc.) that the children engaged in were compared, both in terms of number of minutes spent and percentage of overall time spent, between the autistic and dysphasic groups. The two groups did not differ significantly on any of the various degrees of intensity of interaction. Autistic and dysphasic children experienced almost exactly the same amount (and proportions) of concentrated, continuous, and available interactions with other people.

These findings indicate that the interaction experiences of the two groups of children are very similar in intensity. However, it is also necessary to consider *who* provides the interaction with the children. The data were therefore reanalyzed from the perspective of the *providers* of the interaction rather than the receiving child.

The main difference between the groups in interaction patterns was that dysphasic children had very much greater interaction with siblings and with other children (Table 2). This applied to all intensities of interaction, although the differences were only statistically significant with concentrated and available interactions. Thus, on the average,

TABLE 1
CHILDREN'S ACTIVITIES AS DETERMINED BY
STANDARD DAY ANALYSIS

| | Duration, min/24 hr. | | | |
| | Autistic | | Dysphasic | |
Kinds of Activities	Mean	SD	Mean	SD
Games with people	0.00	0.00	71.43	110.79*
Listening to rhymes and looking at books	97.14	97.36	6.79	10.30
Playing on own	78.21	79.85	17.86	25.25‡
Active playing with toys, riding bikes, etc.	15.36	24.53	72.86	102.28
Sleeping	604.64	66.95	593.21	52.57
School	246.43	226.64	230.00	243.14
Errands and outings	82.14	76.43	113.57	138.67
Television	21.07	48.29	125.00	94.32†
Basic care	151.43	60.27	130.36	46.76
All other activities	143.58	100.51	78.92	66.45
Total	1,440.00		1,440.00	

*$p < .05$
†$p < .002$
‡$p < .02$

siblings and other young people spent three-and-a-half hours a day in concentrated interaction with dysphasic children, in comparison with only half an hour with autistic children. This difference is almost certainly a consequence of autistic children's very serious difficulties in peer relationships.

There were no differences between groups in the pattern of fathers' interactions with the children or in the pattern of other adults' interactions. However, a somewhat different distribution did exist for the mothers. A significantly higher proportion of the time of mothers of dysphasic children was spent in available interaction, whereas the mothers of autistic children spent twice as much time in concentrated interaction (this latter difference fell just short of statistical significance).

TABLE 2
SIBLINGS' AND OTHER CHILDREN'S INTERACTIONS

	Autistic		Dysphasic	
	Mean	SD	Mean	SD
Duration, min				
Concentrated	36.07	50.58	209.64	240.97*
Continuous	86.79	122.34	296.43	471.79
Available	42.86	65.48	290.00	234.59†
Available, not used	10.00	37.42	0.00	0.00
Total	175.72	194.60	796.07	596.46
Frequency, %				
Concentrated	20.53	27.45	26.33	29.10
Continuous	49.39	39.41	37.24	26.76
Available	24.39	17.67	36.43	26.71
Available, not used	5.64	26.46	0.00	0.00
Total "weighted" interaction score	510.36	567.02	2,358.93	1,173.00†

*$p < .02$
†$p < .002$

POSITIVE INTERACTION

Parent-child interaction was also assessed on the basis of parental interview data concerning the frequency of various specified activities that the child might consider positive or pleasurable. The mothers of autistic children spent rather more time reading to them, but there was no significant difference between the groups in the amount of other types of interaction. Nevertheless, although not reflected in these measures, the types of games played were very different in that only the dysphasic children were able to participate in games involving complex rules or prolonged cooperation (Table 1). The groups differed more strikingly in father-child interaction. The fathers in the autistic group spent nearly twice as much time overall with their children. Significantly more time was spent in roughhousing or other forms of boisterous play.

ITTLESON SCALES

Of 36 comparisons on the Ittleson scales (Behrens et al., 1969), only one gave rise to a statistically significant difference (fathers of autistic children were more consistent in emotional relatedness). As this is no more than expected by chance, probably it has no meaning. Both groups of mothers showed a moderately high level of functioning, with an average score of about 5½ (7 is optimal); fathers had slightly higher scores.

TIME-SAMPLED MEASURES OF MOTHER-CHILD INTERACTION

The systematic time-sampled observations provided a very detailed portrait of mother-child interaction. Maternal activities were sub-divided into those that involved the child in some way (through tasks, play, or general care) and those that did not (i.e., mother getting on with her own work, doing things with other people, etc.). In both groups, mothers spent about two thirds of their time involved with the child (Table 3). Most of this involved some kind of "task" (this category included making or building things, completing puzzles, and the like). There were no differences between the groups in this respect. Ratings were also made on the mothers' facial expression during interactions. In both groups, most were classified as neutral, and negative expression was very rarely rated. Again, the groups did not differ in this respect.

Each item of the mothers' speech was classified according to its content (i.e., a frequency analysis rather than a measure of duration). The categories of content were chosen to represent the different types of verbal interaction with respect to their impact on the child. Thus, "that's good, Peter" would be coded as approving; "no, that doesn't go there" as correcting; and "take that out of your mouth" as directing. Most of what was said by the mothers in both groups fell into the neutral or directing/distracting categories, and there were no significant differences with any of the comparisons (Table 4). The total number of maternal communications to the children was similar in the two groups. Not many physical contacts (that is, actually touching the child) by the mothers of either autistic or dysphasic children were made, and almost all of them were positive in tone (i.e., an affectionate arm around the shoulder rather than a smack).

PERSONALITY MEASURES

The Eysenck Personality Inventory yields extroversion, neuroticism, and lie scores. There were no between-group differences for either mothers or fathers on any of these measures.

In view of the frequent clinical observations that the parents of

TABLE 3
MOTHERS' ACTIVITIES AND INTERACTIONS
DURING HOME OBSERVATION*

| | Duration, s | | | |
| | Autistic | | Dysphasic | |
	Mean	SD	Mean	SD
Not involved				
Ignores child	215.71	335.00	130.71	163.92
Does own task	32.14	99.55	87.14	170.76
Is out of room	255.00	443.29	217.14	273.96
Interacts with other family members	235.00	315.10	381.43	364.41
Interacts with observer	58.57	134.73	37.15	114.65
Total	796.42	692.32	853.57	536.44
Involved				
Doing task with child	822.14	688.13	1,231.43	799.56
Playing with child	150.71	321.59	72.14	203.55
Attending to child	273.57	283.24	162.86	253.06
Total	1,603.58	692.32	1,546.43	536.44
Facial expression				
Positive	372.14	378.69	200.71	236.03
Negative	0.71	2.67	10.71	20.56
Neutral	1,230.73	551.74	1,335.01	570.11

*All not significant (Mann-Whitney U test).

autistic children include a disproportionate number with odd personalities, a subjective assessment of this was made. Odd personalities were noted for a minority of parents in both groups, but were somewhat more common in the families with an autistic child (four fathers and two mothers compared with one and one, respectively, in the dysphasic group). The oddities were not the same in all parents of autistic children. Thus, one father was a rather distant, controlled sort of person who showed few feelings and took little part in family activities; another father appeared to be driving, intrusive, and rather touchy;

TABLE 4
MOTHERS' SPEECH AND PHYSICAL CONTACTS
DURING HOME OBSERVATION*

| | No. of Occurrences | | | |
| | Autistic | | Dysphasic | |
	Mean	SD	Mean	SD
Speech				
Approving	3.38	6.67	1.64	3.41
Disapproving	2.36	3.61	2.14	2.54
Neutral	61.21	45.94	89.86	31.98
Directing or distracting	32.50	25.99	38.36	25.20
Confirming	16.50	22.48	12.07	10.07
Correcting	9.07	11.65	8.71	11.49
Gestures	1.57	3.13	0.36	1.08
Total	126.59	71.59	153.14	53.57
Physical contacts				
Positive	12.14	20.35	12.00	24.77
Negative	2.64	5.62	0.14	0.36
Neutral	1.14	2.21	1.79	4.25
Total	15.92	23.30	13.93	24.72

*All not significant (Mann-Whitney U test).

and a mother showed gross hypochondriacal traits together with a decidedly odd pressuring style of social interaction. In the dysphasic group, one father and one mother were observed to have odd personalities. The mother was a socially withdrawn individual with few social contacts or friends, and the father was addicted to amphetamines. These ratings were unstandardized and could not be made blind to whether the child was autistic or dysphasic. Nevertheless, they were generally in keeping with the impressions of those most closely concerned with the children's clinical care.

SOCIAL CLASS DIFFERENCES

The one difference between groups that could have distorted the findings was the greater proportion of professional/managerial families among those with autistic children. This was unlikely to constitute an important bias in that previous studies had shown that the measures used were not strongly associated with social class in ways relevant to our findings. Thus, Lawson and Ingleby (1974) found few social class associations with the standard day measures, although upper-class parents tended to have more intensive interaction with their children over shorter periods of time. Rutter (in press) found no consistent associations between positive interaction and social class in two general population studies. Schlieper (1975) reported very few class differences with respect to mother-child interaction observed at home. Nevertheless, it was important to check for possible social class biases in our own data. The standard day measures, the positive interaction scores, the Ittleson scales scores, and the home observation measures were all compared between upper- and lower-social-class parents. No social class differences were found in any of the measures, and it is clear that controlling for social class would make no substantial difference to the findings.

COMMENT

Our analyses of family life and interaction patterns, using a good range of reliable and sensitive indices, have shown very few differences between families of autistic children and families of dysphasic children. Moreover, the very few differences found reflected either the disparate handicaps of the children or suggested marginally "better" functioning in the families from the autistic group. Thus, the finding that autistic children engaged in no cooperative games and had much less interaction with other children is obviously a consequence of their profound social disability (however that was caused). On the other hand, the greater positive interaction between fathers and children and the more consistent emotional relatedness of fathers could be interpreted as indicating better functioning. However, it would be most unwise to read much into the few differences as the great majority of the comparisons showed the two groups of families to be closely similar. The parents interacted with the children with broadly similar intensity over similar periods of time, there was similar frequency of positive interactions with mothers, a similar quality of family interactions on the Ittleson scales, and similar types and degree of mother-child interaction as assessed by the detailed time-sampled home observations.

Deliberately, our measures were chosen to tap a variety of aspects of family interaction over differing time periods. The time-sampled observations provided a very high-power focus on the minutiae of mother-child interaction over 10-second periods; the standard day interview covered a broader range of everyday interactions; and the positive interaction measure enabled a coverage of a range of weekly activities. Systematic detailed interviewing, standardized home observations, and interpretive clinical judgments were all used to ensure an adequate coverage of the variety of ways in which family interaction might be deviant or maladaptive. Furthermore, every effort was made to use measures that were relevant and clinically sensitive but also reliable and valid. Accordingly, it seems highly probable that our finding of almost no differences in family interaction between autistic and dysphasic groups is a valid and meaningful reflection of the real state of affairs.

Comparisons with previous studies are difficult because of differences both in the definition of groups and in the measures used. Most systematic and well-controlled studies of the families of autistic children have been similarly negative (Pitfield and Oppenheim, 1964; DeMyer et al., 1972; Byassee and Murrell, 1975; Cox et al., 1975; Cantwell, Baker, and Rutter, 1977), although the measures in all cases were rather different from those employed here.

The most directly relevant studies with findings very different to ours are those by Behrens, Meyers, and Goldfarb (Behrens and Goldfarb, 1958; Meyers and Goldfarb, 1961, 1962), which also used home observations of family interaction. They found poor functioning to be much more common in the families of "childhood schizophrenics" than in those of normal children. It is important to consider why the results of the two groups of studies differ.

First, there are diagnostic differences. This study was concerned with infantile autism whereas Goldfarb's group used a broader and more heterogeneous group of "schizophrenic" children, only some of whom were likely to meet the criteria for autism. Almost all of the previous systematic studies that have shown abnormalities in family functioning have been concerned with a widely defined concept of childhood schizophrenia or psychosis. Therefore, it appears likely that, insofar as family pathology is important, it is so for nonautistic psychotic disorders in childhood.

Second, there are sampling differences. The studies of Goldfarb's group have been largely restricted to the families of schizophrenic children in *residential* care, whereas ours have not. It remains uncertain what biasing may have followed this restriction.

Third, Goldfarb's group used a control group of "average" public school children (Meyers and Goldfarb, 1961), which meant that controls did not have any kind of developmental or behavioral handicap. This noncomparability is likely to have introduced important distortions because of the probability that parents will be influenced in their behavior by the characteristics of their children (Bell, 1968, 1971). In contrast, we used a comparison group that was nonautistic and entirely different in behavioral characteristics (Bartak, Rutter, and Cox, 1975), but that shared the features of "patient-status" and of having a handicapped child.

Fourth, Goldfarb's group used only judgmental measures that were open to rater bias. On the other hand, we employed a wide range of measures that were both quantitative and qualitative, objective and subjective. The fact that the results of all measures pointed in the same direction adds considerable confidence to the conclusions.

For all these reasons, we conclude that the families of autistic children are *not* characterized by any particular abnormalities in family life or interaction. Other studies have similarly found that they do not differ in warmth, emotional responsiveness, sociability, parental mental disorder, or early stresses (Cox et al., 1975) and do not differ in patterns of mother-child communication (Cantwell, Baker, and Rutter, 1977). In short, there is considerable evidence *against* the suggestion that autism is psychogenically caused by abnormal family experiences. Of course, it must be said that, necessarily, all the observational data refer to a time *after* the child has become autistic; it could be that there were transient abnormalities in family functioning that *preceded* the onset of autism but did not persist afterwards. On the other hand, there is no satisfactory evidence that anything of this kind occurred.

It should also be added that the finding that autistic children do not seem to have been reared in abnormal families does *not* mean that their family environment is optimal for their development. Handicapped children may require rather special handling different from that needed by normal children. It is perhaps for this reason that treatment methods based on altering the ways autistic children are handled have proved effective (Hemsley et al., 1978).

We also obtained measures on parental personality. These showed that the parents of autistic children did *not* differ in terms of either neuroticism or extraversion. Previous investigations have shown the same results (Kolvin, Garside, and Kidd, 1971; Netley, Lockyer, and Greenbaum, 1975). It has also been found that parents do not differ in obsessionality or neurotic features (Cox et al., 1975) or in thought disorder (Lennox, Callias, and Rutter, 1977). In short, standardized tests have regularly failed to identify any abnormalities of personality in the parents of autistic children. On the other hand, clinical observations have frequently pointed to oddities of personality in a minority of parents. Our own findings are in keeping with this. Of course, the observations have been neither blind nor standardized, and for this reason must be regarded with considerable caution, if not skepticism. On the other hand, the evidence from twin studies (Folstein and Rutter, 1977) suggests that hereditary influences may involve some kind of genetically determined oddity of personality that is associated with autism and that may be found in a few (but only a few) parents of autistic children. However, this has *not* yet been demonstrated and it should be emphasized that it is only a suggestion. If confirmed, it is most unlikely to carry any implications for psychogenesis because of the negative findings on parent-child interaction and family functioning. Rather, it might represent either a response to the very considerable burdens of having an autistic child or some kind of genetic factor.

REFERENCES

Bartak, L., Rutter, M., & Cox, A. (1975), A comparative study of infantile autism and specific developmental receptive language disorder: I. The children. *Brit. J. Psychiat.*, 126:127–145.

——— ——— ——— (1977), A comparative study of infantile autism and specific developmental receptive language disorder: III. Discriminant function analysis. *J. Autism Child Schiz.*, 7:383–396.

Behrens, M. C. & Goldfarb, W. (1958), A study of patterns of interaction of families of schizophrenic children in residential treatment. *Amer. J. Orthopsychiat.*, 28:300–312.

——— Meyers, D., Goldfarb, W., et al. (1969), The Henry Ittleson Center family interaction scales. *Genet. Psychol. Monogr.*, 80:203–295.

Bell, R. (1968), A reinterpretation of the direction of effects in studies of socialization. *Psychol. Rev.*, 75:81–95.

——— (1971), Stimulus control of parent or caretaker behavior by offspring. *Dev. Psychol.*, 4:63–72.

Bender, L. & Grugett, A. (1956), A study of certain epidemiological factors in a group of children with childhood schizophrenia. *Amer. J. Orthopsychiat.*, 26:131–145.

Brown, G. & Rutter, M. (1966), The measurement of family activities and relationships: A methodological study. *Hum. Relat.*, 19:241–263.

Byassee, J. & Murrell, S. (1975), Interaction patterns in families of autistic, disturbed, and normal chilidren. *Amer. J. Orthopsychiat.*, 45:473–478.

Cantwell, D., Baker, L., & Rutter, M. (1977), Families of autistic and dysphasic children: II. Mothers' speech to the children. *J. Autism Child Schiz.*, 7:313–327.

——— ——— ——— (1978a), Family factors in the syndrome of infantile autism. In: *Autism: A Reappraisal of Concepts and Treatment*, ed. M. Rutter & E. Schopler. New York: Plenum, pp. 269–296.

——— ——— ——— (1978b), A comparative study of infantile autism and developmental receptive language disorder: IV. Syntactical and functional analysis of language. *J. Child Psychol. Psychiat.*, 19:351–362.

Cox, A., Rutter, M., Newman, S., et al. (1975), A comparative study of autism and specific developmental receptive language disorder: II. Parental characteristics. *Brit. J. Psychiat.*, 126:146–159.

Creak, M. & Ini, S. (1960), Families of psychotic children. *J. Child Psychol. Psychiat.*, 1:156–175.

DeMyer, M., Pontius, W., Norton, J., et al. (1972), Parental practices and innate activity in autistic and brain-damaged infants. *J. Autism Child Schiz.*, 2:49–66.

Donnelly, E. (1960), The quantitative analysis of parent behavior toward psychotic children and their siblings. *Genet. Psychol. Monogr.*, 62:331–376.

Douglas, J., Lawson, A., Cooper, J., et al. (1968), Family interaction and the activities of young children. *J. Child Psychol. Psychiat.*, 19:157–171.

Esman, A., Kohn, M., & Lyman, L. (1959), The family of the schizophrenic child. *Amer. J. Orthopsychiat.*, 29:455–459.

Eysenck, H. J. & Eysenck, S. (1964), *Manual of the Eysenck Personality Inventory*. London: University of London Press.

Ferreira, A. & Winter, W. (1965), Family interaction and decision-making. *Arch. Gen. Psychiat.*, 13:214–233.

——— ——— (1968), Decision-making in normal and abnormal two-child families. *Fam. Proc.*, 7:17–36.

Folstein, S. & Rutter, M. (1977), Infantile autism: A genetic study of 21 twin pairs. *J. Child Psychol. Psychiat.*, 18:297–321.

Fraknoi, J. & Ruttenberg, B. (1971), Formulation of the dynamic economic factors underlying infantile autism. *J. Amer. Acad. Child Psychiat.*, 10:713–738.

Gittelman, M. & Birch, H. G. (1967), Childhood schizophrenia: Intellect, neurologic status, perinatal risk, prognosis and family pathology. *Arch. Gen. Psychiat.*, 17:16–25.

Goldfarb, W. (1961), *Childhood Schizophrenia*. Cambridge, Mass.: Harvard University Press.

Hemsley, R., Howlin, P., Berger, M., et al. (1978), Treating autistic children in a family context. In: *Autism: A Reappraisal of Concepts and Treatment*, ed. M. Rutter & E. Schopler. New York: Plenum, pp. 379–412.

Holroyd, J. & McArthur, D. (1976), Mental retardation and stress on the parents: A contrast between Down's syndrome and childhood autism. *Amer. J. Ment. Defic.*, 80:431–446.

Kaufman, I., Frank, T., Heims, L., et al. (1959), Parents of schizophrenic children: Workshop, 1958: Four types of defense in mothers and fathers of schizophrenic children. *Amer. J. Orthopsychiat.*, 29:460–472.

Klebanoff, L. (1959), Parental attitudes of mothers of schizophrenic, brain-injured and retarded and normal children. *Amer. J. Orthopsychiat.*, 29:445–454.

Kolvin, I., Garside, R., & Kidd, J. (1971), Studies in the childhood psychoses: IV. Parental personality and attitudes. *Brit. J. Psychiat.*, 118:403–406.

Lawson, A. & Ingleby, J. D. (1974), Daily routines of pre-school children: Effects of age, birth order, sex and social class, and developmental correlates. *Psychol. Med.*, 4:399–415.

Lennox, C., Callias, M., & Rutter, M. (1977), Cognitive characteristics of parents of autistic children. *J. Autism Child Schiz.*, 7:243–261.

Lidz, T., Fleck, S., Alanen, Y. O., et al. (1963), Schizophrenic patients and their siblings. *Psychiat.*, 26:1–18.

Meyers, D. & Goldfarb, W. (1961), Childhood schizophrenia: Studies of per-
plexity in mothers of schizophrenic chilidren. *Amer. J. Orthopsychiat.*,
31:551–564.

———— ———— (1962), Psychiatric appraisals of parents and siblings of schizophrenic children. *Amer. J. Psychiat.*, 118:902–908.

Mishler, E. G. & Waxler, N. E. (1968), *Interaction of Families: An Experimental Study of Family Processes and Schizophrenia.* New York: Wiley.

Netley, C., Lockyer, L., & Greenbaum, G. (1975), Parental characteristics in
relation to diagnosis and neurological status in childhood psychosis. *Brit. J.
Psychiat.*, 127:440–444.

Pitfield, M. & Oppenheim, A. (1964), Child rearing attitudes of mothers of psychotic children. *J. Child Psychol. Psychiat.*, 5:51–57.

Quay, H. & Werry, J., eds. (1972), *Psychopathological Disorders of Childhood.*
New York: Wiley.

Rutter, M. (1971), The description and classification of infantile autism. In:
Infantile Autism: Proceedings of the Indiana University Colloquium, ed.
D. Churchill, G. Alpern, & M. DeMyer. Springfield, Ill: C. C Thomas.

———— (1974), The development of infantile autism. *Psychol. Med.*, 4:147–163.

———— ed. (in press), *The Child, His Family and the Community.* London:
Wiley.

Schlieper, A. (1975), Mother-child interaction observed at home. *Amer. J.
Orthopsychiat.*, 45:468–472.

Singer, M. & Wynne, L. (1963), Differentiating characteristics of parents of
childhood neurotics and young adult schizophrenics. *Amer. J. Psychiat.*,
12:234–243.

Ward, A. J. (1970), Early infantile autism: Diagnosis, etiology and treatment.
Psychol. Bull., 73:350–362.

Developments in
Family Treatment of Schizophrenia

JULIAN P. LEFF

DEVELOPMENTS IN FAMILY TREATMENT OF SCHIZOPHRENIA

Social therapies go through predictable swings of popularity. When a new form of therapy is introduced it takes time to gather momentum. But psychiatrists are avid for new possibilities of helping their patients and popularity grows apace, fed by the publication of enthusiastic single case reports. Any new treatment is usually conceived of in relation to a specific condition, but clinical workers are always anxious to experiment and the new therapy eventually reaches the peak of its popularity as a panacea given to any patient with any one of the whole range of psychiatric illnesses. It may even spread outside the designated sick population and be enthusiastically taken up by the apparently healthy. Psychoanalysis and encounter groups are examples of this overspill. After a time this overexposure breeds its own penalties. Therapists find that many patients fail to respond to the treatment and disillusionment sets in. The popularity of the treatment slumps to an all-time low and is only applied by practitioners who have a great investment in it, either because it reinforces their aetiological theories of psychiatric illness, or because they have spent time and money in acquiring the techniques.

The boom and slump in popularity of a social therapy often extend over several years, because response, or lack of it, in an individual case may not become apparent for many months. It takes even longer for scientific evaluation of social therapies to appear in journals. There are several reasons for this—the methodological problems of this kind of

Julian P. Leff, M.D., M.R.C.P., F.R.C.Psych., is Assistant Director, Medical Research Council Social Psychiatry Unit, Institute of Psychiatry, London, England.

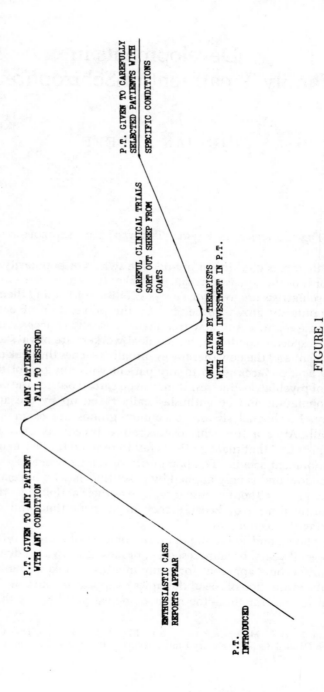

FIGURE 1

The Rise and Fall of Panacea Therapy (P.T.)

research are formidable and not all of them have yet been satisfactorily solved. The research involves a major investment of time and effort and the people with the necessary resources are not the ones who introduce new therapies or in general who even practice them. The attention and interest of serious research workers are not usually captured by new social therapies until they have hit the peak of their popularity. Even then it takes several years to conduct a worthwhile study including follow-up, so that there is a big time lag before the results of such work are brought to the public view (allow at least an additional year for the process of publication). By that time the slump in popularity is well on its way, and may have reached rock bottom.

As time goes by, well-conducted evaluative studies accumulate and increasingly sophisticated methods are employed. It becomes clear that a social therapy does work, but only for specific psychiatric conditions and only with particular kinds of patients. The indications for its use become increasingly well-defined and its popularity rises again, but levels off at a plateau, the limits of which are defined by the proportion of patients shown to benefit from its application.

If we consider particular examples of social therapies, psychoanalysis has gone over the peak in the United States and is now suffering a decline in popularity. However few, if any, evaluative studies have appeared as yet. Behavior therapy is close to its peak, but already evaluative studies are plentiful, probably because treatment takes weeks rather than years. It is becoming clear that schizophrenics are unlikely to derive lasting benefit from social skills training, in contrast to phobic and obsessional patients (Falloon et al., 1977). Such studies are beginning to establish the specificity of behavior therapy. Family therapy is well on its way to the peak of popularity in the United States, although it has only recently been introduced in England. It seems to take at least 10 years for new therapies to cross the Atlantic.

Family therapy was introduced in the 1950s and at that time was mainly concerned with the families of schizophrenic patients (Jackson, 1959). It grew partly out of the theoretical propositions by Bateson on the "double-bind," Lidz on "marital skew" and "marital schism," and Wynne on "pseudomutuality," all of which implicated the family as the prime aetiological agent in the development of schizophrenia. It seemed logical to assume from these theories that correcting the distortions in these families, whether of verbal or emotional communication, or of role performance, would halt the progress of the schizophrenia. As Haley (1962) wrote in his characteristically pithy way, "It became apparent that it was not entirely reasonable to have a child driven mad by his family and then hospitalize him and get him on his feet and send

him right back into his family to be driven mad again." This preoccupation of family therapists with schizophrenia is reflected in the first
volume of *Family Process* issued in 1962. Exactly half the papers (11 out
of 22) in that volume are concerned with schizophrenia. By 1975, 13
years later, the proportion of papers dealing with schizophrenia has
dropped to 10 per cent (3 out of 29). This could reflect two processes: A
disillusionment with the effectiveness of family therapy for schizophrenics, and a broadening of family therapy to include many other
conditions. To determine the relative contributions of these two trends,
we would need to know the absolute numbers of families with members
suffering from schizophrenic and nonschizophrenic illness who received
family therapy in 1962 and 1975. These data are not readily at hand,
but my impression from the literature is that both processes are certainly operating. The disillusionment with family therapy for schizophrenia
is documented in several sources. Massie and Beels (1972) quote Murray
Bowen as declaring in 1969 that he had never changed the fundamental
dynamics of a family with a schizophrenic member, even with years of
contact. Lidz (1975) wrote that conjoint family therapy "can prepare
the way for the reevaluation and intrapsychic reorganization of parental introjects, but it cannot by itself undo the intrapsychic distortions
and disturbances that have resulted from many years of faulty intrafamilial transactions." Rubinstein (1974) went even further in
declaring, "One of our earliest preconceptions, which proved to be unwarranted with the passage of time and our increase in experience, was
that schizophrenic behavior could easily be modified if we treated the
family conjointly, and if we helped the members sort out some of their
distorted interpersonal dynamics." What a contrast between the enthusiasm of the early pioneering family therapists and their current
pessimism. Is this an inevitable consequence of the intransigence of the
families of schizophrenics, or can something be salvaged from the wreck
of these fine hopes? In order to answer this question we need to consider
a number of fundamental issues: (1) Is there any evidence that families
cause schizophrenia? (2) Is it useful to conceive of the family as a
system? (3) What is the aim of family therapy? (4) Does family therapy
work for any kinds of families? (5) Does family therapy work for
families of schizophrenics? These issues are clearly interrelated and not
easily separable, but for the sake of orderliness I shall deal with them
one by one.

1. Is There Any Evidence that Families Cause Schizophrenia?

As family therapy developed largely out of the belief that parents cause schizophrenia in their offspring, it is vital to consider the evidence on this point. Hirsch and Leff (1975) reviewed studies relating to abnormalities detected in the parents of schizophrenics. They surveyed over 200 papers and books including all the major contributions to the field. They found no reliable supporting evidence for the concept of the cold, aloof, hostile "schizophrenogenic mother" (Fromm-Reichmann, 1948). They concluded that no link had been established between schizophrenia and atypical dominance patterns in parents, a hypothesis central to the work of Lidz et al. (1957a, 1957b). They found that the double-bind hypothesis (Bateson et al., 1956) had not been adequately tested experimentally, but the tentative results obtained suggest that double-bind messages are not specific to the parents of schizophrenics. They felt that Singer and Wynne (1964, 1966a, 1966b) had produced the most convincing work on abnormal communication in parents of schizophrenics. Hirsch and Leff (1971, 1975) took pains to replicate the work as carefully as possible, but were unable to repeat the definitive findings of Singer and Wynne. They found that deviant communication was by no means specifically confined to the parents of schizophrenics, but was also relatively common in the parents of neurotic patients. Furthermore, it was strongly linked with the number of words spoken by the subjects, and all their findings could be explained on the basis of the excessive verbosity shown by the fathers of schizophrenics.

So far all the findings reported have been disappointingly negative, but some positive conclusions emerged from the literature review. They are as follows:

1. More parents of schizophrenics are psychiatrically disturbed than parents of normal children, and more of the mothers have schizoid personalities.

2. The parents of schizophrenics show more conflict and disharmony than the parents of other psychiatric patients.

3. The preschizophrenic child more frequently manifests physical ill health or mild disability early in life than the normal child.

4. Mothers of schizophrenics show more concern and protectiveness than mothers of normals, both in the current situation and in their attitudes to the children before they fell ill.

Hirsch and Leff point out that all these findings could be explained on the basis of a common genetic background in both parents and children, finding a partial expression in the parents as abnormal personalities. They could alternatively be explained as parental reactions to the physical illness and disability that characterize the children before they develop frank schizophrenia. The separation of environmental from genetic effects and the detemination of the direction of cause and effect should eventually be achieved by longitudinal studies of children at risk for schizophrenia. A number of these are currently in progress (Garmezy, 1974) but it will take many years for the payoff to materialize. Meanwhile, it is clear that if there are environmental abnormalities in the families of schizophrenics, they differ only in degree, and not in kind, from those found in families with normal offspring and offspring with other psychiatric disorders. As Bleuler (1976) writes: "No *known* particular 'specific' enigmatic *environmental* influence is decisive in the development of schizophrenia; instead the psychological stress that we discover in the life histories of schizophrenics emanates from a combination of worries, stresses, and tensions that by their nature cannot clearly be distinguished from those that afflict all of us at times in one form or another."

It follows from this that the specific nature of schizophrenic symptomatology either stems from a genetic predisposition, or else that schizophrenia lies on a continuum with neurotic disorders and that when a certain level of environmental stress is reached a *qualitative* change in symptoms occurs. The latter explanation implies that we are all potentially schizophrenic and would develop the disease given a sufficient degree of stress. The lack of variation in the incidence of schizophrenia with stressful national events such as major wars weighs against this hypothesis, and furthermore there is now ample evidence for a genetic predisposition for schizophrenia.

The best answer we can currently give to the aetiological question is that a combination of genetic predisposition and environmental stress is involved, but that there is no specific family constellation linked to the appearance of schizophrenia.

2. Is It Useful to Conceive of the Family as a System?

Given the above conclusion, it would still be conceivable for the family to act as a self-perpetuating system, resisting the "cure" of schizophrenia in one of its members once the condition has appeared. In this respect it would not differ from other families with an emotional investment in maintaining "sickness" in a family member, whatever its nature. This view of the family does not illuminate the aetiology of schizophrenia but has far-reaching implications for therapy. In fact, the family as a system is a central concept in family therapy and is the guiding principle of a whole school of family therapists; the system purists (Beels and Ferber, 1969). D. D. Jackson is a member of this school and formulated his views early on. In 1959 he wrote: "Family interaction is a system in which A can also anticipate an effect on B, and this modifies his subsequent behavior; and B in turn modifies his response in anticipation of what he thinks A anticipates." I doubt if anyone would quarrel with the statement that people interact with each other and that they take this into account in the way they behave, but systems theory goes further than this. An essential part of the concept of a system is that it has boundaries with other systems or non-systems which it strives to maintain. Without definable boundaries it would lose its identity as a separate system. Within these boundaries some kind of homeostatic mechanism or mechanisms operate to maintain equilibrium. It is not always clear that these implications are intended when families are referred to as systems. Riskin and Faunce (1972) write that, "The word 'systems' at times does seriously represent a point of view that guides one's thinking and research strategy. At other times it seems to be used as a cliche, almost as a badge of high status." If we try to apply the systems view to the family it is immediately apparent that the family members invariably belong to a number of different systems: the wage-earner is part of a system at work, the schoolchild also belongs to a system at school, and the housewife to a system of neighborhood contacts. Nevertheless they would all agree that they belonged to the same family, although once we stepped outside the household they might not agree as to where the boundary of the family should be drawn. The complex nature of humans as social beings is reflected in their belonging to a whole series of overlapping social systems, of which the family is only one. Change in one system may be counterbalanced by change in another. For example it is well recognized that a child living in a disturbing family environment may behave quite normally at home, and only show disturbed behavior at school. A wage earner subjected to increasing pressures at work may respond by becoming more irritable at home. Due consideration does not seem to have been given to this by systems theorists, with the exception of Hoffman (1971), although the related problem of where to draw the boundary of the family has been tackled by Speck and Rueveni (1969). They include the whole social network of the schizophrenic patient, about 40 persons, in what they call tribe treatment. The term is appropriate since in traditional societies the family is almost always involved in treatment, whether of psychiatric or physical illness. The consultation with the traditional healer usually takes place in the presence of the extended family. Even when the patient is admitted to a modern hospital, the family often camp in the grounds and continue to look after the patient's daily needs. Seen from this historical and transcultural perspective, family therapy could be called a rediscovery. Individual therapy then stands out as the innovative approach, developing out of the fragmentation of social groups by urbanization/ industrialization and the individual-centered theories of illness causation propounded as part of scientific medicine. This refreshing viewpoint is crystallized in Haley's statement that "individual therapy is, in fact, one way of intervening in a family."

However exciting it is to have one's preconceptions shaken up in this way, we have to ask whether this approach actually fits the observable facts and whether it leads to more effective management of problems. There are a number of propositions which follow logically from the systems view of families with a disturbed member, and these can be tested experimentally. Firstly it can be inferred from the systems approach that if a disturbed family member is treated in isolation without attempting to involve the other members of the family, the treatment will not be successful. If we look at schizophrenia, do we find evidence to support this proposition? Very few schizophrenic patients throughout the world have the benefit of family therapy, yet their prognosis has been vastly improved by the use of phenothiazine drugs. A number of studies (Leff and Wing, 1971; Hirsch et al., 1973; Hogarty and Goldberg, 1973) have shown conclusively that phenothiazines not only suppress the florid symptoms of schizophrenia during acute attacks, but prevent recurrences of the illness. Furthermore, very long-term studies like that of Bleuler (1972) have identified a small but exceedingly important group of patients with typical schizophrenic illnesses who recover completely and never have another attack throughout their lives even without further treatment. This is all strong evidence against the above proposition applying to schizophrenia in general. But there is a sizable proportion of schizophrenic patients, amounting to about one third over a year or two, who relapse despite being on regular maintenance treatment with phenothiazines (Leff and Wing, 1971; Johnson, 1976). A series of studies conducted by the Medical Research Council Social Psychiatry Unit in London have demonstrated a significant association between schizophrenic relapse and certain emotional attitudes in the relatives (Brown et al., 1962; Brown, Birley, and Wing, 1972; Vaughn and Leff, 1976a). Patients living with relatives who show either highly critical or emotionally overinvolved attitudes toward them are much more likely to relapse than those living with relatives who do not show such attitudes. Regular maintenance phenothiazines give patients partial protection against the emotional atmosphere generated by the relatives, but the relapse rate is still alarmingly high, about 50 per cent over nine months (Vaughn and Leff, 1976a). Rather less than half the schizophrenic patients living with their relatives are exposed to excessive criticism or overinvolvement.

In such families, the relatives do appear to be maintaining the illness by their emotional attitudes to the patient, and systems theory could well apply. But in the majority of families containing a schizophrenic patient this is not the case and systems theory appears to have nothing to contribute to our understanding of the schizophrenic process.

You may well inquire why schizophrenic patients living in an emotionally "safe" atmosphere relapse at all. The answer appears to lie in the impact of life events on schizophrenia. Brown and Birley (1968) showed that independent life events, which were out of the patient's control, clustered in the three weeks before first onset or relapse of the illness. In fact 46 per cent of patients had experienced an independent life event compared with 14 per cent of a control population. In a recent study of families of schizophrenics (Vaughn and Leff, 1976a), I took a history of life events preceding onset or relapse of schizophrenia. Critical or overinvolved relatives were designated as High EE (Expressed Emotion) and the others as Low EE. The data are shown in Table 1 and indicate that for patients not on maintenance phenothiazine treatment, independent life events cluster when patients are living in Low EE homes, but not when they live in High EE homes. In other words, schizophrenic relapse is associated with *either* certain emotional attitudes in the relatives *or* the occurrence of independent life events.

A second proposition that follows from the systems approach is that alteration in the attitudes or behavior of one family member ought to lead to changes in other family members. A few family researchers have tested this proposition. Reiter and Kilmann (1975) deliberately set out to test the postulate of systems theory that a change in one component of a system has an effect on all other components. They chose to work with the mother on the grounds that she usually spends most time

TABLE 1

INDEPENDENT LIFE EVENTS DURING 3 WEEKS BEFORE RELAPSE
IN PATIENTS OFF REGULAR MAINTENANCE THERAPY

	Life Event	No Life Event	Total
High EE	1 (7%)	14 (93%)	15
Low EE	9 (56%)	7 (44%)	16

$p < .005$

with all family members and hence would be the most effective change agent. Families of children with adjustment difficulties at school were randomly assigned to experimental and control groups. Mothers in the experimental group participated in seven weekly counseling sessions in which they were taught a number of interpersonal skills which they could initiate at home. The aim was to increase positive communication among family members. In fact the experimental mothers did show a significant increase in the number of positive responses in a decision-making task, which was not observed with the control mothers ($p < .01$). The same increase in positive responses was shown by the experimental families as a whole, but not by the control families. However the increase in the families' positive responses was almost entirely due to the mothers' contribution. The fathers' and children's positive responses did not increase significantly. Hence the changes induced in the mothers by counseling did not spread to the other members of the family, and the systems postulate is not supported by this study.

A second study that tested the same postulate is that by Stover and Guerney (1967). In this case two experimental groups of mothers were trained by Rogerian therapists and compared with a control group who received no training. Assessment of effects on mother-child interactions was made by observing mothers in play sessions with children. Rogerian training led to a drop in Directive statements and an increase in Reflective statements by the experimental mothers. The latter increase was significantly greater in the group trained by the more experienced therapist. In the mother-child interactions children's nonverbal aggression increased significantly in both experimental groups, this being the desired and predicted response. However there was no change in children's verbal aggression, verbal leadership, and verbal dependency in any group. Thus a change in mothers' verbal behavior from Directive to Reflective statements was accompanied by an increase in nonverbal aggression in their children. This finding of course supports the systems approach, although to a limited degree since fathers were not included in the study.

The issue of father's role in the family system was specifically investigated by Martin (1977). The clients were children of both sexes with a broad range of behavior disturbances. The families were randomly assigned to father-included, father-excluded, and control groups. For the two treatment groups weekly sessions in which the child participated were conducted. They involved the teaching of conflict resolution and contingency management skills. Modeling and behavior rehearsal were used for parents. No change in children's problem behaviors occurred in the control group, whereas significant decreases occurred in both experimental groups. The same decrease occurred whether or not the father was included in the treatment sessions. The author comments that these results give "little encouragement to a systems point of view that puts an extreme emphasis on family homeostasis and would thus predict that reductions in mother-child problem interactions would be resisted by father." We can but agree with him. He does however add the proviso that there are likely to be some conditions under which father "sabotage" tends to occur, but that such families may be the exception rather than the rule. As emphasized above, this has certainly been our experience with the families of schizophrenics.

The third proposition that follows from systems theory is that treatment of the family as a whole, rather than the designated patient, should lead to the disappearance of the patient's symptoms. This carries us on to questions 4 and 5 about the effectiveness of family therapy, but before dealing with them we need to address ourselves to question 3.

3. What is the Aim of Family Therapy?

This may seem to be self-evident, but this is not the case. As long as treatment is focused on the symptomatic individual the aim is clearly to remove the symptoms. Once the focus shifts to the disturbed family, then the aim becomes to ameliorate the disturbance and return family functioning to normal. Ackerman (1966) states that "the ideal of family therapy is not merely to remove symptoms but to nourish a new way of life." But that immediately faces us with the necessity of deciding what is normal family functioning. Of course there can be no absolute answer to this question. It is relative to the family's social status in society, to the society it is embedded in, and to the era. Who is to say that the Victorian father as epitomized by Mr. Barrat of Wimpole Street, or even by Mr. Charles Dickens, is more normal or abnormal than the father of today, who avoids being labeled as a male chauvinist pig by changing nappies and washing dishes? It is interesting that the relativity of the judgment was recognized by one of the initiators of family therapy, J. E. Bell (1961). He cautioned that the therapist should avoid passing judgment on the behavior of family members, but put a reassuring gloss on what remains a crucial problem. He wrote that "the goals of therapy may represent the values of the therapist, but it is more likely that they emerge primarily from the matrix of cultural norms established within the subculture of which the individual family is a part." This would only be true if the family made it clear to the therapist what their own cultural norms were, as opposed to their actual way of behaving, an almost inconceivable situation. Alternatively the therapist could have available a whole range of norms derived from the subcultures he is likely to encounter against which he could match particular families. This situation is at least conceivable, but I know of nowhere that it exists.

Instead one encounters in the literature statements about normal family functioning which are clearly intended to act as universally applicable standards. McPherson et al. (1974) write that "in an ideal emotionally healthy family, there is no need for stabilized sub-systems, i.e. for splits and alliances within the family." Katz et al. (1975), in their therapy, aimed to produce "a tendency toward the middle range of clarity in expressing content material, an abundance of humor, less topic change, more information sharing rather that commitment demands, freedom to express differences but a high amount of agreement, a wide range of affectivity and a high number of positive relationships."

Other writers recognize that their ideals may not apply to the Mandinka or the Western Sepik, but still take an absolutist stand within their own culture. Jackson (1959) writes, "mature relationships, we label 'parallel' since there are frequent complementary and symmetric crossovers. In the ideal husband and wife relationship each defines areas in which he (sic) determines the nature of the relationship, in which he typically behaves in a symmetric or complementary manner." He adds, however, that the delineation of areas of control is determined by cultural factors. Skynner (1969) considers that in his own culture "families operate best where each parent respects the other and shares responsibility, but where the father is accorded ultimate authority."

These pronouncements fail to take account of the infinite variety found in human families throughout the world, and even in one neighborhood. In my view family structure and functioning are determined partly by cultural expectations and partly by the personalities of the family members. It is the latter that engenders considerable heterogeneity. It is all very well to have a theoretical ideal of normal family functioning to aim at, but it is too often a case of chasing rainbows and may explain the disappointing failure of some family therapy.

4. Does Family Therapy Work for Any Kinds of Families?

The number of scientifically conducted studies of family therapy which include adequate control groups can be counted on the fingers of one and a half hands. Wells et al. (1972) in reviewing the results of family therapy identified only two studies, but in fact they consist of one study and a follow-up of the same patients. More recently Gurman and Kniskern (1978) reviewed the same area and identified an additional 11 studies. Unfortunately four of these are unpublished, and one is not relevant to the concerns of this paper. Of the seven published relevant studies only one included schizophrenic patients and will be considered in the next section. The other six will be briefly reviewed here.

Stover and Guerney (1967) conducted a study (discussed in more detail above) of Rogerian training of mothers of emotionally maladjusted children. The children of the experimental mothers showed an increase in nonverbal aggression which was not seen in the children of the control mothers. This was considered to be a therapeutic change in the experimental children consequent on the Rogerian training of their mothers.

Alexander and Parsons (1973) carried out a well-designed study in which they compared the effects of various kinds of intervention in families of children with delinquent behavior. Families receiving short-term behavioral intervention were compared with families receiving alternative forms of family intervention and a group of families receiving no intervention. Behavioral intervention consisted of the therapists actively modeling, prompting, and reinforcing the desired behaviors for all family members. The alternative forms of family intervention comprised either client-centered didactic group discussions or a psychodynamic family program with an emphasis on insight. The desired changes in family interaction were more equality of talk time, less silence, and more interruptions. These all increased to a significantly greater extent in the families receiving behavioral intervention than in any other group of families. This experimental group also showed a significantly lower recidivism rate in the children than the other groups. This study demonstrates that intervention focused on the quality of communication can produce changes in the desired direction and that these are accompanied by a reduction in the children's delinquent behavior. Dealing with families in other ways less focused on communication did not lead to these changes.

Katz et al. (1975) compared families who received four sessions of family therapy from an experienced therapist with families receiving no therapy. The families were referred by a Mental Health Authority, but no diagnosis of the designated patient or of the family as a whole is given in this paper. The experimental group showed more clear statements and laughter after treatment than the control group, but no comparison of the two groups at initial assessment is reported on. This study is rather lightweight and is inadequately presented, so it does not provide very solid evidence for the effectiveness of family therapy.

Reiter and Kilmann (1975) gave an experimental group of mothers counseling sessions in an attempt to increase positive communication among family members. These mothers and a group of control mothers who received no counseling all had at least one child with adjustment difficulties. Experimental mothers showed an increase in the number of positive responses on a task, which was not shown by control mothers. Experimental mothers and fathers experienced an increase in perceived family integration, whereas control mothers and fathers showed a decrease on this measure. Experimental mothers reported a significant decrease in their children's undesirable behavior, but unfortunately this was not inquired about in the control group. This study shows that mothers can be taught to improve their communication with other family members, but it is not possible to come to any conclusion about the effectiveness of this in changing the children's behavior because of deficiencies in the design.

The last two studies in this section were both conducted by Garrigan and Bambrick (1975, 1977). In the first study families with emotionally disturbed boys were assigned to a treatment group or a control group. The treatment consisted of six weekly sessions using Zuk's (1967) "go-between process." There was a significant gain in family adjustment in the treated group. This reflected the perception of improved interpersonal functioning of the family as a unit by the identified client in areas of communication, decision making, and task accomplishment. However, there was no change in the client's self-concept or in his behavioral problems.

The second study was similar to the first but included female clients as well as male ones and additional assessment methods. This time the parents in the treatment group judged the family as showing better communication, decision making, and task accomplishment, but this change in perception was not shown by the disturbed children in the experimental families. All experimental parents rated their sons and daughters as less timid and less dependent. However, certain behaviors were not affected, namely bizarre cognition, emotional distance, and hyperactive expansive behavior. Family therapy also did not affect the experimental clients' self-concept or transitory state anxiety experienced in school.

The conclusions of this review are that two of the six studies provide equivocal support for the effectiveness of family therapy because of design faults. The remaining four constitute solid evidence that family therapy focused on particular aspects of family transactions can effectively produce some, if not all, of the desired changes. Three of these studies show in addition that changes in family transactions are accompanied by an improvement in the deviant behavior of the identified clients. Since the undesirable behavior itself was not dealt with directly, these findings support the third proposition derived from systems theory, namely, that treatment of the family as a whole, rather than the designated patient, should lead to the disappearance of the patient's symptoms. It is noteworthy, however, that in all six studies reviewed in this section the identified clients were children with behavioral or emotional disturbances. It is conceivable that younger children, being more influenced by their parents than, say, adults are by other adults, are particularly prone to express disturbances in the whole family. Hence systems theory will be more applicable when the client is a disturbed child than when he or she is a psychiatrically ill adult. Unfortunately there is only one published evaluative study of family therapy with adult clients, which will be discussed in the following section.

5. Does Family Therapy Work for the Families of Schizophrenics?

Langsley and his colleagues (Langsley et al., 1968, 1969, 1971) randomly assigned patients referred to Colorado Psychiatric Hospital to hospitalization or to Family Crisis Therapy. The goal of Family Crisis Therapy was to help the entire family to resolve current difficulties. Unfortunately the study was poorly designed and is almost impossible to interpret. The 150 cases in the study included "acutely disturbed schizophrenics, suicidal depressives and other dramatic behavioral disturbances." The authors give no breakdown of findings for the different diagnostic groups. They showed that rehospitalization rates were significantly lower for the first six months in the experimental than in the control group. However from the sixth to the eighteenth month, the difference betwen the groups narrowed. It is a pity they relied on hospitalization, an administrative measure easily influenced by knowledge of the group a patient belongs to, rather than an assessment of symptoms. Further, they state that in the experimental group drugs were used for symptom relief *in any member of the family.* Thus it is impossible to sort out the effectiveness of drugs from that of Family Crisis Theapy, the results for the schizophrenics as a group are not known, and the outcome measure is suspect. We can draw no conclusions from this study about the effectiveness of family therapy for schizophrenics, which means that the issue is wide open since no other study on this topic has been published.

Conclusions and Future Directions

We can conclude from the evidence presented above that systems theory can be applied usefully to *some* families when the identified patient suffers from *certain* conditions. Attempts to change the attitudes and behavior of *one* adult in the family can be successful, but the changes do not necessarily spread to other adults. However, working with the family as a whole can successfully modify deviant behavior when the client is a disturbed child. Various writers have complained (Beels and Ferber, 1969; Walrond-Skinner, 1978) that we do not yet have a well-developed language with which to discuss the operation of systems, particularly at higher levels of complexity. But the work reviewed shows that testable hypotheses can be derived from systems theory and that some of them are supported by scientific evidence. It is true, however, that systems theory engenders a particular approach to families containing a disturbed member, but does not prescribe specific modes of intervention (Alexander and Parsons, 1973). These have been developed from communication theory, behavioral psychology, and group analytic theory. It is difficult, but possible, to test the effectiveness of such interventions in the family, both on the interactional processes between family members and on the symptoms of the identified client. Currently such studies relate entirely to families with behaviorally or emotionally disturbed young children, but there is no reason why they could not be conducted in families containing a psychiatrically disturbed adult. Indeed the time is ripe for work of this kind which should be successful provided certain precautions are observed.

1. Accurate and detailed designation of psychiatric state of identified client.

2. Random assignment of families to treatment and control groups.

3. Intervention focused on specific areas of family transaction which are believed to perpetuate the pathology in the client.

4. Nature of intervention specified as carefully as possible.

5. Avoidance of ideal of "normal family functioning" as aim of intervention.

6. Outcome measured in terms of change in specific areas of family transaction and disappearance or nonrecurrence of client's symptoms.

7. Separation of effect of drugs from effect of social intervention.

We have recently initiated a study of the effectiveness of social intervention in the families of schizophrenics, which is designed to take due account of the above precautions. Schizophrenia is diagnosed on the basis of a standardized clinical assessment of the patients (the Present State Examination; see Wing et al., 1974) in conjunction with a diagnostic computer program, Catego. Only patients living with relatives, mostly parents or spouses, are included and the relatives are assessed by means of the Camberwell Family Interview (Brown and Rutter, 1966; Vaughn and Leff, 1976b). If the relatives are found to be high on Expressed Emotion and the patient is in high social contact with them, two factors indicating a high risk of relapse, then the family enters the study. Once the patient has recovered from the acute episode of schizophrenia, he is put on long-acting injections of fluphenazine and randomly assigned to social intervention or no social intervention groups. Since both groups are known to be receiving medication any reduction of the relapse rate in the experimental group must be due to the social intervention.

The social intervention consists of a package of various strategies which are tailored to the individual family. The strategy of particular relevance to this paper is a form of family therapy. The relatives in the experimental families, *but not the patients*, are included in a group of up to eight members. The patients are excluded for two main reasons. Firstly because the families join the group when the patients are acutely psychotic and we felt that the patients would be in no state to participate in the kind of processes we wished to foster and indeed would act as a distraction from them. Rubinstein (1974) writes that "the schizophrenic patient's behavior can be so disturbing and distracting to the family's daily events that it becomes difficult to make the necessary shift of attention from the individual to the family system. The patient exercises a powerful control over the session and the family. It is difficult to discuss anyone else, or to focus on the relationship between husband and wife, or between parents and any of the children, while the patient acts out without controls either at home or in the middle of the session." The second reason is that we have evidence from a psychophysiological study (Tarrier et al., 1979) that schizophrenic patients are highly disturbed by new situations, and that the presence of High EE relatives does nothing to relieve their disturbance.

Apart from High EE relatives, we do also include a number of Low EE relatives in the group, which is run on a fortnightly basis by two members of the research team. The main aim is to explore coping behavior, that is, what the relatives actually do when faced by everyday practical problems, such as the patient's refusal to take medication, the expression of delusions and hallucinations, and the patient's apathy and inertia. We include Low EE relatives because there is evidence from the psychophysiological study cited above that they are not merely playing a passive, nonirritant role, but are actively assisting patients to cope with stressful situations. We anticipated that helpful coping strategies used by low EE relatives would emerge in the group, both to enlighten the professional members and to instruct the High EE members in better management of the patients. We expected that relatives would find it easier to learn from each other than from professionals.

It is too early to comment on the effectiveness of our form of family therapy, but we have already seen our expectations being fulfilled in the group setting. The High EE relatives are intolerant of the patient's behavior at home, which leads to angry confrontations. By contrast the low EE relatives show a tolerant, even collusive, attitude toward the patient's symptoms and retain a remarkable ability to make light of the most fraught situations. There is no hint of blaming or criticizing the patient. We have already seen modifications of the attitudes of High EE relatives during their participation in the group, which makes us guardedly optimistic about the outcome of this study.

The technique we use to work with the relatives is similar to "multiple family therapy" (Laquer et al., 1964; Blinder et al., 1965). Our exclusion of the patient from the groups is unusual, although we have recently discovered that Waring (1978) has developed the same technique on the basis of our earlier published work. The mainspring of our intervention program has been our discovery that *certain* families do act as systems for the perpetuation of schizophrenia in one member, while others, the majority, do not. This has given us hope that a "deviation-amplifying" family system can be changed into a "deviation-reducing" one (Hoffman, 1971), and that by this means we can substantially improve the prognosis for those unfortunate people suffering from schizophrenia.

REFERENCES

Ackerman, N. (1966), Family psychotherapy—theory and practice. *Amer. J. Psychother.*, 20:405–414.
Alexander, J. E. & Parsons, B. V. (1973), Short-term behavioral intervention with delinquent families. *J. Abnorm. Psychol.*, 81:219–225.
Bateson, G., Jackson, D. D., Haley, J., & Weakland, J. H. (1956), Toward a theory of schizophrenia. *Behav. Sci.*, 1:251–264.
Beels, C. C. & Ferber, A. (1969), Family therapy: A view. *Fam. Proc.*, 8:280–332.
Bell, J. E. (1961), *Family Group Therapy*. Public Health Monograph No. 64. Washington: U.S. Department of Health, Education and Welfare.
Bleuler, M. (1972), *Die Schizophrenen Geistesstörungen*. Stuttgart: Georg Thieme.
——— (1976), An approach to a survey of research results on schizophrenia. *Schiz. Bull.*, 2:356–357.

Blinder, M. G., Colman, A. D., Curry, A. E., & Kessler, D. R. (1965), "MCFT": Simultaneous treatment of several families. *Amer. J. Psychother.*, 19:559–569.

Brown, G. W. & Birley, J. L. T. (1968), Crises and life changes and the onset of schizophrenia. *J. Hlth. Soc. Behav.*, 9:203–214.

_____ _____ & Wing, J. K. (1972), Influence of family life on the course of schizophrenic disorders: A replication. *Brit. J. Psychiat.*, 121:241–258.

_____ Monck, E. M., Carstairs, G. M., & Wing, J. K. (1962), Influence of family life on the course of schizophrenic illness. *Brit. J. Prev. Soc. Med.*, 16:55–68.

_____ & Rutter, M. (1966), The measurement of family activities and relationships: A methodological study. *Hum. Relat.*, 19:241–263.

Falloon, I. R. H., Lindley, P., McDonald, R., & Marks, I. M. (1977), Social skills training of out-patient groups: A controlled study of rehearsal and homework. *Brit. J. Psychiat.*, 131:599–609.

Fromm-Reichmann, F. (1948), Notes on the development of treatment of schizophrenics by psychoanalytic psychotherapy. *Psychiat.*, 11:263–273.

Garmezy, N. (1974), Children at risk: The search for the antecedents of schizophrenia. Part II: Ongoing research programs, issues and intervention. *Schiz. Bull.*, 1(9):55–125.

Garrigan, J. J. & Bambrick, A. F. (1975), Short term family therapy with emotionally disturbed children. *J. Marr. Fam. Counsel.*, 1:379–385.

_____ _____ (1977), Family therapy for disturbed children: Some experimental results in special education. *J. Marr. Fam. Counsel.*, 3:83–93.

Gurman, A. S. & Kniskern, D. P. (1978), Research on marital and family therapy: Progress, perspectives and prospect. In: *Handbook of Psychotherapy and Behavior Change: An Empirical Analysis*, 2nd edition, ed. S. L. Garfield & A. E. Bergin. New York: Wiley.

Haley, J. (1962), Whither family therapy? *Fam. Proc.*, 1:69–100.

Hirsch, S. R., Gaind, R., Rohde, P. D., Stevens, B. C., & Wing, J. K. (1973), Out-patient maintenance of chronic schizophrenic patients with long-acting fluphenazine: Double-blind placebo trial. *Brit. Med. J.*, 1:633–637.

_____ & Leff, J. P. (1971), Parental abnormalities of verbal communication in the transmission of schizophrenia. *Psychol. Med.*, 1:118–127.

_____ _____ (1975), *Abnormalities in Parents of Schizophrenics*. Maudsley Monograph No. 22. London: Oxford University Press.

Hoffman, L. (1971), Deviation-amplifying processes in natural groups. In: *Changing Families*, ed. J. Haley. New York: Grune & Stratton.

Hogarty, G. E.. & Goldberg, S. C. (1973), Drug and sociotherapy in the aftercare of schizophrenic patients. *Arch. Gen. Psychiat.*, 28:54–64.

Jackson, D. D. (1959), Family interaction, family homeostasis and some implications for conjoint family psychotherapy. In: *Individual and Family Dynamics*, ed. J. Masserman. New York: Grune & Stratton.

Johnson, D. A. W. (1976), The expectation of outcome from maintenance therapy in chronic schizophrenic patients. *Brit. J. Psychiat.*, 128:246–250.

Katz, A. J., di Krasinski, M., Philip, E., & Wieser, C. (1975), Change in interactions as a measure of effectiveness in short term family therapy. *Fam. Ther.*, 2:31–56.

Langsley, D. G., Flomenhaft, K., & Machotka, P. (1969), Follow-up evaluation of family crisis therapy. *Amer. J. Orthopsychiat.*, 39:753-759.

———— Machotka, P., & Flomenhaft, K. (1971), Avoiding mental hospital admission: A follow-up study. *Amer. J. Psychiat.*, 127:1391–1394.

———— Pitman, F. S., Machotka, P., & Flomenhaft, K. (1968), Family crisis therapy—results and implications. *Fam. Proc.*, 7:145–158.

Laquer, H. P., La Burt, H. A., & Morong, E. (1964), Multiple Family therapy. In: *Current Psychiatric Therapies*, Vol. 4, ed. J. H. Masserman. New York: Grune & Stratton.

Leff, J. P. & Wing, J. K. (1971), Trial of maintenance therapy in schizophrenia. *Brit. Med. J.*, 3:599–604.

Lidz, T. (1975), *The Origin and Treatment of Schizophenic Disorders*. London: Hutchinson.

———— Cornelison, A. R., Fleck, S., & Terry, D. (1957a), The intrafamilial environment of the schizophrenic patient. I. The father. *Psychiat.*, 20:329–342.

———— ———— ———— ———— (1957b), The intrafamilial environment of the schizophrenic patient. II. Marital schism and marital skew. *Amer. J. Psychiat.*, 114:241–248.

Martin, F. E. (1977), Some implications from the theory and practice of family therapy for individual therapy (and vice versa). *Brit. J. Med. Psychol.*, 50:53–64.

Massie, H. N. & Beels, C. C. (1972), The outcome of the family treatment of schizophrenia. *Schiz. Bull.*, 6:24–36.

McPherson, S. R., Brackelmanns, W. E., & Newman, L. E. (1974), Stages in the family therapy of adolescents. *Fam. Proc.*, 13:77–94.

Reiter, G. F. & Kilmann, P. R. (1975), Mothers as family change agents. *J. Counsel. Psychol.*, 22:61–65.

Riskin, J. & Faunce, E. E. (1972), An evaluative review of family interaction research. *Fam. Proc.*, 11:365–455.

Rubinstein, D. (1974), Techniques in family psychotherapy of schizophrenia. In: *Strategic Intervention in Schizophrenia*, ed. R. Cancro, N. Fox, & L. E. Shapiro. New York: Behavioral Publications.

Singer, M. T. & Wynne, L. C. (1964), Stylistic variables in research on schizophrenics and their families. Unpublished address, Marquette University, Milwaukee, Wisconsin.

———— ———— (1966a), Principles for scoring communication defects and deviances in parents of schizophrenics: Rorschach and T.A.T. Scoring Manuals. *Psychiat.*, 29:260–288.

———— ———— (1966b), Communication styles in parents of normals, neurotics and schizophrenics. *Psychiat. Res. Rep.*, 20:25–38.

Skynner, A. C. R. (1969), A group-analytic approach to conjoint family therapy. *J. Child Psychol. Psychiat.*, 10:81–106.

Speck, R. V. & Rueveni, V. (1969), Network therapy—a developing concept. *Fam. Proc.*, 8:182–191.

Stover, L. & Guerney, B. G. (1967), The efficacy of training procedures for mothers in filial therapy. *Psychother.: Theory, Res. Prac.*, 4:110–115.

Tarrier, N., Vaughn, C. E., Lader, M. H., & Leff, J. P. (1979), Bodily reactions to people and events in schizophrenia. *Arch. Gen. Psychiat.*, 36:311–315.

Vaughn, C. E. & Leff, J. P. (1976a), The influence of family and social factors on the course of psychiatric illness: A comparison of schizophrenic and depressed neurotic patients. *Brit. J. Psychiat.*, 129:125–137.

_____ _____ (1976b), The measurement of expressed emotion in the families of psychiatric patients. *Brit. J. Soc. Clin. Psychol.*, 15:157–165.

Walrond-Skinner, S. (1978), Indications and contraindications for the use of family therapy. *J. Child Psychol. Psychiat.*, 19:57–62.

Waring, E. M. (1978), Family therapy and schizophrenia. *Canad. Psychiat. Assn. J.*, 23:51–58.

Wells, R. A., Dilkes, T. C., & Trivelli, N. (1972), The results of family therapy: A critical review of the literature. *Fam. Proc.*, 11:189–207.

Wing, J. K., Cooper, J. E., & Sartorius, N. (1974), *Measurement and Classification of Psychiatric Symptoms.* London: Cambridge University Press.

Zuk, G. H. (1967), Family therapy. *Arch. Gen. Psychiat.*, 16:71–79.

Assessment of Familial Risks in the Functional Psychoses and Their Application in Genetic Counseling

D. W. K. KAY

Now that the evidence for genetic factors in the major psychoses is very strong but still essentially circumstantial — what is transmitted is unknown — there is a danger that myths about the nonexistence of mental illness may be replaced by equally misleading myths about its inheritance. The need for genetic counseling is therefore likely to increase (counseling is advice given as a result of consultation). Admittedly, the literature on counseling in mental illness is scanty, the author's own experience slight, and the public demand small. Reed (1972) stated that less than 7 per cent of the 3,000 cases seen at the Dight Institute over 20 years were concerned with schizophrenia. Nevertheless, it is probable that much unrequested and ill-informed advice is being given.

Reed (1972) described four particular situations in which genetic counseling may be requested: (1) in adoption cases; (2) to review the desirability of parenthood when one parent is psychotic; (3) in cases of morbid jealousy, to prove paternity; and (4) by relatives asking for the evidence for heredity in mental illness and for estimates as to its importance.

For the present purposes, I shall assume that the consultands consist of a young couple, one being in remission from a psychotic illness, who are seeking to make a rational decision about parenthood. (A consultand is the person about the chances of illness in whose future progeny information is being sought.)

The counselor's role is not to arrive at decisions himself, but to

D. W. K. Kay, D.M., F.R.C.P., F.R.C.Psych., is Professor of Psychiatry, The University of Tasmania, Royal Hobart Hospital, Hobart, Tasmania.

inform, explain, discuss, and support. He needs to clear up gross mis-conceptions as well as to interpret the risks in terms of ordinary ex-perience. The couple may ask him what they can do to reduce the risk, or to give his opinion on the changes in treatment and prognosis which may have occurred by the time the child has grown up and entered the period of risk. He may have to discuss alternatives to child-bearing, such as adoption, family planning, termination of pregnancy, or sterilization, and to deal with the emotional issues involved in these procedures.

GENERAL CONSIDERATIONS

HERITABILITY AND MODE OF TRANSMISSION

One might suppose that knowledge of the mode of transmission and heritability of a trait would be highly desirable if not essential in genetic counseling. (Heritability is the proportion of the total variance of a trait which in a given population is due to genetic variance.) However, in conditions with unknown and possibly complex modes of inheritance, there may be enormous differences between estimates of heritability that are obtained from assumptions of a single gene or a polygene model, and these in turn generate very different estimates of the risk to progeny (Feldman and Lewontin, 1975).

Another difficulty is that in the single major locus (SML) model there are an infinite number of (internal) parameter sets or solutions, which give rise to the same estimated frequencies in relatives (James, 1971). And in practice it is often very difficult to make the distinction between SML and multifactorial MF models solely on the basis of fre-quencies in relatives. Because of these and other problems, as Feldman and Lewontin (1975) point out, heritability estimates are rarely used in genetic counseling, and when good empirical data are available (as for instance, in the case of diabetes mellitus and coeliac disease) predic-tions based on them may be preferable to those derived from an in-ferred complex genetic model.

In disorders in which more than a single threshold can be identi-fied, however, both SML and MF models (Kidd and Cavalli-Sforza, 1973; Reich et al., 1972), can provide a unique "best fit" set of param-eters, and these allow expected prevalences in relatives to be tested against the observed risks.

The concept here is of a *varying liability* to a disorder, continuously distributed throughout the whole population. Gershon et al. (1975a) applied these models to data obtained about affective disorders in the

Jewish population of Jerusalem (Gershon et al., 1975b) on the hypothesis that bipolar (BP) and unipolar (UP) illnesses represented different thresholds on a continuous scale of liability (BP UP) to affective disorder. They found that *both* SML *and* MF models generated solutions which fitted their data, and that neither could be ruled out, in contrast with the currently favored view that BP and UP illnesses are genetically distinct disorders and not merely different in degree of severity. In this article, the risks for BP and UP illness are given separately without implying that their separateness is regarded as proven.

EMPIRICAL RISKS AND SELECTION OF PROBANDS

As genetic counselors we have, therefore, to fall back on empirical morbidity risks. These have been generated by large-scale family studies by investigators who in the hope of working with genetically homogenous conditions, have selected groups of probands who are clinically typical of the disorder being studied. (Probands are the affected individuals through whom the existence of a family with the disorder is brought to attention.) With this method, schizophrenia and manic-depressive disorder have been found to "breed true" with little tendency for both to appear in the same families. But when unselected pairs of relatives, both of whom have been hospitalized for psychosis, are studied, the diagnoses have been discordant (one schizophrenic, one affective) in 30 per cent of pairs (Ödegaard, 1963; Tsuang, 1967).

This suggests that there is a group of conditions which spans the area between chronic schizophrenia and typical manic-depressive illness. Kendell and Gourlay (1970) were in fact unable to discriminate clearly between schizophrenia and affective psychoses from an analysis of symptomatology and historical data, and Tsuang (1967) noted some striking resemblances in symptomatology between related pairs even when their diagnoses were different. For this reason it would be desirable to obtain a full description of the consultand's illness, and not rely only on a diagnosis. The middle ground is occupied by the group of psychoses variously called atypical, reactive, or schizoaffective. Table 1 (Ödegaard, 1972) shows how the diagnoses in the psychotic relatives vary when probands with atypical conditions are included.

ASSESSMENT OF EMPIRICAL RISKS

To return to our consulting couple, one would need to raise questions in five areas before the magnitude of the risk to an offspring and the weight of the burden incurred if he became ill

TABLE 1
DIAGNOSTIC DISTRIBUTION OF INDEX PATIENTS AND THEIR PSYCHOTIC RELATIVES

Patients with	No. of index patients	No. of psychotic[1] relatives	Diagnosis of psychotic relatives			
			Schizophrenia (per cent)	Reactive psychoses (per cent)	Affective psychoses (per cent)	Total (per cent)
Schizophrenia	1205	656	65	16	19	100
with severe defect at follow-up	233	109	78	7	15	100
with slight defect	654	368	70	16	14	100
without defect	318	179	46	23	31	100
Reactive psychosis	278	82	28	48	24	100
Atypical psychosis	96	39	36	28	36	100
Manic-depressive psychosis	99	47	19	11	70	100
All psychoses	1678	824	57	20	23	100

[1] Number at risk not known.

After Ödegaard (1972). From Kaplan, A. R. (1972), *Genetic Factors in Schizophrenia*. Courtesy of Charles C Thomas Publisher, Springfield, Illinois.

could be adequately assessed.

QUESTION 1: THE NATURE OF THE PROBAND'S ILLNESS

In line with what has been said above, the psychosis in the proband, who in this case is one of the consulting couple, will be discussed under the headings Affective, Schizophrenic, and Atypical. In fact, a number of studies have been carried out in the hope of clarifying the genetical relationships between the three groups.

Affective Disorders

The work of Leonhard et al. (1962), Perris (1976), and Angst (1966) in Europe and of Winokur and colleagues (Winokur and Clayton, 1967; Winokur et al., 1969, 1971) in the U.S.A. is mainly responsible for the current practice of subdividing the affective disorders into bipolar (BP) and unipolar (UP) forms. The former corresponds to the traditional circular type of manic-depressive disorder but usually includes patients with manic attacks only, and the latter corresponds to the depressed type of manic-depressive disorder and includes endogenous depression and involutional melancholia.

The reported risks in relatives for all forms of affective disorder fall for the most part (Table 2) within the range 11–16 per cent for relatives of UP probands and 11–25 per cent (i.e., generally somewhat higher) for relatives of BP probands. The differences between authors probably result in part from the definitions used, in part from the methods of study. Winokur's criteria for BP illness (Winokur et al., 1969) for instance, was the occurrence of an attack of mania, while Perris (1976) required both an attack of mania and of depression. UP illness was diagnosed by Winokur et al. (1971) when there had been one or more attacks of depression only, without any manic attacks, but Perris (1976) required three separate episodes of depression without mania; depressions with fewer than three episodes were assigned to a group of "unspecified" affective disorders. Similar criteria were applied to the relatives.

Some authors give the higher risks obtained when "suspected" cases (Videbech, 1975), "related disorders" (Gershon et al., 1975b), or suicides (Angst, 1966) are included. The use of the "family study method" also produces higher risks (Winokur et al., 1969, 1971). (In this method risks are calculated only for the group of relatives who have been personally interviewed.) Other authors use the method in part but do not report the results separately (Gershon et al., 1975b; Helzer and Winokur, 1974). The high risks obtained by Goetzl et al. (1974) were based on relatives' replies to mailed questionnaires.

TABLE 2
MORBIDITY RISKS (MR) FOR UNIPOLAR (UP), BIPOLAR (BP) AND
ALL AFFECTIVE DISORDERS IN FIRST-DEGREE RELATIVES
OF PROBANDS WITH UNIPOLAR OR BIPOLAR ILLNESSES

| | Probands with | | | | | | | General population | |
| | Unipolar illness MR% | | | | Bipolar illness MR% | | | Lifetime MR% | |
	At risk (BZ)	UP	BP	UP + BP	At risk (BZ)	UP	BP	UP + BP	UP	BP
Stenstedt (1952)	432[W]	10	2	12	56[W]	8	5	13		
Perris (1976)	570[S]	7[1]	0.4	8	509[S]	0.6[1]	11	11		
Perris (1976)	570[S]	14[2]	0.4	15	509[S]	9[2]	11	20		
Angst (1966)	341[S]	11[2]	0.3	11	160[S]	14[2]	4	18		
Winokur et al. (1969, 1971)	404[S]	16	−[4]	16	199[S]	24	11	35		
Winokur et al. (1969, 1971)	88[S5]	23[6]	−[4]	23[5]	120[S5]	28	14	42[5]		
Goetzl et al. (1974)	—	—	—	—	141[S]	21	4	25		
Winokur (1974)	—	—	—	—	131[W]	12	5	17[5]		
Mendlewicz & Rainer (1974)	—	—	—	—	585[S5]	21	18	39[5]		
Gershon et al. (1975b)	96[S]	11	2	13	341[S]	7	4	11		
Gershon et al. (1975b)	96[S]	16[6]	2	18	341[S]	14[6]	4	18		
Videbech (1975)	596[S]	5[1]	2	7	367[S]	2[1]	8	11		
Videbech (1975)	596[S]	19	2	22[7]	367[S]	15	9	24[7]		
James & Chapman (1975)	—	—	—	—	265[S]	13	6	20	1.0–2.0	0.2–0.3

[1] three separate episodes of depression. [2] all depression-only illnesses, plus suicides. [3] all depression-only illnesses, not suicides. [4] probands having a manic relative were excluded from this series. [5] family study method (personal interview). [6] includes "related disorders." [7] includes suspected cases. [W]Weinberg's abridged method. [S]Stromgren's method. (See Reid D.D. [1960] Public Health Papers No. 2, Geneva, W.H.O. for an account of these methods. With Stromgren's method the risks tend to be slightly higher than with Weinberg's method.)

Gershon et al. (1975b) relied on the strict criteria of Feighner et al. (1972) which may account for their somewhat low figures (13 per cent for UP and 11 per cent for BP probands). However, the overall prevalence of "affective and related disorders" in this study was about 18 per cent in the relatives of both types of proband.

As Table 2 shows, the overall risks for affective disorders in relatives are usually, but not invariably, found to be higher when the proband illness is BP than when it is UP. An important question is whether these types "breed true." In Perris' (1976) study the risk of UP illness in the relatives of BP probands was only 0.6 per cent according to his preferred criteria, and when Videbech (1975) used the same criteria he also found a low risk. But when other depression-only illnesses were counted, the risks in both studies increased considerably (Table 2). In fact, higher risks for UP than for BP illness have been found in the relatives of BP probands by other authors. All studies agree, however, that BP illness is rare in the families of UP probands, a consensus which has caused some authors to regard the occurrence of a case of BP illness in the family of a proband with UP illness as evidence that the family illness was BP (Cadoret, 1976). The value of this procedure in predicting the risk to the offspring of probands whose own illnesses are UP has not been studied.

The risks shown in Table 2 are those for all first-degree relatives, and not just for offspring. In fact, the very prolonged risk period (15 to 70 years or later) for affective (especially UP) illness makes the calculation of the true age-corrected population at risk (the Bezugsziffer, BZ) particularly uncertain in the case of offspring. The older data indicate, however, that the risks in parents, sibs, and offspring of probands with "manic-depressive" disorder are similar, the median risks derived from various investigations being 10–11 per cent for each class of relative (Zerbin-Rudin, 1967). Of course, the real meaning of the "risks" conveyed to the consultands should be made quite clear.

In considering the risk to a proband's relative one must take account of how the probands themselves in any relevant study were selected. For instance, one could not apply the figures given by Winokur and associates (Winokur et al., 1969, 1971) if our prospective parent's illness had occurred in a setting of bereavement or a serious physical illness or if he was taking drugs known to cause depression, or abusing alcohol or drugs, or if the symptoms appeared to be secondary to another psychiatric illness, including neurosis. The Winokur data are valid only for "primary affective disorder" and risks in relatives of cases with "secondary affective disorders" have not been reported. Accordingly, relatives of patients with a depressive or manic affect accompanying, for instance, hysteria, anxiety neurosis, or alcoholism as the primary condition, cannot be assumed to run exactly the same risk of developing affective illness as those of Winokur's probands. According to Wood et al. (1977) only 45–50 per cent of randomly selected in- or out-patients with affective disorders are suffering from primary disorder. Other recent investigators have generally followed Winokur's criteria or those devised by Feighner et al. (1972).

The main difficulty in applying these criteria in any particular case would seem to be in deciding whether the affective symptoms are or are not "secondary" to a neurosis or to alcoholism. Cases of neurotic depressive reaction are included in the primary category but, presumably, neurotically depressed patients would often be ruled out of the primary category because of the preexistence of neurotic illness often arising presumably on the basis of a markedly anxious or obsessional personality. However, since many patients who *are* diagnosed as unipolar also have anxious or obsessional personalities (Gittelson, 1966; Videbech, 1975), the line of demarcation between primary and secondary affective disorder would not always be clear cut. In the care of alcoholism, a difficulty would be that alcoholism sometimes seems to be an "equivalent" of, or substitute for, affective illness (Winokur et al., 1971).

Schizophrenia

It must be borne in mind that probands with conditions such as paranoia, late paraphrenia, or involutional psychosis would not have been included in the family studies of schizophrenia. The morbidity risks in the first-degree relatives in such cases are, in fact, consistently found to be lower (3–5 per cent) than estimates for relatives of typical schizophrenics obtained from pooled data (9–12 per cent) (Zerbin-Rudin, 1967). Much more important, however, is the existence of a group of symptomatic schizophrenias which arise on an organic basis (Davison and Bagley, 1969). The best established examples are the schizophrenialike states associated with temporal-lobe epilepsy (Slater and Glithero, 1963), amphetamine psychosis, psychoses following penetrating head wounds, and those associated with chronic alcoholism, myxoedema, pernicious anaemia, Huntington's chorea, and possibly deafness (Cooper et al., 1974). Twin studies (Gottesman and Shields, 1972) also have suggested that schizophrenia on an organic basis may occur in a person who is not otherwise specially predisposed. So far as genetic counseling is concerned, it is essential to recognize such cases, because the expectation of illness in the relatives is probably no higher than in the general population (i.e., 1–2 per cent).

Recent studies concerned with psychopathology in the offspring of schizophrenic parents are summarized in Table 3. The risks for schizophrenia (uncorrected for age), when one parent is schizophrenic, range from 6 to 11 per cent, or if borderline states are included (omitting Schulsinger's data) from 7 to 16 per cent. With age correction, the risks for schizophrenia alone increase to 10.5 per cent (Reisby, 1967), 17 per cent (Heston, 1966), and 17 per cent (H. Schulsinger, 1976). There are also some cases of suicide, 10 in all in the pooled data, equivalent to a rate of 1.5 per cent.

The rates for *borderline states* (Column 2, Table 3) vary widely, and one investigation cannot easily be compared with another. Internal comparisons between the control and experimental groups of each author are, however, possible. H. Schulsinger's (1976) unusually large percentage in this category (32 per cent) included "pseudoneurotic" and "pseudopsychopathic" disorders, as well as schizoid and paranoid personality, and conditions which showed "discreet signs of thought disorder, anhedonia and micropsychotic symptoms." Alcohol and drug abuse, which was much commoner in the offspring of the schizophrenic mothers, may have contributed to the occurrence of the micropsychotic symptoms. In the study of Rosenthal et al. (1971) the conditions included under this heading were restricted to borderline schizophrenia or borderline schizophreniform psychosis.

It is still harder in the case of the personality disorders subsumed under column 3 (Table 3), to know if different investigators are comparing like with like. Heston (1966) and Bleuler (1974) both found that these disorders were significantly more common in their experimental than in their control groups, but neither Schulsinger nor Rosenthal et al. (1971) demonstrated significant differences. The Rosenthal data refer only to disorders throught to fall *within the schizophrenic* spectrum. (The "spectrum" comprises schizophrenia and other psychopathological conditions supposedly related to it biologically.) The risk of a spectrum disease (Column 4, Table 3) in that study is 28 per cent in the experimental and 18 per cent in the control group (P > .10). In three of the other five studies about one quarter of the offspring of schizophrenic parents also suffered from conditions falling into the broad category of schizophrenia plus nonneurotic personality disorder (Table 3) but they are probably not identical with Rosenthal's spectrum group. In fact, there is evidence that some nonpsychotic disorders in the offspring of schizophrenics are related to *abnormalities in the coparents,* and that the abnormalities in the coparents in the Danish-American adoption study are different from those found in the coparents in the other studies (see section on assortative mating and

TABLE 3
UNCORRECTED RISKS PER CENT OF VARIOUS DISORDERS IN THE OFFSPRING OF A SCHIZOPHRENIC PARENT

Author	Diagnosis of ill parent	N	Mean ages in years	Condition in offspring						
				Schizophrenia 1	Border-line 2	Nonneurotic personality 3	Col. 4 (1+2+3)	Neurotic disorders	Epilepsy Subnormality Other Psychoses	No definite psychiatric diagnosis
Heston[1] (1966)	Mother schizophrenic	47	36	11	–	17	28	28	9	45
	No psychiatric record	50		0	–	4	4	14	0	80
Rosenthal et al.	Either parent schizophrenic	52	33	6	10	12	28	–	1	–
	Not in Psychiatric Register	67		0	6	12	18	–	–	–
Reisby (1967)	Mother chronic schizophrenic	278	37	6	1	3	10	5	2	80
Bleuler (1974)	Either parent schizophrenic	143	38	7	2	16	25	–	2	73
	General population sample	1077	not given	1	–	5	6	–	–	92
Schulsinger[2] (1976)	Mother severely schizophrenic	173	23½	9	32	16	57	17	1	22
	Not a psychiatric patient	91		1	4	14	19	36	0	42
Fowler et al. (1977)	Either parent chronic schizophrenic	28	>15	4	0	21	25	11	0	64

[1] Child separated from parent early in life.
[2] "Consensus" diagnosis based on agreement between at least two of the 3 methods used.

Table 6).

The generally high rates recorded by Schulsinger may be partly due to the author's wish, in her study of high and low risk children, not to overlook anybody with even minor signs of schizophrenialike psychopathology (H. Schulsinger, 1976).

The results of Schulsinger and Heston disagree about the relative frequency of neurotic disorders in the offspring of schizophrenic and controls, while Heston's findings of a markedly high prevalence of mental deficiency in the former is not borne out in any of the later studies. As regards affective psychoses, these appear to be rare, but the offspring would not yet have passed through the greater part of the risk period for these disorders.

Atypical Psychoses

Clinically, it is usually the mixture of schizophrenic and affective symptoms, or the presence of a precipitant with signs of clouding of consciousness without an organic cause, which constitutes the departure from the "typical." In either case, the onset is nearly always acute and the outcome favorable. Genetically these psychoses might be supposed to be either schizophrenic or affective, or they might be due to the presence of both genotypes. Alternatively, they might be independent entities, or fifthly, they might be a genetically heterogeneous group.

The actual data, summarized in Table 4, give some support to four of these possibilities. Only the view that they are "mixed" psychoses with both schizophrenic *and* manic-depressive heredity seems to be unlikely (McCabe, 1975). Otherwise, the connection with schizophrenia appears to be the weakest. Only Angst (1966) and Mendlewicz (1976) found some increase in risk of schizophrenia in the relatives of their atypical probands. On the other hand, there is a general consensus, with the exception of Perris (1974), that affective disorders are common, though not as common as in relatives of probands with affective disorders. Perris (1974) concluded that "cycloid psychoses" were an independent entity, and McCabe and Stromgren (1975) and McCabe et al. (1971) also found an increase of homologous types of illness in relatives of probands with reactive psychoses and with "good prognosis schizophrenia" respectively. The data of Angst (1966) and of McCabe et al. (1971), however, are also in keeping with some degree of genetic heterogeneity.

To some extent these discrepancies may reflect differences in criteria of selection. For instance, McCabe et al. (1971) included probands who had had *prior episodes of mania or manic-depression*, while

TABLE 4
ATYPICAL PSYCHOSES

Author	Probands' illness	Class of relative and no. at risk	Relatives with			
			Schizophrenia	Atypical psychosis	Affective disorder	Total
			Morbidity risks %			
Angst (1966)	Mixed manic-depressive	190[1] sibs	10	5	5	19.5
McCabe et al. (1971)[2]	Good prognosis schizophrenia	33[1] sibs	3	6	15	24
McCabe and Stromgren (1975)[4]	Reactive psychoses	67[1] sibs	1.5	12	6	19
Perris (1974)	Cycloid psychoses	264.5[3] 1° rel.	0.8	9	1 (4.5)[7]	11 (14.5)[7]
Tsuang et al. (1976)[5]	"Atypical schizophrenia"	(85)[8] sibs	1	—	7	8.5
	Schizophrenia	(200)[8]	1	—	2	3
	Affective disorder	(325)[8] sibs	0.6	—	8	8
Mendelwicz (1976)[6]	Schizo-affective illness	(45)[8] 1° rel.	11 ± 4	—	36 ± 5	47
	Schizophrenia	(45)[8]	17 ± 2	—	9.4	26
	Bipolar illness	(45)[8] 1° rel.	1.4 ± 1	—	41 ± 4	42.4
	Unipolar illness	(45)[8] 1° rel.	3 ± 2	—	29 ± 6	32

[1] Risk-period 15–60. [2] See McCabe & Cadoret (1976). [3] Family history method mainly. Risk-period 15–50. [4] Family histories and review of Central Psychiatric Registry + partial family study. Risk-period 15–60. [5] Case-record study. Method of calculating risks not stated. [6] All available relatives personally interviewed without knowledge of diagnosis of proband. Risk-period 15–70. Probands with schizophrenia, bipolar and unipolar illness matched for age/sex with schizo-affective probands. [7] Includes suicides. [8] Refers to number of probands.

in the study by Mendlewicz (1976) the presence of at least one *schizophrenic episode on a separate occasion,* as well as of manic or depressive episodes, was required for the diagnosis of schizoaffective disorder.

McCabe and Stromgren (1975) excluded probands with prior BP type illness; their *reactive psychoses* were defined as psychoses with acute onset which coincided in time with the occurrence of an emotional trauma, which colored the content of the illness. There was often clouding of consciousness, and good preservation of personality and affect; first rank symptoms of schizophrenia were rare. These authors recognized three subgroups — emotional syndromes, mostly depressive; acute paranoid reactions; and confusional syndromes — but did not report the risks separately.

Tsuang et al. (1976) made a case history study, which produced lower risks. Their probands had a chart diagnosis of schizophrenia, but did not fulfill strict criteria for this diagnosis because the illness was of short duration and of remitting course or showed marked affective symptomatology. Among the conclusions was that the presence of strong manic coloring in patients with some schizophrenic symptoms should make one cautious before diagnosing a schizophrenic illness.

Perris' (1974) *"cycloid psychoses"* seem to have formed only about 5 per cent of all his BP-UP cases (Perris, 1976). They are not to be confused with cyclic manic-depressive illness. The main features are the presence of affective symptoms, varying degrees of confusion, psychomotor disturbances, frequent but transitory delusions and hallucinations, pananxiety, and, occasionally, states of ecstasy. The picture varies within and between episodes. When there are recurrent episodes, which is the rule, the intervals are completely symptom-free. The most striking feature is the acute onset — within a matter of 24 hours — in 87 per cent of episodes. Hardly any cases of schizophrenia or bipolar affective illness were found in the first-degree relatives, but there were 25 cases given the same diagnosis as the probands. There were, however, also nine cases of suicide. The mode of transmission, as inferred from ancestral line research, was probably dominant.

In conclusion, similar psychoses tend to recur in the offspring (and sibs) of probands with schizophrenic, bipolar (BP), or unipolar (UP) disorders of fairly typical kind. The frequency of recurrence reaches some 10–20 per cent by the time the full period of risk is completed.[1] However, of the affected offspring of BP probands, probably fewer than half will ever suffer from a BP illness themselves, the majority

---

[1] This compares with a lifetime risk for affective disorder of about 1.2 per cent for males and 2.2 per cent for females (James and Chapman, 1975), and of 1.0–2.0 per cent for schizophrenia (Slater and Cowie, 1971).

having UP or unspecified depressions, or committing suicide without a diagnosis having declared itself. In the families of chronic schizophrenics there is an increase both of schizophrenia and probably also of borderline states, but the nature, rate of occurrence, and origins of other psychopathological states require further study. As regards the atypical psychoses, affected relatives tend to have either similar disorders or else to suffer from affective psychoses, and chronic schizophrenia rarely occurs.

QUESTION II: SPECIAL FEATURES OF THE ILLNESS

Severity, Course, and Outcome

Is the course and outcome of a proband's illness likely to be reflected in that of an affected relative? Twin studies suggest that heritability is somewhat higher, and therefore that risks to first-degree relatives may be greater, in the more severe forms of both schizophrenia and of affective disorder (Gottesman and Shields, 1972; Bertelsen et al., 1977). Unfortunately, from the point of view of the genetic prognosis, good outcome, at any rate in schizophrenia, is not a consistent feature in familial cases. Larson and Nyman (1974), for instance, found no difference between the relatives of schizophrenic probands whether the outcome was good or bad. But Bleuler (1974) noticed that the course of the schizophrenic illness "tended to be more nearly similar" between parent and offspring than between unrelated pairs, and that episodic illnesses, when followed by remissions, tended to occur in successive generations.

Reisby (1967) concluded that offspring who developed severe or typical schizophrenia had had more prolonged contact with their psychotic parent than those who developed a milder or less typical form of illness, but Bleuler (1974) found little evidence that this factor was important. Although many of the children in Bleuler's study suffered greatly in their home environment, this was sometimes due to living with a cruel foster parent or stepmother, and not necessarily with the ill parent.

McCabe et al. (1971), whose study was conducted blind, showed that the families of probands whose illness was of at least two years' duration and who had failed to return to their premorbid level of functioning, contained more schizophrenia (13 cases), neuroses and overall illness, but less affective disorder (three cases), than the good prognosis families (five cases of schizophrenia and 14 of affective disorder). "Good prognosis schizophrenia" was defined as an illness of less than six months' duration with absence of a preexisting psychiatric illness (other than affective disorder or good prognosis schizophrenia) and a good premorbid personality (good social functioning). Both types of illness showed characteristic schizophrenic symptoms, but (although not a criterion) all the good prognosis probands also had significant affective symptomatology. The authors point to the overlap between their concept of good prognosis schizophrenia and schizoaffective disorder, and Cadoret et al. (1974) found that the good prognosis probands appeared to fit into two subgroups similar in some clinical features to patients with UP and BP affective disorder.

Age of Onset and Subtype

Probably, in general, the earlier the age of onset of illness in the proband, the higher the risk in the relatives. As regards *affective disorders*, Hopkinson and Ley (1969) found the risk was 29 per cent in first-degree relatives of probands whose first affective illness occurred before the age of 40 and 12.5 per cent when the illness began after that age. In a study of unipolar illness ("depressive disease") by Winokur et al. (1971), the risk among first degree relatives was 20 per cent when the onset in the proband was before 40 years, but only 14 per cent when the onset was after 40 years. In his study of involutional melancholia Stenstedt (1959) found that the risk of all forms of affective disorder was only 6 per cent.

A study of bipolar illness by Taylor and Abrams (1973) showed that probands with onset before 30 years had five times as many relatives with affective illness as those with later onset. In both this and Winokur's study, early onset in probands was associated with much alcoholism and sociopathy in the male members of the family. Because of this the term "depressive *spectrum* disease" was introduced to describe the unipolar, early onset disorder. The late onset disorder did not show this feature. Six separate studies of familial illnesses occurring in depressive disease subdivided according to age and sex, summarized by Cadoret (1976), support this distinction. Taylor and Abrams (1973) suggested that, like late onset unipolar depression, late onset *unipolar mania* may be distinct from other forms of manic-depressive illness. Goetzl et al. (1974), however, did not find age-related differences in BP illness.

The distributions of age of onset in BP and UP illnesses based on data from Winokur et al. (1969, 1971) and for cycloid psychosis from Perris (1974) are shown in Table 5. The cumulative percentages may be used to estimate approximately the proportion of the period of risk which a person has passed through.

TABLE 5
CUMULATIVE RISK IN PERCENT FOR AGE OF ONSET
IN UNIPOLAR AND BIPOLAR AFFECTIVE ILLNESSES,
ATYPICAL PSYCHOSES AND SCHIZOPHRENIA

	N	10–19	– 29	– 39	– 49	– 59	– 69	– 79
Unipolar[1]	100	19	39	54	73	87	96	100
Bipolar[2]	150	29	57	79	91	98	100	–
Cycloid[3]	60	17	53	82	95	100	–	–
Schizophrenia[4]	153	10	40	68	86	97	99	100

[1] Winokur et al. (1971).
[2] Data from Winokur et al. (1969), Taylor and Abrams (1973) and Goetzl et al. (1974).
[3] Perris (1974).
[4] Larson and Nyman (1970).

In *schizophrenia* too, the age of onset in the proband seems to influence the magnitude of the risks to the sibs and offspring. In the extreme case of the schizophrenialike psychoses occurring in the elderly, the risk is only 3–5 per cent (Kay, 1963). Such cases are almost exclusively paranoid, and this subtype is of later onset than the nonparanoid types (Winokur et al., 1974; Fowler et al., 1975). Onset in the second half of life may be less unusual than is often supposed. In a study of a birth year cohort, Larson and Nyman (1970) found that 32 per cent of their 153 probands had their first symptoms of overt schizophrenia *after* the age of 40 (Table 5). Of all the offspring born to their probands, two thirds were children of paranoid schizophrenics, whose mean age at onset of illness was 42 years (Larson and Nyman, 1973).

In a study of paranoid and nonparanoid schizophrenics, Fowler et al. (1975) confirmed the earlier work showing that the risk to relatives of paranoid probands was only half the risk to relatives of the younger, nonparanoid probands (7 versus 14 per cent). There was a significant correlation in age of onset between probands and relatives, but none as regards subtype (which seemed to exclude the possibility of genetic heterogeneity). Unlike earlier studies, which showed a modest degree of subtype resemblance between related pairs, the relatives' illnesses were diagnosed blind. Tsuang et al. (1974) concluded that the observed difference in morbidity risk between relatives of paranoid and nonparanoid schizophrenics is accounted for at least partly by age of onset differences. Age of onset may reflect degree of liability to the illness, but unfortunately few systematic attempts to link it with morbidity risks in relatives appear to have been made.

In conclusion, an earlier age of onset in both affective disorder and schizophrenia is associated with higher risks and with earlier onset of illness in relatives. In schizophrenia the higher risk in non-paranoid compared with paranoid schizophrenia may be related to the generally lower age of onset in the former but no definite conclusion about this question can at present be drawn. Generally speaking, the aspects of a schizophrenic parent's illness which are most likely to be replicated in that of his offspring seem to be the presence of marked affective coloring, and a remitting course. A biological affinity between some types of atypical psychoses, BP illnesses and so-called "good prognosis schizophrenia" has been postulated.

QUESTION III: THE PROBAND'S RELATIVES

Ideally, of course, the counselor would like to have a complete dossier of the family histories (unlikely to be available except in Scandinavia) and also to be able to make a *family study* of the close relatives. In practice he is not likely to get more than a family history from the proband and one relative, supplemented by hospital records when these exist, and Winokur et al. (1969) have shown that information so obtained is considerably less complete and reliable than with the family study method.

Psychiatric information about the close relatives would be important for several reasons. (1) The presence of one or more cases of the same illness would go far to establish that the illness in question was heritable and not sporadic or symptomatic. (2) Empirically, the presence of an affected relative in addition to the proband seems to increase the risk to other members of the family. (3) The occurrence of BP illness in a relative of a UP proband would suggest that the family illness was bipolar and that the risk of BP illness in offspring would be increased (Winokur et al., 1971; Taylor and Abrams, 1973). (4) The presence of alcoholism (or sociopathy) in a male relative of a proband with early onset affective disorder of either type might be regarded as an "affective equivalent" rather than as an unconnected condition. (5) Finally, individual pedigrees may be scrutinized for the presence of inherited characters which might serve as "markers" for the presence (or absence) of the gene causing the psychiatric illness. This will be discussed below in the section on X-linked inheritance.

If the consultand is concerned about a brother or sister he can be told that the chances of a sib falling ill is increased when a parent is similarly affected. For schizophrenia the risk increases from about 10 to 17 per cent (Slater and Cowie, 1971) for affective disorder from about 12 to 16 per cent (Stenstedt, 1952). Winokur and Clayton (1967), however, found that the risk for the sibs of probands when a parent was ill rose from 12 to 26 per cent (BP and UP illnesses were not separated). Ödegaard (1972) found that the presence of psychotic aunts and uncles also increased the chances of the sibs of schizophrenic probands falling ill by a factor of more than two. When a parent *and* uncles or aunts were psychotic, the all-diagnosis rate in sibs rose to 61 per cent (Gottesman and Shields, 1976). The risks to the consultand's offspring may be expected to increase in a similar fashion when his sibs, who, of course, will be the aunts and uncles of the next generation, are affected. However, recently Essen-Möller (1977) has reported failure to replicate Ödegaard's results and has pointed out some methodological problems.

Risks to the Second-Degree Relatives of an Ill Person

If the couple are not themselves ill, but are concerned about passing on a psychotic illness in a parent or sib to their own offspring, they may be advised that the empirical risks in second-degree relatives of probands (e.g., grandchildren or nephews and nieces) are only 3–5 per cent. Bleuler (1974) remarked that this low risk offered hope to the children of schizophrenics who, tortured by doubts, sought advice as to whether they should marry and have children of their own. However, in the given case, what really matters is the genetic makeup of the would-be parent (our consultand), and this should be assessed as carefully as possible. For example, how much of the period of risk for the psychosis has he himself passed through? Could he, while not actually ill, have a disorder of personality which falls within its "spectrum"? However, if by any chance the ill sib was the consultand's monozygous twin, then the consultand's own offspring would run the same risk as if he had been the proband (Fischer, 1973).

QUESTION IV: THE COPARENT AND THE IN-LAWS;
CONSANGUINITY AND ASSORTATIVE MATING

It has long been known that when the *spouse* of a psychotic person is also psychotic the risk of the offspring becoming psychotic is in the region of 35–45 per cent (Slater and Cowie, 1971). With one parent suffering from schizophrenia and the other from manic-depressive disorder, these conditions will appear with equal frequency among the offspring. When one parent has a typical, the other an atypical psychosis, some of the affective offspring will resemble one parent, some the other (rather than having a mixed type of illness). About 30 per cent of the nonpsychotic offspring of two schizophrenics will be abnormal in some other way, but only about 10 per cent of the offspring of two manic-depressive parents. Whatever the condition in the parents is, 40–50 per cent of the offspring are reported to be clinically normal.

Now that many patients are being treated outside hospitals, fertile marriages between two psychotic or formerly psychotic people may be becoming more common. The possibility of marriage between related individuals also arises. However, assortative mating (i.e., the tendency for mated pairs to be more similar in genetically influenced liability to psychosis than for random pairs) is probably only slightly commoner if the couple are first cousins, and first cousin marriages are therefore only slightly more likely than marriages between unrelated pairs to produce mentally ill offspring.

Assortative Mating in the Affective Disorders

Previous studies of hospital admissions (for references, see Gershon et al., 1973) have found a tendency for both members of a married couple to be hospitalized for affective disorder at greater than expected frequencies. There are four recent studies of the health of the spouses of probands suffering from affective disorders. In 144 spouses of patients admitted to research wards of the NIMH over a 10-year period, Gershon et al. (1973) found an increased prevalence of affective disorder in wives (20 per cent) but not husbands. There was also increased risk of affective disorder in the first-degree relatives of the wives. In a study of 127 patients attending the Lithium Clinic of the New York State Psychiatric Institute, Donner et al. (1976) found an increase of affective disorder (with morbid risk of 30 per cent) in the wives of males with UP illness. There was no increase of affective illness among the relatives of the wives compared with relatives of controls. In a third study, carried out in Jerusalem, Gershon et al. (1975b) found no evidence of assortative mating. Thus two out of three of these studies suggest that assortative mating in affective disorder is occurring.

The fourth study was focused on the spouses of schizophrenics (Fowler and Tsuang, 1975) but included two comparison groups with affective disorder. It was found that psychiatric abnormalities, the majority of them personality disorders or alcoholism, were significantly less frequent in the spouses of schizophrenics (39 per cent) than in the spouses of bipolar or unipolar depressives (17 per cent). There was no difference between the spouses of manics and the spouses of UP depressives.

Assortative Mating in Schizophrenia

Interest has recently revived in the health of the spouses of schizo-phrenics. If the risk to the offspring is about 40 per cent in the rare in-stance of both parents being schizophrenic, what is the effect when one parent has schizophrenia and the other a spectrum defect, and how often do such marriages occur?

Rosenthal (1974) presented data from the Danish-American Adop-tion Study (the coparent study) on the condition of the spouses of psy-chotic parents who had given up a child for adoption at an early age. Limiting ourselves to the spouses of the chronically schizophrenic parents, only two had a "hard spectrum" diagnosis (i.e., borderline or chronic schizophrenia, questionable or definite), but altogether nine (38 per cent) fell into the spectrum as a whole (which includes ques-tionable or definite acute schizophrenia and personality disorders of in-adequate, paranoid, or schizoid types). A further five (21 per cent) of the spouses suffered from psychopathic disorders.

These parents were of course unrepresentative in that they had given up a child for adoption. The spouses of patients admitted to men-tal hospitals with schizophrenia have been studied by Bleuler (1974), Fowler and Tsuang (1975), and Fowler et al. (1977). The results of these and of Rosenthal's study are summarized in Table 6. Pooling the data, only 3 per cent of the spouses in the nonadoption studies fell into the spectrum, but 30 per cent had *other* disorders or eccentricities, chiefly undiagnosed psychiatric disorders and alcoholism.

When the diagnoses in the offspring were related to the diagnoses in the coparents, the results were as follows. When, in the Rosenthal study, the coparent had a spectrum diagnosis, the offspring were three to five times more likely to have a spectrum diagnosis than when the coparent had another diagnosis or was normal (the diagnoses were made blind). In the study by Fowler et al. (1977), in which assortative matings were far less frequent than in the Rosenthal study but other diagnoses in the coparent were common, there was an increased risk of psychiatric disturbance in the offspring when the spouse was also abnor-mal. The commonest diagnosis in the offspring was definite or suspected antisocial personality, the commonest diagnosis in the spouse was alcoholism. Fowler and Tsuang (1975) pointed out that having an alcoholic or sociopathic parent had been shown (Robins, 1966) to be one of the strongest predictors of adult antisocial behavior, and the possi-bility therefore arose that certain of the abnormalities in the children of schizophrenics were perhaps more likely to be related to the illnesses of the spouses, than to be a form of schizophrenia transmitted from the

TABLE 6
PSYCHOPATHOLOGY IN THE SPOUSES OF SCHIZOPHRENICS

Author	Schizophrenia (definite or suspected) or schizoid personality N (%)	Alcoholism (definite or suspected) N (%)	Antisocial personality (definite or suspected) N (%)	Feeble-minded N (%)	Other and undiagnosed psychiatric illness and suicide N (%)	Total ill N (%)	Total well N (%)
Bleuler (1974)	4	9	–	7	17[1]	37 (30)	83 (70)
Fowler et al. (1975)	1	5	2	3	7	18 (37)	31 (63)
Fowler et al. (1977)	1	6	1	0	5	13 (37)	22 (63)
Total	6 (3)	20 (10)	3 (1.5)	10 (5)	29[1] (14)	68 (33)	136 (67)
Rosenthal (1974)[2] (Adoption Study)	9[3] (37.5)	–	5 (21)	–	8 (33)	22 (92)	2 (8)

[1] Includes three suicides.
[2] Spouses of chronic schizophrenics.
[3] Two in 'hard,' seven in 'soft' spectrum.

schizophrenic parent.

In a controlled study of psychiatric morbidity among schizophrenic families (Stephens et al., 1976) a high risk of personality disorder was found among the male sibs of schizophrenics. Kay et al. (1976b) suggested that this might be connected with the psychopathic abnormalities found in many of the fathers, and be unrelated to the schizophrenic trait itself. Since, apparently, some forms of psychopathic disorder have a hereditary basis (F. Schulsinger, 1972; Crowe, 1975), this kind of mating might be called "cross-assortative," i.e., selective mating between people of *different* genotypes (but sharing certain social and phenotypical characteristics).

QUESTION V: SEX OF PROBAND AND X-LINKAGE; SEX OF OFFSPRING.

When Reich et al. (1969) found virtually no ill father-ill son pairs in their patients with bipolar illness, they revived the earlier hypothesis of dominant X-linked transmission. This hypothesis is eminently testable; it predicts absence of male-to-male transmission. A number of instances of male-to-male transmissions have in fact been reported, notably by Perris (1976), but also by Donner and Fieve (1975), Goetzl et al. (1974), and Loranger (1975). The theory also predicts that mothers and daughters of male probands will invariably possess the gene; the actual morbidity risk, depending on the rate of manifestation, would be probably in the 30–40 per cent range. Brothers and sisters of male probands would both run only about half this risk of falling ill.

By including brothers, some control is provided for the nonspecific effect of sex on the manifestation of the disorder. The theoretical ratios would be 0:2:1 for the risks in fathers and sons, mothers and daughters, and brothers, respectively. As Table 7 shows, the observed rates in fathers and sons are much lower than those in mothers and daughters. But they are not significantly lower than the risks in brothers. Overall, there are clearly too many affected fathers and sons of male probands to fit the model of X-linkage though X-linked transmission might still be occurring in some families.

Some ill fathers-ill son pairs could be explained by supposing that a depressive illness in the father belonged to the UP type of illness. However, instances of undoubted bipolar illness in both members of a pair have been reported, and have included cases where there was no evidence that transmission could have been via the mother (assortative mating) (Donner and Fieve, 1975; Van Grieff et al., 1975; Mendlewicz and Rainer, 1974; Hays, 1976).

TABLE 7
RISK OF AFFECTIVE DISORDER IN MALE AND FEMALE
RELATIVES OF MALE PROBANDS WITH BIPOLAR ILLNESS

	Fathers and Sons		Mothers and Daughters		Brothers	
	No. ill		No. ill		No. ill	
	No. at risk	MR%	No. at risk	MR%	No. at risk	MR%
Total from pooled data[1]	32/229	14	93/222	41.7	64/358	17.9
Observed ratios	0.78		2.33		1.00	
Theoretical ratios assuming X-linked dominant transmission	0		2		1	

[1] Data from Perris (1969), Winokur et al. (1969), Cadoret et al. (1970), Goetzl et al. (1974), Helzer and Winokur (1974), Mendlewicz and Rainer (1974), and Gershon et al. (1975b).

Genetic Markers

The other line of evidence for X-linkage in bipolar illness is its apparent linkage with the known X-linked traits, color blindness and the Xg blood group (first reported by Winokur and coworkers in 1969). The most recent reports come from Mendlewicz et al. (1974) who analyzed the evidence in 29 "informative families" belonging to both bipolar and unipolar probands. (An "informative family" is one which includes a mother who is heterozygous for both traits and who has two or more sons.) Evidence was found for close linkage between bipolar illness and both deutan and protan color blindness, and somewhat less close linkage between bipolar illness and the Xg blood group. There was no measurable linkage between unipolar illness and either protanopia or the Xg blood group. Mendlewicz (1976) also reported data consistent with X-linkage in three or four families with schizoaffective illness, and suggested that in view of the known occurrence of male transmission in some families, bipolar affective psychoses might be regarded as genetically heterogeneous, with some genetic relationship to schizoaffective syndromes.

These conclusions were criticized by Gershon and Bunney (1976) who pointed out that the data so far reported showed an *association* between bipolar illness and color blindness *across* families, whereas linkage involves either a state of coupling or of repulsion *within* families. The latter had not so far been demonstrated. In a review of family study data, Gershon and Bunney (1976) considered that the excess of affectively ill female over male parents and offspring of probands was probably a reflection of the influence of autosomal and environmental factors on the sex ratio in affective disorders in general. The nature of the apparent association of BP illness with color blindness and with the Xg blood group required further study.

In the case of our consulting couple, if there was a family history of male-to-male transmission, the X-linked dominant model could clearly not be applied. In the absence of male-to-male transmission, an extensive pedigree showing good evidence of linkage between the BP illness and X-linked traits would allow a counselor to postulate that the model could be applied to that particular family and to suggest which members might or might not be at risk. However, families with these possible marker genes are too rare for this method to be of any practical importance in genetic counseling (Cadoret, 1976).

The Influence of the Environment

A future article should take account of the environment. The empirical risks are the resultant of both heredity and environment and of the interaction between them. Unfortunately, at present, if our consulting couple asked, as they very reasonably might, what they could do during the first 15 years of life to reduce the risks of their offspring falling ill, we would hardly know what advice to give. For example, in regard to antenatal care, the reports of higher rates of pregnancy and birth complications (PBCs) among the offspring of psychotic women (Sameroff and Zax, 1973) have not been confirmed (Mirdal et al., 1977) though Mednick et al. (1971) suggested that children of schizophrenic parents might react differently to PBCs than children of normal parents, and Rieder et al. (1977), in a study of IQ in the offspring of schizophrenics, found evidence compatible with the idea that such children may have a specific susceptibility to certain perinatal events.

In a Swedish study an unfavorable environment in childhood was reported to increase the liability to the disorder in manic-depressive families (Stenstedt, 1952) but Rosenthal et al. (1975), in the Danish study of adopted children and their parents, found that rearing patterns apparently had only a modest effect on individuals who had a genetic liability to schizophrenia (but an appreciable effect on persons without such a background). In another study using the crossfostering technique, Wender et al. (1974) found more psychopathology among the adopted-away children of schizophrenics (reared by normal parents) than among the children of normal parents who were reared by schizophrenic adoptive parents.

Although schizophrenogenic family patterns have been described (e.g., Lidz, 1973; Laing, 1960), it is not clear how far they are independent of, or result from interaction with, hereditary factors. Scharfetter's study (1970) of folie à deux between nonconsanguineous individuals suggested that a degree of liability to psychosis was already present in the induced subjects. It is to be hoped that the current research on children at high risk for schizophrenia will eventually throw light on the antecedents of illness and suggest strategies of prevention (see Garmezy [1974] for a review).

The responsiveness of an eventual illness to treatment and the factors affecting the rate of relapse are also relevant in genetic counseling, since they are measures of the burden to be borne. Life event research (e.g., Brown et al., 1973) appears to hold out the possibility of being able to anticipate and so perhaps prevent depressive or schizophrenic episodes, particularly in predisposed individuals (Abe, 1966). Identifiable events (especially postpartum and physical) have been found to be most frequent before episodes of schizoaffective, next before UP affective illness, less so before BP illness, and least frequent before episodes of schizophrenia (Tsuang et al., 1976). It is possible, however, that the low social class environment which many schizophrenics are born or drift into may interact with their genetic make-up to increase the risk of psychotic illness (Kohn, 1976), and the same may be true of the impairment of hearing with which paranoid psychoses occurring in the elderly are often associated (Kay et al., 1976a). At present, however, the most (and often the only) effective and practicable way of "environmental manipulation" is by the use of appropriate drugs, which of course can only be given after the illness has declared itself. The nature of the interaction between drug, inherited liability, and emotional relationship with key figures, as described by Brown et al. (1973), needs to be elucidated before the factors affecting the course of illness can be properly understood (Leff, 1975).

Conclusions

To a couple concerned about the risk of a psychotic illness in one of them being transmitted to their offspring, the counselor would have to base his advice on the risks derived from the numerous family studies which are now available. While these "empirical risks" must be regarded as the resultant of environmental as well as of inherited factors, it appears that little useful advice can be given as to how, by taking thought for the future, the risk might be reduced. At the present time, therefore, the magnitude of the risk has to be assessed on the basis of factors already existing in the parent and coparent, and in their families.

When the parent's illness is typical (schizophrenia or affective psychosis), the illness in the offspring is likely to be similar in kind, and when the parent's illness is atypical (schizoaffective, reactive, cycloid), illnesses in the offspring, though more varied in form, will also tend to be atypical. When the parent suffers from a schizophrenic illness showing the features predictive of good prognosis—acute onset, affective content, and remission—these will tend to be repeated in the next generation, though unfortunately the degree of resemblance does not always extend to the eventual outcome. The offspring of a parent with paranoid schizophrenia will run only about half the risk of becoming psychotic as the offspring of a parent with a nonparanoid form of schizophrenia. Among affective disorders, bipolar illness carries a higher risk for affective disorders of all kinds than unipolar illness, and bipolar disorder would be virtually restricted to children of bipolar parents. Instances of male-to-male transmission have been reported, but this does not preclude dominant X-linked inheritance as the mode of transmission of bipolar disorder in some families.

Generally speaking, the risk of a psychosis occurring at some time in the life of an offspring of a psychotic parent falls within the range 10–15 per cent, but related conditions detected by personal interviews occur more frequently. Factors which tend to reduce the risk are: (1) evidence of gross organic aetiology in the parental illness; (2) an onset late in life; (3) an absence of affected relatives; (4) an absence of any psychotic illness on the coparent's side of the family. The opposite factors would tend to increase the risk, which would reach a maximum of about 45 per cent in the case where both parents were or had been psychotic.

Empirically, the offspring of a schizophrenic parent are found to be prone to psychopathological disorders of a nonpsychotic kind. However, it is not yet clear to what extent these disorders (the "spectrum" of schizophrenia) are genetically related to schizophrenia and are transmitted through the ill parent. Even when he or she is not psychotic, the psychopathological state of the coparent appears to have an important effect on the risk of psychiatric abnormality in the offspring and on the form it will take.

REFERENCES

Abe, K. (1966), Suspectibility to psychoses and precipitating factors: A study of families with two or more psychotic members. *Psychiatrie et Neurologie*, 151:276–290.

Angst, J. (1966), *Zur Atiologie und Nosologie Endogener Depressiver Psychosen*. Berlin: Springer.

Bertelsen, A., Harvold, B., & Hauge, M. (1977), A Danish twin study of manic-depressive disorders. *Brit. J. Psychiat.*, 130:330–351.

Bleuler, M. (1974), The offspring of schizophrenics. *Schiz. Bull.*, 8:93–107.

Brown, G. W., Sklair, F., Harris, T. O., & Birley, J. L. T. (1973), Life events and psychiatric disorders. Part I: Some methodological issues. *Psychol. Med.*, 3:74–87.

Cadoret, R. J. (1976), The genetics of affective disorder and genetic counselling. *Soc. Biol.*, 23:116–122.

_____ Fowler, R. C., McCabe, M. S., & Winokur, G. (1974), Evidence for heterogeneity in a group of good-prognosis schizophrenics. *Compr. Psychiat.*, 15:443–450.

_____ Winokur, G., & Clayton, P. J. (1970), Family history studies: VII. Manic depressive disease versus depressive disease. *Brit. J. Psychiat.*, 116:625–635.

Carter, C., Evans, K., Fraser-Roberts, J. A., & Buck, A. (1971), Genetic clinic: A follow up. *Lancet*, 1:281–285.

Cooper, A. F., Curry, A. R., Kay, D. W. K., Garside, R. F., & Roth, M. (1974), Hearing loss in paranoid and affective psychoses in the elderly. *Lancet*, ii:851–860.

Crowe, R. R. (1975), An adoptive study of psychopathy: Preliminary results from arrest records and psychiatric and hospital records. In: *Genetic Research in Psychiatry*, ed. R. R. Fieve et al. Baltimore: Johns Hopkins.

Davison, K. & Bagley, C. R. (1969), Schizophrenia-like psychoses associated with organic disorders of the central nervous system: A review of the literature. *Brit. J. Psychiat.*, Special Publication No. 4, pp. 113–184.

Donner, D. L. & Fieve, R. R. (1975), Psychiatric illness in fathers of men with bipolar primary affective disorder. *Arch. Gen. Psychiat.*, 32:1134–1137.

_____ Fleiss, J. L., Addonizio, G., & Fieve, R. R. (1976), Assortative mating in primary affective disorder. *Biol. Psychiat.*, 11:43–51.

Essen-Möller, E. (1977), Evidence for polygenic inheritance in schizophrenia? *Acta Psychiat. Scand.*, 55:202–207.

Feighner, J. P., Robin, E., Guze, S. B., Woodruff, A. R., Jr., Winokur, A., & Munoz, R. (1972), Diagnostic criteria for use in psychiatric research. *Arch. Gen. Psychiat.*, 26:57–63.

Feldman, M. W. & Lewontin, R. C. (1975), The heritability hang-up. *Science*, 190:1163–1168.

Fischer, M. (1973), Genetic and environmental factors in schizophrenia. *Acta Psychiat. Scand.*, 238(suppl.).

Fowler, R. C. & Tsuang, M. T. (1975), Spouses of schizophrenics: A blind comparative study. *Compr. Psychiat.*, 16:4, 339.

_____ _____ & Cadoret, R. J. (1975), A clinical and family study of paranoid and non-paranoid schizophrenics. *Brit. J. Psychiat.*, 124:346–359.

———— ———— ———— (1977), Psychiatric illness in the offspring of schizophrenics. *Compr. Psychiat.*, 18:2, 127.

Garmezy, N. (1974), Children at risk: The search for the antecedents of schizophrenia. Part 1. Conceptual models and research methods. *Schiz. Bull.*, 8:14–90.

Gershon, E. S., Baron, M., & Leckman, J. F. (1975a), Genetic models of the transmission of affective disorders. *J. Psychiat. Res.*, 12:301–318.

———— & Bunney, W. E. (1976), The question of X-linkage in bipolar manic-depressive illness. *J. Psychiat. Res.*, 13:99–117.

———— Dunner, D. L., Sturt, L., & Goodwin, F. K. (1973), Assortative mating in the affective disorders. *Biol. Psychiat.*, 7:63–74.

———— Mark, A., Cohen, N., Belison, N., Baron, M., & Knobe, K. (1975b), Transmitted factors in the morbid risk of affective disorders: A controlled study. *J. Psychiat. Res.*, 12:283–300.

Gittelson, N. L. (1966), Depressive psychosis in the obsessional neurotic. *Brit. J. Psychiat.*, 112:883–887.

Goetzl, U., Green, R., Whybrow, P., & Jackson, R. (1974), X-linkage revisited. *Arch. Gen. Psychiat.*, 31:665–672.

Gottesman, I. I. & Shields, J. (1972), *Schizophrenia and Genetics*. London: Academic Press.

———— ———— (1976), A critical review of recent adoption, twin and family studies of schizophrenia: Behavioural genetics perspectives. *Schiz. Bull.*, 2:360–401.

Hays, P. (1976), Etiological factors in manic-depressive psychoses. *Arch. Gen. Psychiat.*, 33:1187–1188.

Helzer, J. E. & Winokur, G. (1974), A family interview study of male manic depressive. *Arch. Gen. Psychiat.*, 31:73–77.

Heston, L. L. (1966), Psychiatric disorders in foster home reared children of schizophrenic mothers. *Brit. J. Psychiat.*, 112:819–825.

Hopkinson, G. & Ley, F. (1969), A genetic study of affective disorder. *Brit. J. Psychiat.*, 115:917–922.

James, J. W. (1971), Frequency in relatives for an all-or-none trait. *Ann. Hum. Genetics*, 35:47–49.

James, N. M. & Chapman, C. J. (1975), A genetic study of bipolar affective disorder. *Brit. J. Psychiat.*, 126:449–456.

Kallmann, F. J. (1956), Psychiatric aspects of genetic counselling. *Amer. J. Hum. Genet.*, 8:97–101.

Kay, D. W. K. (1963), Late paraphrenia and its bearing on the aetiology of schizophrenia. *Acta Psychiat. Scand.*, 39:159–169.

———— Cooper, A. F., Garside, R. F., & Roth, M. (1976a), The differentiation of paranoid from affective psychoses by patients' premorbid characteristics. *Brit. J. Psychiat.*, 129:207–215.

———— Roth, M., Atkinson, M. W., Stephens, D. A., & Garside, R. F. (1976b), Genetic hypotheses and environmental factors in the light of psychiatric morbidity in the families of schizophrenics. *Brit. J. Psychiat.*, 127:109–118.

Kendell, R. E. & Gourlay, J. (1970), The clinical distinction between the affective psychoses and schizophrenia. *Brit. J. Psychiat.*, 117:261–266.

Kidd, K. K. & Cavalli-Sforza (1973), An analysis of the genetics of schizophrenia. *Soc. Biol.*, 20:254–265.

Kohn, M. L. (1976), The interaction of social class and other factors in the etiology of schizophrenia. *Amer. J. Psychiat.*, 133:177–180.

Laing, R. D. (1960), *The Divided Self.* London: Tavistock.

Larson, C. A. & Nyman, G. E. (1970), Age of onset in schizophrenia. *Hum. Hered.*, 20:241–247.

—— —— (1973), Differential fertility in schizophrenia. *Acta Psychiat. Scand.*, 49:272–280.

—— —— (1974), Schizophrenia: Outcome in a birth year cohort. *Psychiat. Clinica*, 7:50–55.

Leff, J. P. (1975), The maintenance of schizophrenic patients in the community. *Studies of Schizophrenia, British Journal of Psychiatry Special Pub. No. 10*, pp. 132–141.

Leonhard, K., Korff, I., & Schulz, H. (1962), Die Temperamente in den Familien der Monopolaren und Bipolaren phasischen Psychosen. *Psychiatrie u. Neurologie* (Basel), 143:416–434.

Lidz, T. (1973), *The Origin and Treatment of Schizophrenic Disorders.* New York: Basic Books.

Loranger, A. W. (1975), X-linkage and manic-depressive illness. *Brit. J. Psychiat.*, 127:482–488.

McCabe, M. S. (1975), Reactive psychoses: A clinical and genetic investigation. *Acta Psychiat. Scand.*, 239(suppl.):1–133.

—— & Cadoret, R. J. (1976), Genetic investigations of atypical psychoses. I. Morbidity in parents and siblings. *Compr. Psychiat.*, 17:347–352.

—— Fowler, R. C., Cadoret, R. J., & Winokur, G. (1971), Familial difference in schizophrenia with good and poor prognosis. *Psychol. Med.*, 1:326–332.

—— & Stromgren, E. (1975), Reactive psychoses. *Arch. Gen. Psychiat.*, 32:447–454.

Mednick, S. A., Mura, E., Schulsinger, F., & Mednick, B. (1971), Perinatal conditions and infant development in children with schizophrenic parents. *Soc. Biol.*, 18:103–113.

Mendlewicz, J. (1976), Genetic studies in schizoaffective illness. In: *The Impact of Biology on Modern Psychiatry*, ed. E. S. Gershon, R. H. Belmaker, S. S. Kety, & M. Rosenbaum. New York: Plenum.

—— & Fleiss, J. L. (1974), Linkage studies with X-chromosome markers in bipolar (manic-depressive) and unipolar (depressive) illnesses. *Biol. Psychiat.*, 9:261–294.

—— & Rainer, J. D. (1974), Morbidity risk and genetic transmission in manic depressive illness. *Amer. J. Hum. Genet.*, 26:692–701.

Mirdal, G. M., Rosenthal, D., Wender, P. H., & Schulsinger, F. (1977), Perinatal complications in off-spring of psychotic parents. *Brit. J. Psychiat.*, 130:494–505.

Ödegaard, Ö. (1963), The psychiatric disease entities in the light of a genetic investigation. *Acta Psychiat. Scand.*, 169(suppl.):94–104.

—— (1972), The multifactorial theory of inheritance in predisposition to schizophrenia. In: *Genetic Factors in Schizophrenia*, ed. A. R. Kaplan. Springfield, Ill.: C. C Thomas, pp. 256–275.

Perris, C., ed. (1976), A study of bipolar (manic depressive) and unipolar recurrent depressive psychoses. *Acta. Psychiat. Scand.*, 194(suppl.).

_____ (1974), A study of cycloid psychoses. *Acta. Psychiat. Scand.*, 253 (suppl.).

Rainer, J. D. (1975), Genetic knowledge and heredity counsellings: New responsibilities for psychiatry. In: *Genetic Research and Psychiatry*, ed. R. R. Fieve, D. Rosenthal, & H. Brill. London: Johns Hopkins.

Reed, S. C. (1972), Genetic counselling in schizophrenia. In: *Genetic Factors in Schizophrenia*, ed. A. R. Kaplan. Springfield, Ill.: C. C Thomas, pp. 315–324.

Reich, T., Clayton, P. H., & Winokur, G. (1969), Family history studies: V. The genetics of mania. *Amer. J. Psychiat.*, 125:1358–1369.

_____ James, J. W., & Morris, C. A. (1972), The use of multiple thresholds in determining the mode of transmission of semi-continuous traits. *Ann. Hum. Genetics*, 36:163–184.

Reisby, N. (1967), Psychoses in children of schizophrenic mothers. *Acta Psychiat. Scand.*, 43:8–20.

Rieder, R. O., Broman, S. H., & Rosenthal, D. (1977), The offspring of schizophrenics: II. Perinatal factors and I. P. *Arch. Gen. Psychiat.*, 34:789–799.

Robins, L. N. (1966), *Deviant Children Grow Up*. Baltimore: Williams & Williams.

Rosenthal, D. (1974), The concept of subschizophrenic disorders. In: *Genetics, Environment and Psychopathology*, ed. S. A. Mednick, F. Schulsinger, J. Higgins, & B. Bell. Oxford: North-Holland.

_____ Wender, P. H., Kety, S. S., Welner, J., & Schulsinger, F. (1971), The adopted-away offspring of schizophrenics. *Amer. J. Psychiat.*, 128:307–311.

_____ _____ _____ Schulsinger, F., Welner, J., & Rieder, R. (1975), Parent-child relationships and psychopathological disorder in the child. *Arch. Gen. Psychiat.*, 32:466–476.

Sameroff, S. J. & Zax, M. (1973), Perinatal characteristics of the schizophrenic woman. *J. Nerv. Ment. Dis.*, 157:191–199.

Scharfetter, C. (1970), On the hereditary aspects of symbiotic psychoses: A contribution towards the understanding of the schizophrenia-like psychoses. *Psychiat. Clin.*, 3:145–152.

Schulsinger, F. (1972), Psychopathy: Heredity and environment. *Internat. J. Ment. Hlth.*, 1:190–206.

Schulsinger, H. (1976), A ten-year follow-up of children of schizophrenic mothers: Clinical assessment. *Acta Psychiat. Scand.*, 53:371–386.

Slater, E. & Cowie, V. (1971), *The Genetics of Mental Disorders*. London: Oxford University Press.

_____ & Glithero, E. (1963), The schizophrenia-like psychoses of epilepsy. III: Genetical aspects. *Brit. J. Psychiat.*, 109:130–133.

Stenstedt, A. (1952), A study in manic-depressive psychoses. *Acta Psychiat. Scand.*, 79(suppl.).

_____ (1959), Involutional melancholia: An aetiological, clinical and social study of endogenous depression in later life. *Acta Psychiat. Scand.*, 127(suppl.).

Stephens, D. A., Atkinson, M. W., Kay, D. W. K., Roth, M., & Garside, R. F. (1976), Psychiatric morbidity in parents and sibs of schizophrenics and non-schizophrenics. *Brit. J. Psychiat.*, 127:97–108.

Taylor, M. & Abrams, R. (1973), A genetic study of early and late onset affective disorders. *Arch. Gen. Psychiat.*, 28:656–658.

Tsuang, M. T. (1967), A study of pairs of sibs both hospitalised for mental disorder. *Brit. J. Psychiat.*, 113:283–300.

_____ Dempsey, G. M., & Rauscher, F. (1976), A study of "atypical schizophrenia." *Arch. Gen. Psychiat.*, 33:1157–1160.

_____ Fowler, R. C., Cadoret, R. J., & Monnelly, E. (1974), Schizophrenia among first-degree relatives of paranoid and non-paranoid schizophrenics. *Compr. Psychiat.*, 15:295–302.

Van Grieff, H., McHugh, P. R., Stokes, P. E. (1975), The familial history in 16 males with bipolar manic-depressive illness. In: *Genetic Research in Psychiatry*, ed. R. R. Fieve, D. Rosenthal, & H. Brill. London: John Hopkins.

Videbech, T. (1975), A study of genetic factors, childhood bereavement, and premorbid traits in patients with anancastic endogenous depression. *Acta Psychiat. Scand.*, 52:178–222.

Wender, P. H., Rosenthal, D., Kety, S. S., Schulsinger, F., & Welner, J. (1974), Cross fostering: A research strategy for clarifying the role of genetic and experimental factors in the etiology of schizophrenia. *Arch. Gen. Psychiat.*, 30:121–128.

Winokur, G., Cadoret, R., Dorzab, J., & Baker, M. (1971), Depressive disease. *Arch. Gen. Psychiat.*, 24:135–144.

_____ & Clayton, P. (1967), Family history studies. I. Two types of affective disorders separated according to genetic and clinical factors. In: *Recent Advances in Biological Psychiatry*, Vol. 9, ed. J. Wortis. New York: Plenum, pp. 35–50.

_____ _____ & Reich, T. (1969), *Manic Depressive Illness*. St. Louis: Mosby.

_____ Morrison, J., Clancy, J., & Crowe, R. (1974), Iowa 500: The clinical and genetic distinction of hebephrenic and paranoid schizophrenia. *J. Nerv. Ment. Dis.*, 159:12–19.

Wood, D., Othmer, S., Reich, T., Viesselman, J., & Rutt, C. (1977), Primary and secondary affective disorder. 1. Past social history and current episodes in 92 depressed inpatients. *Compr. Psychiat.*, 18:201–210.

World Health Organization (1969), *Genetic Counselling*. World Health Organization Technical Report Series No. 416.

Zerbin-Rudin, E. (1967), Endogene Psychosen. In: *Humangenetik: Ein Kurzes Handbuch*, Vol. 2., ed. P. E. Becker. Stuttgart.

Family Psychotherapy

Family psychotherapy is one of the two major divisions of family treatment, vector therapy being the other. In interview psychotherapy the tool that fashions change is the personality of the therapist or therapists. One form of family psychotherapy is commonly employed, this being conjoint family therapy (sometimes simply termed family therapy), which involves the whole family meeting with the therapist or therapists.

In this section, two papers discuss techniques — the use of paradox and the use of explanation. Another paper discusses co-therapy. Of the last three, two papers discuss multiple family therapy and the concluding paper in this section, fittingly, is an evaluation of therapy.

Paradox as a Therapeutic Technique: A Review

PATRICIA H. SOPER
and LUCIANO L'ABATE

Paradox has been a philosophical curiosity since Epimenedes of Megara devised the paradox of the liar and Zeno of Elea produced the paradoxes of infinity (Hughes and Brecht, 1975). Interest in paradox waned until the late-nineteenth-century revival of logic (Edwards, 1967). Recently, family therapists have developed an interest in pragmatic paradoxes, leaving logical and semantic paradoxes to the domain of philosophers and linguists.

A paradox is defined as a "contradiction that follows correct deduction from consistent premises" (Watzlawick, Beavin, and Jackson, 1967). Watzlawick et al. (1967) viewed pragmatic paradoxes as most important in the study of human interaction because these paradoxes arise in ongoing interactions and determine behavior. Haley (1955) pointed out that a paradoxical behavior has two levels of abstraction. One level denies the assertion of the other; the second statement of the paradox is about the first but is at a different level of abstraction. Haley went on to say that this type of paradox is inevitable in the process of communication.

This paper is concerned with the nature of paradox as a therapeutic intervention from an historical and theoretical perspective. Included is a review of types of paradoxical interventions as well as a brief review of related approaches with heavy paradoxical overtones. Major emphasis is on the use of paradox in family therapy through relevant individual approaches such as paradoxical intention and hypnosis.

Patricia H. Soper, M.A., and Luciano L'Abate, Ph.D., both teach at Georgia State University, Atlanta, Georgia.

The Therapeutic Double Bind

The Palo Alto group (including both the Bateson project and the Mental Research Institute) is credited with the recognition of pathological aspects of paradoxical communication in their work on the double bind (Bateson, Jackson, Haley, and Weakland, 1956, 1963; Watzlawick, 1963). The direct outgrowth of their work is the therapeutic double bind which is a mirror image of the pathological bind (Watzlawick et al., 1967). The therapeutic double bind presupposes an intense relationship between the therapist and client. The therapist enjoins the client to change while remaining unchanged with the implication that the injunction is the agent of change. The client is in the position either of changing and demonstrating control over his pathology or of resisting by behaving nonsymptomatically. Thus, the client is bound to change. The therapeutic setting dissuades the client from leaving the field by withdrawing or commenting on the paradox (Watzlawick et al., 1967; Feldman, 1976).

Prescribing the Symptom and Reframing

Varieties of therapeutic double binds that are closely associated with the Palo Alto group are: (1) prescribing the symptom and (2) reframing. Prescribing the symptom is quite simply instructing the client to maintain or exaggerate his symptomatic behavior. Watzlawick et al. (1967) view making the client behave as he has been behaving as applying a "be spontaneous" paradox. If the client is asked to display his symptom which is a nondeliberate, spontaneous behavior, then he cannot be spontaneous any more since the demand precludes spontaneity.

A number of practitioners report the use of this paradoxical instruction to bring about change in clients. Farrelly and Brandsma (1974) frequently encourage their clients to continue with their symptoms to an absurd degree to "prove" the clients' irrational contentions about themselves. Montalvo and Haley (1973) report that the child therapist may even encourage a symptom as a means of bringing about change. Fischer (1974) and Prosky (1974) make reference to the usefulness of enlisting the family's oppositional feelings against the therapist. Andolfi (1974) reports that Jackson utilized prescribing the symptom with paranoid patients by teaching them to be more suspicious. In families disrupted by divorce, Peck (1974) instructs the partial family to take their incompleteness more seriously, which resolves the members' ambivalence.

Feldman (1976) cites the usefulness of the technique of prescribing the symptom in dealing with a depressed client. The therapist may *implicitly* encourage the client to remain depressed by commenting, "It's a wonder you aren't more depressed." The client can respond by remaining depressed, and thus acknowledging control over his symptom, or evidence decreased depression, which also acknowledges control over his symptom. The therapist can follow through by trying to change or to circumscribe the situation further, suggesting, for instance, that the client spread out his depression throughout the week as opposed to being depressed only on the weekends.

Weakland, Fisch, Watzlawick and Bodin (1974) gave an example of a client who was complaining of headaches. She was told to make every effort to have more headaches at specified periods in the coming week. Again, regardless of whether the headaches got worse or disappeared, the client was bound to demonstrate that the apparently unchangeable problem could change. Weakland et al. (1974) reported that the most effective manner to give such paradoxical instructions is to play one down or to act ignorant or confused in order to have the advice accepted. When the therapist came on strong with the paradoxical instructions, the client tended to ignore the advice.

An additional example of prescribing the symptom is a case involving a middle-aged woman and her schizophrenic son who were in a power struggle over the son's allowance (Fisch, Watzlawick, Weakland, and Bodin, 1972). The mother was reluctant to hand over much money due to her son's unstable mental state while the son was never sure he was able to meet expenses. The mother judged the amount of money she gave the son by the amount of psychotic behavior she perceived in him. The therapist instructed the son to use his psychotic behavior deliberately with the mother who was even more fearful of an expensive rehospitalization of the son than she was of his possible squandering of his allowance. The mother came through with a larger amount paid on a regular basis from which the son saved enough money to buy himself a car, thus giving himself greater independence from his mother.

Reframing, also a therapeutic double bind, involves changing the entire meaning of a situation by altering both or either its conceptual and/or emotional context in such a manner that the entire situation is experienced as completely different, i.e., the situation has been placed in a new frame (Watzlawick, Weakland, and Fisch, 1974). The therapist may frame the therapy procedures so he can work effectively, reinterpret messages from family members in a positive light (Jackson and Weakland, 1961), take a psychotic client's metaphors literally and interpret them as evidence of his sanity (Kantor and Hoffman, 1966), define all events as being for the good of the family (Haley, 1962), and turn a family member into an observer (Minuchin, 1965). Haley (1963) used the term relabeling which essentially is a synonym for reframing. He makes the point that relabeling maladaptive patterns (or reframing) in couples therapy makes continuing those patterns more of an ordeal than changing.

The concept of reframing may be further clarified by the following examples. DeShazer (1975) reports the tactic of having an uninvolved father formally assigned the chore of keeping score in fights between the mother and child. In another case (Andolfi, 1974), a young couple whose relationship was characterized by frequent fighting was told that their fights were demonstrations of their love. They were directed to fight on a regular schedule. The couple was determined to prove the therapist was wrong, ceased fighting, and consequently began to get along better.

Luthman (1974) reports a case involving a family where the father was progressively going blind. She inquired whether he was learning Braille. The father defensively replied he was "as good a man as anyone else." She asked him, "How does it come about that the possible adding of new knowledge and skills to your repertoire would make you feel less in some way?"

The therapist may employ reframing in his own family. Guerin (Guerin and Fogarty, 1972), a Bowen trainee, reversed his usual tactic of interrogating his wife about what was the matter when she was distant. He began commenting to her that it sure is peaceful to live with someone who does not burden me with personal thoughts and feelings. Or he said, "I cannot stand people who are always talking about their troubles." He would immediately leave the room before she could reply. His wife began to broach the issues that were bothering her to her husband.

TASKS

The therapeutic double bind may be in the form of an assignment or task. The therapist utilizes his client's resistance when assigning a task (Jackson and Weakland, 1961; Camp, 1973). Haley (1973a) presents a case of Erickson's involving the breaking of an overinvolved mother-son dyad. The son wet his bed almost on a nightly basis. The exasperated mother brought him to Erickson who assigned a task to the two of them. The mother was to get up between 4:00 A.M. and 5:00 A.M. each morning to check her son's bed. If it was wet, he had to get up and practice his handwriting with his mother supervising him. If the bed was dry, his mother still had to get up and check. The boy went along with the task because his mother would like it less than he. The boy ended up with a dry bed, beautiful handwriting, an admiring mother, and even increased involvement with his father who now played ball with him. Hare-Mustin (1975) used a similar strategy with a four-year-old boy who threw spectacular and frequent temper tantrums. She instructed the boy to continue having his tantrums but only in a special tantrum place at home. The child and his family decided on the specific location. In the following session, the child picked a time of day he would tantrum. By the third session the tantrums had decreased to a bare minimum. Hare-Mustin expressed concern over the rapid change and asked the child to choose a day for a tantrum the following week. The child had no further tantrums.

DeShazer (1974) presents an excellent example of a task in his use of the functions of the presenting symptom in the family's interaction. A family brought in their 14-year-old son who had a stealing problem. The therapist instructed the father and son as a team to hide five one-dollar bills around the house. If the son resisted stealing the money for one week, he was to be allowed to come in for a previously denied private session with the therapist. Otherwise the whole family was to come in. The son did come in alone and received instructions to steal two of the bills but to delay his usual dramatic confession until the next family session. At this time the son went through a dramatic display of guilt and sinfulness gaining the full attention of his family, but this time the father's open complicity was known to all. The father was able to recognize his part in his son's stealing episodes as were other family members.

The junior author remembers a difficult case with a couple where the husband demanded intercourse two or three times a week from his wife who felt resentful and angry at being used. Intercourse had become an ordeal for both. Other courses of action such as treatment of sexual attitudes and behaviors had failed. The husband was instructed to give up sex completely for the time being. The husband was reluctant, but the wife expressed great enthusiasm at the idea. For this couple the advantages of the husband's curtailment of his sexual behavior began to become apparent: (1) the pressure would be off both parties to perform sexually; (2) the wife could feel loved for herself rather than for her body; (3) the husband would be forced to think about his sexual behavior in relationship to his wife rather than take the usual route of unreflectively following his impulses; (4) by lowering the husband's dominance the couple could establish equilibrium in the relationship; and (5) the wife, who had been protesting that it was not sex *per se* that turned her off, but the manner in which her husband approached her for intercourse, would be on the spot. It would now be up to her to initiate any sexual activity.

WRITTEN INSTRUCTIONS

Both Selvini-Palazzoli, Boscolo, Cecchin, and Prata (1975) and L'Abate and colleagues (1976) have experimented with the effectiveness of using paradoxical written messages for presentation to the clients generally at the end of a session. The advantages of such a procedure are: (1) the message can be systematically thought out in advance and would serve as the major, important interpretation of the session; (2) the message would be more difficult to distort or forget by the clients than a verbal interpretation and thus assure repercussions in marital or familial homeostasis; and (3) copies of the messages could serve as progress notes for the therapist as well as a source of research data. For instance, a paradoxical message was presented to a couple whom the junior author and his wife had seen in therapy for approximately one year with minimal results. Previously, the couple had been in therapy numerous times over the years with a variety of therapists in different towns.

Dear B and J:

On the basis of our detailed and prolonged observation of your marriage and after a great deal of thought and deliberation, we have come to the conclusion that you both love each other so deeply and so dearly that any change for the better in the other is interpreted as a sign of rejection and a demonstration of disloyalty. You both are so loyal to each other that neither one can change for fear of disappointing the other one.

We can see and understand then, how it is impossible for each of you to change for the better, since changing for the better would be a sign of disloyalty and rejection. We really wonder whether each of you can change for the better without disappointing the other.

We would like for each of you to read this note each day but not to talk about it too much. We will talk about it next time we meet.

Cordially yours,

Luciano L'Abate and Bess L. L'Abate

Positive Interpretation

With this technique the therapist takes the stance of stressing the positive aspects of behaviors rather than the negative aspects (L'Abate, 1975; Otto, 1963). Stressing the positives is a form of relabeling or reframing.

Selvini-Palazzoli and her coworkers (1974, 1975) make use of positive connotation in their work with families. The therapists declare themselves as allies of the family and approve the behaviors of the family members — particularly those traditionally considered scapegoated — by making them the family heroes, i.e., "By drawing attention to himself Giovanni has protected the whole family and especially father and mother, from looking at themselves and how they behave."

Change is produced by the therapists' paradoxically aligning themselves with the family's homeostatic tendency (Selvini-Palazzoli et al., 1974, 1975). They report a case in which the martyrlike mother of a schizophrenic six-year-old boy declares herself as changed in an early session and no longer wanting to suffer. The therapist expressed concern over her premature change and described the importance of her suffering as a commendable virtue without which she would be at a severe loss. The therapist further described the husband and son as protecting the mother from suffering more than she had to, i.e., keeping her at the status quo. In essence, the therapist posed a paradox which was a metacommunication or confirmation of the pathogenic paradox by prescribing the symptom. Since the family always tries to disqualify the therapist, they must now change their game.

L'Abate (1975) writes of the choice available to the therapist in interpreting behaviors to the family and to himself. He may choose a traditional, negative orientation based on the pathology being presented to him and view the behaviors as a deficit or liability. On the other hand, the therapist may also choose to view the behaviors in terms of assets or strengths. The family expresses many strengths if the therapist is open to recognizing them and pointing them out to the family: Asking for help is a strength, expressing hurt through tears is a strength, caring for oneself and one's family is expressed by the family's presence in the therapist's office, and sharing hurt is a sign of caring. Paradoxically, the use of positive labeling can disrupt fixed, negative views the family takes for granted. For example, the parents of a 10-year-old girl complained that she is making new demands on them. Since she was initially shy and undemonstrative, the therapist praised her new demands as an indication of her positive self-assertion and increased self-esteem.

Paradoxical Intention

Paradoxical intention, a technique devised by Frankl (1965, 1975a, 1975b) has been used successfully in the treatment of phobias, obsessive-compulsive disorders, and anxiety states (Gerz, 1962; Solyom, Garza-Perez, Ledwidge, and Solyom, 1972; Hand and La-Montagne, 1974). The technique is similar to that of prescribing the symptom. The therapist instructs the client to train himself to experience his symptom to an extreme degree as frequently as possible. The symptom has run its course when the client recognizes its absurdity and gains sufficient self-detachment to laugh at the symptom. Frankl (1975a, 1975b) described the viciously circular nature of a symptom which brings forth a fear of recurrence or anticipatory anxiety. The anxiety provokes the symptom whose recurrence reinforces the anxiety or fear. The technique of paradoxical intention is aimed at the phobic's flight from his fear and the obsessive's tendency to fight his fears. In short, the client is instructed to give up the mechanisms of resistance he has developed to avoid giving in to his fears and to face his fears head on. Frankl (1975b) reported the case of a woman who had suffered from severe claustrophobia for 15 years. She feared riding in all modes of transportation and entering buildings. She would become anxious and would fear that she would suffocate and die upon entry into a closed, confined space. As part of her desensitization treatment, she was encouraged to let the symptoms become as bad as possible and to seek out places where her symptoms had previously occurred. Within a week, she was able to enter symptom-free innumerable places, first with her husband and then by herself, that she had previously been under considerable duress to enter.

Hypnosis

Hypnosis employs many of the paradoxical procedures mentioned in this article. The hypnotist uses reframing, emphasizing the positive, resistance, and a variety of double binds. A paradoxical injunction is given to the subject by the hypnotist who communicates two levels of messages: (1) do as I say; (2) don't do as I say but behave spontaneously. The subject adapts to the conflicting set of directives by undergoing a change and behaving in a way described as trance behavior (Sander, 1974; Andolfi, 1974; Haley, 1963, 1973b). The hyponotist's techniques are very similar to those of the therapist who first directs his client to do things he can voluntarily do and then requests or communicates an expectation of spontaneous change (Haley, 1973b).

Erickson and Rossi (1975) have identified a number of double binds used in hypnosis as well as in therapy. The first involves offering a free choice among comparable alternatives, one of which must be chosen (i.e., "Would you like to go into a trance now or later?"). In a second, rather complex double bind, a request ostensibly made at the conscious level effects a change at the unconscious or subconscious level (e.g., "If your unconscious wants you to enter a trance, your right hand will lift. Otherwise your left hand will lift."). A third double bind uses time as a binding agent (e.g., "Do you want to get over that habit this week or next? That may seem too soon. Perhaps you'd like a longer period of time like three or four weeks?"). The fourth double bind—the reverse set double bind—is frequently used by Erickson in enabling patients to reveal material by enjoining them not to. The fifth therapeutic double bind used by Erickson is the *nonsequitur* double bind where he casually inserts a variety of increasingly absurd comments in a binding form. There is a similarity in the content of the alternatives offered by no logical connection (e.g., "Do you wish to take a bath before going to bed, or would you rather put your pajamas on in the bathroom?").

Not every case involves formal hypnosis. Joe, the eight-year-old son of a divorcee, had become the neighborhood and family terror (Erickson, 1962). His mother brought him to see Erickson who assured Joe he would change his behavior "all by himself." His mother would be told some simple things she could do so he could change himself, and he was to guess what they were. The next day, Joe arose, demanded breakfast, and when it was not forthcoming, began to tantrum. His mother prepared for the occasion with books and food for herself, sat on Joe explaining she would get up when she thought of a way to change his behavior, but unfortunately as the day progressed, she did not think she would come up with anything so it was all up to him. Joe struggled, pleaded, screamed all to no avail for most of the day. He was sent to bed without supper since he had missed lunch and breakfast had to be eaten before lunch. The next day, Joe was fed oatmeal which he hated for breakfast and had the leftover oatmeal for lunch. He accepted it gratefully. That day he spontaneously cleaned his room, canvassed the neighborhood, apologizing to the neighbors for his past behavior and making arrangements for amends. He spent the rest of the day with his schoolbooks and voluntarily went to bed. The mother explained to him she expected him to behave like a normal eight-year-old boy. All went well with the exception of one relapse dealt with by Erickson several months later. Otherwise, Joe behaved like a normal eight year old.

RELATED APPROACHES

Other therapists use paradoxical approaches without labeling their techniques as being paradoxical per se. Nelson and her colleagues (1968) used the term "paradigm" to denote the interactions in which the therapist attempts to foster insight in the client by siding with his resistance and avoiding making interpretations. Sapirstein (1955) emphasized the importance of unconscious processes in the maintenance of paradoxical behavior. Farrelly and Brandsma (1974) labeled their brand of therapy as "Provocative Therapy" using symptom prescription and other double binding maneuvers.

Many of Rosen's (1953) techniques of direct therapy with psychotics involved a therapeutic double bind. When Rosen felt sufficient progress had been made, i.e., the client begins to let the therapist into his unconscious, a variety of techniques acknowledging the psychosis were initially employed. When a client began to make unsuccessful efforts at stopping his visions or voices, Rosen used magical gestures to stop the voices (e.g., repetitive strokes in the air, jumping and shouting, or drawings of antiwitchcraft figures posted on the wall). The client was intent on what Rosen was doing and did not hear the voices. After the client achieved some sense of reality, Rosen employed the technique of reductio ad absurdum which is an outright attack on the delusional system or suicidal impulses. He would observe loudly and with annoyance in front of the client who still insisted on dressing as Christ, "Isn't this the fourth Jesus Christ who's been here today?" He would portray the suicide attempt to the client who was no longer suicidal as the most absurd action he could have possibly taken. Both Haley (1955) and Andolfi (1974) viewed this technique in terms of a deliberate confusion of the symbol and the object symbolized. Rosen took his client's metaphorical statements seriously and then insisted they do the same. This technique dramatized the differences between metaphorical and literal messages leading to a clarification of the situation for the client who learned to discriminate between the two levels of messages. Haley (1955) emphasized the importance of reframing in this technique. A second technique employed by Rosen was reenacting an aspect of the psychosis that bears some similarity to prescribing the symptom. Rosen would instruct a client who no longer heard voices but who was still in a rather shaky state to hear the voices again. The client, if all went well, insisted he did not hear anything while Rosen insisted he did. The client's coming back indignantly was a sure sign of a cure.

The Status of Paradox — Theoretical and Other Considerations

Paradox as a therapeutic technique appears to have spotty recognition. In several recent reviews of psychotherapy, paradox was not mentioned (Usdin, 1975; Barten and Barten, 1973; Bergin and Garfield, 1971). Even more surprising is the absence of mention of paradox in recent family therapy publications (Bell, 1975; Howells, 1975; Glick and Kessler, 1974; Andrews, 1974; Zuk, 1971). Fox (1976) also did not mention paradox as a therapeutic technique but does mention the pathological double bind as a historical note. Friedman (1974) did, however, mention prescribing the symptom and relabeling in his alphabet of family therapy techniques. Dolliver (1972) also recognized the importance of paradoxical techniques in the conceptualization of opposites in psychotherapy.

The Why of Using Paradox

Regardless of the recognition or lack of recognition by psychotherapists, important questions surround the usage of paradoxical techniques: How are paradoxes formed; how does one deliver a paradox successfully; and theoretically, why do paradoxes work? Practitioners and theorists offer a variety of answers to the questions posed which will be briefly reviewed in this section.

The basic appeal of paradox is novelty. Straightforward interpretations by the therapist, particularly with families, have little chance of "shaking-up" the family system. Straightforward interpretations are frequently expected, and, therefore, easily ignored. A paradoxical communication, by presenting the familiar in a new unexpected light, has a greater chance of being heard and, by virtue of this novelty, has a greater potential for evoking change.

A second characteristic of a paradoxical communication is the apparent craziness of the suggestion. The communication seemingly goes against common sense and can even be termed nonsense. How can a client or clients be persuaded to follow a nonsensical directive? One obvious predisposing condition is the desperateness of the client(s). Hare-Mustin (1975) reports spending a great deal of time with her inquiry about the details of the presenting symptom. After laying this groundwork, she begins prescribing the symptom. Rossi (1973) points out that the therapist sets up binding conditions prior to the paradoxical prescription. For example, the client promises in advance he will follow the therapist's directive without protest. Weakland et al. (1974) comment that a high pressure approach to presenting the paradox does not work, but a confused, ignorant stance on the part of the therapist seems to facilitate client compliance. Selvini-Palazzoli et al. (1975) observe that paradoxical interventions are more effective if spaced out over time.

There are many theoretical explanations as to how paradoxes work. Social psychology contributes some explanations. Attribution theory (Jones, 1971) is concerned with how an individual explains his world. People tend to think in terms of a linear, cause-effect context and employ social consensus as a criterion for validation of explanations. The presentation of a paradox in therapy provides an alternate, circular explanation or attribution of meaning for a given event. This "reframing" affects the client's subsequent feelings and behavior about that event. The therapist and changed reactions of other family members are the social context for validating the new explanation of the event.

Laing's use of attribution and mystification in pathological situations (1965, 1971) can be translated into therapeutic paradoxes. The therapist attributes an alternate explanation of the behavior sequence at hand and then offers a cryptic prescription which he refuses to elaborate upon. The attribution denies the family's usual negative explanations of the given behavior and the mystification of the prescription keeps the clients in a state of confusion which circumvents their ignoring of what the therapist has said. Whitaker (1975) writes of the potency of the therapist's use of obscurity and absurdity in family therapy.

Transactional Analysis (TA) utilizes a straightforward approach to therapy. Steiner (1974) commented that the use of permission giving by the therapist in TA is criticized on the grounds that the client may react paradoxically and do the opposite of what the therapist indicates he should do. Steiner denies that this will result if the therapist is speaking from his Adult. Berger (1976) contends that in a deliberate paradoxical approach, an effective paradoxical message comes from the therapist's positive Parent and the client's Child does not dare comment that the message does not make sense. Hartman and Narboe (1974) reported on the protective aspects of certain pathological catastrophic injunctions.

The most widely held explanation for why the paradox works is based on the idea that some clients come to the therapist for help but are resistant to any help offered, in addition to provoking the therapist to try and fail (Andolfi, 1974). The use of paradox enables the therapist implicitly to tell the client to change by asking him not to change. This paradoxical communication, as derived from the Russellian paradoxes in classification systems (Ruesch and Bateson, 1951; Haley, 1963) is not a contradiction in the sense that two levels of communication are involved. The higher level or metacommunication is an attempt to control the definition of the relationships (Anderson, 1972; Jackson, 1967). Thus, the therapist is perceived by the couple or family (each of whom has been resisting the other's attempts at defining the relationship already) as trying to define the relationship and unite to resist the therapist. To transcend this circular resistance, the therapist must use circular language (Selvini-Palazzoli et al., 1975). He makes his double binding request at the primary conscious level but effects change on the unconscious or metalevel (Erickson and Rossi, 1975).

The criticism can still be leveled that paradox, regardless of the preceding theoretical explanations, still lies outside of adequate theoretical explanation. Weisskopf-Joelson (1975) points out that aspects of Frankl's technique of paradoxical intention remain outside the existential tenets of Logotherapy.

Conclusion

From this review about the use of paradoxical practices in family therapy, it is easy to see that most evidence is still impressionistic, incomplete, anecdotal, and hence, questionable. One of the greatest needs in the use of paradoxical practices lies in finding more tenable theoretical, clinical, and empirical bases.

References

Anderson, E. K. (1972), A review of communication theory within the family framework. *Fam. Ther.*, 1:15–34.

Andolfi, M. (1974), Paradox in psychotherapy. *Amer. J. Psychoanal.*, 34:221–228.

Andrews, E. E. (1974), *The Emotionally Disturbed Family and Some Gratifying Alternatives*. New York: Aronson.

Barten, H. H. & Barten, S. S. (1973), *Children and Their Parents in Brief Therapy*. New York: Behavioral Publications.

Bateson, G., Jackson, D. D., Haley, J., Weakland, J. H. (1956), Toward a theory of schizophrenia. *Behav. Sci.*, 1:251–264.

———— ———— ———— ———— (1963), A note on the double bind—1962. *Fam. Proc.*, 2:154–161.

Bell, J. E. (1975), *Family Therapy*. New York: Aronson.

Berger, M. (1976), What is done in trust: Conditions underlying the success of paradoxical interventions. Unpublished manuscript, Georgia State University.

Bergin, H. E. & Garfield, S. L. (1971), *Handbook of Psychotherapy and Behavior Change: An Empirical Analysis*. New York: Wiley.

Camp, H. (1973), Structural family therapy: An outsider's perspective. *Fam.*

Proc., 12:269–277.

DeShazer, S. (1974), On getting unstuck: Some change-initiating tactics for getting the family moving. *Fam. Ther.*, 1:19–26.

———— (1975), Brief therapy: Two's company. *Fam. Proc.*, 14:79–93.

Dolliver, R. H. (1972), The place of opposites in psychotheapy. *J. Contemp. Psychother.*, 5:49–54.

Edwards, P. (1967), *The Encyclopedia of Philosophy.* New York: Free Press.

Erickson, M. H. (1962), The identification of a secure reality. *Fam. Proc.*, 1:294–303.

———— & Rossi, E. L. (1975), Varieties of double bind. *Amer. J. Clin. Hypnos.*, 17:143–157.

Farrelly, F. & Brandsma, J. (1974), *Provocative Therapy.* Fort Collins, Col.: Shields.

Feldman, L. B. (1976), Processes of change in family therapy. *J. Fam. Counsel.*, 4:14–22.

Fisch, R., Watzlawick, P., Weakland, J., & Bodin, A. (1972), On unbecoming family therapists. In: *The Book of Family Therapy*, ed. A. Ferber et al. New York: Science House, pp. 597–617.

Fischer, J. (1974), The Mental Research Institute on family therapy: Review and assessment. *Fam. Ther.*, 1:105–140.

Fox, R. E. (1976), Family therapy. In: *Clinical Methods in Psychology*, ed. I. B. Weiner. New York: Wiley, pp. 451–515.

Frankl, V. E. (1965), *The Doctor and the Soul.* New York: Knopf.

———— (1975a), Paradoxical intention and dereflection. *Psychother.: Theory, Res. Prac.*, 12:226–237.

———— (1975b), Paradoxical intention and dereflection: Two Logotherapeutic techniques. In: *New Dimensions in Psychiatry: A World View*, vol. 1, ed. S. Arieti et al. New York: Wiley, pp. 305–326.

Friedman, P. H. (1974), Outline (alphabet) of 26 techniques of family and marital therapy. *Psychother.: Theory, Res. Prac.*, 11:259–264.

Gerz, H. O. (1962), The treatment of the phobic and the obsessive-compulsive patient using paradoxical intention. *J. Neuropsychiat.*, 3:375–387.

Glick, I. D. & Kessler, D. R. (1974), *Marital and Family Therapy.* New York: Grune & Stratton.

Guerin, P. & Fogarty, T. (1972), Study your own family. In: *The Book of Family Therapy*, ed. A. Ferber et al. New York: Science House, pp. 445–467.

Haley, J. (1955), Paradoxes in play, fantasy, and psychotherapy. *Psychiatric Research Reports of the American Psychiatric Association*, 2:52–58.

———— (1962), Wither family therapy? *Fam. Proc.*, 1:69–100.

———— (1963), *Strategies of Psychotherapy.* New York: Grune & Stratton.

———— (1973a), Strategic therapy when a child is presented as the problem. *J. Amer. Acad. Child Psychiat.*, 12:641–659.

———— (1973b), *Uncommon Therapy.* New York: Ballantine.

Hand, I.. & LaMontagne, Y. (1974), L'intention paradoxale et techniques comportementales similaires en psychotherapie à court terme. *Canad. Psychiat. Assn. J.*, 19:501–507.

Hare-Mustin, R. T. (1975), Treatment of temper tantrums by a paradoxical intervention. *Fam. Proc.*, 14:481–485.

Hartman, C. & Narboe, N. (1974), Catastrophic injunctions. *Trans. Anal. J.*, 4:10–12.

Howells, J. G. (1975), *Principles of Family Psychiatry*. New York: Brunner/ Mazel.

Hughes, P. & Brecht, G. (1975), *A Panoply of Paradoxes: Vicious Circles and Infinity*. New York: Doubleday.

Jackson, D. D. (1967), The individual and the larger contexts. *Fam. Proc.*, 6: 139–147.

_____ & Weakland, J. H. (1961), Conjoint family therapy: Some considerations on theory, technique, and results. *Psychiat.*, 24:30–45.

Jones, E. E. (1971), *Attribution: Perceiving the Causes of Behavior*. Morristown, N.J.: General Learning Series.

Kantor, R. E. & Hoffman, L. (1966), Brechtian theater as a model for conjoint family therapy. *Fam. Proc.*, 5:218–229.

L'Abate, L. (1975), A positive approach to marital and familial intervention. In: *Group Therapy 1975*, ed. L. R. Wolberg & M. L. Aronson. New York: Stratton, pp. 63–75.

_____ O'Callaghan, J. B., Piat, J., Dunne, E. E., Margolis, R., Prigge, B., & Soper, P. H. (1976), Enlarging the scope of intervention with couples and families: Combination of therapy and enrichment. In: *Group Therapy 1976: An Overview*, ed. L. R. Wolberg et al. New York: Stratton, pp. 62–73.

Laing, R. D. (1965), Mystification, confusion, and conflict. In: *Intensive Family Therapy*, ed. I. Boszormenyi-Nagy & J. L. Framo. Hagerstown, Md.: Harper & Row.

_____ (1971), *The Politics of the Family*. New York: Pantheon.

Luthman, S. (1974), Techniques of process therapy. *Fam. Ther.*, 1:141–162.

Minuchin, S. (1965), Conflict-resolution family therapy. *Psychiat.*, 28:278–286.

Montalvo, B. & Haley, J. (1973), In defense of child therapy. *Fam. Proc.*, 12:227–244.

Nelson, M. C., Nelson, B., Sherman, M. H., & Strean, H. S. (1968), *Roles and Paradigms in Psychotherapy*. New York: Grune & Stratton.

Otto, H. A. (1963), Criteria for assessing family strength. *Fam. Proc.*, 2: 329–338.

Peck, B. B. (1974), Psychotherapy with fragmented (father-absent) families. *Fam. Ther.*, 1:27–42.

Prosky, P. (1974), Family therapy: An orientation. *Clin. Soc. Work J.*, 2: 45–56.

Rosen, J. N. (1953), *Direct Analysis*. New York: Grune & Stratton.

Rossi, E. L. (1973), Psychological shocks and creative moments in psychotherapy. *Amer. J. Clin. Hypnos.*, 16:9–22.

Ruesch, J. & Bateson, G. (1951), *Communication: The Social Matrix of Society*. New York: Norton.

Sander, F. M. (1974), Freud's "A case of successful treatment by hypnotism (1892–1893)": An uncommon therapy? *Fam. Proc.*, 13:461–468.

Sapirstein, M. R. (1955), *Paradoxes of Everyday Life*. New York: Random House.

Selvini-Palazzoli, M., Boscolo, L., Cecchin, G. E., & Prata, G. (1974), The treatment of children through brief therapy of their parents. *Fam. Proc.*, 13:429–442.

_____ _____ _____ (1975), Paradox and counterparadox: A new model for the therapy of the family in schizophrenic transaction. Paper presented at the Fifth International Symposium on Psychotherapy of Schizophrenia, Oslo, August 14–18.

Solyom, L., Garza-Perez, J., Ledwidge, B. L., & Solyom, C. (1972), Paradoxical intention in the treatment of obsessive thoughts: A pilot study. *Compr. Psychiat.*, 13:291–297.

Steiner, C. M. (1974), *Scripts People Live.* New York: Bantam.

Usdin, G. (1975), *Overview of the Psychotherapies.* New York: Brunner/Mazel.

Watzlawick, P. (1963), A review of the double bind theory. *Fam. Proc.*, 2: 132–153.

_____ Beavin, J. H., & Jackson, D. D. (1967), *Pragmatics of Human Communication.* New York: Norton.

_____ Weakland, J., & Fisch, R. (1974), *Change: Principles of Problem Formation and Problem Resolution.* New York: Norton.

Weakland, J. H., Fisch, R., Watzlawick, P., & Bodin, A. M. (1974), Brief therapy: Focused problem resolution. *Fam. Proc.*, 13:141–168.

Weisskopf-Joelson, E. (1975), Logotherapy: Science or faith? *Psychother.: Theory, Res. Prac.*, 12:238–240.

Whitaker, C. A. (1975), Psychotherapy of the absurd: With a special emphasis on the psychotherapy of aggression. *Fam. Proc.*, 14:1–16.

Zuk, G. H. (1971), *Family Therapy: A Triadic Based Approach.* New York: Behavioral Publications.

Susan Smiled: On Explanation in Family Therapy

ALBERT E. SCHEFLEN

One day a group of us was watching a videotape of a family therapy session. At one point the daughter, whom I will call "Susan," smiled in an enigmatic way. This smile provoked a prolonged discussion among the observers. In all, six quite different kinds of explanations were offered of the incident.

I think it is worthwhile to recount this experience and share it with family therapists. I think it typifies the problems of framework and doctrine that characterize clinical practice and theory.

EXPLANATIONS OF SUSAN'S SMILE

One member of our group conjectured about what feelings Susan's smile could express. He felt she was experiencing hostility. Another group member suggested she felt amused or possibily sarcastic.

But someone else said that Susan *was* sarcastic. This explanation attributed the smile to a lasting trait of Susan rather than to a feeling state that could have been transient. Other group members made inferences about Susan's personality traits too. Another group member cast the issue in diagnostic terms. He said Susan might be hebephrenic. From his point of view, Susan's smile was a symptom of her "illness."

A lot of other inferences could have been made about Susan's traits or conditions. Someone could have argued that her smile reflected her genetic constitution, her regional or cultural origins, or her social role, for instance.

Albert E. Scheflen, M.D., is Professor of Psychiatry, Albert Einstein College of Medicine, and Psychiatrist, Harlem Valley Psychiatric Center, Wingdale, New York.

All explanations of this sort have something in common. They assume that the smile expressed some feeling or trait of Susan. If one makes this assumption there is a next question: "What is being expressed?" There are as many possible answers as there are theories about individual states and traits. There are genetic theories and psychological ones and social ones. Even in the field of psychology there are learning theories, cognitive theories, and many kinds of psychodynamic ones. So the assumption that something is being expressed turns us to our favorite theory about individuals and what goes on inside them.

One can take this pathway in explaining any kind of behavior. One can observe a depressive posture, for example, and infer that some feeling of sadness or some state of loss or deprivation is being expressed. One can observe a strange behavior, label it schizophrenic, and proceed to elaborate one or another of the many theories of schizophrenia.

Expressional modes of explanation are very ancient in Western thought. Aristotle is reputed to have explained the acceleration of falling bodies in this way. He said that they fall faster as they approach the earth because they get more and more anxious to get home. Darwin explained the behavior of animals and man as an expression of emotion he attributed to inheritance. As the scientific revolution of 1860 was elaborated with genetic theories and became part of common culture, we attributed human behavior to bad or good seed and to genes. After the turn of the century, psychological theories of expression came more and more into common usage. We said that a person acted in a given way because he wanted to or had a motivation or drive in that direction. Or we attributed an action to the way someone felt or was. In any version of an expression paradigm, a person's actions are attributed to something *within* the person.

Our group of videowatchers did not get into a long argument about what Susan was expressing with her smile. We had often gotten into doctrinal arguments about the nature of the people on the videoscreen, and we knew it was fruitless to argue about what was going on in Susan. Instead one member of the group pointed out that Susan had smiled just after her father had turned to her, held out his hands, and said: "I think Susan loves us. We certainly love her."

One member of our group had a theory about this. He said that Susan must have considered her father's approach absurd or ironic. Someone else conjectured that Susan had to withdraw from the approaches of her father because she distrusted him. We talked about Susan's smile as a defensive behavior. We could have made a great many conjectures about the father-daughter relationship.

Each of these explanations fall into a different class of attribution. Each countenances the idea that father's behavior has something to do with the smile. The smile is now seen as a response. It is no longer only an expression of Susan's qualities or internal states.

Notice the mechanics of observation we have used in arriving at the idea of Susan's smile as a response. We looked at father's action, *and then* we looked at Susan's smile. After doing this we reappraised our explanatory mode. By this route we saw father's approach as a stimulus, and we employed a stimulus-response paradigm to formulate an explanation.

We can use a formulation like this to explain any behavior. Nowadays we speak of schizophrenia as a reaction. Freud (1917) formulated depression as a reaction to some loss. And Kaufman and Rosenblum (1967) showed that infant macaques, when experimentally separated from their mothers, show a posture and a facial expression that seem identical to those in human depressive patients.

In visualizing Susan's smile as a response, we can get into another kind of argument. If we are not careful, we can attribute a causality to the stimulus. We can blame Susan's smile on her father's behavior. Now we have jumped from the frying pan into the fire. We previously relied upon an oversimplified model in which we explained Susan's smile as a function of Susan's states or traits. Now we could attribute it, in an equally oversimplified way, to her father. We are only a step away from arguing about which of them *caused* the smile or who was to blame.

Switching from one of these explanatory modes to the other provides a basis for the politics of everyday experience. The arguing couple provides a ready example. Each one claims that the other one is expressing something or other while holding that their own behavior is a response. Each shifts the blame. Our court system operates this way too, and so do most institutions of Western culture.

It seems obvious that Susan's smile is an expression *and* a response. The difference arises from options in our way of looking at the sequence. This idea emerged in the scientific revolution that occurred about 1900. Freud (1933) described behavior as a learned or psychically determined response to some life situation. This paradigm came to be known as "psychodynamic." The learning theorists of that era also countenanced a synthesis between expression and response. They added the symbol "o" to the S-R paradigm to take account of the role of past experience or conditioning (Hull, 1943; Pavlov, 1927). Modern anthropology emerged in that revolution too. The concept of culture does not allow for a dichotomy between expressions and reactions. It describes, instead, what people learn to do in given situations in given traditions.

So the revolution after 1900 brought us an important synthesis between some old splinter views. To the idea that people simply expressed inherited characteristics, a view of learning was added. The notion that people either expressed or responded was supplanted by the idea that they expressed-in-reacting. The simplistic notions that followed Darwin and the scientific revolution after 1860 were replaced by a more integrated paradigm of behavior in the revolution that took place two generations later.

So we were freed two generations ago from simple dichotomies such as instinct versus learning and expression versus response. But we still use these. We argue whether smiling or depression or schizophrenic behavior is a consequence of "internal" or "environmental" forces. We use the lingo of psychodynamics, but usually we then go on simply to speculate about what is expressed. Or we argue about whether some behavior is an expression *or* a response.

Cultural traditions die hard. Four centuries after Copernicus, we still say the sun rises and sets.

BEHAVIOR AS STIMULUS

We talked about these matters. Then one of the group members made another observation that again forced us to change our frame of reference. After Susan smiled, her mother turned to her and said, "Susan you never appreciate what we try to do for you."

A new round of suggestions occurred. One group member inferred that Susan's smile annoyed her mother. Another person embellished this idea and called Susan's smile provocative.

We had looked at mother's reprimand as a response to Susan's smile, and then we looked back and reassessed the smile as a stimulus. There was, then, an S-R chain involving Susan's and mother's behavior too. And we had to agree now that Susan's smile was a stimulus as well as an expression and a response. The adjective "provocative" carried an additional implication. It suggested that Susan's smile had a motive. Maybe she smiled in order to provoke her mother. If so, we could argue that an expected reprimand from mother was also a cause of Susan's smile. Now our causal arrows run both forward and backward in time.

An implication like this appears in the psychodynamic concept of secondary gain and in the concept of conditioning, but this mode of explanation was made explicit in the next scientific revolution, which began after 1940. After the shift in viewpoints, yet another explanation of depression appeared. Kaufman and Rosenblum (1967) also demonstrated that the depressive posture of the lonely macaque infant elicited adoption behavior in some species and the protection of a senior male in another species. Clinicians began to say that depressive patients thereby manipulated members of their family in order to ward off an object loss. And schizophrenic behavior was said to be a way of double binding instead of merely a reaction to double binds (Bateson, 1955).

We should notice that each time we shifted our viewpoint, we came up with a different mode of explanation for Susan's smile. The first time around we looked only at Susan and ignored what her parents were doing. When we did so, we came up with an expressional or Aristotelian type of explanation. We had no data on which to base an explanation about anything but Susan's internal state.

The next time around we looked at the father-daughter relationship and noticed a sequence in which father's approach came just before the smile. We could then see Susan's smile as a response, but we also used a mode of explanation that put together the responsive and expressional formulations.

On our third look, we focused on the daughter-mother relationship and hence saw a sequence in which Susan's smile preceeded a maternal reprimand. From this data base, we saw Susan's smile as a stimulus or cue.

So the mode of explanation we are justified in using depends upon the focus and the scope of our conscious observation. But we can turn this interdependent relation around. If we wish to feature a particular mode of explanation, we can *manipulate what we consciously see.* We can look at one person alone or a particular dyad or at a sequence of three people's behavior. And we can look forward from what just happened to what happened next or backward from what is happening to what just did occur.

There are several reasons for making a manipulation like this. Maybe we wish to prove that some particular person is doing or causing something or other. By changing the way we look at the sequence above, we can alternately produce evidence that schizophrenics are provocative or that their mothers are reprimanding or that they react with withdrawal from the fathers, and so on.

By the same token we can foster some theory or other by the way we establish our observational field, e.g., a theory of depression. If we favor biochemical or intrapsychic explanation, we should see depressive patients in isolation. If we favor a reactive explanation, we should only enquire what happened before they got depressed. Our clients will help us to guide our focus. A husband may tell us only about his wife's rejection and conceal the fact that his depressive behavior compels her to stay with him.

Where are we in this thesis? So far we have seen Susan's smile as an expression, then as a response, and then as a cue. Obviously it is all of these, but it is often convenient for us to see it as one or the other. We can manipulate our way of looking at the sequence and argue that a behavior is an expression *or* a response *or* a stimulus.

All three of these views have something in common. All of them focus on Susan. All of them focus on the behavior of one person. It is true that father and mother's behavior was taken into account in explaining the smile as a response and as a cue, but still the focus was upon Susan. In the scientific revolution of the 1940s, another paradigm of explanation emerged. In this paradigm each group member's behavior is explained by reference to the others. The participants are said to *interact*. And they are hence seen as causing each other's behavior. We should go back to our videotape to see what we do in arriving at such an explanation.

So far we have been describing a sequence of behavior in which father made an approach, Susan smiled, and then mother began a reprimand. But other behaviors appeared in this sequence.

One of our observing group pointed out two of these. When Susan smiled, her father dropped his head, turned his face away from her, moved back in his chair, and fell silent. When mother began her reprimand, Susan acted in a similar way. She turned away, dropped her head, and fell silent. In short, father reacted to Susan's smile with a withdrawal, and Susan withdrew at her mother's reprimand.

First of all, we wondered why we missed these behaviors on our first go-around. I think a reason is to be found in our customary way of observing a human encounter. *Ordinarily we look at those who speak or at those who act in a gross or unexpected way.* Maybe this is because we have a selective attention to speech behavior and to behavior that poses a potential threat. In any event, we first looked at father when he spoke, at Susan when she smiled, and then at mother when she spoke. We overlooked the silent withdrawal behaviors of father and Susan.

Our notice of these two behaviors changes our picture of what happened. Father, Susan, and mother did act in that sequence, but father also responded to Susan's smile, and Susan responded to her mother's reprimand. Said in another way, *father and Susan acted and reacted to each other, and Susan and her mother did the same thing.* In the parlance of one social view, we can say that father and daughter *interacted*, then daughter and mother *interacted*.

We observe the data for this point of view when we look backward at the silent performances of those who have previously spoken or previously acted in an eye-catching way. An interactional formulation was given a basis when we reversed the usual tendency to look from one speaker to the next as each took turns. We looked back instead at those who *had been* more noisy a moment ago but who were now silent.

When we look back and forth from one participant to the next we can say that each is providing stimuli or cues for the other one's responses. We can say, for example, that father and Susan cued each other or caused each other's behavior. And we can say that Susan and mother did this too.

An interactional view changes our conception of cause and responsibility. If each person responds to the others, we cannot hold that one person's behavior causes the interaction. It seems, instead, that each person is responsible for the course of events.

But an interactional explanation also has some serious shortcomings. The members of a group do not respond only to what some other member has just said and done. They respond to all sorts of other human business, including events they expect to come next. And as we have already agreed, the participants do not merely respond. They express and cue as well. They initiate, change, provoke, maneuver, and manipulate their relationships. So we will have to greatly expand our notion of interaction or try yet another viewpoint if we are to gain a more holistic explanation of Susan's smile and the sequence in which it occurred.

Susan's Smile as Patterned Response

One member of our observational group noticed something that opened up another frame of reference. This person said that the same sequence had occurred earlier in the session. We played back the tape in search of this incident. All in all we found three sequences somewhat like the one we have already described. In two of these father approached, Susan smiled, and mother reprimanded her daughter. In one of them mother made the approach, Susan smiled, and father scowled.

The father also told a story that seemed relevant to this pattern of behavior. He said that his wife had laughed when he first proposed marriage to her. The wife corroborated the story and smiled as she did so.

It appeared, then, that a sequence like this occurred again and again in this family. The one I have described was not an isolated or unique experience. Instead there seemed to be a pattern of smiling or laughing at any approach, followed by a withdrawal and reprimand.

It was as though these family members did this as a customary or traditional way of relating. If so, we can argue that the pattern is scripted or preprogrammed. The sequence must be guided by an unwritten agenda or script. Each member must be playing his or her part in a minidrama. I have elsewhere described such sequences as programmed interactions (Scheflen, 1968, 1973).

The idea that a customary pattern was being enacted is strengthened by the observation that the participants can change roles. Either parent can make the approach, be smiled at, and withdraw. We did not, to be sure, see Susan take the approaching role. We can invoke a series of observations about this point. Maybe Susan had learned what happens to the person who takes that part. Maybe this is what earned her behavior the label schizophrenia.

We have now arrived at yet another sort of explanation for Susan's smile. We have claimed that it is customary enactment in a customary sequence of shared behavior. In this case we can say that Susan smiled because it was time to do so. Her contribution was cued by an approach and a past experience with what happens next. Susan smiled because she was expected to contribute her part.

This possibility forces us to another kind of explanation. If these people go through this sequence again and again, it must be traditional for them to do so. They are doing something customary. If so, there must be an unwritten score or agenda or program that is being enacted. Each one is playing his or her part in a family drama.

This notion was strengthened by another observation. The sequence of approach, smile, and reprimand occurred each time just after the therapist pointed out that the family members seemed to act separately with little affiliation or mutual involvement. Just after this interpretation was made, the father turned to Susan and made his approach. And after the mother's reprimand, each family member turned again to the therapist and resumed their separate accounts. It was as though the three of them were enacting a script to rectify the state of affairs that the therapist pointed out or to show that it could *not* be rectified. On one such occasion, both parents complained to the therapist saying, in effect, "You see there is nothing we can do to get to this girl."

Where are we, then, in our modes of explanation? Each participant's enactment in the sequence may cue and signal the next expected part, but we cannot so simply argue that each one caused the other ones to act that way. We can observe the famous stabbing of Polonius in Hamlet and argue about Hamlet's motives in stabbing or Polonius' motive in rustling the curtain and giving away his presence. But we should not forget that the scene is called for by Shakespeare's script. Like the members of Susan's family, the actors in *Hamlet* are interacting in response to a preexisting scenario.

We do not know how this sequence evolved or how it was learned. One member of our group said that this sequence also appeared in Albee's play, *Who's Afraid of Virginia Woolf*. Someone else conjectured that such sequences often occurred in families with a schizophrenic member. Someone else conjectured that Susan's mother must have learned such a sequence in her family of origin since she was already enacting her part in it before she got married.

It these guesses are so, the script for this sequence must be handed down from generation to generation and learned by some people for enactment in certain situations. Doing this sequence, then, is like playing baseball or *Hamlet* or *Semper Fidelis*. If so, the sequence is a bit of culture, and we are using a cultural rather than a social or individual-centered kind of explanation.

An explanation like this has an integrative usefulness. It provides a basis for claiming that participants respond to what has happened and to what they know will happen next. It provides a framework for explaining the course of an interaction. It allows us to see that each enactment is an expression of role and cognitive process as well as a response and a cue. But this paradigm has not taken cognizance of all of our concerns. What about feelings, for instance? And what about individuality and the prospects of change in a view of stereotyped role enactments? And what is the function or purpose of this sequence?

We can make some guesses about these aspects of the scene, but so far we lack the data to confirm them. If we are not to ignore this issue we must take yet another step. I am sure we are weary of this effort, but we have at least learned the direction we must take. To gain a broader explanation of Susan's smile, we moved to a view of the pattern in which it occurred. We broadened the scope of our observation, we took account of further items of behavior, and we looked at the larger picture.

SUSAN'S SMILE AS METARESPONSE

One observer argued as follows: Susan's smile was a response to father's approach, but it was not a response in kind. In Bateson's language the smile was meta to the approach (Bateson, 1955).

What does this jargon mean? I can best explain it by starting with a contrary case—one in which the response to an approach is a response in kind. Consider the case of a traditional, programmatic interaction like at greeting. I wave at you, and you wave back. Then I say, "Hello," and you say something similar. Or suppose you move toward me, and I move toward you or else back off a bit. I tell a story, and then you tell one. Or I ask a question, and you answer. Each of us is behaving in an analogous way. The behaviors of these interactions are of a common type.

But suppose I wave at you and you say, "Why are you waving?" Or suppose you move toward me, and I interpret your motives for doing so. Or suppose I tell a story, and you criticize the story instead of countering with another one. Or suppose I ask a question to which you respond with a look of disdain. In these instances the second behavior of the interaction is a judgment or an interpretation rather than a response in kind. The response is not to or with the first action. It is *about* or meta to it.

To behave about or meta to what is going on one steps out of the usual programmatic structure of a customary interaction, takes a judgmental position, and indicates this. Metareactions like this can change the shape of succeeding events. Adverse metareactions can shoot down an incipient involvement. They can ward off its escalation.

This is what we first thought about Susan's smile. It seemed that she derailed father's offer of involvement. It seemed that her smile ridiculed or suggested an absurdity about father's behavior. The smile was, you will remember, followed by a withdrawal of father and a reprimand from mother.

If we suppose that Susan derailed an affiliative sequence, we are back again to assigning blame. The classical theorist of schizophrenia could say, "See, the schizophrenic is afraid of involvement. Susan prevented the attempts to reach out to her."

But not so fast. Mother's reprimand was a metacommunication too. She commented on what her daughter had done. So two parts in the sequence were metacommunicational.

What about father's approach? Was he an innocent victim? And was Susan's smile a behavior of ridicule? We argued about smiling and laughing in general. A smile often indicates that a behavior is not to be taken as hostile. It often defuses an escalating panic or a mounting confrontation. Is it possible that Susan was not ridiculing her father? Maybe she was cueing someone that father's approach was not what it seemed. As a matter of fact, some members of our group had questioned father's sincerity earlier in the discussion. We were cued to look further. So we replayed the videotape and took a more careful look at father's approach.

Grossly, father's movement toward Susan was like most invitations to involvement. He turned toward his daughter, leaned closer to her, and stretched out his hands in the posture of gesticulation as he began to talk. But an important element was omitted from father's approach. His face was held in deadpan, and his voice was flat. Therapists use this set when they are stepping out of an interaction in kind and preparing an interpretation. So the father's face and intonation were not those of an involvement in kind.

An incongruent cue was also added to father's approach. He held his eyebrows in an elevated position as one does in raising a question. It seemed that he was testing or questioning or wondering rather than making an affirmation. There was yet another incongruity. Father looked at Susan and used the third person as if he were talking *about* his daughter rather than to her. He said, "I think Susan loves us."

So father's approach too was metacommunicational. In fact the whole sequence was carried out in the metacommunicational mode. It is not surprising, then, that Susan did not meet father with a warm smile or an approach. It was not simply that Susan shot down an attempt at family affiliation. She did, in fact, react in kind to what happened and to what happened next.

So we have now offered a sixth kind of explanation of Susan's smile. We have viewed it as a comment on the ongoing events. But this explanation does not preclude the others we have used. That the sequence was carried out in a metacommunicational mode does not preclude the idea that it was programmed and customary. And an interaction is still an interaction, even if it does not escalate to some expected stage. And each behavior of the sequence can still be viewed as an expression, a response, and a cue.

But we still do not know the meaning of the sequence. We have still not explained its occurrence. But we have labeled it a commentary about family relationships rather than an attempt to effect a mutual involvement. Its failure — its repetitive failure — to bring about an involvement now makes sense. The outcome also gives us a hint about its meaning or purpose. We confirmed our hunch by taking a broader view of the context in which it occurred.

The sequence occurred just after the therapist made an interpretation about the separateness or disaffiliation of the family members. On each of the three occasions when she did this, one parent turned to Susan and the sequence was repeated. And after each repetition all three family members turned again to the therapist and resumed their separate accounts of the family. So the sequence seemed to be provoked by a recognition of separateness. It seemed to maintain that separateness while appearing to change it. Maybe the family members

go through this ceremony each time they are confronted with their separateness. Maybe other families do this too, and maybe some of these
families have schizophrenic members too. But I am getting off the
track.

Susan's Smile as Intrapersonal Expression

I saw one of the participants in our discussion a few days later. He
offered me a doubting proposition. He speculated that Susan had simply drifted off into her own thoughts and smiled at some thought she
had. In this case, he said, her smile had nothing to do with the events
we have described.

Maybe so. Or maybe she drifted off and smiled at that very thought
anytime *anyone* approached her. Or maybe she did this only when people approached her as tentatively as her father did.

When I was writing this paper, I thought of a famous smile that
reminded me of Susan's. It was the smile of the Mona Lisa. Then I
thought of another one — the smile of the sphinx. If the sphinx was, as
legend has it, smiling at the paradox of the ages, we can make
another speculation about what Susan thinks about. She may smile at
the paradox of schizophrenia as it enfolds in her family and in a
psychotherapy session. Few phenomena have evoked so many possible
explanations.

The Use of Explanation in Clinical Practice

Whenever we make an interpretation, we have made use of some
mode of explanation. And even when we do not verbalize our interpretation, we think of one. Our stance on the matters at hand will
manifest themselves in some subtle way in our deportment, and our
metapositions influence the course of psychotherapy. After all, this is
one of the things we are paid to do. Sometimes, at least, we are supposed to step back from our involvements, find explanations, and im-
part what we can discover. How and when we share these with our
clients or patients is a matter of art and experience that I will not go
into here. But I do want to make a few comments on our choice of explanatory mode.

Obviously our judgments can make a difference. Our choice of explanations and our values in such matters can trip the scales and alter
the balance of power in a family. If our viewpoints and explanations
thus serve to dominate, control, or manipulate the members of a family, we are acting in a political way. I am not suggesting that we can

or should avoid this. The metaposition is inescapably political in the broad sense of that word. Any effort to involve, change, and teach effects a modicum of control. But we can be aware of the political implications of our explanatory stances and avoid carrying them out in a relentless, inflexible way.

I believe that explanations are sometimes used unwittingly in family therapy in an almost purely political way; i.e., they serve the purpose of maintaining control over one or more of the family members *for the duration of the course of therapy.* Here is an example. Suppose most family members blame their problems on one member — mother, for example. If the therapist persistently explains the mother's behavior as an expression, he or she will reinforce a set of inferences. The idea can be sustained that the others simply react and that mother initiates and causes the patterns of family behavior. Somewhat paradoxically this view may also maintain mother's influence, for a scapegoat is still a center of attention.

If a therapist persistently sees one family member's behavior as a reaction, this selective approach can also support a proclivity to blame one's behavior on other people or on fate of circumstance. An overly worked interactional or programmatic explanation, too, can free family members from taking responsibility for their contributions to a family problem.

I do not think family therapists usually plug only one mode of explanation in order to foster blame or keep some balance of power in the family. They are instead merely following the explanatory fashions of the doctrinal school in which they were trained. But in doing so they are also indoctrinating their patients or at least confirming the existing biases of certain family members. In the long run, however, one-explanation therapists serve to withhold alternative viewpoints. Their patients and students as well may not learn how to probe the larger contexts of their experience. They look only to their thoughts or only to the actions of villains or only to traditions to explain their fates.

This criticism opens the possibility of using explanations on purpose. A therapist can choose a particular sort of explanation and use this mode for a particular and conscious purpose. Once the point has been made, another mode of explanation can be employed. In this way various modes can be employed as temporary tactics in a long-term strategy.

Consider an example. Suppose a family member habitually blames his or her behavior on external circumstances or on other people. In this case, a therapist might avoid explaining this person's behavior as a reaction and explain it as an expression. When this family member begins to take responsibility for his or her contributions, the therapist might discontinue an expressional mode of explanation. Conversely, a reactional explanation could be tactically employed toward those who are always explaining their actions as expressions that have no relationship to the behavior of other family members. Later on an interactional explanation could be favored until each family member takes cognizance of the behaviors of others and assumes some responsibility for his or her contributions to the whole. Said in another way, explanatory modes can be used to alter habitual tendencies to deny, ignore, project, and blame.

The clinician can think of many variants of this idea. If family members persistently attribute their problems to some member's traits or feelings, the therapist can tactically use expression theory in a paradoxical way. For example, conjectures can be carried out until such blaming is reduced to absurdity. Or a therapist may tactically shift the blame to those who make the most accusations and thus restore a balance of power in which new approaches can be explored.

The idea of tactical uses helps us to formulate a strategic use of explanation. I think each of us needs to know that there are many possible explanations of human behavior. Each of these has its usefulness, its political value, and its limitations. Each of us needs to be able to view multiple aspects of the contexts of our behavior in order to know what we are facing. And we must know that there can be multiple sources of difficulty. If we can learn one way of looking and explaining and then another and another, we can achieve a more comprehensive ability. I think our parents, our teachers, and our therapists should help us to learn this. Then we should pass it on. In the course of family therapy our clients can learn multiple approaches from us and end up with a more flexible and comprehensive strategy for viewing and making sense of their experience.

REFERENCES

Bateson, G. (1955), The message, 'This Is Play.' In: *Group Process*, vol. 2, ed. B. Schaffner. New Jersey: Madison.

Freud, S. (1917), Mourning and melancholia. *Standard Edition*, 14:243–258. London: Hogarth Press, 1957.

———— (1933), New introductory lectures on psycho-analysis. *Standard Edition*, 22:5–182. London: Hogarth Press, 1964.

Hull, C. L. (1943), *Principles of Behavior*. New York: Appleton-Century.

Kaufman, I. C. & Rosenblum, L. A. (1967), The reaction to separation in infantile monkeys. *Psychosom. Med.*, 29:648–675.

Pavlov, I. P. (1927), *Conditioned Reflexes.* London: Oxford.
Scheflen, A. E. (1968), Human communication: Behavioral programs and their
     integration. *Behav. Sci.,* 13:45–55.
_____ (1973), *Communicational Structure.* Bloomington, Ind.: Indiana Uni-
     versity Press.

The Uses and Abuses of Co-Therapy

AXEL RUSSELL and LILA RUSSELL

The literature produced over the last 20 years reflects an increasing interest in conjoint therapy. Two or more therapists have been used to treat single patients, couples, families, or groups. A considerable number of variations and permutations of co-therapy have been reported. There is a paucity of literature on peer co-therapy. Most papers describe training and supervision under the guise of co-therapy with trainees, students, and participant observers moving in and out.

We will report our own co-therapy experiences, which facilitated the development of certain techniques. The constructive use of our co-therapy relationship to maximize results will be described. Advantages, disadvantages, and abuses perceived will be noted.

OVERVIEW

Rice, Fey, and Kepecz (1972) listed studies that claimed 30 or so advantages for the use of two therapists in marital therapy and made the point that the procedure finds "many advocates and relatively few detractors." A few male-female co-therapy teams have related the joys and sorrows of their joint therapeutic experiences. The Appels (1975), Sonne and Lincoln (1965), Bellville, Rath, and Bellville (1969), and the Lows (1975) have related the vicissitudes of co-therapy team functioning and underlined the crucial need for unity of this "symbolic marriage." This analogy was used to describe the dynamic operative in the co-therapy relationship and the serious, even disastrous, consequences of any splits for the therapy situation.

Axel Russell, M.D., F.R.C.P.(C), M.R.C. Psy., is Consultant Psychiatrist and former Medical Director, Oxford Regional Centre, Woodstock, Ontario, Canada, and a member of the Department of Psychiatry, University of Western Ontario, London, Ontario, Canada.

Lila Russell, M.S.W., F.A.A.M.F.T., is with the Department of Psychiatry, Victoria Hospital, South Street, London, Ontario, and Faculty of Social Work, Wilfred Laurier University, Kitchener, Ontario.

To maintain unity and the "nascent creative potential" implicit in the team relationship requires the ability to "work through" any difficulty present and the use of remarkable coping skills (Arieti, 1975). This suggests the kind of ego strength, flexibility, reality sense, and resolution of neuroticism which only a coming to terms with one's own present family situation and that of one's family of origin might give. Given the need for this capacity, it was suggested that co-therapists are likely to benefit from a course of family and/or couple or marital therapy for themselves even more than would other psychotherapists. Our assumption is that trained interveners are likely to be more objective in assessing their own involvement than some of their clients are. It is apparent that this is not always so, posing a problem not easily resolved. Scientific, professional, or personal biases can interfere.

Rice, Fey, and Kepecz (1972) and Rice, Razin, and Gurman (1976) point out that in over 20 years there have been no published studies which directly tested the effects of co-therapy as contrasted with treatment by one therapist. Most studies were written from a clinical viewpoint; the cases reported were too few in number for meaningful statistical analysis. Rabin (1967), writing from a group psychotherapist's point of view, appears to have been the only investigator to use a large enough sample. The 38 group therapists he surveyed agreed that co-therapy had value in that it led to more therapeutic movement and "working through."

Masters and Johnson use a co-therapy procedure to treat sexual problems. In terms of trying to evaluate the effect of such a procedure, no analyzable comparative data appear to have been generated.

Rice, Razin, and Gurman (1976) found that experienced and inexperienced therapists as a group do have preferences as to the style desired in a co-therapist; that they do have different therapy styles: blank screen, paternal, transactional, authoritarian, maternal, and idiosyncratic; that subjectively rated effectiveness of co-therapy correlated with the degree of comfort felt by the therapist in the relationship and by the acceptance of the other co-therapist. There might be a point of diminishing return in co-therapy satisfaction with an increase in the number of couples seen. Carl Whitaker, in his commentary appended to their study, explains this finding as a honeymoon phenomenon. Co-therapy may be suited for only a small percentage of therapists. There are as yet no answers to such conundrums. Another unanswered question asks, "What effects, if any, does the united stance of spouse-therapists have on clients?" Other puzzling in-session behaviors of co-therapists need exploration.

Spouse Co-Therapists

Several spouse co-therapists described the unique manner in which their marriage influenced their conjoint clinical work. Lazarus, also a spouse co-therapist, reported on his experiences, reviewed the literature, discussed advantages as well as disadvantages facing a husband-wife team, and made comparisons with a "colleaguel," non-related, co-therapy-team model. We agree with Lazarus (1976) that being married provides a pre-existing base of complementary interaction, adds support of loving involvement with one's family, lessens the tendency to argue about treatment events, adds time for resolution of differences, and provides healthy role models. We concur with his caution that the spouse co-therapy model offers no guarantee for therapeutic effectiveness. His impressions tally with our clinical observations and recall phases in our own development as co-therapists. Therapeutic effectiveness depends on the co-therapists' style of communication, maturity, and complementarity and not on whether the co-therapists are married to each other.

Tabulating the current state of the art is bound to be incomplete. It helped us map out our position and supplied us with reference points to understand and define our own situation.

Advantages of Co-Therapy

(1) *A good teaching method.* Participation gives the trainee a more intimate understanding of the process of therapy, while at the same time permitting ongoing, continuous supervision. It teaches sensitivity, openness, playing in tune, development of inter-therapists' signaling systems, and a better timing of interventions. One Canadian Psychiatric Residency Training Program encourages each trainee to try out as many as several dozen co-therapists in one year to find a suitable one before being allowed to choose a relatively permanent partner. This was found useful with sexual-therapy trainees.

(2) *A useful device to role-model didactically.* It offers the possibility for extensive role-modeling and role-playing (demonstrating active-passive, directive-nondirective, giving and taking). One therapist can act as interpreter, the other as listener. Therapists substitute for absent parents or reconstitute parental power (Peck and Schroeder, 1976). It provides an opportunity to modify male or female role expectations, demonstrate open and honest communication, role-play marital and family "democracy," and teach role flexibility.

(3) *Provides a source of support in the face of powerful psycho-*

pathology. Co-therapists can sometimes better understand the assault of delusional systems, prevent psychotic contamination, and maintain the attention of senile patients and chronic psychotics. A united front is produced. Two therapists are likely to be more objective; in tricky situations they can bale each other out. Massive misconceptions and distortions of reality are more easily avoided. The co-therapist serves supportively and as an ally and may pick up cues the other might have missed. Couples are likely to feel that they each have an ally.

(4) *Dilutes the emotional drain caused by very pathological couples, groups, or families.*

(5) *Affords continuity of care. If one therapist has to be away, the other is still present.* This is a controversial point. Therapists' blind spots cancel each other out. It improves the possibility of catharsis, reality testing, and insight development.

(6) *Clarifies transference and countertransference problems.* It ensures greater objectivity, prevents over-involvement and clarifies the transference situation. It offers the potential for projective identification with the co-therapists.

(7) *Co-therapists act as a mirror, foil, and sonar screen.* Distortions are minimized. A co-therapist facilitates the therapeutic process by providing feedback in post-interview rap sessions and on-the-spot peer supervision. Mutual support outweighs increased complexity of the in-session situation. It helps overcome initial resistance and breaks up destructive behavioral sequences.

DISADVANTAGES OF CO-THERAPY

(1) *Diluted or confused transference.*

(2) *It is an expensive use of badly needed therapeutic time.* It is too wasteful economically. A definite cost-benefit analysis, however, has not been done.

(3) *It increases the possibility of forming counterproductive alliances.*

(4) *The choice of co-therapist is frequently involuntary.* A pairing may not be a workable match and there is the possibility of prolonged inter-therapists conflict which destructively interferes with the therapy. It may increase complexity, create resistances and resentments. Inter-therapist conflicts based on different orientations are said to be on the increase. Pitfalls and mistakes threaten the unwary. Friction between co-therapists is seen as a great potential hazard. The co-therapist can be an obstacle to treatment.

(5) *Erotic issues in co-therapy arise and need to be dealt with*

(Dickes and Dunn, 1977).

ABUSES OR MISAPPLICATION OF CO-THERAPY

Co-therapy is misapplied in the following instances:

(1) It is indulged in merely to lessen the insecurity of individual therapists. This practice meets only the needs of the therapist. If a co-therapist is upstaged, patronized, leaned on, or put down, this represents abuse.

(2) Therapists allow the client(s) to play court room. Some may collude with the couple, engage in oblique interpretations, and exhibit narcissistic or bizarre behaviors. Co-therapists have inappropriately bullied clients or the other therapist, pranced, shown off, pontificated, competed. Co-therapists abuse by sarcastic manners and improper stances, which are as unprofessional as they would be in any other form of psychotherapy.

(3) Therapists do not know what the co-therapist is up to at any given moment and no feedback is asked for, or given. Co-therapy is no place for ego trips, for "tricks," or authoritarian "solo-playing." If an inexperienced co-therapist is meant to be used as an observer only, this should be made explicit. While this procedure is a valid teaching instrument, it is not co-therapy. Co-therapy needs the interplay of equals.

CLINICAL EXAMPLES

Examples from our own case material demonstrate our method. We work as co-therapists only when we feel this to be indicated; otherwise we work as individual therapists. Ideally, it would be comfortable to have a perfectly matching co-therapist always there. However, apart from the appropriate suggested use of co-therapy as outlined above, many families and couples are not that pathological or do not need role-modeling by two therapists. Their problems can often be managed quite adequately by one therapist. It is important to emphasize that we did not always regard each other as the perfectly matching co-therapist. This evolved slowly, often painfully, through the years. As we went through our own developmental crises in our family life cycle, we have had about eight or nine different marriage contracts with each other. We never work together at times of personal stress and conflict. Frequently it was necessary to work through these conflicts in another forum.

It might have been tempting to use the families we were treating to solve our own problems. Fortunately, our own growth and our consultants prevented such a potential misuse. We must all face this hazard squarely.

CASE EXAMPLE A

A couple in their mid-forties found their traditional marital relationship was no longer satisfying their needs. The husband was, and saw himself as, a successful, self-made man. They both found they were suffering from identity diffusion. They were confused regarding their sexual roles. Old intrapsychic conflicts reappeared in each of them and their drawn-out fights were becoming like wars. It appeared that they were out for the kill. They both felt threatened and fearful of being abandoned. Both experienced feelings of great insecurity and a profound sense of loss. The wife, no longer interested in being his helpmate, was threatening divorce.

He, being a self-professed "male chauvinist," felt threatened by any "smart woman." The husband accused the male author of being a "pretty passive fellow; a real jerk; as anyone would be who had such an effective, successful, and aggressive wife."

During the weeks of therapy, they learned how to fight without attacking each other's character, to admit their dependency needs to each other, to negotiate about this, to renew their sexual relationship, and, most important, to give and receive support based on a tolerant understanding of each other. They began to reveal a delightful sense of humor, an ability to reassure each other gently, and then become less embarrassed when demonstrating how close and loving they could be.

In our final session (held weekly for four months), we asked them what had helped them. They revealed that co-therapy had a real meaning for them. Our role-modeling had enabled them to accept and respect each other's differences. Hence, they could give up their need for constant competition with each other. Finally, the power struggle ceased altogether. We had used a cognitive approach in some of the sessions. They told us that this helped them modify their stereotyped attitudes regarding male and female roles. She, as wife, could now accept her husband's feelings of insecurity, allowing him to become much less defensive. The husband no longer had to attack her or discount her desire for some independence, autonomy, and self-assertion.

CASE EXAMPLE B

In case B, co-therapy was used to help a couple establish controls and to counteract and minimize transference distortions. They were in their early fifties, married for 25 years, with grown children living away from home. The wife had submerged herself in the role of wife and homemaker in a marriage to a man with a history of chronic alcoholism, who was suspicious, possessive, and domineering. She claimed naïvete, being unaware that life could ever be different for her. Under the mounting impact of the Women's Liberation Movement, she adopted an independent stance, unknowingly feeding into her husband's jealousy. With threats of separation hanging over his head, he joined A.A. He had been dry for a year. His thwarted dependency needs reinforced his possessive, demanding, and, sometimes, physically abusive behavior. This precipitated the wife's urgent request for marital therapy. The family physician, who had reached an impasse with the couple, described them as "impossible, manipulative, and psychopathic." We made a decision to see them jointly.

In the first interview both attacked and counterattacked in a vicious, destructive manner which bordered on severe paranoid distortion of reality. We elicited feelings of depression and despair, which we helped them label as indicators of a frustrated caring. They agreed that they cared and listed positive feelings, focused largely on parenting roles and the sexual relationship.

The gross suspicions expressed by both were due to profound threats of abandonment and loss. The husband had tried to escape these feelings through alcohol, the wife through a frantic attempt at emotional separation through working and developing her own private business in a new role as a career woman. She thus compensated for her frustrated dependence on a man who let her down continuously. Her revenge was to attack him in his manhood, which hurt him deeply. He counterattacked by calling her a slut, which hurt her. Each tried to prove the other crazy. A crucial intervention occurred when Lila told Axel during a particularly chaotic moment, half-way into the first interview, that she thought both were crazy. This caused the couple to stop short. They began supporting each other. We shall describe this interaction sequentially as it demonstrates our co-therapy technique. By the end of the interview they had gone so far as to hold hands as they sat together on the couch. They asked at the end whether "there is any hope for us?" They remained sufficiently relaxed long enough to tolerate the shift from each as an individual to focusing on their relationship.

We felt we would have gotten stuck in a therapeutic impasse, ten or fifteen minutes into the session, had we been there as individual therapists. While we might have extricated ourselves alone, it was much easier to establish control early in the interview and more comfortable to carry it through with a co-therapist present. The interaction referred to above, in playback, is as follows: while they were fighting each other viciously in a primitive manner, they used psychiatric jargon in a pseudo-sophisticated manner, and both appealed to Axel as the "doctor" to confirm the diagnostic labels they put on each other. The wife insisted Axel agree with her in referring to her husband as a "psychopathic, paranoid, and alcoholic liar," while he called her an "hysterical, obsessive, depressive sociopath." Lila then intervened, while Axel was trying to cope with mounting counterhostility, by saying gently: "I think it is so sad to see them in this crazy way; eh, Doc?" Axel: "How so?" Lila then encouraged the husband to admit that he was indeed a jealous, suspicious husband. This was accepted as understandable on the basis of his long exposure to women who were untrustworthy. Turning to the wife, Lila then said, "As you are so aware of what his mother did to him, how come you continue to feed his jealousy by omission rather than by commission?" Axel: "Ah, I see what you mean by calling their behavior crazy." The couple began to cry. They then supported each other and became benign and constructive.

This example reflects the use of co-therapy with an extremely dependent couple, prone to distort reality and each partner profoundly needing an alliance with an all-forgiving parent. Co-therapy cut short the ongoing battle.

We use our verbal in-session communication as a powerful strategic device to interrupt the destructive maladaptive behavior of our clients and help them to develop more adaptive communication patterns. We have found this to be an effective strategy for overcoming resistance. In the last three years we have treated 29 couples together. Only one withdrew from therapy prematurely. This represents a great improvement over previous years.

Although there may be other variables to our co-therapy style and techniques which we changed subtly, this is the one variable we are aware of changing drastically and consciously. We came to the conclusion that couples have a right to information and to the feedback we used to keep for our post-interview, rehash sessions.

Discussion and Conclusions

Mounting interest in the theories of group processes, general systems and communications, and their technical application, as these help us understand the emotional functioning of families, of couples, and of groups, has led to a renewed interest in co-therapy. Presently, there is some agreement on the advantages and disadvantages pre-

sented by the co-therapy procedure and limited agreement on indications and contraindications for its use (Holt and Greiner, 1975).

Co-therapy remains a controversial method in the sense that it has
not yet been demonstrated to be more effective than treatment by one
therapist. Critical comparative studies to test the effects of co-therapy as
contrasted with individual therapies need to be mounted. These should
include research efforts on outcome, follow-up, and cost benefits.

Co-therapists are selected for various reasons, for complementarity
of styles, proximity to treatment centers, training purposes, crisis intervention, and prevention of psychiatric hospitalization.

Valid indicators and contraindicators, potential hazards, and clinical advantages of co-therapy need to be further studied. The pros and
cons of working with a co-therapist of the same or opposite gender, of
the usefulness of spouse co-therapists versus unrelated therapists also
require further investigation. Some abuses mentioned could be prevented by using experienced, matching, peer co-therapy teams.

A glossed-over question is that of how professional hierarchies and
status affect co-therapy behavior. Frequently, the senior professional,
often a male psychiatrist, is a neophyte. He leads a psychologist, psychiatric nurse, or social worker, often female, who is clearly a more experienced couples' therapist. Such unresolved hierarchical problems
lead to abuse of co-therapy.

Haley (1975) has suggested that the introduction of innovative procedures often via social work or psychology into traditional training
and treatment centers and departments of psychiatry, which emphasize the medical model and individual psychotherapy, tends to
create dysfunction, disequilibrium, and general upset. Misapplied co-
therapy can be such a one.

The literature reveals claims made for and against co-therapy as a
treatment procedure which run across the whole spectrum. Protag-
onists have claimed too much for too little.

It is not yet possible to make a balanced judgment. We recommend
the holding of seminars and workshops to examine the pros and cons of
co-therapy per se, and to investigate its current use by "colleaguel" and
spouse co-therapists who would like to participate in such efforts.

Lastly, when we have a more satisfactory and specific marital- and
family-problem taxonomy of treatments, including co-therapy, we
should be able to specify answers to the questions raised.

REFERENCES

Appel, C. & Appel, M. (1975), The journey of spouse co-therapists. Paper presented at A.A.M.F.C. Meeting, Toronto.

Arieti, S. (1975), Creativity and its cultivation, In: *American Handbook of Psychiatry*, vol. 6, ed. S. Arieti. New York: Basic Books, pp. 230–250.

Bellville, T. P., Rath, O. N., & Bellville, C. J. (1969), Conjoint marriage therapy with husband-wife team. *Amer. J. Orthopsychiat.*, 39:473–483.

Dickes, R. & Dunn, M. D. (1977), Identifying and managing erotic elements in co-therapy. (Paper presented at 2nd Annual S. E. Regional Conference, A.A.S.E.C.T., Ashville.) *J. Sex Mar. Ther.*

Haley, J. (1975), Why a mental health clinic should avoid family therapy. *J. Marr. Fam. Counsel.*, 1:2–13.

Holt, M. & Greiner, D. (1975), Co-therapy in the treatment of families. In: *Family Therapy, Theory and Practice*, ed. P. J. Guerin, Jr. New York: Gardner Press, pp. 414–431.

Lazarus, L. W. (1976), Family therapy by a husband-wife team. *J. Marr. Fam. Counsel.*, 2:225–233.

Low, P. & Low, M. (1975), Treatment of married couples in a group run by a husband and wife. *Internat. J. Group Psychother.*, 25:54–66.

Peck, B. B. & Schroeder, D. (1976), Psychotherapy with the father-absent military family. *J. Marr. Fam. Counsel.*, 2:3–31.

Rabin, H. (1967), How does co-therapy compare with regular group therapy? *Amer. J. Psychother.*, 21:244–255.

Rice, D. G., Fey, W. F., & Kepecz, J. G. (1972), Therapist experience and 'style' as factors in co-therapy. *Fam. Proc.*, 11:227–241.

_____ Razin, A. M., & Gurman, A. S. (1976), Spouses as co-therapists: 'Style' variables and implications for patient-therapist matching. *J. Marr. Fam. Counsel.*, 2:55–62.

Sonne, J. C. & Lincoln, G. (1965), Heterosexual co-therapy team experiences during therapy. *Fam. Proc.*, 4:177–197.

Multiple Family Therapy Systems

ANNA BETH BENNINGFIELD

Just as a family is viewed as a system by therapists, so every form of therapy can also be viewed as a system (Laqueur, 1966). By inference then, therapy is the intervention in one system by another. Foley (1974) described four types of intervention in family systems: conjoint family therapy, multiple impact therapy, network therapy, and multiple family therapy. Differences among the four are primarily in practice rather than in theory. In multiple family therapy (MFT), which is the focus of this paper, several families meet together with the therapist(s) simultaneously.

The relationship of MFT and conjoint family therapy has been described as analogous to the relationship between group therapy and individual treatment (Glick and Hessler, 1974). However, the therapeutic approach known as multiple family therapy includes a variety of reported groupings including weekend marathons, a group composed of three to 30 families (Glick and Hessler, 1974), five or six families meeting once a week for 60 to 75 minutes (Laqueur, 1973), three identified patients and their parents (Barcai, 1967), a time-limited group for adolescents and their parents (Donner and Gamson, 1971), and three families, including children of all ages (Leichter and Schulman, 1968). Clearly MFT as a modality encompasses diverse settings and structures. Although some family therapists work with MFT groups composed entirely of couples, this paper will report only on multiple family therapy which includes two generations.

HISTORICAL DEVELOPMENT

The development of MFT as a treatment method closely paralleled the development of family therapy. Essentially, MFT combined emerging family therapy with established group therapy both in theory and practice.

Anna B. Benningfield, M.A., is a Clinical Psychologist, Doctoral Candidate, University of Texas; Clinical Member AAMFT, in private practice, Dallas, Texas.

The primary impetus for family therapy came from several unrelated observations by researchers during the 1950s. What was repeatedly discovered in various hospital settings was that the patients' home environments, that is, the quality of their relationships with their families, were a contributing factor in their illness. Furthermore, the maintenance of therapeutic gains in treatment depended on the behavior and attitudes of family members toward the patient. Evidence from many researchers made it clear that families must be included in the treatment plan to help the patient (e.g., Laqueur et al., 1971; Levin, 1966).

In contrast to the carefully researched evidence for family therapy, MFT was born of that "mother of intervention," necessity. There were simply not enough therapists to go around in the hospitals. Consequently, therapists in the 1950s and 1960s began meeting with groups of families. Laqueur (1973) credited his colleague Carl Wells, who had been active in MFT groups with Laqueur since 1951, with inventing the name "multiple family therapy." Laqueur, then at Creedmoor Hospital in New York, first reported on MFT as a treatment modality in 1964 and is generally acknowledged as its leading pioneer (Leichter and Schulman, 1974; Papp, 1974). However, in 1964 Carroll reported that Dr. Rudolf Dreikurs in Chicago had combined family therapy and group therapy, and Berman (1972) maintained that MFT was first described in 1961 by Detre, Kessler, and Sayers. Perhaps, as in the case of family therapy, innovative therapists were discovering, independently of each other, the same treatment mode.

The increasing interest in multiple family therapy was a natural outgrowth of the ever-widening concept of what constitutes a therapeutic system. Reports of beneficial changes in family systems attributed to MFT led to its inclusion in many inpatient and outpatient treatment programs as shown in column three of Table 1.

LITERATURE REVIEW

Table 1 is a representative but not an exhaustive summary of the reports in the literature on MFT. It is intended to indicate the range and scope of these reports.

In column two it becomes obvious that families from diverse populations have been included in multiple family therapy systems. The groups have included families with a hospitalized adult or adolescent, families with a problem adolescent, families with an adolescent drug addict, deprived families, and "well" families. The third column describes where the groups met or the context of the multiple family

TABLE 1
A REVIEW OF MFT SYSTEMS

Author	Population	Setting	Conclusions or Outcome
Bader, 1976	5 families	Intensive workshop	Positive changes in individuals family systems
Barcai, 1967	Parents with schizophrenic sons	Day center	Alliances between sons and parents in group
Bartlett, 1975	Families with adolescent drug addict	Hospital	Found MFT helpful in reversing trend for families in crisis and at point of decision
Berman, 1972	Families with hospitalized member	Hospital	Readmission rate = 0
Blinder, Colman, Curry, & Kessler, 1965	Families with hospitalized schizophrenic	Hospital	Family involvement in patient's treatment Conflicts worked through
Coughlin & Wimberger, 1968	10 families with adolescent boys	Child psychiatric clinic	Decreased conflict Improved family relations Satisfactory completion of school year by boys
Curry, 1965	Families with hospitalized schizophrenic	Hospital	Opportunity to observe interaction in other families
Davies, Ellenson, & Young, 1966	Families with member in day center	Day center	Improved communication within families Less scapegoating of patient
Donner & Gamson, 1971	Families with problem adolescent	Community psychiatric clinic	Families showed adjustment to revelation of strong feelings
Durrell, 1969	4 families with problem adolescent males	Junior high school	Better achievement and behavior by adolescents Increased communication within families

TABLE 1—Continued

Author	Population	Setting	Conclusions or Outcome
Jansma, 1971	9 families in control 9 families in ind. family therapy 9 families in MFT	Research design	Improved family concepts for two groups in therapy MFT group showed more conceptual changes
Julian, Ventola, & Christ, 1969	Mothers and schizophrenic adolescents	Hospital	Extraordinary cohesion within Adolescents discharged Mothers used group for therapy
Kimbro, Taschman, Wylie, & MacLennan, 1967	3 families with adolescent males	NIMH community unit	Advantages of group and family therapy Extrafamilial adolescent-adult relationships
Laqueur, 1966 1971 1972a 1972b	Families with hospitalized schizophrenic (900 families over 17 years)	Hospital	Improved communication Reduction in frequency and length of hospitalization Restructured intra-familial relations for greater understanding in families
Leichter & Schulman, 1968 1972 1974	3 or 4 families	Jewish Family Service	Forum for reality testing Decreased alienation and isolation between generations
Levin, 1966	Families with hospitalized schizophrenic	Hospital	Increased understanding of hospital life by family Some families more open in MFT than in single family therapy
Lewis & Glasser, 1965	Families with day-hospitalized member	Day treatment center	Greater family interaction Family members accepted responsibility for part of problem
Lurie & Ron, 1971	17 families with schizophrenic young adults	Community center	None of ex-patients rehospitalized

TABLE 1 — Continued

Author	Population	Setting	Conclusions or Outcome
Papp, 1974	Families applying for treatment	Nathan Ackerman Institute	Effective for "hopeless" families Families learned from other families
Papp, Silverstein, & Carter, 1973	"Well" families	Church or home	Structuring enhanced release of feelings Teaching concepts discouraged intellectualizing Limited group interaction intensified quality of interaction
Paul & Bloom, 1970	5 families	Outpatient	Concluded MFT effective intervention
Pellman & Platt, 1974	3 families	Jewish Family Service	Isolation decreased Boundaries of color, age, culture crossed
Powell & Monahan, 1969	Deprived families	Child Guidance	Improved communication Children more open and direct
Sullivan, 1972	5 target families in group of 12 families	Hospital	Significant increase in frequency and total duration of utterances Increase in individual's proportional contribution to family total frequency of utterances within MFT Correlation between interfamilial and intrafamilial interaction in MFT No differences between families who remained in MFT and those who dropped out in fewer than 10 sessions in frequency and duration measures Disproportionte amount of therapist activity
Vogel, 1972	Parents and adolescents	Community center	Improved communication Less tension and hostility

therapy. In all these settings MFT itself functions as a living system. It comes into being, exists for a while, and ceases. It has a program and style. Within the suprasystem of the hospital, clinic, and community is the MFT system which has several subsystems: the therapist, co-therapists, observers, the family, and individuals (Laqueur, 1966).

The last column indicates that writers who have reported on MFT believe it is an effective treatment modality. Available data regarding hospital readmission of patients participating in MFT also suggest its effectiveness. However, what is most evident in the fourth column is the paucity of research in multiple family therapy systems. Three reports were based on actual research of MFT, and three other reports gave data regarding reduced rate of readmission for patients who participated in MFT. All other reports of outcome and/or conclusions have been based on clinical impressions or observations of the authors.

Characteristics of Multiple Family Therapy

Multiple family therapy has some of the features of both group therapy and family therapy. Its characteristics can be delineated by an overview of the elements of change attributed to it, a description of the stages of development in MFT groups, the role of the therapist, and the special problems of this treatment method.

Elements of Change Attributed to MFT

Laqueur (1972a) has identified what he believes to be the "mechanisms of change" in MFT groups. Other writers suggest similar change-producing elements (Davies et al., 1966; Kimbro et al., 1967; Leichter and Schulman, 1968; Papp, 1974).

The use of families as co-therapists in the group is the first mechanism of change. For example, if four families are together, usually at least one family can understand the therapist's signal and make it comprehensible to other families. Also, families do not have to cope with the "authority" of the therapist in isolation but can absorb obliquely from their peers. The group's size tends to diffuse an attack upon an individual and provide many possible sources of support. Laqueur (1973) has said that the motto of MFT is to teach families to help each other.

The second mechanism of change is the competition which exists among families in the group. Such competition produces changes in the internal power distribution and behavior of a family. Families with very little motivation are encouraged by other families whose motivation is stronger.

A third mechanism is the delineation of the field of interaction. Multiple family group members begin to understand that the behavior of an individual family member must be understood in the context of the total field of interaction. Papp (1974) explained that the goal for each family member was to help him/her understand that s/he is constantly reacting to many different systems, that his/her inner system is conditioned by forces flowing through the larger ones, and s/he is contributing to that flow.

Learning by analogy is the fourth mechanism of change in MFT. Laqueur (1972b) has described a multiple family therapy system as "*a tool to teach individual families* a great deal about their behavior by *setting up mirrors...*" (p. 633). Berman (1972) reported that one family's problem rapidly involved all families.

Learning through identification is the fifth change-producing mechanism in MFT. Such identification produces shifting alliances within the group. Also, group members have an opportunity to explore how roles are handled similarly or differently within families. Lewis and Glasser (1965) reported greater diffusion in the identification of "patient" and "relative." In fact, group members could not distinguish the two in new families admitted to the MFT group.

The sixth mechanism, learning through the identification constellation, is probably unique to multiple family therapy systems (Laqueur, 1972a). Identical family configurations lead to extremely rapid identification. Also, the identification of one situation with another can produce a "tuning-in" which promotes change within a family. The presence of other families provides an opportunity for recognizing patterns of interaction in other families which are repetitive of patterns within one's own family.

A seventh mechanism of change is the opportunity to learn through trial and error. MFT offers a safe place for reality testing. For example, the "dumb" child in a family was seen by the group as one with valuable contributions, challenging the family's perception. Barriers between individuals and families can be transcended in MFT and used to therapeutic advantage.

The eighth mechanism is the use of models. The healthier aspects of one family are used as an example and a challenge to other families in order to motivate change. "Usually the persons with the most severe symptoms are the first members of an MFT group to profit from the use of models" (Papp, 1974, p. 21). Leichter and Schulman (1974) observed that parents in MFT groups became parent substitutes for children other than their own, thus showing each other how to parent.

The final mechanism of change is the amplification and modulation of signals. A patient can pick up a signal from the therapist, amplify it for his/her family, who in turn amplifies it for other families. Rather than a therapist confronting a single family system, the therapist confronts a group of systems. Within the group, systems confront other systems, and parts of systems confront parts of other systems.

Multiple family therapy systems may sound formidable to many therapists. If one family is difficult to work with, how much more three or four would be! Such reasoning overlooks the group process which engages families with one another.

STAGES OF DEVELOPMENT IN MFT

Several writers have commented on the stages of development found in multiple family therapy groups (Coughlin and Wimberger, 1968; Curry, 1965; Donner and Gamson, 1971; Laqueur, 1973).

The first stage of MFT is often one of relief. There is an expectation, to some degree unreal, that "something is to be done," which in turn generates a spark of hope. On the other hand, the first stages of treatment also may involve a denial of problems by the families followed by feelings of being blamed for causing the patient's illness. There may be divisions among group members in the initial stage according to familial structure of identified-patient status.

Laqueur's second stage (1973) corresponds to later stages described by other writers. He described the second stage as "resistance to treatment" wherein the individual sees that change is required from him/her, who "for one thousand and one good reasons behaves in such a way that misunderstanding and rejection came about" (p. 79). Behavior of individuals and families during this stage is often hesitant, reluctant, and argumentative. They may doubt that a person can change or be afraid of losing what little good relationship they do have when they open up and confront the real problem in their lives. This writer's experience suggests that families are more likely to terminate at this point than at any other. Also attributed to the second stage are the examination of feelings of guilt, failure, and helplessness; increased group interaction; and more direct communication among family members.

The final stage as described by Laqueur is characterized by individuals' and families' openness and increased self-confidence. Some faults are accepted in an attitude of "you can't win them all." Families in this stage are more helpful to other families in distress. Group members relate as human beings, and roles of parent or child are less important.

Role of the Therapist

The therapist in multiple family groups has been compared to the conductor of an orchestra (Laqueur, 1972b). S/he must know her/his score and have both short-term and long-term plans for the interaction s/he plans to produce.

With families, the therapist is more active than in peer group therapy, and in multiple family therapy s/he is even more active than with one family. The therapist may have to intervene frequently in the beginning to promote interaction and prevent some families from "visiting"; however, lively communication occurs much faster in MFT than in peer group therapy, and the therapist will "more often have to deal with a mild free-for-all than with dullness or silences" (Laqueur et al., 1971, p. 89).

The therapist provides descriptive information about hurt expressions, signs of rejection, or rebellion. S/he attempts to elicit feelings and make those that are covert manifest. S/he locates and displays for the group the dyadic and triadic alliances and counteralliances which are continually forming and reforming. The therapist considers all interactions to be essentially symmetrical, and s/he does not take sides. S/he is sensitive and perceptive to the needs of *all* group members. The therapist also functions as a model of communication and "proper distance" in the group (Coughlin and Wimberger, 1968). S/he helps the group to focus on basic messages, sometimes multiple messages or double binds, but does not get caught up in them emotionally or become intellectual about them.

The therapist must have a variety of techniques available. S/he must keep the group from avoiding issues or feelings through intellectualizing or shallow humor, but at the same time s/he must avert excessive probing which might be uncomfortable for group members not yet ready for such disclosures. Since complicated therapeutic interactions are going on at all times, flexibility and creativity are required of the therapist.

Special Problems

There are limitations or difficulties in treating several families at one time (Blinder et al., 1965; Laqueur, 1972; Leichter and Schulman, 1974). MFT, like other group therapies, does not focus on restructuring individual personality but on relationships between individuals. Whether or not this is a limitation or an asset might be argued by therapists.

Some families may be resistant to the idea of meeting with other families, and individual or conjoint sessions are needed initially to prepare family members for MFT. Leichter and Schulman (1972) have been puzzled by the resistance to further treatment following MFT of some of the "problem children" who are active and enthusiastic participants in MFT. These authors have also stated that multiple family therapy is contraindicated for chaotic families in which the children drown out any meaningful discussion and transaction (1974). Also, families who have an important fact as a secret which the keepers of the secret insist on maintaining, are also misplaced in MFT. Families in which another person besides the primary patient is very unstable or likely to become sick do not belong in MFT groups.

A group composed of families has distinct disadvantages. The question of how many family members should be in the group is a difficult one, and attendance and absences must be considered. The termination of an entire family from an ongoing group will be experienced by the group as a severe loss. An imbalance of sex in the group's composition can inhibit and block participation.

Some of the difficulties in groups of multiple families are typical of groups in general. Over-identification may make it hard for group members to express their feelings. "Me-too-ism" in the confession of small "sins" can be used to avoid dealing with important concerns. Group members may seek escape into irrelevant discussions to avoid the target issue. Playing down the importance of emotional events avoids real change in the family. Token emotional reaching out may be substituted for meaningful interaction. Secret codes may be used to communicate important messages to others.

However, the most significant problem the therapist must deal with is countertransference (Laqueur et al., 1971). Since the MFT group is filled with persons of all ages, unresolved problems in the therapist's own relationships with parents, siblings, or children may interfere with his functioning as a participant-observer in the group. An observer can perceive countertransference and discuss it with the therapist. Audio and videotapes can also document patterns of countertransference. Such information is important in order to give the therapist a reasonably complete record of the session.

Implications for Research and Conclusions

A significant obstacle to adequate research for the evaluation of multiple family therapy systems is the lack of measurement tools. The first task, therefore, may be to find or develop tools and techniques to evaluate family systems within the MFT format. Assuming that measurement instruments will be developed, important clinical questions offer many opportunities to future researchers in MFT. A few such questions will suggest the magnitude of the research that is needed.

Does MFT expedite certain stages, such as the beginning and ending, of family therapy? Families who are initially resistant to therapy in general may progress more rapidly in MFT. Multiple family therapy systems may be a more effective means for consolidating gains in a family system approaching termination of treatment.

Does MFT have any specific advantages over conventional therapeutic treatment in institutions such as schools, prisons, churches, and hospitals? MFT may offer an effective and economical therapeutic program for these institutions. Perhaps MFT would foster cooperation between representatives of the institution and the families who are affected by that institution. It may be that MFT would also provide a support system for persons within the institution. A research design could easily include a group who received treatment as usual and the experimental group who received MFT. The significance of MFT as a treatment method would be measured by selected dependent variables.

The signal research, from the clinician's viewpoint, should focus on the effectiveness of MFT as compared to individual family therapy. Selected intrafamilial dependent variables such as cohesion, expressiveness, patterns of communication, or role relations within the family could be treated in two experimental groups, one using conjoint family therapy and the other using multiple family therapy. Written measurement techniques and/or reports from observers, perhaps through the use of videotapes, would yield results. Interfamilial dependent variables, such as interaction, patterns of communication, or role relations could also be investigated in the same way. There are many unanswered questions regarding MFT and conjoint family therapy. Does multiple family therapy retain all the advantages of conjoint family therapy? Are there any characteristics which are unique to MFT? Do family systems change in the same way in both treatments? Do both methods achieve the same degree of change in family systems? Is one any faster or more economical than the other? Only when a clinician knows how the two treatment modalities compare in effectiveness and the advantages and disadvantages of each can s/he make a responsible decision concerning their usage.

It is evident that those who have reported on MFT in the literature consider this treatment method to be effective. The fact that MFT is now included in many hospital treatment programs also suggests that it is useful. Although there is a scarcity of research to substantiate scientifically the clinical impression of therapists, there seems little room for doubt that MFT can be a valuable therapeutic intervention for changing family systems. Significantly, the literature contains no negative reports about MFT. Neither is there a report which raises any doubts about its value as a form of treatment. To date the claims of the therapists who report MFT's effectiveness remain unchallenged.

The elements of MFT which promote change in the family system were discussed earlier. To recapitulate, the essential element is the presence of other families in the group. The multiple family therapy system seems to be more powerful than a single family system and more potent than a peer group system. Predictably, a therapist will probably be more active in MFT than in single family or peer group therapy because of the multiple levels of interaction; s/he may also be less powerful and less central in the MFT group than with a single family because the group is the primary mechanism for changing the family system. The group becomes a mirror in which the family sees itself. The group encourages, challenges, supports, and reflects so that the family members can become who they want to be in relationship to each other.

Special problems encountered in MFT groups seem to be related either to the group's composition or to the therapist. Which family members should attend remains an open question. Some families may not be suited for MFT. The therapist may get caught in countertransference and interfere with the group's process. The therapist must be flexible and have a variety of techniques at his/her disposal.

Multiple family therapy seems to offer distinct benefits. There is the opportunity for the therapist to learn more about a family. S/he sees and hears them interact as a family with other families as well as with each other. There may be less pressure on the therapist to induce change in a family's system within the group context. Families may also be less resistant to change in the presence of other families. The group can provide motivation for change. Families are able to learn from other families who share similar problems. Within the MFT system there is also the potential for a greater number of relationships and thus for expanded socialization.

Multiple family therapy systems have existed for a long time. Families have helped other families in various ways and have learned from each other since the beginning of family life. It is a natural process. Most families who are functioning well today probably rely on a system of support and information which includes other families. Those families who are not functioning well require help in learning how to live more constructively with each other. Multiple family therapy groups can offer such assistance.

REFERENCES

Bader, E. (1976), Redecisions in family therapy: A study of change in an intensive family therapy workshop. Unpublished dissertation, California School of Professional Psychology.

Barcai, A. (1967), An adventure in MFT. *Fam. Proc.*, 6:185–192.

Bartlett, D. (1975), The use of multiple family therapy groups with adolescent drug addicts. In: *The Adolescent in Group and Family Therapy*, ed. M. Sugar. New York: Brunner/Mazel.

Berman, K. (1972), Multiple family therapy: Its possibilities in preventing readmission. In: *Family Therapy: An Introduction to Theory and Technique*, ed. G. Erickson & T. Hogan. Monterey, Calif.: Brooks/Cole.

Blinder, M., Colman, A., Curry, A., & Kessler, D. (1965), MCFT: Simultaneous treatment of several families. *Amer. J. Psychother.*, 19:559–569.

Carroll, E. (1964), Family therapy — Some observations and comparisons. *Fam. Proc.*, 3:178–185.

Coughlin, F. & Wimberger, H. (1968), Group family therapy. *Fam. Proc.*, 7:37–50.

Curry, A. (1965), Therapeutic management of multiple family groups. *Internat. J. Group Psychother.*, 15:90–96.

Davies, I., Ellenson, G., & Young, R. (1966), Therapy with a group of families in a psychiatric day center. *Amer. J. Orthopsychiat.*, 36:134–146.

Donner, J. & Gamson, A. (1971), Experience with multi-family, time-limited, outpatient groups at a community psychiatric clinic. In: *Brief Therapies*, ed. H. Barton. New York: Behavioral Publications.

Durrell, V. (1969), Adolescents in multiple family group therapy in a school setting. *Internat. J. Group Psychother.*, 19:44–52.

Foley, V. (1974), *An Introduction to Family Therapy*. New York: Grune & Stratton.

Glick, I. & Hessler, D. (1974), *Marital and Family Therapy*. New York: Grune & Stratton.

Jansma, T. (1971), Multiple vs. individual family therapy: Its effects on family concepts. Unpublished dissertation, Illinois Institute of Technology.

Julian, B., Ventola, L., & Christ, J. (1969), Multiple family therapy: The interaction of young hospitalized patients with their mothers. *Internat. J. Group Psychother.*, 19:501–509.

Kimbro, E., Taschman, H., Wylie, H., & MacLennan, B. (1967), A multiple family group approach to some problems of adolescence. *Internat. J. Group Psychother.*, 17:18–24.

Laqueur, H. P. (1966), General systems theory and multiple family therapy. In: *Handbook of Psychiatric Therapies*, ed. J. Masserman. New York: Grune & Stratton.

_____ (1972a), Mechanisms of change in multiple family therapy. In: *Progress in Group and Family Therapy*, ed. C. Sager & H. Kaplan. New York: Brunner/Mazel.

_____ (1972b), Multiple family therapy. In: *The Book of Family Therapy*, ed. A. Ferber, M. Mendelsohn, & A. Napier. New York: Jason Aronson.

_____ (1973), Multiple family therapy: Questions and answers. In: *Techniques of Family Psychotherapy: A Primer*, ed. D. Bloch. New York: Grune & Stratton.

———— Laburt, H., & Morong, E. (1971), Multiple family therapy: Further developments. In: *Changing Families: A Family Therapy Reader*, ed. J. Haley. New York: Grune & Stratton.

Leichter, E. & Schulman, G. (1968), Emerging phenomena in multifamily group treatment. *Internat. J. Group Psychother.*, 18:59–69.

———— ———— (1972), Interplay of group and family treatment techniques in multifamily group therapy. *Internat. J. Group Psychother.*, 22:167–176.

———— ———— (1974), Multi-family group therapy: A multi-dimensional approach. *Fam. Proc.*, 13:95–110.

Levin, E. (1966), Therapeutic multiple family groups. *Internat. J. Group Psychother.*, 16:203–208.

Lewis, J. & Glasser, N. (1965), Evolution of a treatment approach to families: Group family therapy. *Internat. J. Group Psychother.*, 15:505–515.

Lurie, A. & Ron, H. (1971), Multiple family group counseling of discharged schizophrenic young adults and their parents. *Soc. Psychiat.*, 6:88–92.

Papp, P. (1974), Multiple ways of multiple family therapists. *The Family*, 1:20–25.

———— Silverstein, O., & Carter, E. (1973), Family sculpting in preventive work with "well families." *Fam. Proc.*, 12:197–212.

Paul, N. & Bloom, J. (1970), Multiple-family therapy: Secrets and scapegoating in family crisis. *Internat. J. Group Psychother.*, 20:37–47.

Pellman, R. & Platt, R. (1974), Three families in search of a director. *Amer. J. Orthopsychiat.*, 44:224.

Powell, M. & Monahan, J. (1969), Reaching the rejects through multi-family group therapy. *Internat. J. Group Psychother.*, 19:35–43.

Sullivan, P. (1972), Intrafamilial and interfamilial interaction in multiple family therapy: A descriptive study. Unpublished dissertation, University of Vermont.

Vogel, L. (1972), Mediation within a group of multiple families. In: *Adolescents Grow in Groups: Experiences in Adolescent Group Psychotherapy*, ed. I. Berkovitz. New York: Brunner/Mazel.

Multiple Family Groups as Aftercare

MELVIN R. LANSKY, CAROL R. BLEY, GENEVA G. McVEY, and BONNIE BROTMAN

Multiple Family Group Therapy (MFGT) has emerged as a treatment modality in the last decade or so as a fusion of group and family therapy techniques. It developed at a time when family therapy had begun to move away from its origins in the study of the family of the schizophrenic and toward being a discipline in its own right. The major proponents of MFGT have been family therapists whose views strongly reflect a rebellion against what has been called the medical model of symptoms or disease (Davies et al., 1966; Laqueur, 1969, 1972, 1973). There is a de-emphasis on viewing psychiatric disorders as sickness residing in an individual patient and an emphasis on symptomatology as indicating a disturbance in the entire family system. The technical stance of not regarding symptomatology as residing exclusively in the person manifesting a disruption is evident from the interactional terminology prevalent in the writings of family therapists: "double binding" (Bateson et al., 1956), "family projection processes" (Bowen, 1966), "scapegoating" (Bell and Vogel, 1967), and so forth. Although this technical attitude has been extremely profitable in many instances, the resulting lack of attention to psychiatric symptoms, diagnoses, and diseases has led to a failure to distinguish genuine morbid phenomena from the context in which it is precipitated or the use to which it is put by all concerned. Behavioral disruption and regression

Melvin R. Lansky, M.D., is Adjunct Associate Professor of Psychiatry, UCLA School of Medicine; Staff Psychiatrist, Brentwood VA Hospital, Los Angeles, California.

Carol R. Bley, M.S.W., is on the Social Work Service, Brentwood VA Hospital, Los Angeles, California.

Geneva G. McVey, R.N., is on the Nursing Service, Brentwood VA Hospital, Los Angeles, California.

Bonnie Brotman, M.S.W., is on the Social Work Service, Brentwood VA Hospital, Los Angeles, California.

are rarely distinguished from front-rank signs of psychosis, almost to the total exclusion of the latter. As a result, it is difficult to assess what was addressed in what sort of patient and with what outcome. Progress tends to be seen not in terms of symptom remission or even of ego strength, but in terms of increased individuation of family members and of the attainment of more direct levels of communication among family members. The literature on MFGT is dominated by reports of younger patients securely lodged in their families of origin, especially those whose disturbance is described in terms of aberrant behavior — addiction, misbehavior, or underachievement (Barcai, 1967; Hendricks, 1971; Millard and McLagen, 1972; Powell and Monahan, 1969).

The rebellion against the medical model has led to almost total lack of appreciation for recent research into the major psychiatric disorders stimulated by the advent of the phenothiazines, the tricyclic antidepressants, and lithium carbonate. Offhanded and sloppy methods of diagnosis so prevalent even a decade ago are beginning to give way to a strong movement to relate diagnosis to manifestations of the patient's condition with significance for prognosis and treatment response (Feighner et al., 1972; Taylor, 1972; Woodruff et al., 1974). The resulting impetus has been diametrically opposed to that of the family therapy movement: the establishing of a firm medical model with a resulting de-emphasis on interpersonal aspects of disease or the significance of symptoms; both of these, if not denied altogether, tend to be seen as epiphenomena of the disease process rather than as of primary importance.

As a result of the polarized position of the family therapy model and the medical model or neo-Kraepelinian attitude toward psychiatric illness, gains in technique and knowledge do not complement each other as they should and do not combine to lead to more effective treatment, better health care delivery systems, and new knowledge and research hypotheses. Both points of view tend to neglect the question of residual illness; family therapists because they do not speak of illness; and neo-Kraepelinians because they rarely go beyond medication-induced remission of illness.

This report is a preliminary communication on the use of MFGT to minimize residual illness and prevent relapse — that is to say, as after-hospital care or tertiary prevention (Caplan, 1964) in patients about to be discharged or already discharged from a small family-oriented inpatient unit and maintained on medication. Our concern with tertiary prevention made us aware that neither employment of the family systems model nor the medical model resulted in remission without residual illness, and we have drawn freely from both as the particular situation demanded.

The Setting and the Choice of MFGT

The groups draw patients from a twenty-bed, male inpatient unit at Brentwood VA Hospital (Lansky, 1977). The unit involves families of every patient. Two types of patients are most common: schizophrenics in their mid-to-late twenties and men in their forties and fifties with affective disorders, usually unipolar depressions. Schizophreniform psychoses are rare in our population, and patients with exclusive diagnoses of addictive disorders are usually sent to other specialty units within the hospital. The program began two years ago. The staff includes a ward psychiatrist (M.R.L.), two social workers (C.R.B., B.B.), a head nurse (G.G.M.), about fifteen other nursing personnel, and various staff in training. The treatment philosophy views the family as central to the event of hospitalization. Family involvement is mandatory and ongoing family meetings are begun early in treatment. Most patients are medicated. Aftercare is administered as resources permit, and rehospitalized patients return to our unit. The population is local and relatively stable, so sustained contact is the rule.

One reason for the choice of MFGT was simple expediency. The family-oriented approach, developing in many cases into family psychotherapy for inpatients, posed a staffing problem, since the recognized need for family psychotherapy far exceeded our resources to provide it. Staff time became a critical issue because only the more experienced members of the staff see families as outpatients and because it is usually necessary to accommodate outpatient treatment to working schedules of at least one family member. Most of the groups are late afternoon or evening groups.

But there were reasons apart from expediency to select MFGT as a treatment modality. We found disturbance not only within the families but in the relation of families to the outside world. Concepts such as the "rubber fence" (Wynne et al., 1958), the limitations of extrafamilial socialization (Lidz et al., 1965), and the tertiary injunction of the double bind (preventing the victim from leaving the field) (Bateson et al., 1956) all point to the extreme isolation of many families with disturbed members from what might be supportive and corrective interplay with the outside world (Leichter and Schulman, 1974).

We found also that, in individual family sessions, family members tend to be so concerned with protecting their self-esteem that the emerging process of therapy with very disturbed patients and their families may produce uncontrollable anxiety. In times of family turmoil, particularly if one or more members of the family are psychotic, the therapists may be unable to maintain a sufficiently supportive atmosphere. The situation is less difficult in groups of families in which persons occupying the same role may provide more support and more constructive criticism than anyone designated a therapist or any family member could without raising issues of who was siding with whom. This is one aspect of what Laqueur (1969, 1972, 1973) has called identification constellations — the fact that family members tend to identify with those in other families occupying similar positions. Another aspect of the same observation is that family members in MFGT may see behavior or try out behavior with members of another family which they are not yet ready to see or try with members of their own families. For example, a father may express rage at the son of another family when his anger at his own son is repressed or suppressed, or a mother might see infantilizing in another mother's behavior and then begin to reflect on this unacknowledged part of her own activities as a mother.

The Evolution of Homogeneous Groups

Since the unit has two treatment teams, each responsible for ten beds, it seemed reasonable at first to begin MFGT with families or members from each team staying together, that is, to have two groups heterogeneous for diagnosis of the index patients. Problems rapidly developed. Manic patients dominated the groups in non-productive ways and were excluded. The few patients with addictive disorders succeeded in getting the groups to view almost every difficulty in terms of addiction. Families of depressives and those of schizophrenics seemed to be talking about withdrawal of a different magnitude. Married schizophrenics and their mates were mute. Parents of schizophrenics colluded in moralizing at their sons. In short, resistances to seeing the family as a unit emerged without a common theme and in therapeutically unmanageable ways. Furthermore, the extent to which troublesome behavior could be considered controllable or negotiable varied to such an extent that the members in one family became confused responding to those in another, and issues of responsibility did not emerge clearly. Alcoholics treated all pathology as defectiveness of will power. Families of patients with organic brain syndromes became depressed at any attitude that suggested conflict resolution or improvement of the patient. Accordingly, we soon developed the conviction that more homogenous groups would present an opportunity for families in similar predicaments to meet on a common ground. Thus, groups were arranged so that predicaments and possibilities of the families were comparable.

Groups relatively homogeneous as to diagnosis were begun with inpatients with the intention that the groups remain as the major psychotherapeutic follow-up care for the families as outpatients. The groups are ongoing and the composition is fairly closed; new families are added only if families drop out. There are three to seven families and several co-therapists in a group. In the event of rehospitalization families continue in the same group. Most index patients remain on medication and come at a different time for prescriptions.

As clinicians, our roles were complex. We continued work begun while the patient was hospitalized but always with an eye on posthospital adjustment in or out of the family. Residua of illness, incipient relapse, mounting family tensions, reluctance to attend sessions or take medications were as legitimate issues for the group as were issues of individuation of all group members, family members as well as index patients. In every case, clinical judgment prevailed over any preconceived notion of what therapy should be like (Norton et al., 1963). The groups also served as ongoing research instruments from which we sought to learn from diagnostically similar patients about the course of chronic illness as experienced by the patients themselves and those in close relationship to them.

The Groups Themselves

Schizophrenics and Families of Origin

These groups were the first homogeneous groups to be tried. A total of ten patients and their families have been treated, some for almost two years. All index patients were male and varied in age from midtwenties to early thirties. Not all lived with their families of origin, and several separated from them while hospitalized. One patient had married and divorced; the rest had never married. Only one patient was a first admission. All were poor-prognosis and had had manifest illness for at least several years prior to hospitalization on our unit. The index patients, one of more parents, and occasional siblings and girl friends attended. All patients were maintained on major tranquilizers after hospitalization.

The groups started after preparation of patient and family in individual family sessions. For the families, fears of being blamed and fears of having demands made on them were quite near the surface in members reluctant to attend. Once families started coming, attendance was regular, and families almost unanimously preferred MFGT to individual family sessions and agreed to stay in the groups after discharge.

The tendency for parents of several families to unite around discussing the difficulties of one identified patient proved a tenacious resistance to the groups' looking at families as units. When the family as a whole came into focus, it was common for patients to be accompanied by one parent one week and the other the next. Parents responded to sons in a condescending, if not totally unsupportive, way. Mothers offered considerable support to mothers, so much so that issues of overprotectiveness could begin to surface without undue defensiveness. The index patients were very reluctant to respond to each other, even to fellow patients whom they had known for months and with whom they occasionally socialized. A striking exception to this observation occurred when one patient assailed another for the latter's refusal to take medication.

Much of the business of the group had to do with practical issues of living independently or with parents: with jobs, parental demands, provocation, house rules, and so forth. These could be seen in terms of conflicts about dependency and independence. Scapegoating and the tendency of the identified patient to accept that role were prominent, and all families tended to collude with the scapegoating process. At times when scapegoating appeared, either by the attack of the group on a seemingly innocent victim or in reaction to the provocation of a disrupted patient, it seemed to be entirely the staff's concern to stop it. Bizarre communicative patterns typical of what were once called "schizophrenogenic" mothers were striking but infrequent.

We were struck by the necessity to handle certain aspects of the patient's problems within the group at face value rather than as aspects of scapegoating. Families had a tendency to speak of illness as "depression" or as the consequence of, say, marijuana smoking and to sermonize about will power and clean living. At such times, we spoke of "psychosis" or "tendency to psychosis" — in our opinion, much to the relief of the group, which proceeded to raise and discuss quite genuine perplexities about the condition they were faced with: questions about relapse and prevention, possibility of ultimate recovery, and the problem of whether and under what circumstances the patients were to be seen as defective or as responsible. These considerations had quite a different flavor from the scapegoating maneuvers. It was only after the group had been meeting for a great while that one patient ventured to say that he still had delusions of influence that he knew others believed to be crazy. Gradually other patients began to talk of residual psychotic phenomena and their fear of being rehospitalized if they discussed them. These situations, unlike provocative behavioral disruptions and scapegoating maneuvers, were again treated at face value as serious issues for discussion. The therapists felt free to respond either with information about the illness, or, on occasion, with judiciously selected material from the patients' pasts to fill the rest of the group in.

The effect of these groups on the members has been quite favorable. All but one of the index patients improved beyond the remissions they had achieved in previous hospitalizations, and, for most of these, the post-hospital adjustment period was considerably more successful. So far there has been only one readmission. Several went on to vocational and educational pursuits from which they had formerly been distracted by years of relapsing psychosis. Only two of the patients showed evidence of reluctance or refusal to take medication; one of these was the readmitted patient. Many patients expressed great relief at coming to the group — often verbalized only when initiating a new family — and a number of parents went on to enrich their lives outside of the family or to remarry. Siblings generally watched in quiet awe and said little in the groups despite the fact that they attended regularly.

SCHIZOPHRENICS AND THEIR WIVES

This group was started because of the failure of married schizophrenics to participate in other multiple family groups. The group started with great difficulty, and only after many months of preparation and encouragement did more than two couples appear. Index patients were diagnostically clear-cut, poor-prognosis schizophrenics with a long course of illness. Ages varied from mid-twenties to late forties. Unlike the group just described, these patients had been erratic in taking medication and forming any kind of treatment alliance with the hospital staff. None worked. In fact, there seemed to be agreement among husbands and wives that the patient was not to be expected to meet any responsibilities whatsoever. Most patients stayed at home except when accompanied by their wives. Wives tended to be the same age as husbands and without symptomatic psychiatric illness in evidence. At first, they showed great commitment to the relationship and a willingness to overfunction in the presence of a completely dysfunctional spouse, but after the group got going, wives complained of almost complete withdrawal of their husbands from any human contact. There was no socializing, no going out, little if any sex, and constant fear of violence. Husbands were more inclined to speak of their fears and to relate to each other than were schizophrenics in groups with their families of origin. There seemed to be a great inclination on the part of the husbands to maintain the dependent, regressive marital relationship. Wives were highly ambivalent about the marriages, voicing anger at their husbands' constricted life styles, regressive behavior, drawing relatives (siblings especially) into the marriage, and threats of violence or actual violence when the wives threatened to leave.

It would be premature to estimate the long-term effects of the group. So far, wives have been most motivated to insist on changes or to talk of leaving or living apart. Husbands have had fewer relapses due to drug discontinuance but have shown little inclination or ability to regard themselves as other than totally disabled and irresponsible.

DEPRESSED MEN AND THEIR WIVES

Several groups of couples manifesting severe marital disharmony formed easily in response to the staff's suggestion in individual family sessions. In many cases individual family meetings continued. Index patients had depressive symptomatology usually somewhat responsive to antidepressants but with characterologic residua that became issues for therapy. Many index patients met research requirements for the diagnosis of unipolar affective disorder, but in several diagnosis was not as clear-cut as it was for the schizophrenic index patients discussed above. Age varied from late twenties to mid-fifties. Most of the patients had had some degree of vocational success at one time or another. Most were first hospitalizations. All were first marriages for the husbands. All had children. Even in pictures presenting as so-called "endogenous depression" most index patients showed neurotic depressive traits after medication took effect. Most wives later appeared to be neurotic depressives also. Husbands were maintained on tricyclic antidepressants. Hospital regulations precluded medicating the wives.

Patterns unfolded quickly in the groups. Blaming transactions dominated the early phases of the group, and, at first, it was the wives who banded together to blame one of the husbands. Other husbands would often join in unsupportive criticism so that one husband would become the group scapegoat. As the group progressed, spouses seemed more and more like each other despite the surface transactions involving blame, withdrawal, misconduct (drinking, infidelity). Spouses usually agreed that the particular marital patterns evident in the group had characterized their relationship for years, often at the expense of everything else. Such patterns as blame, criticism, withdrawal into preoccupation with work or children, or well-timed misbehavior or irresponsibility served as distancing maneuvers to avoid intimacy. Projection of disowned traits onto the spouse was evident to the therapists when such communication patterns prevailed. It was not infrequent to find more noticeably disturbed husbands protecting quite seriously disturbed wives by accepting these projections. As the group progressed, a number of the couples were able to let the support and dependency gratification bolster their self-esteem enough to look at their part in the difficulties. Many comments that would have been poorly timed and perceived as critical coming from therapists were accepted from patients in similar plights. For example, a patient who recently left the hospital and who had begun to make changes at home pointed out that another hospitalized patient was looking for excuses not to go home and face his difficulties.

These groups were more like traditional psychotherapy groups than were the groups with schizophrenics. The therapists' comments were grasped more easily, and often comments about one couple were applied to other couples. Responsibility for the group was taken by the patients with greater ease, and they were, in general, receptive to the therapists' remarks about communication. We did not bring information about patients gained from other sources to the group. There was less need to explain psychopathology; blaming, misbehavior, criticism, preoccupation, or withdrawal usually served a communicative and distancing function that we did not see in the persistent withdrawal of schizophrenics.

The groups were comfortable for the therapists and easy to run. There was unquestionable success in locating and studying psychopathology unrelieved by tricyclic antidepressants. Success in reversing or minimizing the pathology was less clear-cut. About one-third of the twelve couples were able to bask in the support and dependency gratification in the group enough to effect constructive changes in the marriage and, in turn, in their own feelings of well-being. Two marriages terminated, and, since we do not regard continuation of marriage as a goal of treatment, outcome is hard to assess. Several couples dropped out of the groups. Four marriages failed to improve, as did both partners in the marriages. In three of these cases, the index patient seemed to be greatly affected by the group, took considerable responsibility for his part in the unsatisfactory marriage, and pleaded with his wife to work on making changes. The wives failed to respond. Dread of intimacy and criticisms emerged as major issues with these women. These cases highlighted our findings of dovetailing and interlocking maladaptive patterns that so ubiquitously characterized the marriages of the depressed men in our sample.

Conclusions

Our experience with MFGT confirms findings reported previously: that issues of autonomy and individuation are prominent, that scapegoating is common in families with a disturbed member, that communication in disturbed families is often indirect and aberrant, and that at least some of these difficulties can be addressed by the treatment modality using identification constellations, learning by analogy, group support, and metacommunicative insights. As with other such reports, our follow-up is too short and our sample size too small to permit any but anecdotal observations. The phenomena observed in all of the groups took different forms in the different homeogeneous groups. Scapegoating, for example, arose to prevent the constant battling of the depressed couples from either resolving itself in threatening intimacy or in separation. In the group of married schizophrenics, however, the husband remained an identified defective, presumably with some advantages in his so being to both spouses. Schizophrenics in their families of origin would more often become scapegoats to divert attention from other trouble spots in the family. Withdrawal varied from the preoccupation with work and children in depressed couples to the pervasive anhedonia of even well-functioning schizophrenics in their families of origin, to the housebound, terror-filled withdrawal of the totally dysfunctional married schizophrenic. Communication patterns also differed. Schizophrenics in their families of origin were prey to more ambivalent, indirect, and bizarre communication than were married schizophrenics, whose communication was more straightforward and even emphatic and dominated by motifs of terror and violence. Marriages of depressives were dominated by dovetailing neurotic patterns including blame, criticism, distancing maneuvers to fend off intimacy. In all of the families, socialization outside of the nuclear family was severely restricted or absent.

Our use of MFGT as tertiary prevention has made us painfully aware of the crippling residua of so-called successful hospital treatment. When the floridly psychotic episode of schizophrenic illness or the neurovegetative signs of depression remit after medication takes effect, the patient is rarely normal: there are withdrawal patterns, hidden delusions, maneuvers to distance unmanageable intimate relationships, damaged self-esteem, and vocational handicaps rampant in our population. In our attempt to minimize the residual morbidity and provide support for the all-important first year after hospitalization we have had to deal with these problems. It has been necessary for us to become not only psychotherapists but psychopathologists exploring the longitudinal manifestations of illness and the predicaments of patients with such illnesses and their families. The use of MFGT combined with continued medication as the principal method of aftercare has allowed us to mobilize staff and other families with considerable effectiveness in locating previously ignored difficulties and some effectiveness in responding to them. It has also drawn our attention to many aspects of the family system of the disturbed patient that do not unfold quickly enough for use to see them on a short-term inpatient unit. We have learned more about various types of withdrawal, dovetailing, and interlocking neurotic patterns of blaming and criticism, sexual dysfunction, and the manifestations of residual psychiatric disorders which patients themselves or even families seen alone are unwilling or even unable to tell us about. Awareness of these difficulties and of the shortcomings of models based on secondary prevention in recognizing them is prerequisite to doing something about them. The use of MFGT provides us with a laboratory for human attachment behavior, and, as such, is not only a treatment modality, but also a source of new information and hypotheses for research.

REFERENCES

Barcai, A. (1967), An adventure in multiple family therapy. *Fam. Proc.*, 6:185–192.
Bateson, G., Jackson, D., Haley, J., & Weakland, J. (1956), Toward a theory of schizophrenia. *Behav. Sci.*, 1:251–264.
Bell, N. & Vogel, E. (1967), The emotionally disturbed child as the family scapegoat. In: *The Psychosocial Interior of the Family*, ed. G. Handel. Chicago: Aldine Atherton.
Bowen, M. (1966), Family theory in clinical practice. *Compr. Psychiat.*, 7:345–374.
Caplan, G. (1964), *Principles of Preventive Psychiatry*. New York: Basic Books.
Davies, I., Ellenson, G., & Young, R. (1966), Therapy with a group of families in a psychiatric day center. *Amer. J. Orthopsychiat.*, 31:134–146.
Feighner, J. et al. (1972), Diagnostic criteria for use in psychiatric research. *Arch. Gen. Psychiat.*, 26:57–63.
Hendricks, W. (1971), Use of multifamily counseling groups in treatment of male narcotic addicts. *Internat. J. Group Psychother.*, 21:84–90.
Lansky, M. R. (1977), Establishing a family-oriented inpatient unit. *J. Operational Psychiat.*, 8:66–74.
Laqueur, H. P. (1969), General systems theory and multiple family therapy. In: *General Systems Theory and Psychiatry*, ed. W. Gray et al. Boston: Little, Brown, pp. 409–433.
_____ (1972), Mechanisms of change in multiple family therapy. In: *Progress in Group and Family Therapy*, ed. C. Sager & H. Kaplan. New York: Brunner/Mazel.
_____ (1973), Multiple family therapy: Questions and answers. In: *Techniques*

of Family Therapy, ed. D. Bloch. New York: Grune & Stratton.

Leichter, E. & Schulman, G. (1972), Interplay of group and family treatment techniques in multifamily group therapy. *Internat. J. Group Psychother.*, 22:167–176.

————— ————— (1974), Multiple family group therapy: A multidimensional approach. *Fam. Proc.*, 13:95–110.

Lidz, T. et al. (1965), The limitaton of extrafamilial socialization. In: *Schizophrenia and the Family*. New York: International Universities Press, pp. 336–350.

Millard, J. & McLagen, J. (1972), Multifamily group work: A hopeful approach to the institutionalized delinquent and his family. *Compar. Group Studies*, 3:117–227.

Norton, N., Detre, T., & Jarecki, H. (1963), Psychiatric services in general hospitals: A family-oriented re-definition. *J. Nerv. Ment. Dis.*, 136:475–484.

Powell, M. B. & Monahan, J. (1969), Reaching the rejects through multiple family group therapy. *Internat. J. Group Psychother.*, 19:37–47.

Taylor, M. (1972), Schneiderian first-rank symptoms and clinical prognostic features in schizophrenia. *Arch. Gen. Psychiat.*, 26:64–67.

Woodruff, R. A. et al. (1974), *Psychiatric Diagnosis*. New York: Oxford University Press.

Wynne, L. et al. (1958), Pseudomutuality in the family relations of schizophrenics. *Psychiat.*, 21:205–220.

The Effectiveness of Family Therapy:
A Review of Outcome Research

KATHRYN NASH DeWITT

The field of family therapy first received attention during the 1950s and has grown in popularity during the last two decades. In a survey of the field conducted between February, 1966 and February, 1967, the Group for the Advancement of Psychiatry (1970) found that 90 per cent of those surveyed listed "the desire to treat people more effectively" as their primary reason for using family therapy. The authors report that "It seems to be an almost universal feeling among the respondents that family therapy is more effective and that results can be seen more quickly and often more clearly" (p. 539). The authors consider it unfortunate that no comprehensive studies of the comparative effectiveness of family therapy had been reported at that time.

To date, four authors have published reviews that examine the available evidence on the effectiveness of family therapy. Olson (1970) provided a narrative description of five studies as part of a general discussion of issues in marital and family therapy. He paid special attention to the type of outcome measures that were used but did not summarize the evidence from all five studies. On the basis of his review, Olson concluded that little attention has been paid to the systematic evaluation of outcome in family therapy.

Winter (1971) described fourteen studies of the outcome of family treatment. He separated the studies into groups according to the type of outcome measure used (clinical estimates of improvement, with or without explicit criteria, and extra-therapeutic test procedures) and whether a control group was included. He too did not provide a general summary of the evidence, but did conclude that "the results are not

Kathryn Nash DeWitt, Ph.D., is a member of the Department of Psychiatry, University of California School of Medicine, San Francisco, California.

encouraging" (p. 113). Winter noted the lack of specification of the quality of the treatment in the studies and problems with the identification of proper criteria for improvement. He pointed to the need for development of treatment techniques designed to change specific target behaviors in families.

Wells et al. (1972) reviewed seventeen studies of family therapy. Although they reported on eighteen studies, two of these (Langsley et al., 1968, 1969) were actually reports of the same study. The studies were classified as "inadequate" (fifteen studies), "borderline" (one study), and "adequate" (one study) on the basis of their research designs. Studies in the inadequate group were further separated into three subgroups on the basis of the outcome measure used, i.e., termination evaluations by therapists or patients, follow-up evaluations by therapists or patients, and methods other than clinical judgments. Wells et al. found that the studies with borderline and adequate designs reported results in favor of family treatment. In addition, the authors provided tables summarizing the success rates from those inadequate studies that provided clinical evaluations stated in a form that can be tabulated. Results were reported separately for studies with "identified patients" who were adults, and those who were children and adolescents. The summary figures of 69 per cent improvement for adults and 79 per cent improvement for children and adolescents were found to compare favorably with results reported by reviewers of individual treatment of adults and of children and adolescents. Wells et al. concluded that although the quality and quantity of the data supporting family treatment were disappointing, this was to be expected given the complexity of the task. They expressed the hope that more and better evidence would follow.

Finally, Massie and Beels (1972) reviewed eight studies of the family treatment of schizophrenia. They provided a detailed description and evaluation of each study using seven criteria of adequate research. The criteria assess the adequacy of description of theory and technique, patient characteristics, therapist characteristics, context of intervention, process of treatment, outcome and follow-up, and data gathering. These evaluations are summarized in tabular form. On the basis of their review, Massie and Beels concluded that "outcome studies in the family treatment of schizophrenia are relatively limited and inadequate in scope" (p. 35). They did not believe that it would be appropriate to contrast the results of family treatment of schizophrenia with individual treatment of similar patients on the basis of the data available at that time. However, they did think that family therapy has been shown to be effective in restoring patients in a crisis of acute decompensation to a functional level that was equal to, or better than, their pre-crisis condition.

In all, previous reviewers have all noted that the research evidence as to the efficacy of family therapy was disappointing in terms of both quantity and quality. Winter (1971) has found that the results that have been reported are not an encouraging support for the use of family treatment, whereas Wells et al. (1972) and Massie and Beels (1972) found that the results do show that family treatment may have promise. All of these authors call for more and better research on this question.

METHOD

This article combines and re-evaluates all of the evidence on the effectiveness of family therapy contained in the four previous reviews and updates it by adding studies that have been missed by previous reviewers or that have appeared since these reviews were published. Studies included cover a period from 1961 through December, 1974. A total of 31 studies are reviewed. References were obtained from previous reviews, a search of the *Psychological Abstracts*, and from comprehensive bibliographies published by Glick and Haley (1971), Aldous and Dahl (1974), and Olson and Dahl (1975).

Studies that are included in this review are limited to those that provide explicit evaluation of the results of the conjoint treatment of two or more families. Some authors, such as Montalvo and Haley (1973), have pointed out that changes in the family system can be made by treating only one, or some subgroup, of its members. However, the conjoint treatment of entire families represents a clear break with treatment tradition, a break that was initiated by, and is associated with, the family therapy movement. Collaborative and concurrent treatment of family members have been in use in the field of child therapy for years and are reviewed elsewhere (Levitt, 1957, 1963, 1971).

To qualify as an example of conjoint family treatment, all relevant members of the family must have been treated together as a unit for all or a major portion of the treatment. "Relevant family members" have been defined as at least the identified patient and available parents or the identified patient, spouse, and children. Studies that report on the collaborative, separate treatment of individual family members by different therapists, and on the concurrent, separate treatment of family members by one therapist have been excluded. Also excluded are studies that discuss the family in systems terms but that report on

TABLE 1
LIST OF STUDIES INCLUDED IN THIS AND PREVIOUS REVIEWS

Authors	Date	Reviewers					Reason for Exclusion
		Olson (1972)	Winter (1971)	Wells et al. (1972)	Massie & Beels (1972)		
A. Studies reviewed elsewhere but excluded from this review							
Ayers	1965		x				parents only
Bellville et al.	1969			x			couples only
Carroll et al.	1963			x			couples only
Chance	1959		x				concurrent treatment
Fitzgerald	1969		x	x			couples only
Friedman & Lincoln	1965	x	x	x			results not reported
Greenberg et al.	1964			x	x		results confounded
Kirby & Priestman	1957				x		mother-daughter only
Pittman et al.	1968			x			couples only
Shellow et al.	1963	x					results not reported
B. Studies reviewed elsewhere and included in this review							
Bowen	1961			x	x		
Coughlin & Wimberger	1968			x			
Esterson et al.	1965				x		
Ferreira & Winter	1966		x				
Ferreira & Winter	1968		x				
Freeman et al.	1964			x			
Haley	1964		x				

Jackson & Weakland	1961				x
Kaffman	1963		x	x	x
Langsley	1971[1]		x	x	x
Laqueur et al.	1964				x
MacGregor et al.	1964[2]		x	x	
Martin	1967		x	x	
Minuchin et al.	1967	x	x	x	
Safer	1966			x	
Schreiber	1966	x		x	
Sigal et al.	1967[3]	x		x	
Spiegel & Sperber	1967		x	x	
Wells	1971		x	x	

C. Studies not reviewed elsewhere but included in this review

Alexander & Parsons	1973
Baird	1973
Burks & Serrano	1965
Cutter & Hallowitz	1962
Donner & Gamson	1968
Esser	1971
Evans et al.	1971
Hendricks	1971
Jansma	1972
Liebman et al.	1974
Parsons & Alexander	1973
Rosenthal et al.	1974

[1] Interim results reported in Langsley et al. (1968, 1969).

[2] Interim results reported in MacGregor (1962).

[3] Results also reported in Postner et al. (1971).

treatment that has a unidirectional rather than an interrelational focus. Examples are treatment programs in which parents are trained to change their approach to child-rearing without also considering the effect of the current or altered behavior of the child on the parent. Finally, studies that report on the treatment of marital couples alone have also been excluded. Although many of these studies are examples of conjoint family treatment, they have been reviewed recently by Gurman (1973) and will, therefore, not be covered here.

Table 1 gives a list of the studies that have appeared in previous reviews and those that are reviewed here. The studies have been separated into the following three categories: studies reviewed elsewhere but excluded from this review (N = 10); studies reviewed elsewhere and reviewed here (N = 19); and studies not reviewed elsewhere but reviewed here (N = 12).

Luborsky et al. (1971) in a general review of the factors affecting the outcome of individual psychotherapy with adults, consider separately the effect of the patient, the therapist, and the treatment on the outcome. Numerous other reviewers (Bergin, 1971; Kiesler, 1966; Malan, 1973; Paul, 1967) have written on the importance of evaluating the effect of each of these factors on the outcome of treatment. These authors have emphasized the need for increased specificity in the selection and description of each of these factors.

The present review begins with a description of studies of conjoint family treatment. Included in this description is a summary and evaluation of the results that they report. Following this description, each of the three factors, patient, therapist, and treatment, that may affect the outcome of psychotherapy are discussed. Special attention is given to issues involved in these factors that are specific to the family treatment approach. Finally, the problem of identifying the proper criteria for measuring improvement in family treatment is discussed briefly.

SURVEY OF OUTCOME STUDIES

Studies of the outcome of family therapy report on the treatment of a variety of clinical problems, using a range of methods. Table 2 gives a summary of the characteristics of patients and treatment reported in these studies. Patient populations are generally described in these studies in terms of the characteristics of the identified patient, i.e., the family member on whose behalf the treatment was originally sought. Since studies that report on the treatment of marital couples alone are not included in this review, the majority of these studies report on the treatment of families in which the identified patient is a child or an

TABLE 2

SUMMARY OF CHARACTERISTICS OF IDENTIFIED PATIENTS
AND OF TREATMENT IN STUDIES OF CONJOINT FAMILY THERAPY

	No. of Studies
Identified Patients	
Age group	
Child	7
Child and adolescent	2
Preadolescent	1
Adolescent	11
Adolescent and adult	4
Adult	2
Not reported	4
Clinical diagnosis	
Behavior disorder	10
Neurotic	3
Neurotic and psychotic	6
Psychotic	6
Addict	2
Intractable asthma	1
Not reported	3
Patient status	
Outpatient	21
Outpatient and inpatient	3
Inpatient	6
Not reported	1
Treatment	
Type	
Conjoint	14
Conjoint with hospitalization	6
Conjoint with other outpatient	8
Multifamily group	2
Multifamily group with hospitalization	1

TABLE 2 — Continued

	No. of Studies
Duration	
Short (1–3 mo.; 1–12 sessions)	10
Medium (3–6 mo.; 13–24 sessions)	12
Long (<6 mo.; <24 sessions)	4
Not reported	5

adolescent. The most common clinical problem is some form of behavior disorder, variously described as "delinquent," "character disorder," "behavior problem," or "behavior disorder." Problems range in severity from "neurotic outpatient" to "chronic schizophrenic inpatient." Most identified patients are classified as outpatients. Other characteristics about the identified patient such as sex, socioeconomic status, and race are mentioned too infrequently to warrant their inclusion in Table 2.

Information about the general type and duration of treatment is also summarized in Table 2. Most studies used conjoint family treatment alone or in combination with some other form of inpatient or outpatient treatment. Three studies reported on the use of multifamily group treatment in which three or more families were seen at one time. The average treatment duration reported was six months. Treatment ranged from two full days of crisis intervention to more than two years of weekly sessions.

The quality of the information provided about the therapists who participated in the treatment reported in these studies is too poor to supply any general description of their characteristics. Fifteen of the 31 studies reported no information about the therapists at all, including the number who participated in the treatment. Only one study reported on the sex of the therapists; three noted that some or all of the therapists were students. No other information was included.

Studies of the outcome of conjoint family therapy vary considerably in the adequacy of their research designs. Bergin has noted that "There have been more articles written describing how ideal outcome research should be done than there are studies attempting to match the described designs" (1971, p. 252). Since these issues have received abundant attention elsewhere (Bergin, 1971; Goldstein et al., 1966; Malan, 1973; Paul, 1967), they will not be reviewed here. However, the design adequacy of the studies reviewed here is evaluated as it affects the quality of the results reported.

Studies of the outcome of conjoint family treatment can be separated into two main categories on the basis of their research design. There are 23 studies in one category that lack comparison groups of any kind. In general, these studies also lack other important elements of good research procedures, such as the random selection of subjects, the use of both pre-tests and post-tests, the use of follow-up measures, and the use of statistical tests for the evaluation of results. The eight studies that do have comparison groups compose the second category. These studies usually show a general knowledge of adequate research procedures. Since the quality of the information reported by these two types of studies is so different, and because they report their results differently (per cent improvement vs. statistical tests), the results will be summarized and evaluated separately in the following section.

OUTCOME STUDIES WITHOUT COMPARISON GROUPS

Table 3, adapted from Gurman (1973), provides a summary description of each of the 23 studies without comparison groups. Goldstein et al. (1966) point out that untreated "normals" do not constitute a proper comparison group for the effects of psychotherapy; therefore, studies by Ferreira and Winter (1966, 1968), Haley (1964), and Minuchin et al. (1967) have been classified here as studies without comparison groups. Results that are reported in these studies are listed in the following five categories of improvement: dropout, worse or no change, some improvement, moderate improvement, and definite improvement. These classifications were made by this author in cases where the results were reported in the form of narrative descriptions. Bergin (1971) has discussed the problems involved in attempting to interpret and summarize the results of outcome studies without comparison groups. There is considerable between-study variability in the number and definition of categories of improvement, which makes the comparability of classifications of cases highly doubtful. The discussion by Massie and Beels (1972) of the criteria of improvement used by Bowen (1961) and others, highlights this problem:

> Bowen's concept of significant change involved fundamental interpersonal alterations, and this is not the basic criterion for change used by most of the family therapists whose efforts we are reviewing here. Most are content, even triumphant, if they can simply help families [with a schizophrenic member] function in a smoother fashion with fewer crises [p. 28].

TABLE 3
FAMILY TREATMENT STUDIES WITHOUT COMPARISON GROUPS

Author	Date	No. of Families	Characteristics of Identified Patient	Type of Treatment	Length of Treatment	No. of Therapists	Random	Follow-Up	Pre-Post	Statistics	Author ≠ Therapists	Source	Focus	Measures	Drop-Out	Worse or No Change[5][6]	Some Improvement	Moderate Improvement	Definite Improvement	Total	Not Reported
Bowen	1961[†]	15	adolescent and adult psychotic inpatient and outpatient	conjoint only (whole family live in hospital)	6-33 months	5	no	some	yes	no	no	T	P,C,F	evaluation of symptoms and system	---	4(33)	5(42)	2(17)	1(8)	12	3
Burks & Serrano	1965	25	adolescent psychotic and neurotic inpatient	conjoint with hospitalization,- IP & individual : M,F,IP	less than 2 months	NR	no	12 mths.	yes	no	no	T	P,C,F	evaluation of treatment objectives	2(9)	6(26)	5(22)	---	10(43)	23	2
Coughlin & Wimberger	1968	10	adolescent character disorder outpatient	conjoint with concurrent	18 sessions	4(co) 3M,IF	no	no	no	no	no	T,IF	F	termination comments	1(10)	1(10)	---	1(10)	7(70)	10	---
								6 mths.				F	I	follow-up questionnaire		1(20)			4(80)	5	5
Cutter & Hallowitz	1962	56	adolescent character disorder outpatient	conjoint with some individual	NR (some in progress)	NR	no	no	no	no	NR	T	P,F	evaluation of symptoms and family relations		8(14)		14(25)	34(61)	56	---
Donner & Gamson	1968	30	adolescents not psychotic or retarded outpatient	multifamily groups of 3-4 families	10-30 sessions	2(co)	no	no	no			T	P	symptoms family relations and treatment complete	---	10(33)	---		20(66)	30	30
								"several mths."				F	F		---	12(40)	4(13)		11(37)	30	30
								"several mths."				F	P	follow-up, 4 criteria		3(38)			5(62)	8	24
												B	P	post-treatment trouble with law or school	3(10)	6(20)			24(80)	30	---
Esser	1971	14	adults alcoholic inpatient	conjoint only	13 months average	NR	no	unstated interval	no	no	NR	T	P,F	general improvement drinking behavior	---	2(14)	4(29)	5(36)	3(21)	14	14
									yes			B	P								
Esterson, Cooper, & Laing	1965	42	adolescent and adult schizophrenic inpatient	conjoint with hospitalization (no individual, shock, leucotomy, heavy drugs)	3 months average	NR	no	12 mths.	no	no	NR	B	P	obtained and maintained employment	---	10(24)	4(10)	2(05)	26(62)	42	42
								12 mths.				B	P	re-hospitalization	---	7(17)	---	---	35(83)	42	42
Ferreira & Winter[1]	1966	10	child schizophrenic, neurotic, or delinquent	conjoint only	6 months (some in progress)	NR	no	no	yes	yes	yes	B	F	spontaneous agreement decision time choice fulfillment	---	---	10(100)	---	0(00)	10	---
Ferreira & Winter[2]	1968	10	child schizophrenic, neurotic, or delinquent	conjoint only	6 months (some in progress)	NR	no	no	yes	yes	yes	B	F	amount of silence units of opinion	---	10(100)	---	---	0(00)	10	---

TABLE 3 (Continued)

Author	Date	No. of Families	Characteristics of Identified Patient	Type of Treatment	Length of Treatment	No. of Therapists	Random	Follow-Up	Pre-Post	Statistics	Author ≠ Therapist	Source	Focus	Measures	Drop-Out	Worse or No Change [5]	Some Improvement	Moderate Improvement	Definite Improvement	Total	Not Reported
Freeman, Klein, Rieman, Lukoff, & Heisey	1964	13	adolescent behavior problem outpatient	conjoint only	NR	NR	no	no	no / yes	no	NR	T / F	P / I	15 point scale questionnaire on role expectations and perceptions	--- / ---	2(16) [7] / 13(100)	--- / ---	--- / ---	11(85) / 0(00)	13 / 13	--- / ---
Haley [1]	1964	6	child schizophrenic, neurotic, or delinquent	conjoint only	6 months (some in progress)	6 (4 students)	no	no	no / yes	no	NR	T / B	F / F	evaluation of change talking order	---	6(100)	---	---	0(00)	6	---
Jackson & Weakland	1961	18	adolescent and adult schizophrenic inpatient and outpatient acute and chronic	conjoint with some hospitalization	12 months average	NR	no	no	no	no	NR	T	P	symptoms, communication, social adaptation	---	3(17)	---	---	15(83)	18	---
Kaffman	1963	29	child neurotic, behavior disorder, or schizophrenic outpatient	conjoint with some individual	10 sessions average	NR	no	no	no	no	NR	T	I, F	5-point scale with criteria	---	5(17)	---	4(14)	20(69)	29	---
Laqueur, LaBurt, & Morong	1964	80	adolescent and adult schizophrenic inpatient, then outpatient	multifamily groups of 4-5 families with hospitalization	6-8 months	14	no	no / no / 12 mths.	no	no	NR	F / T / B	F / F / P	communication / general improvement / rehospitalization	--- / --- / ---	10(13) / 18(23) / 8(10)	17(21) / 26(33) / ---	--- / --- / ---	53(66) / 36(45) / 72(90)	80 / 80 / 80	--- / --- / ---
Liebman, Minuchin, & Baker	1974	7	intractable asthma outpatient	conjoint only	NR	NR	no	some	yes / no	no	no	B / T / T	P / P / F	drug use, school or work attendance, hospitalization / physical activities / peer group relations / family characteristics	---	---	---	1(14)	6(86)	7	---
MacGregor, Ritchie, Serrano, & Schuster	1964	62	adolescent severely disturbed outpatient (not retarded, organic gross psychotic behavior)	conjoint with individual and couple	2 full days (20 hours)	6(co)	no	6 mths. 18 mths.	yes / no	no	no	T	P, F	outline rating characteristics	---	13(21)	---	11(18)	38(61)	62	---
Minuchin, Montalvo, Guerney, Rosman, & Schumer	1967	12	adolescent delinquent (more than one family) outpatient	conjoint with group for parents and children	30 sessions	7(co)	no	no	yes, yes / no	yes	no	B / T	F / F	number and direction of communications in Wiltwyck Family Task / clinical impressions criteria varied	---	12(100) / 5(42)	---	---	0(00) / 7(58)	12 / 12	--- / ---

TABLE 3 (Continued)

Author	Date	No. of Families	Characteristics of Identified Patient	Type of Treatment	Length of Treatment	No. of Therapists	Design: Random	Follow-Up	Pre-Post	Statistics	Author ≠ Therapists	Criteria[3]: Source	Focus	Measures	Results[4]: Drop-Out	Worse or No Change[5]	Some Improvement	Moderate Improvement	Definite Improvement	Total	No Reported
Rosenthal, Mosteller, Wells, & Rolland[1]	1974	5	child behavior problem (more than one/family) outpatient	conjoint in home and in clinic with some couple or child	24 months or more	NR	no	no	no	no	no	T T	P F	behavior in home and community tension in home	---	1(17)	---	---	5(83)	6	1
Safer	1966	29	child and adolescent behavior disorder outpatient	conjoint with child	6 sessions average	NR	no	4-16 mo.	no	no	NR	T	P	symptoms	---	5(17)[8]	12(41)	---	12(41)	29	---
Schreiber[2]	1966	72	child and adolescent behavior problem outpatient	conjoint with individual	4.3 months average	11	no	some[2]	yes	no	yes	T	F,I	scale by Satir (at 3 mths.) (at more than 3 mths.)	--- ---	39(54)[9] 9(12)	--- ---	--- ---	33(46) 63(88)	72 72	--- ---
Sigal, Rakoff, & Epstein	1967	20	child not psychotic outpatient	conjoint only	5-44 sessions	9	no	no	yes	no	yes	T&I	F	judge gave 6 pt. rating to change seen in therapist ratings via questionnaire	---	5(26)	---	9(47)	5(26)	19	1
Spiegel & Sperber	1967	7	child not psychotic outpatient	conjoint only	6 sessions	NR	yes	6 mths.	yes	no	NR	P P,C T	P P P	Leary's ICL, symptom checklist behavior in sessions	---	---	5(71)	---	2(29)	7	---
Wells	1971	9	outpatient	conjoint only	NR	12	no	no	no	no	no	T,P	F	termination report follow-up NR	---	3(33)	4(44)	---	2(22)	9	---

on 3/12

[1] Studies by Ferreira & Winter (1966, 1968) and Haley (1964) are on the same subjects. If not, they are on different groups of randomly selected subjects from the same sample of treated families.

[2] Schreiber (1966) lists results at three months and at over three months. Some cases may have been terminated during those intervals and are, therefore, follow-up at the time of post-testing.

[3] Criteria are described in terms of the source (i.e., who supplied the information), focus (i.e., who was the object of the information), and measure. Symbols in the Source column should be interpreted as follows: T = therapist, F = all family members, P = identified patient, B = observable behavior, I = independent judge. Symbols in the Focus column should be interpreted as: P = identified patient, C = parental couple, F = entire family as a system, I = all individual family members. Information in the Follow-up and Pre-Post columns under Design indicates when the measurements were made. In cases where more than one measure was used, the information for each measure on which results were reported is listed separately. When only one set of results is listed but multiple measures are described, the results represent a judgment based on all of the measures in combination.

[4] Figures in parentheses are percentages of the total number of cases on which results were reported. Some studies reported results in the form of narrative descriptions of changes in each patient or family. In these cases, families were assigned to improvement categories by the author.

[5] Only one study (Freeman et al., 1972) included a category for "worse," in the description of results.

[6] Burks and Serrano (1965) report that three cases were switched by their therapists from family treatment to individual treatment. These cases have been included in the "no change" column.

[7] Freeman et al. (1972) report that one family was judged to be worse at termination and one showed no change.

[8] Safer (1966) lists three cases as "symptomatic remission"; these have been included in the "No Change" category.

[9] Schreiber (1966) reports results in percentage terms on six separate outcome categories. Percentages of improvement at three months range from 31-61%, at more than three months they range from 80-96%. The figures listed here are averages of the six percentages. Since the author does not list the number of families on whom each percentage is based, they have been assumed to be the total sample of 72. This may well be a false assumption.

Table 4 gives an attempt to arrive at a general estimation of the effectiveness of conjoint family therapy, based on the information contained in these studies. Results of studies using more than one measure of improvement have been simplified by calculating the arithmetic mean of the results reported for the various measures. An alternate method for summarizing results from multiple measures would be to select the most valid measure of improvement; however, I know of no *a priori* basis for making such selections. Results reported on only a small portion of the sample, such as the follow-up data reported by Coughlin and Wimberger (1968) and Donner and Gamson (1968), were not included in these calculations.

Bergin (1971) discusses the variation in estimates of success and failure that can be reached depending on the categories of improvement that are included in each group. Different figures can be obtained depending on whether dropouts are excluded from the calculations or included as failures. The classification of cases with slight improvement as successes or failures also yields different estimates of effectiveness. Bergin concludes that either position on both issues is defensible, depending on the subjective biases of the reviewer. A list of these categories is given in Table 4 in uncombined form so that readers can make their own interpretations.

Based on the data in these studies, the general success rate of conjoint family therapy is estimated to be 72 per cent with cases classified as "slight improvement" included, and 64 per cent without such cases included. These figures compare favorably with the figures of 67 per cent, 65 per cent and 66 per cent success reported by Eysenck (1966) and Bergin (1971) for individual treatment of adult patients and by Levitt (1971) for non-conjoint treatment of children and adolescents, respectively. Given the problems with classification and interpretation of the aforementioned results, these figures should be interpreted as at best a gross indication of the success of conjoint family therapy.

Much discussion has been devoted to the identification of the proper estimate of improvement in persons with psychological problems who do not receive formal psychotherapy. Eysenck (1952), Kiesler (1966), and Bergin (1971) all discuss the problem of determining the rate of "spontaneous remission" and provide estimates. Malan concludes that attempts to arrive at a proper estimate "probably lead into a cul-de-sac" (1973, p. 723) because of variations in the types of patients included and the criteria of improvement. He points out that these problems are best remedied through the use of studies with comparison groups that eliminate them via research design.

TABLE 4

SUMMARY OF RESULTS OF STUDIES WITHOUT COMPARISON GROUPS

	Results[1]					
	Dropout	Worse or no change	Some improvement	Moderate improvement	Definite improvement	Total
Bowen (1961)	–	4	5	2	1	12
Burks & Serrano (1965)	2	6	5	–	10	23
Coughlin & Wimberger (1968)	1	1	–	1	7	10
Cutter & Hallowitz (1962)	–	8	–	14	34	56
Donner & Gamson (1968)	1.5	11	2	–	15.5	30
Esser (1971)	–	2	4	5	3	14
Esterson et al. (1965)	–	8.5	2	1	30.5	42
Ferreira & Winter (1966)	–	10	–	–	–	10
Freeman et al. (1972)	–	7.5	–	–	5.5	13

Haley (1964)	—	6	—	—	—	6
Jackson & Weakland (1961)	—	3	—	—	15	18
Kaffman (1963)	—	5	—	4	20	29
Laqueur et al. (1964)	—	12	14.3	—	53.7	80
Liebman et al. (1974)	—	—	—	1	6	7
MacGregor et al. (1964)	—	13	—	11	38	62
Minuchin et al. (1967)	—	8.5	—	—	3.5	12
Rosenthal et al. (1974)	—	1	—	—	5	6
Safer (1966)	—	5	12	—	12	29
Schreiber (1966)	—	24	—	—	48	72
Sigal et al. (1967)	—	5	—	9	5	19
Spiegel & Sperber (1967)	—	—	5	—	2	7
Wells et al. (1971)	—	3	—	4	2	9
Total (%)	4.5 (1)	153.5 (27)	49.3 (8)	52 (9)	316.7 (55)	576 (100)

[1]Results of studies using more than one measure of improvement have been simplified by calculating the arithmetic mean of the results reported for the various measures. Results reported on only a small portion of the sample were not included in these calculations.

OUTCOME STUDIES WITH COMPARISON GROUPS

Table 5 provides a summary description of each of the eight family treatment studies with comparison groups. These studies can be separated into three subgroups on the basis of the comparisons being made.

Conjoint treatment vs. no treatment. Studies by Alexander and Parsons (1973), Baird (1972), Jansma (1971), Martin (1967), and Parsons and Alexander (1973) compare conjoint family therapy with no treatment or minimal treatment. All five studies report results favoring conjoint family treatment.

However, problems in four of these studies limit the interpretations that can be made from them. Shapiro (1971) has emphasized the need to certify that the results of any treatment under study are due to its specific, active elements rather than the nonspecific effects of all treatment approaches. Nonspecific treatment effects can be assessed by including attention-placebo comparison groups or by performing long-term follow-up assessments. Four of the five studies included in this subgroup (Alexander and Parsons, 1973; Baird, 1972; Jansma, 1971; Martin, 1967) do not include such procedures. Therefore, although all of them report results favoring conjoint family treatment over no treatment, these results cannot necessarily be attributed to specific elements of the conjoint treatment approach.

In addition, the studies by Baird (1972) and Martin (1967) have other weaknesses. Both studies have extremely small samples that seriously limit the generalizability of results. Baird uses a subject-as-own-control design that does not control for the effect of the order of presentation of the treatments. (Goldstein et al. [1966, pp. 23–24] outline the problems with this type of research design.) The study by Baird also lacks between-group comparisons so that no conclusions as to the relative effectiveness of the treatments can be drawn.

Only the study by Parsons and Alexander (1973) provides clear evidence of the effectiveness of conjoint family therapy over no treatment. Parsons and Alexander use a four-group design that includes controls for the effects of attention and for reactive testing procedures. Their results show that treated families are superior to nontreated families on all three target behaviors.

Conjoint treatment vs. hospitalization. One study by Langsley et al. (1968, 1969, 1971) compares the outpatient treatment of severely disturbed patients and their families with the normal inpatient hospital regimen. The authors report an initial reduction in post-treatment hospital admissions among identified patients treated by conjoint family therapy, but the difference between this group and those treated by the standard hospitalization program disappears over time. Langsley (1971) comments that hospital admissions in the conjoint group had probably risen because the family-crisis services were no longer available to this group. This comment, in combination with the lack of between-group differences on the other measures of improvement, indicates that it is possible that no substantial changes had taken place in the families treated by conjoint family therapy; rather, they had substituted the family-crisis treatment for hospitalization as a method of coping with recurring crises. Although this outcome may have benefits in terms of the cost of treatment and the extent of disruption to the lives of identified patients and their families, it does not show that conjoint family therapy is a more effective treatment method.

Hospitalization plus conjoint treatment vs. hospitalization alone. Two studies, Evans et al. (1971) and Hendricks (1971), compare the combination of hospitalization and conjoint treatment with hospitalization alone. Both studies report results that favor combined treatment. However, Evans et al. (1971) did not include the follow-up evaluation needed to control for nonspecific treatment effects. In contrast, the results of Hendricks (1971) do provide a strong case for the effectiveness of the combined treatment. They find that identified patients who were given the additional treatment differed substantially on target behaviors twelve months after termination.

Although all eight studies reviewed in this section report results favoring conjoint family therapy, only the studies by Parsons and Alexander (1973) and Hendricks (1971) provide solid evidence for the effectiveness of this treatment approach.

The evidence on the general effectiveness of conjoint family treatment presented here leads to the following conclusions. First, outcome studies without comparison groups appear to give similar results to those achieved by other types of treatment. However, since these studies do lack comparison groups, only gross contrasts in terms of per cent of patients who benefit can be made. Better information on the types of patients who benefit and how they benefit is needed. Second, of the eight studies with comparison groups, five compare conjoint family therapy with no treatment or minimal treatment. Although these studies have some weaknesses, they show that, in general, conjoint family treatment is superior to no treatment at all. This finding is similar to that reported by Luborsky et al. (1975) for studies of non-conjoint treatment approaches. Third, of the three studies that compare conjoint family treatment with non-conjoint methods, only that of Hendricks (1971) provides solid evidence of the superiority of conjoint family therapy. The experience of the review of Luborsky et al.

TABLE 5
FAMILY TREATMENT STUDIES WITH COMPARISON GROUPS

Author	Date	No. of Families	Characteristics of Identified Patient	Type of Treatment	Length of Treatment	No. of Therapists	Random	Follow-Up	Pre-Post	Statistics	Author # Therapists	Source	Focus	Criteria¹ Measures	Research Design	Results
Alexander & Parsons	1973	40	adolescent delinquent outpatient	conjoint behavior mod w/comm. conjoint client-centered conjoint dynamic	12–15 sessions	20 (18 students)	yes	no	no	yes	NR	B	F	within-family var. in amount speech, amount silence, no. interruptions	T_1 = Behav. Mod. N 20 / T_2 = Client-Cent. 10 / T_3 = No Treat. 10	T_1 sig. superior to T_2 and T_3 on all measures. T_2 sig. superior to T_3.
		86					yes	6–18 mo.	yes	yes	NR	B	P	recidivism	T_1 = Behav. Mod. 46 / T_2 = Client-Cent. 19 / T_3 = Dynamic 11 / T_4 = No Treat. 10	T_1 sig. superior to T_2, T_3, T_4. T_3 = 26% T_3 = 73% T_2 = 47% T_4 = 50%
Baird	1972	4	adolescent outpatient	conjoint only	6 weeks	NR	no	6 wks.	yes	NR	NR	I	F	discussion content ratings via categories in Leavy's ICL	subject as own control / 6 wks. Period I Test Treat / Test Period II Treat Test / 6 wks. Period III Test	changes in all periods Period I – all 4 attributed to external reasons Period II – all 4 consistent with treatment goals Period III – 1 regressed, 3 progressed No between period comparisons mode
Evans, Chagoya, & Rakoff	1971	100	adolescent schizophrenic, depressive, character disor. inpatient	conjoint hospitalization with individual and drugs	6 months average	23	no	no	yes	yes	yes	I	P	symptoms from chart, 3 categories with criteria	T_1 = conj. + hosp. N 50 / T_2 = hosp. alone 50	T_1 sig. superior to T_2 chg N 1 2 / Obvious 32 23 / Slight 14 5 / None 4 22
Hendricks	1971	85	adult narcotic addicts inpatient	multifamily groups of 8 families hospitalization with daily group therapy + recreation and vocational training	5.5 months average	11 teams (co–)	no	12 mo.	yes	no	yes	B	P	drug use	T_1 = fam grp. + hosp N 85 / T_2 = hosp. alone NR (all outpatients released in 1967)	T_1 41% drug free T_2 21% drug free

TABLE 5 (Continued)

Author	Date	No. of Families	Characteristics of Identified Patient	Type of Treatment	Length of Treatment	No. of Therapists	Random	Follow-Up	Pre-Post	Statistics	Author ≠ Therapists	Source	Focus	Measures	Research Design	Results
Jansma	1971	27	NR	conjoint multifamily groups	NR	NR	yes	no	yes no	yes	NR	F C T	I C I	Vander Veen's Family Unit Inventory Locke Marital Adjustment Test general rating	T_1 = conj. T_2 = multi-fam. grp. T_3 = No Treat. N 9 9 9	measures analyzed separately for each family member. 9/23 compar. sig. $8T_1$ over T_3; $1T_2$ over T_3 $7T_1$ over T_2; $2T_2$ over T_1
Langsley, Flomenhaft & Machotka	1969	300	severely disturbed inpatients	conjoint crisis with office, home, phone, and collateral hospitalization with individual, group, milieu, drug	24.2 days average 28.6 days average	4 NR	yes	6 & 18 mos.	yes	yes	no	B I	P I	hospitalizations post treatment Social Adjustment Inventory, Personal Functioning Scale	T_1 = conj. crisis T_2 = hosp. N 150 150	T_1 fewer hosp. than T_2 during 0–6 mos. gap reduces over time mo. 1 2 0–6 13% 26% 6–12 13% 18% 12–18 12% 17% Both T_1 & T_2 improved on SAI and PFS; no between-group diff.
Martin	1967	4	preadolescent behavior problem outpatient	conjoint with communication training focus	6 sessions	1	match 3 wks.	yes	no		B I	F P	number of blaming statements school behavior using Peterson's Problem Checklist	T_1 = conjoint T_2 = No Treat. N 2 2	T_1 greater reduction blaming than T_2; T_1 & T_2 both reduced problems, T_1 greater reduction than T_2
Parsons & Alexander	1973	40	adolescent delinquent outpatient	conjoint with communication training focus	8 sessions	20 students	yes	no	yes	yes	yes	B I	F F	amount silence, speech distribution, frequency and duration of speech spontaneous agreement	T_1 Pre-Treat–Post T_2 — Treat–Post T_3 Pre — Post T_4 — Atten–Post N 10 10 10 10	T_1 & T_2 sig. superior to T_3 & T_4 on all behavior measures T_1 & T_2 no dif. T_3 & T_4 on spontaneous agreement

¹See Table 3 footnote for explanation of symbols.

(1975) of comparative treatment studies clearly indicates that a single study is very difficult to use as a basis for generalization.

Since many reviewers of outcome research (Kiesler, 1966; Malan, 1973; Paul, 1967) have expressed dissatisfaction with the quality of information obtained when examining the effectiveness of any general treatment approach, attention is turned next to the available information on the specific factors that affect the outcome of conjoint family therapy.

FACTORS AFFECTING OUTCOME

Each of the three main ingredients of psychotherapy (patient, therapist, and treatment) has an important effect on the results obtained. This section provides a brief description of the quantity and quality of information on these factors contained in the studies of conjoint family therapy reviewed here.

PATIENT FACTORS

The studies included in this review report on the treatment of a varied collection of families. Some of the main characteristics of these families are summarized in Table 2. The quality of the information on family characteristics varies considerably from study to study. Some studies, such as the study by Wells (1971), provide almost no information on family characteristics, while others, such as MacGregor et al. (1964), provide extensive descriptive information. Although many studies include family descriptions, only two of the 31 studies relate any characteristics of families or of individual family members to the outcome of treatment. MacGregor et al. (1964) separate the families in their sample into four groups depending on the level of psychosocial development of the adolescent identified patient. Results are reported separately for each family group and are found to vary among them. Sigal et al. (1967) examine the relationship between certain interactional characteristics of families measured at intake and their response to treatment. They find no effect of these characteristics on treatment success.

Some additional information on this question can be found in studies that examine factors that affect premature termination from conjoint family therapy. Families who do not remain in treatment until it is completed probably do not receive its full benefits. Sager et al. (1968) report that race, socioeconomic status, current marital status of parents, and initial treatment requests of families are related to the probability that they will continue in treatment, whereas religion is not a factor. Slipp et al. (1974) find that a family's socioeconomic status, method of requesting treatment, and scores on the F-scale have an effect on commitment to treatment, whereas age, point in family life cycle, family status of identified patient, and severity of disturbance of identified patient do not. Such analyses do not indicate how these family characteristics have an effect on commitment and whether this effect is specific to conjoint family therapy or applies to psychotherapy in general. Clearly, the quantity and quality of research information on the relationship between patient characteristics and the outcome of conjoint family therapy is poor. (The opinions of family therapists on this question are found in discussions of the indications and contraindications for conjoint family therapy by Ackerman [1966, 1967], in the Group for the Advancement of Psychiatry report [1970], and in the work of Guttman [1973], Offer and VanderStoep [1975], Skynner [1969], and Wynne [1971]. Avallone et al. [1973] report on a survey of the criteria used by practicing therapists in their assignment of patients to conjoint family therapy and other forms of treatment.)

THERAPIST FACTORS

Only minimal information is available on the characteristics of the therapists who participated in the conjoint family therapy reported in the studies reviewed here. No study provides any analysis of the effect of any therapist characteristic on the outcome of treatment. Beels and Ferber (1969) have analyzed the styles of family therapists. They separate them into two main types, described as "reactors" and "conductors." It would be interesting to examine the differential effectiveness of therapists in each group. Examination of this question, and of the effect of any other characteristic of family therapists on treatment, awaits future research.

TREATMENT FACTORS

Alexander and Parsons point out that the conjoint family approach to treatment is not necessarily associated with universally defined treatment techniques:

> ...systems theory represents more of a model, or points of view than a specific theory, and does not include a set of clearly derived specific techniques for changing maladaptive patterns of family interaction [1973, p. 220].

The studies in this review support this point of view. They range widely in variety and type of treatment procedures. Studies by Alexander and Parsons (1973) and Jansma (1971), reviewed earlier, found differential effectiveness of various forms of conjoint family therapy. Alexander and Parsons found that conjoint treatment that is focused on changing specific communication behaviors is more effective in altering these behaviors than is conjoint treatment using a client-centered or a dynamic approach. Jansma found that the conjoint treatment of a single family unit is more effective than multifamily groups. More research of a similar type is needed.

In all, little attention has been devoted, thus far, to the analysis of the effects of the characteristics of patient, therapists, and treatment on the outcome of conjoint family therapy. Two studies examine the impact of characteristics of family or identified patient; two look at variations in treatment; none examines the effect of therapist characteristics. Three of four of these studies report substantial results. Although these results are promising, much more research on the specific active elements of effective family therapy is needed.

CRITERIA OF CHANGE

The importance of selecting the proper instruments for measuring change and the problems involved in their selection have received abundant attention in the area of individual psychotherapy. A recent publication by Waskow and Parloff (1975) contains an extensive discussion of these issues by leaders in the field. These authors stress the need for between-study comparability in the measures used and suggest a standard battery of instruments that includes devices for measuring the patient's behavior and experience from the point of view of self, therapist, independent evaluator, and relevant others.

The assessment of change in conjoint family therapy adds a new level of complexity to this already difficult issue. With few exceptions, studies of the outcome of family treatment describe their patient families in terms of the characteristics of the identified patient. Whereas change in the identified patient is one focus of such treatment, change in the entire family system is often mentioned by the authors as another. Treatment that has the stated objective of making changes at the family-system level should make an attempt to describe families in these terms.

Bowen (1961) discusses the difficulties encountered by therapists in the switch from focusing on individuals to focusing on family systems. He finds that this problem is reflected in the difficulty of arriving at family-system descriptions. Some authors use the device of changing labels from the individual diagnosis of schizophrenic, for example, to the family diagnosis of "schizophrenic-producing family." Such changes are fine if accompanied by substantive descriptions of the characteristics of families labeled in this manner. Without such descriptions, they are nothing more than labeling changes. The studies by Singer and Wynne (Singer and Wynne, 1965; Wynne, 1968; Wynne and Singer, 1963) on the characteristics of families of schizophrenics are examples of progress in this area.

Of the authors reviewed here, only Bowen (1961) and MacGregor et al. (1964) made a concentrated attempt to provide family-system descriptions. Studies by Ferreira and Winter (1966, 1968), Haley (1964), Minuchin et al. (1967), Alexander and Parsons (1973), and Parsons and Alexander (1973) include some measure of family interaction. These studies assess the impact of conjoint family therapy on interaction variables that have been shown to discriminate between disturbed and normal families. This is a promising trend that deserves continued attention. (Jacob [1975]) provides an extensive review of studies that have examined differences in interaction between disturbed and normal families.)

Two additional points deserve mention. Since conjoint family therapy is offered as an alternate method for alleviating the problems of the identified patient, studies that assess its impact should include measures of change in both the family system and in the identified patient. In addition, the use of multiple measures of improvement in both the family and the identified patient is important when attempting to compare the benefits of different forms of treatment. It holds out the hope that it will be possible to distinguish among types of outcomes even when percentages of patients who benefit from the different treatments are not significantly different. This point is made by Luborsky et al. (1975) in their review of comparative studies of non-conjoint treatment.

COMMENT

The results of the 31 outcome studies of conjoint family therapy reviewed here can be summarized as follows. First, the 23 studies without comparison groups appear to give results that are similiar to those obtained by other non-conjoint methods. Second, of eight studies with comparison groups, five find that conjoint family therapy is superior to no treatment, and one of three that contrast conjoint family therapy with non-conjoint methods reports a lasting advantage for conjoint treatment. Third, three of the four studies that examine factors affecting the outcome of conjoint family therapy find that variations in patient or treatment characteristics have an impact on results. No studies have examined the effect of therapist characteristics.

Although the quantity and quality of these results are not impressive in an absolute sense, research in this area is just beginning. The field of family therapy itself has a short 25-year history. The earliest research study reviewed here was reported by Bowen in 1961, just fifteen years ago. Since that time, there have been some noticeable trends toward improvement. Only one of the 20 studies published during the 1960s included a comparison group; seven of the eleven studies reported during the 1970s did. Three of the four studies that examined factors affecting the outcome of conjoint family therapy appeared during the last five years.

Much work remains to be done, however. The conjoint approach was developed to provide more effective treatment for individual patients who had been found to be unresponsive to traditional approaches. Whether this promise is being fulfilled, for whom, and under what conditions is not clear at this time.

It is important to remember that the defining characteristic of the family treatment approach is a refocusing of attention on the family as a system. This shift calls for theoretical and technical developments that are just beginning. There is a crucial need for better methods of describing family functioning and for measuring system-level change. (Cromwell et al. [1976] provide a discussion of current progress in this area.) Both the methods of intervention and therapist characteristics need to be examined in greater detail. Finally, the problem of the effect of values on the development and definition of family problems and on the prescription of treatments should be examined at length.

Bowen (1961) is of the opinion that significant change in families with severe disturbance may take two or three years, if it takes place at all. Yet others, like Kaffman (1963), Burks and Serrano (1965), Esterson et al. (1965), report on the use of relatively short-term (ten weeks to three months) treatments with similar families. Just what changes can be expected with what kinds of input over what period of time is yet to be determined. Whitaker (1967) has said that working with families requires special talents and stamina on the part of the therapist. Whether this is true and just what therapist characteristics are needed has not been established.

If future research is to provide answers to these and other important questions, certain changes must be made. The characteristics of families, therapists, and treatments should be described in detail. Specific family features to be changed should be identified in advance. Outcome assessment should include information on changes in all family members (whether identified patients or not, treated or not) and on the family system as a whole. Without such changes, researchers will find themselves in the all-too-familiar position of having rooms full of fascinating data that simply tell them what they already know, that family therapy works for some people and not for others.

Researchers can experience the huge amount of work involved in making such discoveries as an exercise in futility. The demanding nature of family research is sufficient to dampen the enthusiasm of the most committed researcher. However, it is hoped that the potential for nihilism in the mental health establishment will remain dormant unless the results of programmatic and meticulously executed family research warrant turning attention to other treatment methods. This research, although difficult, is crucial. It is also doable.

REFERENCES

Ackerman, N. W. (1966), *Treating the Troubled Family*. New York: Basic Books.
——— (1967), The uses of family psychotherapy. *Amer. J. Orthopsychiat.*, 37: 391–392.
Aldous, J. & Dahl, N. (1974), *International Bibliography of Research in Marriage and the Family, 1965–1972*, vol. 2. St. Paul: University of Minnesota Press.
Alexander, J. E. & Parsons, B. V. (1973), Short-term behavioral intervention with delinquent families: Impact on family process and recidivism. *J. Abnorm. Psychol.*, 81:219–225.
Avallone, S., Aron, R., Starr, P., et al. (1973), How therapists assign families to treatment modalities. *Amer. J. Orthopsychiat.*, 45:767–773.
Ayers, E. G. (1965), A study of conflict between parents in clinic and non-clinic families. Unpublished thesis, University of Kansas.
Baird, J. P. (1972), Changes in patterns of interpersonal behavior among family members following brief family therapy. Unpublished thesis, Columbia University, New York.
Beels, C. C. & Ferber, A. (1969), Family therapy: A view. *Fam. Proc.*, 8:280–318.
Bellville, T., Raths, O. N., & Bellville, C. J. (1969), Conjoint marriage therapy with a husband and wife team. *Amer. J. Orthopsychiat.*, 39:473–483.
Bergin, A. E. (1971), The evaluation of therapeutic outcomes. In: *Handbook of Psychotherapy and Behavior Change*, ed. A. E. Bergin & S. L. Garfield. New York: Wiley, pp. 217–270.
Bowen, M. (1961), The family as the unit of study and treatment. *Amer. J. Orthopsychiat.*, 31:40–60.
Burks, H. & Serrano, A. (1965), The use of family therapy and brief hospitalization. *Dis. Nerv. Syst.*, 26:804–806.
Carroll, E., Cambor, G. C., Leopold, J. V., et al. (1963), Psychotherapy of marital couples. *Fam. Proc.*, 2:25–33.

Chance, E. (1959), *Families in Treatment*. New York: Basic Books.

Coughlin, F. & Wimberger, H. C. (1968), Group family therapy. *Fam. Proc.*, 7:37–50.

Cromwell, R. E., Olson, D. H., & Fournier, D. G. (1976), Tools and techniques for diagnosis and evaluation in marital and family therapy. *Fam. Proc.*, 15:1–50.

Cutter, A. V. & Hallowitz, D. (1962), Diagnosis and treatment of the family unit with respect to the character-disordered youngster. *J. Amer. Acad. Child Psychiat.*, 1:605–618.

Donner, J. & Gamson, A. (1968), Experience with multifamily, time limited, outpatient group at the community psychiatric clinic. *Psychiat.*, 31:126–137.

Esser, P. D. (1971), Evaluation of family therapy with alcoholics. *Brit. J. Addict.*, 66:251–255.

Esterson, A., Cooper, D., & Laing, R. (1965), Results of family-oriented therapy with hospitalized schizophrenics. *Brit. Med. J.*, 2:1462–1465.

Evans, H. A., Chagoya, L., & Rakoff, V. (1971), Decision-making as to the choice of family therapy in an adolescent in-patient setting. *Fam. Proc.*, 10:97–109.

Eysenck, H. J. (1952), The effects of psychotherapy: An evaluation. *J. Consult. Psychol.*, 16:319–324.

———— (1966), *The Effects of Psychotherapy*. New York: International Science Press.

Ferreira, A. J. & Winter, W. (1966), Stability of interactional variables in family decision-making. *Arch. Gen. Psychiat.*, 14:353–355.

———— ———— (1968), Information exchange and silence in normal and abnormal families. *Fam. Proc.*, 7:251–276.

Fitzgerald, R. V. (1969), Conjoint marital psychotherapy: An outcome and follow-up study. *Fam. Proc.*, 8:261–271.

Freeman, V. J., Klein, A. F., Rieman, L. M., et al. (1964), Results reported by Wells, R. A., Dilkes, T. C., & Trivelli, N. (1972), The results of family therapy: A critical review of the literature. *Fam. Proc.*, 11:189–208.

Friedman, A. S. & Lincoln, G. (1965), Quantitative family evaluation measures. In: *Psychotherapy for the Whole Family*, ed. A. S. Friedman et al. New York: Springer, pp. 146–164.

Glick, I. D. & Haley, J. (1971), *Family Therapy and Research: An Annotated Bibliography*. New York: Grune & Stratton.

Goldstein, A. P., Heller, K., & Sechrest, L. B. (1966), *Psychotherapy and the Psychology of Behavior Change*. New York: Wiley.

Greenberg, I. M., Glick, I., Match, S., et al. (1964), Family therapy: Indications and rationale. *Arch. Gen. Psychiat.*, 10:7–24.

Group for the Advancement of Psychiatry (1970), The field of family therapy. *Group for the Advancement of Psychiatry Reports*, 7:519–546.

Gurman, A. S. (1973), The effects and effectiveness of marital therapy: A review of outcome research. *Fam. Proc.*, 12:145–170.

Guttman, H. A. (1973), A contraindication for family therapy: The prepsychotic or postpsychotic young adult and his parents. *Arch. Gen. Psychiat.*, 29:352–355.

Haley, J. (1964), Research on family patterns: An instrument measurement. *Fam. Proc.*, 3:41–65.

Hendricks, W. J. (1971), Use of multifamily counseling groups in treatment of male narcotic addicts. *Internat. J. Group Psychother.*, 21:84–90.

Jackson, D. D. & Weakland, J. H. (1961), Conjoint family therapy: Some considerations on theory, techniques, and results. *Psychiat.*, 24(suppl. 21):30–45.

Jacob, T. (1975), Family interaction in disturbed and normal families: A methodological and substantive review. *Psychol. Bull.*, 82:33–65.

Jansma, T. J. (1971), Multiple vs. individual family therapy: Its effects on family concepts. Unpublished thesis, Illinois Institute of Technology, Chicago.

Kaffman, M. (1963), Short-term family therapy. *Fam. Proc.*, 2:216–234.

Kiesler, D. J. (1966), Some myths of psychotherapy research and the search for a paradigm. *Psychol. Bull.*, 65:110–136.

Kirby, K. & Priestman, S. (1957), Values of a daughter and mother therapy group. *Internat. J. Group Psychother.*, 7:281–288.

Langsley, D. G. (1971), Avoiding mental hospital admissions: A follow-up study. *Amer. J. Psychiat.*, 127:1391–1394.

_____ Fromenhaft, K., & Machotka, P. (1969), Follow-up evaluation of family crisis therapy. *Amer. J. Orthopsychiat.*, 39:753–760.

_____ Pittman, F. S., Machotka, P., et al. (1968), Family crisis therapy: Results and implications. *Fam. Proc.*, 1:145–158.

Laquer, P., LaBurt, H., & Morong, E. (1964), Multiple family therapy. *Curr. Psychiat. Ther.*, 4:150–154.

Levitt, E. E. (1957), The results of psychotherapy with children: An evaluation. *J. Consult. Psychol.*, 21:189–196.

_____ (1963), Psychotherapy with children: A further evaluation. *Behav. Res. Theory*, 60:326–329.

_____ (1971), Research on psychotherapy with children. In: *Handbook of Psychotherapy and Behavior Change*, ed. A. E. Bergin & S. L. Garfield. New York: Wiley, pp. 174–194.

Liebman, R., Minuchin, S., & Baker, L. (1974), The use of structural family therapy in the treatment of intractable asthma. *Amer. J. Psychiat.*, 131:535–540.

Luborsky, L., Auerbach, A. H., Chandler, M., et al. (1971), Factors influencing the outcome of psychotherapy: A review of quantitative research. *Psychol. Bull.*, 75:145–185.

_____ Singer, B., & Luborsky, L. (1975), Comparative studies of psychotherapies. *Arch. Gen. Psychiat.*, 32:995–1008.

MacGregor, R. (1962), Multiple impact psychotherapy with families. *Fam. Proc.*, 1:15–29.

_____ Ritchie, A., Serrano, A., et al. (1964), *Multiple Impact Therapy with Families*. New York: McGraw-Hill.

Malan, D. H. (1973), The outcome problem in psychotherapy research. *Arch. Gen. Psychiat.*, 29:719–729.

Martin, B. (1967), Family interaction associated with child disturbance: Assessment and modification. *Psychother.: Theory Res. Pract.*, 4:30–35.

Massie, H. N. & Beels, C. C. (1972), The outcome of the family treatment of schizophrenia. *Schiz. Bull.*, 6:24–36.

Minuchin, S., Montalvo, B., Guerney, B. G., et al. (1967), *Families of the Slums*. New York: Basic Books.

Montalvo, B. & Haley, J. (1973), In defense of child therapy. *Fam. Proc.*, 12:227–244.

Offer, O. & VanderStoep, E. (1975), Indications and contraindications for family therapy. In: *The Adolescent in Group and Family Therapy*, ed. M. Sugar. New York: Brunner/Mazel.

Olson, D. H. (1970), Marital and family therapy: Integrative review and critique. *J. Marr. Fam.*, 32:501–530.

_____ & Dahl, N. S. (1975), *Inventory of Marriage and Family Literature*, vol. 3. St. Paul: University of Minnesota Press.

Parsons, B. V. & Alexander, J. F. (1973), Short-term family intervention: A therapy outcome study. *J. Consult. Clin. Psychol.*, 41:195–201.

Paul, G. L. (1967), Strategy of outcome research in psychotherapy. *J. Consult. Psychol.*, 31:109–118.

Pittman, F. S., Langsley, D. G., & DeYoung, C. D. (1968), Work and social phobias: A family treatment approach. *Amer. J. Psychiat.*, 124:1535–1541.

Postner, R. S., Guttman, H. A., Sigal, J. J., et al. (1971), Process and outcome in conjoint family therapy. *Fam. Proc.*, 10:451–473.

Rosenthal, P. A., Mosteller, S., Wells, J. L., et al. (1974), Family therapy with multiproblem multichildren families in a court clinic setting. *J. Amer. Acad. Child Psychiat.*, 13:126–142.

Safer, D. J. (1966), Family therapy for children with behavior disorders. *Fam. Proc.*, 5:243–255.

Sager, C. J., Masters, Y. J., Ronall, R. E., et al. (1968), Selection and engagement of patients in family therapy. *Amer. J. Orthopsychiat.*, 38:715–723.

Schreiber, L. E. (1966), Evaluation of family group treatment in a family agency. *Fam. Proc.*, 5:21–29.

Shapiro, A. K. (1971), Placebo effects in medicine, psychotherapy, and psychoanalysis. In: *Handbook of Psychotherapy and Behavior Change*, ed. A. E. Bergin & S. L. Garfield. New York: Wiley.

Shellow, R. S., Brown, B. S., & Osberg, J. W. (1963), Family group therapy in retrospect. *Fam. Proc.*, 2:52–66.

Sigal, J. J., Rakoff, V., & Epstein, N. B. (1967), Interaction in early treatment sessions as an indication of therapeutic outcome in conjoint family therapy. *Fam. Proc.*, 6:215–266.

Singer, M. T. & Wynne, L. C. (1965), Thought disorder and family relations of schizophrenics: IV. Results and implications. *Arch. Gen. Psychiat.*, 12:201–212.

Skynner, A. C. (1969), Indications and contraindications for conjoint family therapy. *Internat. J. Soc. Psychiat.*, 15:245–249.

Slipp, S., Ellis, S., & Kressel, K. (1974), Factors associated with engagement in family therapy. *Fam. Proc.*, 13:413–427.

Spiegel, D. & Sperber, Z. (1967), Clinical experiment in short-term family therapy. *Amer. J. Orthopsychiat.*, 37:278–279.

Waskow, I. E. & Parloff, M. B. (1975), *Psychotherapy Change Measures*. No. ADM 74-120, U.S. Department of Health, Education, and Welfare, Public Health Service, Alcoholism, Drug Abuse and Mental Health Administration.

Wells, R. A. (1971), The use of joint field instructor-student participation as a teaching method in casework treatment. *Soc. Work Educ. Rep.*, 19:58–62.

_____ Dilkes, T. C., & Trivelli, N. (1972), The results of family therapy: A critical review of the literature. *Fam. Proc.*, 11:189–207.

Whitaker, C. A. (1967), The growing edge. In: *Techniques of Family Therapy*, ed. J. Haley & L. Hoffman. New York: Basic Books.

Winter, W. D. (1971), Family therapy: Research and theory. In: *Current Topics in Clinical and Community Psychology*, vol. 3, ed. C. D. Spielberger. New York: Academic Press, pp. 95–121.

Wynne, L. C. (1968), Methodological and conceptual issues in the study of schizophrenics and their families. *J. Psychiat. Res.*, 6(suppl. 1):185–199.

_____ (1971), Some guidelines for exploratory conjoint family therapy. In: *Changing Families: A Family Therapy Reader*, ed. J. Haley. New York: Grune & Stratton.

_____ & Singer, M. T. (1963), Thought disorder and family relations of schizophrenics: I. A research strategy. *Arch. Gen. Psychiat.*, 9:191–198.

Vector Therapy

In vector therapy the family interview should skillfully guide a process of therapy that takes place outside the interview by a repatterning of the pattern of vectors both inside and outside the family.

Some of the obvious measures open to the vector therapist are demonstrated here — day care, wife employment, and adoptions. One paper concerns itself with the problems that follow family fragmentation. The last paper throws light on the evaluation of a type of family — the multiproblem family — which is usually unresponsive to interview psychotherapy, but which can respond to vector therapy.

The Effects of Day Care
on Attachment and Exploratory
Behavior in a Strange Situation

JAIPAUL L. ROOPNARINE
and MICHAEL E. LAMB

Recent sociopolitical and economic changes have brought about a dramatic increase in the number of mothers in the labor force (cf. Bronfenbrenner, 1975). This in turn has stimulated research on the effects of these changes on the psychological development of young children. Unfortunately, as most reviewers have noted, much of the research on the effects of maternal employment (Hoffman, 1974) and on the effects of day care (Bronfenbrenner, 1975) has been flawed by methodological ineptitude and conceptual naïvete. As a result, the research has been inconclusive and contradictory.

The primary focus in the research on day care has been upon mother-child attachment. In general, studies involving infant subjects or subjects who entered day care in infancy have reported that day care has no adverse effects on the mother-child relationship (Bronfenbrenner, 1975; Ricciuti, 1976; Schwarz, 1975). By contrast, Blehar (1974) reported that after five months in day care, 2½ and 3½ year-old children showed "maladaptive" patterns of interaction with their mothers. It is possible that children who have been subjected to daily separations from their mothers after attachments had been formed,

Jaipaul L. Roopnarine, Ph.D., is a postdoctoral fellow at the Mailman Center for Child Development, University of Miami, Coral Gables, Florida.

Michael E. Lamb, Ph.D., is Professor of Psychology, Pediatrics, and Psychiatry at the University of Utah, Salt Lake City, Utah.

This report is based on Masters research conducted by the first author under the direction of the second. The research was supported by funds from the Graduate School Research Committee of the University of Wisconsin at Madison. Hildy Feen and Diane Grinnell assisted in the collection of the data.

but before they had matured, might be at greater risk than children who have experience with multiple caretakers from earlier in their lives. Other data, however, do not support this interpretation (cf. Feldman, 1973, 1974; Ragozin, 1975). Reconciliation of the conflicting findings is made especially difficult by the fact that Blehar (1974) attempted to characterize the *quality* of mother-child attachment in the manner described by Ainsworth and Wittig (1969), whereas researchers such as Feldman (1973, 1974) and Ragozin (1975), who have studied children of comparable ages, have not focused on similar qualitative aspects.

These differences notwithstanding, Blehar's results were strangely counterintuitive. Using the Ainsworth and Wittig (1969) Strange Situation procedure, Blehar reported that children who had been in day care cried in response to separation considerably more than home-reared children; were significantly less friendly toward a strange adult; and responded maladaptively to reunion. Specifically, the younger day care children tended to avoid their mothers on reunion whereas the older children evinced angry, resistant behavior on reunion. Both resistance and avoidance were absent in the home care groups. The present study sought to replicate these "effects."

Unfortunately, none of the studies in this area have observed the same children both before and after day care experience. "Effects of day care" have been inferred from differences between children who are and those who are not enrolled in day care programs. One might question how reasonable it is to assume that the families seeking day care differ in no important respects from those choosing to rear their children at home. If they do.differ, the differences that one observes in any post-test procedure may reflect initial or background differences, rather than "effects" of the day care experience. Alternately, an interaction between day care experience and initial variables may account for observed group differences or similarities. These factors may be responsible for the inconsistency noted earlier.

In order to address these issues directly, we designed a study in which a group of three-year-old children was observed in the Strange Situation immediately prior to admission to day care and again three months later. Their behavior was compared with that of another group of children, matched in all respects except for the fact that their parents had no plans to enroll them in day care. We focused on three major questions: (1) Do children who *are* and those who *are not* destined to be enrolled in day care have different relationships with their parents, are they exposed to different child-rearing philosophies, and are they perceived differently by their parents? (2) In comparing their behavior before and after the day care treatment, can one demonstrate significant changes in the attachment behavior of young children? (3) Do these changes resemble those reported by Blehar in her controversial study?

METHOD

SUBJECTS

Twenty-three white three-year-olds ($\overline{X}$ = 3.1 years at the start of the study) and their mothers participated in this study. All of the children had been cared for at home by their mothers prior to the first observation. Twelve of the children (five boys) were about to enter day care at the time of the first observation, while eleven (six boys) continued to be raised by their mothers at home. The two groups did not differ on demographic, sex, age or family-status variables. About 60 per cent of the eligible child-mother pairs contacted for either group agreed to participate.

The day care group was recruited through three private centers in an affluent suburb of Madison, Wisconsin. The caretaker-child ratio in all centers was 1:6–7. The names of the children who were scheduled to enter day care were obtained from the centers prior to enrollment. Parents were contacted by means of a letter followed by a phone call.

The home care group was obtained by selecting from published birth records the names of children whose families resided in the same neighborhood as the day care group. Again, parents were contacted via an introductory letter and follow-up phone call.

The day care children were observed in a standardized situation during the week preceding their enrollment in day care. They were observed in the same setting three months later. The home care children were observed twice in the same circumstances, except that they were not, of course, enrolled in day care during the intervening three-month period.

PROCEDURE

Behavioral Observations

The children and their mothers were observed in an experimental procedure (the Strange Situation) originally described by Ainsworth and Wittig (1969). This procedure involves a series of separations and reunions of mother and child, and two entrances by a stranger. The

TABLE 1
THE STRANGE SITUATION PROCEDURE

Episode No.	Duration	Participants	Description of Episode
1	3 min.	Mother, child	Mother takes child to center of room, and encourages him/her to explore or play.
2	3 min.	Stranger, mother, child	Stranger enters, sits quietly for 1 minute, interacts with mother (1 min.), then with child (1 min.).
3	3 min.[a]	Stranger, child	Mother leaves. Stranger remains with child; responses to his/her advances or comforts him/her if necessary.
4	3 min.	Mother, child	Stranger leaves as mother enters. Mother comforts child if s/he is distressed, then reinterests him/her in toys.
5	3 min.[a]	Child	Mother leaves child alone in room.
6	3 min.[a]	Stranger, child	Stranger enters. Attempts to comfort child if distressed. Returns to her chair.
7	2 min.	Mother, child	Mother enters as stranger leaves. Mother behaves as in episode 5.

[a]The duration of these episodes was curtailed if the child became very distressed.

sequence of episodes, and a description of the procedure, are contained in Table 1. The observation room (6 × 7.5 m) was equipped with a one-way window along one wall, in front of which were placed two chairs (2.5 m apart) in which the mother and stranger sat. Twenty toys were provided for the children to play with; with the exception of one large toy between the two chairs, all of the toys were more than 2.5 m from the chairs. Taped lines on the floors indicated a radius of 3 feet (0.9 m) from each of the chairs.

At the beginning of Episode 1, the child was taken by its mother to a designated spot in the center of the room. The children were then filmed from behind the one-way window. Two young females alternated in the role of stranger; both were completely unfamiliar to the children and to the mothers.

The mothers and strangers were instructed to refrain from initiating interaction with the children, but were asked to respond normally when the children initiated interaction with them. When leaving the room the mothers were instructed to say "bye bye." On returning they were free to say what they wished.

Both time-sampled, frequency-count, and presence-absence measures were used to cull data from the videotapes. Three measures— *exploratory manipulation, crying,* and *oral behavior*— were scored on a time-sampled basis: for each 15 second unit, the coders determined whether the behavior had occurred or not. Thus these behaviors could occur 12 times in the 3-minute episodes, and 8 times in the brief seventh episode. Instances of *distance interaction,* by contrast, were recorded each time they occurred. The definitions of these four behaviors were derived from those of Blehar (1974). Exploratory manipulation involved shaking, banging, turning over, or otherwise contacting a toy. Oral behavior involved chewing or sucking fingers or toys. Crying was defined to include all distress vocalizations, while distance interaction consisted of instances of smiling, showing/offering toys, and vocalizing to an adult. Interaction with stranger and mother was tabulated separately. Separate tallies of these four behaviors were kept for each episode.

The coding system designed by Ainsworth, Bell, and Stayton (1971) to record "social interactive behaviors" in the separation (Episodes 3, 5, 6) and reunion (4, 7) episodes was substantially modified, since we converted their rating procedure into one involving merely a determination of the presence or absence of each behavior regardless of degree. In the reunion episodes and in the "stranger" episodes we coded *proximity seeking, contact seeking, interaction avoidance, proximity avoidance, interaction resistance, contact resistance,* and *greeting* with either a smile or cry. Besides the measures listed in the preceding paragraph, *search behavior* was monitored in the separation episodes. Proximity seeking was scored when the child approached to within 3 feet (0.9 m) of its mother within the first 15 seconds of each reunion episode. Contact seeking was scored when the child actively attempted to attain physical contact by clambering, gesturing to be picked up, or resisting being put down. Interaction avoidance was coded when the child ignored or looked away from an adult when she attempted to interact with it, whereas proximity avoidance was scored if the child deliberately moved away from an adult as she entered the room. Contact resistance was manifest in attempts by the child to push away, hit, or kick its mother, or by attempts to squirm away when its mother tried to soothe it. Interaction resistance, by contrast, was scored when the child angrily rejected attempts by the mother to interact with it. Smiling or crying greetings were scored only if they occurred within the first 15 seconds. Searching was deemed to have occurred if the child followed mother to the door and attempted to open it, or went to the mother's chair. "Social interactive behaviors" directed toward the stranger were searched for, but none were ever observed.

   Reliability. The videotaped records were coded by the first author. Prior to coding the tapes, he and an assistant independently coded several similar records until interscorer agreement (computed in the manner described below) exceeded .85 in all scoring categories. The same assistant (who was unaware of the group membership of the subjects) thereafter recoded 25 per cent of the records within each condition (before-after: home-day care) in order to ensure that adequate interscorer reliability was maintained. The tapes on which reliability checks were conducted were randomly selected from the corpus. Finally, a third scorer randomly selected and recoded four of the tapes, and attained reliability coefficients similar to those obtained in the other checks. Reliability in the scoring of exploratory manipulation (.88), crying (.99), oral behavior (.99), and distance interaction (.92 for mother, .82 for strangers) was determined by computing correlations between the total per-episode scores. For the presence-absence measures, reliability refers to the proportion of occasions on which the same decision was made by both coders. Coefficients ranged from .80 (proximity seeking) to 1.0 (interaction and contact resistance).

QUESTIONNAIRE MEASURES

   At the time of the first observation the mothers were asked to complete the Parent's Report (PR) and the Childhood Personality Scale (CPS) inventories developed and standardized by Cohen, Dibble, and Grawe (1977a, 1977b). The Parent's Report contained 20 items relating to the child's autonomy, parental control techniques, consistency, child-centeredness, and parental involvement. The Childhood Personality Scale was a 20-item inventory relating to the child's attentiveness, behavior modulation, zestfulness, sociability (extroversion-intraversion), verbal expressiveness, and mood.

   The inventories were scored by using the factor-scale scoring procedures described by Cohen et al. Scores on each scale ranged from 0 to

24. High scores on the CPS would describe a child with the following perceived characteristics: extreme attentiveness, hyperactivity, marked intraversion and talkativeness, extreme apathy, and markedly positive mood. High scores on the PR would indicate that the mother saw herself as having much respect for the child's autonomy, often employing guilt or anxiety as methods of control, being extremely consistent and child-centered, and frequently involved in the child's activities.

Results

All group comparisons were computed using t-tests. The significance values reported below refer to two-tailed tests.

Proximity- and interaction-avoidance and contact and interaction resistance occurred so infrequently that no statistical comparisons could be made. Their rarity is reflected in Table 2. As noted earlier, none of the "social interactive behaviors" were directed to the stranger in any episode. Thus, with the exception of one measure—distance interaction to stranger—all mean values and all analyses refer solely to behaviors directed toward the mothers. Since the procedure was designed by Ainsworth and her colleagues to elucidate individual differences in the responses to separation and reunion, our analyses focused on measures derived from the separation (3, 5, 6) and reunion (4, 7) episodes.

Questionnaire Measures

Maternal perceptions of children in the two groups were compared in order to determine whether there were initial group differences with respect to parental attitudes or perceived child characteristics. There were no differences on the CPS scores, and there was only one difference on the PR scores. Mothers of children in the day care group reported that they were somewhat more child-centered ($\overline{X}$s = 17.3, 14.5; $p < .05$) than mothers in the home care group.

Observational Measures

At the time of the first observation, there were several differences between the children who were destined to enter day care, and those who would continue to be cared for at home. As the data in Table 2 indicate, the home care children appeared to be substantially less distressed by separation than the day care group, and consequently, their reunions tended to be less intense. All of the differences observed were

TABLE 2

MEAN SCORES, CHANGES, AND SIGNIFICANT DIFFERENCES
ON THE OBSERVATIONAL MEASURES FOR THE TWO GROUPS

Behavior	First Observation		Second Observation		Longitudinal Changes	
	Day Care	Home Care	Day Care	Home Care	Day Care	Home Care
Exploratory manip.[a]	14.67***	29.64	29.92	30.18	*	
Crying[a]	4.08	2.63	0.00*	1.18	*	
Oral behavior[a]	6.16†	1.72	0.83	1.36	*	
Distance int-mother[b]	44.58	36.90	40.16	39.73		
Distance int-stranger[c]	18.50	19.09	20.83	33.90		*
Proximity seeking[b]	1.16**	0.27	0.25	0.18	*	
Search[b]	1.42**	0.36	0.66	0.63		
Contact seeking[b]	0.25**	0.09	0.00**	0.18	*	
Greet with smile[b]	0.42*	0.63	0.75	0.90		
Greet with cry[b]	0.33**	0.09	0.00	0.00		
Interaction avoid.[b]	0.00	0.00	0.00	0.00		
Interaction resist.[b]	0.00	0.00	0.00	0.00		
Proximity avoid.[b]	0.00	0.00	0.00	0.00		
Contact resist.[b]	0.00	0.00	0.00	0.00		

Asterisks indicate significant differences in the relevant comparisons.
[a] Scores summed across 3 separation episodes (3, 5, 6).
[b] Scores summed across 2 reunion episodes (4, 7).
[c] Scores summed across 2 stranger-present separation episodes (3, 6).
*** $p < .005$
** $p < .01$
* $p < .05$
† $p < .10$

consistent with this interpretation. Compared with the home care group, the day care group explored less, searched more, were more likely to seek contact with or proximity to their mothers on reunion, and were more likely to cry on seeing them, whereas the home care children were more likely to smile.

By the time of the second observation, few differences between the groups were evident. Comparisons revealed that the day care children were less likely to seek contact on reunion, and less likely to cry during the separation episodes. These behaviors occurred very rarely, so that the statistical significance tends to exaggerate the size of the group differences. The relevant data are presented in Table 2.

Comparisons of the changes across time generally indicated that the behavior of the home care group was relatively stable, while the day care group changed significantly in several respects (see Table 2). In the separation episodes, the day care children explored more, cried less, and showed less oral behavior in the second observation than in the first, whereas there were no comparable changes in the home care group. There were fewer significant changes in the reunion episodes; those that did occur showed the day care group seeking less proximity and contact after group care than before. Again, no comparable changes took place in the home care group. The only significant change in their behavior was an increase in interaction with the stranger.

DISCUSSION

Since this was the first study to have observed the same children both before and after enrollment in day care, we were especially interested in determining whether there were differences between children who were and those who were not destined to enter group care settings for the first time. We found no differences in the perceived personalities of the children, a minor difference in the maternal attitudes (with the mothers of day care enrollees being more "child-centered"), and several differences in the children's behavior. In general, the day care group was far more concerned about the brief separations than the home care children. This was evident in their responses to both separation and reunion. As a result of the day care experience, however, these group differences disappeared. All analyses indicated that it was the behavior of the day care children, not the home care children, that changed across time, so that on the occasion of the second observation there were fewer group differences, with the home care group marginally more distressed by separation and thus more intense in their greetings.

The initial group differences were unexpected. While they could be

interpreted to indicate that the children in the day care group initially
had anxious and insecure attachments to their mothers (cf. Blehar,
1974), we believe that they probably represent temporary (rather than
permanent) anxiety on the part of children whose parents are preparing them for the entry into group care the next week. Their behaviors,
then, would reflect their uncertainty and some anticipatory anxiety.
We intend to investigate this interpretation in subsequent research by
observing day-care-bound children several months before as well as
immediately before enrollment. Unfortunately, no data relevant to this
were gathered in the present investigation.

Our pre-test, post-test design yields conclusions regarding "the
effects of day care" very different from Blehar's (1974) post-test comparisons between home care and day care groups. Where her day care
group "came to" protest more, ours protested less; where her subjects
"became" less friendly toward (indeed resistant and avoidant of) the
stranger, ours became more sociable. None of our subjects displayed
either resistant or avoidant behavior in interaction with the stranger.
Where six of Blehar's ten day care three-year-olds were rated as resistant, we observed no resistant behavior. And whereas she found both
older and younger day care groups avoiding their mothers more than
home care children, we observed no avoidant behavior. We should emphasize that we observed no behavior that could be considered even
remotely or minutely avoidant or resistant, so that the discrepancy cannot merely be attributed to the fact that Blehar used a 7-point rating
scale while we used a present-absent categorization procedure.

The reason(s) for the discrepancies between Blehar's findings and
our own are not immediately apparent. The caretaker-child ratios in
the day care centers sampled were comparable, as was the age at time
of admission to day care. The only obvious difference is that Blehar's
subjects had been in day care for five months, whereas ours were observed after three months in day care. It seems unlikely that this could
account for the vastly different results. Instead, we would suggest that
Blehar's anomalous findings might best be attributed to differences in
the mother-child relationships antedating her subjects' admission to
day care. Even this statement must be qualified, however. The Strange
Situation procedure used by Blehar and by the present authors was designed to assess the quality of mother-*infant* attachment, and there is
no evidence yet available to indicate that it provides a reliable or valid
measure of the quality of the relationships between mothers and three-
year-olds. Research is needed to validate the procedure as well as to develop alternative methodologies for the assessment of social skills in
pre-schoolers.

The results of the present study and those reviewed by Bronfenbrenner (1975) and Ricciuti (1976) suggest that day care experiences do not have predictably adverse effects on psychosocial development. For both practical and theoretical reasons, however, it is important that researchers now begin to determine what types of children are likely to benefit/suffer as a result of day care experience, and what types of substitute care arrangements are best suited to facilitate the psychosocial development of children with different characteristics and differing social backgrounds. Clearly, researchers must shift from studying "the (detrimental) effects of day care" to investigating the positive and negative effects of different types of substitute care on different types of children with differing family needs.

REFERENCES

Ainsworth, M. D., Bell, S. M., & Stayton, D. J. (1971), Individual differences in strange situation behavior of one-year-olds. In: *The Origins of Human Social Relations*, ed. H. R. Schaffer. London: Academic.

———— & Wittig, B. A. (1969), Attachment and exploratory behavior of one-year-olds in a strange situation. In: *Determinants of Infant Behavior*, vol. 4, ed. B. M. Foss. London: Methuen.

Blehar, M. C. (1974), Anxious attachment and defensive reactions associated with day care. *Child Develop.*, 45:683–692.

Bronfenbrenner, U. (1975), Research on the effects of day care. Unpublished manuscript, Cornell University.

Cohen, D. J., Dibble, E., & Grawe, J. M. (1977a), Fathers' and mothers' perceptions of children's personality. *Arch. Gen. Psychiat.*, 34:480–487.

———— ———— ———— (1977b), Parental style. *Arch. Gen. Psychiat.*, 34:445–451.

Feldman, S. S. (1973), Some possible antecedants of attachment behavior in two-year-old children. Unpublished manuscript, Stanford University.

———— (1974), The impact of day care on one aspect of children's social-emotional behavior. Paper presented to the American Association for the Advancement of Science, San Francisco, California.

Hoffman, L. W. (1974), Effects of maternal employment on the child: A review of the research. *Develop. Psychol.*, 10:204–228.

Ragozin, A. (1975), Attachment in day care children: Field and laboratory findings. Paper presented to the Society for Research in Child Development, Denver, Colorado.

Ricciuti, H. N. (1976), Effects of infant day care experience on behavior and development: Research and implications for social policy. Unpublished manuscript, Cornell University.

Schwarz, J. C. (1975), Social and emotional effects of day care: A review of recent research. Paper presented to the Society for Research in Child Development, Study Group on the Family, Ann Arbor, Michigan.

Role Allocation, Family Structure, and Female Employment

MAXIMILIANE E. SZINOVACZ

The situation of working wives and mothers has often been characterized as one of overload, stress, and role conflict (Chombart de Lauwe et al., 1963; Laub-Coser and Rokoff, 1971; Pfeil, 1961). Although the degree of overload and the amount of stress might vary from case to case, the gainful employment of a wife typically results in some reorganization of household and child-rearing responsibilities. Such adjustments can be achieved by the re-allocation of tasks within the nuclear family, the delegation of tasks to persons other than immediate family members (e.g., relatives, friends, neighbors), or by hiring paid help and services.

A large number of studies have dealt with the socioenvironmental conditions affecting role-allocation patterns in families with employed women and with the consequences of various solutions in terms of family structure and family interaction patterns (cf. Bailyn, 1970; Fogarty et al., 1971; Hoffman and Nye, 1974). Despite this emphasis during the last two decades on the conditions and effects of female employment, only a few attempts have been made to relate this existing knowledge to the results obtained in studies on family structure and kin relations (e.g., Hoffman and Nye, 1974). This failure to relate findings from different studies has led researchers to some precipitate conclusions regarding the effects of female employment on family structure. One general conclusion is that regardless of the specific arrangements chosen by employed wives to reduce their family responsibilities, fe-

Maximiliane E. Szinovacz, Ph.D., is Assistant Professor of Human Development and Family Economics, Division of Individual and Family Studies, Pennsylvania State University, University Park, Pennsylvania.

The author would like to thank Ted Huston and Ira Reiss for their comments on earlier drafts of this paper. Data for this study were collected during the winter of 1968–1969.

male employment will result in more sharing of family functions by the spouses (Blood and Wolfe, 1960; Hoffman, 1963; Lamousé, 1969; Leplae, 1968; Michel, 1970a, 1970b; Musil, 1971; Pfeil, 1968; Piotrowski, 1971; Powell, 1963; Safilios-Rothschild, 1970a; Silverman and Hill, 1967). However, most of these studies did not rely on multivariate and causal analyses to test the validity of this assumption. In order to gain a more accurate description of family structure in relation to female employment, comprehensive analyses both of the factors influencing the role-allocation patterns between the spouses and of the factors relating to the availability and effectiveness of outside help are necessary.

Social-environmental conditions and subcultural value patterns have been shown to have some impact on both the prevalence of segregated or joint role-allocation patterns in nuclear families and the availability and willingness of relatives to provide help for young families. Sharing of family responsibilities by the spouses is more readily accepted and implemented by urban than by rural families and by middle and higher status groups as compared to lower status families (cf. Haavio-Mannila, 1972; Komarovsky, 1964; Silverman and Hill, 1967; Straus, 1975).

Contacts with relatives play a major role in providing social and emotional gratifications and/or economic support for young couples or families (Adams, 1964, 1968; Hill, 1965; Michel, 1970a; Sussman and Burchinal, 1962; Tallman, 1969). Participation of relatives in household and child-care tasks seems particularly important and quite effective in decreasing the work load of gainfully employed wives and mothers (cf. Pfeil, 1961). Some research evidence suggests that availability of kin and/or intensive contacts with relatives are furthered by a family's residence in a small community as opposed to a metropolitan area (Michel, 1970a; Straus, 1969; Winch and Greer, 1968). While contacts with and support from kin are of relatively high importance in families of low socioeconomic status, the absolute amount of help provided by relatives might be higher for families in middle and higher status groups (cf. Blood, 1970).

Another set of studies indicates the existence of interrelationships between the type of family social network and/or the amount of emotional gratification and instrumental support provided by extrafamilial sources and the internal structure of family relations: couples with close-knit social networks and/or with extra-familial relationships providing emotional gratification and instrumental support, particularly to the wives, are more likely to have segregated role-allocation patterns than are couples with loose-knit networks and/or without intensive contacts with or support from other members of their community (Bott, 1957; Harris, 1969; Straus, 1975; Toomey, 1971; Turner, 1970).

According to these research results, it can be hypothesized that a woman's gainful employment will have differential effects on family structure, depending on the relative availability and the relative effectiveness of family-internal and family-external support, as well as subcultural norms regarding the role-allocation patterns within the nuclear family and the maintenance of close kinship ties. Thus, sharing of family responsibilities between the spouses will occur primarily within those families of employed women in which the wives' traditional household and child-caring tasks can only be reduced by the re-allocation of these tasks among members of the nuclear family. In this case, role-allocation patterns between the spouses will depend on subcultural norms as well as the spouses' relative availability and their relative effectiveness in performing specific family tasks (cf. Holmstrom, 1972; Silverman and Hill, 1967). Although help given by relatives to working wives and mothers effectively decreases these women's work loads, it might also have latent functions by slowing down changes toward joint role-allocation patterns between the spouses. In other words, as long as relatives are able and willing to help working wives, husbands are less likely to share household and child-rearing responsibilities with their employed wives than if no such help were available. Social-environmental conditions and/or subcultural norms will determine whether or not help given by the relatives and support provided by the husband will represent alternative rather than complementary sources of support for employed wives. Complementary patterns of support will result if subcultural norms favor joint role-allocation patterns between the spouses; if subcultural norms support high role segregation between the spouses, help provided by relatives will provide an exclusive source of support for employed wives.

High role segregation between the spouses has been shown to be related negatively to marital satisfaction (Leplae, 1968; Michel, 1970a, 1970b). Thus, while employed women might receive very effective help from relatives, these close kin interactions and their implications for the role-allocation patterns between the spouses can result in low marital satisfaction. Of course, the husband's reluctance to help in the household and/or his dissatisfaction with the marriage might also lead employed women to increase their reliance on kin support.

DATA AND METHODS

The material presented in this paper is part of a larger research project on employed wives. The data are based on questionnaires completed by women during their working hours. The sample consists of 1,370 blue- and white-collar working wives and mothers, aged 20 to 30 years. The inquiry included white-collar workers employed in several large industrial organizations, insurance companies, banks, and large stores, and blue-collar workers employed in different lines of industry (e.g., textile, clothing, and metal factories). Some of these firms were located in small communities and middle-sized towns in lower Austria and the Burgenland, and others were located in Vienna. The sample of white-collar workers consisted of Viennese women only. These women were working as saleswomen and clerks. A replication of some of the findings of this study in the Austrian microcensus did reveal similar results, particularly for questions regarding household help to employed women (cf. Szinovacz, 1975).

The data on family task allocation are based on one general question concerning major help in the household, as well as a series of questions regarding help with specific household tasks. In both cases, the women were asked to indicate the person or persons who helped in the household.

The family's decision-making structure was measured by a series of eight questions regarding the relative participation of the spouses and other persons in the following decision areas: decisions concerning the family budget; changes in the furniture and household equipment; invitations and visiting; the place where vacations are to be spent; major expenditures in general; the purchase of a car; and the choice of a newspaper. The women were asked to state if these decisions were carried out by themselves, by their husbands, by both spouses jointly, or by other persons. The women's answers to these questions were computed to scores of mean numbers of decisions carried out by the husband, the wife, or by both spouses jointly. These scores were differentiated for feminine and masculine decision areas, based on whether decisions were more often carried out by the women or by the men in the majority of the families included in the sample. Computation of these scores was chosen because they seemed more likely to reveal the family's decision-making structure than husband's mean power scores, and because of serious shortcomings noted in regard to these latter scores (cf. Safilios-Rothschild, 1970b). As questions concerning the relative importance of these decisions were not included in the questionnaire, high scores on joint participation in family decision making do not necessarily imply egalitarian role relations between the spouses.

The data on marital satisfaction were gathered by a single question regarding the women's evaluations of their marital happiness. Marriages described as "very happy" or "happy" were classified as "happy." The category of "unhappy" marriages includes all cases in which the marriage was characterized as "average," "unhappy," or "very unhappy."

It should be pointed out that the answers given to all of these questions are subjective in that they represent the women's subjective definitions of the situation, rather than an objective picture of their family-life patterns (cf. Safilios-Rothschild, 1969). Furthermore, the data presented in this paper do not allow for causal analyses. Thus, further studies are necessary in order to adequately account for the causal relations implied in the following interpretations.

RESULTS

SOCIAL-ENVIRONMENTAL CONDITIONS AFFECTING HELP WITH HOUSEHOLD TASKS

In this sample, the wife's occupational position, regional background, and type of residence account for most of the variations in the amount and type of household help received by the women.

As indicated in Table 1, household help by the husband is more often reported by women in urban than in rural areas, by women in white-collar rather than blue-collar positions, and by women living separated from rather than with relatives. This trend toward joint role-allocation patterns in the urbanized areas and in the middle and higher status groups is in accordance with the evidence reported for other European countries (e.g., Haavio-Mannila, 1972). Relatives play a major part in reducing the women's overload problems in small communities, in the group of white-collar workers, and particularly in the group of young families who maintain a common residence with relatives. These differences in type of household help according to regional background, occupational position, and type of residence are significant at the .01 level.

Since white-collar families in urbanized areas are most likely to accept egalitarian norms (cf. Haavio-Mannila, 1972), availability of kin support should result in complementary help patterns by the husband and by the relatives. The Austrian data give support to this assumption. Only white-collar workers report a noteworthy amount of help by several persons, indicating participation of both the husband and the relatives in household activities. Furthermore, it is this group of women who are least likely to receive any help with their household duties. Among the women in smaller communities and in blue-collar

TABLE 1
GENERAL HELP WITH HOUSEHOLD TASKS BY WIFE'S OCCUPATIONAL POSITION, REGION, AND TYPE OF RESIDENCE

		Help with household tasks from:						
		Mother	Mother-in-law	Husband	Several persons	No help	(N)	χ^2
Blue-Collar Workers								
Small Communities[a]	Common residence[b]	33[c]	34	15	4	14	(124)	47.9
	Separate residence	22	4	34	7	33	(105)	p<.01
	Total	29	20	24	5	22	229	
Middle-Sized Communities	Common residence	41	16	19	7	17	(86)	57.8
	Separate residence	12	6	46	1	35	(209)	p<.01
	Total	20	9	38	2	31	296	
Vienna	Common residence	31	24	12	12	21	(33)	68.3
	Separate residence	4	3	47	1	45	(162)	p<.01
	Total	9	6	43	2	40	200	
Saleswomen	Common residence	36	19	14	14	17	(42)	43.7
	Separate residence	12	3	52	4	29	(129)	p<.01
	Total	18	7	43	6	26	215	
White-Collar Workers	Common residence	46	10	18	18	8	(48)	42.0
	Separate residence	15	2	49	12	22	(280)	p<.01
	Total	19	4	44	12	21	328	

Chi Square
For region, total 65.7; p<.01;
For occupational groups (only Vienna, total) 44.1; p<.01

[a] Communities with a population of 2,000 or less were defined as "small communities"; communities with a population of 20,000 or more were defined as "middle-sized communities."

[b] The category "common residence" includes all couples or families living together with relatives, usually the wife's parents or parents-in-law. The category "separate residence" refers to all women living only with members of the nuclear family.

[c] Percentages.

positions, on the other hand, help by the husband and help by relatives seem to represent exclusive rather than complementary sources of support.

Subcultural variations in the availability of relatives and in the relatives' and husbands' readiness to participate in these tasks lead to substantial differences in the situation of employed women. In urban blue-collar families, adherence to a more traditional family ideology (high role segregation) and some isolation from the kin group account for 40 per cent of the women reporting no help with household tasks. In urban white-collar families, on the other hand, with a more egalitarian family ideology and close relations with relatives, only 21 per cent of the women receive no help with household tasks. In rural blue-collar families, the husband's reluctance to help in the household is at least partly compensated for by the high participation of relatives: only 22 per cent of these women report no household help as compared to 40 per cent of the Viennese blue-collar workers.

TASK ALLOCATION AND FAMILY STRUCTURE

Both common residence with relatives and participation of kin in the household tasks of young families are positively related to high role segregation between the spouses. This pattern does not only emerge in task allocation among family members, but also in the spouses' relative participation in family decision making.

The data shown in Table 2 clearly indicate that common residence with relatives contributes to a partial withdrawal of the husband from household tasks: women who live with relatives are less likely to report sharing these functions with the husband than women living only with members of the nuclear family. This pattern is particularly pronounced for those tasks moderately stereotyped as traditional "feminine" responsibilities (washing the dishes, vacuum cleaning, and in the case of blue-collar workers, also purchases of gifts, going to public offices, cleaning shoes). It is less pronounced for highly stereotyped female tasks (e.g., cooking). The division of "masculine" tasks (e.g., small repairs in the house) between the spouses seems not to be influenced by type of residence.

Thus, common residence with relatives appears to reduce the husbands' willingness to share some feminine household tasks with their wives; regardless of the type of residence, husbands rarely assume full responsibility for "feminine" household activities. This pattern cannot be fully explained by the fact that relatives assume major responsibility for these functions. If this were the case, wives living with kin would

TABLE 2
DIVISION OF SPECIFIC HOUSEHOLD TASKS AMONG FAMILY MEMBERS AND RELATIVES BY WIFE'S OCCUPATIONAL STATUS AND TYPE OF RESIDENCE

Usually carried out by:	Shopping for daily needs	Purchases of gifts	Cooking	Washing dishes	Vacuum cleaning	Going to public offices	Small repairs in the house	Cleaning shoes
Blue-Collar Workers								
Common Residence								
Wife	58[a]	69[a]	58[a]	69[a]	81[a]	36[a]	8[a]	74[a]
Husband	1	–	–	1	2	30	80	8
Jointly	7	30	2	10	5	24	11	12
Mother, Mother-in-law	34	1	40	20	12	10	1	6
(N)	(262)	(258)	(254)	(253)	(243)	(259)	(235)	(262)
Separate Residence								
Wife	79	53	90	73	83	29	3	64
Husband	2	1	1	1	3	47	88	14
Jointly	13	46	4	22	13	22	9	21
Mother, Mother-in-law	6	–	5	4	1	2	–	1
(N)	(497)	(498)	(489)	(487)	(482)	(490)	(460)	(500)
White-Collar Workers								
Common Residence								
Wife	59	52	72	65	61	37	2	34
Husband	–	–	–	–	8	37	88	36
Jointly	13	46	–	11	12	26	10	25
Mother, Mother-in-law	28	2	28	24	19	–	–	5
(N)	(46)	(50)	(47)	(46)	(49)	(49)	(42)	(44)
Separate Residence								
Wife	73	50	93	62	58	25	3	43
Husband	2	1	–	2	17	41	84	31
Jointly	20	49	5	35	23	33	12	26
Mother, Mother-in-law	5	–	2	1	2	1	1	–
(N)	(282)	(285)	(280)	(281)	(276)	(284)	(262)	(281)

[a]Percentages.

have to be much less involved in household activities than the data suggest.

In should be noted, however, that the husband's reluctance to help in the household where common residence with relatives is maintained does not necessarily lead to more overload problems for the wife. In fact, women living with relatives are less likely to state that some traditional feminine tasks are mainly carried out by themselves (e.g., shopping and cooking) than those women living separated from kin. Additional data from the same study also indicate that help from relatives is usually more efficient than help from husbands: while relatives tend to take full responsibility for some of the young women's household tasks, husbands are more likely to perform these activities together with their wives (Rosenmayr et al., 1973; Szinovacz, 1975).

These materials provide some further evidence that availability of relatives contributes to the spouses' maintenance of segregated rather than joint role relations even in families of employed women.

If the assumption that availability of relatives and/or actual help provided by relatives tend to further high role segregation between the spouses is correct, this relationship should not only hold for the couple's division of labor, but for other interaction patterns as well.

Interrelations between the spouses' decision-making patterns and type of residence, as well as type of domestic help, are summarized in Tables 3 and 4. The data show that women living with kin and women receiving household help from relatives are less likely to report joint decision making than women who live separated from their relatives and women receiving domestic help primarily from their husbands. Although a similiar trend appears for feminine and masculine decisions, statistically significant differences are obtained only for the feminine decision areas.

Finally, it should be pointed out that it is joint decision making, in particular, which is reduced by common residence with kin or domestic help from relatives. In families living with kin or receiving domestic help from relatives, husbands are somewhat more likely to take full control of some feminine decision areas and wives are more likely to assume full responsibility for some of the masculine decision areas.

Thus, availability of relatives and actual participation of relatives in the household tasks of young employed wives seem not only to be related to the husbands' reluctance to participate in household activities, but also to their reluctance to share decision-making responsibilities with their wives.

TABLE 3

FAMILY DECISION MAKING BY WIFE'S OCCUPATIONAL
POSITION AND TYPE OF RESIDENCE[a]

| Mean number of decisions carried through by | Family lives: | | T-test (two-tailed) |
	Together with relatives	Separate from relatives	
Blue-Collar Workers			
Feminine decisions			
Wife	1.02	0.80	t = 2.41; p < .05
Husband	0.32	0.19	t = 2.38; p < .05
Jointly	2.66	3.01	t = 3.13; p < .01
(N)	(225)	(461)	
Masculine decisions			
Wife	0.34	0.29	t = 0.76; n.s.
Husband	1.02	1.05	t = 0.30; n.s.
Jointly	2.64	2.66	t = 0.21; n.s.
(N)	(172)	(387)	
White-Collar Workers			
Feminine decisions			
Wife	0.84	0.49	t = 1.78; p < .05
Husband	0.27	0.16	t = 1.05; n.s.
Jointly	2.89	3.35	t = 2.29; p < .05
(N)	(45)	(283)	
Masculine decisions			
Wife	0.22	0.17	t = 0.45; n.s.
Husband	1.12	0.95	t = 0.99; n.s.
Jointly	2.66	2.88	t = 1.11; n.s.
(N)	(41)	(254)	

[a] Masculine decision areas include the decisions on place of vacations, major purchases, choice of newspaper, and choice of car; feminine decision areas include the decisions on family budgeting, purchases of furniture, invitations, and visiting.

MARITAL SATISFACTION AND FAMILY STRUCTURE

High role segregation between the spouses has been shown to relate negatively to marital happiness (cf. Leplae, 1968; Michel, 1970a, 1970b). As can be seen from Table 5, the Austrian data indicate a similar relationship. Both blue-collar and white-collar workers whose

TABLE 4

FAMILY DECISION MAKING BY WIFE'S OCCUPATIONAL POSITION
AND GENERAL HELP WITH HOUSEHOLD TASKS

| Mean number of decisions carried through by: | Domestic help is given mainly by: | | T-test (two-tailed) |
	Relatives	Husband	
Blue-Collar Workers[a]			
Wife	1.11	0.59	t = 5.31; p < .01
Feminine Husband	0.25	0.21	t = 0.69; n.s.
decisions Jointly	2.64	3.20	t = 4.73; p < .01
(N)	(227)	(244)	
Wife	0.40	0.21	t = 3.05; p < .01
Masculine Husband	0.98	1.04	t = 0.59; n.s.
decisions Jointly	2.62	2.75	t = 1.02; n.s.
(N)	(182)	(204)	
White-Collar Workers[a]			
Wife	0.72	0.38	t = 2.81; p < .01
Feminine Husband	0.24	0.14	t = 1.41; n.s.
decisions Jointly	3.04	3.48	t = 3.41; p < .01
(N)	(95)	(143)	
Wife	0.20	0.11	t = 1.28; n.s.
Masculine Husband	1.08	0.92	t = 1.41; n.s.
decisions Jointly	2.72	2.97	t = 1.62; n.s.
(N)	(84)	(123)	

[a] N's are lower for the relationships with domestic help as women receiving other or several forms of help or no help were omitted from this analysis.

husbands do not help in the household and who report segregated rather than joint participation of the spouses in specific family decisions (first and fifth columns in Table 5) more often describe their marriages as unhappy than do all other groups. Although the relationship between marital happiness and pattern of family decision making varies with decision area, this tendency appears consistently for all decision areas included in Table 5. Women who report some participa-

TABLE 5
MARITAL SATISFACTION BY TYPE OF HOUSEHOLD HELP AND TYPE OF DECISION MAKING

Household help by: Decision making is:[a]	Mother, Mother-In-Law		Husband		No help		χ^2
Marriage is:	Segregated	Joint	Segregated	Joint	Segregated	Joint	
Blue-Collar Workers							
Decision on Family Budgeting[c]							
Very Happy	20[b]	19[b]	26[b]	20[b]	14[b]	21[b]	19.9
Happy	47	49	53	60	46	49	p<.05
Unhappy	33	32	21	20	40	30	
(N)	(136)	(88)	(97)	(134)	(118)	(99)	
Decision on Major Purchases							
Very Happy	7	24	34	17	17	16	34.2
Happy	50	47	53	61	44	50	p<.01
Unhappy	43	29	13	22	39	34	
(N)	(68)	(152)	(55)	(170)	(54)	(158)	
Decision on Choice of Newspaper							
Very Happy	20	15	23	22	15	20	21.3
Happy	41	57	56	60	50	48	p<.05
Unhappy	39	28	21	18	35	32	
(N)	(120)	(98)	(121)	(103)	(124)	(88)	
Decision on Family Car							
Very Happy	13	21	21	19	16	19	22.8
Happy	44	53	54	64	46	46	p<.05
Unhappy	43	26	25	17	38	35	
(N)	(80)	(111)	(76)	(119)	(78)	(102)	

White-Collar Workers

Decision on Family Budgeting						
Very Happy	18	29	33	20	30	18.8
Happy	50	53	43	46	55	p < .05
Unhappy	32	18	24	34	15	
(N)	(54)	(38)	(55)	(35)	(33)	
Decision on Major Purchases						
Very Happy	—	28	31	—	34	23.3
Happy	61	49	58	74	42	p < .01
Unhappy	39	23	11	26	24	
(N)	(18)	(73)	(118)	(19)	(50)	
Decision on Choice of Newspaper						
Very Happy	18	27	33	24	26	14.2
Happy	50	54	48	45	58	n.s.
Unhappy	32	19	19	31	16	
(N)	(50)	(41)	(57)	(38)	(31)	
Decision on Family Car						
Very Happy	17	27	32	26	21	13.2
Happy	50	58	56	48	56	n.s.
Unhappy	33	15	12	26	23	
(N)	(40)	(41)	(50)	(31)	(34)	

a Segregated decision making implies that decisions are made separately by either spouse.
b Percentages.
c The other decision areas could not be included in this table because the N's were too small for some subgroups.

tion of the husband in either household activities or family decisions are less likely to describe their marriages as unhappy than those women whose husbands fail to help in the household and do not share decision making responsibilities with their wives. All of these relationships are significant except for decisions concerning the newspaper and the family car in the case of white-collar workers.

These findings might imply that a working woman's reliance on kin for help in order to deal effectively with her various duties not only discourages the husband from engaging in household tasks and routine family decisions, but also can produce some stress in the relationship between the spouses. However, some of the interrelationships between kin participation in household activities and women's marital happiness might, in fact, be accounted for by the husbands' reluctance to share family responsibilities with them.

Conclusion

Earlier research on the situation of working women has centered on the effects of female employment on family structuring as well as on the overload problems of, and types of help provided to, employed women. However, connections between these two problem areas, as suggested by the work of Bott (1957) and others, have rarely been analyzed; this neglect has led researchers to some precipitate conclusions regarding various effects of female employment.

Data on 1,370 Austrian blue-collar and white-collar families indicate a clear link between specific social-environmental or subcultural conditions and the specific help received by working women. The data also reveal differences in the effectiveness of this support and, thus, in the general situation of different groups of employed women. Reliance upon outside help from relatives is positively related to high role segregation in the spouses' division of labor and in their participation in family decisions. Furthermore, some stress in the marital relationship occurs among those families who maintain close contacts with kin.

Several implications can be drawn from these results. First they provide some evidence that female employment does not necessarily lead families to develop egalitarian life styles. Rather, the consequences of female employment on family task-allocation patterns will depend on a number of subcultural and situational factors; e.g., the role expectations of each family member, previous role-allocation patterns within the family, the normative orientations of members of the family's social network, and the availability and relative effectiveness of different sources of support.[1] Changes toward joint task allocation between the spouses as a consequence of the wife's employment are least likely to occur if egalitarian norms are strongly rejected both by the members of the nuclear family (at least the husband) and by the community, and/or if relatively effective outside help is available. If outside help is available, families accepting egalitarian norms will tend to establish complementary help arrangements, while families favoring more traditional norms will tend to maintain a segregated division of labor by relying on extra-familial help as the main source of support for the wife.

It seems likely that employed women's needs for effective help with their family duties increase the relatives' readiness to provide such help, particularly if subcultural and social-environmental conditions favor close kin relations and/or discourge immediate re-allocation of family tasks between the spouses. Thus, some familial and socio-structural conditions which enable women to deal quite effectively with the burden of their double role might hinder the development of joint role relations between the spouses.

Common residence with kin and household help from relatives are not only related to the spouses' task-allocation patterns, but also to their relative participation in family decisions. It should be noted that high occurrence of segregated decision-making patterns and/or relatively high control over major family decisions by the husbands among some groups of employed women do not necessarily contradict resource-theoretical assumptions regarding the effects of female employment on the family power structure (cf. Bahr, 1974; Blood and Wolfe, 1960; Centers et al., 1971; Lamousé, 1969; Lupri, 1969; Michel, 1967; Safilios-Rothschild, 1967, 1970a; Weller, 1968). Even if employed women generally tended to favor joint decision making and had the power to implement this pattern, exertion of such power might be too costly. Enforcement of joint decision making despite strong resistance by the husband and/or within a mainly traditionally oriented social network might be very costly for the wife. In addition, assuming major responsibility for specific household tasks (even if they are usually carried out by relatives) will increase the wife's interest in control-

[1] Within this sample of families with both spouses working full time, relative availability or relative time of the spouses can be considered to be relatively constant. In fact, correlations with some time-related variables (e.g., the husband's working overtime or having a part-time occupation) did not reveal any significant differences in the families' task-allocation patterns. It can be assumed, however, that this factor plays a major part in explaining differences in task-allocation patterns among families with full-time employed wives, part-time employed wives, and housewives, as well as differences in the families' reliance upon outside help (cf. Blood and Wolfe, 1960; Silverman and Hill, 1967).

ling related decision areas (cf. Safilios-Rothschild, 1969). Thus, even if gainful employment does increase the wife's relative power position in the marital relationship, maintenance of traditional role expectations by the husband and by members of the wider community, as well as high segregation in the spouses' task-allocation patterns, will lead wives to refrain from enforcing joint decision-making patterns in their families. It might be this particular situation that contributes to the relatively low marital satisfaction of employed wives reporting high role segregation.

Second, the data further support the request for development and application of general strategies in solving specific family problems. It is clear that allowing females to deal with these problems by themselves might result in latent effects that hinder rather than further social change. Such latent effects are to be expected if social policies designed to further equality between the sexes through higher involvement of women in the labor force are not combined with specific programs which help families adjust to the social innovations resulting from these policies and which provide solutions reinforcing the intended direction of change. Longitudinal studies seem necessary in order to ascertain the causal relationships implied in this interpretation.

Finally, the Austrian data show subcultural differences in the relative difficulties that women might experience when entering the labor force. In Austria, it is certainly the group of urban blue-collar working women who face serious problems due to their work load. Similar studies in other countries might provide useful information on where societal and community help is most needed.

References

Adams, B. N. (1964), Structural factors affecting parental aid to married children. *J. Marr. Fam.*, 26:327–331.
——— (1968), *Kinship in an Urban Setting*. Chicago: Markham
Bahr, S. J. (1974), Effects on power and division of labor in the family. In: *Working Mothers*, ed. L. W. Hoffman & F. I. Nye. San Francisco: Jossey-Bass, pp. 167–185.
Bailyn, L. (1970), Career and family orientations of husbands and wives in relation to marital happiness. *Hum. Relat.*, 23:97–113.
Blood, R. O. (1970), Social change and kinship patterns. In: *Families in East and West: Socialization Process and Kinship Ties*, ed. R. Hill & R. Konig. Paris & The Hague: Mouton, pp. 189–201.
——— & D. M. Wolfe (1960), *Husbands and Wives: The Dynamics of Married Living*. New York & London: Free Press.
Bott, E. (1957), *Family and Social Network*. New York: Free Press.
Centers, R., Raven, B. H., & Rodrigues, A. (1971), Conjugal power structure:

A re-examination. *Amer. Sociol. Rev.*, 36:264–278.

Chombart de Lauwe, M. J., Chombart de Lauwe, P. H., Huguet, M., Perroy, E., & Basseret, N. (1963), *Le Femme dans la Societe. Som Image dans Differents Milieux Sociaux*. Paris: CNRS.

Fogarty, M. P., Rapaport, R., & Rapaport, R. (1971), *Sex, Career, and Family*. New York: Sage.

Haavio-Mannila, E. (1972), Cross-national differences in adoption of new ideologies and practices in family life. *J. Marr. Fam.*, 34:525–537.

Harris, C. C. (1969), *The Family: An Introduction*. London: Allen & Unwin.

Hill, R. (1965), Decision-making and the family life cycle. In: *Social Structure and the Family: Generational Relations*, ed. E. Shanas & G. F. Streib. Englewood Cliffs, N.J.: Prentice-Hall, pp. 113–139.

Hoffman, L. W. (1963), Parental power relations and the division of household tasks. In: *The Employed Mother in America*, ed. F. I. Nye & L. W. Hoffman. Chicago: Rand McNally, pp. 215–230.

———— & Nye, F. I. (1974), *Working Mothers*. San Francisco: Jossey-Bass.

Holmstrom, L. L. (1972), *The Two-Career Family*. Cambridge, Mass.: Schenkman.

Komarovsky, M. (1964), *Blue-Collar Marriage*. New York: Vintage.

Lamousé, A. (1969), Family roles of women: A German example. *J. Marr. Fam.*, 31:145–152.

Laub-Coser, R. & Rokoff, G. (1971), Women in the occupational world: Social disruption and conflict. *Soc. Prob.*, 18:535–554.

Leplae, C. (1968), Structure des tâches domestiques et du pouvoir de décision de la dyade conjugale. In: *La Dyade Conjugale*, ed. P. de Bie, K. Dobbelaere, C. Leplae, & J. Piel. Bruxelles: Les Editions Vie Ouviére, pp. 13–49.

Lupri, E. (1969), Contemporary authority patterns in the West German family: A study in crossnational validation. *J. Marr. Fam.*, 31:134–144.

Michel, A. (1967), Comparative data concerning the interaction in French and American families. *J. Marr. Fam.*, 29:337–344.

———— (1970a), La famille urbaine et la parenté en France. In: *Families in East and West: Socialization Process and Kinship Ties*, ed. R. Hill & R. Konig. Paris & The Hague: Mouton, pp. 411–441.

———— (1970b), Wife's satisfaction with husband's understanding in Parisian urban families. *J. Marr. Fam.*, 32:351–359.

Musil, J. (1971), Some aspects of social organization of the contemporary Czechoslovak family. *J. Marr. Fam.*, 33:196–206.

Pfeil, E. (1961), *Die Berufstätigkeit von Müttern*. Tübingen.

———— (1968), *Die 23-Jährigen*. Tübingen.

Piotrowski, J. (1971), The employment of married women and the changing sex roles in Poland. In: *Family Issues of Employed Women in Europe and America*, ed. A. Michel. Leiden: E. J. Brill, pp. 73–90.

Powell, K. S. (1963), Family variables. In: *The Employed Mother in America*, ed. F. I. Nye & L. W. Hoffman. Chicago: Rand McNally, pp. 231–240.

Rosenmayr, L., Haller, M., & Szinovacz, M. (1973), Barrieren im beruflichen Aufstieg. Studien über die junge Arbeitnehmerin im Spannungsfeld von Beruf, Haushalt und Familie. Schriftenreihe zur sozialen und beruflichen Stellung der Frau 2. Vienna: Bundesministerium für Soziale Verwaltung.

Safilios-Rothschild, C. (1967), A comparison of power structure and marital satisfaction in urban Greek and French families. *J. Marr. Fam.*, 29:345–352.

———— (1969), Family sociology or wives' family sociology? A cross-cultural examination of decision-making. *J. Marr. Fam.*, 31:290–301.

———— (1970a), The influence of the wife's degree of work commitment upon some aspects of family organization and dynamics. *J. Marr. Fam.*, 32:681–691.

———— (1970b), The study of family power structure: A review 1960–1969. *J. Marr. Fam.*, 32:539–552.

Silverman, W. & Hill, R. (1967), Task allocation in marriage in the United States and Belgium. *J. Marr. Fam.*, 29:353–359.

Straus, M. A. (1969), Social class and farm-city differences in interaction with kin in relation to societal modernization. *Rural Sociol.*, 34:476–495.

———— (1975), Husband-wife interaction in nuclear and joint households. In: *Explorations in the Family and Other Essays: Professor K. M. Kapadia Memorial Volume*, ed. D. Narain. Bombay: Thacker, pp. 134–150.

Sussman, M. B. & Burchinal, L. (1962), Parental aid to married children: Implications for family functioning. *Marr. Fam. Liv.*, 24:320–331.

Szinovacz, M. E. (1975), Entscheidungsstruktur und Aufgabenverteilung in jungen Familien. Unpublished doctoral dissertation. Vienna.

Tallman, I. (1969), Working-class wives in suburbia: Fulfillment or crisis? *J. Marr. Fam.*, 31:65–72.

Toomey, D. M. (1971), Conjugal roles and societal networks in an urban working class sample. *Hum. Relat.*, 24:417–431.

Turner, C. (1970), Conjugal roles and social networks. In: *Readings in Kinship in Urban Society*, ed. C. C. Harris. Oxford: Braunschweig, pp. 245–260.

Weller, R. H. (1968), The employment of wives, dominance, and fertility. *J. Marr. Fam.*, 30:437–442.

Winch, R. F. & Greer, S. A. (1968), Urbanism, ethnicity, and extended families. *J. Marr. Fam.*, 30:40–45.

Adoption:
Legal Resolution or Legal Fraud?

ROBERTA G. ANDREWS

Adoption as a statutorily created parent-child relationship is under attack from those it was designed most of all to benefit: the dependent child. Adopted adults, no longer dependent, are winning increasing community and legal support in their efforts to unseal adoption records. One of the arguments of individual adopted young people and organizations of adoptees is that their constitutional rights to equal protection, due process of law, freedom of speech, and freedom from involuntary servitude are violated by a hard-line system of secrecy and confidentiality. They argue that this cuts them off from their roots and from resolving their identity needs. In that they had no part in the earlier decisions that transferred parental rights and responsibilities, they feel free to challenge the adoption contract between the biological parent and the adoptive parents.

In 1977, a state superior court judge in New Jersey, Philip A. Gruccio, ruled in a landmark decision that four plaintiffs did not have a constitutional right to know the identities of their natural parents; on the other hand, Judge Gruccio issued guidelines to adoption agencies to respond to the compelling psychological needs of these plaintiffs as well as other adopted adults by assisting in a search under certain prescribed conditions.

Adoption agencies for decades have been in an ambiguous position regarding the revealing of information to a child about his or her adoption status. Whereas agencies have urged honesty about a child's adoption status, they have also insisted that the identity of the biological family not be made known. Taken at face value, this position repre-

Roberta G. Andrews, M.S.S., A.C.S.W., is Associate Director, Children's Aid Society of Pennsylvania, Philadelphia, Pennsylvania.

sents a contradiction. It illustrates one of the many complexities of the adoption process and of the feelings and needs of the different people involved. In this period of dramatization of experiences in searching for roots, broadening civil rights, and establishing identity, it is under-standable that adopted persons may feel victimized and discriminated against. Locating and meeting a biological parent may become built up in fantasies as the answer to feelings of worthlessness, helplessness, uncertainty about themselves and their future. The experience of the Children's Aid Society of Pennsylvania is that a search can be extremely helpful to the individuals involved, but that it can be, equally, a trau-matic, unsatisfactory experience.

A Legal Perspective

Adoption agencies have considered that with the granting of a de-cree by a court of law, a contract between the biological and adoptive parents becomes a binding fact. A contract is defined in the dictionary as an agreement between two or more people to do something; it is an agreement, usually written, enforceable by law. If a contract applies to a marriage or a divorce, it should apply to an adoption, if not com-pletely, at least in part. By means of an adoption contract, parental rights and responsibilities are transferred from the biological parents to the adoptive parents by court decree. Either the biological parents had voluntarily relinquished the child or lost their rights to the child by judicial action, as in abandonment. By contrast, the adoptive parents assume full legal rights and responsibilities. Only if a child to be adopted has reached the age of twelve is his or her consent required at the time of a hearing, at least according to the Pennsylvania Adoption Statute. The adoption decree marks a complete break, except for the matter of inheritance. It is a curious fact that the same law that pro-vides for the sealing of records provides for the right of an adoptee to inherit from the biological family. In some states, an adoptee does not have the same right of inheritance as natural children, another in-teresting contradiction.

Rights Versus Compelling Need

Respect for the adoption contract and ethical concern for the confidentiality of records caused agencies, courts, Bureaus of Vital Statistics, and hospital record rooms to maintain a rigid stance against disclosure with adopted adults who had compelling reasons to search. Their need became lost in an entrenched system of secrecy. The Child

Welfare League of America reviewed the practices of member agencies in 1976 and issued a revision of the Standards for Adoption Service with regard to the confidentiality of records. While reaffirming the principle of confidentiality, the revised statement opened up the possibility that under certain conditions biological parents could waive the right to privacy and authorize the disclosure of their identity to the adopted adult.

In Pennsylvania, the Adoption Regulations of the State Department of Public Welfare, issued in 1975, state: "Information in adoption records that identifies the child's natural parents or family shall not be disclosed to anyone after legal adoption, without consent of the court. When all parties to the adoption agree, in writing, to disclose identifying information, the court's consent will not be necessary." This statement has provided a framework for agencies to follow in response to requests for assistance in searching. However, in June of 1977, the Pennsylvania Attorney General's Office issued an opinion that "A birth certificate is *not* one of the documents...to be impounded by the court," with the result that the original birth certificate may be released to a "mature adoptee" by the Bureau of Vital Statistics. Whereas the Child Welfare League of America, in its revision of a section of the Standards for Adoption, respects the right of biological parents to privacy, the Pennsylvania Attorney General's Office weakens the adoption contract as well as state regulations by ruling that the original birth certificate is not to be considered one of the documents to be impounded.

Had agencies and courts been more responsive to the principle of compelling need, the ruling of the Attorney General's Office and its erosion of the adoption contract might not have occurred. In all of the emotional and legalistic controversy regarding the unsealing of records, little has been said about the rights and feelings of both adoptive and biological parents. Instead, there is a rapidly accelerating identification with the right of an adult adoptee to have identifying data and, thereby, means of locating the biological family.

The philosophical and practical approach of the Children's Aid Society, as is true of most enlightened professional adoption services, has been to respond to requests for either brief information or intensive counseling from adoptive parents, natural parents, and the adopted child. In that the adoption experience shifts as children grow and families change, an agency needs to be available to offer post-adoption informational and counseling services. The fact of a court decree does not resolve all conflicts or concerns about the giving up or taking in of a child.

For decades this agency has worked with adult adoptees, in addition to adoptive families, and has responded to the compelling need of some adult adoptees for genealogical material, and for help in understanding themselves in relation to their origins as well as in relation to their experience with the adoptive family; in a few instances, the agency has assisted in a search for the biological family. The agency has also responded to communications from biological parents asking for information about the child or adding medical data to the file; in a few instances there have been requests for help with a reunion.

In line with Judge Gruccio's decision, the agency has conducted searches for biological parents, giving the parents the right to agree or refuse to meet the child they had surrendered for adoption. Where there was agreement to a reunion, the agency gave psychological preparation to both the biological parents and adoptee before the actual meeting took place. The consent of the adoptive parents, if they were available, was obtained. Counseling during and after a reunion often helped the adoptees sort out what they had been looking for, what they had found, and what they perceived to be the meaning of the event for them. Often this experience helped adoptees grow closer to the adoptive family as the caring, nurturing family.

A Theoretical Framework

Four theories from psychiatry and psychoanalysis became incorporated into a clinical approach to adoption practice in the 1940s and 1950s. They can be summarized as follows:

1. Separations are traumatic and produce anxieties that affect ego development in a child.

2. A crucial interactional process between infant and mother, based in part upon the infant's patterns of reactivity and the mother's confidence in her mothering capacities, will influence their ongoing relationship and determine the kind of identification the child will develop.

3. Unresolved feelings resulting from narcissistic wounds received in childhood can create intense feelings of disappointment and deprivation at the inability to produce a biological child, thus impairing the parenting capacity of the adopters.

4. When the child is told of his or her adoption, what he or she is told and how the information is communicated are important determinants in how the child resolves identity problems.

Adoption practitioners studied the psychiatric literature with respect to traumatic separations and disorders of nonattachment.

Agency procedures as a result began to stress the importance of an infant's placement with adopters before a strong object attachment had taken root. The importance of a permanent, gratifying interaction with a "feeding" mother to satisfy normal, healthy, narcissistic needs and to establish patterns of identification was accepted as essential to the psychological well-being of a young child. The assessment of the adoption applicant couple was virgin territory, for the literature provided few guidelines as to how to predict successful parenting, particularly parenting of a child not born to a couple. The courts and the wider community tended to stress external sociological qualities, such as character, morals, income, providing a religious upbringing, etc. These were important qualifications, but a far cry from assessing defense mechanisms, narcissistic wounds, anxieties and tensions of a married couple who in most instances were childless and probably feeling many of the deprivations and disadvantages of being childless. Their problems could be psychological, familial, social. Practitioners tried to avoid placing a child to hold a marriage together or to satisfy neurotic narcissistic needs; stress was placed upon proof by the couple of physiological infertility because it was considered inadvisable to place a child in order to help a couple overcome their infertility; applicant couples with extreme ideas about child rearing and discipline were screened out; couples had to agree to tell a child at an early age that he or she was adopted.

Practitioner sensitivity, psychological perceptiveness, and professional confidence in assessing the personalities of an applicant couple, their marriage and their motivation, have proven to be important determinants in the outcome of an adoption. Research studies show that when practitioners intuitively and clinically choose couples with maturity and warmth, the adoption is more likely to turn out well, as found by Lawder et al. (1969).

In the area of adoption education and dialogue, agency practitioners, lacking a model in the literature, developed their own psychological frame of reference at variance with the concerns of psychiatrists and child analysts. Practitioners reasoned in this way:

1. The stated unwillingness of an adoption couple to initiate dialogue with a child about his or her adoption status, or the couple's obvious tension about the subject, could indicate a lack of resolution of narcissistic wounds concerning their infertility. Adoption would thus become an anxious, uncomfortable secret, undiminished by time.

2. The opposite extreme of a couple repeatedly labeling the child as adopted could indicate a lack of sensitivity and perhaps a derogation of the child's status.

3. If a couple took the position of not opening up dialogue until asked or pressed by the child or in conjunction with some important maturational event or family crisis, it could be reasoned that the use of denial and conscious secrecy would militate against a frank, comfortable dialogue that could be meaningful and helpful to a child.

It was known by adoption practitioners that many loving, accepting families, not burdened with narcissistic injury in being childless and not paragons of perfection, families able to care, nurture, and learn from mistakes, were plagued by uncertainty as to how to deal with the subject of illegitimacy. Many approached adoption education on tiptoes, ready to cover up and retreat if a child asked too many leading, difficult questions. The perplexities and uncertainties in opening up and sustaining a meaningful dialogue caused many adopters to seek advice and help from clinicians and to join in group discussions with other adoptive families.

At the same time that agencies were gaining in clinical knowledge and experience, clinicians who were treating adopted children began to question the wisdom of opening up a dialogue about adoption with a young child. Adopted children were viewed as being particularly vulnerable to stress, and the timing and manner of being told of adoption was considered a major source of psychological trouble. Several clinicians believed a child could split his identification between good natural parents and bad adoptive parents and for this and other reasons have difficulty in resolving oedipal issues and in achieving a healthy identity.

IDENTITY AND ADOPTION

Adopted children and natural children have similar developmental stages to master; each group has no greater or fewer family problems to contend with than the other. The difference is in the concept of adoption and its psychological impact. It can be dealt with in as low key and sensible a manner as any family matter that is successfully resolved, or it can become an ambivalent, secretive, and emotional issue that builds up persistent fantasies. The adoptee, instead of viewing his or her adoption as a happy, wanted event, begins to suspect that something bad was connected with his or her birth and placement; or he or she may be given a negative image of the biological parents. If a child does not feel fully accepted and important for what he or she has added to family purpose and contentment, a sense of difference and separation can hurt and grow into a compelling need to know the truth about his or her origin, whatever it may be.

The adoptive family needs to be a particularly secure one, able to deal with the feelings of family members and friends about the adoptive parents' barrenness, if such was the case. Pain and anxiety can be inflicted on a child by peers who will say, "She's not your real mother, you're adopted." If a natural child is born after adoption, one of the most usual and least sensitive comments to adopters can be, "At last you have one of your own." Many adopted children have heard this and other comments biased in favor of natural birth.

Despite the fierce partisanship of innumerable parents who dearly love and value their children and have waged a campaign against negative biases, to build a family by adoption is generally considered second best. There may be rejoicing when a child comes into a family as a cure to barrenness, but also feelings of "too bad they couldn't have had one of their own." One wonders if adoptive families who choose childlessness through contraception have found it easier to begin and maintain an open dialogue with the adopted child. Many such families have chosen to adopt a child who otherwise might not have a permanent family in name and fact. Perhaps adoption works best when it is visibly and clearly different from the outset. In such instances, the parent-child relationship does not need to be patterned on a biological tie but rather on a nurturing one.

Those who have grown up with a compelling need to uncloak secrets argue that a sense of identity is impossible without a direct knowledge of biological roots. This may be true for those whose adoption status left too much unanswered and unresolved. For the majority of adoptees whose parents were nurturing, accepting, and secure enough, a sense of identity does develop from their importance to their parents. It should not be forgotten that many adopted children have made life richer, more meaningful, and more rewarding for their parents. This experience can surround the adoption with a positive aura strong enough to bind parents and child through identification and mutual need. The bonds of identification become stronger than the need for biological identity. Identity can be built on the experience of identification.

Erikson (1968) states:

> ...the fate of childhood identifications...depends on the child's satisfactory interaction with trustworthy representatives of a meaningful hierarchy of roles as provided by the generations living together in some form of family. Identity formation, finally, begins where the usefulness of identification ends. It arises from the selective repudiation and mutual assimilation of childhood identifications...in a new configuration...dependent on the process by

which a society... identifies the young individual, recognizing him as somebody who had to become the way he is and who, being the way he is, is taken for granted [p. 159].

Whereas this clear definition of identity applies to natural children growing up with their families, it has also been observed by practitioners and researchers in working with adopted children and their families. A deep-seated need to search for natural parents can result from a poor or split identification with the adoptive family. If a child received mixed messages about himself and important questions were unanswered or received with obvious tension, then a natural curiosity would be piqued by questions about origin and the reasons for being given away. Natural childen can grow up with secrets and humbling comparisons to disparaged relatives. For the adopted child, there exists the escape route of projecting and blaming unhappiness on the ready-made peg of adoption. The fact that there are other parents — somewhere — can weaken or split an identification with adoptive parents. The narcissistic hurt of feeling or of being told there is something wrong with one's origin and placement can lead to an all-consuming need and drive to search for the biological parents or family in order to find where one truly belongs.

Schechter (1960), in reviewing the cases of sixteen adoptive children treated between 1948 and 1953, found "... the feature of their adoptive status playing a significant role in the underlying dynamics of the problem" (p. 21). A girl of ten told the therapist of trying to find the hidden birth certificate and having fantasies regarding the real parents; a boy of twelve fantasized his "real" mother had red hair; a five-year-old had anxieties about being "sent away" (she was placed with adoptive parents at seventeen months); a boy first seen when seven, adopted at four weeks, had symptoms of restlessness and thumbsucking. He asked many questions about birth and adoption, talked about his "other" parents. He seemed angry at being "given away." At a later time in treatment when he was older, he had aggressive fantasies of a violent nature.

Schechter noted that the adoptive parents, having tried for years to have a child, were older than other parents in his clinic's cases, and that the mothers had feelings of inadequacy regarding womanly functions. Because the adopted child reminded them of their barrenness, the mothers had a strong need to use the story of the "chosen child." In addition to conflictual feelings about their infertility, these parents fantasized abut sexual promiscuity in the biological mother, using this as a possible explanation of the child's behavior.

Schechter, among others, doubted the wisdom of telling a child of his adoption during the ambivalent oedipal period when a child would have a ready-made reason to fantasize about other parents. "The adoptive child has a chance, however, of splitting the image of his parents and attributing the good elements to one set and the bad to the other. Since they really have two sets of parents, they are capable of keeping the good and the bad images diffused, with a subsequent grave problem of superego and ego ideal formation" (p. 29).

Toussieng (1962) comments that the possibility of unconscious opposition to pregnancy could interfere with the parent-child relationship and impair a capacity to be close to the child, a significant factor in how the child would perceive his adoption status. Mothers who feel "damaged" in not giving birth and are in conflict about mothering the adopted child, in telling the child about adoption, "will be less sensitive to the child and will be apt to choose the wrong time or do it in a way that may push the child further into emotional difficulties" and into "fantasies regarding the real parents or into more disastrous forms of unreality" (p. 64).

Lawton and Gross (1964) reviewed many thorny and inconclusive questions raised by the literature on adoption. They doubted that adopted children constitute a significant number of those treated for psychiatric problems, as stated by several clinicians; however, they referred to clinical "hunches" that even though the symptoms described by parents of both natural and adopted children sounded similar, there appeared to be a difference: "as a group they [adopted children] were extremely disturbed" (p. 639).

Concern about an adopted child's splitting his identification between biological and adoptive parents has raised speculation as to whether the universal "family romance" would further a splitting phenomenon. However, as Lawton and Gross point out, without further clinical research there is inadequate data to know whether such fantasies occur only in relation to biological parents or can be observed in relation to adoptive parents as well. Following the two-part construct theory about the "family romance" developed by Freud, a child can split his perceptions of his parents after becoming aware of the father's role in procreation; in this instance, it could be the adoptive father about whom there are fantasies and whom the child exalts.

As to the concern of many psychiatrists about a child's being told of adoption before the oedipal conflict is resolved, Lawton and Gross point out that the oedipal phase is not finally resolved until at or near puberty. They feel that learning about being adopted "need not be traumatic or anxiety-evoking unless the parents communicate to the child that this is a highly anxious topic and indicate that they expect problems. . . . reasonably secure adoption parents can tell the preschool child about his adoption without necessarily providing the stimuli for negative emotional reaction" (p. 640).

Between the years of 1959 and 1971, the Children's Aid Society of Pennsylvania, jointly with Bryn Mawr College, conducted three studies of the functioning of adoptive families and children: the first study (Lawder et al., 1969) analyzed and described the functioning of 200 white adoptive families who had adopted 250 children; the second (Hoopes et al., 1969) studied a random sample of 100 of the 250 children living with the 200 families; the third (Lawder et al., 1971) studied the functioning of black adoptive families and children.

The first study found that satisfaction in parental role, warmth, and affection toward the child and acceptance of adoptive role were more important variables regarding outcome than marital satisfaction, communication of adoption, or role compatibility. No child factors stood out as being significant. Family functioning was rated as: poor, 10 per cent; fair, 27 per cent; good, 49 per cent; superior, 14 per cent.

The second study involved a random sample of 100 adopted children from ten to sixteen years of age and a control group matched for age, race, and social class. Independent teacher ratings were obtained for both the adopted and natural children, in addition to tests conducted in the schools; further tests were given to several groups of adopted children, eight at a time, in the offices of the Children's Aid Society.

The research team conceptualized several areas of fantasy material that might differentiate the adopted group, and a Thematic Apperception Test (TAT) was devised to elicit fantasy material. The findings of this study indicated that there was no evidence of greater emotional disturbance or psychopathology in the sample of 100 adoptees than in the control group living with biological families, nor were the fantasied responses significantly different. The children compared closely in IQ, performance on the TAT Projection Test and the California Tests of Mental Maturity and Personality.

The third study of black adoptive families analyzed the functioning of 82 children between ages three and six in 76 families. Families who had adopted in a traditional way were compared with those who had received a subsidy from the time of placement up to legal finalization, a practice called the Quasi-Adoption Service. More children with risk factors such as age, health, development, and number of previous placements were in the Quasi-Adoption group. The families were interviewed both in their homes and in the office of Children's Aid Society; the children were given a battery of tests by psychologists.

The study found that children in both groups were developing well with a minimum of problems. The adoptive families, as was true of the first study, functioned with a good degree of warmth, affection, acceptance, and satisfaction. There were no statistically significant differences between the traditional and subsidized families.

These three studies do not support the concern that adopted children are more vulnerable to stress. For the most part, these were happy families, coping well, unconflicted about adoption. The parents were educated by the agency to begin a warm, simple dialogue about adoption by the time the child was three or slightly older, perhaps using the word earlier.

The issue of being told about adoption is far from resolved. Wieder (1977), in describing his analysis of three adoptees, believes that telling children under the age of three has a deleterious effect. Knowing that they have two set of parents produces conflicts of identification, but he also states that the image of their biological parents from the adoptive parents was "structured on meager, secretive and inherently socially derogative information." It is unfortunate that psychiatrists build theory on the basis of treating a few maladjusted adoptive families and individuals, but it is also helpful to have reports of the analysis of adopted adolescents and young adults. Wieder's description of how his three patients were told of their adoption may at least partially explain their psychological problems.

Peter, adopted in early infancy, was fifteen months old when a second child was adopted. Beginning at age two and following agency advice, Peter was told he was adopted. It is doubtful that an agency would have recommended the following explanation: "Mother and father wanted a baby very much but something was wrong with mother's insides and she couldn't make a baby. Another mother bore you. She was a young girl who made you with a soldier. They couldn't take care of you. We found you through a doctor who helped your mother and made arrangements for us to take you home" (p. 3).

Jim was told of being adopted when two and a half: "He had been told that his biological mother, a young girl living near a military base, had been impregnated by a naval officer...[who] was sent overseas and the mother was unable to care for her baby" (p. 8). Because the adoptive father "couldn't make a baby," the parents found him and took him home from the hospital. Jim was three when his parents adopted a sister.

Jeannie, adopted at eight days old, was told at age two and a half: "The lady who bore you had died, and no one was available to raise you. Mother and father had wanted a baby very much but were unable to make one" (p. 12). When Jeannie asked why her mother could not "make her," she was told there was something wrong with the mother's "insides." She was also told they could not adopt another child because "it takes too much money" (p. 13).

The parents of all three adoptees reported problems after they were told of their adoption. Peter became intolerant of separation from his mother, becoming excessively dependent on her. Jim changed from a contented, easy child to one who could not sleep well, could not sit still, ran away, and could not bear any discussion of adoption. Jeannie's sleep became disturbed, and, as was true of Peter, she became overly dependent on her mother.

In their analyses, each one described bad feelings about their adoption. Peter associated adoption with abandonment. He revealed distorted fantasies of a sadistic nature about a young girl, a whore who enticed men to have sex with them and then got rid of them or the bastard baby. Incestuous fears developed in his fifth to seventh years "when he had been allowed and even urged to share his adoptive mother's bed 'to cuddle' before going to sleep" (p. 6).

Jim fantasized several things about his biological mother: that she was a whore, or that she was married and both parents were killed, or that she was too young. But he also wondered why blood relatives had not cared for him. He began to feel that there was something flawed and damaged about him.

Jeannie, feeling a loss of self-esteem, as had Peter and Jim, became hostile toward her adoptive mother, complaining that she was being starved. Because of her behavior, she was placed in a special class, which was humiliating and was like being sent away. Jeannie was angry about being adopted, confused about having two sets of parents, and had fantasies about a bad biological mother.

Wieder believes his patients demonstrate the traumatic effect of early communication. However, if all adoptees reacted as did his patients, adoption agencies would be guilty of gross incompetence and insensitive practice. Neither experience nor research support such a dismal view. It is less the age at which a child begins to learn of his adoption than the feelings behind the choice of words that creates psychological problems.

The parents of Peter, Jim, and Jeannie conveyed to the children the sense that something was wrong with the adoptive parents, with their insides, as well as something wrong with their biological mothers. The theme of saving a baby from abandonment was stressed. In each instance, the telling may have been accompanied by anxiety; the choice of words was anxiety-provoking. These parents did not cushion the harsh reality of adoption, or stress the joy it brought to them. The children thus became anxious about any kind of separation and had distorted fantasies of a cruel and negative kind about the biological mother. Despite damage to their self-esteem, none of the three patients expressed a desire to search for the biological parent; they appeared attached to the adoptive family.

POST-ADOPTION SERVICES

Post-adoption services should be available to the three parties to an adoption; the biological parents, adoptive parents, alone or with the child, and the child at whatever age he or she may be. At times, requests come from a sibling or siblings of the adoptee for help with a reunion.

In its nearly 100 years of existence, the Children's Aid Society of Pennsylvania has arranged over 5,000 adoptions. For the past two to three decades, adoptive families have been encouraged to keep in touch about happy and significant events and, as needed, to request counseling help or information from the records. The agency's point of view has been that problems occur in all families. Resolving them is what matters.

During the three research studies, and following their publication between 1969 and 1971, an increasing number of families requested assistance for a number of reasons, such as a review of the child's medical history, counseling regarding a child's background and how to discuss it with him or her, counseling regarding family interactional problems, school and/or developmental problems in a child.

A number of parents have called the adoption service for an appointment for an older child, either alone or with one or both parents, to discuss his or her adoption, biological family background, and placement history. Many parents have freely confessed to the child and agency that they had forgotten some or most of the details given them. Quite possibly the agency also had omitted specific information at the time of placement, knowing that the excitement and tension of becoming parents would color what they were told. Data of a sordid or too identifying nature would be withheld. The time between placement and legal finalization could be used to review a child's background, but since a majority of parents still are experiencing an adjustment to parenthood, they are not psychologically ready to face the task of telling a child about her or his biological family; also, a majority of the children would be too young to be told. However, forgetting and other forms of avoidance are different from secrecy or distortion. Adoptees, by and large, particularly after they have passed through adolescence, can understand avoidance, for many worry about hurting their parents in searching. In many instances, adoption workers have urged parents to be more courageous and forthright when they have missed the point of a child's verbal and behavioral messages. For example, a panicked, distraught mother phoned from western Pennsylvania to report that her ten-year-old daughter had told a school friend her biological father had approached her on the street and that he and her biological mother were to pick her up at school that very afternoon. The adoptive mother thought it was a fantasy or "story," as she put it, but also asked, "Could the natural parents have traced her?" She and her husband had alerted the local police just in case.

Enough details were obtained to indicate that the parents had avoided a discussion of the child's biological parents, although she had known of being adopted from her toddler years. The mother's words in describing her daughter were warm and accepting. The daughter's development and adjustment seemed good.

The worker asked for time to immediately review the records before discussing the matter further. An hour's counseling session on the phone was used to allay anxiety about the daughter's story to her friend and to review what the mother remembered of the daughter's background. The few details she recalled were colored with anxiety. The worker asked that she get paper and pencil to make notes as family background details were presented and interpreted. There was an active interchange on the phone with the mother expressing emotional relief and agreement that she and her husband must find ways of talking with their daughter about her parentage. The worker invited them to visit the agency's office if this would add to the reality and meaning of their daughter's adoption. Eighteen months have elapsed with no further contact.

Approximately 40 to 50 requests are received each year for post-adoption services. Whereas these requests have been divided fairly evenly among brief service information, counseling regarding a child's adjustment, and questions about background, in the past five years more adult adoptees and members of the biological family are approaching the agency.

Searching is not a new phenomenon in adoption. What is different is the changing climate toward opening adoption records or making the original birth certificate available to an adult adoptee. It is unlikely that this remarkable shift in attitude and response would have come about without the emotional and dramatic impact of published accounts by adopted adults. Whereas adoption was designed to "rescue" the needy, dependent child, now society, through its laws, may "rescue" the adopted adult from his adoptive family. One must hope that the present momentum for unsealing records or birth certificates will slow down, giving agencies and courts time to examine and change their policies and procedures. As one reads about and works with those who are searching, it is clear that many have a compelling need to fill a painful void in their lives; for others it is a developmental crisis, in part related to adoption and in part to other experiences. Both agencies and courts must be ready to respond with appropriate assistance.

Searching — A Developmental Crisis

Although many adolescent and adult adoptees have a normal curiosity about the details of their backgrounds and want a factual and psychological explanation of their birth, relinquishment, and placement, a smaller group feel they must search for and locate a biological mother in order to satisfy their curiosity more completely.

John was nineteen when he phoned for an appointment to review and discuss his biological background. He had been placed at a few weeks of age and grew up in a sophisticated family that believed in keeping adoption an open subject of discussion. He and his sister were told they could, if they wished, look for their natural parents when eighteen. There were problems in the marriage only slightly improved by family therapy. John was increasingly resented by his father and protected by an adoring mother. He had had a series of adolescent problems such as drinking, drugs, breaking and entering, failing in school. Psychiatric treatment in time helped John to complete high school and plan a career.

His approach to the agency was cautious, for he was risking a great deal in asking for an appointment and obviously feared a negative or disappointing response. Details about his background and placement filled out and added to the general information he had received. He seemed pleased and reassured. The adoption worker speculated that John had worried about his heredity, perhaps having received a suggestion from his father that his behavior was unstable because of problems in his biological family.

Bolstered by knowledge of a sound, stable background, John asked for help in locating his biological mother. The worker made a contract with him, namely, that she would conduct a search if he would let his parents know and obtain their consent to a reunion. The reunion, when it occurred about one month later, did not exclude his adoptive parents. He first met his biological mother, who had agreed to travel to Philadelphia, and then introduced her to his parents. He followed the worker's advice of keeping his adoptive family, including grandparents, fully informed of his telephone talks with his biological mother, her husband, and children prior to the actual reunion.

For John, this experience was reassuring and ego-building, for he coped in a grown-up way with several emotional relationships and the potential for great distress to his adoptive parents. He has enjoyed getting to know his biological family, a large gregarious one, but remains involved with and attached to his adoptive family.

Developmental crises can and do occur at any age, usually associated with the loss of parents or spouse; with taking a significant step toward greater independence; or with failing in school, job, or relationships. Requests for a review of family background and help in locating the maternal family can come from adults in their middle years.

A bachelor of 50 in a civil service position, after the death of both adoptive parents, established phone and mail communication with the adoption service. He felt his parents had been secretive about something. For example, when he entered a room in which they were talking with each other or another party, conversation would stop or quickly change. He had built a "family romance" kind of fantasy of being "well-born" and "well-connected." He hoped to locate a biological mother (who, if living, would have been in her mid-seventies) or cousins to expand his limited family contacts. The adoption worker shared information from his file as he asked for it. The data indicated there were economic and social problems in the maternal family during the depression years when he was born. Much to his astonishment, he learned that he was illegitimate, a fact his parents had concealed and which in all likelihood was the family secret he sensed in his growing up. Family surnames on the maternal side had a "class" quality he valued. It is interesting that he at no time asked about his natural father whose ethnic origin was southern European.

Efforts by the agency to locate maternal relatives came to a dead end. After two years, he is continuing to do some desultory searching on his own. He maintains contact with the adoption worker, phoning or writing from time to time about his job, social life, and trips abroad. It is a meaningful contact for him, well worth supporting and encouraging, for the agency, having an *in loco parentis* function, can provide a parental concern.

It is assumed that "family romance" fantasies are always romantic. As described by Wieder (1977), a number of adopted young people fantasize that the natural mother was promiscuous, a prostitute, and that their background is sordid and lower class. This kind of negative identity may not be solely the result of what they were told by their adoptive parents. The parents may have pursued a benignly constructive approach to adoption education but may have missed entirely an important aspect of their family life.

In one case, the parents and extended family were so proud of their own genealogy, the adopted son began to feel "left out and put down." He managed to develop a number of irritating, attention-getting habits and difficult behavior, including failing in school. Treatment at the agency involved the fifteen-year-old in individual sessions with a therapist. As part of treatment, his biological family background was discussed. A disbelieving lad learned that his biological parents, unwed, grew up in substantial professional families. His fantasy that the biological mother was no good and a prostitute could be put at rest by the facts of her relationship with his father and subsequent events in her life.

This lad was attached to his adoptive family and needed continued treatment outside the agency for dependence-independence struggles and a resolution of oedipal conflicts. At present in his mid-twenties, he is an interesting, competent young man. He has not returned to the agency for help in searching.

In thinking of developmental crises facing adopted children and adults, it must be remembered that adoption education is received from many sources other than the nuclear family. The attitudes of extended family, teachers, peers, and neighbors can be hurtful to self-esteem. Often in a classroom, children are asked to write the story of their lives with details as to where they were born and exact hour of birth. One lad, age ten, in response to the question of where he was born, wrote "in bed." It is not as easy to clown about repeated comments by new family acquaintances who often exclaim and point out how much an adopted child looks like one or both parents. In pointing out similarities, differences can be accentuated. At times, this writer, after some 35 years of adoption experience, believes most people are surprised when an adopted child does well, reflecting the values society places on biological parenthood and keeping one's child. In a sense, it is the entire adoptive family that is under stress, not the adoptee alone. How well the parents can build a child's self-esteem and sense of worth is critical to the need to search as a resolution of developmental stages and crises.

Searching — To Fill a Void

Searching is as complicated and diverse in its ramifications as are the persons involved. The need to search can arise for several reasons: (1) to satisfy a strong and persistent curiosity as to one's roots; (2) to act out a festering resentment of the adoptive family and the need for more independence and autonomy; (3) to find a parent to become attached to, either in a dependently regressed way or in a healthier, interactional way.

When the search becomes desperate, it is the experience of the Children's Aid Society that the adoptive experience was a negative, humiliating one, or that the child, placed at an older age, never completely gave up the psychological parent. In either situation, fantasies of a lost mother, less often a father, persist.

Florence Fisher (1973), in her dramatic story of finding her biological parents, describes the traumatic way in which she first learned at five years of age that there was a secret about her birth certificate when her mother sent her out of the teacher's room on the day she was being registered for school. At age seven she found a paper in a dresser drawer with the word "adopted" on it and the name "Anna Fisher." Her mother, when confronted, could not bring herself to admit that her child was adopted. A bright, determined little girl began her search from that point on. Unfortunately, as a young adult she received no help in trying to unravel the mystery of her life until a hospital record clerk, perhaps in ignorance or out of compassion, gave her the family names from her card.

Betty Jean Lifton (1975) in her "psychological detective story" of years of searching described being sick and feverish with scarlet fever at age seven. Her mother chose that time to tell her she had been adopted when two and a half years old. "We wanted a child and so we drove to New York and found you. You were so plump and pretty, like a Campbell's soup baby" (p. 8). But having told the child, the mother sealed the confession by making the child promise never to tell anyone, "especially your father...He wants to think he is your real daddy" (p. 8). So fantasies of biological birth are sealed in a secret by the adopters. In later years, Mrs. Lifton, as did Florence Fisher, persisted in the grueling experience of locating her natural parents.

This agency has had many years of experience in working with young and older adults whose compelling need to search has ended in mixed results.

One young man, recently married, came east on a business trip. He spoke warmly of his adoptive parents who valued him. His adoption was not a secret; what hurt his self-image was being told that his biological mother was sexually promiscuous. A review of his records indicated a very different set of circumstances. Apparently, an insecure adoptive mother, afraid the son would not continue to love her and later attempt to locate the biological mother, set up a self-fulfilling prophecy by telling him his mother was no good, a whore. The records dispelled this fantasy on her part. Later, through his own efforts (for the agency failed to bring about a reunion) he confronted his biological mother in the anonymous privacy of a busy department store. He was able to talk with her and, as he explained in a phone call, "I touched her." The adoption staff, while wondering about his mother's feelings, felt relieved he had achieved his mission of finding her; it is often not easy to be cooly objective about the feelings of a person who has a need to search.

Although some searches have a story-book ending, others are less satisfactory. Marie was adopted by the foster parents with whom she had been placed in early infancy. She described the death of her father, with whom she had felt close, in contrast to her mother, who could be warm at times, hostile and punishing at other times. After the father's death, Marie, now 22, and her siblings, one natural and one adopted, left home.

Marie, a high-school graduate, was able to obtain clerical work. She lived with a man who fathered her two-year-old son. Since early childhood, she had been told her mother was "a rich white woman," her father, a "no-good black." Marie was given family background that was middle class and mercantile for her mother; little was known of her father except that he was black and worked in a store. When Marie asked for help in finding her mother, the worker told her of a phone call from a state psychiatric hospital eight years previously; her mother, a patient, had wanted to know if the child she relinquished was "all right."

In collaboration with the hospital staff, a reunion was arranged. The hospital setting was grim, the mother chronically depressed but nicely groomed and pleased to embrace her daughter. Marie had taken her son with her. Her mother answered questions as well as she could and urged Marie to come again soon. Telephone numbers were exchanged.

Since the meeting in the hospital Marie has not responded to her mother's phone entreaties to see her again. The adoption worker has not been able to reach her to discuss the meeting with her mother and the disappointment she must feel.

Marie appears to be a narcissistic young woman whose needs were not met by a chronically ill mother, herself very needy.

Richard was seven when he was uprooted from a large, lively foster home to be placed with an older, childless couple because it was felt that he should have a permanent adoptive home. Richard was lonely and homesick; his parents in a dutiful, conscientious way tried to console the child. They never supplanted the boy's attachment to the foster family. Incompatibility led to increasing friction, culminating in Richard's being "thrown out" of the house at seventeen. A neighbor took him in and helped Richard complete high school before he joined the Marines to serve in Vietnam. He became a licensed electrician and creative wood carver as a profitable hobby.

The adoption service has worked with Richard for over ten years in his search for a family to whom to belong. A reunion with the biological father, his wife, children, and extended family has not ended his searching. He has a deep-seated yearning to find the biological mother of whom no trace can be found. Each year he dusts off his efforts to find her; his father has hinted, if not actually told him, she was a prostitute. This only makes him more desperate to find her, to rescue, and take care of her. Unmarried, and with few if any close friends, Richard supports himself, but has longer periods of intense depression. The void in his life is not diminishing.

OTHER KINDS OF REQUESTS

The placement of a child at an older age who retains memories of biological parents or foster parents and at times of siblings, differs in many respects from the placement of a young infant. Some placements fail because a child cannot become attached to the adoptive parents; the primary attachment is to previous psychological parents. If such an adoption becomes final, the child at an older age may ask help in restoring earlier relationships. In a truly enlightened "modern" adoption, these relationships are not cut off by court decree.

Frequently, siblings will approach an agency for assistance in locating a brother or sister, often the youngest in a family group and the only one to have been adopted.

Although biological parents from time to time have approached the agency with new medical information or to ask about a child's well-being, an increasing number are registering their willingness to be involved in a reunion or are actively pressing for a reunion. The Adoption Service is no less responsive to their requests than any other, but follows the guideline of involving the adoptive parents, and through them the adoptee, in the decision-making process.

COMMENTS

A changing climate in society toward more openness in discussing sex, marriage, childbirth in and out of wedlock, and family problems may free adoptive parents to be less tense in discussing adoption. Illegitimacy no longer is as difficult to understand and discuss. Adoption applicants have become less reserved in describing their marriages and are freer to admit to problems. Infertility is not as narcissistically hurtful in that many couples in the general population are preventing conception. It no longer is a fixed value that people should grow up to marry and have children. Many alternative arrangements are acceptable, indeed, preferred by some.

Adopted adults have grabbed the tail of the civil rights and liberation movements and are pushing hard to overcome what they perceive to be a deprivation and handicap in being adopted. For a minority of adoptees, their experience has been an unhappy or troubled one. The experiences of several unhappy adoptees have been publicized in dramatic accounts by the press and national media. Their cry is the need for identity, an emotional issue shared by many who have grown up in their family of origin: genealogical research has become a national pastime as more and more Americans, white and black, search for records of ancestors here and abroad.

The problem with the emphasis on identity is that it is less important who one is than what one is and how one feels about oneself in relation to family and friends. Finding a biological parent may provide answers to secrets but does not necessarily help an identity crisis. One of the most positive results of searching may be to put split identifications back together. Also, a person with an extensive genealogical tree can feel just as deprived, inadequate, and lonely as an adoptee who grew up feeling cut off from his roots. Many people growing up in their biological families complain that they were an "accident," not really wanted, or "second fiddle" to a favored sibling; many have had traumatic separations and rejections. The adoption secret is not the only kind of secret many families struggle with.

What then is so different for the adopted? It appears to be the amount of psychic energy engendered both by secrets about their birth and adoption or negative and distorted statements about their biological parents. Narcissistically hurt, these adopted children begin to feel different and, feeling different, they need to search for what they are like and can truly belong to.

A majority of adoptive families, as research studies have shown, are strong, healthy ones; a small percentage are rated as poor, which does not always mean that the children growing up in these families have serious problems. Reports by clinicians in private practice, child guidance clinics, and adoption services indicate that a lack of resolution of feelings about barrenness and possibly jealousy of the mother who could bear and give up a child color the manner in which the adopters tell a child about his or her adoption. The words used, affect behind the words, time and place, make a strong imprint on a child's mind and feelings and create more psychological difficulties than telling a child he is adopted at an early age.

SUMMARY

Research studies in adoption confirm that it can be a satisfactory resolution of the needs of natural parents, adoptive parents, and a dependent child. Adoption is a contract by which parental rights and responsibilities are permanently transferred by court decree. One of the advantages of adoption over foster care is supposed to be permanence and belonging. However, psychological stress within the adoptive family, exacerbated by community and family biases towards biological parenthood, in a minority of adoptions has created tension, secrecy, and distortion in the vitally important area of adoption education. Adopted adults, feeling cut off from their roots and impaired in their identities, are crusading for the constitutional right to have access to identifying facts about themselves. An increasing number are searching for biological parents in an attempt to resolve a developmental crisis or fill an aching void in their lives.

Because adoption has always been a sensitive, complex, and highly individualized human process, agencies and courts as the main instruments in this process should respond to the compelling needs of the adoptee and the biological and adoptive parents. The lack of sufficient response has created the present crisis with respect to opening records. It is unfortunate that a rigid application of confidentiality has denied understanding professional service to needy persons.

If the adoption contract is attacked and in effect nullified by legislative acts, both biological and adoptive parents will have good reason to feel that for them adoption has become a legal fraud. There are remedies short of full disclosure that can repair damaged self-esteem and assist adopted persons in sorting out their tangled identifications and identity struggles.

REFERENCES

Erikson, E. H. (1968), *Identity, Youth and Crisis*. New York: Norton.
Fisher, F. (1973), *The Search for Anna Fisher*. New York: Arthur Fields.
Hoopes, Sherman, Lawder, Andrews, & Lower (1969), *A Follow-Up Study of Adoptions, Vol. II: Post-Placement Functioning of Adopted Children*. Child Welfare League of America.

Lawder, Hoopes, Andrews, Lower & Perry (1971), *A Study of Black Adoption Families: A Comparison of a Traditional and a Quasi-Adoption Program.* Child Welfare League of America.

Lawder, Lower, Andrews, Sherman, & Hill (1969). *A Follow-Up Study of Adoptions. Vol. I: Post-Placement Functioning of Adoption Families.* Child Welfare League of America.

Lawton, J. J. & Gross, S. Z. (1964), Review of psychiatric literature on adopted children. *Arch. Gen. Psychiat.*, 11:635–644.

Lifton, B. J. (1975), *Twice Born: Memoirs of an Adopted Daughter.* New York: McGraw-Hill.

Schechter, M. D. (1960), Observations on adopted children. *Arch. Gen. Psychiat.*, 3:21–32.

Toussieng, P. W. (1962), Thoughts regarding the etiology of psychiatric difficulties in adopted children. *Child Welfare*, 41:59–71.

Wieder, H. (1977), On being told of adoption. *Psychoanal. Quart.*, 46:1–22.

Evaluating Families
with Custody or Visitation Problems

ANDREW P. MUSETTO

Divorces are increasing. The breakup of a family presents a crisis to all its members. The children involved in these families often feel helpless, abandoned, blameful, angry, fearful, or betrayed. While some families separate in a way that minimizes the inclusion of their children in the marital struggles, too often children become or continue to be the center arena in which the marital battles take place. Then, disputes over custody or visitation become prevalent.

When one parent accuses the other of being unfit for custody or visitation of the children, or if both parents compete for custody, the courts can be called upon to decide the outcome. Mental health professionals are increasingly being asked to help the courts with these decisions. It is vital that the mental health professional work closely and cooperatively with the court, since it makes the final decision. A well-informed court decision, one that honors all family members as much as possible, can have profound effects on the further development of the children and the well-being of the entire family. This article will focus on how these evaluations can be done, including a theoretical position and the goals and methods of intervention.

There are many reasons why parents do not agree about custody or visitation. First of all, out of concern for their children, parents may wish to continue their involvement with them as closely as possible. On another level, separation may be very painful for both parents and children alike. Other parents may regard getting custody or visitation as a sign of their competence, as a justification of their position vis-à-vis their spouse, or as a method of revenging hurts accumulated in the marriage.

Andrew P. Musetto, Ph.D., is Senior Clinical Psychologist, Camden County Health Services Center, Community Mental Health Program, Lakeland, N.J.

Furthermore, parents are reluctant to give up custody of children they have parentified. About parentification Boszormenyi-Nagy and Spark (1973) write that it "... implies the subjective distortion of a relationship as if one's partner or even children were his parent. Such distortion can be done in a wishful fantasy or, more dramatically, through dependent behavior" (p. 151). These parentified children are desperately held on to; loss of their support is threatening and may evoke on the part of parents recollections of their own earlier deprivation, exploitation, or neglect. A divorce or physical separation, then, does not necessarily end an emotional relationship.

Children are especially vulnerable to the stress of a divorce or separation. They depend on others for their emotional well-being. Their feelings for their parents are usually intense. The blood ties they have with their parents can never be dissolved by the courts. Even if a biological parent ceases to be or has never been a loving and caring parent, loyalty ties between parents and children still bind them together on some level (Boszormenyi-Nagy and Spark, 1973).

Systems Theory

Rearing children is multifaceted. In one sense, it is a relationship between parents and children. That relationship is partially determined by the quality of the parent's marital relationship. And the viability of a marital relationship is greatly influenced by the extent to which each spouse has negotiated prior commitments and obligations to his or her family of origin. Since people tend to carry over into their marriages past feelings and yearnings originating with their own parents, marriage and childrearing then becomes an intergenerational matter.

The family is usually the most powerful emotional system to which a person belongs. Rule-governed and change-resistant, the family regulates the interpersonal life of its members. Over several generations the family evolves norms and expectations for the behavior of its members. These usually implicit expectations, felt as obligations or entitlements, shape personality development. They include but transcend intrapsychic forces and individual motivations.

Assessing individual dynamics alone or evaluating the competence of one individual to be a parent without taking into account the multi-person systems' aspect of parenting is inadequate. Looking at the individuals alone neglects the context in which parenting takes place. It puts aside the leverage a mental health professional may have in assisting the family (and not just one individual) in generating solutions to their relationship conflicts. Taking what one individual says alone can also be meaningless or misleading; parents can allege many things about each other, the truth of which may become clear only in a family-evaluation interview. In fact, only in a face-to-face interview does the true nature of a family's functioning come to light.

Seeing the family as a unit both actually and theoretically rests on the systems-theory assumptions that emotional functioning is interdependent and reciprocal, that the causes of behavior are circular and not linear, that powerful motivating factors involve the covert expectations and loyalty obligations implicit in being a member of a family.

Inherent in all personal relationships are the polarities of distance and fusion, "I" and "we," differentiation and conformity. Neither element exists without the other. Since all parts of a system or family are vital to maintain the status quo, causality is circular, not linear. No one person is wholly responsible for the marriage or family being what it is; each person plays his or her appointed and accepted roles. For example, if there is distance between father and the children, one wonders what part the mother plays in maintaining this distance. If mother and son are locked into a fused relationship, one may inquire into how distant father is from mother and how both spouses contributed to this setup.

The above description of the relationships between mother, father, and children highlight another tenet of systems theory, namely, that emotional relationships tend to form triangles (Bowen, 1976). In order to preserve their relationship, two people (for example, parents) divert the tension that exists between them onto a third person (for example, a child), or issue (for example, custody). Then the emotional relationship between the spouses is maintained at the expense of the third party, a child, whose resultant dysfunction keeps the family ties alive, even though the family may be physically separate. Out of loyalty to the family, children triangled into the morass of marital discord accept their roles and give up or fail to develop parts of their functioning or emotional autonomy. Children's failure to grow emotionally and therefore to separate from parents can allay the anxiety of other family members who depend on these children for emotional satisfaction.

Despite overt pronouncements of uninvolvement, actual separation, or divorce, the marital and family relationships can endure, often in the form of custody/visitation disputes.

GOALS OF INTERVENTION

The ideal goal of interviewing a family involved in a custody/visitation problem is not simply to detect pathology in individual members. More importantly, it is to provide the family with an opportunity to generate a solution to the conflict, hostility, and bitterness. Intervention surpasses pure evaluation. Not looking for blame, the interviewer tries to understand the family as a multiperson system, with its intergenerational commitments, loyalty ties, roles, triangles, reciprocal functioning, repetitive and circular patterns of behavior. The mental health professional broaches the idea that all the family has contributed to the current dysfunction. Each family member, especially the parents, needs to explore more constructive alternatives than the dispute over custody/visitation.

Cooperation between the court and the mental health professional is crucial. The court insures the attendance of whatever family members are necessary for the evaluation. The mental health professional tries to give the court a recommendation that is as explicit as possible and that also has the definite endorsement of both parents and the family. A valuable service is rendered to the court if the evaluation can bring about an agreement within the family regarding custody/visitation. It is the spirit in which the court's final decision is carried out which is more important than the specific custody/visitation arrangement.

Systems concepts are introduced into the sessions. Blame is put aside in favor of circular causality and reciprocal functioning. Past mistakes, anger, and revenge should give way to accountability and responsibility. Rather than continuing to bicker over custody/visitation, the parents are encouraged to understand that loyalty ties to both parents are present. The children will have great difficulties constructively maintaining these ties unless both parents permit them to. As the parents become aware that it is their conflict over the children that affronts the children's loyalty toward both parents, and therefore the healthy development of their personalities, it becomes the parents' responsibility to try to minimize the conflict.

Children need to be reassured of consistent parenting, regardless of which parent is granted custody. Both parents are encouraged in their responsibilities as parents. Noncustodial parents especially need this reinforcement to avoid their abandoning the children and violating the children's trust in human relationships. Without object constancy and the gratification of dependency needs, the children's self-esteem will be jeopardized. Furthermore, lack of involvement with the children can also lead noncustodial parents into feeling guilty and drive them further away.

With children present during some of the sessions, it is important that they understand that neither parent is solely responsible for the breakup of the family. Neither parent should be scapegoated or idealized.

Children are not the judges of the rightness of their parents' positions regarding the marital problems. Nor should a relationship with a child be used as a way of getting revenge by one parent against another. Through the evaluation process, the children can be given a chance to mourn the separation from the noncustodial parent.

During the interviews the mental health professional pays attention to whether placement with one or the other parent will exploit the children through parentification, neglect, abuse, or scapegoating. At the same time, the interviewer searches out whether or not at least one parent is a psychological parent, one who wants and appropriately cares for the children according to their ages and needs.

There are cases where custody is not contested, but there is a sharp disagreement about visitation. Usually the custodial parent alleges that visitation with the noncustodial parent is harmful. These charges by the custodial parent (often ranging from saying that the children are upset by seeing the noncustodial parent to alleging that they are being sexually abused by that parent) must be weighed carefully against the importance of the children being allowed to continue to see the noncustodial parent. Explicit abuse may eliminate or severely restrict visitation opportunities (for example, having a person appointed by the court to supervise visitation), but sometimes the children's protests about seeing their absent parent merely echo the implicit and perhaps unconscious objections by the custodial parent. In the latter case, the task of the interviewer becomes that of helping the custodial parent give permission to the children to maintain their relationship with the other parent, despite what may be incorrigible marital problems.

The mental health professional is not the judge of which parent is right or wrong. The interviewer is there to help find an alternative that does not endanger the children's implicit loyalties to their parents. Nor should the recommendation be unjust to either parent. This alternative should promote the children's commitments to their families and age-appropriate individuation at the same time. As the interviewer stresses the accountability of parents to children, it is essential not to overlook the children's obligations to their parents. In this way, parents can be confirmed in their roles and responsibilities as parents, and children can be afforded a constructive way of repaying their parents for what they have received from them.

Practical Considerations

The repetitive and reciprocal patterns present in the marriage are likely to appear in the family interviews. Alert to these patterns erupting, the interviewer should be in charge of the sessions. Fighting and bickering are discouraged. Communication and compromise are stressed. The interviewer tries to help the parents put aside their hurts, for the sake of the children at least, and work out a compromise or solution to the dispute if possible. The purpose of the interview is not to resolve the marital and family problems, but to settle the custody/visitation issue in the least harmful way to the children and parents. A contract for marital or family therapy can be agreed to if the family is willing to go beyond the custody/visitation evaluation.

Resolving a custody/visitation dispute is an arduous, at times impossible task. The problems are usually chronic and severe or the family would have found a solution before being sent by the court for the evaluation. One parent may have been absent or marginally involved with the children for many years. Emotional investment in revenge or vindication against this parent can be enormous. Communication is punctuated with bitterness, accusations, and disappointments.

The goal of the interview is not to find the ideal solution; the fact of a divorce or separation and the conflict over custody/visitation are far from ideal and often harmful to the children. The severity of the family dysfunction and the likelihood that the conflicts will not be easily resolved, if at all, mean that the best that can be hoped for is the "least detrimental alternative" (Goldstein et al., 1973).

The author typically begins the family evaluation by seeing the parents and children together. Each parent may be seen separately, however, if at first the anxiety level of the family is too strong. Both husband and wife are notified ahead of time that the interview may be a conjoint one. This prepares them for the face-to-face encounter which may have been avoided for a long time. This method of seeing the family together also stresses from the start that the problem is a joint one and underlines the family's responsibilities in bringing about a solution to the problem if possible. This approach may be especially helpful to the noncustodial parent, who often feels defensive or accused. A family may be angry or upset insofar as the court has insisted that they come for the evaluation. One or both parents may take this to be a commentary on their inadequacy or failure. These feelings can be lessened by the interviewer talking to the family about their joint responsibility, not individual blame. The family is advised that the court has ordered the evaluation because of the family conflict over custody/visitation and not necessarily because of any suspected individual pathology.

Several sessions are usually required to complete the evaluation.

The family dysfunction may be so great that a compromise solution is never arrived at. In that case, the mental health professional recommends to the court what seems to be the least detrimental alternative, advising the court of the difficulty of the situation and the absence of a compromise solution.

The children are part of the evaluation. They should be given a chance to hear both parents' points of view and are encouraged to express their own feelings about custody/visitation. While their preferences are not the deciding factor, their desires regarding custody/visitation are important and should be heard. Regardless of the outcome, children should be given permission by both parents to have, if possible, a positive relationship with each parent, even if one parent does not respond favorably to the children's efforts.

The Final Recommendation

The final recommendation regarding custody favors the parent who has demonstrated being in fact a psychological parent. If one parent already has custody and is a psychological parent as well, it is the responsibility of the parent who seeks to disrupt this relationship to show that continuing the present arrangement would be more harmful to the children than making a change. If one parent is not able or willing to be a psychological parent, then, of course, that parent should not be granted custody. It is important, however, to keep in mind that the other parent may be scapegoating this individual, before deciding on an individual's unfitness to have custody. It is very difficult to tell, at times, whether abuse has actually taken place as one parent may allege. What the children say about possible abuse can be what one parent has prompted them to tell.

Psychological parents want their children and are able to care for their needs. They provide support, stimulation, guidance, and limits. They take care of their children's physical well-being. They help the children master their instinctual urges and provide the children with a motive for incorporating a moral conscience and concern for the rights and feelings of others. They provide models for identification. They value the children as members of the family and as individuals in their own right.

Psychological parents recognize the importance of affirming their children's intrinsic loyalty ties to both parents; they encourage as positive contact as possible with the noncustodial parent. Psychological parents do not use their children to further their own aims: to seek revenge on the other parent; to justify their own position; to serve as a mediator between parents; to parentify children into emotionally caring for them or taking on the primary responsibility for other children; to scapegoat children for the marital failure or personal unhappiness. Psychological parents encourage their children's connectedness with grandparents and extended family on both sides.

Psychological parents are willing to acknowledge their own contribution to the family problems. They allow their children to express genuine feelings even if these feelings may be painful to the parents. Psychological parents accept the responsibility for being parents and expect some fair consideration from their children for their efforts, neither infantalizing them into fixed dependent positions, nor parentifying them into roles that surpass their capabilities. Nor do psychological parents want custody in order to force an unwilling spouse to stay in the marriage; nor to secure financial aid; nor to replace another child lost by death or separation.

In the case of young children, it is especially important for the court to make a decision swiftly, since what may be considered short periods of time by adults is for a child much longer and more disrupting. With urgent instinctual and emotional needs, a child's sense of time is different from that of an adult's (Goldstein et al., 1973). Postponement of gratification and tolerance of frustration occur far less in children than in adults. Hence, children have a great sensitivity to the lengths of separation. Being egotistical, children are more likely to react to a separation as if it were a profound personal loss. They are governed more by their anxieties, fears, and impulses. Children are less able than adults to respond to a threat to their emotional security, such as a separation or a conflict regarding with whom they will live.

In cases where the question is limited to visitation, it is often necessary for the court to outline the times and places of visitation, so as not to allow the parents to continue their conflict by capriciously altering the visitation setup. It is not infrequent that a parent will arrive for visitation and be told repeatedly that a child is sick, absent, unwilling, or unavailable. Although the custodial parent has been given the day-to-day responsibility to care for the children, the importance of the children's contact with the noncustodial parent separate from the control of the custodial parent needs the court's encouragement. In short, visitation should not be under the whims of the custodial parent. The noncustodial parent's financial commitment to the children should also be emphasized.

Summary

In evaluating and intervening in custody/visitation disputes for the court, the mental health professional can be guided by the following ideas:

1. A custody/visitation dispute is a marital and family problem. An understanding of these situations requires a family evaluation and not just the assessment of the individuals involved. The family is primarily an emotional system, and emotional systems outlast legal relationships. Loyalty ties continue despite physical separation.

2. The mental health professional tries to have the family accept responsibility for the problem and for resolving the dispute, but in a way that encourages the parental responsibilities of both parents. The recommendation should not endanger the loyalty ties of the children to either parent or place the children in a position of being neglected, scapegoated, parentified, or triangled in some other way. Nor should the recommendation be unjust to the parents or activate the guilt of either parent, thus encouraging abandonment or neglect of the children or undermining their roles as parents.

3. The recommendation for custody is in favor of the parent who appears to be a psychological parent as described above.

4. Both parents are accountable as parents regardless of which one is granted custody.

5. The mental health professional stresses accountability, reciprocal functioning, and circular causality rather than blame, scapegoating, vindication, or side taking.

6. The recommendation for custody should be seen as the least detrimental alternative, since the divorce or separation and the conflict over custody/visitation are far from ideal and often harmful.

REFERENCES

Boszormenyi-Nagy, I. & Spark, G. (1973), *Invisible Loyalties*. New York: Harper & Row.

Bowen, M. (1976), Principles and techniques of multiple family therapy. In: *Family Therapy*, ed. P. Guerin. New York: Gardner Press.

Goldstein, J., Freud, A., & Solnit, A. (1973), *Beyond the Best Interests of the Child*. New York: Free Press.

The Multiproblem Family Presents in a Children's Outpatient Psychiatric Clinic

MATTHEW SCHIFF and NEIL KALTER

The term "multiproblem family" was popularized in the mid-1950s following a significant study of these families in St. Paul, Minnesota (Geismer, 1958). Descriptions and definitions of multiproblem families have not undergone significant alteration since the term was introduced into the literature. The Minnesota study described these families as

> extremely troublesome to the community. By reason of child neglect, crime, dependence on relief, truancy, delinquency, problem drinking, and many other deviant kinds of behavior, they represent the threat of financial burden to the community. Second, they are troubled people, unhappy and suffering, whose feelings of self-worth are low. In many subtle (and unsubtle) ways they have been told they are failures as family providers, as parents, as neighbors, etc., and have heard this so often that they have come to believe it themselves. It is not surprising that they are defensive and mistrustful, seeing society in all its parts, including social workers, as a threat.

They have been aptly described by Polanski et al. (1972) in their book about West Appalachian multiproblem families as people who breathe apathy and futility.

The following characteristics are seen as most important in defining the nature of multiproblem families (Cohen and Bernard, 1961;

Matthew Schiff, M.D., is Director of Child Psychiatry at Monmouth Medical Center, Long Branch, New Jersey, and Assistant Professor of Psychiatry at Hahnemann Medical School, Philadelphia, Pennsylvania.

Neil Kalter, Ph.D., is Associate Professor of the Departments of Psychology and Psychiatry, University of Michigan, Ann Arbor, Michigan.

Geismer, 1958; New York City Youth Board, 1952):

1. *Multiplicity of problems:* There should be two or more recent problems involved in the case.

2. *Chronicity of need:* There is a history of consistent and recurrent multiple difficulties producing family and individual disorganization.

3. *Resistance to treatment:* This may range from an inability to ask for or use help appropriately to rejection of help offered.

4. *Handicapping attitudes:* This includes lack of understanding of the meaning and value of formal education or modern medical care (Cohen and Bernard, 1961).

In referring to the various attempts to intervene with multiproblem families in the area of mental and physical health care and school and job counseling, Cohen and Bernard (1961) note:

> In these very families that need it most, agency services tend to be either rejected, or if begun, discontinued. This resistance to treatment — or in some instances, outright rejection of treatment — may take the form of not making use of suggested casework services, of failing to act on early symptoms of cancer, diabetes or tuberculosis, of breaking probation, of school drop-outs, of failure to follow up on suggested opportunities for employment. Since traditional concepts of agency service are based on "client initiative," conventional casework approaches either do not reach these people or fail to "take."

An examination of several studies of multiproblem families reveals that a large number of children in these families are at risk psychiatrically due to disturbing rates of interpersonal and emotional difficulties among parents and/or parent surrogates, and a high incidence of disrupted, broken homes. These families tend to be isolated from their communities and mental health workers. Their child-care practices, economic situations, household practices, and physical and mental health are generally inadequate (Brown, 1968; Geismer, 1958; New York City Youth Board, 1952). Many studies agree that these families drain up to 36 per cent of the resources spent and given to correctional, health, mental health, and public-relief services, despite the fact that they represented only approximately five per cent of the total families in a community (Brown, 1968; Curtis, Simon, Boykin, et al., 1964; Geismer, 1958).

Multiproblem families differ with respect to national norms for families along many dimensions. In the St. Paul study the average size of the family was 7.4 members compared to 5.5 members in the general population. Approximately 50 per cent of their families were one-parent families. Over 30 per cent of multiproblem families contained a woman who married at under eighteen years of age. The national average in the late 1950s was 18 per cent. Approximately 70 per cent of these families received significant financial aid (Geismer, 1958). The New York Youth Board families were similar to those studied in Minnesota with respect to use of financial welfare aid, court systems, and protective services. In both samples over 75 per cent of both sets of these families were involved with these agencies (Geismer, 1958; New York City Youth Board, 1952).

A further elaboration of the types of significant parental difficulty was done in the New York study. A total of 236 parents were studied: 54 had physical disease; 26 had diagnosed mental deficiency or disease; 34 had severe drug abuse problems; 36 had physically abused or neglected their children; and 64 were out of the home because of death or desertion. These figures are described as minimal estimates (New York City Youth Board, 1952). Howells' (1966) study of hard-core families in England revealed an incidence of significant emotional pathology in 98 per cent of these families as compared to 30 per cent in the general population. He defined "significant" as multiple symptomatology with only a fair chance of amelioration even with long-term psychotherapy.

Generally, many factors seemed to interrelate and compound one another in a negative fashion. The poorer the family solidarity, the greater the chance of individual socially or mentally disordered behavior. All of these factors negatively influenced money management and the state of individual and family health. These families seemed to pick different agencies and present in "different" crises. These crises seem predictable. They can all be understood through one's knowledge and understanding of the multiproblem family (Geismer, 1958).

While research on multiproblem families has carefully described the range and depth of difficulties confronting these families, there is little literature concerning psychiatric aspects of the children of multiproblem families. To examine this issue the first 50 cases referred for evaluation at a large outpatient children's psychiatric facility were studied.

Procedure

A psychiatric evaluation at this clinic consisted of an average of two interviews with the designated child patient, two appointments with the child's parents or guardians, and an interpretive, feedback interview with the parents/guardians.

Data on these 50 cases included general demographic and socioeconomic information as well as material elicited in the psychiatric interviews. The former consisted of parents' or guardians' age, race, religion, education, occupation, and income, and the child's age, sex, and grade in school. Interview data included the number of caretakers and households involved in the child's life, the overall mobility and intactness of the family, contacts that all known members of the immediate family had with helping agencies and/or professionals since January, 1971, and the data on intrapsychic and family assessment of conflicts and problems.

RESULTS

The first step in analyzing these data involved developing an empirical definition of the multiproblem family. We thought that the number of helping agencies and/or professionals contacted by family members in the most recent three-year period would reflect the chronicity and multiplicity of problems that other investigators have noted as a major characteristic of multiproblem families. An inspection of the distribution of this variable in our sample showed that contact with six or more agencies and/or helping professionals provided a natural cutting point. In addition, an index of lack of family stability, another important aspect of the multiproblem family condition, was sought. Thus it was decided that if the child patient had lived in two or more households over the three-year period prior to the evaluation, it would be an indication of family instability. Both of these criteria were applied to the 50 families, and nine families met both criteria. The median number of helping agencies and/or professionals contacted by the multiproblem families was seven; for the non-multiproblem families, three. The median number of households in which the multiproblem child patients had lived was four; the corresponding figure for the non-multiproblem children was one. The fact that as many as eighteen per cent of the sample came under our operational definition of a multiproblem family was in itself an interesting and surprising datum.

The next step was to compare the multiproblem (MP) and non-multiproblem (NMP) families with respect to five sets of variables: demographic, socioeconomic, family health, family stability, and evaluation-related variables. In each instance the dependent variable was dichotomized, yielding a two-by-two contingency table (i.e., MP vs. NMP and the two elements of the dichotomized dependent variable). A Fisher exact test was performed for each table to determine if differences between the MP and NMP families were statistically significant. Table 1 summarizes these analyses.

An inspection of Table 1 shows that MP families differed signifi-

TABLE 1

COMPARISON OF MULTIPROBLEM AND NON-MULTIPROBLEM
FAMILIES ON DEMOGRAPHIC, SOCIOECONOMIC, FAMILY
HEALTH, FAMILY STABILITY, AND EVALUATION VARIABLES

	Per cent of Families among MP vs. NMP		Significance
Demographic			
Age of child patient (13–17 years old)	44	41	N.S.
Sex of child patient (male)	67	56	N.S.
Race (non-white)	33	10	N.S.
Number of siblings and/or step-siblings (>2)	56	15	*
Socioeconomic			
Mother's education (<12 years)[1]	100	27	**
Father's education (<12 years)[2]	100	23	**
Receiving ADC (yes)	89	2	**
Family Health			
One or both parents hospitalized within the last three years	44	2	**
Child patient's siblings and/or stepsiblings with clear psychiatric problems[3]	88	11	**
Family Stability			
Number of moves (>2)	89	12	**
Not currently living with either biological parent	78	5	**
Evaluation			
Referral by DSS or court	67	2	**
Length of evaluation (>6 weeks)	89	37	**

* = p < .05
** = p < .01

[1] Based on 6 multiproblem families and 38 non-multiproblem families.
[2] Based on 5 multiproblem families and 37 non-multiproblem families.
[3] Based on 8 multiproblem families and 36 non-multiproblem families.

cantly from NMP families on nearly all the variables examined. The exceptions were race, sex, and age (teen vs. preteen) of the child patient. There does not seem to be any relationship between these demographic measures and coming from an MP family.

A picture of the MP families emerges from the analysis of the remaining quantitative data. Contrasted with the NMP group, MP families were larger, poorer, less well-educated, and less healthy. These differences were striking. Eighty-nine per cent of the MP families were receiving Aid to Dependent Children (ADC), and none contained a parent who had completed a high school education. Fully 44 per cent of the MP families had a parent who had been hospitalized for a psychiatric and/or medical problem within the past three years. Among the eight MP families where the designated child patient had a sibling and/or stepsibling, seven contained another child with clear-cut psychiatric problems. Thus, the two relatively straightforward criteria used to identify MP families seemed to locate these families efficiently in our sample.

Differences between the two family groups with respect to the evaluation process were also in evidence. Sixty-seven per cent of the MP families as opposed to only two per cent of the NMP group had the target child patient referred by the courts or the Department of Social Services rather than the more common sources such as school, family physician, or the child's parents or guardians. And evaluations took considerably longer to complete for children of MP families. Eighty-nine per cent of the MP families had evaluations that extended beyond six weeks, while only 37 per cent of the evaluations of NMP families took this long. Many MP families bring their children for an outpatient psychiatric evaluation when under some pressure from a social agency to do so. And the evaluation process is unusually prolonged often due to missed appointments which need to be rescheduled and the complexity of the task of collecting relevant information from a large number of community agencies and professionals.

In addition to the quantitative differences between MP and NMP families, there were clinical dissimilarities as well. Among our 41 NMP families, two types of problems were prevalent. The first was an essentially neurotic difficulty occurring within an intact family. These included instances of enuresis, phobias, learning inhibitions, behavioral problems, and so forth. A second pattern of difficulties consisted of acute developmental or environmental crisis cases. Included in this group were adolescent adjustment problems (e.g., school truancy, runaway behavior, and drug taking), reactions to birth of a sibling, and custody cases. In contrast to these kinds of psychiatric and behavioral problems, the children of MP families seemed to present with smoldering, chronic difficulties occurring in a family setting that lacked definition and cohesion. The child's problem, itself, rarely could be clearly defined. An atmosphere of chaos and uncertainty pervaded the material. And evaluators often felt confused and helpless in the face of long and tortuous histories of family difficulties and multiple social agency contacts.

CASE STUDIES

CASE 1

The case of John J., a twelve-year-old boy, had an unsatisfactory resolution. John was referred by the Department of Social Services for evaluation and disposition. He had been in five different residences in the three years prior to his evaluation, including placements in a group home, a juvenile boys' home, and a children's psychiatric hospital. In between placements he had stays of various lengths with his biological mother and stepfather, and his biological father. His six siblings in his two families were just as dispersed and fragmented in their living arrangements as was John. Previous evaluations noted marked disturbed and antisocial behavior. The list of difficulties included enuresis, fire setting, fighting, stealing, poor school adjustment with a normal IQ, and physical abuse of his siblings and biological mother.

John was taken to another state precipitously, but with the state's permission, by his biological father; this solved the disposition problems. It obviously did not touch on the dilemma of beneficial management for John, his siblings, or his sets of parents. This evaluation lasted eight weeks and was mostly focused on liaison with social agencies that had had contact with this family in order to gather pertinent historical information. Neither John nor his parents were ever seen as part of the evaluation.

CASE 2

Lucretia G. is an eight-and-a-half-year-old girl whose difficult but successful evaluation took 21 weeks to complete. Much of this time was spent compiling data and mobilizing services 70 miles away from the clinic. This task involved liaison work with the seven agencies that had had contact with the G.'s over the last three years. These agencies included Aid to Dependent Children, Department of Social Services, Protective Services, three medical hospitals, and many helping resource people at Lucretia's school.

Lucretia was described by various medical, helping, and school personnel as sleepy, lethargic, hyperactive, retarded, abused, and just plain confused. People who attempted to diagnose her difficulties further felt frustrated and overwhelmed as they uncovered the existence of two homes (the mother's and grandmother's), an absent and previously abusing father, and a mother and grandmother who seemed to shift their feelings toward and responsibility for Lucretia. In addition, a difficult diagnostic assessment was needed that called for pediatric and neurological review and psychological testing.

The evaluation proceeded with the patient being brought in on the wrong hour of the wrong day. When she finally was seen, Lucretia had difficulty leaving the evaluator's office. In all three interview sessions she left drawings for the evaluator. These pictures and specimens of her writing indicated the presence of some problem in perceptual-motor integration. It was already known that she was myopic and had significant nerve hearing loss in her left ear. Difficulties in the use of language were also present. Her enunciation of words made it difficult to understand her vocabulary and its syntax. She also had difficulty hearing and particularly integrating instructions. When Lucretia wanted to learn to use the office dictaphone, verbal and nonverbal instructions had to be repeated many times before she learned to master this activity. But, despite obvious difficulties in perception and particularly integration, she could clearly communicate a sense of her psychological world. Her object hunger and her wish for people to stay involved with and not abandon her were poignantly obvious. She made it clear despite her somewhat damaged equipment that she wanted to and would communicate with people if she had the chance. She would only get angry and flail out at people when she felt that they were not understanding her. This anger and oppositional behavior would provoke negative reactions from peers and adults, thus sustaining her feelings of being a damaged, abused, and worthless girl.

Lucretia's family circumstances, past and present, contain chaotic, frightening events. Mrs. G., a blustery woman, tried to lead with a show of force. She would yell and chide the secretaries and the evaluator about all the things the clinic had done wrong. Underneath this exterior, there was a very passive, dependent, frightened, ill (diagnosed tuberculosis) woman who had herself been abandoned by her father as a child. She still required her mother to drive on almost all trips no matter how brief. Often she would leave responsibility for the supervision of her children to her mother. This was gladly accepted; the grandmother preferred to keep her daughter childlike and helpless. In fact it took both "parents" to give any semblance of a developmental history for Lucretia. It was filled with moves, unfortunate surprises, and unexpected happenings. Lucretia had to face at two and a half her father's hospitalization for alcoholism manifested by destructive and abusive behavior toward his children and family, at three her mother's hospitalization for tuberculosis, at four a fire in their house in a southern state while they were vacationing in Chicago, and, at various ages, four moves.

It was decided that the interpretive interview with the school, its social worker, and its learning disability team, and the interview with the mother and grandmother, would be held in the small town where the referral originated. Together with a number of school specialists, a program for this perceptually and emotionally damaged youngster was established. Lucretia is now learning in her resource room at school with a minimum of behavioral difficulties. The epilogue to this 21-week adventure was a call to the evaluator some six months later about a second child in this family of three siblings who was having sudden problems with sexual identity. The G.'s seemed more trusting and more willing to cooperate in helping this second child than they initially had been in Lucretia's case. The integrated, active effort of several helping professionals seemed to leave its mark upon the G.'s.

DISCUSSION

The first step in developing practices for the useful psychiatric evaluation of children from multiproblem families is to recognize such children when they present at a clinic or community agency. Without the realization that one is dealing with a child from a multiproblem family and without the concept of such a family, the evaluator can often feel inundated by the amount of time, energy, and patience that is required in compiling relevant historical data and developing a constructive diagnostic assessment of the current psychological and situational difficulties. If one proceeds on a case-by-case basis without this perspective, feelings of frustration and helplessness soon beset the evaluator.

In our sample, a constellation of characteristics was descriptive of MP families. The family's having had extensive (six or more) contacts with helping agencies and/or professionals in the most recent three-year period and the child patient's having lived in two or more households proved to be relatively straightforward indicators of a multiproblem family. These "signs" were associated with a host of socioeconomic, family, health, and family stability characteristics. Demographic variables, however, such as age, sex, and race of the child patient, were not aspects that differentiated children of MP from those of NMP families.

While parents of MP families were consistently poorer and less well educated than NMP parents, low socioeconomic status is not to be equated with being a multiproblem family. Rather, it seems that family instability and long-standing physical and/or psychiatric problems of family members are the key features of a multiproblem family. In the sample studied, all MP families were of low socioeconomic status, but it seems that this compounds the problems MP families face rather than causing them (Howells, 1966; Polanski et al., 1972).

Once a particular family is recognized as being a multiproblem family, the helping professional should be prepared for an evaluation that is longer than usual and that involves contacting numerous agencies and professionals. Often the evaluator is confronted by crises in at least two areas, within the families and among the helping agencies. With respect to the latter, the agencies are frequently unaware of one another's involvements. Thus, an important early step in the evaluation process is to collate relevant data from multiple sources. When the integrated information is communicated to each of the agencies, a recognition of the extent and nature of the difficulties serves to decrease the global sense of futility and paralysis separately and yet mutually experienced by those who have been in contact with the multiproblem family. A concerted plan for intervention can then be devised through a cooperating team of professionals drawn from the several agencies involved (Curtis, Simon, Boykin, et al., 1964; Enzer and Stackhouse, 1968). Such an effort recognizes the need for effective intervention to be multifaceted and drawn from several resources when helping a multiproblem family. In the case of Lucretia G., intervention included coordinating the efforts of several educational specialists as well as attention to Mrs. G.'s medical problems. The intervention plan rested on knowledge of the psychological, cognitive, and neurological aspects of Lucretia's functioning and on mother's past medical history. Thus a number of helping agencies and professionals were involved including school personnel, a pediatric neurological unit at a hospital, and medical personnel who had previous contact with the G.'s and especially with Lucretia.

Concurrent with the coordination among the several agencies and helping professionals involved, the family and child should be seen as quickly as possible. Delay of even a week can lend support to the family's feeling that agencies are basically unresponsive to their needs and increase their resistance to being helped. Further, such families will often act precipitously, thus aborting the evaluation process as in the case of John J. Home visits or meeting the family elsewhere in its community can be particularly effective in demonstrating a commitment to be helpful to the family and where speed in seeing the family is crucial

(Meyer, 1963; Polanski, Borgman and Desaix, 1972).

We have found it helpful in evaluating multiproblem families to emphasize to the family the potential strengths the child has and the *specific* steps that can be undertaken to aid the child and other family members. Here one's role as a coordinator of multiple services involving several agencies or institutions is important. What is stressed is clear-cut action that will take place in the near future. Multiproblem families often cannot afford the luxury, nor do they usually have the inclination, to observe themselves at length in a psychologically minded fashion with no tangible action planned. And in most instances they are correct in feeling that such highly visible actions are what the situation requires.

Multiproblem families present special difficulties in the psychiatric evaluation of children. And our sample findings suggest that children of these families may be appearing in substantial numbers at large outpatient psychiatric facilities. The recognition of these families and the problems they face lends a perspective to the evaluation of these children that is in itself useful to the mental health professional. An emphasis on coordinating information from and resources of the numerous agencies involved with the multiproblem family seems essential in arriving at a constructive assessment and plan for intervention. Quickly seeing the family and emphasizing readily observable actions to help with the difficulties they are experiencing can prove effective in delivering service.

References

Brown, G. E. (1968), *The Multiproblem Dilemma.* Metuchen, N.J.: Scarecrow Press.

Cohen, W. & Bernard, S. E. (1961), *The Prevention and Reduction of Dependency.* Ann Arbor, Mich.: Washtenaw County Department of Social Services.

Curtis, J. L., Simon, M., Boykin, F. et al. (1964), Observations on 29 multiproblem families. *Amer. J. Orthopsychiat.*, 34:510–516.

Enzer, N. B. & Stackhouse, J. (1968), A child guidance clinic approach to the multiproblem family. *Amer. J. Orthopsychiat.*, 38:527–538.

Geismer, L. L. (1958), Families in trouble. Family Centered Project, Greater Saint Paul Community Chest and Councils, Inc., St. Paul, Minnesota.

Howells, J. (1966), The psychopathogenesis of hard-core families. *Amer. J. Psychiat.*, 122:1159–1164.

Meyer, C. (1963), Individualizing the multiproblem family. *Soc. Casework*, 44:267–272.

New York City Youth Board (1952), *Reaching the Unreached.* Monograph 1. New York: Author.

Polanski, W. A., Borgman, R. A., & Desaix, C. (1972), *Roots of Futility.* San Francisco: Jossey-Bass.

Name Index

545

Subject Index

Rorschach test, 129–133, 257

Scapegoat, 13, 80, 169, 397, 425, 430, 432, 434, 529
Schizophrenia
  in aboriginal populations, 205
  borderline, 12
  childhood, 296, 308
  corrective parent, 135–136
  double bind, 389
  environmental factors, 358–359
  family contributing factors, 11, 46–47, 106, 114, 116–117, 119–134, 204, 330, 351–353, 359, 393, 459
  family psychiatric histories, 351–352
  family therapy, 3, 4, 6–9, 313, 320, 328–330, 438–439
  fathers of, 317
  genetic factor, 130, 335, 359
  morbidity risk of offspring and relatives, 342–360
  multiple family aftercare therapy, 429–432, 434
  organic basis, 342
  psychopharmacology, 320, 329
  as reaction, 387, 392, 394, 396
  recovery from, 320
  relapse, 320–321
  spouses of, 353–356
  stress, 318
  therapy, 315
Schools
  and elective mutism, 146
  and families, 41
Scripts, family, 392–393
Sculpting, family, 257
Separation anxiety
  and abandonment fears, 280–284
  in adopted children, 502, 510
  in child custody, 530
  intergenerational abandonment, 285
  in mutists, 143
  prevalence of, 279
Sexual abuse, 188–189, 191
Sexual dysfunction, 15, 67
Signal amplification, 417–418
Society

and cultural norms, 324
and elective mutism, 145–146, 154–155, 160
and labeling theory, 203–204
Stereotypes, 69
Stress
  adoptees' vulnerability to, 509
  and child abuse, 183–184, 186
  and disease, 43–44
  family coping patterns, 54
  and family violence, 174–178, 180
  schizophrenia, contributing to, 318
Stuttering, 203
Suicide
  double bind therapy, 378
  family therapy, 10–11
  morbidity risk of relatives, 339, 343, 347–348, 355
Symbiosis
  from abandonment fears, 283
  and adolescent violence, 164–165
  in borderline disorders, 12
  in elective mutism, 143, 145, 147, 152–153, 155
  in families, 82
Symptom prescribing, 370–371, 376, 378–379
Symptomatology, 12, 425–426

Tantrums, 373
Tasks
  family, 75–76
  therapy, use of, 372–374
Team-family evaluation, 185
Thematic Apperception Test (TAT), 129, 131–132, 508
Therapist
  anxiety in, 11, 280, 286–287
  co-therapist, 405
  countertransference, 420
  distance, 209
  ethics, 65, 67–70
  legal position, 67–68
  personal experience, 372, 402–403, 405–406
  professional privilege, 67–68, 224–225
  record keeping, 221–222, 225
  resistance to, 380–381
  role, 419–420, 422